Tort Law
for Paralegals

ASPEN PUBLISHERS

Tort Law for Paralegals

Third Edition

Neal R. Bevans, J.D.

Western Piedmont Community College

Wolters Kluwer

Law & Business

AUSTIN   BOSTON   CHICAGO   NEW YORK   THE NETHERLANDS

Aspen Publishers
Attn: Permissions Department
76 Ninth Avenue, 7th Floor
New York, NY 10011-5201

To contact Customer Care, e-mail customer.care@aspenpublishers.com, call 1-800-234-1660, fax 1-800-901-9075, or mail correspondence to:

Aspen Publishers
Attn: Order Department
PO Box 990
Frederick, MD 21705

Printed in the United States of America.

1 2 3 4 5 6 7 8 9 0

ISBN 978-0-7355-7873-9

Library of Congress Cataloging-in-Publication Data

Bevans, Neal R., 1961-
  Tort law for paralegals / Neal R. Bevans. — 3rd ed.
      p.   cm.
  Includes index.
  ISBN 978-0-7355-7873-9
  1. Torts — United States. 2. Legal assistants — United States — Handbooks, manuals, etc. I. Title.

  KF1250.Z9B48 2009
  346.7303 — dc22

                                                      2009013510

About Wolters Kluwer Law & Business

Wolters Kluwer Law & Business is a leading provider of research information and workflow solutions in key specialty areas. The strengths of the individual brands of Aspen Publishers, CCH, Kluwer Law International and Loislaw are aligned within Wolters Kluwer Law & Business to provide comprehensive, in-depth solutions and expert-authored content for the legal, professional and education markets.

CCH was founded in 1913 and has served more than four generations of business professionals and their clients. The CCH products in the Wolters Kluwer Law & Business group are highly regarded electronic and print resources for legal, securities, antitrust and trade regulation, government contracting, banking, pension, payroll, employment and labor, and healthcare reimbursement and compliance professionals.

Aspen Publishers is a leading information provider for attorneys, business professionals and law students. Written by preeminent authorities, Aspen products offer analytical and practical information in a range of specialty practice areas from securities law and intellectual property to mergers and acquisitions and pension/benefits. Aspen's trusted legal education resources provide professors and students with high-quality, up-to-date and effective resources for successful instruction and study in all areas of the law.

Kluwer Law International supplies the global business community with comprehensive English-language international legal information. Legal practitioners, corporate counsel and business executives around the world rely on the Kluwer Law International journals, loose-leafs, books and electronic products for authoritative information in many areas of international legal practice.

Loislaw is a premier provider of digitized legal content to small law firm practitioners of various specializations. Loislaw provides attorneys with the ability to quickly and efficiently find the necessary legal information they need, when and where they need it, by facilitating access to primary law as well as state-specific law, records, forms and treatises.

Wolters Kluwer Law & Business, a unit of Wolters Kluwer, is headquartered in New York and Riverwoods, Illinois. Wolters Kluwer is a leading multinational publisher and information services company.

For my sisters, Lisa Burnett and Tara Bevans

Summary
of Contents

Contents

CHAPTER 4: INTRODUCTION TO NEGLIGENCE   95

CHAPTER 6: BREACH OF DUTY UNDER NEGLIGENCE LAW   153

I. INTRODUCTION   153

II. WHO BREACHED A DUTY IN THE CHUMLEY CASE?   154

CHAPTER 10: STRICT LIABILITY AND PRODUCTS LIABILITY

XI. FOLLOW-UP ON THE SHAREHOLDER'S SUIT   ·   **441**

Preface

INTRODUCTION TO THE THIRD EDITION

The topic of civil injuries or torts continues to be in the forefront of civil practice. With this third edition of *Tort Law for Paralegals,* the author has updated the materials to reflect new trends in technology while continuing to emphasize bedrock principles of tort law. The author continues to provide in-depth discussion of civil injuries law while at the same time giving the paralegal student a solid foundation in the practicalities of daily legal work. The reader is introduced to the important concepts of negligence, intentional torts, products liability, and business torts, among others. However, the author also places great emphasis on the practical aspects of tort law, including understanding how law firms function, assessing cases for settlement value, investigating claims, billing hours, and evaluating automobile insurance policies, among many other topics.

In this newest edition, the author has updated specific areas of law to reflect recent changes, while still laying out the traditional foundation of tort element analysis and providing students with "real world" examples to help them make an intellectual and, to some extent, emotional connection with the material. This new edition follows in the footsteps of previous editions by emphasizing the essential elements of specific torts and explaining them in an easy-to-understand manner, while also providing real-life case examples and interview excerpts with working paralegals about their day-to-day activities.

Running through almost every chapter, and providing a sense of continuity, is a hypothetical case that the author uses to illustrate various points. The case involves a collision between a car and a train, resulting in the death of a passenger and severe, permanent injuries to the driver. Discussions about the case help develop the differences in civil injury law among the various jurisdictions. A complete file on this case is also provided in the appendix.

FEATURES

The third edition has many features that emphasize the topics and is designed to appeal to various learning styles. Many of its components give the text a solid, visual appeal.

- **Chapter Objectives**
  Each chapter begins with clearly stated learning objectives to guide readers in their studies.

Issue at a Glance
Scattered throughout each chapter are small synopses of the issues discussed. Students can see a brief summary of the topic and the critical points to be gleaned from the material.

Definitions
As each new term is introduced, it is also defined for the student. These on-the-spot definitions provide a handy reference and save the reader time.

Figures, Tables, and Diagrams
The chapters have been updated with new figures, tables, and diagrams designed to assist students with the topics and to emphasize the material in different ways.

Practical Advice
Practical examples and advice about topics as varied as drafting legal documents, interviewing clients, and billing hours are provided.

Case Excerpts
In addition to discussing the legal theory and practical applications, the author has updated the case excerpts in most chapters to reflect newer case law and recent trends in tort law.

Litigation Facts
Various figures and tables presenting a wide variety of interesting facts about negligence and personal injury cases in the United States are found throughout the text.

Skills You Need in the Real World
In many ways, the text achieves a balance between theoretical discussions and practical applications. The "Skills" sections, which come at the end of each chapter, emphasize a particular skill that all paralegals should develop. Whether discussing investigating a claim, billing hours, or conducting Internet research, this section is designed to assist paralegals in their actual, day-to-day duties.

The Life of a Paralegal
To provide additional interest, a section in each chapter highlights the work of an actual paralegal. Here, the reader hears in the paralegal's own words what working in the legal field is like and the types of activities they engage in. This section also contains tips for students about to embark on a paralegal career.

Ethical Issues for the Paralegal
Ethics is an important concern in any legal course, and it is emphasized throughout the text. Near the end of each chapter, the author discusses

topics as diverse as attorney-client privilege and avoiding insurance fraud.

Chapter Summary
At the conclusion of each chapter, a condensed overview of the material covered is provided, helping students focus on the key points raised.

Web Sites
The third edition has been updated to reflect the new and expanding offerings for students on the World Wide Web with legal sites devoted to legal issues. As before, these Web sites help the students by emphasizing topics covered in the chapters and giving the student additional resources to explore on their own.

Forms and Court Documents
This end-of-chapter section reproduces actual court pleadings that pertain to the issues discussed in the chapter, following the text's balance between concepts and practicality.

Key Terms
The author also provides a list of key terms used in the chapter.

Review Questions
Extensive review questions are provided to test the student's understanding of the important concepts raised in the chapter and to serve as a springboard for classroom discussions.

Applying What You Have Learned
This section gives students another opportunity to test their practical skills. Students are presented with problems and asked to prepare appropriate pleadings and other documents to address these concerns.

Non-Gender-Specific Language
In recognition of the impact of gender-specific language, the author has adopted the following convention in the text: each even-numbered chapter uses "he" in general discussions and examples, while the odd-numbered chapters use "she" for the same purposes.

INSTRUCTOR'S MANUAL

The instructor's manual is provided for the newest edition and contains the following much-needed resources:

Suggested Syllabi

Chapter Lecture Outline and Discussion
Each section contains some introductory remarks about the chapter and a complete chapter outline.

■ **Additional Web Resources**
These additional Web sites provide other resources for classroom discussion and assignments.

■ **Additional Assignments**
These assignments are in addition to the assignments listed in the text.

■ **Answers to Review Questions**
The end-of-chapter review questions are answered in detail.

■ **Answers to Applying What You Have Learned**
Each chapter contains a section entitled "Applying What You Have Learned." These sections are designed to provide practical, hands-on assignments for the students. This section of the Instructor's Manual lists the answers to these assignments.

■ **Test Bank**
The test bank provides a variety of test questions, including:
Essay questions (5 per chapter)
Short answer (10 per chapter)
Multiple choice (25 per chapter)
True-False (10 per chapter)

■ **Additional Features on Instructor's Manual CD**
PowerPoint Slides
The author has prepared a PowerPoint presentation for each chapter of the text.

■ **Additional Cases**
Additional cases are provided for classroom discussion. These can be used in a variety of ways, including as lecture handouts and additional assignments.

ACKNOWLEDGMENTS

The author would like to thank the following people for their assistance in preparing this book: Paula Barnes, Betsy Kenny, Richard Mixter, Debra Holbrook, Linda McCurry, Lisa McHugh, Wendy Seagle, Christina Lynn, Gwyn Huffman, Pamela Tallent, Celeste Jenks, Elizabeth Adams, Renae Elam, Christina Truitt, John Purvis, Leah Laidley, and Jane Huffman.

Neal R. Bevans

March 2009

Tort Law
for Paralegals

An Introduction to Tort Law

Chapter Objectives

- Explain the foundations of tort law
- Show the distinction between tort law and other branches of law
- Describe the differences between tort law and criminal law
- Explain the basic steps involved in a civil trial
- Describe the basic court system, including appellate court structure

INTRODUCTION TO A TORTS CASE

They had spent the day shopping. Charles Chumley, 60 years old, was driving while Julia, his wife of 35 years, was in the passenger seat beside him. They had visited a larger town about 30 miles away and had spent the day at the mall. Now they were heading home. They had lived in the town of Cling for almost 20 years. Charles had a job nearby as a shift supervisor at a plant that made wooden chairs and tables. Julia had worked for city hall as a secretary until she retired last year. For the past few months, they had enjoyed taking little shopping trips together on the weekends. Charles was looking forward to his retirement. He used to joke to her that they would get a camper and drive all over the country. Julia didn't like driving, especially long trips, but she would play along with him. Around 4:30 that Saturday afternoon, they reached the outskirts of town and turned down their street. Morgan Street hadn't changed much in 20 years. Just short of their house, a railroad track crossed Morgan Street. There wasn't a stop sign or a mechanical gate, just one "cross-buck" sign that read "Rail Road Crossing." Charles had driven across that track at least twice a day, five days a week for 20 years. The thick evergreen trees that grew near the intersection made it hard for him to see down the track.

What happened next has been pieced together from the facts. There is no dispute that when the Chumley car crossed the tracks, it was struck broadside by a 32-ton train, owned by National Railroad Company. The impact sounded like a small bomb going off, as some neighborhood people said later. The car was impaled on the front of the locomotive engine and pushed about 100 yards down the track, before the car finally rolled off the front of the railroad engine and slid into a ditch. Charles was severely injured and Julia was killed instantly.

Fortunately for Charles, a fire station was only two blocks away and it was equipped with an ambulance. Fire and rescue got to the scene in less than three minutes. They cut Charles out of the car, but there wasn't anything they could do for Julia. Charles was airlifted from the scene to a nearby city and spent several months in the hospital there. Although he almost died in intensive care, he managed to pull through. He has no memory of the collision. He walks with a cane now. He has severe, permanent injuries that prevent him from ever returning to work or even driving a car again. His wife is dead. His life has been devastated.

Charles Chumley has just walked into your law office. He wants to sue the railroad.

This is a torts case.

The term *tort* refers to any case involving a physical, financial, or emotional injury. Many states have gradually phased out this term, replacing it with the more general term *civil injury*.

Throughout this book, we discuss the many fascinating aspects of tort law, but we never stray far from this case. Because no matter how interesting a particular point of law may be, tort law in its final analysis is always about people. People get injured; people bring lawsuits; people win or lose at trial. People, like Charles Chumley, want to know what their legal options are.

A. "CAN I SUE?"

Clients always want an answer to that question. That's what Charles Chumley asks the day he walks into the law office. Mr. Chumley doesn't have any legal training, so he doesn't realize that he is asking the wrong question. The real question is: Has Mr. Chumley suffered a legal wrong for which he can receive damages?

Case type	Total trials*		Percent disposed through jury trial
	Number	Percent of total trials	
All cases	**26,948**	**100.0%**	**68.3%**
Tort cases	**16,397**	**60.8%**	**90.0%**
Motor vehicle	9,431	35.0	92.1
Medical malpractice	2,449	9.1	98.7
Premises liability	1,863	6.9	93.8
Intentional tort	725	2.7	78.3
Other or unknown tort	664	2.5	71.6
Conversion	378	1.4	46.3
Product liability	354	1.3	93.5
Asbestos	87	0.3	95.5
Other	268	1.0	92.7
Slander/libel	187	0.7	64.2
Professional malpractice	150	0.6	59.9
Animal attack	138	0.5	80.6
False arrest, imprisonment	58	0.2	63.9
Contract cases	**8,917**	**33.1%**	**36.0%**
Seller plaintiff	2,883	10.7	16.6
Buyer plaintiff	2,591	9.6	44.1
Fraud	1,114	4.1	50.2
Rental/lease	605	2.2	19.2
Other employment dispute	558	2.1	62.9
Employment discrimination	319	1.2	91.2
Mortgage foreclosure	249	0.9	3.5
Other or unknown contract	245	0.9	52.2
Tortious interference	152	0.6	61.7
Partnership dispute	119	0.4	32.3
Subrogation	82	0.3	7.4
Real property cases	**1,633**	**6.1%**	**26.4%**
Title or boundary dispute	963	3.6	15.0
Eminent domain	542	2.0	50.7
Other or unknown real property	129	0.5	9.0

FIGURE 1-1

Civil Trials in State Courts, by Case Type, 2005

Note: Detail may not sum to 100% because of rounding.
*Trial cases include all bench and jury trials, trials with a directed verdict, judgments not withstanding the verdict, and jury trials for defaulted defendants. See *Methodology* for case type definitions.

Bureau of Justice Statistics, Special Report, Civil Bench and Jury Trials in State Courts, 2005.

B. TORTS ARE LEGAL WRONGS

A tort is a legal wrong or legal injury that entitles the victim to compensation. Later we discuss how a torts case is different from a criminal case and other types of law, but there is one major element to a torts case: If a person has suffered a legally recognized wrong, then she may be entitled to compensation from the person who injured her. A tort, or a civil injury, gives the injured party a legal right. Having said that, however, not every injury entitles a person to compensation.

C. CAUSE OF ACTION

Cause of action
A legal injury on which a lawsuit can be based

Before a person can sue, he or she must have a **cause of action.** Simply put, this is an injury that is recognized at law. Say, for instance, that you are going out to your car in the parking lot. It's been a long day, and you're looking forward to getting home and relaxing a bit. However, a strange man is standing close to your car. As you walk up, you begin to feel a little apprehensive. You nod at the man, but he doesn't nod back. Feeling even more apprehensive, you reach for your car keys to unlock your door and you realize that the man is actually glaring at you. He has a very angry look on his face. You consider asking him a question, but instead you wisely get into your car. The man continues to stare at you as you start your car. You can feel his eyes on you as you back up and leave the area. Throughout this situation, the man has neither said anything nor moved, but you can *feel* his maliciousness. You drive home and although you never see the man again, you suffer from nightmares that he is coming after you.

Do you have a cause of action? Or, put another way, does the law of your state authorize a lawsuit based on these facts?

The answer, barring any additional facts, is no. Because the man didn't actually do anything and you never saw him again, there is no legally recognized claim you could bring against him. There are some things in life that people simply have to put up with. A glaring stranger is one of them. The law only permits people to bring lawsuits against others when the victim has suffered some legally recognized wrong. The fact that you felt that the man had an evil purpose, or that he gave you a mean look, does not mean that his actions rise to a legally recognized wrong. Without a wrong, or a cause of action, there can be no case. This is as true with evil looks as it is for multimillion-dollar losses. If there is no legal wrong, there is no tort.

Now take the same scenario and change one fact: As you get into your car, the man takes a swing at you and misses, then runs away. Do you have a legally recognized cause of action against him? Yes, absolutely. The man has just committed the tort of assault (discussed in Chapter 2). The important point is that the man did something that the law recognizes as a legal wrong. In some cases, as we see in later chapters, when the man fails to act, or fails to act in a reasonable manner, you may also have a cause of action against him for negligence.

D. THE BASIS OF A LAWSUIT IS A CAUSE OF ACTION

Does Charles Chumley have the basis for a lawsuit? On the face of it, the answer would seem to be yes. The state where he was injured, like all states, allows a person injured in a car wreck to sue the person who caused the wreck. The basis of the cause of action is the other person's negligence. In this case, Mr. Chumley claims that a train caused his injuries by acting in a negligent manner. Mr. Chumley is not saying that the railroad engineer deliberately or intentionally set out to hurt him. Instead, Mr. Chumley is saying that he was hurt through the carelessness of the engineer, and through him, the railroad company that he works for. The first answer we can give Mr. Chumley, at this stage, is yes, a lawsuit can be brought on these facts. That doesn't necessarily mean that the lawsuit *should* be brought. That's a different question. First, we must answer the question: How is a torts case different from other kinds of cases? Then we can outline the steps that a torts case follows.

TORT LAW COMPARED TO OTHER FORMS OF LAW

Tort law is a field of law that is as specialized in its own way as criminal law, tax law, or divorce law. Let's explore the basic differences between a torts case and a criminal case, using the scenario of the glaring stranger that we mentioned earlier.

A. WHO BRINGS THE CASE?

A torts case is brought by the individual who has suffered some legally recognized wrong. If this were a criminal case, for example, a prosecutor would bring the case. Prosecutors are the representatives of the government and seek criminal indictments against people who break the law. The prosecutor does not represent the victims; the prosecutor represents society. Although a prosecutor may work closely with the victims, the victims do not have any authority over the prosecutor. On the other hand, when a victim brings a civil suit, she often hires a lawyer to represent her interests. This lawyer works directly for the victim and must follow her instructions.

Tort case	Criminal case	**FIGURE 1-2**
Individual	Prosecutor	**Who Brings the Case?**

FIGURE 1-3	Tort case	Criminal case
Who Represents the Parties?	Civil Attorney	Prosecutor

FIGURE 1-4

Changes in the Tort Caseloads of U.S. District Courts Primarily Related to Litigation Involving Asbestos and Other Product Liability Claims

Number of tort cases terminated in U.S. district courts

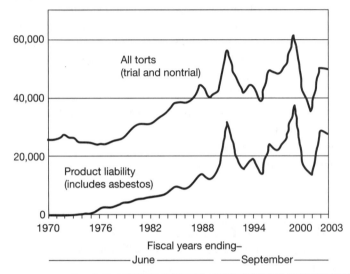

Fiscal years ending– June ——— September

■ U.S. district courts terminated approximately 512,000 civil cases during fiscal years 2002-03. Nearly 20% or 98,786 of these cases were torts in which plaintiffs claimed injury, loss, or damage from a defendant's negligent or intentional acts.

■ Of the 98,786 tort cases terminated in U.S. district courts in 2002-03, about 2% or 1,647 cases were decided by a bench or jury trial.

■ An estimated 9 out of 10 tort trials involved personal injury issues — most frequently, product liability, motor vehicle (accident), marine, and medical malpractice cases.

■ Juries decided about 71% of all tort cases brought to trial in U.S.

district courts; judges adjudicated the remaining 29%.

■ Plaintiffs won in 48% of tort trials terminated in U.S. district courts in 2002-03. Plaintiffs won less frequently in medical malpractice (37%) and product liability (34%) trials.

■ Eighty-four percent of plaintiff winners received monetary damages with an estimated median award of $201,000.

■ Plaintiffs won more often in bench (54%) than in jury (46%) tort trials. The estimated median damage awards were higher in jury ($244,000) than in bench ($150,000) tort trials.

Bureau of Justice Statistics, Federal Tort Trials and Verdicts, 2005.

In addition to the differences outlined above, the terminology we use to describe these parties is also different. When a person brings a civil suit, he or she is called a *plaintiff*. When the government brings a criminal case, it is usually referred to as the *state*, or the the *people*. One thing that often contributes to confusion about these terms is that we use the same term to refer to the other side in civil and criminal cases. That person is called the *defendant*.

B. THE PLEADINGS

Another important difference between torts cases and criminal cases has to do with the documents that begin the suit, commonly referred to as the **pleadings.** In a civil case, the plaintiff files a **complaint.** This document sets out the legal wrong that the plaintiff suffered. It also requests that the defendant pay the plaintiff monetary damages.

A criminal case usually begins with a warrant, followed by an **indictment** issued by a grand jury. The indictment details the defendant's actions and how these actions violate the law. The indictment doesn't ask for monetary damages. In fact, if the defendant loses the criminal case, she will usually go to prison.

C. CIVIL AND CRIMINAL CASES OPERATE INDEPENDENTLY OF ONE ANOTHER

When the strange man waiting by the car took a swing at you and missed, he committed the tort of assault. He may also have committed a crime. For example, if you got into your car and called the police, criminal law would be triggered and the man might get arrested. Does this mean that you cannot also sue him? Absolutely not. You can bring your lawsuit whether or not a criminal case has also been brought against the man. Civil cases and criminal cases operate independently of one another. The plaintiff's attorney doesn't work with the prosecutor. The plaintiff's attorney doesn't have to wait until the criminal case is over before bringing a civil suit. A civil suit can be brought before, during, or after a criminal case. One reason why these two cases can proceed independently of one another is that the burden of proof is different in both cases.

D. PROOF IN A CIVIL CASE IS PREPONDERANCE OF EVIDENCE

When a plaintiff brings a complaint against a defendant, she must prove her case by a preponderance of evidence. This means that the plaintiff has to prove that her allegations are "more likely than not" true. Another way of thinking about this standard is to imagine an old-fashioned, two-sided scale. If the plaintiff presents enough evidence to tilt the scales in her favor, she is entitled to win. However, the proof required in a criminal case is very different.

Pleadings
Documents that describe the legal injuries and counterclaims raised by the parties in a civil case

Complaint
Document drafted by the plaintiff's attorney and served on the defendant. It details the personal or financial injury suffered by plaintiff

Indictment
Official document issued by the grand jury, accusing the defendant of a criminal act

Sidebar
When a person chooses to represent himself without an attorney, it is referred to as proceeding pro se *(by oneself). Less than 3 percent of litigants in tort cases represent themselves.[1]*

Torts case	Criminal case	**FIGURE 1-5**
Complaint	Indictment	**Bringing the Charges**
↓	↓	
Details plaintiff's injury	Details defendant's crime	

The burden of proof in a civil case is preponderance of the evidence, which means that the plaintiff must prove that his version of the facts is true "more likely than not."

In a criminal case, the government must prove its case "beyond a reasonable doubt." The problem with this standard is that it is hard to explain. It is certainly higher than the civil requirement of preponderance of evidence, but how much more? Most commentators explain "beyond a reasonable doubt" as the requirement that the government prove its case to the point where the jury would have no commonsense objections to the government's version of what occurred.

E. TERMS ARE DIFFERENT

Damages
Money that a court orders the losing side in a civil case to pay to the other side

Liable
A finding that one of the parties in a civil case is obligated to pay damages to the other party

Guilt
The jury's determination that the defendant in a criminal case is responsible for committing a crime

In addition to a different standard of proof, the terms that we use in a torts case are different from what we use in criminal cases. At the end of a civil case, if the jury decides that the defendant should pay **damages** to the plaintiff, the defendant is held to be **liable.** At the end of a criminal case, if the jury decides that the government has proven its case against the defendant, the defendant is **guilty.** In the case of the man who took a swing at you, he could be prosecuted by the government and sued by you at the same time. Civil torts and criminal cases, although based on the same facts, actually have very little to do with one another.

TORT LAW COMPARED TO OTHER AREAS OF LAW

Obviously, tort law has many differences from (and similarities to) criminal law. How does tort law compare to other forms of civil law — for instance, business law, corporate law, and patent law, to name a few other subspecialties in law? Tort law is actually quite different from these other areas of law, as well. When parties to a contract sue one another, the cause of action is usually based on some unfulfilled promise contained in the contract. People who are parties to a contract have a relationship with one another and it is that relationship that gives rise to the suit. In a torts case, on the other hand, there is usually no requirement of relationship. A plaintiff is not even required to know the defendant. The important issue is whether the defendant's actions injured the plaintiff. In corporate law, for example, the focus is on the creation and legal obligations of various forms of businesses, from sole proprietorships to major corporations. In this book we address the topic of business torts, but other than that small overlap, there are few similarities between tort law and corporate law. As you can see, tort law is a distinct subspecialty of law and has its own rules, concepts, and historical roots.

Tort law is often referred to by the more descriptive title of "civil injuries." Actually, that title makes a great deal of sense. Torts involve physical, emotional, or financial injuries. The civil courts provide a framework for victims to attempt to receive compensation for these various injuries. Just as there are various kinds of crimes, there are various kinds of torts. This book focuses on one of the largest areas of tort law: personal injury cases. The reason for this is simple — personal injury cases are common. A paralegal is far more likely to become involved in a car wreck case than a class action product liability case. In fact, many firms limit their entire practice to car wreck cases. There is never a shortage of business.

However, this is not to say that the other kinds of torts are not important. One of the largest jury verdict awards came in a torts case but did not involve a car wreck. That verdict resulted from the foundering of the Exxon *Valdez* off the coast of Alaska. The resulting oil spill ruined miles of beaches and killed untold thousands of fish and animals. The jury that heard the negligence suit awarded punitive damages against Exxon of over $9 billion. To date, that remains the largest jury verdict in history. Whether Exxon will actually have to pay out $9 billion is another matter. At least one appellate court has said that the punitive damage award is too large and should be reduced.

 ## A SHORT HISTORY OF TORT LAW

Although the development of tort law over the past 2,000 years makes an interesting treatise on its own, we dispense with a great deal of it in this book. However, we focus attention on certain historical developments in tort law, if for no other reason than some of these legal concepts are still around today and continue to have an impact on modern lawsuits.

A. AN EYE FOR AN EYE

One of the ancient concepts in tort law had to do with the legal principle of "an eye for an eye." Under this principle, if a person intentionally cut off another person's hand, the injured man would be entitled to require amputation of the offender's hand. The practical difficulties of such a system seem apparent to us, and probably became readily apparent to the participants. Such a system does not promote a peaceful society. It also does not encourage people to use the court system to work out their differences.

B. MONEY FOR AN EYE

The concept of "an eye for an eye" quickly changed to a more modern concept of legal payment for injuries. Under this system, the various parts of a person's body were given monetary value, and damage (or loss of use) of any of these parts would require a monetary payment by the offender. Eyes and hands had the greatest value, while toes had the least. Facial scars carried more monetary value than scars on other parts of the body. Although this system seems terribly outdated, it is in fact the system that is in use today in most worker's compensation statutes. Today, when a worker is injured on the job, a dollar amount is set for damage or loss of use of a hand, an arm, or an eye, just as it was done over a thousand years ago.

This system of assigning monetary value to parts of the body also applies to negligence cases. Although there is no printed schedule stating exact amounts for body parts, the idea remains the same. One of the things that the jury will determine during the course of its deliberations is how much value to attach to the plaintiff's injuries caused by the defendant's negligence. This determination is one of the main duties of the jurors when they retire to the jury room to deliberate. First they determine if the plaintiff should win, then they determine how much the plaintiff should receive.

C. THE DEVELOPMENT OF TORT LAW IN THE UNITED STATES

Sidebar

The survivors of the sinking of the RMS Titanic had little success in negligence suits brought against the White Star Line for the disaster that occurred in 1912.

Tort law developed very slowly in the United States. Early legal treatises either neglect it entirely, or mention tort law only as a minor consideration. This situation changed dramatically with the coming of the Industrial Revolution to both England and the United States. Suddenly, there were dangerous machines operating everywhere and they were injuring people. One particular machine, the railroad locomotive, generated more lawsuits than anyone could have imagined. The law of negligence suddenly took center stage, with workers and passengers bringing suits against negligently operated railroad engines. The courts, always slow to recognize massive changes in social institutions, at first sided with the railroad companies. Recoveries were denied in the face of obvious negligence. However, this situation slowly changed over the decades, until the courts developed new theories of negligence to take into account the negligence of a public carrier. In these days of ubiquitous lawsuits brought against airline companies and others for accidents, it is difficult to comprehend that similar railroad disasters of 150 years ago spawned few cases and even fewer recoveries.

BRINGING A TORT CASE

Plaintiff
The legal title of the person who brings a complaint

The person or corporation who files a lawsuit is called the **plaintiff.** The person or corporation who is sued is called the **defendant.** Sometimes both parties have claims against one another. How do we determine who is the

Type of tort cases	Jury and bench trials terminated	
	Number	Percent
All tort trials	**1,647**	**100.0%**
Personal injury		
Total	1,464	88.9%
Airplane	16	1.0
Assault/libel/slander	37	2.2
Federal employers' liability	79	4.8
Marine	169	10.3
Motor vehicles	335	20.3
Medical malpractice	163	9.9
Product liability	210	12.8
Airplane	2	0.1
Marine	5	0.3
Motor vehicles	27	1.6
Asbestos	1	0.1
Other	175	10.6
Other personal injury	455	27.6
Property damage		
Total	183	11.1%
Fraud	66	4.0
Truth-in-lending	11	0.7
Product liability	30	1.8
Other property damage	76	4.6

Note: Detail may not sum to total because of rounding.
Source: Federal Judicial Center, Integrated Data Base (Civil), fiscal years 2002-03.

Bureau of Justice Statistics, Federal Tort Trials and Verdicts, 2005.

FIGURE 1-6

The Nature of Suit in Tort Trials Terminated in U.S. District Courts, 2002-03

plaintiff and who is the defendant? The answer is simple: Whoever files a complaint first is the plaintiff. But there is a lot more to a civil case than simply filing a complaint. In our case, before a complaint can be filed, the lawyer representing the plaintiff, Charles Chumley, has to launch an investigation to make sure that the claim Mr. Chumley is raising is valid.

Defendant
The legal title of the person who is served with the complaint

A. INVESTIGATING THE CAUSE OF ACTION: RULE 11

Not only is investigating a claim prior to filing a lawsuit a good idea, the rules of civil procedure may require it. For instance, Rule 11 of the Federal Rules of Civil Procedure (a rule that is closely followed in most states) requires that a reasonable inquiry be made into the factual basis of the lawsuit before a complaint is filed. The rule was developed as a way to attempt to reduce the number of frivolous lawsuits. Investigation can take many forms, but always focuses on discovering the facts of a claim.

B. LITIGATION CHART

One item that helps in investigating a case is a litigation chart. This chart shows all of the essential elements of the lawsuit. Prepared either for the plaintiff or the defense, this chart shows all the elements of the claim, the evidence necessary to support that claim, and the identity of the witness or evidence that will prove this claim.

Obviously the litigation chart will look different depending on which side prepares it. When the plaintiff prepares a litigation chart, the essential elements include all of the basic claims of the complaint. When the defense side prepares a litigation chart, it focuses on disproving the essential elements of the plaintiff's claim and whatever defenses will be raised at trial.

C. SOURCES OF PROOF

As the legal team investigates a claim to develop a case for trial, one aspect of the case remains paramount: evidence. Because an attorney cannot testify at trial, the only way to prove or disprove a claim is through testimony or evidence. A witness will testify either through deposition or on the witness stand about the facts of the case. Exhibits will be used to bolster or support this evidence. In other situations, evidence may be presented to disprove a claim.

| **FIGURE 1-7**

Rule 11, Federal Rules of Civil Procedure | **Rule 11. Signing Pleadings, Motions, and Other Papers; Representations to the Court; Sanctions**

(a) Signature.
Every pleading, written motion, and other paper must be signed by at least one attorney of record in the attorney's name — or by a party personally if the party is unrepresented. The paper must state the signer's address, e-mail address, and telephone number. Unless a rule or statute specifically states otherwise, a pleading need not be verified or accompanied by an affidavit. The court must strike an unsigned paper unless the omission is promptly corrected after being called to the attorney's or party's attention.

(b) Representations to the Court.
By presenting to the court a pleading, written motion, or other paper — whether by signing, filing, submitting, or later advocating it — an attorney or unrepresented party certifies that to the best of the person's knowledge, information, and belief, formed after an inquiry reasonable under the circumstances:
(1) it is not being presented for any improper purpose, such as to harass, cause unnecessary delay, or needlessly increase the cost of litigation;
(2) the claims, defenses, and other legal contentions are warranted by existing law or by a nonfrivolous argument for extending, modifying, or reversing existing law or for establishing new law;
(3) the factual contentions have evidentiary support or, if specifically so identified, will likely have evidentiary support after a reasonable opportunity for further investigation or discovery; and
(4) the denials of factual contentions are warranted on the evidence or, if specifically so identified, are reasonably based on belief or a lack of information. |

This is a sample litigation chart from a car wreck case. The allegations come directly from the complaint.

FIGURE 1-8

Litigation
Chart

Allegation	Witness	Testimony (summary)	Physical evidence
That, on or about the 19th day of October 2000, at approximately 9:40 A.M., plaintiff was operating a motor vehicle traveling west on Maple Street in Anytown, Mason County, North Carolina	Plaintiff: Jane Smith	That she was driving that day, on that street	None
The defendant driver admitted at the scene that she did not see plaintiff's vehicle before pulling out into the intersection	Officer: John Doe	Taking the statement from defendant after being called to the scene	None
That plaintiff was operating her vehicle below the posted speed limit of 35 mph	Plaintiff: Jane Smith	Ms. Smith's testimony	None
	Accident reconstructionist: Dave Jones	His study of the scene; skid marks, point of impact from glass shards	Photographs, diagrams made by Dr. Jones

In either event, it is important to know both who the witnesses are, what they are going to say, and what type of evidence the attorney intends to introduce at trial. Much of this evidence and witness testimony can be discovered long before a complaint is ever filed. We explore the types of investigations and other trial preparation issues throughout this book.

D. FILING A COMPLAINT

Once the investigation is complete, the next step in a civil suit is drafting the complaint and serving it on the defendant. Keep in mind that not all states use the same terminology. In fact, this is a good place to point out that the law in each state is unique, with its own rules, terminology, and procedures. We address the basic law of torts that can be found in all states, but always remember to check the laws of your state for differences. These differences apply to everything from the names of courts to the titles of documents in a lawsuit. For simplicity's sake, we use the same terminology throughout. We

Answer
The name of the
document that the
defendant serves on
the plaintiff, outlining
his defenses and any
claims he may have
against the plaintiff

refer to the document that sets out the plaintiff's cause of action — and begins the lawsuit — as the complaint. When the defendant responds to the complaint, he or she files a document that is usually called an **answer.**

DISCOVERY IN CIVIL CASES

Once the pleadings have been filed and served on the opposing parties, the case moves into a new phase: discovery. During the discovery phase, both sides are encouraged to learn as much about the claim in the case as possible. Courts have gradually liberalized the rules surrounding civil discovery under the theory that the more that both sides know about the case prior to trial, the more likely they are to settle the case before taking it to a jury. To that end, parties may do any or all of the following:

- Issue interrogatories
- Depose witnesses
- Request the production of documents
- Request the other side to admit to certain facts
- Request a physical and/or mental examination of a party

A. INTERROGATORIES

Interrogatories are written questions posed by one side to the other. These questions can cover a wide range of issues concerning the case and other matters. For instance, a party is permitted to ask the other side for the names, addresses, and telephone numbers of the witnesses the other side plans to call at trial, and about the general nature of the testimony, the existence of written reports about the incident, etc. As is true with all discovery requests, courts are very liberal in permitting questions and ordering the other side to provide answers.

B. DEPOSITIONS

Unlike interrogatories, depositions are oral questions of a witness. A deposition occurs weeks or even months prior to trial. At the beginning of the deposition, the witness is sworn, and is then asked questions by the attorneys. The entire deposition is conducted before a court reporter, who takes down everything that is said by the witness and the attorneys. Later, the court reporter produces a typed transcript of the questions and answers that the attorneys may review prior to trial.

C. REQUEST FOR PRODUCTION OF DOCUMENTS

Discovery rules also permit both sides to request the other side to produce documents. These requests for documents can include reports or almost any other written material relating to the incident that forms the basis of the suit.

D. REQUEST TO ADMIT FACTS

In addition to permitting either side to a suit to ask questions of the opposition, the discovery rules also allow one side to request that the other side admit to the truth of certain matters. For instance, the firm representing Mr. Chumley might serve a request to admit on the defendant railroad company requesting that it admit that it is a duly authorized corporation in the state of Placid. When a party admits to certain facts, it means that further proof is no longer required. An admitted fact is taken as true.

E. REQUEST FOR PHYSICAL AND/OR MENTAL EXAMINATION OF A PARTY

When the plaintiff's physical injuries are in dispute in a case, as they usually are in personal injury (tort) cases, the defendant is permitted to request that the plaintiff submit to a physical examination performed by a doctor chosen by the defense. In the case of Mr. Chumley, his extensive injuries are the basis of a substantial monetary claim. In this case, the defendants may very well request a physical examination by their doctor to help them determine Mr. Chumley's health.

 ## THE TRIAL OF A CIVIL CASE

When it comes to the actual trial of a civil case, there are remarkably few differences between how this trial is conducted and the way that any other trial, including a criminal case, is carried out. In fact, if you happened to enter a courtroom on any given day of the week, it might take you several minutes before you could figure out if you were watching a criminal case or a civil case. The reason for this is simple: All jury trials proceed in much the same way. The first phase of a jury trial is the selection of a jury.

A. JURY SELECTION

The parties to a civil case select a jury from a panel of citizens who have been summoned to the court for jury duty. This panel, also called the *venire,* is filled with people who are citizens of the county or state. These people come from all walks of life and all types of backgrounds. The only limitation is that a convicted felon is not allowed to sit on a jury. Short of that, there are very few limitations on who is allowed to sit on a jury.

When jury selection begins, both parties question the panel and use the answers as the basis for removing panel members until 12 jurors remain. This process is called **voir dire** or "striking" the jury, named after the process of striking off a person's name from a list. Each side in a civil case has the right to strike panel members. They usually take turns as each panel member's name is called out, either announcing that they strike or that they accept a panel member. As soon as the requisite number of jurors is selected (in some states, six-person juries can be seated), the rest of the panel is excused. At this point, the people who have been selected to sit on the jury are put into the jury box.

Voir dire
(French) "Look speak"; the process of questioning a juror to discover bias or prejudice, or who would make an acceptable juror to hear a case

B. OPENING STATEMENT

Once the jurors are seated in the jury box, the next phase in most jury trials is the opening statement. In an opening statement, the attorneys for the plaintiff and the defendant are permitted to address the jury and explain their basic positions in the case. The plaintiff's attorney goes first. He or she often begins by explaining to the jury what the case is about. After that, the attorney explains how the plaintiff was injured by the defendant's actions and how that injury entitles the plaintiff to receive monetary damages from the defendant. Once the plaintiff's attorney has addressed the jury, the defendant's attorney has the right to address the jury. Obviously, the defense opening will be very different from the plaintiff's opening. The defendant's attorney often tells the jury that the plaintiff's case is unjustified and that the plaintiff is not entitled to receive any money from the defendant. The jury has to decide which version of these two diametrically opposed viewpoints is the more reasonable.

Sidebar

On television, attorneys are often seen screaming and yelling at witnesses, or sometimes at each other. In the real world, this seldom happens. For one thing, most judges would never put up with such behavior. For another, a trial is a very formal affair, conducted by professionals. As a general rule, the attorneys are very courteous to each other and the witnesses.

C. PRESENTATION OF THE PLAINTIFF'S CASE

Once opening statements are over, the plaintiff presents her case. The plaintiff must prove the allegations she has raised in her complaint. If she has claimed that the defendant was reckless or negligent, she has to present evidence to support that claim. Proof comes in the form of witness testimony and physical exhibits. The plaintiff's attorney calls witnesses to the stand and asks them questions under oath. The purpose of this questioning, called direct examination, is to prove the claims in the complaint. The plaintiff's attorney asks the witnesses about what they saw on the day of the accident (if they are eyewitnesses) or about the plaintiff's medical troubles (if they are medical professionals). Whatever claim the plaintiff raises, she has to prove it through witnesses and exhibits. These exhibits often consist of items such as photographs, videos, documents, and medical records, among others.

Once the plaintiff's attorney has finished asking the witness questions, the defendant's attorney has the right to ask questions. This is called cross-examination. The purpose of cross-examination is very different from direct examination. In cross-examination, the defendant's attorney often attempts to show that the witness has a bias for the plaintiff or that the evidence could be interpreted in some other way, etc.

The plaintiff's case proceeds from witness to witness, exhibit to exhibit, until the plaintiff has presented all the evidence and the attorney believes that the claim has been proven. At this point, the plaintiff's attorney announces that she "rests." This announcement means that the plaintiff's case is over. At this point, the defendant will usually ask for a directed verdict.

D. MOTION FOR DIRECTED VERDICT

When the plaintiff's case is over and the plaintiff has rested, the defense normally asks the judge for permission to argue a **directed verdict motion.** At this point the jury is sent out of the courtroom and the defendant's attorney will present an argument to the judge that the plaintiff has failed to prove her case. Most defense attorneys make this argument, even if the evidence in the case has been extensive. The defense attorney has nothing to lose by making the request and everything to gain. If the judge agrees with the defense, the case will be dismissed and the defendant will pay no damages. If the judge sides with the plaintiff, the case will proceed and the defendant is in no worse a position than he was when he started.

Motion for directed verdict
A motion brought by the defense at the end of the plaintiff's case, asking that the case be dismissed because the plaintiff has failed to prove the claims raised in the complaint

E. THE DEFENSE CASE

The case for the defense closely resembles the presentation of the plaintiff's case. The defense is attempting to prove that the plaintiff has no basis for her suit, either because the defendant did not do anything wrong, or because the plaintiff was not as injured as she claimed, etc. The defense calls witnesses to the stand and these witnesses are questioned in exactly the same way as the plaintiff's witnesses were. The defense may also present exhibits. All of this evidence is designed to disprove the plaintiff's case. The plaintiff's attorney has the same right to cross-examine the defense witnesses as the defense attorney had to cross-examine the plaintiff's witnesses.

When the defendant has presented all his testimony and evidence, he makes the same announcement as the plaintiff made when she finished her case: "Your Honor, the defense rests." At this point, the trial of the case is over. No additional witnesses will testify and no other exhibits will be offered. The case is not over, however. There are still at least two more phases before the trial is complete: the closing argument and jury charge.

In some cases, the plaintiff may have the opportunity to dispute specific facts raised by the defense during its presentation. This right is called rebuttal.

F. CLOSING ARGUMENT

When the evidentiary phase of the trial is over, the attorneys have the right to address the jury one more time during closing argument. A closing argument resembles an opening statement, but only superficially. The attorneys speak directly to the jurors, explaining what they believe the evidence in the case proved. Obviously, the plaintiff will argue that the evidence proved her points. The defense attorney will just as obviously claim that the testimony and exhibits support his view of the case. Unlike an opening statement, attorneys are permitted to draw conclusions, appeal to the jurors' emotions, or argue the consequences to the community of a particular verdict.

G. THE JURY CHARGE

Once the closing arguments are complete, the judge addresses the jurors. She tells the jurors what they are supposed to do once they retire to the jury room. The judge tells the jurors how they should go about deciding the case. She also reads them the crucial legal points that factored in the case. For instance, a judge might instruct the jurors that, "One of your first duties upon retiring to the jury room will be to select one member to act as jury foreperson. This person will conduct the proceedings and alert the court when you have reached a verdict." These instructions are called *jury charges,* and provide direction for the jury about what the law on particular points is and what weight they can give to certain types of evidence.

H. THE VERDICT

Verdict
The jury's final decision in the case in which they decide questions of fact raised in the case

When the jury charge is complete, the jurors are told to leave the courtroom and sequester themselves in the jury room, where they can talk about the case. The jurors are also told that once they make up their minds, their decision, or **verdict,** should be announced to the court. The jury's verdict in a civil case often boils down to a decision about who should win. If the jury decides that the defendant should win, the verdict will be "we, the jury, find for the defendant." If they decide that the plaintiff should win, the verdict will be "we, the jury, find for the plaintiff." If the jurors find for the plaintiff, they are also instructed to decide how much money the defendant should have to pay to the plaintiff.

The basic steps in a civil trial are:

Jury selection	Closing arguments
Opening statements	Jury charge
Direct and cross-examination	Jury deliberation
of witnesses	Verdict

 **ALTERNATIVE DISPUTE RESOLUTION**

So far, our discussion has focused on the stages of a civil trial. This should not create the impression that civil cases are not settled prior to trial. In fact, most civil cases are disposed of prior to trial, either through the efforts of the parties to negotiate some mutually acceptable resolution, or through alternative dispute resolution.

A. WHAT IS ALTERNATIVE DISPUTE RESOLUTION?

Over the past two decades, alternative dispute resolution and mediation have become increasingly popular with overwhelmed court systems. The term *alternative dispute resolution,* or ADR, is shorthand for any of a variety of non-trial methods to resolve differences in civil cases. Among these methods are arbitration and mediation.

Some types of cases are not required to go through arbitration/ mediation. These include class action lawsuits or demands for injunctive relief.

Arbitration is a process in which two or more parties voluntarily agree to submit their dispute to an impartial third person for resolution. Arbitration can be either binding or nonbinding. When the parties voluntarily submit a case to an arbitrator, there is usually a stipulation in the agreement that the parties agree to be bound by the arbitrator's decisions in the case. Many states also have programs in place that force litigants in most civil cases to go through an arbitration or mediation process. The rules governing arbitration and mediation are set out in the state statutes. In North Carolina, for instance, court-ordered, nonbinding arbitration has been authorized in certain civil cases since 1989.

B. ARBITRATION VERSUS MEDIATION

When parties enter into arbitration, they agree to submit certain disputed issues to a third party. They also agree that they will follow the ruling of the arbitrator, whatever the final decision may be. Mediation, on the other hand, is an informal process designed to assist the parties to resolve their disputes among themselves. Unlike arbitrators, mediators do not make an award or render a judgment on the merits of the action.

Arbitrators decide contested issues; mediators help the parties resolve their contested issues.

APPEALS

When one or more parties to the case are dissatisfied with the jury's verdict, they are permitted to appeal their case. Appellate courts are courts of limited jurisdiction, meaning that they can only address certain issues and make certain, limited rulings. When a party appeals her case, the appeal is not conducted as a new trial. Appellate courts do not hear witness testimony or consider evidence. They review what occurred at the trial and read the briefs submitted by the parties. In almost all cases, an appellate court is limited to three possible decisions on an appeal; the court can **affirm, reverse,** or **remand** a case.

Affirm
The appellate court agrees with the verdict, or some ruling, entered in the trial and votes to keep that decision in place

When an appellate court affirms a decision, it agrees with the lower court's decision in the case. If the decision is reversed, it means that the appellate court is changing the decision of the lower court. A reversal at the first appellate court would mean that whoever won the case in the trial court would now be the loser. A remand directs the case back to the trial court for an additional hearing on some issue. Remands are relatively rare, but when they occur, they are usually the result of some new allegation. Because the appellate court has neither the facility nor the legal authority to carry out a hearing, the only option is to send the case to a court that does have such power.

Reverse
To reverse a decision is to set it aside; an appellate court disagrees with the verdict, or some ruling, in the trial, and overturns that decision

The appellate court's decision means that one party wins and one party loses. In order to justify its decision, and to explain its reasoning, the appellate court publishes its decision in an opinion. The opinion states the important facts, law, and rationale for the court's decision. This published opinion becomes extremely valuable for legal researchers, because it explains the court's view on a particular topic. The body of published decisions is known as case law.

Remand
The appellate court requires additional information or an evidentiary hearing; it cannot conduct such a hearing itself, so it sends the case back to the trial court for the hearing, and then considers the appeal based on that hearing

A. THE IMPORTANCE OF CASE LAW

When a client asks about the "law" on a particular topic, he usually fails to realize that for legal professionals, there are several different kinds of law. For instance, statutes are created by the legislature and signed into existence by the state governor. Administrative rules and regulations are created by governmental agencies and are often considered to be just as binding as a statute. (If you are in doubt about that statement, just consider the rules and regulations of the Internal Revenue Service.) However, most clients are not aware of the fact that prior decided cases are just as binding on the legal system as are statutes.

Case law
The body of cases decided by judges who have interpreted statutes and prior cases

Case law refers to the body of judicial decisions stretching back for centuries. Appellate courts such as the U.S. Supreme Court have been deciding cases since our legal system was created. This body of legal decisions creates a vast, and sometimes confusing, body of law.

When a case goes up on appeal, the appellate courts are often called upon to interpret statutes. The court's interpretation of a statute is binding on all future litigants. The U.S. Supreme Court makes such rulings many times a year. For instance, when the U.S. Supreme Court rules that a specific type of evidence is admissible (medical narratives, for instance), this ruling is binding on the entire nation. An understanding of judicial interpretations, or case law, is critically important to a legal professional. In an area of law such as tort law, which is rich in case law but has relatively few applicable statutes, case law takes on an even more prominent role.

1. HOW IS CASE LAW CREATED?

To discuss how case law is created, we review the facts of a hypothetical case: John Doe sues Richard Roe over a car wreck. John was sitting in his car at a red light when Richard Roe, who was traveling in the same direction, rear-ended Mr. Doe. This is a pretty straightforward case, but it will help to illustrate how case law is created. At trial, Richard Roe argues a rather novel idea: that John Doe's car, which is an import with a radically different design from any other car in this country, is built so low to the ground that a driver in a more standard car would have trouble seeing it. The judge only allows Richard Roe to offer limited testimony along these lines before cutting him off. Richard Roe is allowed to use this idea as his defense to the jury, but the jury decides against him and finds for the plaintiff, John Doe. Rather than pay the damages assessed by the jury, Richard Roe takes his case up on appeal. In the court of appeals, he argues that the judge unfairly limited his right to produce evidence about the design of John Doe's car. Roe is essentially saying to the court of appeals, "If I had been allowed to present this testimony, I might have won."

B. STARE DECISIS

The court of appeals considers this argument. Because all courts are bound by the principle of **stare decisis,** their consideration of this argument takes a standard format. Stare decisis is the Latin term for *stand by decided cases.* It is an old but still very useful concept. When a court states that it will stand by decided cases, it is saying that if there is a prior decision by a court that dealt with this same issue, this court will rule the same way as that prior court, even if this court doesn't like the ruling. Stare decisis is really an issue of continuity. Judges abide by stare decisis to give everyone who appears before them some sense of predictability about what the court will do. If a judge decides that she will not follow the decision in the prior case, she must show how this case is different from the prior case. With a different case, you can have a different ruling.

> **Stare decisis**
> The principle that courts will reach results similar to those reached by courts in prior cases involving similar facts and legal issues

Let's get back to the case of *Doe v. Roe.* The court of appeals has been asked to decide if the trial judge unfairly curtailed Roe's ability to present evidence about the design of Doe's car. The first question that the judges in the court of appeals will ask themselves is: Has this same issue ever come up before? If it has, the principle of stare decisis dictates that they must rule the same way as that prior case. In researching the law, the judges discover that ten years ago, the state supreme court had a similar case before it in which a party raised a very similar claim. In that case, the state supreme court said that there was nothing improper in limiting the presentation of this evidence, so long as the party was allowed to present the defense to the jury.

This case seems very similar to the current case on appeal. The judges in the court of appeals decide to affirm.

With an order affirming the trial court's decision, Richard Roe now faces a decision. He can appeal to the state supreme court, but his chances of winning there are much lower. For one thing, most state supreme courts have the requirement of **certiorari,** or cert. Cert refers to that court's power to decide which cases it will hear on appeal. In most states, the court of appeals (or whatever name it is called) lacks the power of cert. However, most state supreme courts, and certainly the U.S. Supreme Court, have the power to decline to hear an appellate case by denying cert. Generally speaking, the state supreme court, like the U.S. Supreme Court, will only decide to hear cases that the court considers to be significant or that will help clear up some cloudy issue of the law.

Richard Roe's attorney files a request for cert with the state supreme court and, as in most cases appealed to that court, cert is denied. At this point, unless Roe thinks that he has a chance with the U.S. Supreme Court, his options are over.

At every stage of this process, Roe's attorney has had his paralegal researching the case law to see if there are any legal issues that she can raise with the court that might be successful. John Doe's legal team has also been busy reviewing the case law, but their focus has been to make sure that the decision stands.

Certiorari (cert)
The power of a court to decide which cases it will hear and which it will not

C. AN EXAMPLE OF CASE LAW

In each chapter of this book, you will find at least one case reported. In this first chapter, an appellate case is presented that is similar to the facts of the Chumley case with which we began the chapter.

CRABTREE v. JOHNSON
752 N.W.2d 36 (2008)

Vaitheswaran, J.

A dog bite precipitated a lawsuit and a subsequent directed verdict in favor of one of the defendants. The plaintiffs appeal that directed verdict ruling. We affirm in part, reverse in part, and remand.

I. Background Facts and Proceedings

Mark Johnson's girlfriend gave him a German Shepherd puppy named Cotton. Mark later moved into an apartment house owned by his father, Raymond Johnson. The house adjacent to the apartment house was separated by a field and was occupied by Wanda Crabtree and her son Christopher.

Mark sometimes chained Cotton in the yard of the apartment house. On one occasion, the dog broke loose and bit Wanda Crabtree. After this incident, Mark applied for and was granted a permit to build a fence around the back yard of his father's apartment house. Mark built the fence with some help from his father. The fence was six feet tall and had a steel door that locked with a padlock. When the fence was built, Raymond asked Mark to give up Cotton. Mark declined to do so. Raymond expressed concern about having the dog on his property.

Mark was jailed on matters unrelated to Cotton. Mark's girlfriend remained in the apartment house with Cotton. Eventually, Raymond evicted her. Cotton was left in the fenced-in back yard. Raymond informed Mark he wanted Cotton removed from the property. Mark responded by threatening to commit suicide, and Raymond relented.

Mark's girlfriend occasionally came by and threw food over the fence, as did Raymond. An animal control service was called more than once, in response to complaints that no one was caring for the dog.

After some time, Wanda Crabtree's brother, Bill Frey, moved into the apartment house and began caring for Cotton. One day, while Frey was feeding the dog, the canine escaped and ran directly toward Wanda's son, Christopher, who was leaving his house. The dog severely bit Christopher.

Wanda filed a lawsuit against Mark and Raymond Johnson on behalf of herself and her son. She urged three theories of liability: (1) a dog owner's liability under Iowa Code §351.28 (2005), (2) a landowner's liability, and (3) negligence. Later, Clinton National Bank, conservator for Christopher, was substituted as a plaintiff.

The district court granted a directed verdict in favor of Raymond on all three claims. A jury found against Mark and awarded Christopher and Wanda damages of almost $240,000.

The sole issue on appeal is whether the district court erred in directing a verdict in favor of Raymond Johnson. *Yates v. Iowa West Racing Ass'n*, 721 N.W.2d 762, 768 (Iowa 2006) ("We review the district court's rulings on motions for directed verdict for correction of errors at law.").

II. Analysis

A. Statutory Liability under Iowa Code §351.28

Iowa Code section 351.28 provides that a dog owner is strictly liable for injuries caused by the dog:

> The owner of a dog shall be liable to an injured party for all damages done by the dog, when the dog . . . is attacking or attempting to bite a person, except when the party damaged is doing an unlawful act, directly contributing to the injury. This section does not apply to damage done by a dog affected with hydrophobia. . . .

Iowa Code §351.28. The plaintiffs argue Raymond effectively became the dog's owner after Mark went to jail, subjecting him to strict liability under this statutory provision.

The problem with their argument is that an "owner" has been narrowly defined as "the person to whom the dog legally belongs." *Alexander v. Crosby*, 143 Iowa 50, 53, 119 N.W.2d 717, 718 (1909). In Alexander, the court specifically stated "nothing in other decisions indicates a construction of the word 'owner' as including those who may harbor dogs." Id.

Here, the evidence established as a matter of law that Mark Johnson, not Raymond, was Cotton's legal owner. Specifically, it was undisputed that Mark received the dog as a gift and did not transfer ownership of the dog to anyone else. Because (1) section 351.28 only holds "the owner" strictly liable for dog bites, (2) case law defines "owner" as "legal owner," and (3) Raymond was not the legal owner, the district court did not err in granting Raymond's motion for directed verdict on this claim.

B. Common Law Dog Bite Claim

Although pled as a "landowner's liability" claim, the plaintiffs next raise a common law claim based on harboring a dangerous dog. Specifically, they argue "the trial court should have allowed the jury to decide whether Raymond Johnson was strictly liable . . . because he kept a dog which he knew or should have known to have dangerous tendencies on his property. . . ." To support their argument, they rely on dicta contained in *Wenndt v. Latare*, 200 N.W.2d 862, 869-70 (Iowa 1972). There, the court stated, "The owner or keeper of domestic animals is liable for injuries inflicted by them only where . . . the injuries are the result of known vicious tendencies or propensities." Wenndt, 200 N.W.2d at 869-70. As a preliminary matter, we must address Johnson's argument that "Wenndt did not create an alternative theory of liability," and "liability is appropriately addressed by §351.28." The district court rejected this argument noting "the common law theory survives if properly pled and proven." We agree with this reasoning because our supreme court has addressed common law theories of liability in addition to the statutory theory of liability set forth in section 351.28. Returning to the common law theory articulated in Wenndt, the plaintiffs note that the language on which they rely is consistent with the Restatement (Second) of Torts, section 509. That provision states:

> (1) A possessor of a domestic animal that he knows or has reason to know has dangerous propensities abnormal to its class, is subject to liability for harm done by the animal to another, although he has exercised the utmost care to prevent it from doing the harm.
> (2) This liability is limited to harm that results from the abnormally dangerous propensity of which the possessor knows or has reason to know.

The comments to this section are instructive. Comment c states:

> One who keeps a large dog which he knows to be accustomed to fawn violently upon children and adults is liable under the rule stated in this Section for harm done by its dangerous playfulness or over-demonstrative affection.

Comment d states:

> One who keeps a domestic animal which to his knowledge is vicious, or which though not vicious possesses dangerous propensities that are abnormal, thereby introduces a danger which is not usual to the community and which, furthermore, is not necessary to the proper functioning of the animal for the purposes that it serves.

Comment f states:

> Although dogs, even hunting dogs, have no material utility comparable to cattle, horses and other livestock, they have from time immemorial been regarded as the friends and companions of man. The great majority of dogs are harmless and the possession of characteristics dangerous to mankind or to livestock are properly regarded as abnormal to them. Consequently the possessor of a dog is not liable for its biting a person or worrying or killing livestock unless he has reason to know that it is likely to do so.

Comment g states:

> A dog is not necessarily regarded as entitled to one bite. It is enough that the possessor of the animal knows that it has on other occasions exhibited such a tendency to attack human beings or other animals or otherwise to do harm as should apprise him of its dangerous character. Restatement (Second) of Torts §509 at 15-18 (1965).

This Restatement provision is consistent with the common law of our state. Applying the provision, we are convinced the plaintiffs generated a fact question on this claim. Although Raymond was not an owner of Cotton, a reasonable fact finder could conclude he was a "possessor" of the dog after Mark left the apartment house and Raymond evicted Mark's girlfriend. Raymond allowed the dog to stay in the pen, fed and watered it sometimes, and responded to calls from animal control services. He did not remove the dog after the animal control service visited his property, but instead attempted to feed and water Cotton more regularly. Frey testified he agreed to care for the dog in return for Raymond's $50 deduction in his rent. Raymond provided the food for Cotton. Frey further testified Raymond gave him a key to the pen that Cotton lived in. Raymond admitted he was concerned about keeping Cotton on the property after the dog bit Wanda Crabtree. Based on this evidence, we conclude the claim should have been submitted to the jury for resolution. Accordingly, we reverse the district court's grant of a directed verdict as to this issue.

C. Negligence

Finally, the plaintiffs argue the court erred in directing a verdict in Raymond's favor on his negligence claim. To establish negligence, the plaintiffs had to prove (1) the existence of a duty, (2) breach of that duty, (3) proximate cause, and (4) damages. *Raas v. State,* 729 N.W.2d 444, 447 (Iowa 2007).

We begin with the duty element. The plaintiffs cite *Allison v. Page,* 545 N.W.2d 281, 283 (Iowa 1996) for their assertion that a duty existed. There, the court was asked to decide whether "a landlord is liable for an injury inflicted by a tenant's dog when the landlord knew or had reason to know that the dog was dangerous." The court was asked to apply Restatement (Second) of Torts section 379A, which subjects a lessor to liability for harm to persons off the land "caused by activities of the lessee or others on the land after the lessor transfers possession," but only if,

> (a) the lessor at the time of the lease consented to such activity or knew that it would be carried on, and
> (b) the lessor knew or had reason to know that it would unavoidably involve such an unreasonable risk, or that special precautions necessary to safety would not be taken.

Restatement (Second) of Torts §379A at 283 (1965). The court "declined the plaintiffs' invitation to apply section 379A to animals not owned or controlled by the landlord." Allison, 545 N.W.2d at 283. Finding that the landlords "did not own or harbor the dog," the court concluded they "owed no duty to third persons to protect them from the dog." Id. at 284.

The duty addressed under section 379A applies to lessors, and differs in kind from the duty alluded to in Wenndt and articulated in Restatement (Second) of Torts section 509. However, the evidence supporting a duty under 379A overlaps the evidence supporting a duty under section 509. Without detailing that evidence, we conclude the plaintiffs generated a fact question as to whether Raymond owed a duty as lessor under section 379A.

This does not end our inquiry, however, because the plaintiffs also had to show a breach of that duty by Raymond. On this element, the plaintiffs alleged Raymond acted negligently by: (1) allowing a dangerous dog to remain on his property, (2) allowing the dog to be neglected, (3) failing to properly confine Cotton, (4) failing to properly instruct Bill Frey as to how to care for Cotton and keep the dog from escaping, (5) failing to warn Frey of Cotton's dangerous propensity, and (6) placing Cotton in the care of a person "not suitable to care for the dog." The district court concluded the plaintiffs did not present sufficient evidence to generate a fact issue on any of these specifications.

We agree with the court that the plaintiffs failed to generate a fact issue on three of the six specifications of negligence. Specifically, the plaintiffs presented no evidence on the third specification of negligence that Raymond failed to properly confine Cotton. In fact, the undisputed evidence establishes that Raymond helped erect a six-foot fence around the yard with a padlocked door. The plaintiffs also presented scant, if any, evidence on the fourth specification of negligence that Raymond failed to properly instruct Bill Frey as to how to care for Cotton and keep him from escaping. Finally, the plaintiffs did not present evidence on the sixth specification of negligence that Frey was "not suitable to care for the dog." Therefore, the district court did not err in directing a verdict in favor of Raymond on these specifications of negligence.

Turning to the first and fifth specifications of negligence, we conclude the plaintiffs generated a fact issue that required submission to the jury. Specifically, a reasonable fact-finder could conclude Raymond allowed a dangerous dog to remain on his property, and failed to warn Frey of Cotton's dangerous propensity.

This brings us to the proximate cause element. We conclude the plaintiffs did not generate a fact question on the second specification of negligence, whether Raymond allowed the dog to be neglected. Although there was evidence of neglect, there was no evidence that the neglect was the proximate cause of the dog bite. Therefore, the district court did not err in directing a verdict for Raymond on this specification. We conclude the plaintiffs generated a fact question on whether the breaches alleged in the first and fifth specifications of negligence were the proximate cause of Christopher Crabtree's damages. See *Rieger v. Jacque*, 584 N.W.2d 247, 251 (Iowa 1998) (stating proximate cause ordinarily for jury to decide absent exceptional circumstances). Accordingly, we reverse the grant of a directed verdict in favor of Raymond on these specifications.

III. Disposition

We affirm the district court's grant of a directed verdict in favor of Raymond Johnson on the statutory liability claim. We reverse the district court's grant of a directed verdict in favor of Raymond Johnson on the claim styled "land-owners' liability" and remand for further proceedings on this claim. We reverse the district court's grant of a directed verdict in favor of Raymond Johnson on the first and fifth specifications of the plaintiffs' negligence claim and remand for further proceedings on those specifications.

AFFIRMED IN PART, REVERSED IN PART, AND REMANDED.

Questions about the case:

1. What are the facts leading up to the dog bite in this chapter's case excerpt?
2. Is a dog owner strictly liable for the injuries caused by his or her dog?
3. Under Iowa law, who is considered to be the "owner" of a dog?
4. According to the court, what liability does a dog owner have when the dog is known to be vicious?
5. Is it possible that Raymond could be liable for the dog bite in this case?

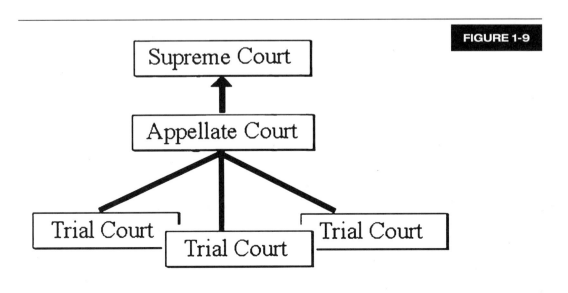

FIGURE 1-9

 SKILLS YOU NEED IN THE REAL WORLD

How a Paralegal Can Do Some Basic Investigative Work

Most paralegals are not trained to carry out investigations. Many would be surprised to learn that knowing basic investigative techniques could be a real asset in the marketplace. When a firm needs basic information about a case, the most common method of obtaining it is for the attorney to investigate the basic details and then rely on discovery to ferret out additional details. However, there are times when this process is not efficient. Some cases do not have the financial resources to justify an attorney's time. In such a situation, the other alternative — a private detective — may also be too costly. Not all clients can afford the added expense of a private investigator. However, a paralegal who knows some basic investigative techniques can learn a great deal about a case, with less of a cost investment, and that paralegal will become even more indispensable to the firm in the process.

What Facts Do You Need?

Before a paralegal can begin to investigate a claim, she must first decide what facts are the most important to discover. For a plaintiff's firm, the most important facts are those that support the cause of action. Without that support, there can be no valid claim.

Using Public Records to Gather Information

Suppose your firm is investigating the defendant (or the person who will be the defendant if the lawsuit is actually filed). What public records can help a paralegal learn more information about this person? The best place to start is the local courthouse.

The Courthouse

The local courthouse is a gold mine of information, if you know where to look. Consider the following resources:

- **Clerk's Office**   The local clerk's office maintains records about all civil and criminal cases in the county. Using the computer databases, a paralegal can learn whether someone has been sued, divorced, or convicted of a crime.
- **Deed Room or Registrar's Office**   Sometimes called the registrar's office, or the land office, the deed room is where all records of real estate transactions are stored. In this office, a paralegal can find out what real estate a defendant owns (useful in evaluating the likelihood of enforcing a judgment against him).
- **Tax Office**   The tax office is required to keep extensive records about real estate and other items. In some tax offices, you can even see a digital photo of the house. In larger counties, such as metropolitan areas, this information is available at public access terminals. A picture of the house and all of the details are just a mouse click away.

Internet

The Internet also offers some valuable research tools. There are numerous sites that allow you to search out a person's address, telephone number, e-mail address, and other information. However, there are also questionable sites that claim to provide you with a complete background on a person for a nominal fee. Unless the site is one that you recognize as a reputable company, you should avoid such sites. There is a great deal of free information available about persons, but if you plan on paying for research, the best bet is still a private detective.

Keep these sources in mind if you are ever called upon to do some basic investigative work in a case.

THE LIFE OF A PARALEGAL

Going to Court with the Attorney

When I go to court, I give the attorney my point of view and input with regard to jury selection. It can be very important. For one thing, it helps to keep all of the witnesses' information straight and keep up with their testimony. The attorneys often find that it's helpful to have another person in the courtroom who is listening for all sorts of things. [One] of the other things that I do is to keep the witnesses prepared and on standby, coordinating when they need to be called to come on in. I also keep the exhibits straight and the file in order so that I can put my hands on anything that the attorney might require without having to shuffle through an unorganized file.

Debra Holbrook, Paralegal

ETHICAL ISSUES FOR THE PARALEGAL: AN INTRODUCTION

Paralegals must have a finely developed sense of ethics. For one thing, a solid basis in ethical standards will keep a paralegal from violating an attorney's ethics. When a paralegal engages in unethical practices, this reflects on the attorney. The attorney may get sanctioned by the state bar and be sued for legal malpractice. In recent years, paralegals have also been named in such suits. Throughout this text, we explore ethical issues for paralegals involved in civil cases.

To begin with, a paralegal should read and understand the ethical obligations of the attorney. These rules can be found in the state bar's handbook, on the bar Web site, or in the published court rules. An hour or two spent with these rules can save a paralegal a great deal of heartache later on.

Chapter Summary

A tort is a legal wrong that gives the wronged party the right to seek redress in court. When a person files an action claiming a civil injury, she is seeking damages or other compensation for a wrong carried out by another. Tort law is civil in nature and differs from other areas of law, such as criminal law, in several important ways. When a plaintiff initiates a case against a defendant, both the pre-trial procedures and the trial itself follow a predictable pattern from the filing of the complaint to the jury's verdict. Once the jury has decided the case and rendered a verdict, the dissatisfied party is permitted to appeal his case. On appeal, an appellate court can affirm the trial court's decision, reverse the decision, or remand for further determinations. The appellate court's decision is recorded in an opinion that is published for all others to read and forms the basis of case law, one of the foundations of judicial interpretation.

Web Sites

- **Lexis-Nexis**
  http://www.lexisnexis.com/

- **Legal resource links on personal injury cases**
  http://www.legalresourcelinks.com/group8

- **Understanding mass personal injury litigation**
  http://www.rand.org/publications/RB/RB9021/RB9021.word.html

- **Personal Injury and Tort Law Cornell University**
  http://www.law.cornell.edu/topics/torts.html

- **Westlaw**
  http://www.westlaw.com

- **Harassment/emotional distress links**
  http://www.lawlib.state.ma.us/harassment.html

- **What is tort law? Locke Institute**
  http://www.thelockeinstitute.org/journals/tortlaw3.html

- **Jurist: Tort Law Guide**
  http://jurist.law.pitt.edu/sg_torts.htm

Forms and Court Documents

You will find this section at the conclusion of each chapter of this book. It is designed to provide you with examples of actual court documents, pleadings, and other relevant topics. Your first form consists of a basic negligence complaint. This complaint involves a car wreck — one of the most common forms of personal injury torts.

IN THE SUPERIOR COURT OF GANNETT COUNTY
STATE OF PLACID

John Doe,	)	CASE NO. CV 2003-0034
Plaintiff	)	
	)	
vs.	)	
	)	
Rhonda Roe,	)	
Defendant	)	

Complaint

COMES NOW, the plaintiff, John Doe, and complaining of the defendant alleges the following:

1.

The Plaintiff is a citizen and resident of Gannett County, Placid.

2.

The Defendant is, upon information and belief, a citizen and resident of Union County, Placid.

3.

On or about February 2, 2002, at approximately 10:30 A.M., the Plaintiff, John Doe, was operating a 1999 Honda Civic automobile, which was owned by the Plaintiff, in a general westerly direction along US Highway 22, within the County of Gannett in the state of Placid.

4.

At the time and place and on the occasion stated in paragraph #3, the defendant was operating a 1994 Ford pickup truck in a westerly direction along the same road as that being traveled by the Plaintiff, John Doe, approaching the location of the Plaintiff, John Doe.

5.

It is further alleged upon information and belief that at all times relevant hereto, the Defendant owned the 1994 Ford vehicle being driven by the Defendant.

6.

At the time and place stated above, the Plaintiff, John Doe, had slowed and stopped his 1999 Honda automobile in respect and in obedience to a traffic light emitting a signal compelling him to stop.

7.

At the time and place stated above, the 1994 Ford being operated by the Defendant did, without justification, and without warning, drive into and collide with the rear of the vehicle operated by the Plaintiff, while the Plaintiff's automobile was at a complete stop in obedience and in conformity with the traffic signal.

8.

The defendant was negligent in that she:
a. Failed to keep reasonable and proper control of her vehicle
b. Failed to keep and maintain a reasonably safe and proper lookout in her direction of travel
c. Drove her vehicle carelessly and in willful and wanton disregard of the rights and safety of others including the Plaintiff, John Doe.

9.

That as a proximate cause of the Defendant's negligence, the Plaintiff, John Doe, suffered severe and permanent injuries in excess of $10,000.00.

WHEREFORE, the Plaintiff prays that the Court:
1. That the Plaintiff, John Doe, have and recover a judgment against the Defendant in an amount in excess of $10,000.00 for personal injuries.
2. That the Plaintiff have and recover of the Defendant a sum to be determined at trial, but in any event, no less than $10,000.00 for damage to personal property.
3. That prejudgment interest be awarded as provided by law.
4. That the costs of this action be taxed against the Defendant.
5. That all issues raised be tried before a jury.
6. For such other and further relief as the Court may deem just and proper.

This the _____ day of May, 2003.

_____

Clarence D. Arrow
Attorney for Plaintiff, John Doe
State Bar No. 000-998

Key Terms

Affirm	Cause of action	Damages
Answer	Certiorari	Defendant
Case law	Complaint	Guilt

Indictment	Plaintiff	Stare decisis
Liable	Pleadings	Verdict
Motion for directed verdict	Remand	Voir dire
	Reverse	

Review Questions

1 What is a cause of action?
2 How is tort law different from criminal law?
3 What are the names of the parties who bring a civil suit?
4 Explain the difference between a complaint and an answer.
5 Explain the difference between the burden of proof in a civil case and a criminal case.
6 What is a litigation chart and how does it help the parties prepare for trial?
7 What are some of the public records that can provide helpful information in investigating a case?
8 How is case law developed? Why is it important?
9 Explain stare decisis.
10 List and describe the basic steps of a civil trial.

Applying What You Have Learned

1 Search the Internet for general sources about tort law. How many sites can you find that provide guidance about the general law of torts, especially for such issues as the history of tort law, arbitration, and trials of civil cases?
2 Refer to your local newspaper for examples of recent automobile accidents or other actions that may result in a tort action. Summarize the facts involved, and identify the potential parties in a civil tort action.
3 How is your local courthouse organized? What types of public records are available there? What records could you use to investigate a potential defendant?

Endnote

[1]Bureau of Justice Statistics, Department of Justice, Civil Justice Survey of State Courts, 1992, p. 2.

Intentional Torts

Chapter Objectives

- Introduce the basic elements of intentional torts
- Show how intentional torts differ from torts involving negligence
- Point out the important types of information that a paralegal should obtain from a client
- Describe the elements of intentional torts to property
- Explain how an intentional tort is proved at trial

 **THE CHUMLEY CASE**

Unlike almost every other chapter in this book, we do not begin this chapter with a discussion of the Chumley case. The simple reason is that the Chumley case does not involve an intentional tort. An **intentional tort** is one in which the defendant acted purposefully to injure the plaintiff. Most car wreck cases involve acts of negligence. As we see in later chapters, lawsuits involving negligence revolve around the issue of proper care and reasonable conduct, but not intentional actions. If a defendant intentionally runs over the plaintiff

Intentional tort
A civil action based on a defendant's purposeful, intentional act that causes harm, as opposed to a defendant's act that causes harm through negligence

35

with his car, that is not a negligence case. That is a case involving an intentional tort. If a defendant fails to stop for a red light and by so doing causes a car wreck with the plaintiff, the result will be action for negligence. We spend several chapters discussing negligence cases, primarily because the vast majority of court cases involve negligence. But in this chapter, we discuss intentional torts.

THE PROBLEM WITH INTENTIONAL TORTS

Most civil lawsuits do not involve intentional torts. The vast majority of civil lawsuits involve car wreck cases, otherwise known as personal injury cases. On any given day in a courthouse anywhere in America, you are far more likely to see a civil trial that involves a car wreck or a divorce than a trial involving intentional torts. This is not because people do not intentionally injure each other. Unfortunately, people hurt, maim, and kill each other every day. The problem with intentional torts is that there is a large overlap between this area of law and criminal law. In fact, when you use the term *assault* most people will jump to the conclusion that you are talking about the crime of assault, not the tort of assault.

Personal injury cases refer to lawsuits involving negligence, such as car wrecks, slip and fall cases, and product liability cases.

As we mentioned in the first chapter, there is a good deal of overlap in terminology and procedure between criminal cases and civil cases. This overlap is even more striking when we examine intentional torts. Not only is there a great deal of overlap in terminology, but when we discuss many intentional torts the elements — the basic points of proof — are identical between crimes and intentional torts. As you can imagine, this often causes a great deal of confusion.

In the first chapter, we used the example of a person taking a swing at you while you are getting into your car. This is the crime of assault. It is also the tort of **assault.** The person who took a swing at you could be prosecuted for a crime, but you could also sue him civilly for the tort. The important difference in these two lawsuits involves the outcome of the case. A criminal prosecution could land the man in jail, while the civil case could compel him to pay you monetary damages.

Before discussing these specific intentional torts, we should take a few moments to address some of the specific problems with intentional torts. One problem is that intentional torts often sound like crimes. For instance,

Case type	Total trials	
	Number	Plaintiff winners*
All cases	**23,445**	**56.4%**
Tort cases	**15,428**	**51.6%**
Animal attack	125	75.2
Motor vehicle	8,844	64.3
Product liability (asbestos)	82	54.9
Intentional tort	609	51.6
Conversion	296	48.3
Other or unknown tort	606	41.1
Slander/libel	175	39.4
Professional malpractice	143	39.2
Premises liability	1,827	38.4
Medical malpractice	2,397	22.7
Product liability (other)	265	19.6
False arrest, imprisonment	58	15.5
Contract cases	**8,016**	**65.6%**
Mortgage foreclosure	245	89.4
Seller plaintiff	2,610	74.6
Partnership dispute	102	65.7
Rental/lease	531	62.5
Buyer plaintiff	2,252	62.3
Employment discrimination	307	60.9
Tortious interference	146	60.3
Other or unknown contract	214	59.3
Fraud	1,041	59.1
Other employment dispute	519	50.9
Subrogation	51	27.5

FIGURE 2-1

Percent of Plaintiff Winners in Civil Trials in State Courts, by Case Type, 2005

Note: Data on plaintiff winners were not applicable to real property cases. Data on plaintiff winners were available for 99.6% of all tort and contract trials.
*Includes cases in which both the plaintiff and defendant won damages and the plaintiff award amount was greater than the defendant award amount. Excludes the 1,884 bifurcated trials in which the plaintiff litigated only the damage claim.

Civil Bench and Jury Trials in State Courts, 2005, October 2008, U.S. Department of Justice.

there is the crime of battery and there is the tort of **battery.** As we have already seen in Chapter 1, a civil case can proceed before, during, or after a criminal case has been brought. Intentional torts are all based on the premise that the defendant knowingly and intentionally caused the action that harmed the victim.

Battery
When the defendant causes harmful or offensive contact to the plaintiff

ASSAULT AND BATTERY

The torts of assault and battery are often intertwined and sometimes confused. However, it is important to keep the **elements** of each clearly delineated. We begin our discussion with the tort of assault.

Elements
The points raised by the plaintiff in his complaint that must also be proved at trial; failure to prove these points will often result in a dismissal of the plaintiff's case

A. THE ELEMENTS OF ASSAULT

In order to prove the tort of assault, the plaintiff must show:

- that the defendant intentionally caused the plaintiff to have
- fear or apprehension of a
- harmful or offensive contact.

When we discuss the elements of a particular tort, we are really talking about what the plaintiff must prove in order to win a trial. For instance, in the tort of assault, the plaintiff must prove that the defendant did knowingly and intentionally cause fear or apprehension to the victim of a harmful or offensive contact. If we break these elements down and list them separately, we come up with a table that looks like this:

Element	Proof
Defendant did knowingly and intentionally	Testimony that the defendant acted voluntarily
Cause apprehension	Plaintiff's testimony about his reaction to the defendant's actions
Of a harmful or offensive contact	Plaintiff's testimony about what the contact defendant did

Prima facie
(Latin) "At first sight"; the party has presented adequate evidence to prove a particular point

As you can see from the table, each of these elements stands separate and apart from the other elements. If the plaintiff presents evidence about each element, he has made a **prima facie** or basic case against the defendant. If the plaintiff fails to prove one of the essential elements, the case against the defendant will fail. The plaintiff must present sufficient evidence to prove each and every allegation against the defendant. By failing to prove that the defendant acted knowingly and intentionally, the plaintiff has failed to meet his burden. A plaintiff can present evidence or testimony to establish any of these elements. However, it is always up to the jury to decide whether the plaintiff has presented enough evidence. In cases where a judge acts as the jury, such as in a bench trial, it is the judge's responsibility to determine if the plaintiff has presented enough evidence. If the plaintiff fails to present sufficient evidence, the jury is authorized to find for the defendant. In other words, the jury will vote that the defendant is not liable. Later in this chapter, there is a checklist that you can use to help establish the basic facts for any intentional tort. We also discuss some of the investigative techniques that paralegals use to investigate defendants and other witnesses.

When a person assaults another person, he causes the victim to undergo fear or apprehension that he is about to receive a harmful or offensive contact. There is no touching in an assault. When a person swings a fist at the plaintiff and misses, this is an assault and the plaintiff can bring a civil suit against the attacker. Let's examine the elements of the tort and explain how these elements become important during the trial.

1. THE DEFENDANT'S ACTIONS ARE INTENTIONAL

Although this sounds like a very obvious point, it is worth mentioning that the defendant's action must be intentional. The word *intent* carries a very specific meaning in law. When a person acts intentionally, it does not mean that he had a specific result in mind. A child will often say, "I didn't intend to hurt you," when he hits his friend with a stick. Although that defense may work on the playground, it won't work in the courtroom. The test of the defendant's intent is not what the ultimate result is; the test for intent is whether the defendant acted voluntarily and knowingly. Suppose you are in a crowded movie theater and the man next to you has an epileptic seizure. As he flails about, his hand strikes your face. Most people would agree that the man's actions are not intentional, that is, that he did not voluntarily and knowingly strike you, so he should not be held accountable for the damage he caused. This is the standard we use to determine intent.

2. FEAR OR APPREHENSION

In an assault, actual fear is not a requirement. The victim must simply be apprehensive of the contact. Because awareness is a requirement, a victim cannot be assaulted if he or she is unconscious. Unconscious people cannot be fearful or apprehensive, so an assault cannot be committed against them.

The defendant must have the apparent ability to carry through the threat of violence. If, for instance, a man is holding a baseball bat and screams at a woman passerby, "I'm going to hit you with this bat!," this may constitute an assault. If the man swings the bat and misses the woman, an assault has certainly occurred. However, if the man is standing on the other side of a tall fence, with no way to get to the woman, and he repeats the same threat, he now lacks the apparent ability to put the threat into action and no assault has occurred.

The threat must be imminent and cannot be a future threat, such as "I'll hit you with this bat at 3 o'clock!"

Sidebar

Of the 3,356 tort cases disposed of in 1994-95 in the federal court system, 1.8 percent involved assault and battery.[1]

3. HARMFUL OR OFFENSIVE CONTACT

Assault involves the fear or apprehension of contact. However, the intended contact must be harmful or offensive. There is no requirement that the intended victim would have been seriously injured had the contact occurred. Because different people have different standards about what they consider "offensive" touching, most states approach this issue from the hypothetical reasonable person standard. The question becomes, would a reasonable person have considered this attempted contact to be harmful or offensive? If the answer is yes, an assault has occurred. The law does not take into account the subjective feelings of a particular victim.

The reasonable person standard is a guideline that courts use as an alternative to the subjective viewpoints of the parties involved.

ISSUE
AT A
GLANCE

B. THE ELEMENTS OF BATTERY

If an assault is an attempted battery, battery is a completed assault. In a lawsuit over battery, the plaintiff must prove that the defendant made knowing and voluntary, intentionally offensive, or harmful contact with the plaintiff.

To prove the tort of battery, the plaintiff must show:

- that the defendant intentionally
- made contact with the plaintiff that was
- harmful or offensive.

1. DEFENDANT ACTED INTENTIONALLY

In all intentional torts, the plaintiff must prove that the defendant acted voluntarily and knowingly. Just as we saw with assault, if the defendant inadvertently strikes another person, such as when someone bumps into you in a crowded restaurant, because the person did not act intentionally, there is no tort of battery.

2. WHAT DO WE MEAN BY "CONTACT"?

In battery, the term *contact* refers to any contact with the plaintiff, no matter how slight. This contact can consist of the defendant actually reaching out and touching the plaintiff with his hands. It can also be accomplished by other means. If a person throws a rock at you and strikes you on the head, that certainly qualifies as contact. Under the strict interpretation of the law, though, because the person who threw the rock is not holding it when it strikes you, can this qualify as a battery? Both law and common sense say yes. Battery can occur by physical touching and it can occur through other means, too.

a. Making Contact with Weapons or Other Objects

The law recognizes that when a defendant uses a weapon to make contact with the plaintiff, this is as much of a battery as when the defendant uses his own hands. The same rule applies to other objects. Harmful or offensive contact with the plaintiff through any object that the defendant uses qualifies as a battery, as long as the defendant acted intentionally.

b. The Connection Between the Defendant's Actions and Ultimate Harm

Proximate cause
Proof that the defendant's actions were the legal cause of the plaintiff's injuries (see Chapter 7)

This is a good place to discuss one other point that we return to in several other chapters: **proximate cause.** For example, let's suppose that two men get into an argument at their sons' hockey game. One man attacks the other and beats him severely. We'll call the victim John and the attacker Steve. In this scenario, there is no question that a battery has occurred. An ambulance arrives and takes John to the hospital. On the way there, the ambulance driver, who is drunk, gets into a wreck and John is injured even more severely. The issue becomes, is Steve liable for these new injuries to John? This is the concept of proximate cause. As we see in later chapters, proximate cause is a doctrine in tort law that requires a strong connection between the defendant's actions and the ultimate harm to the plaintiff. Closely tied to proximate cause is the issue of **foreseeability.** The law of proximate cause dictates that Steve will be liable for all foreseeable injuries to John, but will not be liable for injuries that were not foreseeable. In this scenario, Steve will be liable for the injuries he caused to John, but will probably not be liable for Steve's additional injuries caused by the car crash. We discuss proximate cause in much greater detail in Chapter 7.

Foreseeability
The legal requirement that the plaintiff be a person who would likely be injured by the defendant's conduct

The importance of proximate cause to society arises from the recognition that there should be an eventual termination of a person's liability. Here is another example: Marcy sees Barbara in the parking lot of a grocery store and shoves a shopping cart at her, hoping to knock her over. The shopping cart misses Barbara, but because the incident causes her some fear, she has an action for assault. The shopping cart continues to roll across the parking lot, and because it is on the side of a hill, it continues to roll to the street. Several drivers swerve to miss the shopping cart and one of them hits a telephone pole. The shopping cart comes to rest in a vacant lot. Several years later, Rick is surveying the lot and trips over the shopping cart and breaks his leg. Under proximate cause, which of these people has an action against Marcy?

Let's take it one by one. First of all, Barbara certainly has an action against Marcy for assault, because the incident meets all of the elements for that tort. What about the driver who swerved to miss the shopping cart and struck the telephone pole? Because there is a strong connection between the harm to the driver and Marcy's actions, the law would probably allow an action by the driver against Marcy. What about Rick, the surveyor? There doesn't seem to be a close connection between Marcy's actions and Rick's broken leg. Proximate cause was developed to give some closure to a person's liability. We have all done things in the past that could come back to haunt us decades later. Under proximate cause, Rick's lawsuit against Marcy (assuming that he could even figure out who caused the shopping cart to be there in the first place) would probably be dismissed at trial because of the causation problem. After all, there should come a point in a chain of events when the original person is no longer responsible for what happens.

Proximate cause **is the term for the legal standard courts use to determine the liability of the defendant's actions. Only if the defendant's act (or failure to act) is the proximate cause of the injuries to the plaintiff will he be liable.**

ISSUE
AT A
GLANCE

FIGURE 2-2

Plaintiff Award
Winners in Civil
Trials in State
Courts, by
Case Type,
2005

Case type	Number of trials with plaintiff winner	Median final award amount	Percent of plaintiff winners with final awards				
			<$10,000	$10,001-$50,000	$50,001-$250,000	$250,001-$1 million	>$1 million
All cases	**14,170**	**$28,000**	**28.7%**	**33.0%**	**24.1%**	**9.9%**	**4.4%**
Tort cases	**8,455**	**$24,000**	**32.7%**	**30.6%**	**21.3%**	**10.4%**	**5.0%**
Product liability	99	567,000	4.0	17.2	13.1	35.4	30.3
Asbestos	47	682,000	2.1	0.0	19.1	53.2	25.5
Other	52	500,000	5.8	32.7	7.7	17.3	36.5
Medical malpractice	584	400,000	0.7	5.3	29.1	43.8	21.1
False arrest, imprisonment	8	259,000	37.5	0.0	12.5	12.5	37.5
Professional malpractice	63	129,000	3.2	31.7	22.2	28.6	14.3
Premises liability	666	98,000	5.6	30.9	32.9	23.3	7.4
Other or unknown tort	305	83,000	36.1	8.9	27.2	12.5	15.4
Intentional tort	429	38,000	28.7	23.8	36.1	7.0	4.4
Conversion	148	27,000	24.3	31.8	37.2	4.1	2.7
Slander/libel	80	24,000	22.5	40.0	2.5	22.5	12.5
Animal attack	107	21,000	37.4	32.7	29.0	0.9	0.0
Motor vehicle	5,964	15,000	40.0	34.8	17.7	5.4	2.1

Civil Bench and Jury Trials in State Courts, 2005, October 2008, U.S. Department of Justice.

3. HARMFUL OR OFFENSIVE CONTACT

The last element of the tort of battery is that the contact must be harmful or offensive. Everyone has a different standard about what would be considered harmful or offensive. Because this standard shifts dramatically from one person to another, the law does not use a subjective standard to determine this element. Put another way, the determination of harmful or offensive contact is not based on the individual plaintiff. We don't ask the plaintiff if the contact was harmful or offensive to her. Instead, we use the reasonable person standard.

4. THE REASONABLE PERSON STANDARD

We return to this hypothetical reasonable person many times throughout this book. The reasonable person standard was developed as a way to address incidents where the parties could have very different interpretations about what happened. Here's an example: Andy is Carol's supervisor. One day, he walks into her office and while speaking with her about her job performance, he touches her in a place that she considers to be inappropriate. Andy doesn't think that his action is wrong; in fact, he thinks that Carol secretly wanted him to touch her. Carol brings a battery lawsuit against Andy. Will she win? If we relied on Andy's interpretation of the events, there would be no cause of action at all. On the other hand, Carol's interpretation of the events may not be conclusive either. For instance, if Andy touched Carol on the shoulder as a way of emphasizing a point he was making, Carol may find this contact offensive, but would a hypothetical, reasonable person? Probably not. However, change the facts and you get a different result. Instead of touching her shoulder, Andy touches her thigh or her breast. Would a hypothetical reasonable person find that to be offensive contact? The answer would almost certainly be yes.

 **FALSE IMPRISONMENT**

When a plaintiff brings a suit for false imprisonment, he is saying that he was intentionally, unlawfully restrained against his will by the use of force or the threat of force. Although this tort sounds as though it involves some form of incarceration, what the plaintiff is really saying is that he was restrained from moving about freely by the defendant.

Most false imprisonment lawsuits are brought by people who are detained in stores or malls under suspicion of committing shoplifting. A person who is wrongfully detained by store personnel can bring this suit against the people who restrained her and the store that employs them.

A. THE ELEMENTS OF FALSE IMPRISONMENT

- Intentional
- Unlawful
- Restraint of a person
- By the use of force or threats

1. DISCUSSING THE ELEMENTS: RESTRAINT MUST BE INTENTIONAL

It is not false imprisonment if the defendant in the lawsuit did not realize that he or she was confining someone. Suppose that John is in a bathroom in the mall and comes out to find that the mall has closed and he is locked inside. Because the people who were locking up had no reason to know that John was inside, his lawsuit for false imprisonment will almost certainly fail.

2. UNLAWFUL RESTRAINT

When a person acts without legal authority to detain someone, the detained person has a cause of action for false imprisonment. However, the reverse is also true. If a person acts with lawful authority, there is no suit for false imprisonment. How does someone acquire lawful authority to detain someone else? A police officer has such authority when he makes an arrest. But other people can also legally restrain a person. We have already mentioned shoplifting. Suppose that Mary is a security guard at a large retail store and she sees Carl hiding merchandise inside his clothes. Carl walks toward the exit, looks around, and then walks out. Mary chases him, tackles him, and holds him until the police arrive. Can Carl sue Mary for false imprisonment? If Mary has acted unlawfully, the answer is yes. But has she? Does Mary have the right to detain a person who has committed a crime? Yes. In fact, a person can lawfully restrain another person for any of the following:

- To stop someone from injuring himself or others
- To stop someone from damaging property
- To prevent someone from committing a crime or to detain him if he has already committed a crime

Sidebar

Most claims of false imprisonment arise from suspected shoplifting cases.

In the scenario above, Mary has seen Carl commit the crime of shoplifting and therefore has the right to restrain him. Such a rule makes sense — merchants should be able to prevent people from stealing. However, suppose Mary is wrong. What if Carl wasn't the right person? This is an entirely different scenario. Now, Mary has unlawfully restrained a person. Her lawful right was based on the fact that the person she restrained had committed a crime. If he hasn't committed a crime, Mary has no lawful right to restrain. Carl can bring a false imprisonment suit against her and will probably win.

3. BY THE USE OF FORCE OR THREATS

In the scenario we outlined above, Mary tackles Carl and holds him until the police arrive. False imprisonment can certainly be achieved through force. The force required does not have to be quite as spectacular as Mary's tackle. Simply putting a hand on a person's elbow and guiding him to the security office is sufficient. What if the person is never touched at all? Mary sees a young woman acting suspiciously and apparently stuffing items into a shopping bag. Mary approaches her, accuses her of shoplifting, and asks her to come to the security office. When the woman hesitates, Mary says, "If you don't come, I'll have to drag you there." Is this threat enough? Under the law, the answer is yes. Mary's threat of force is enough to justify a false imprisonment suit, assuming that the other elements of the tort are met.

4. HOLDING PERSONAL PROPERTY HOSTAGE

What if Mary simply takes the young woman's car keys and walks to the security office? She hasn't threatened the young woman and certainly hasn't used force on her either. Would this justify a suit for false imprisonment? Most jurisdictions would agree that it does. After all, without her car keys, the young woman is stranded at the store. Mary has effectively restrained the woman's movements, but has not resorted to physical violence to do so.

B. DEFENSES TO FALSE IMPRISONMENT

Do Mary and her employer have any defenses to the claim of false imprisonment? We have already seen that so long as Mary acts in a lawful manner, a claim of false imprisonment is not justified. That is one defense, but there are several others.

1. CONSENT

If the plaintiff voluntarily accompanies Mary back to the security office to "clear the matter up," and agrees to remain in the office until the police arrive, she has consented to the restraint and has effectively waived her right to complain about it later. Consent is only a defense when the person does not act voluntarily. Consent cannot be the result of force, threats, or trickery. In Chapter 3, we discuss in greater depth the many other defenses available in a torts action. Consent is also a defense to assault and battery cases. Consent is also a crucial issue when a person is having a medical procedure performed, as discussed in the following case excerpt.

RAND v. CITY OF GLENDALE
2008 WL 5383363

MEMORANDUM DECISION

DOWNIE, Judge.
Plaintiffs/Counter-Defendants/Appellants Neil Rand and Shirlene Fant Rand
appeal the superior court's grant of summary judgment in favor of Defendant/
Counter-Claimant/Appellee City of Glendale ("City"). For the following reasons, we affirm.

Factual and Procedural Background
In January 2002, the Rands and the City entered into an "Office Lease Agreement" (the "Lease") for two suites in an office building located in Glendale,
Arizona. The Lease, which was to commence on August 1, 2002, and expire on
July 31, 2007, stated that the leased premises would be Suites 250 and 252,
located on the second floor of the building. The Rands later claimed that they
only agreed to sign the Lease because the City orally promised that they could
move from Suite 252, which they found unsuitable, to Suite 150.

In November 2002, the Rands vacated Suite 252 and withheld rent due
under the Lease as a protest of the City's refusal to provide their desired office
space. They continued to occupy Suite 250 and, in February 2003, paid a
portion of the rent due under the Lease as payment for four months' occu-
pancy of that suite. The Rands ceased all rent payments in March 2003.

On May 2, 2003, the City sent a letter to the Rands advising that they were
in arrears and that the City would exercise its right under the Lease to lock
them out of the premises if they did not make full payment by May 9, 2003.
Shirlene Rand telephoned Glendale City Attorney Rick Flaaen to advise that
she was out of town and to request a meeting upon her return. Shirlene claims
Mr. Flaaen agreed to such a meeting. On May 9, 2003, Assistant City Attorney
James M. Flenner wrote to the Rands stating that, based on Shirlene's
conversation with Mr. Flaaen, the City would grant them an extension
until May 16, 2003, to pay the full arrearage amount.

On May 19, 2003, the City had not received payment from the Rands and
entered the premises to perform a lock-out. Shirlene was present in Suite 250
and refused to leave. The City called Glendale police officers to the scene. The
officers explained to Shirlene that she had been evicted and must vacate the
premises or face arrest for trespassing. She disputed that she had been evicted
and refused to leave. The officers arrested Shirlene for trespassing, handcuffed
her, and escorted her down the stairs of the building and out to a marked
police car in the parking lot. They then took her to the police station, where
she was cited and released.

On September 12, 2003, Neil Rand sent a notice of claim letter to the City
pursuant to Arizona Revised Statutes ("A.R.S.") section 12-821.01 (2003). He
alleged that the City had wrongfully and maliciously seized property exempt

from execution that was in Suite 250 at the time of the lock-out. Neil offered to settle his claim against the City for $5,000,000.

Neil subsequently initiated a lawsuit against the City, alleging that the City breached the Lease by failing to allow the Rands to occupy Suite 150 or to provide suitable alternative premises as promised, tortiously interfered with contracts he had with business customers and advertisers, and converted his business and personal property after the lock-out. He claimed entitlement to a set-off/recoupment against any rent he owed to the City because the City had wrongfully deprived him of the use of Suite 150 or a suitable alternative and had interfered with his possession and beneficial enjoyment of the premises. Neil also requested relief under the equitable theory of unjust enrichment for wrongful retention of his business and personal property. The City counter-claimed for breach of contract due to Neil's failure to pay amounts owed under the Lease.

The City moved for summary judgment on all of Neil's claims, alleging: (1) the contract-based claims were barred because Neil failed to disclose them in his notice of claim; and (2) all other claims failed as a matter of law. Neil responded to the City's motion and filed a cross-motion for partial summary judgment on his breach of contract, conversion, and unjust enrichment claims. The trial court granted summary judgment to the City on all of Neil's claims. On September 30, 2005, the court entered judgment for the City and included finality language pursuant to Rule 54(b), Arizona Rules of Civil Procedure. Neil did not timely appeal that judgment.

In the interim, on September 16, 2003, the City received a notice of claim letter from Shirlene Rand. It alleged that the Glendale Police Department, through gross negligence and willful and malicious action, falsely arrested her without probable cause on May 19, 2003. Shirlene stated she would settle her claim against the City for $150,000,000.

On December 3, 2003, Shirlene filed a complaint against the City in superior court in which she alleged, pursuant to 42 U.S.C. §1983 (1996), that the City's actions on May 19, 2003, violated her civil rights; she also pled additional state law claims. The City removed the action to federal district court, and Shirlene amended her complaint to allege a civil rights violation under 42 U.S.C. §1983, battery, gross negligence, false arrest/imprisonment, negligence, intentional infliction of emotional distress, negligent infliction of emotional distress, negligent supervision, breach of contract, tortious interference with contract, punitive damages, and set-off/recoupment (the "Federal Court Action"). The district court granted summary judgment to the City on Shirlene's civil rights claim, ruling that Shirlene had not offered any proof to support her claim that the City promulgated a policy or established a custom that caused her to be subjected to a deprivation of her constitutional rights. The court ruled that it lacked supplemental jurisdiction over the remaining state law claims and dismissed them without prejudice.

Shirlene filed a new complaint in the superior court, alleging twelve counts against the City: violation of due process, battery, false arrest/imprisonment, negligence, intentional infliction of emotional distress, negligent infliction of emotional distress, negligent supervision, punitive damages, breach of contract, tortious interference with contract, set-off/recoupment, and promissory estoppel. The City counterclaimed for breach of contract arising out of Shirlene's failure to pay amounts due under the Lease. Shirlene's lawsuit was consolidated with Neil's action, where only the City's counterclaim for breach of contract remained.

The City moved for summary judgment on all of Shirlene's claims. The City argued that Shirlene's claim for intentional infliction of emotional distress failed as a matter of law because no reasonable person could find the alleged conduct to be extreme and outrageous. The court granted summary judgment to the City on all of Shirlene's claims.

Issues

Shirlene challenges the trial court's grant of summary judgment to the City on each of her claims. The Rands also appeal the trial court's judgment in favor of the City on its counterclaim for breach of contract.

Discussion

In reviewing a grant of summary judgment, our task is to determine de novo whether any genuine issues of material fact exist and whether the trial court incorrectly applied the law. We review the facts in the light most favorable to the Rands, against whom summary judgment was entered. Summary judgment is appropriate "if the facts produced in support of the claim or defense have so little probative value, given the quantum of evidence required, that reasonable people could not agree with the conclusion advanced by the proponent of the claim or defense." We will affirm the entry of summary judgment if it is correct for any reason.

Negligent Infliction of Emotional Distress

In support of her claim for negligent infliction of emotional distress, Shirlene alleged that the City's failure to exercise reasonable care caused her "to incur severe and grievous mental and emotional suffering, fright, anguish, shock, nervousness, and anxiety. In Arizona, a plaintiff may not recover for negligent infliction of emotional distress unless the shock or mental anguish is accompanied by or manifested as a physical injury."

The trial court granted summary judgment after finding that Shirlene offered no evidence of a physical injury resulting from the City's actions. Shirlene argues on appeal that she did introduce evidence of physical manifestations of her stress resulting from the alleged wrongful arrest, citing notes of her physicians that she has suffered anxiety attacks and muscle weakness due to the incident.

As the trial court noted, the only admissible evidence Shirlene submitted on this issue was her deposition testimony that she had not suffered any physical injuries as a result of the arrest. Although Shirlene also sought to rely on her physicians' reports in the trial court, they were not admissible because they were unsworn and merely contained the physicians' descriptions of Shirlene's hearsay statements that she suffered muscle aches and other physical symptoms. We therefore assume that the trial court did not consider these reports. As Shirlene produced no admissible evidence that her purported emotional distress and mental anguish manifested as a physical injury, the superior court properly granted summary judgment to the City on this claim.

Intentional Infliction of Emotional Distress

The trial court ruled that Shirlene's claim for intentional infliction of emotional distress failed as a matter of law because the conduct alleged to be atrocious did not constitute "extreme" or "outrageous" conduct. Arizona has adopted the Restatement (Second) of Torts ("Restatement") §46 (1965), which sets forth the elements of an intentional infliction of emotional distress claim:

> First, the conduct by the defendant must be "extreme" and "outrageous"; second, the defendant must either intend to cause emotional distress or recklessly disregard the near certainty that such distress will result from his conduct; and third, severe emotional distress must indeed occur as a result of defendant's conduct.

Ford v. Revlon, Inc., 153 Ariz. 38, 43, 734 P.2d 580, 585 (1987).

Whether a defendant's conduct may be regarded as extreme and outrageous is initially examined by the court as a matter of law. Restatement §46 cmt. h.

To prove a claim for intentional infliction of emotional distress, "a plaintiff must show that the defendant's acts were so outrageous in character and so extreme in degree, as to go beyond all possible bounds of decency, and to be regarded as atrocious and utterly intolerable in a civilized community." *Mintz v. Bell Atl. Sys. Leasing Int'l, Inc.,* 183 Ariz. 550, 554, 905 P.2d 559, 563 (App.1995). We agree with the trial court that Shirlene's allegations, taken as true, do not support a claim for intentional infliction of emotional distress as a matter of law. The conduct Shirlene attributes to the City — arresting her for trespass without probable cause and holding her for less than one hour — does not "go beyond all possible bounds of decency" and therefore does not state a claim for intentional infliction of emotional distress.

Nevertheless, Shirlene contends that a reasonable jury could find that the City acted outrageously because she was "handcuffed, although she was not a threat to the police, and she was dragged down the stairs and into the public parking lot where she was then forced into a marked police car in front of several witnesses." This description of the arrest is not supported by the record. Shirlene admitted during her deposition that she was not dragged down the stairs or forced into the police car and that she knows of only one witness who actually saw the arrest. She conceded that the officers were polite, did not harm her, yell at her, or make racial comments. Given these facts, Shirlene cannot satisfy the first of the three required elements for her intentional infliction of emotional distress claim, and the trial court properly granted summary judgment to the City.

Conclusion

For the foregoing reasons, we affirm. The City requests an award of costs and attorneys' fees on appeal pursuant to Article 31.6 of the Lease, which provides that the prevailing party in an action to enforce an obligation under the Lease shall be entitled to recover his or her costs and reasonable attorneys' fees. We enforce a contractual provision for attorneys' fees according to its terms and have no discretion not to award fees. *Chase Bank of Ariz. v. Acosta,* 179 Ariz. 563, 575, 880 P.2d 1109, 1121 (App.1994). Accordingly, we award the City its reasonable attorneys' fees and taxable costs on appeal subject to compliance with Arizona Rule of Civil Appellate Procedure 21.

Questions about the case:

1. Why did the City move to evict Shirlene Rand?
2. What is the basis of Shirlene's claim for intentional infliction of emotional distress?
3. What legal defense did the City offer to Shirlene's claim of intentional infliction of emotional distress?
4. According to the court, what is the difference between negligent and intentional infliction of emotional distress?
5. What are the elements of intentional infliction of emotional distress, as set out by the court?

ALIENATION OF AFFECTIONS

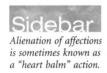
Alienation of affections is sometimes known as a "heart balm" action.

The tort of alienation of affections is based on a third party's interference with a marriage, usually by committing adultery with one of the spouses. In many states, this action is no longer authorized. Most parties prefer to handle the allegation as part of a divorce action and do not bring a separate action for alienation of affections. In some states, the tort has been merged with other torts and does not exist as a separate cause of action. At least one recent case has brought this tort back into nationwide prominence. In North Carolina, the wife of a man who had an affair brought suit against the mistress, basing her claim on alienation of affections. Her verdict for $1 million renewed interest in this tort.

The elements of alienation of affections are:

- Interference with the marriage by the defendant
- Subsequent loss of affection by one spouse for another
- Loss of affection caused by this interference
- Interference was motivated by malice

INTENTIONAL INFLICTION OF EMOTIONAL DISTRESS

Lawsuits involving the intentional infliction of emotional distress are far more common than claims for alienation of affections. In this tort, the injured party is claiming that either through intentional actions or recklessness, the defendant caused the plaintiff severe emotional distress through some outrageous behavior.

A. ELEMENTS OF INFLICTION OF EMOTIONAL DISTRESS

- Intentional or reckless conduct
- Caused the plaintiff severe emotional distress
- By defendant's outrageous conduct

Here's an example: Stan is a photographer who is down on his luck. If he can get a photograph of a celebrity, preferably an unflattering one, he knows he can sell it to a national tabloid. He gains access to the home of a famous actress by posing as a police officer. When the actress appears, Stan says, "I'm sorry to tell you this, but your son has been killed." He whips out his camera and takes her photograph just as she reacts to this news. Although he gets the photograph published in the tabloid, he also gets served with a complaint alleging intentional infliction of emotional distress. We use this example to discuss the elements of this tort.

1. INTENTIONAL OR RECKLESS CONDUCT

In order to be liable for this tort, the defendant must act with the specific intention of inflicting emotional distress on the plaintiff or act with such utter recklessness that emotional distress would naturally result. Stan's actions point to his intention of causing emotional distress. An example of recklessness is when someone reports a very damaging fact as true, without bothering to check it for accuracy. For instance, if Stan had announced the son's death on television without investigating whether it was true, his conduct would be reckless.

2. BYSTANDER EMOTIONAL DISTRESS

In some jurisdictions, a bystander or a witness to a horrific event may be entitled to bring a claim of "bystander emotional distress." For instance, a child might be permitted to bring a claim of bystander emotional distress if she witnesses injuries to her mother.[2]

3. CAUSATION

We have discussed the legal term *causation* before, but another word or two about it here is also required. The plaintiff has to prove that there is a direct connection between the emotional distress and the defendant's actions. If a plaintiff was already suffering from sleeplessness and anxiety, she couldn't allege that these conditions were caused by the defendant's actions, no matter how cruel they were.

B. EMOTIONAL DISTRESS: WHAT IS IT?

The biggest problem with this tort is the last element: emotional distress. Like love, hate, pain, or joy, emotional distress is impossible to measure and varies considerably in intensity from one person to another. The fact that it is so difficult to define makes it very difficult to prove at trial. As in the case of assault and battery, the hypothetical, reasonable person comes to our aid again.

In order to prove emotional distress, the plaintiff must show that the defendant's actions were such that a hypothetical, reasonable person would have suffered emotional distress if he had been subjected to the same conduct. We do not look to the subjective reaction of the plaintiff. Instead we judge it by an objective standard. What about Stan's actions? Would a hypothetical, reasonable person suffer emotional distress because of what Stan did? Most juries would probably answer yes. His actions would seem designed to cause anyone a great deal of emotional distress. However, there is still one requirement that the plaintiff must prove: outrageousness.

Sidebar

In most jurisdictions, the best practice when pleading intentional infliction of emotional distress is to tie the claim to some specific injury. Many jurisdictions have trouble assessing damages for emotional distress when the injury is purely psychological.[3]

1. THE DEFENDANT'S ACTIONS WERE OUTRAGEOUS

Many would argue that the last element of the tort of intentional infliction of emotional distress is outrageousness. What do we mean by *outrageous?* Courts have defined this term in many ways, but the most common definition states that the defendant's actions must be "intolerable" or "beyond society's accepted standards of decency and morality." Why include this element at all? If the plaintiff can prove that the defendant's actions were intentional, that they were a direct cause of the plaintiff's emotional distress, isn't this enough? For most jurisdictions, the answer is no.

FIGURE 2-3

Examples of Situations That Meet the Standard for Intentional Infliction of Emotional Distress

■ Plaintiff is 11 years old, and the defendant, a 40-year-old neighbor, harasses the child and continually tells him that a freckle on the back of his neck is cancer, that he's going to die very soon, and that his mother is planning on abandoning him.

■ Plaintiff is particularly susceptible to loud noises; defendant knows this and sets off a firecracker in plaintiff's chair at work.

FIGURE 2-4

■ Defendant curses and insults the plaintiff.
■ Plaintiff is particularly nervous or susceptible to loud noises; defendant sets off a firecracker during the Fourth of July celebration.

Examples of Situations That Do Not Meet the Standard for Intentional Infliction of Emotional Distress

The most common reason given for requiring the element of outrageousness is that it will help limit frivolous lawsuits. We must all suffer our fair share of emotional distress; there is no way to go through life without it. This tort is not intended to address the tragedies that affect everyone. Instead, this tort was created to give plaintiffs some redress against a person who goes out of his way to cause emotional distress to another person.

What about Stan, the photographer? If our hypothetical, reasonable person considers Stan's actions to be outrageous, the actress has proved her case against him. Under these circumstances, Stan will probably lose this lawsuit. In a later chapter, we discuss the kinds of damages (or monetary payments) the actress may be entitled to receive against Stan. He will probably end up losing a lot more money than he gained by taking the photograph.

Intentional infliction of emotional distress is a cause of action asserted by plaintiffs who have suffered emotional or psychological damage because of the defendant's outrageous actions.

ISSUE AT A GLANCE

 **MALICIOUS PROSECUTION**

Malicious prosecution is a tort designed to punish people who use the court system as a way to harass or intimidate other people. When a person brings a baseless criminal charge against someone, or continues to press charges knowing that the person is innocent, the innocent party has the right to sue.

A. THE ELEMENTS OF MALICIOUS PROSECUTION

- Defendant brings or continues a criminal charge against the plaintiff
- The case terminates in the plaintiff's favor
- The defendant acted with malice in bringing the charge
- There was no probable cause for the charge

1. DEFENDANT BRINGS OR CONTINUES A CRIMINAL CHARGE AGAINST THE PLAINTIFF

*Can police or prosecutors be sued for malicious prosecution? Prosecutors, police, and judges cannot be sued for malicious prosecution as long as they are acting within their duties. This tort is only authorized against private individuals who try to use the criminal justice system for their own ends. If a prosecutor or a police officer brings charges against an individual, no matter what the ultimate outcome of the case, that government official is **immune** from suit. The rules of immunity were specifically designed to prevent people convicted of a crime from trying to sue government officials for doing their jobs. If the official is acting out of personal malice, however, the immunity may not apply. In a similar way, people who call in suspicious activities cannot be sued for malicious prosecution because they are not responsible for continuing the prosecution. That duty falls to the prosecutor.*

Immunity
A legal protection that prevents a person from being liable in a civil suit

Malicious prosecution is based on the idea that a private citizen is using the court system for unlawful purposes, such as harassment or intimidation. These cases normally originate when a private citizen appears before a magistrate, swears to certain facts, and as a result of this sworn testimony the magistrate issues a warrant for a person's arrest. If the sworn statement turns out to be false, the person who is arrested (whom we call the plaintiff from now on) has a cause of action against the other person (whom we call the defendant).

2. THE CASE TERMINATES IN THE PLAINTIFF'S FAVOR

Under malicious prosecution, it does not matter whether the allegation involved a misdemeanor or a felony. However, the plaintiff can only bring this suit when he can prove that the criminal action ended in his favor. If the prosecutor or judge dismisses the case against the plaintiff, he can prove this element. However, if his case goes to trial and the jury finds him not guilty, he cannot. What is the difference? In the first example, the case was dismissed for lack of probable cause (the basic requirement for any criminal charge). However, in the second example, the jury must find a person guilty of a crime beyond a reasonable doubt. Many juries have been convinced of a person's guilt but have failed to return a guilty verdict because they believed that the state had failed to meet its burden. By requiring that the case end favorably to the plaintiff before it goes to the jury, courts do not have to inquire into the jury's actions in the criminal case.

3. THE DEFENDANT ACTED WITH MALICE IN BRINGING THE CHARGE

Another requirement that the plaintiff must establish is that the defendant acted with malice in bringing the charge in the first place. How does the plaintiff prove malice? The plaintiff can present evidence that the defendant knew the criminal case was baseless but pressed for prosecution as a way of "getting even" with the plaintiff. The plaintiff can show that the defendant was biased against him or hated him.

4. THERE WAS NO PROBABLE CAUSE FOR THE CHARGE

The requirement that there was no probable cause for the criminal charge is a way of preventing frivolous lawsuits. If the plaintiff can prove that probable cause was lacking in the criminal case, he can prove his civil case. However, the requirement of lack of probable cause discourages many lawsuits from individuals who believe that they have been wronged by the criminal justice system, but have either pled guilty to a charge or been convicted at trial.

Malicious prosecution is a civil suit authorized when the defendant uses the court system as a means of unwarranted, private retaliation against the plaintiff.

TORT IMMUNITY FOR FAMILIES

We have already mentioned the concept of immunity in the context of a prosecutor's immunity from suit for malicious prosecution. There are many other forms of immunity (also known as privileges) that essentially prevent certain individuals from being sued for specific torts. We saw earlier that a police officer has the right to touch a suspect in order to arrest him. The suspect cannot sue the officer for this touching, even though technically it is a battery. The officer is protected by immunity (as long as he is acting within his official capacity). There is also something known as intra-family tort immunity. Simply put, family members are protected from lawsuits filed by other family members. Although there are some important exceptions to this rule, children cannot, for example, sue their parents for a spanking. Although the spanking is again a technical battery, the law does not permit this suit, because to do so would contribute to disharmony inside the family. Imagine the legal hornets' nest that would open up if children could sue their parents for activities they think are unfair. In later chapters, we explore specific immunities as they arise in the context of the material discussed.

INTENTIONAL TORTS INVOLVING PROPERTY: TRESPASS

We are all familiar with the term *trespass,* but we may not know the exact nature of the legal elements of this tort. At law, trespass consists of:

- the (intentional), unprivileged
- entry onto the plaintiff's real property
- without permission.

A. DISCUSSING THE ELEMENTS: INTENT

Trespass is an unusual tort in that many states do not require intent on the defendant's part before he can be liable for the tort. Put another way, trespass can be viewed as a strict liability tort. A strict liability tort is one in which the intent of the defendant is irrelevant to the issue of liability. There are very few strict liability torts. Under the common law, trespass to another person's property, no matter what the reason, was actionable, even if the defendant had a very good reason for committing the tort. The common law rule opened up a wide range of problems. Consider the following scenario: It is a stormy night and John Doe loses control of his car and crashes through Jane's fence. Jane can sue him for trespass, simply because he entered onto her property without permission. You can see why many states have amended their trespass laws to require an intentional action on the defendant's part.

1. UNPRIVILEGED

If the trespass occurred through operation of law, or because of public safety concerns, a civil suit for trespass will fail. For example, a police officer is pursuing a fleeing suspect and chases him through Jane's backyard. Although this seems to meet the elements of trespass, Jane's suit against the officer will fail because the officer is protected at law by a privilege that allows him to use reasonable means to apprehend a fleeing suspect, even if this means that he carries out a trespass to do so.

2. ENTRY ONTO THE PLAINTIFF'S REAL PROPERTY

Real property refers to land. If you imagine an invisible wall that rises up along the boundaries of the property, then the defendant commits trespass when he breaks through this imaginary boundary.

a. Proving "Entry"

Although "entry" would seem to be an easy element to prove, it can involve some very complicated issues. It's one thing to find someone on your property, and another to claim that a low-flying aircraft has trespassed on your property. Under the law, entry usually means the physical entry of the defendant onto the plaintiff's land. The defendant can also enter using some extension of his body, such as tools, or objects, such as thrown rocks or debris. However, the law is clear that it is not trespass if light or sound from the defendant's house filters over to the plaintiff's property. The same thing is true for odors. The plaintiff can sue for these unpleasant situations, but not because they are trespasses. (See nuisances, below.) What about air traffic? Surely every time that a plane flies overhead, it is crossing over the physical boundaries of hundreds, perhaps thousands, of individual pieces of property. Is this trespass? No. Under the law, entry onto the plaintiff's property occurs within the "immediate reaches" of the surface of the property. This can also mean the space above the surface of the property that the plaintiff can reasonably be expected to use. Above that, it is no trespass even when an airplane passes over the plaintiff's property lines.

3. WITHOUT PERMISSION

This is perhaps the easiest element of trespass to prove. If the defendant has permission from the property owner, he has the privileged right to enter the defendant's property. However, who exactly has permission may sometimes be more complicated than one would imagine. What about the men and women who read electric meters? When you first moved into your house, did someone from the local electric company come out and ask for permission to read your meter? Because they did not, why can't you sue them for coming onto your property? There are two problems: (1) The meter reader is privileged (they provide the service to your home and it would go against public policy to allow them to be sued), and (2) you have given implied permission to allow them to come onto your property to maintain your service. You might be surprised to learn just how many different people, from water company representatives to the cable company, have access to your property.

 ## NUISANCE ACTIONS

Suppose a person does not actually trespass onto John's land, but the fumes, odors, or noises reaching his property make it impossible for him to enjoy his own property. John can bring a **nuisance** action against the person producing the fumes. This action alleges that a person is doing something off the property that is affecting a person's ability to enjoy or use features on the property. It is commonly seen in situations where fumes, liquids, or other substances are leaking from one person's property onto another's.[4]

Nuisance
A cause of action that is authorized when the defendant's behavior results in a loss of enjoyment or value in the plaintiff's property

A. PUBLIC NUISANCE VERSUS PRIVATE NUISANCE

The law recognizes two different kinds of nuisances: public and private. A public nuisance is some condition that affects the rights of citizens in general. This condition could be a health risk or a general annoyance. When a condition is classified as a public nuisance, the local government must take a hand. Individuals are usually prevented from bringing a claim under public nuisance; such actions are generally reserved for the government. Placing such limitations on public nuisance lawsuits is a direct reflection of the fact that there are many things in life that we must all put up with and allowing a private person to bring a public nuisance suit for any of these things would cause the legal system to grind to a halt. However, these limitations disappear when the allegation is a private nuisance.

1. PRIVATE NUISANCE

John lives inside the city limits. His next-door neighbor, Sam, has recently acquired about 30 chickens and keeps them in his backyard, where he allows them to roam free. Sam doesn't clean up after the birds and the resulting odors are overpowering. John has asked Sam to remove the birds,

FIGURE 2-5	▪ Defendant's factory, located close to plaintiff's residence, produces terrible odors and fumes	at all hours of the night and involves the use of heavy equipment, with loud noises and bright lights that keep the plaintiff up all night
Examples of Situations in Which Courts Have Found Private Nuisances	▪ Defendant's business causes the ground to tremble constantly at plaintiff's residence ▪ Defendant's long haul business involves trucks coming and going	▪ Defendant pumps untreated sewage across the plaintiff's property

but Sam has refused. John can't sit in his backyard anymore because the prevailing winds come across Sam's backyard and onto John's property. Can John bring a private nuisance lawsuit against Sam? Let's take a look at the elements.

a. Elements of a Private Nuisance Action

▪ The defendant maintains a condition that
▪ Substantially interferes with the plaintiff's right
▪ To use and enjoy his property.

Sam's chickens would seem to satisfy the elements for a private nuisance action. If John brings suit, what damages is he entitled to receive? John could receive monetary payments to compensate him for the decreased use of his property, but what John really wants is someone to force Sam to get rid of the chickens. Although we discuss damages in much greater detail in a later chapter, a quick word may help explain the situation.

2. DAMAGES AND INJUNCTIONS

Can a court order Sam to get rid of his chickens? Yes. The court can order Sam to remove the chickens through its power to issue injunctions. An injunction is a court order that tells a person to either stop carrying out a specific action, or, in some cases, to do a specific thing. If the person refuses to follow the court's order, she can be held in contempt by the judge. A finding of contempt means that the judge could order a monetary fine assessed against the person or even order that she spend time in jail.

B. NEW LAWSUITS UNDER ENVIRONMENTAL THEORIES

New federal statutes have made the use of nuisance actions even more valuable to those claiming that large corporations are polluting groundwater or dumping hazardous waste. Working through the EPA, many agencies use these various federal statutes to force companies to pay for the complete cost of cleaning up a site that has been designated as hazardous.

TORTS TO PERSONAL PROPERTY: TRESPASS TO CHATTELS

So far our discussion has focused on real property. However, there is a wide range of other torts that involve personal property or "things." The main category under this heading consists of trespass to **chattels.** A chattel is an ancient term for personal property. *Trespass to chattels* is a suit based on the defendant's interference with the owner's rights to his personal property. This interference could come in the form of theft (permanently removing the property from the plaintiff's possession), conversion (retaining someone's property without permission), and damage to property (depriving the plaintiff of the use of the property). Here are the general elements of trespass to chattels:

Chattel
Personal property, including animals

- Intentional
- Unprivileged interference with the
- Plaintiff's personal property
- That results in damages to or loss of the property.

Example: Rick sneaks onto Steve's property one night and pours sugar into Steve's car's fuel tank. What type of action does Steve have against Rick?

Actually, Steve may have two actions against Rick. Steve can sue Rick for trespass, because he entered onto Steve's property without permission. Steve can also sue Rick for trespass to personal property, because Rick's actions resulted in damage to Steve's car.

A trespass to chattels case can also be based on the theory of **conversion.** When a person converts property, it means that he initially had legal right to use or possess the property, but then failed to return it. The unlawful detention amounts to theft, thus permanently depriving the owner of use of the property.

Conversion
The exercise of control over the property and removal of it from the possession of the rightful owner

SKILLS YOU NEED IN THE REAL WORLD

Keeping Track of Your Time

Whether you are working for a plaintiff's firm or a defense firm, it is usually important for you to keep track of your billable hours. As we see in a later chapter, plaintiffs' firms are generally only paid when the case settles. The amount of payment does not depend on the hours billed, so why would it be important to keep track of the hours you spend working on a particular case? The simple answer is that by keeping track of your hours you can have a better idea of where you are spending the majority of your time and whether your activities ultimately benefit the firm. You may find, for example, that most of your time is spent dealing with clients on the telephone. Keeping track of your activities and the amount of time you spend on those activities gives you a better idea of how to streamline your workday and to eliminate some of the nonproductive periods. This helps you to be a better paralegal and consequently even more indispensable to the firm.

Billable Hours at Defense Firms

When a paralegal works for an insurance defense firm, keeping track of billable hours is often the only way to ensure that the firm is paid for its time. Insurance defense firms are not paid based on the ultimate settlement amount. Instead, most insurance defense firms bill their clients with an hourly charge. In such a situation, the attorneys working at the firm want to make sure that they bill for every possible activity. Some firms do this by requiring you to keep track of your activities and assigning not only how much time you spent on these particular activities but for whom the activity was carried out. For instance, you may have spent a half hour writing a letter on the *Joe Doe v. Sue Doe* case. Most firms bill their clients on the basis of one tenth of an hour. One tenth of an hour equates to six minutes. There- fore, if you spend half an hour working on a letter, your time would appear as .5 hours. Insurance defense firms spend a great deal of time and energy making sure that all activities at the firm are billed to the appropriate client.

In the real world, attorneys realize that they cannot over-bill their clients. For instance, billing three hours for a two-minute telephone call would not only be unethical, it might also be illegal. This is why it is important not to exaggerate the hours you spend on a particular task. In some firms, you hand in your worksheets at the end of each week. These days, it is far more common for paralegals to keep track of their time with software. Using software, a paralegal can bill each and every activity to the appropriate client as well as assign a time value depending on how long it took to complete that particular activity. Paralegals who routinely bill high amounts of hours are often the ones who receive bonuses and pay raises.

Dealing with Clients on the Telephone

When you are dealing with clients on the telephone, always keep a handy reference about the client nearby. This could be as simple as a three-by-five card listing the client's complete name and other important information. Your information card should contain the client's full name, address, and all relevant telephone numbers, as well as some personal information. For instance, you should keep track of the client's spouse's name. Also list the names of any children. When you are talking to a client, refer to this card. Work the child's name into the conversation. Your client will be favorably impressed that you remember, not realizing that you had the infor- mation on a card—a little detail that can mean a lot.

Returning Phone Calls

The biggest source of frustration for a client is when the client fails to get a return phone call from the attorney. Clients do not like leaving several phone messages without a return call. One way that you can deal with this problem is to return the client's call as soon as possible, even if you don't have any information for the client. You may have a natural tendency to hold off returning the phone call until you can tell the client something of interest. This is a mistake. Often a client will appreciate a telephone call even when you don't have any news to report. Sometimes the client will be reassured just by hearing another person's voice.

Talkative Clients

Everyone has had the experience of speaking with someone on the phone who simply won't stop talking. If you have a client who calls you frequently or doesn't stop talking after a reasonable amount of time, you have to develop some new strategies to get off the phone. For example, arrange a hand signal with a co-worker to let the co-worker know that he or she should call you and give you an excuse to hang up. Some people prearrange to have their cell phone ring after a certain period of time, which also gives them the excuse to pick up the other line.

In situations where the client has been particularly talkative, you may be able to arrange with the attorney a policy that dictates the client will be billed personally for all phone calls. This has a tendency to keep talkative clients off the telephone.

Billable Hour Software

There are numerous programs available these days that allow you to track your time. Billable hours are important for insurance defense firms, but they are also becoming increasingly important for plaintiffs' firms as well. (It helps the firm track how it spends its time and helps to improve overall efficiency.) Billable hour software comes in a vast array of forms, from standard programs that come bundled in office management software to individual programs that can be uploaded to a digital assistant, Palm Pilot, or Blackberry. No matter what software you choose, there are some features that should be present. The program should be easy to use, both in entering information and assigning it to a particular client's file. It should be able to interface with other computer systems to allow you to print out the final version and e-mail to others in the firm. Finally, it should be flexible enough to allow for additional notes or other materials that you might need to enter about a particular activity.

THE LIFE OF A PARALEGAL

Having a Good Relationship with the Courthouse Personnel

A lot of paralegals don't realize how important it is to have a good relationship with the people at the courthouse. They're obligated to provide information and to do certain things whether you have a good rapport with them or not, but they're just so much more helpful if you've got a good relationship. I don't abuse that. Anything I can look up myself, I absolutely will. I only call on them when I need to know something now and don't have the time to run over to the courthouse and check it out.

There are even times when they'll provide information to you just to put you on notice of something that's happened. Sometimes the court schedule gets changed around or things have been delayed. A lot of times, a clerk will actually call you and fill you in on recent developments. The courthouse people have to deal with a lot of jerks; showing them some respect and kindness goes a long way with them.

Linda McCurry, Paralegal

 ETHICAL ISSUES FOR THE PARALEGAL:
STATUTES OF LIMITATION

When dealing with intentional torts, the most pressing issue is often the statute of limitations. Many people fail to realize that they often have a very short period during which they must bring their suit or have it barred forever. On your first meeting with the client, you should establish this date as precisely as possible. The more likely that the date is going to be an issue, that is, that the statute is going to run soon, the more you should do to make sure that the client understands the importance of that date. You should also let the attorney know that the statute may "run" shortly. How do you do this? Note it prominently in the file. Send a letter to the client noting this date as a major point in the letter. Send a memo to the attorney, again noting the importance of this date. That way, you've covered the legal point (and yourself) from every angle you can think of.

Chapter Summary

Intentional torts are a small and very distinct category of tort law. As the name implies, intentional torts involve deliberate actions by the defendant. Assault, for instance, consists of causing fear or apprehension to the plaintiff. On the other hand, battery is intentional, harmful, physical contact between the defendant and the plaintiff. In both circumstances, the defendant has not acted in a negligent manner, but in a deliberate and intentional manner. Intentional torts are judged from the reasonable person standard, that is, would a reasonable person believe that the defendant's actions were harmful or offensive? This objective standard prevents actions based on the subjective feelings of the plaintiff. Other intentional torts include false imprisonment, alienation of affections, and malicious prosecution. In each of these torts, the defendant is taking some action to affect the freedom, rights, or relationships of the plaintiff. Intentional torts can also consist of interfering with the plaintiff's rights to his property. Trespass to chattels involves the defendant's intentional actions to prevent the plaintiff from exercising control over his own property. This intentional interference with the plaintiff's property covers not only personal property (things), but real property (land) as well. When the defendant interferes with the plaintiff's use or enjoyment of his real estate, it is called a nuisance action.

Web Sites

National Center for State Courts
http://www.ncsconline.org

Time-Tracking Software
http://www.timepanic.com

▨ **Wikipedia — Intentional Torts**
   http://en.wikipedia.org/wiki/Intentional_torts

▨ **Mega Law**
   http://www.megalaw.com

Forms and Court Documents

This complaint is for an allegation of battery in a bar fight.

IN THE SUPERIOR COURT OF GANNETT COUNTY
STATE OF PLACID

Richard Coe,	)	CASE NO. CV 2002-1101
Plaintiff	)	
vs.	)	
Terry Zoe,	)	
Defendant	)	

Complaint for Personal Injury

COMES NOW, the plaintiff, Richard Coe, and complaining of the defendant alleges the following:

1.

The Plaintiff is a citizen and resident of Gannett County, Placid.

2.

The Defendant is, upon information and belief, a citizen and resident of Gannett County, Placid.

3.

On or about August 13, 2000, at approximately 11:00 P.M., the Plaintiff, Richard Coe, was in an establishment known as Tilly's Tavern, 123 Highway 92, Florence City. The defendant, Terry Zoe, was also present in the same establishment.

4.

As the plaintiff was sitting quietly at the bar of the establishment, the Defendant, Terry Zoe, without warning and without any provocation, struck the Plaintiff with a bar stool. The Plaintiff had had no prior contact with the Defendant, and had neither instigated nor encouraged any physical altercation with the Defendant.

5.

Defendant's actions were an intentional, unjustified, unprovoked, and violent battery on the person of the Plaintiff, Richard Coe.

6.

After being struck by the Defendant, the Plaintiff lost consciousness and was later transported to the Memorial Mission Hospital for treatment.

7.

That as a proximate cause of the Defendant's intentional battery on the person of the Plaintiff, said Plaintiff suffered severe, debilitating, and permanent injuries in excess of $10,000.00.

WHEREFORE, the Plaintiff prays that the Court:
1. That the Plaintiff, Richard Coe, have and recover a judgment against the Defendant in an amount in excess of $10,000.00 for personal injuries.
2. That the Defendant be assessed with punitive damages as permitted by law.
3. That prejudgment interest be awarded as provided by law.
4. That the costs of this action be taxed against the Defendant.
5. That all issues raised be tried before a jury.
6. For such other and further relief as the Court may deem just and proper.

This the _____ day of June, 2002.

_____

Clarence D. Arrow
Attorney for Plaintiff, Richard Coe
State Bar No. 000-998

Key Terms

Assault	Elements	Nuisance
Battery	Foreseeability	Prima facie
Chattel	Immunity	Proximate cause
Conversion	Intentional tort	

Review Questions

1 How does assault differ from battery?
2 Explain what is meant by the term *elements of proof.*
3 Explain the reasonable person standard. Why is it used?
4 Why can't an unconscious person be assaulted?
5 What are the elements of false imprisonment?
6 What is the justification for continuing to allow lawsuits for interference with private property? Couldn't these situations simply be resolved through the criminal courts?

7   How does a "private nuisance" differ from a "public nuisance"?

8   Explain the elements of alienation of affections. Should such a civil injury continue to provide a cause of action for plaintiffs? Why or why not?

9   What are chattels? Why is there a tort for trespass to chattels?

10 What are some of the methods a paralegal can use to maintain good client relations?

Applying What You Have Learned

1   Rick is a fully competent adult who has decided that he doesn't want critical medical attention that would clearly save his life. His doctor decides to treat Rick anyway. Has the doctor committed the tort of battery?

2   Nora was originally admitted into Happy Dale Nursing Home without incident. However, after she'd been there for a day, she decided that she wanted to go home. The management of the nursing home facility refused to release her to her son when he arrived to take her home, because it was Nora's daughter who had arranged for Nora's admission to Happy Dale. Does Nora have a valid claim for false imprisonment?

3   Claudia's daughter, Rachel, goes out on a date one night with Ross. While they are driving, Ross loses control of the car and runs off the road. Rachel is killed. Ross drags her body several hundred feet from the scene of the accident and arranges Rachel's body to make it look like a car struck her while she was walking. The next morning, Ross calls Claudia and accuses Rachel of stealing his car and worries that something may have happened. Draft a complaint for intentional infliction of emotional distress based on these facts.

Endnotes

[1] Federal Tort Trial and Verdicts, 1994-1995. Bureau of Justice Statistics, U.S. Department of Justice.

[2] *Klein v. City of Stamford*, 669 A.2d 644 (1994).

[3] Am. Jur. 2d, Negligence.

[4] *Bousquet v. Com.*, 374 Mass. 824, 372 N.E.2d 257 (1978).

Defenses to Intentional Torts

Chapter Objectives

- Be able to explain the components of various defenses

- Explain how and under what circumstances a defense is triggered

- Describe how and under what circumstances self-defense is an available defense

- Explain how age or mistake can affect liability analysis

- Define the insanity defense

WHAT IS A DEFENSE?

We have already seen that when the plaintiff brings suit against the defendant, the plaintiff's complaint spells out in detail exactly what injury the defendant caused and why the plaintiff is entitled to recover damages from the defendant. When the defendant files an answer, he states that he is not responsible for the plaintiff's injuries and is not liable to pay damages. This is a simple denial. However, a defendant can also raise a defense. A defense seeks to mitigate, explain away, or completely remove liability. Some defenses are known as absolute defenses, meaning that if the jury or judge believes the defense, the defendant will not be liable to the plaintiff as a matter of law. Most defenses are designed to mitigate the defendant's responsibility. In civil law, these defenses often take the form of: "I did it, but . . . ."

A defense is a legal claim raised by a defendant that either seeks to mitigate or completely exonerate him from liability.

SELF-DEFENSE

Self-defense
When a person uses force (sometimes deadly force) to protect himself from an attack

In our first example, **self-defense,** the defendant is admitting that he used violence against the plaintiff, but offers an explanation. The "but" in this example is the very core of the defense. The defendant is claiming that he used force only to protect himself or someone else.

Here's an example: Ron and Ramon are at a bar. Ron doesn't know Ramon, but, as sometimes happens in a bar, Ron takes an immediate dislike to Ramon. After making a few insulting comments, Ron grabs a beer mug and rushes toward Ramon, swinging the mug over his head. Ramon, believing that he is about to be struck by the beer mug, kicks a chair in Ron's way. Ron falls over the chair and breaks his leg. Later, Ron sues Ramon for battery. Does Ramon have a legal defense? Yes, absolutely. Ramon, like anyone else, has the right to defend himself against physical attack. Ramon doesn't have to wait until someone actually strikes him before he has this right.

A. THE RESPONSE MUST BE EQUAL TO THE THREAT

Sidebar

In one case, a police officer fired his gun at and injured a motorist who was backing up his car in the officer's direction at 2 miles per hour. The court found that the use of deadly force was unreasonable, noting that the officer could have easily stepped out of the way of the car. The officer was found liable to the motorist for the torts of assault and battery.[1]

Can Ramon successfully raise self-defense if, instead of pushing a chair in Ron's way, he takes out a gun and shoots Ron? Put another way, just how far does self-defense go? Common sense alone would say that Ramon has overreacted. Shooting someone who is about to hit you with a beer mug doesn't seem to be a fair response. Interestingly enough, this is exactly what the law requires in self-defense. When you are defending yourself, you must use force that is approximately equal to the threat. If you are threatened with minimal force, you must respond with minimal force. On the other hand, if you are threatened with deadly force, you can respond with deadly force. Suppose that Ron had a knife in his hand instead of a beer mug. Could Ramon successfully claim self-defense if he shoots Ron? Under these circumstances, the answer would be yes. It would be silly to require Ramon to respond with exactly the same kind of force (a knife instead of a gun). Because a knife and a gun are both deadly weapons, Ramon can use deadly force to protect himself.

B. LIMITATIONS ON SELF-DEFENSE

The law also recognizes that there are certain situations in which a person is not permitted to use self-defense as a legal defense to a civil suit. We have already discussed one such example: when the victim of the attack responds with **excessive force.** But there are other situations as well.

Excessive force
Force used in self-defense that is clearly disproportionate to the threat posed

1. NO SELF-DEFENSE FOR AGGRESSORS

Suppose in our example that Ramon had actually started the fight by attacking Ron. Ron then responds with the beer mug maneuver. Can Ramon still claim self-defense? As a general rule the answer would be no. People who start fights (called "aggressors" under tort law) do not have the legal defense of self-defense available to them.

Sidebar

In some jurisdictions, a homeowner is required to warn a trespasser before resorting to force.[2]

a. Self-Defense Claim if Aggressor Voluntarily Stopped Fighting

However, this exception has its own exception. Ramon can successfully raise self-defense if he voluntarily stopped fighting, even though he was the aggressor, but Ron continues to fight.

2. NO SELF-DEFENSE FOR MARTIAL ARTISTS

We've all heard the expression "his hands were classified as deadly weapons." People with special training or abilities have a greater responsibility under the law and less opportunity to raise self-defense.

Sidebar

At the time of the writing of the Declaration of Independence, the area of tort law was poorly developed and remained so for many years. The 1700s saw many legal treatises on criminal law, evidence, and other issues, but the first treatise on tort law did not appear until 1850, and it was a British publication.[3]

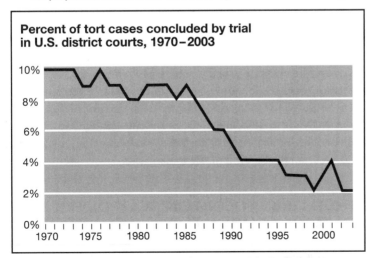

Most federal tort cases are not concluded by trial.
The proportion of tort cases concluded by trial has been declining.

Percent of tort cases concluded by trial
in U.S. district courts, 1970–2003

FIGURE 3-1

**Federal
Tort Cases
Concluded
by Trial**

Federal Tort Trials and Verdicts, 2002-03, NCJ 208713. Bureau of Justice Statistics, www .ojp.usdoj.gov/bjs/glance/tortperctrial.htm.

ISSUE
AT A
GLANCE

People who have specialized training in martial arts have a greater responsibility to exercise care in using this knowledge. When they do use their skills, they are held to a higher standard than people who do not have such training.

Example: Ron threatens Ramon and they fight. Ramon is a black belt in a particularly lethal form of martial arts. He easily defeats Ron and causes him severe injuries. When Ron sues Ramon over his injuries, Ramon claims self-defense. The court rules against Ramon. Why? Ramon's special training essentially makes him a deadly weapon. We've already seen that responding with excessive force removes the claim of self-defense. When Ramon uses his hands, he is automatically responding with deadly force. Unlike most people, Ramon has stricter limits placed on him because of his training.

C. CLAIMING SELF-DEFENSE WHEN DEFENDING OTHERS

Can a person use self-defense as a legal defense when he uses violence against someone who is threatening a third person? The answer is yes, with some obvious limitations. Under the old common law rule, no longer applicable in most states, a person could only use violence to protect him- or herself and immediate family. The old rules did not extend this legal protection when a person used force to protect a stranger. That rule has been changed in almost every jurisdiction. These days, a person can use deadly force to protect a stranger, so long as the stranger is being threatened with deadly force.

The limitations on this defense are more practical than legal. In the first place, the person raising this defense has to show that the violence was necessary.

Example: Stan is walking through the park and he hears a man scream, "You devil! I'll fix you now!" He rounds a corner to see a man in flowing robes choking a woman while others look on and do nothing. Stan rushes forward, pulls out a gun, and shoots the man.

How would you analyze this situation from a legal perspective? Is the man using deadly force against the woman? Yes. Can Stan respond with deadly force when another person is being threatened with deadly force? Yes. The legal defense of self-defense should be available to Stan, but in this situation, it is not. Why? Because the man and the woman were actors, performing the last act of *Othello*. This is what we mean by the practical difficulties that are raised by defense of others. The person using force to save another has to be sure that he has a correct understanding of the situation.

D. OTHER LIMITATIONS ON SELF-DEFENSE: NO DEADLY FORCE TO PROTECT PROPERTY

A person cannot use self-defense when he uses deadly force to protect property. At law, "property" refers to anything that can be owned. Real property refers to land and the houses permanently attached to it; personal property refers to everything else: cars, candy, cannonballs, etc. If a person is threatening to destroy personal property, the owner is not permitted to use deadly force to stop it.

Example: Around 2 A.M. one morning, Andy finally gives up trying to go to sleep and wanders around his house. He happens to look out his window and he sees a man splashing gasoline inside Andy's car. Andy gets his gun and runs outside. The man lights a match and is just about to throw the match inside Andy's car and set it on fire. Andy shoots the man. When the man sues him for battery, Andy claims self-defense. Will he be successful?

No. Andy cannot use deadly force to protect his car.

(Note: Andy does have an action against the man for damaging his car, so even if the jury reaches a verdict favorable to the man Andy shot, they will probably also reach a verdict awarding damages to Andy for the damages the man caused to Andy's car.)

Example: Joanna is walking her beloved dog one evening when a man staggers out of his house, aims a gun at her dog, and shouts that he is going to kill it. Joanna pulls out a gun and shoots the man. Can she claim defense of others or self-defense?

No. Under the law, dogs are considered to be property, just like cars and jewelry and fountain pens. If Joanna cannot use deadly force to protect those items, she cannot use deadly force to protect her dog either. A person is always entitled to use *reasonable* force to protect property, such as forcibly stopping someone from stealing a car, but a person cannot use deadly force in such a situation.

E. MUTUAL COMBAT

Closely related to self-defense, a claim of **mutual combat** is a defense that claims the plaintiff voluntarily entered into a fight with the defendant. If the plaintiff did agree to fight the defendant, he cannot then claim that the defendant battered him, especially while he was carrying out a battery himself. However, there are limitations on how far the defense of mutual combat goes. For instance, if the plaintiff voluntarily enters a fistfight with the defendant, and the defendant then escalates the violence by pulling out a gun, the defense of mutual combat will no longer be available to the defendant.

Mutual combat
When the parties to a fight voluntarily engage in violence

 ## CONSENT

The defense of consent is based on the premise that the plaintiff agreed to whatever injury he received from the defendant. A plaintiff can consent to a wide range of injuries, including physical, emotional, and financial injuries. In order to prevail on a claim of consent, the defendant must show that the plaintiff voluntarily gave consent once he knew the possible consequences.

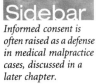
Informed consent is often raised as a defense in medical malpractice cases, discussed in a later chapter.

This defense is not available when the defendant tricks the plaintiff into giving consent or when the plaintiff consents without knowing the full facts.

Not everyone is legally capable of giving consent. Children cannot give consent, because the law considers them to lack the maturity and knowledge necessary to understand what is happening. Other people who cannot give consent include people who have been declared mentally incompetent or who are acting under the influence of drugs or alcohol.

DURESS, NECESSITY, COMPULSION, AND COERCION

When a defendant raises any of the defenses of duress, necessity, compulsion, or coercion, the defendant is essentially admitting that he committed a particular action, but that he had no choice in the matter.

Duress
When the defendant uses force, threat, or intimidation to overcome the plaintiff's will or to compel the plaintiff to do (or not to do) some action

A. DURESS

When a defendant pleads **duress** in his answer, he is saying that he was forced to carry out the act because someone was threatening his physical safety. Duress overcomes the person's will and unduly influences his behavior. This influence can come about through threats, intimidation, or other means. Whatever form it takes, the duress must be something that reasonable people would agree would cause someone to feel that they must commit a tort. It is not duress if the defendant "felt like" someone was pressuring him. The pressure brought to bear on the defendant must be something that an average person would consider to be compelling.[4]

Sidebar

Duress is based on the claim that the defendant was forced by someone else to carry out the intentional act.

Sidebar

When a defendant intends to raise the defense of duress, he must plead it with specificity. His answer must clearly spell out all the elements of duress before the court will consider it.[5]

B. COERCION

In most situations, duress and coercion are so closely related that there is no essential difference between them. When a person claims coercion, she is admitting that she committed the act, but that she was forced to do so by physical or other type of threat. As is true with all of these defenses, the defendant must satisfy the jury that the facts support the defense. The jury is usually informed that the defendant must prove that she acted in a reasonable manner. Coercion, like duress, is judged from the standpoint of a reasonable person, not the subjective viewpoint of the defendant.

Sidebar

A claim of coercion is closely associated with the claim of duress; the defendant is claiming that he was forced to commit an intentional tort.

C. NECESSITY

Necessity is similar to duress. When a defendant claims necessity, he admits that he carried out the wrong to the plaintiff, but that he did so only to avoid some greater catastrophe. Example: John is out in the woods when a sudden snowstorm strands him miles away from home. He trespasses onto Jim's land and breaks into his barn to seek shelter. Later, Jim brings suit against John for the damages he caused in breaking in. John can legally raise the defense of necessity as a defense to the allegation.

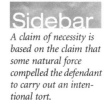

A claim of necessity is based on the claim that some natural force compelled the defendant to carry out an intentional tort.

Necessity is a defense in which the person claims that he committed one type of harm to avoid a more serious harm.

ISSUE
AT A
GLANCE

D. COMPULSION

The defense of **compulsion** actually goes to the mental state of the defendant at the time that he committed the tort. Mary sues Stan because Stan has stolen figurines she entrusted to him to clean. Stan claims that he has a compulsion called kleptomania. Whenever Stan sees figurines, he cannot help himself; he feels an overwhelming desire to take them. Compulsion is closely related to the defense of insanity, which we discuss later in this chapter.

Compulsion
An overwhelming or irresistible impulse to commit some action

A claim of compulsion is a form of insanity plea; the defendant is essentially saying that he could not prevent himself from carrying out the intentional tort.

 **INTOXICATION**

When a person raises the claim of intoxication, he is essentially seeking to excuse his behavior on the grounds that he was not in his right mind. As such, intoxication is a form of insanity. At law there are two types of intoxication: voluntary and involuntary.

A. VOLUNTARY INTOXICATION

When a person claims intoxication as a defense, he is actually saying that because of alcohol or some other drug, he lacked the ability to carry out intentional actions. However, a person can't use this defense if he voluntarily got intoxicated before carrying out the action.

Example: Stan wants to beat up Carl. Stan goes to a local bar, imbibes a lot of alcohol, and when Carl shows up, Stan attacks him. Carl sues Stan for battery and Stan claims that he was so intoxicated that he didn't know what he was doing. However, because Stan's own actions created his intoxication, the judge refuses to allow Stan to use this defense.

B. INVOLUNTARY INTOXICATION

Although a defendant is not permitted to use voluntary intoxication as a defense, the reverse situation can be a defense. If a person becomes intoxicated without her knowledge or intent, she may be allowed to use it as a defense. First of all, how does someone get "involuntarily intoxicated"? In the cases in which this defense has been used successfully, the defendant is usually exposed to chemicals or fumes that throw off her mental balance. That is the kind of involuntary intoxication the law recognizes as a valid defense.

 **MISTAKE**

Mistake can be a valid defense, in which the defendant's actions would have been permissible but for his legitimate misunderstanding.

Example: A group of friends is playing a game of tackle football at the local park. Ron, who is not a member of the group, and is not playing football, is wearing a jersey very similar to one of the team members. Rick sees Ron out of the corner of his eye, and believing Ron to be carrying the ball, tackles him. Ron is badly bruised and brings a battery lawsuit against Rick. Rick raises the claim of mistake and has a good chance of winning the suit.

Mistake is a defense seen far more often in contract law cases or business torts than in intentional torts.

 **AGE**

In almost all jurisdictions, a child under the age of seven is not considered to be responsible for his actions. If the child commits a battery, or any other tort, the law will not permit an action against the child. The reason for this prohibition is simple: A child, especially a young child, often does not understand the consequences of his actions. The law works hard to protect children, including placing more responsibility on adults to take precautions when children are involved. Allowing lawsuits against children would fly in the face of that social policy. Later, we discuss some situations in which a suit is allowed against a child's parents for actions carried out by the child.

Children receive special protection under the law and are often barred from consenting to actions to which an adult could legally give consent.

 **INSANITY**

A. OVERVIEW

When a person raises the defense of insanity, he is saying that he is not legally responsible for his actions. The law will not allow a legally insane person to be found liable in a civil suit. Insane people do not have to pay judgments to plaintiffs. However, this begs the question: What is legal insanity? In most jurisdictions, the standard for determining legal insanity is that the defendant, at the time that he carried out his actions, did not know the difference between right and wrong. It should be noted that a person can be mentally disturbed to a great degree and still not be considered legally insane.

Why would the law protect an insane person by prohibiting suits against him? The idea behind the protection is that an insane person is no more able to control his actions than is a child. An insane person, like a child, does not understand the consequences of his actions. In such a situation there would be very little gained, and a good deal lost, if we permitted suits against those who are insane. Legally incompetent people receive special protection in our society. This is true for children and it is also true for the legally insane. The law of insanity is essentially a manifestation of public policy. However, this is not to say that we have always had the same approach to liability of the legally insane.

In previous decades, the standard for determining legal insanity has swung from one extreme to the other. In some periods, even marginal cases of mental disturbance were given the greatest protection, while in others, this protection was only given to the most disturbed of individuals.

B. THE INSANITY DEFENSE

A defendant in an intentional tort action may claim that he or she was insane at the time that the tort was committed. A defendant who claims insanity at the time of the action at one time might have been insulated from the effects of his or her actions in the same way that a criminal defendant who is legally insane cannot be convicted of a crime. However, the civil rule has changed across most of the United States to the effect that a legally insane person will be liable to another for an intentional tort whether the defendant was legally insane or not. State after state has adopted an approach that places the burden of the legally insane person's torts squarely on the shoulders of the person who committed it. In this way, legal insanity varies considerably between civil and criminal cases.

Some states have gone so far as to make a legally insane person liable for both intentional and negligent actions in the same way that a legally sane person would be. Although making a legally insane person liable for intentional torts has obvious societal implications such as preventing potential fraud by those claiming insanity, there are different considerations for the insanity defense and negligence cases. As we will see in the next chapter, a claim of negligence involves establishing that the defendant was aware of a duty to another and subsequently breached that duty. Proving these elements against a legally insane person can present practical difficulties. For instance, is it fair to ascribe fault to a person who is incapable of controlling himself?

"Where one of two innocent persons must suffer a loss, it should be borne by the one who occasioned it."[6]

When it comes to imposing damages for an insane person's actions, there are still some important differences that hold over from original case law stating that an insane person would not be liable. Punitive damages are designed both to punish an individual for actions that he or she knew were reckless or grossly negligent and to provide an example to society of behavior that will not be tolerated. However, because an insane person cannot by definition know, understand, or control his or her behavior, there would seem to be little point in imposing them. This is the rule followed in many jurisdictions: A legally insane person can be liable for intentional and even negligent actions but cannot have punitive damages imposed for those actions. Similarly, some jurisdictions also limit damages in cases where malice or specific intent are required, such as slander.

IMMUNITY

Immunity
An exception or privilege granted by the law to an action that ordinarily would result in a cause of action

The claim of **immunity** is a defense that states that the plaintiff is legally barred from suing the defendant. When a person is immune from suit, it means that the lawsuit brought by the plaintiff must be dismissed. Immunity is reserved for people in specific professions or for specific circumstances.

Example: Last year, Judge South ruled against Ron in Ron's divorce action. The result was that Ron had to make high alimony payments to his ex-wife. Ron believes that the judge was wrong in her ruling and brings suit against her for intentional infliction of emotional distress, claiming that the high alimony payments have caused him to lose sleep and have left him generally irritable and cranky. Judge South's attorney, before addressing the questionable merits of Ron's lawsuit, files a motion to dismiss the suit, claiming judicial immunity. All jurisdictions have statutes that specifically bar suits against sitting judges when they act within the limits of their discretion in deciding cases before them. Ron has not alleged that Judge South exceeded her discretion or performed some action outside the scope and duties of her position. Without such an allegation, Ron has failed to show how the judge's actions are outside the protections of the immunity statute. Therefore, Judge South is immune from suit. The current judge will dismiss the lawsuit against Judge South.

The premise behind immunity is that government officials deserve protection from lawsuits for carrying out duties that are often unpopular with someone. Every time a police officer makes an arrest, at least one person (the arrestee) is upset with the officer's decision. When a judge makes a ruling in a case, it usually means that one side will lose. Protecting these officials with immunity allows these officials to act independently. Otherwise, they would be hampered by worrying about who would sue them for doing what they have been hired and trained to do. Immunities only apply when the official is acting in her professional capacity. When the person is "off duty," she has no greater protection against suit than anyone else.

Professions protected by immunity include police officers, judges, members of the legislature (for comments they make during debate), and others.

 PRIVILEGE

When defendants raise the claim of **privilege,** they are agreeing that they did commit the act but the act is protected from lawsuits by a statute or other law.

Example: Ron has a valid arrest warrant outstanding against him. Officer Steve, arresting Ron on this valid warrant, takes Ron's hands and puts them behind Ron's back and then handcuffs him. Ron believes that he has been battered, and when he later makes bond on the arrest charge, he goes to his attorney and asks that the attorney file a lawsuit against Officer Steve for battery.

After the complaint is filed and served on Officer Steve, the officer moves for a dismissal, raising the claim of privilege. He points out that police officers in his state are specifically protected under a statute that permits them to touch a suspect, even to use reasonable force, to make an arrest. The judge dismisses Ron's complaint. Others may enjoy a limited privilege, such as the limited privilege given to store employees to use reasonable force to subdue a shoplifter, as outlined in the case excerpt below.

> **Privilege**
> A protection or advantage given to a class of persons for actions taken by them

---

WILLIAMS v. KEARBEY
13 Kan. App. 2d 564, 775 P.2d 670 (Kan. App. 1989)

Syllabus by the Court

1. An insane person who shoots another may be held civilly liable in damages for his or her tort. Following *Seals v. Snow,* 123 Kan. 88, 254 P. 348 (1927).

2. A finding of insanity does not preclude a finding that a defendant acted intentionally. A jury may find that an insane person acted intentionally if he intended to do what he did, even though his reasons and motives were entirely irrational.

Before LEWIS, P.J., and DAVIS and GERNON, JJ. DAVIS, Judge:

In this case, we are asked to update Kansas tort law by holding that a 1927 Kansas Supreme Court decision no longer states the current tort law in Kansas. That decision held that "an insane person who shoots and kills another is civilly liable in damages to those injured by his tort." *Seals v. Snow*, 123 Kan. 88, Syl. ¶1, 254 P. 348 (1927). We conclude that *Seals v. Snow* is well grounded in sound public policy and expresses the unanimous view of all jurisdictions considering this question. Thus, we affirm the decision of the trial court.

Defendant Alan Kearbey, a minor, shot and wounded plaintiff Don Harris and plaintiff Daniel Williams, also a minor. Plaintiffs brought this action against Kearbey for battery. The jury found for plaintiffs. It also found, in answer to a special question, that Kearbey was insane at the time. The trial court entered judgment for plaintiffs and Kearbey appeals, arguing: (1) that an insane person should not be held civilly liable for his torts; and (2) that an insane person cannot commit a battery because he is incapable of forming the necessary intent.

Highly summarized, the material facts are as follows: On January 21, 1985, Alan Kearbey, who was then 14 years old, shot several people at Goddard Junior High School. The principal was killed and three other people were wounded. Among the wounded were plaintiff Don Harris, a teacher at the school, and plaintiff Daniel Williams, a student at the school. Both were shot in the leg. Harris and Williams brought this action against Kearbey, his parents, and the Goddard School District (U.S.D. No. 265). The trial court held that Harris' claim against the school district was barred by the Kansas Workers' Compensation Act and, at the close of plaintiffs' case, granted the school district's motion for a directed verdict against plaintiff Williams based on governmental immunity. These rulings were not appealed. The jury was allowed, however, to apportion fault to the school district. The court denied Alan Kearbey's motion for a directed verdict on the grounds of insanity.

The jury apportioned 80% of the fault to Alan Kearbey, 0% to his parents, and 20% to the school district. It found that Harris' damages were $66,637.68, and Williams' damages were $44,402.80. The trial court reduced the damages to reflect the percentage of fault attributed to Alan Kearbey and entered judgment in favor of Harris for $53,310.14 and in favor of Williams for $35,522.24.

1. Whether an Insane Person Should Be Held Civilly Liable for His Torts.

In 1927, the Kansas Supreme Court held that "an insane person who shoots and kills another is civilly liable in damages to those injured by his tort." *Seals v. Snow*, 123 Kan. 88, Syl. ¶1, 254 P. 348 (1927). In 1940, the Supreme Court reaffirmed this holding in dicta, saying: "It is definitely settled in this state that the defendant, Toepffer, if in fact insane, would have been civilly liable in damages for his torts." *Toepffer v. Toepffer,* 151 Kan. 924, 929, 101 P.2d 904 (1940). The appellate courts of this state have not spoken on this subject since 1940.

The tort liability of insane persons presents a policy question. In resolving this question, American courts have unanimously chosen to impose liability on an insane person rather than leaving the loss on the innocent victim. *Seals v. Snow* is a leading case in support of this view.

In *Seals v. Snow,* Martin Snow shot and killed Arthur Seals. Seals' widow brought an action for wrongful death. Snow answered that he had acted in self-defense. The jury returned a general verdict for the plaintiff, and found in answer to special questions that Snow had not acted in self-defense, that he was insane when he shot Seals, and that he was not able "to distinguish right from wrong" at the time he shot Seals. 123 Kan. at 88-89, 254 P. 348.

On appeal, Snow argued that he should not be held liable for his torts since he was insane. The court responded:

> It is conceded that the great weight of authority is that an insane person is civilly liable for his torts. This liability has been based on a number of grounds, one that where one of two innocent persons must suffer a loss, it should be borne by the one who occasioned it. Another, that public policy requires the enforcement of such liability in order that relatives of the insane person shall be led to restrain him and that tort-feasors shall not simulate or pretend insanity to defend their wrongful acts causing damage to others, and that if he was not liable there would be no redress for injuries, and we might have the anomaly of an insane person having abundant wealth depriving another of his rights without compensation.

123 Kan. at 90, 254 P. 348.

Kearbey argues (1) the loss should fall upon plaintiffs rather than himself since he was not capable of avoiding his conduct and, hence, was not at fault; (2) it no longer makes sense to impose liability on an insane person in order to encourage his relatives to confine him since public policy no longer favors confinement of the mentally ill unless the insane person presents a danger to other people, in which case liability should be imposed directly on the insane person's relatives for failing to confine him, rather than on the insane person himself; and (3) concern over feigned insanity is no longer warranted since psychiatrists and psychologists now have improved methods of proving or disproving insanity.

Taking up Kearbey's arguments in reverse order, it is obvious that Kearbey's confidence in modern psychiatry is not widely shared. Comments to the Restatement (Second) of Torts list several valid reasons why liability is still imposed on insane persons. These reasons include:

> the unsatisfactory character of the evidence of mental deficiency in many cases, together with the ease with which it can be feigned, the difficulty of estimating its existence, nature and extent; and some fear of introducing into the law of torts the confusion that has surrounded the defense of insanity in the criminal law.

Restatement (Second) of Torts §895J comment a (1977).

Next, Kearbey argues that liability should not be imposed on an insane person in order to encourage his relatives to confine him since public policy no longer favors confinement of the mentally ill. We agree that this is not a particularly strong reason for imposing liability. It is also clear, however, that removing this rationale would not have changed the court's decision in *Seals v. Snow.*

The main rationale of *Seals v. Snow* and the one which keys our affirmance of the trial court in this case is that, as between an insane person who injures another and an innocent person, it is more just for the insane person to bear the loss he caused than to visit the loss on the injured person. As stated in *Seals v. Snow:*

> Undoubtedly, there is some appearance of hardship, even of injustice, in compelling one to respond for that which, for want of the control of reason, he was unable to avoid; that it is imposing upon a person already visited with the inexpressible calamity of mental obscurity an obligation to observe the same care and precaution respecting the rights of others that the law demands of one in the full possession of his faculties. But the question of liability in these cases, as well as in others, is a question of policy; and it is to be disposed of as would be the question whether the incompetent person should be supported at the expense of the public, or of his neighbors, or at the expense of his own estate. If his mental disorder makes him dependent, and at the same time prompts him to commit injuries, there seems to be no greater reason for imposing upon the neighbors or the public one set of these consequences, rather than the other; no more propriety or justice in making others bear the losses resulting from his unreasoning fury, when it is spent upon them or their property, than there would be in calling upon them to pay the expense of his confinement in an asylum, when his own estate is ample for the purpose.

123 Kan. at 90-91, 254 P. 348 (quoting 1 Cooley on Torts 172 3d ed. 1906).

Although the above language is somewhat dated, the reasoning is still well grounded in sound public policy. Someone must bear the loss and, as between the tortfeasor, the injured party, and the general public, sound public policy favors placing the loss on the person who caused it, whether sane or not.

2. Whether an Insane Person Is Capable of Forming the Intent of Bringing About a Harmful or Offensive Bodily Contact That Is Necessary to the Tort of Battery.

Kearbey argues that he did not commit the tort of battery because his insanity prevented him from forming the intent necessary for that tort. The prevailing American view as set forth above is that a finding of insanity does not preclude a finding that a defendant acted intentionally. A jury may find that an insane person acted intentionally if he intended to do what he did, even though his reasons and motives were entirely irrational. Restatement (Second) of Torts §895J comment c (1977); Prosser & Keeton on Torts §135, p. 1074 (5th ed. 1984).

The requirements of the prevailing American view for imposing liability for an intentional tort are satisfied in this case. In finding for the plaintiffs, the jury necessarily found that Alan Kearbey touched or struck the plaintiffs "with the intent of bringing about either a contact or an apprehension of contact, that is harmful or offensive." The fact that Kearbey did not "understand the nature of his acts" or did not "understand that what he was doing was prohibited by law" does not preclude the jury from finding that Kearbey acted intentionally in discharging a weapon in Goddard Junior High School.

Affirmed.

Questions about the case:

1. What is the central question for the court in this case?
2. What actions were carried out by Alan Kearbey?
3. According to the court, is an insane person liable for his actions in a civil action? Why or why not?
4. What is the public policy justification for the court's decision in this case?
5. According to the court, is an insane person capable of forming the intent to commit a battery?

STATUTES OF LIMITATION

All tort actions have statutes of limitation, that is, time limits in which the case must be brought or be forever barred. The limitation periods are usually set by the legislature and can be found in the various state and federal codes. For intentional torts, the time periods are usually short. For example, a battery action has a one-year statute of limitation in some jurisdictions. This means that if a battery suit is not brought within one year of the incident, the plaintiff cannot bring the action at all. Statutes of limitation are designed to provide some sense of closure to potential legal claims. Defendants can be secure that if a case is not brought within the applicable statute of limitation, it will not be brought at all. These statutes also encourage plaintiffs to bring actions as soon as possible, when witness memories are still clear and before the evidence is lost or destroyed.

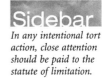

In any intentional tort action, close attention should be paid to the statute of limitation.

DEFENSES AVAILABLE TO CODEFENDANTS

Among the defenses available to a defendant is the right to apportion blame against a codefendant. In cases in which there is more than one defendant, each defendant has the right to assess the blame for the plaintiff's injuries against the other defendant. When there is more than one defendant, the plaintiff is often in the difficult position of assessing blame against both. How does a plaintiff specify which injuries were caused by which defendant?

Example: Ted is attacked and beaten by two men: Carl and Stanley. During the attack, Ted is knocked unconscious. When he regains consciousness, he has severe injuries but is unable to say which of the two men caused them. What does he do? He takes advantage of the legal principle of joint and several liability.

A. JOINT AND SEVERAL LIABILITY

The doctrine of joint and several liability was created for just such a situation as the one confronting Ted. Under this doctrine, a plaintiff who has been injured by more than one defendant is permitted to sue both and seek his total damages against them individually and as codefendants. Ted can sue Carl and Stanley and recover his entire damages from just one of them. Joint and several liability is based on the premise that between the plaintiff and the defendants in this scenario, the person who should be given the greatest consideration is the injured plaintiff. Ted can obtain judgments against both or against each man individually. If Carl ends up paying the full amount of Ted's injuries, Carl can seek reimbursement from Stanley in a separate legal action. Joint and several liability has come under criticism in recent years by those who claim that plaintiffs use it as a way to sue everyone in sight, on the off chance that someone will have enough funds to pay for the plaintiff's injuries. There are some important limitations on joint and several liability. The plaintiff can only sue defendants who are potentially liable. A plaintiff is not allowed to sue anyone who might have "deep pockets," that is, someone who has financial resources. The person or corporation sued must be liable for some of the plaintiff's injuries. Another important limitation is that the plaintiff is not allowed to recover more than his claimed injuries. For instance, Ted can't recover twice the monetary damages he requests by having Stanley and Carl both pay him the total amount.

In joint and several liability, when two or more defendants contribute to the plaintiff's injuries, they remain individually liable to the plaintiff for the total amount of the plaintiff's injuries.

B. VICARIOUS LIABILITY

We have seen that when there is more than one defendant, a plaintiff is permitted to sue all those who have injured him and can recover his entire damages against any one of them. Another principle closely associated with joint and several liability is vicarious liability. Under most situations, a person is solely responsible for her actions. However, there are times when the law allows suits against others, even people not present when the plaintiff's injuries occurred. In vicarious liability one defendant is held liable for the actions of another. This is true even when the second defendant didn't actually do anything to injure the plaintiff.

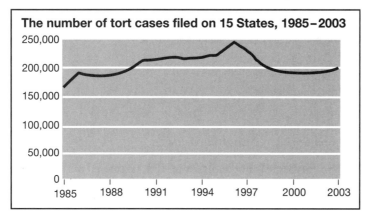

The number of tort cases filed in 15 states increased through 1996, then decreased but stabilized recently.

The number of tort cases filed on 15 States, 1985–2003

Bureau of Justice Statistics, www.ojp.usdoj.gov/bjs/glance/tortperctrial.htm.

FIGURE 3-2

Number of Tort Cases Filed in 15 States, 1985-2003

1. EMPLOYER/EMPLOYEE LIABILITY (*RESPONDEAT SUPERIOR*)

The most common form of vicarious liability is the liability of an employer for the actions of an employee.

Example: Ron works for a local furniture store and is driving the delivery truck to deliver some furniture. He runs a red light and strikes Mary. Mary brings suit against Ron and Ron's employer, the furniture store. Her suit can proceed against Ron, as an individual, and against Ron's employer for Ron's actions.

The theory behind employer/employee liability is based on an ancient doctrine that said a slave's misdeeds could be assessed against his master. Under more modern interpretation, the principle continues to be used because the employee was acting within the scope of his employment at the time that he caused injury to the plaintiff. Since the defendant was working for a company, his negligence is imputed to his employer. This principle is also known as ***respondeat superior,*** a Latin term that translates, "Let the master respond."

Respondeat superior
Liability imposed on an employer for the actions of the employee, when the employee is carrying out his duties for the employer

Pro:
Joint and several (J/S) liability is the only way to make sure the plaintiff receives a full monetary recovery and can return to something resembling a normal life.

Con:
J/S liability allows unscrupulous plaintiffs to sue everyone, hoping that someone will have the financial resources to enrich the plaintiff, even if a defendant isn't the main culprit.

Pro:
Of the people involved in the lawsuit, the plaintiff is the one who has been injured and is often in no shape to know which of the defendants actually injured him.

Con:
Defendants in J/S liability cases often settle cases before going to trial out of fear that the jury will assess huge verdicts against them.

FIGURE 3-3

Arguments For and Against the Joint and Several Liability Doctrine

FIGURE 3-4

**A Summary
of Vicarious
Liability**

■ One person is found to be liable because someone else has acted unreasonably.
■ The unreasonableness of one person is assessed against another, even though
   this other person didn't do anything wrong.

The most common examples of vicarious liability are

■ Employer/employee
■ Joint enterprise
■ Family purpose doctrine

a. Limitations on *Respondeat Superior*

Obviously, an employer is not liable for all actions carried out by an employee.
For instance, Ron gets off work and goes home. As he is driving his own car,
he runs another red light and hits Betty. Betty sues Ron and Ron's employer.
The furniture store files a motion to be dismissed from the case and the judge
agrees. After all, Ron was not acting within the scope of his employment at
the time of his accident.

Scope of Employment

As long as the employee is acting within the scope of his employment at the
time that he injures the plaintiff, his employer will be liable for his actions.
However, "scope of employment" has proved to be a difficult term to define.
For instance, suppose that at the time that Ron is driving the delivery truck in
his accident with Mary, he is actually running a personal errand. Because this
errand has nothing to do with his job, his employer claims that she should not
be liable under *respondeat superior.* Two clear exceptions have developed over
time to protect employers from such situations.

Frolic and Detour

When an employee is out running a personal errand, or actually away from his
job without permission, the employer will not be liable for his actions. When
an employee is on a "frolic," he is no longer acting for his employer; he is
carrying out personal business or simply having fun. When an employee
deviates from his job duties to carry out personal business, this "detour"
will also relieve his employer of liability for his actions. These two exceptions
developed out of a need to restrict the doctrine of *respondeat superior* to the
employee's actual job duties. Without such limitations, an employer would
essentially be liable for all the employee's actions, even when the employee was
not carrying out company business. Courts have consistently ruled that
expanding the doctrine of *respondeat superior* to this extreme would place
too high a burden on businesses. On the other hand, when the employee is
acting within the scope of his duties, he is furthering the company's interests.
In some cases, the employee's actions may actually have been caused by the
company's policies.

Example: Mary works for a local pizza restaurant that guarantees a pizza
delivery within 30 minutes of the time that the order is placed or the pizza

is free. Local managers tell their drivers that any free pizzas will be deducted from the driver's paycheck. This has the natural effect of encouraging the drivers to deliver the pizzas as fast as possible. They often drive faster than the posted speed limit and even run traffic lights. Managers realize that the drivers are doing these things, but do not change their policy. One evening, Mary is rushing to deliver a pizza before the 30-minute deadline and she runs a red light. She crashes into another car driven by Amy. Amy is severely injured. She brings suit against Mary and the pizza restaurant. Her allegation is based on the fact that (1) Mary was working for the pizza restaurant at the time of the accident; (2) Mary was acting in furtherance of the restaurant's business; and (3) Mary's haste (and recklessness) was based on the restaurant's 30-minute policy, which encouraged the drivers to drive too fast.

When Amy's case is heard, her theory of *respondeat superior* is found to be valid and her suit proceeds against both Mary and the restaurant.

Under the doctrine of vicarious liability, third parties can be liable for the actions of others. The most common example is when an employer is liable for the actions of her employee. This is also called *respondeat superior*.

ISSUE
AT A
GLANCE

Independent Contractor

When a person is classified as an independent contractor, he is not an employee and there is no *respondeat superior* claim. How does the law define an independent contractor? An independent contractor is a person who is usually some form of specialist. When a person is an independent contractor, he controls his day-to-day decisions and actions, as opposed to an employee who works under the direct supervision of a supervisor. An independent contractor might be someone like a software expert, who is called in to help de-bug new computer programs. This person will often work under his own initiative, decide how to proceed, and will ultimately declare when he has completed his task. In such a situation, this person is not an employee. The theory of *respondeat superior* has been specifically limited to employees. The principle behind *respondeat superior* is that the employee has very little discretion in what he does. The employee obeys the employer and is, at least in this regard, an extension of the employer. However, an independent contractor operates on his own, without supervision and direct control. Therefore, *respondeat superior* does not apply to him.

What makes an independent contractor?
Worker has control over job duties = IC
Worker has discretion in how the job is carried out = IC
Worker is hired to do a specific job = IC

ISSUE
AT A
GLANCE

2. OTHER SITUATIONS IN WHICH VICARIOUS LIABILITY IS AUTHORIZED: FAMILY PURPOSE DOCTRINE

The so-called family purpose doctrine allows a plaintiff to sue the parents of a driver who causes injury, even though the parent wasn't present in the car at the time of the accident. Although this doctrine is not recognized in all jurisdictions, in the ones where it is, the doctrine essentially allows plaintiffs to sue parents for the actions of their children.

To bring a lawsuit under the family purpose doctrine, the plaintiff must show:

1 That the parent owns the car involved in the accident
2 That the parent makes the car available to family members for family use
3 That the driver is a member of the defendant's immediate family
4 That the driver was using the car for a family purpose
5 That the driver had express or implied permission to use the car

When the plaintiff can establish each of those elements, the plaintiff can recover damages from the car owner, even though the owner wasn't involved in the car wreck.

Example: Fred is injured in an accident in which Jimmy runs a stop sign and strikes Fred's car. Jimmy is 16 years old and is driving the family car. Fred brings suit against Jimmy and Jimmy's parents under the family purpose doctrine. Jimmy's parents file a motion to dismiss them from the suit. The judge rules against them, stating that the case clearly falls within the family purpose doctrine.

3. OTHER SITUATIONS IN WHICH VICARIOUS LIABILITY IS AUTHORIZED: JOINT ENTERPRISE

The third situation in which a person may be liable for the actions of another is the joint enterprise doctrine. This doctrine allows a plaintiff to bring suit against one business partner for the actions of the other. However, to take advantage of this doctrine, the plaintiff must show:

1 That there was an express or implied agreement among the defendants to carry out a business
2 That the defendants had a common purpose in carrying out the business
3 That the defendants each had the right to control the business (i.e., that one member wasn't an employee of the other)

SKILLS YOU NEED IN THE REAL WORLD

Evaluating a Case

One of the most important skills a legal professional can acquire is the ability to evaluate a case objectively. Like any skill, getting good at evaluating a case takes time. Why should you invest this time? The simple answer is that the better you are at evaluating cases, the better you are at your job (and the more indispensable you become to the firm). An evaluation of any case takes into account the following factors:

- The nature of the claim
- The type of injuries
- The quality of the opposing counsel
- The judge's temperament and several other factors

Step One: Evaluate the Facts

The facts of the case are perhaps the single most important item in a case evaluation. This is true whether you are working for the plaintiff or the defendant. Before evaluating the plaintiff's injuries, there are some preliminary questions that must be answered. One of the questions that should be answered early on in the case evaluation process is "Just how liable is the defendant?" If the case against the defendant is shaky, this affects the rest of your evaluation. On the other hand, if the case against him is one of clear and obvious liability, you can feel much more secure in your evaluation. As such, the facts of the case are the most important aspect of the evaluation. Find out all the details and write them down. Make sure that you have a solid (and objective) view of the facts. Here is where having sympathy for the plaintiff could be your downfall. Take a cold, hard look at the case. If the answer to "Just how liable is the defendant?" is "not very," you don't have a strong case, no matter how many injuries the plaintiff has.

Step Two: Evaluate the Opposition

In theory, all attorneys know the rules and will do a good job in court. However, the reality is starkly different. Some attorneys are master trial advocates and others are plainly terrible. A skilled adversary is obviously more of a challenge than a novice. Veteran attorneys can almost always justify a higher settlement in a case than recent law school graduates. One thing you can do is to find out how long the opposing attorney has been practicing. You could point out to your own attorney the skill level of the opposition (if he or she does not already know it). Find out what others in the legal community think about the opposition. What type of reputation does this attorney have? Is the attorney noted for excellent trial skills? If so, you can bet that this attorney will be a real challenge and you must prepare accordingly.

Step Three: Evaluate the Likelihood of Recovery

The plaintiff always wants to know how much money he or she will get from the defendant. Frankly, there is no way to know that prior to the actual settlement. You should never promise a client that he is "guaranteed" to get at least x amount of dollars. There are times when the defendant's liability is not in question, but he has no assets. (In Chapter 8, we discuss the importance of asset searches.)

Step Four: Evaluate the Injuries

The plaintiff's injuries are a crucial part of any case evaluation. For instance, suppose that the defendant is clearly at fault, but the plaintiff has not been injured in any significant way. In such a case, the recovery amount will be low. Conversely, where the plaintiff's injuries are severe, and the defendant's liability is obvious, the recovery is likely to be large.

Step Five: Evaluate the Law

How does the applicable law affect the case? Some jurisdictions follow the rule of contributory negligence (see Chapter 9). This rule provides that the plaintiff is not entitled to any recovery if he can be shown to have contributed to his own injuries. Other jurisdictions follow a comparative negligence rule, in which the plaintiff's recovery is reduced by the amount of his own negligence. The rule followed in your jurisdiction has a profound impact on the evaluation of the case.

 THE LIFE OF A PARALEGAL

Assisting in Jury Selection

When I attend trials, I often take notes during jury selection. I will watch the people on the panel, looking at their facial expressions, their body language. Sometimes people will shake their heads or frown at something the lawyers say. I feverishly write down as many comments as I can. Usually, I'm looking for the people who aren't going to be sympathetic to our side. We dismiss those people.

I prepare a seating chart of the jury panel during jury selection, so we can remember who is sitting where. I'll write any important notes about the person right on the chart. It's good to have a woman's perspective during jury selection. I usually work with a male attorney, and once during jury selection on a case, the juror had answered the plaintiff's attorney's questions very sweetly, but then when my attorney started asking questions, she totally copped an attitude with him. When the attorney asked me what I thought, I said that he should get rid of her. "She doesn't like you," I told him. He said, "Really? I didn't pick up on that." He needed a woman's perspective on that juror.

Lisa Mazzonetto, Paralegal

ETHICAL ISSUES FOR THE PARALEGAL: AVOIDING A CLAIM OF UNAUTHORIZED PRACTICE OF LAW

Many times during your paralegal career, you will be asked by a client for advice about a legal topic. A client could, for example, ask you about the merits of the defense he is raising in his answer. A paralegal should always be careful to avoid any allegation of unauthorized practice of law (UPL). Paralegals who give legal advice are practicing law without a license. When they do, they run into two immediate problems. The first problem is that UPL is illegal in all states. Paralegals who give legal advice can end up in jail. The second problem is that paralegals who give legal advice can end up being named in legal malpractice suits brought against the attorney. If the attorney loses the suit, she could end up having to pay monetary damages to the former client.

Does giving an opinion about the client's legal defense constitute UPL? Probably. The safest course to follow is: When in doubt, assume the worst. If you aren't sure if the answer you are about to give is legal advice, assume that it is. Pause for a moment and reflect. Perhaps this answer should come from someone else, such as the attorney? Perhaps it is time for a disclaimer? Gently remind the client that you're not an attorney and you can't give legal advice. Remember that the client who is smiling now could be an adversary in a lawsuit next year.

Chapter Summary

When the plaintiff brings a claim of intentional tort against a defendant, the defendant is allowed to raise one or more defenses against the claim. The various defenses include self-defense, defense of others, or consent. These defenses essentially admit that the action occurred, but that it was excused, either because the defendant was protecting himself or protecting others, or because the plaintiff agreed to the action. Other defenses raise the specter of the defendant's will overcome by other forces. The defendant might claim duress, that is, that he committed the action because of pressure or undue influence of another. Similar defenses are necessity, compulsion, and coercion. Insanity is also a defense to a tort. In an insanity defense, the defendant is claiming that he did not know the difference between right and wrong at the time that he carried out the action. When more than one defendant is involved, both may be liable to the plaintiff under the theory of joint and several liability. The defendant's employer may also be liable under certain circumstances, under the theory of *respondeat superior*.

Web Sites

▓ **University of Minnesota Law School**
   http://www.law.umn.edu/library/tools/pathfinders/verdicts1.html

▓ **Cornell Law**
   http://www.law.cornell.edu/topics/torts.html

▓ **Hieros Gamos**
   http://www.hg.org

▓ **Intimate Partner Violence, 1993-2001**
   http://www.oip.usdoj.gov/bjs/abstract/ipv01.htm

Forms and Court Documents

This form shows an answer to the complaint in Chapter 2.

IN THE SUPERIOR COURT OF GANNETT COUNTY
STATE OF PLACID

Richard Coe,	)	CASE NO. CV 2002-1101
Plaintiff	)	
	)	
vs.	)	
	)	
	)	
Terry Zoe,	)	
Defendant		

Answer

The Defendant answers the Plaintiff's Complaint as follows:

1.

Admitted.

2.

Admitted.

3.

The defendant admits that he was present in Tilly's Tavern on the evening of August 13, 2000. To the best of his knowledge, plaintiff was also present.

4.

The defendant admits that he struck the Plaintiff, but that he did so in self-defense to prevent the plaintiff from severely injuring him with a weapon. The remainder of the allegations contained in Plaintiff's Complaint Paragraph 4 are denied.

5.

Denied; defendant acted in self-defense and his actions were, therefore, justified under the law to protect himself from a vicious, unwarranted, and unjustified violent attack by the Plaintiff.

6.

Defendant is without sufficient information to either deny or admit the allegations contained in Paragraph 6.

7.

Defendant is without sufficient information to either admit or deny the allegations contained in Paragraph 7, except to deny that he is responsible in any way for the Plaintiff's claimed damages.

First Defense

8.

The defendant realleges and incorporates by reference his responses to Paragraphs 1 through 7 of the Complaint as if fully set forth.

9.

Defendant's actions on the evening of August 13, 2000, in striking the Plaintiff were motivated entirely by his desire to avoid Plaintiff's offer of violence and Plaintiff's unwarranted and unjustified threat of physical violence to the defendant by use of a weapon, most likely a knife, which Plaintiff had in his possession at the time of the incident alleged in the Plaintiff's complaint.

Having fully answered each and every allegation of the complaint, the defendants request the court:

1. That plaintiffs have and recover nothing of the defendants by way of this action.
2. That the costs of this action be taxed against the plaintiffs.
3. For a trial by jury of all triable issues of fact.
4. For such other and further relief as the court may deem just and proper.

This the _____ day of July 2002.

Respectfully submitted,

By: _____
Attorney for Defendant

Key Terms

Compulsion	Immunity	*Respondeat superior*
Duress	Mutual combat	Self-defense
Excessive force	Privilege	

Review Questions

1 When does a defendant lose the right to raise the defense of self-defense?

2 Explain "excessive force."

3 Under what circumstances can a person use deadly force to protect personal property?

4 Describe a situation in which the defendant's claim of consent would be legally invalid.

5 Explain the differences between duress, necessity, coercion, and compulsion.

6 When is a person permitted to raise the defense of "involuntary intoxication"?

7 What is the legal definition of insanity?

8 Give an example of a situation in which the defense of mistake would be appropriate.

9 Describe a class of persons who could be protected by immunity under tort law.

10 Explain joint and several liability.

11 What is vicarious liability?

12 When does a person qualify as an "independent contractor"?

13 What is the justification for *respondeat superior?*

14 What is the family purpose doctrine?

15 What are some of the important points to consider when evaluating a case?

Applying What You Have Learned

1 Ted is a police officer. One day, he pulls over a driver for speeding and begins writing a ticket. Stan, the driver, puts the car in reverse while Ted is writing the ticket and backs up toward Ted, who is standing between Stan's car and Ted's patrol car. Stan's car is moving about one mile per hour. Ted pulls his service revolver and shoots Stan though the back window, killing him. When Stan's relative brings a civil action against Ted, does Ted have a valid claim of self-defense?

2 A group of foreign guests at a local hotel decide that the service has not been acceptable. When the manager refuses to refund their money, they threaten him and the other staff members and then force them into the manager's office and refuse to allow them to leave. Does the doctrine of *respondeat superior* provide a claim for the manager and staff against the hotel for the guests' conduct?

3 John owes $10,000 to a local businessman. Jerry, the businessman, becomes angry when John fails to pay back the money. He sends John a letter that says, in part, "If you don't pay back the money, I'll release certain facts to the press and your friends and family that you won't find very flattering." Draft a complaint alleging duress based on these facts. Feel free to create your own dates for these specific actions, but make sure that your complaint meets the legal requirements for duress.

4 Does your state differentiate between defenses such as duress and coercion? If so, what are the elements of these defenses in your state?

5 Is "compulsion" recognized in your state? If so, is it a form of the insanity defense, or is it organized under some other defense?

6 Why did the court in the *Kearby* case rule that an insane person could be liable for his actions?

Endnotes

[1] *Taran v. State,* 186 A.D.2d 794, 589 N.Y.S.2d 74 (1992).

[2] *Scheuermann v. Scharfenberg,* 163 Ala. 337, 50 So. 335 (1909); *Cornell v. Harris,* 60 Idaho 87, 88 P.2d 498 (1939).

[3] A History of American Law by Lawrence Friedman, Simon and Schuster, New York, p. 261 (1973).

[4] *Wilson v. Wilson,* 642 S.W.2d 132 (1982).

[5] *Bennett v. Auto. Ins. Co.,* 646 A.2d 806 (1994); *Imperial Refineries Corp. v. Morrissey,* 119 N.W.2d 872 (1963).

[6] *Seals v. Snow,* 123 Kan. 88, 254 P. 348, 349 (1927).

Introduction to Negligence

Chapter Objectives

- Explain the four elements of a negligence action
- Explain how negligence is different from other forms of torts
- Describe how a new file is created
- Explain the methods used to gather information from the client
- Identify the important features found in a negligence complaint

NEGLIGENCE: WHAT MAKES IT DIFFERENT?

A negligence case is very different from the intentional tort cases that we discussed in the previous chapter. In a negligence action, the plaintiff is not claiming that the defendant intentionally injured him. Instead, the plaintiff is claiming that his injuries are the result of the defendant's carelessness — his failure to pay attention or failure to take adequate measures to protect others. In an intentional torts case, the plaintiff must show that the defendant acted knowingly and voluntarily. In negligence cases, the elements of proof are very different.

THE HISTORY OF NEGLIGENCE

Although some commentators argue that the body of negligence law originated in the Middle Ages, others claim that the real impetus to negligence as a
separate (and highly specialized) area of law arose in the twentieth century.
That century saw huge social and economic upheavals and the development of
vast new industries. These new chemical, industrial, and electronic developments had unseen potential dangers. And earlier, the dangers of the Industrial
Revolution had had a profound impact on the development of legal principles
of negligence. We discuss the historical development of negligence in the
chapters specifically devoted to each of the four basic elements.

In negligence cases there are four elements that must be satisfied before
the defendant can be found liable: the establishment of a legal duty, proof that
the defendant breached that duty, a causal connection between the breach
and the plaintiff's injuries, and damages suffered by the plaintiff that can be
assessed against the defendant. For simplicity's sake, we abbreviate these four
elements as duty, breach, causation, and damages.

The basic elements of a negligence case
In any negligence claim, the plaintiff must prove four elements:
    Duty   **Causation**
    Breach   **Damages**

In this chapter, we explore the basic principles of each element, explaining
them in general terms and providing examples. In the next four chapters, we
examine each of these elements in depth. We also examine how a negligence
case first reaches a firm and the important information that must be gathered
early in the process. But first, we show how the elements of negligence factor
into a discussion of the Chumley case.

THE CHUMLEY CASE

To remind you of the basic details of the Chumley case, Mr. and Mrs. Chumley
were driving home when they were struck broadside by a train owned and
operated by National Railroad Company. The engineer who was driving the
train is a man named Stanley Blue. The basic contention that Mr. Chumley
raises is that the intersection was dangerous. According to him, it was difficult,
if not impossible, for a motorist stopping at the intersection to see down the
railroad tracks because there were thick evergreen trees growing along the
track. Because the track curved, these trees blocked the view of any oncoming

train. Remember that Mr. Chumley was severely injured in the crash and his wife was killed. He wants to sue the railroad.

If our firm is going to take this case, we must first determine if the wreck falls into the category of a negligence case. In other words, we must go through each element of a negligence case and make sure there is enough evidence to support each element.

THE FOUR ELEMENTS OF NEGLIGENCE

As we discuss each of the four elements that must be proved by the defendant, consider why the courts would impose such elements in the first place.

A. DUTY

The first element of a negligence claim is **duty.** To prove a negligence claim, the plaintiff must prove that the defendant owed a duty to the plaintiff and that he failed to live up to that duty. How does a person come to owe a duty to another person? A duty can arise out of a relationship, such as the duty of a parent to a child. Duty can also arise out of legal obligation, such as the obligation of a police officer to take care of a suspect once he has been placed under arrest. In fact, the defendant doesn't even have to know the plaintiff to owe him a duty. People who drive on the public highways have a general duty to other drivers not to drive in a careless manner.

Duty
An outcome that a person should have known or been able to anticipate or predict based on certain facts

In the chapter on duty, we discuss the issue of foreseeability. This term encompasses the concept that, for the defendant to have a duty to the plaintiff, it must be foreseeable for the plaintiff to be a person who could be injured by the defendant's actions.

Duty can also be established through court-created doctrines. Courts frequently have created exceptions to the equation: duty + breach + proximate cause + damages = negligence. One such exception occurs because courts agreed that a duty could be created by a contractual agreement. Court doctrines can affect every step of the negligence equation, often supplying a missing or tenuous element.

Is negligence a question of fact or law? The answer is that it is both. A court can hold that a defendant is not negligent as a matter of law and dismiss the lawsuit, but only after finding that no reasonable jury could find negligence, based on the facts presented in the case.[1]

We begin our overview of duty by taking a look at an excerpt from the Chumley Complaint in Figure 4-2.

Notice that until paragraph 15 nothing in the complaint refers to the duty owed by the various defendants. A complaint must build its case by asserting facts. Once the facts are presented, the plaintiff can allege the defendants' duty. In later chapters, we examine this complaint and subsequent pleadings in detail, explaining how Mr. Chumley must set out each of the elements of negligence in his complaint and how the defendants in this case will attack those same elements.

FIGURE 4-1

The Four
Elements of a
Negligence
Action

■ Duty   ■ Causation
■ Breach   ■ Damages

FIGURE 4-2

The Complaint
in the Chumley
Case

| STATE OF NORTH CAROLINA | | SUPERIOR COURT DIVISION |
| COUNTY OF HALEY | | FILE NUMBER: |

CHARLES CHUMLEY,   )

        Plaintiff,   )
)

        vs.   )   <u>COMPLAINT</u>
)   <u>JURY TRIAL DEMANDED</u>

NATIONAL RAILWAY COMPANY   )
TOWN OF CLING,   )
and STANLEY W. BLUE,   )

        Defendant.   )
)
_____   )

Plaintiff, by and through his attorneys, complains of the defendant as follows:

1. Plaintiff is, and all times hereafter was, a citizen and resident of the Town of CLING, County of HALEY, State of North Carolina.
2. Plaintiff alleges upon information and belief that the defendant National Railroad Company (Railroad) is, and at all times hereafter was, a corporation organized and existing under the laws of the State of Virginia, licensed to do business, and in fact doing business, in the State of North Carolina and having a registered agent for the service of process by the name of Richard Robin located at 1221 North Bolstridge Ave., Suite 2000, Lakesboro, North Carolina, 27401.
3. Plaintiff alleges upon information and belief that the defendant Town of CLING (Town) is a duly chartered municipality in the County of HALEY and the State of North Carolina.
4. Plaintiff alleges upon information and belief that the defendant STANLEY W. BLUE is a citizen and resident of the County of Buncombe, State of North Carolina.
5. That at all times relevant to this Complaint the defendant STANLEY W. BLUE was an agent, servant, and employee of the defendant National Railroad Company (Railroad) and was acting within the course and scope of his employment with it.
6. The plaintiff is informed and believes and therefore alleges that the Town has waived any sovereign immunity that it otherwise might have through the purchase of liability insurance, thereby affording its residents and residents of other communities the right to sue for negligent acts that it might commit.
7. Railroad, at the time of the accident, owned, maintained, and used a set of railroad tracks laid in an east-west direction and passing through the Town.
8. Morgan Street is a public street in the Town that runs in a north-south direction crossing the tracks.
9. Plaintiff alleges, upon information and belief, that at the time of the accident, Railroad owned, maintained, and used the railroad tracks at railroad crossing

FIGURE 4-2

(continued)

number 728339E, which tracks cross and intersect with Morgan Street, in the Town of CLING, County of HALEY, North Carolina.

10. On August 23, 2002, at approximately 4:30 P.M., plaintiff was driving his automobile south on Morgan Street approaching the railroad crossing. A train belonging to and being operated by Railroad, its agents, servants, and employees, was approaching the crossing from an easterly direction.

11. At the crossing in question at the time of the accident, there were no mechanical devices to warn motorists of an approaching train; no blinking lights, automatic gates, bells or gongs, or stop bars were installed at the crossing.

12. The northeast quadrant of the grade crossing, at the time of the accident, contained vegetation and trees in such a position that they obstructed and/or severely restricted the view of the tracks or an approaching train by a motorist approaching the crossing. Upon information and belief, defendants, Railroad, Town, and STANLEY W. BLUE, were under a duty to maintain the area in question.

13. That as the plaintiff approached the crossing, he stopped and looked both ways; however, he was unable to see the train approaching because of the vegetation and overgrowth, which both the Town and the Railroad had negligently allowed to remain upon the right of way, until such time as he was on the tracks and a collision was inevitable.

14. Railroad's train struck plaintiff's automobile with great force as plaintiff attempted to cross the railroad track, knocked the car off the tracks in a southwesterly direction and dragged the car 100 yards from the point of impact, upon which the car rolled into a ditch.

15. The Town and Railroad owed to the plaintiff a duty of due care to reasonably and safely maintain the tracks and the area surrounding such tracks, particularly at crossings, in order to provide adequate sight distance for motorists operating automobiles on streets that intersect such crossings.

B. BREACH

Once the plaintiff has established that the defendant owes a duty, the next step is to show how the defendant violated that duty. When a defendant **breaches** a duty, he violates a standard of care or acts in a careless or reckless way. Just as there are doctrines that affect the analysis of duty, so too there are similar doctrines that affect how we view breach of that duty.

One such court-created doctrine allows the plaintiff to establish a breach simply because the defendant violated a safety statute at the time that he injured the plaintiff. This doctrine of **negligence per se** allows the plaintiff to establish a presumption of negligence when the defendant violates a traffic law when he injures the plaintiff.

Breaches
When the defendant fails to live up to a legal standard, or violates a duty

Negligence per se
Negligence in and of itself; the principle that the violation of a safety statute establishes a presumption of breach of duty in a negligence action

The second element of a negligence claim is a showing that the defendant breached a duty to the plaintiff. Without proof of a breach, the other elements of a negligence case are meaningless.

ISSUE
AT A
GLANCE

FIGURE 4-3

Excerpt from the Chumley Complaint: Breach

16. The Town *breached* this duty of due care by the following acts of negligence (emphasis added):

a. it failed to close the crossing pursuant to state law, when it knew, or in the exercise of due care should have known, that the crossing constituted an unreasonable hazard to vehicular or pedestrian traffic;

b. it failed to require the installation, construction, erection, or improvement of warning signs, gates, lights, stop bars, or such other safety devices when it knew or should have known in the exercise of reasonable care that such devices were necessary;

c. it allowed the crossing to remain in use with absolutely no safety devices with total, wanton, and reckless disregard for the safety of vehicular and pedestrian traffic;

d. it allowed the vegetation and trees adjacent to the tracks to obstruct the view by motorists of the tracks and approaching trains when it knew, or in the exercise of due care should have known, that such vegetation and trees constituted an unreasonable hazard to vehicular and pedestrian traffic;

e. it failed to keep the public street free from unnecessary obstructions in violation of State law.

Notice how the complaint in Figure 4-3 details the exact nature of the defendants' breach of the duty. In a later chapter, we explore the legal concept of breach of duty in greater detail.

C. CAUSATION

Proximate causation
The facts that show the defendant's legal responsibility for the injuries to the plaintiff, also known as legal cause

Once the plaintiff has proved that the defendant had a duty to him and the defendant breached that duty, the next step is that the plaintiff must prove that there is a factual connection between what the defendant did (or failed to do) and the resulting injuries to the plaintiff. This connection is referred to as **proximate causation.** This legal term requires a strong connection between the defendant's actions and the plaintiff's harm. Without this strong connection, the plaintiff cannot recover damages from the defendant.

Causation refers to the link between the defendant's actions (or failure to act) and the subsequent injury to the plaintiff.

D. DAMAGES

Damages
Monetary payments designed to compensate the plaintiff for an injury

After the plaintiff proves duty, breach, and causation, he must still prove that he suffered some form of physical or financial loss. Without this final element, a negligence case will fail. **Damages** are awarded as a way to attempt to put the plaintiff back into the condition he was in before the injury (or as close as possible). There are several different categories of damages, including damages for pain and suffering, lost wages, future medical payments, and many others, which we examine in greater depth in a later chapter.

19. That the negligence of the defendants Town of CLING, National Railway, and STANLEY W. BLUE joined and concurred and combined in point of time and place *proximately to cause* the collision between plaintiff's vehicle and Railroad's train.

FIGURE 4-4

Excerpt from the Chumley Complaint: Causation

. . . plaintiff's resulting serious, painful, and permanent injuries and damages, all of which exceed the sum of Ten Thousand Dollars ($10,000.00), and which include, without limitation, the following:

1. bodily injury and resulting pain and suffering;
2. medical expenses, including the costs of therapy;
3. loss of earnings and earning capacity;
4. punitive damages as a result of the defendants' reckless and wanton conduct.

FIGURE 4-5

Excerpt from the Chumley Complaint: Damages

To see a complete version of the Chumley Complaint, please refer to the appendix.

Damages refer to the plaintiff's monetary losses, such as lost time from work and the medical expenses incurred due to the defendant's negligence.

ISSUE AT A GLANCE

Here we see an example of how the various elements of a negligence case come together.

VAN HORN v. WATSON
2008 WL 5246046, 7 (Cal. 2008)

MORENO, J.

Under well-established common law principles, a person has no duty to come to the aid of another. If, however, a person elects to come to someone's aid, he or she has a duty to exercise due care. Thus, a "good Samaritan" who attempts to help someone might be liable if he or she does not exercise due care and ends up causing harm. The Legislature has enacted certain statutory exceptions to this due care requirement. One such statute, Health and Safety Code section 1799.102, immunizes any "person who . . . renders emergency care at the scene of an emergency . . ." from liability for civil damages.

In this case, defendant Lisa Torti removed plaintiff Alexandra Van Horn from a vehicle involved in an accident and, by so doing, allegedly caused Van Horn to become paralyzed. In the resultant suit for negligence, Torti argued that she had provided "emergency care at the scene of an emergency" and was immune under section 1799.102. The trial court agreed and granted her motion for summary judgment, but the Court of Appeal reversed. We granted review to determine the scope of section 1799.102. We hold that the Legislature intended for section 1799.102 to immunize from liability for civil damages any person who renders emergency *medical* care. Torti does not contend that she rendered emergency medical care and she may not, therefore, claim the immunity in section 1799.102. Accordingly, we affirm the judgment of the Court of Appeal.

I. Background

During the evening of October 31, 2004, plaintiff, Torti, and Jonelle Freed were relaxing at Torti's home where plaintiff and Torti both smoked some marijuana. After defendants Anthony Glen Watson and Dion Ofoegbu arrived, they all went to a bar at around 10:00 P.M., where they consumed several drinks. They remained at the bar until about 1:30 A.M., at which point they left.

Plaintiff and Freed rode in a vehicle driven by Watson; Torti rode in a vehicle driven by Ofoegbu. Watson lost control of his vehicle and crashed into a curb and light pole at about 45 miles per hour, knocking a light pole over and causing the vehicle's front air bags to deploy. Plaintiff was in the front passenger seat. When Watson's vehicle crashed, Ofoegbu pulled off to the side of the road and he and Torti got out to help. Torti removed plaintiff from Watson's vehicle. Watson was able to exit his vehicle by himself and Ofoegbu assisted Freed by opening a door for her.

There are conflicting recollections about several critical events: Torti testified at deposition that she saw smoke and liquid coming from Watson's vehicle, and she removed plaintiff from the vehicle because she feared the vehicle would catch fire or "blow up." Torti also testified that she removed plaintiff from the vehicle by placing one arm under plaintiff's legs and the other behind plaintiff's back to lift her out. Others testified, on the other hand, that there was no smoke or any other indications that the vehicle might explode and that Torti put plaintiff down immediately next to the car. Plaintiff testified that Torti pulled her from the vehicle by grabbing her by the arm and yanking her out "like a rag doll."

Emergency personnel arrived moments later and plaintiff and Freed were treated and transported to the hospital. Plaintiff suffered various injuries, including injury to her vertebrae and a lacerated liver that required surgery, and was permanently paralyzed.

Plaintiff sued Watson, Ofoegbu, and Torti. Plaintiff asserted a negligence cause of action against Torti, alleging that even though plaintiff was not in need of assistance from Torti after the accident and had only sustained injury to her vertebrae, Torti dragged plaintiff out of the vehicle, causing permanent damage to her spinal cord and rendering her a paraplegic. Torti and Watson cross-complained against each other for declaratory relief and indemnity. After some discovery, Torti moved for summary judgment, arguing that she was immune under section 1799.102. The trial court granted Torti's motion.

The Court of Appeal reversed. It held that the Legislature intended for section 1799.102 to apply only to the rendering of emergency *medical* care at the scene of a *medical* emergency and that Torti did not, as a matter of law, render such care. Such a construction, the Court of Appeal explained, is consistent with the statutory scheme of which section 1799.102 is a part. We granted review.

II. Discussion

Our primary duty when interpreting a statute is to "'determine and effectuate'" the Legislature's intent. To that end, our first task is to examine the words of the statute, giving them a commonsense meaning. If the language is clear and unambiguous, the inquiry ends. However, a statute's language must be construed in context, and provisions relating to the same subject matter must be harmonized to the extent possible. With these principles of statutory construction in mind, we turn to the language of the provision.

Section 1799.102 provides, "No person who in good faith, and not for compensation, renders emergency care at the scene of an emergency shall be liable for any civil damages resulting from any act or omission. The scene of an emergency shall not include emergency departments and other places where medical care is usually offered." The parties identify two possible constructions of this provision: Torti urges us to conclude that it broadly applies to both nonmedical and medical care rendered at the scene of any emergency; plaintiff, on the other hand, argues that section 1799.102 applies only to the rendering of emergency *medical* care at the scene of a *medical* emergency. While section 1799.102 is certainly susceptible of Torti's plain language interpretation, a "literal construction should not prevail if it is contrary to the legislative intent apparent in the statute. The intent prevails over the letter, and the letter will, if possible, be so read as to conform to the spirit of the act." We conclude for several reasons that, when the statutory language is viewed in context, the narrower construction identified by plaintiff is more consistent with the statutory scheme of which section 1799.102 is a part.

The Statutory Scheme and Related Provisions
1. Purpose of the Scheme in Which Section 1799.102 Is Located
Section 1799.102 is located in division 2.5 of the Health and Safety Code. That division, titled "Emergency Medical Services" by the Legislature, was enacted as the Emergency Medical Services System and the Prehospital Emergency Medical Care Personnel Act (Act). (§1797; Stats.1980, ch. 1260, §7, p. 4261.) One can infer from the location of section 1799.102 in the Emergency *Medical* Services division, as well as from the title of the act of which it is a part, that the Legislature intended for section 1799.102 to immunize the provision of emergency *medical* care at the scene of a medical emergency.

Additionally, apart from the name of the division and the Act, the Legislature made clear in numerous other statutes that it intended for the statutory scheme to address the provision of emergency *medical* care. For example, in section 1797.1, the Legislature declared that it is the intent of the Act "to provide the state with a statewide system for emergency *medical* services. . . ." (Italics added.) In section 1797.6, subdivision (a), the Legislature declared that it is "the policy of the State of California to ensure the provision of effective and efficient emergency *medical* care." (Italics added.) Indeed, nowhere in the Act's general provisions (Health & Saf.Code, div. 2.5, ch. 1, §§1797-1797.8) is there any indication that the Legislature intended to address or affect the provision of *nonmedical* care.

2. Definition of "Emergency" in Section 1797.70

Chapter 2 of division 2.5, Emergency Medical Services, contains definitions which govern the provisions of the division. (§1797.50; see §§1797.52-1797.97.) Of particular relevance is section 1797.70, which defines "emergency" as meaning "a condition or situation *in which an individual has a need for immediate medical attention,* or where the potential for such need is perceived by emergency personnel or a public safety agency." (Italics added.) Section 1799.102, the provision at issue here, immunizes persons who render "*emergency* care at the scene of an *emergency. . . .*" (Italics added.) Section 1797.70 thus makes clear that the phrase "scene of an emergency" in section 1799.102 refers to the scene of a *medical* emergency.

Torti's Broad Interpretation Would Undermine Well-Established Common Law Principles

Torti's expansive interpretation of section 1799.102 would undermine long-standing common law principles. As we previously noted, the general rule is that "one has no duty to come to the aid of another." As explained in the Restatement Second of Torts, "The origin of the rule lay in the early common law distinction between action and inaction, or 'misfeasance' and 'nonfeasance.'" (Rest.2d Torts, §314, com. c, p. 116.) Courts were more concerned with affirmative acts of misbehavior than they were with an individual "who merely did nothing, even though another might suffer serious harm because of his omission to act."

While there is no general duty to help, a good Samaritan who nonetheless "undertakes to come to the aid of another . . . is under a duty to exercise due care in performance. . . ." As we explained in *Artiglio v. Corning,* "it is ancient learning that one who assumes to act, even though gratuitously, may thereby become subject to a duty of acting carefully, if he acts at all."

The broad construction urged by Torti — that section 1799.102 immunizes *any* person who provides *any* emergency care at the scene of *any* emergency — would largely gut this well-established common law rule. As we recently noted, "we do not presume that the Legislature intends, when it enacts a statute, to overthrow long-established principles of law unless such intention is clearly expressed or necessarily implied." Torti does not identify anything that would overcome the presumption that the Legislature did not intend to work such a radical departure.

Broad Interpretation Would Render Other "Good Samaritan" Statutes Unnecessary Surplusage

As the Court of Appeal points out, Torti's sweeping construction of section 1799.102 would render other "Good Samaritan" statutes superfluous. For example, Government Code section 50086 immunizes anyone with first aid training who is asked by authorities to assist in a search and rescue operation and who renders emergency services to a victim. The statute defines "emergency services" to include "first aid and medical services, rescue procedures, and transportation or other related activities."

III. Disposition

In light of the foregoing reasons, we conclude that the Legislature intended for section 1799.102 to immunize from liability for civil damages only those persons who in good faith render emergency medical care at the scene of a medical emergency. We accordingly affirm the judgment of the Court of Appeal.

Questions about the case:

1. What were the circumstances that led to the accident?
2. In what way does the plaintiff allege that Torti was negligent?
3. What is the "Good Samaritan" statute?
4. How does the statute define "emergency"?
5. Why would Torti's definition of the Good Samaritan statute undermine the law, at least according to the court?

 **THE LAWYERS WHO REPRESENT PLAINTIFFS AND DEFENDANTS**

Any discussion of negligence cases should include the lawyers who actually represent either side in the action. Plaintiffs' lawyers and defendants' lawyers have different financial arrangements with their clients, have different strategies, and frequently have firms that are structured in dramatically different ways. Paralegals who work for these firms should understand the important differences between lawyers who regularly represent plaintiffs and those who regularly represent defendants.

A. BECOMING A LAWYER

Whether a lawyer eventually represents a plaintiff or a defendant in a particular case, the initial training is the same. To become a lawyer, a person must attend a law school and pass an examination called the bar exam. These days, to be allowed to take the bar exam, the future attorney must graduate from an American Bar Association-approved school. The ABA does not directly regulate attorneys. Instead, the ABA approves law schools by reviewing professors' qualifications, the quality of instruction, and even the law school's physical facility. The ABA stamp of approval is essential to a law school and helps maintain the high standard of legal education.

Once the law student completes what is almost always a three-year program of study, she graduates from law school and then takes the bar exam. (In some states, a third-year law student can take the bar exam shortly before graduation.) The bar exam is administered by the state bar. If a law student receives a passing grade on this exam, she can then be admitted to the bar. Admission to the bar means that a graduate now has a license to practice law and is entitled to give legal advice, receive compensation for services, and carry out any other action permitted of a fully licensed attorney.

To be admitted into law school, an applicant must have already earned a bachelor's degree. Law school curricula are designed to last for three years.

B. THE ECONOMICS OF LAW FIRMS

It is important for any legal professional to understand the economics of a law firm. Attorneys who represent people in negligence cases almost always work in private firms. This firm may consist only of the attorney (called a sole practitioner) or hundreds of attorneys in branch offices across the nation. In either situation, client fees pay the attorney's salary.

Our example is a 25-person firm that handles primarily defense work. This means that the firm represents people who have been sued by others. There is no prohibition against a firm handling both plaintiff and defense work—as long as the ethical rules are followed—but as a practical matter, most firms specialize in one or the other. Our hypothetical firm has six partners and nineteen associates. An associate is usually a relatively new lawyer who is hired to work for the firm. This associate earns a set salary, which, unlike what you often see on television, is not high. Even at big firms, the starting salary for an associate is often the same as the manager of a local retail store. Partners split the profits of the law firm once everyone else has been paid. Paying the associates, secretaries, and paralegals a fixed salary means that if the firm is particularly profitable, the partners will split these huge profits among themselves. It also means that when times are lean, the staff will continue to earn the same salary and the partners will have less to share among themselves.

If an associate does not make a large salary, why work for a large firm? The answer is simple. Associates know that if they work long hours, generating as much income as possible to impress the partners with their work ethic, they may be offered a partnership of their own. "Making partner" at a profitable firm is the ticket to wealth for an attorney.

An associate generates income by working on cases, hopefully bringing them to a successful conclusion and then billing the client for the time spent on the case. The more that an associate bills, the more money he brings in for the firm. An associate who fails to generate income will eventually be fired.

C. PLAINTIFFS' FIRMS

Large plaintiffs' firms resemble their defense counterparts in many ways. The financial arrangements among associates and partners are often identical. However, while defense firms bill by the hour, often setting an hourly rate of $150 or more (for a large firm), plaintiffs' firms operate on an entirely different system. A plaintiffs' firm represents people who may have a claim for injuries against someone else. The most common type of personal injury claim is one arising from a car collision. Plaintiffs' firms generally do not bill by the hour. Instead, they work on a contingency fee.

Plaintiffs' firms represent people who have been injured by others' negligence. **Defense firms** represent people who have been sued.

ISSUE AT A GLANCE

Plaintiffs' firms are normally paid out of the ultimate settlement in the case. Many firms charge a standard rate (33 percent of the total recovery, for instance). This means that whatever amount the plaintiff ultimately gets in the case will be reduced by the firm's payment of one-third.

Example: Ron's case has finally settled and the defense has agreed to pay him $100,000 to settle all claims. Ron ultimately receives $66,000, while the firm that represented him receives $33,000 (give or take a few hundred).

If the plaintiff ends up getting nothing because the jury entered a verdict in favor of the defendant, the firm gets no money. This often puts financial stress on plaintiffs' firms. They must decide not only if each case has merit, but also what the possibility of recovering any money is. No matter how great the case, if there is no possibility of recovering damages from the defendant, there is no incentive for the firm to take the case.

D. DEFENSE FIRMS

Insurance companies regularly pay the fees for firms that specialize in defense work. When a motorist is sued, his insurance policy often contains a provision that guarantees an attorney will represent him. Many firms have standing arrangements with insurance companies that they will represent all people in a geographic area who are sued. These attorneys normally charge an hourly rate, as opposed to the contingency fee arrangement followed by most plaintiffs' firms. The firm bills the insurance company at the end of each month, or in whatever interval the insurance company and the firm have decided on. In some cases, the insurance company will pay a flat fee to the firm to handle a certain kind of a case, for example, a basic car wreck case.

The two pay arrangements would seem to put the two types of firms in different philosophical approaches to a case. If the plaintiffs' firm only gets paid when the case is over, that firm would want to settle the case as soon as possible. On the other hand, the defense firm is paid by the hour and therefore would seem not to want to end the lawsuit quickly. Although this is somewhat of an oversimplification, it is an accurate picture of the different viewpoints these two firms bring to the case.

E. CONTRACTING WITH A LAW FIRM

When a client engages a law firm, whether to represent him as a plaintiff in a suit, or to defend him in a suit, the firm enters into a contract with that client. In insurance defense cases, the contract is actually between the insurance company and the firm, but it accrues to the benefit of the insured party.

F. CONTRACT IN THE CHUMLEY CASE

For instance, suppose that a firm has decided to represent Mr. Chumley in his lawsuit against the railroad company. When it agrees to take the case, an attorney for the firm enters into a signed contract with Mr. Chumley. This contract of representation spells out the details of the arrangement between the plaintiff and the firm. One major item in the contract is the provision that authorizes the firm to receive one-third of the eventual settlement, if any. But the contract does more than simply deal with payment; it details what each party will do for the other, as shown in the sample contract form in Figure 4-6.

FIGURE 4-6	

Contract of Representation	THIS AGREEMENT, made this _____ day of _____, 200 _____ is between _____ the foregoing named person(s) being herein called Client, and Clarence D. Arrow, herein called "Attorney(s)." It is understood that litigation can be expensive, and that the Attorneys are prohibited by law from becoming liable for its costs, expenses, disbursements, and deposits. These may be advanced, but Attorneys cannot become ultimately liable for them. The Client and the Attorneys have agreed as follows:
	
	WITNESSETH
	
	1 The Client this day retains, employs, and authorizes the Attorneys:
	   (a) To prosecute, administratively and judicially, if necessary in their judgment, each of the Client's claims; and
	   (b) To prosecute or defend any and all appeals that may be taken in connection with the Client's claims; and
	   (c) To receive and collect any final recovery that may be realized on the Client's claims and to satisfy the same upon the records of the appropriate agency or court. The words *final recovery* when used anywhere in this Agreement

means the total gross amount of any and all monies, property, and compensation of any and every kind whatsoever realized or received by any Client for any claim, whether realized as the result of settlement or litigation or otherwise, and shall include, but not be limited to, any and all monies, funds, awards, verdicts, judgments, determinations, damages, principal, interest of every kind and nature, penalties, allowances, costs, and any and all compensation of every kind, nature, and description; and

(d) To deduct and retain their Attorneys' fees out of the proceeds of the final recovery, and to remit the balance, less their costs, expenses, disbursements, and deposits, to the Client.

2 The Client agrees to pay the Attorneys, and the Attorneys agree to accept for all of the legal services rendered in accordance with this Agreement, the following fee:

(a) A retainer, paid over and above the contingent fee and within ten (10) days of execution of this Agreement, as follows: $_____; or

(b) A contingent fee, paid within thirty (30) days of a final recovery or any portion thereof, computed as follows: percent (_____%) of any final recovery obtained if the claim is settled without suit; or

(c) A contingent fee, paid within thirty (30) days of a final recovery or any portion thereof, computed as follows: percent (_____%) of any final recovery obtained after commencement of suit;

The final Attorneys' fees shall be due and shall be paid to the Attorneys at an earlier time if the Attorneys execute and tender delivery of their waiver of Attorneys' lien to the Client. In the event of an appeal to an Appellate Court from the Trial Court, an additional Attorneys' fee for such work shall be negotiated between the parties at the time a decision to pursue an appeal is made.

3 The Client agrees to pay, reimburse, and hold the Attorneys harmless from any and all costs, expenses, disbursements and deposits incurred and/or paid by the Attorneys, and same shall be due and paid to the Attorneys at any time when billed by the Attorneys. Examples of such costs, expenses, disbursements, and deposits are as follows: court and court reporter charges; document processing and copying costs; mail and delivery costs; telecommunications and research database expert fees and expenses; witness fees and expenses; computer costs; paralegal and consultant costs; photography, videotaping, and other visual aid costs; and investigation charges and reports.

In the event of a recovery, the Client agrees that the Attorneys may pay any unpaid bills from the Client's share of recovery. Should the Client recover nothing, it is understood that the Attorneys are not bound to pay any of the costs, disbursements, expenses, and deposits incurred or deemed necessary by the Attorneys handling the Client's case, and that the Client remains liable for their payment.

A cost deposit of $_____ is due and payable within ten (10) days after execution of this Agreement.

4 The Client hereby assigns to the Attorneys the portion of any final recovery realized or recovered by the Client which represents the Attorneys' fee computed in accordance with this Agreement, and an additional portion sufficient to cover all costs, expenses, disbursements, and deposits billed by Attorneys and unpaid by Client.

5 The Client reserves the absolute right to discharge the Attorneys at any time. Likewise, the Attorneys, in their absolute discretion, may withdraw at any time. If the Client discharges the Attorneys, or if the Attorneys withdraw for justifiable cause, all costs, expenses, disbursements, and deposits incurred by the Attorneys, as well as compensation to the Attorneys for the fair and reasonable value of services, to be determined as follows:

(a) If the Attorneys are discharged or justifiably withdraw before any settlement or similar understanding is effected or any verdict, award,

FIGURE 4-6

(continued)

(continued)

FIGURE 4-6

(continued)

determination, or judgment is rendered, the compensation of the Attorneys shall be paid within thirty (30) days of discharge and shall be computed on a time basis at the rate of One Hundred Fifty Dollars ($150.00) per hour, which rate the Client agrees is fair and reasonable for services rendered. The Attorneys, in the event of such discharge and upon the Client's request, shall furnish the Client with a statement of their services, which shall be binding on all parties. In lieu of payment pursuant to this similar understanding regarding Client's claims, or a verdict, award, determination, or judgment in Client's favor, at which point in time the Attorneys may select payment pursuant to either subparagraph 2(b) or 2(c);

(b) If the Attorneys are discharged by the Client or justifiably withdraw after a settlement or similar understanding is effected or after a verdict, award, determination, or judgment is rendered in favor of the Client, the compensation of the Attorneys shall be computed in accordance with the non-discharge provisions of this Agreement, just as if the settlement, verdict, award determination, or judgment had actually been collected in full hereunder for the Client;

(c) In case of discharge or justifiable withdrawal, the Attorneys shall not be obligated to return any of the Client's papers or property to the Client until the Attorneys' fees, computed as set forth in this paragraph, together with all costs, expenses, disbursements, and deposits, are fully paid to the Attorneys.

6 The Client agrees not to compromise the claim without the Attorneys' consent and the Attorneys are not authorized to do so without the Client's consent. It is mutually agreed that if the Client does settle his claim or cause of action without the consent of the Attorneys, the Client agrees to pay the Attorneys, within thirty (30) days of the settlement, all of the costs, expenses, disbursements, and deposits incurred and/or paid by him, together with their Attorneys' fee, computed in accordance with the terms of this Agreement, based upon the final recovery realized or received by the Client in such settlement, unless the Attorneys exercised their option hereby granted to be paid on that basis. If by the terms of such settlement it is agreed by the party making the same that he or she will also pay for the services of the Client's Attorneys, such percentage of the Attorneys' fee shall be computed on the amount of such Attorneys' fee agreed to be paid to the Client's attorney.

7 All monies due and payable to Attorneys by Client, which have been due and payable for at least thirty (30) days following the date a statement of the account is rendered by Attorneys to Client, will incur a finance charge of one and one-half percent (1.5%) per month calculated on the amount owed from the date upon which it became due and payable until paid.

8 The Client agrees to cooperate in the preparation and trial of the case, to appear on reasonable notice for conferences, medical examinations, video-taping, depositions and court appearances, and to comply with all reasonable requests made of Client in connection with this legal representation.

9 Client hereby gives Attorneys Client's power of attorney to execute all documents connected with the claim for the prosecution of which Attorneys are retained, including pleadings, contracts, commercial paper, settlement agreements, compromises and releases, verifications, dismissals, orders, settlement checks or drafts, and all other documents that Client could properly execute. The Client hereby authorizes the Attorneys to turn over all information, documentary and otherwise, to the defendant and others, as discretion of the Attorneys may dictate.

10 The Client agrees that the Attorneys have given no guarantees, promises, or representations regarding the successful termination of the Client's claim or cause of action relative to the Client's claim or reimbursement are only matters of their opinion given in good faith. No representation has been made as to what amounts, if any, the Client may be entitled to recover in this case.

FIGURE 4-6

(continued)

11 The Attorneys shall have general, possessory, and retaining liens, and all special and charging liens known to the common law, in addition to any statuary lien, including upon the Client's cause of action, upon any recovery in the Client's favor, and to the proceeds thereof in whatever hands they may come. The Attorneys shall not be obligated to waive their Attorneys' lien until their Attorneys' fees and any and all of their costs, expenses, disbursements, and deposits hereunder have been fully paid. The Attorneys shall not be liable to the Client for any loss the Client may incur or suffer because of the Attorneys' exercising their Attorneys' lien in order to secure full payment of legal fees and costs, expenses, disbursements, and deposits under this Agreement.

12 The Attorneys shall receive no compensation in any manner or form in connection with this claim or cause of action other than that provided for in this Agreement, except by written modification of this Agreement.

13 The Attorneys, in their sole discretion, may employ or contract with other counsel in the prosecution of the Client's claims. The other counsel's fee will be covered by the Attorneys' fee herein for which Client is responsible, while the costs, expenses, disbursements, and deposits of the other counsel will be the Client's responsibility.

14 This Agreement shall be binding upon the heirs, executor, administrators, successors, and assigns of each of the parties hereto, and constitutes the entire Agreement between the parties hereto. Should any provision be rendered inoperative, the other provisions shall remain in full force and effect.

15 This Agreement is to be construed according to state law and all parties are agreed that the sole personal jurisdiction and venue for the resolution of any dispute hereunder shall be Anytown, New York, USA, and that any and all judgments rendered shall be enforceable in the jurisdictional residence of the Client.

　　IN WITNESS WHEREOF, the parties have executed this Agreement the day and year first above written.

Sworn to and subscribed before me
this _____ day of _____, 200___

_____
Notary Public

_____
Unofficial Witness

_____
CLIENT

VI OBTAINING INFORMATION FROM THE CLIENT

Once the contract has been signed, there are some additional issues that should be addressed. One of them is the information that the firm should always get from the client. The Client Questionnaire in Figure 4-7 has an extensive list of questions that should be asked of clients, regardless of whether the firm represents plaintiffs or defendants.

As you can see in Figure 4-7, the firm requires a great deal of information from the client, including her full name, address, and all telephone numbers. You need all of this information so that you can contact your client, especially on short notice, so having access to all of this information can be crucial.

FIGURE 4-7

Client Interview— Personal Injury Case

Client's Name:
    Address:
    Phone # Work:
    Phone # Home:
How long at present address?:
With whom does client live?:
    SPOUSE: _____   AGE: _____
    CHILDREN: _____   AGE: _____
    _____   AGE: _____

Other Prior Residences:

Persons Client Supports: _____   AGE: _____
    _____   AGE: _____

Client's Age:
Client's Date of Birth:
Client's Social Security Number:
Client's Place of Birth:
Client's Educational Background:
Client's Employment History:

Client's Current Employment:
    Employer:
    Address:
    Supervisor:
    Type of Work:
    Length of Employment:
    Present Job Still Available?:
    Pay:

Military History:

Client ever treated by psychiatrist or been in Mental Institution?:

Physical Ailments?:

Physical Ailments of Family Members?:

Other names by which client has been known?:

Brief explanation of what happened:

Prior Accidents/Lawsuits?:

YEAR	COURT	DISPOSITION	PARTY

A. AUTHORIZATIONS FROM THE CLIENT

In addition to signing a contract of representation, the firm will usually need a signed medical authorization from the client as well. A medical authorization is a legal document that allows the firm to get copies of the client's medical or other records. Because this material is confidential, most medical professionals will refuse to release the records without an authorization signed by the client. Many firms have the client sign several copies of authorizations. The authorization form provided in Figure 4-8 is for the release of medical records,

---

TO:

FROM:

You are hereby authorized and directed to permit the examination of, and the copying or reproduction in any manner, whether mechanical, photographic, or otherwise, by my attorney or such other person as my attorney may authorize, all or any portions requested by my attorney of the following:

1. Hospital records; x-rays; x-ray readings and reports; laboratory records and reports; all tests of any type and character and reports thereof; statement of charges; and any and all of my records pertaining to hospitalization, history, condition, treatment, diagnosis, prognosis, etiology, or expense;
2. Medical records, including patient's record cards; x-rays; x-ray readings and reports; laboratory records and reports; all tests of any type and character and reports thereof; statements of charges; and any and all of my records pertaining to medical care, history, condition, treatment, diagnosis, prognosis, etiology or expense.

You are further authorized and directed to furnish oral and written reports to my attorney, or his delegate, as requested by him for any of the foregoing matters.

By reason of the fact that such information you have acquired as my physician or surgeon is confidential to me, you are also requested to treat such information as confidential and requested not to furnish any of such information in any form to anyone without written authorization from me. I hereby revoke any previously dated medical authorization.

I also authorize my attorney(s) or their delegate(s) to photograph my person while I am present in any hospital.

I further authorize the sending of medical and hospital bills to my attorney, and in the event of recovery by trial or settlement to allow my attorney to withhold an amount sufficient to cover these bills and to make payment directly to you and to deduct the same from any recovery which may be due me. I agree that a photostatic copy of the authorization shall be considered as effective and valid as the original.

Client

Sworn to and subscribed
before me this _____ day
of _____, 200____

Notary Public

FIGURE 4-8

Medical Authorization and Patient's Request for Confidential Treatment of Medical Information

but it could just as easily be directed to an employer or anyone else who keeps confidential records that the firm may need to prove its case.

B. OTHER INFORMATION FROM THE CLIENT: FACTS AND PHOTOS

In addition to a signed contract of representation and signed authorizations, you as the paralegal may also be called on to gather additional information from the client at the first meeting. What types of questions should you ask? You should not neglect obvious points. Does the client know of any witnesses to the collision? Has anyone taken photos of the car he was driving? Does he

FIGURE 4-9

Photos of Mr. and Mrs. Chumley

know if the local press did a story about the wreck? The only way you can find out this information is by asking. You should also acquire photographs of the plaintiff before the accident, preferably showing him smiling and happy.

SKILLS YOU NEED IN THE REAL WORLD

Meeting with the New Client

When a person walks through the firm's front door, he or she is usually anxious and is often in trouble. People who have had no previous experience with lawyers and paralegals only know what they have seen on television — and that is often grossly inaccurate. What actually happens when a lawyer meets with a new client and what procedure does the firm use to investigate the claim, accept the case, and open a new file?

The First Step: Getting the Information

When Mr. Chumley walks through the door, the lawyer and the paralegal meet with him and get the basic facts. He is able to tell you some of the details of the accident, but not very many, because he has amnesia concerning the actual event. He may have brought documentation with him, but most clients do not. What kind of documentation would you like to see at this point?

- The police report (helps determine any statute of limitations problem)
- Any investigative report
- Police accident-reconstructionist report (if any)
- Any correspondence between Mr. Chumley and the potential defendants and their insurance companies

Information About the Court Process

Information gathering is not a one-way street. Remember that the client may not have any experience with the court system and so may not understand many of the procedures. For instance, clients are often confused and frustrated by the length of time it takes from filing the complaint to actually trying the case. They don't understand why this process can take a year or more. Explaining it to them at this stage often prevents a lot of frustration later on.

Many times a client won't ask a question because he thinks it makes him sound stupid. Give the client a handout or brochure about the legal process to take home with him and read. This brochure should spell out in uncomplicated terms exactly what happens at each stage of the lawsuit. A well-written brochure can also serve as publicity for the firm. When the case ends successfully, Mr. Chumley may give the brochure to a friend who needs legal assistance.

FIGURE 4-10

Number of Tort Trials Terminated in U.S. Courts

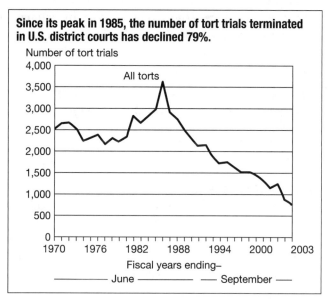

Since its peak in 1985, the number of tort trials terminated in U.S. district courts has declined 79%.

Number of tort trials

Fiscal years ending–
June — September

Federal Tort Trials and Verdicts, 2002-03, Bureau of Justice Statistics, U.S. Department of Justice.

Videotapes

Firms can now purchase professional-quality videotapes that discuss all phases of civil litigation. You might consider buying some of these tapes to show to clients at the initial meeting. They answer most of the common questions raised by new clients.

 THE LIFE OF A PARALEGAL

Putting Together a Settlement Package

When I put together a settlement package that we intend to send to the claims adjuster or opposing counsel, I follow a set pattern. Once I've gotten in all of the medical bills and all medical records and the client has been released from his doctors, I type up a first page cover sheet. It's usually called a "settlement packet for Client X." After the cover sheet, the first section is the police or accident report. The next section is the itemized statement of bills, which includes everything but our fee. These itemized charges could be things like copying costs for medical records, notes from physicians, and any other bills. Then, the next section is the medical bills. I put copies of all of the medical bills in the settlement package. I confirm what bills have been paid by insurance and which ones remain unpaid. I make sure that the outstanding balances are correct. I do a summary on each one, stating whether or not this bill has been paid, or if there has been some reimbursement to the insurance company, things like that. After the medical bills, the next section is Discovery. Typically, this section contains witness statements, statements from anyone in the car with them at the time of the accident and any other type of discovery (interrogatories, deposition transcripts, etc). If it's a big case, there's usually a private investigator involved and his report will go in this section. If the case involved a wrongful death, we would include any information about other pending lawsuits from the same action. After the Discovery section, I'll include photographs. Typically, I'll include photographs of the scene. If they ran off an embankment, for instance, I'll have photographs of the area, showing skid marks, obstructions, things like that. I usually take photographs of the scene. Then, I take photos of the car. Sometimes I have to go out to junkyards or body shops to find the car. In some cases, we include pictures of the client's injuries. I tell our clients, "If you haven't taken pictures of your injuries, do it immediately." We take photos of their injuries to show scarring or other injuries.

After the photo section, I include a copy of our representation letter, showing that we do, in fact, represent the client. Right next to that, I usually put in a copy of the medical releases, showing that we obtained the medical bills under the client's authority. The next section is the demand section (setting out the client's demand for settlement). Typically, in a demand letter we review the facts, list any serious bodily injuries and any permanent injuries and then our quote for demand. We always put what we demand, then we put in, "or best settlement offer." We always get closer to our demand if there is a lot of information. I believe that adjusters think, "Well, they've really done their homework; it's going to be worth our while to settle this case before taking it to trial."

Wendy Seagle, Paralegal

ETHICAL ISSUES FOR THE PARALEGAL: INITIAL CLIENT MEETING

One area that is filled with potential problems concerns the initial meeting with the client. We have already mentioned the dangers involved in unauthorized practice of law. This meeting is the most common time for a client to ask you a legal question, such as "Does my case look good?" There is almost no way to answer this question without getting into some form of legal advice. When this question comes up, the safest course is to simply say that you can't give legal advice and leave it at that. However, not all clients will let the issue go so easily. They ask what you think because they really want some assurance that things are going to work out all right. If you understand that the reason behind this question is to seek assurance, you can speak to the client's real concerns and still avoid giving legal advice.

Chapter Summary

There are four elements to a negligence action: duty, breach, causation, and damages. Each of these elements must be proved at trial before the plaintiff can succeed on his claim. These elements build on one another. When you evaluate the facts of a negligence case, you should proceed from one element to the other in order. If the plaintiff fails to prove duty, for instance, there is no point in proceeding to the other elements. The plaintiff's failure to prove one of the elements brings the negligence action down like a house of cards. A negligence complaint must state these four elements in clear language. In addition to understanding the elements of a negligence action, it is also important to understand the practical aspects of gathering information about the case and the people involved.

Web Sites

■ **Causation/Damages**
http://home.pon.net/wildrose/column4.htm

■ **Find Law**
http://www.findlaw.com

■ **Juris Dictionary: Law of Negligence**
http://www.jurisdictionary.com/SidePages/Samples/pLanguage.pdf

Forms and Court Documents

This form shows a typical automobile collision negligence complaint.

STATE OF PLACID   IN THE SUPERIOR COURT
COUNTY OF BARNES   FILE NUMBER: _____

Lisa Burnett,   )
)
Plaintiff   )
)
vs.   )
)
Marvin John Quartermain, and   )
Delia Xavier Quartermain,
Defendants

Complaint

COMES NOW THE PLAINTIFF, Lisa Burnett, and complaining of the defendants, alleges the following:

1.

That plaintiff Lisa Burnett (hereafter "plaintiff") is a citizen and resident of Barnes County, Placid.

2.

Upon information and belief, defendant Delia Xavier Quartermain (hereafter "defendant driver") is a citizen and resident of Barnes County, Placid.

3.

Upon information and belief, defendant Marvin John Quartermain (hereafter "defendant owner") is a citizen and resident of Barnes County, Placid.

a. Further, upon information and belief, defendant owner was the registered owner of the vehicle involved in the collision at issue in this case, said vehicle being a 2001 Ford, license plate number LZK 245.

b. That, at all times mentioned herein and upon information and belief, defendant driver was operating and using aforementioned vehicle with authority, consent, permission, and knowledge of defendant owner, and defendant driver's operation and use of the vehicle was under the direction and control of defendant owner.

c. Furthermore, at all times mentioned herein and upon information and belief, defendant driver was a member of the family or household of defendant owner and was living in such person's home; that the vehicle driven by defendant driver was owned, provided, and maintained for the general use, pleasure, and convenience of the family; and that the vehicle was being so used with the express or implied consent of defendant owner. Therefore, any negligence on the part of the defendant driver in causing the plaintiff's injuries should be imputed to defendant owner under the family purpose doctrine.

4.

That, on or about the 19th day of October, 2002, at approximately 9:40 A.M., plaintiff was operating a motor vehicle traveling west on East Union Street in Placid City, Barnes County, Placid.

5.

That, at the same time and place, defendant driver was operating the aforementioned 2001 Ford motor vehicle and traveling south on Kirk Drive in Placid City, Barnes County, Placid.

6.

That defendant driver entered plaintiff's lane of travel, thereby causing a collision with plaintiff's vehicle.

7.

That defendant driver at the scene stated that she did not see plaintiff's vehicle before pulling out into the intersection.

8.

That defendant driver was negligent in that she:

a. While operating a motor vehicle on the public streets and highways, failed to keep a reasonable and proper lookout in plaintiff's direction of travel.

b. Failed to maintain the vehicle that she was operating under proper control and drove the vehicle in such a manner so as to deprive the defendant driver of such control over the vehicle as a reasonable and prudent person would maintain under the circumstances then existing.

9.

That, as a direct and proximate cause of the negligent conduct of defendant driver, plaintiff was seriously injured, causing her great pain and suffering, medical expenses, lost wages, physical and mental anguish, and permanent injuries.

10.

That, as a direct and proximate result of the aforementioned negligence of defendant driver, plaintiff has sustained damage to her person in an amount in excess of Ten Thousand Dollars ($10,000.00), representing damage to plaintiff's person, medical bills, pain and suffering, lost wages, mental anguish, and permanent injuries.

WHEREFORE, the Plaintiff prays that the Court as follows:
1. That the Plaintiff have and recover a judgment against the Defendants in an amount in excess of $10,000.00 for personal injuries.
2. That the Defendants be assessed with punitive damages as permitted by law.
3. That prejudgment interest be awarded as provided by law.
4. That the costs of this action be taxed against the Defendants.
5. That all issues raised be tried before a jury.
6. For such other and further relief as the Court may deem just and proper.

This the _____ day of June, 2003.

_____

Clarence D. Arrow
Attorney for Plaintiffs
State Bar No. 000-998

Key Terms

Breach	Duty	Proximate causation
Damages	Negligence per se	

Review Questions

1 How are negligence cases different from intentional tort cases?
2 What are the four basic elements of a negligence case?
3 Under what circumstances does a person owe a duty to another?
4 When we use the term *causation,* what do we mean?
5 What are some of the differences between plaintiffs' firms and defense firms?

6 Is there a philosophical difference between plaintiffs' firms and defendants' firms?

7 What is a contingency fee?

8 What are the basic steps involved in investigating a new case?

9 List and explain some crucial information that you should obtain from a new client.

10 What is a medical authorization and when would it be required?

11 List some ways of organizing a client's file.

12 Why is a settlement package necessary and what is one way that it is put together?

13 What are some other methods for obtaining information about the cause of action?

14 When we discuss negligence, are we using this term as it is used in common parlance, or does it have a specific legal meaning? If so, define it.

Applying What You Have Learned

1 X, an 11-year-old boy, brings a suit against a priest alleging that the priest sexually assaulted him. His action is based on a claim of clergy malpractice and negligence. Does he have a valid negligence claim? Show how this claim would satisfy the basic elements of a negligence action.

2 Sally and Bill dated for several weeks. After they broke up, Sally discovered that Bill was HIV positive and failed to tell her. She has had herself tested and although she doesn't test positive for AIDS or HIV, she brings a suit against Bill based on a negligence claim. Is this a valid claim under a negligence theory?

3 Bill and Ted are police officers. While they are chasing an escaped mental patient, they are both injured. They file a negligence claim against the hospital from which the mental patient escaped. Will their claim succeed?

4 Prepare a chart showing the significant differences between intentional tort law, criminal law, and negligence law.

5 How are firms in your area organized? Are there several large plaintiffs' firms, or many smaller firms?

Endnote

[1]*Cook v. Continental Casualty Co.,* 180 Wis. 2d 237, 509 N.W.2d 100 (1993).

Duty

Chapter Objectives

- Describe how a duty arises and the legal consequences when it does

- Describe how certain special relationships give rise to a higher standard of care

- Explain the concept of "premises liability"

- Explain the different duties imposed on laypersons, professionals, and specialists

- Explain the "attractive nuisance" doctrine

 ## THE CHUMLEY CASE: A DANGEROUS INTERSECTION?

The train tracks that intersect with Morgan Street run through two other intersections in the town of Cling. Both of the other intersections have warning lights and gates that descend whenever a train is approaching. The Morgan Street intersection has only a sign. When a motorist approaches the intersection from one direction, he immediately notices that there are tall, thick evergreen trees growing along the track. These trees are so thick that they

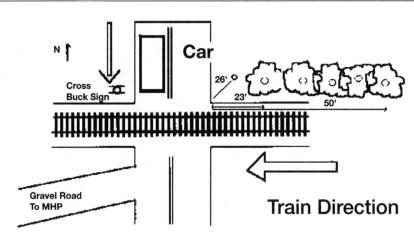

FIGURE 5-1

Map of Accident Site

Morgan Street

are impossible to see through. Mr. Chumley claims that in order to look past these trees and down the tracks for an oncoming train, he would have had to inch forward until the front of his car was almost on the tracks before he could see far enough to tell if a train was coming. See Figure 5-1.

In his suit, Mr. Chumley claims that National Railroad Company had a **duty** to keep the intersection safe and failed to meet that duty. Mr. Chumley claims that the intersection was dangerous and that the company failed to take any action to make it safe. He cannot be sure if the railroad company or the town had a duty to trim the trees, so he is suing both. Just to be safe, he is also suing the engineer, Stanley Blue, who was at the controls of the train that day.

As we have already seen, the first step in bringing a negligence suit is to show that there was a duty. If the defendant does not owe the plaintiff a duty, there can be no case. We explore the concept of duty throughout this chapter.

Duty
An obligation imposed by statute or common law

THE LEGAL DEFINITION OF DUTY

Courts have used a wide variety of terms to describe and define the term *duty*. At its simplest, duty refers to a person's obligation to conform his conduct to a particular **standard of care.** It is often defined as an obligation to protect someone else from an unreasonable risk of harm. In negligence cases, duty often simply means the obligation of a person to act in a reasonable manner. We often use the terms standard of care and *duty* interchangeably. The reason for this is that duty refers to the legal obligation and standard of care refers to how this obligation is put into practice. Put another way, duty is *why*; standard of care is *how*.

Standard of care
The standard used to determine if a party has acted negligently in a particular case

A. WHEN DOES A DUTY ARISE?

This simple question has been the focus of an amazing amount of litigation. In general terms, a duty arises when one person has the power to injure another and can only avoid injuring this other person by acting in a reasonable, prudent, and cautious way. The problem with that general definition is its generality. In any given situation, how do we know if defendant *B* has a duty to plaintiff *A?* We must look to the facts of the case for an answer. Here is the most common question the courts ask to determine duty:

Was the injury to the plaintiff reasonably foreseeable?

Example: Jamal is driving his car and fails to stop at a red light. Is it reasonably foreseeable that by running the red light he could collide with another car? Most people would agree that it is. When Jamal does, in fact, collide with Rick's car, Rick can claim that Jamal had a duty and breached it by failing to act in a reasonable and prudent manner.

When we determine foreseeability, we are really asking: "Just how likely was it that the plaintiff would be injured?" Foreseeability does not mean a "mere possibility," but a clearly recognized danger.[2] By addressing the issue of foreseeability, the courts attempt to establish some clear guidelines to establish duty. If the injuries were foreseeable, it is more likely that the defendant owed a duty to the plaintiff to keep him from harm. In situations in which the plaintiff's injuries are not foreseeable, courts generally rule that the defendant had no duty.

Duty → Breach → Causation → Damages. Without duty, you cannot move on to the other three elements of a negligence claim.

ISSUE AT A GLANCE

B. USING FORMULAS TO DETERMINE DUTY

In the past, some judges have attempted to come up with complex rules (some of them resembling algebraic formulas) to determine if a defendant in a case owed a duty to the plaintiff. However, most of these rules and formulas have disappeared over time. The reality of most cases does not lend itself to such rigidity, no matter how appealing such rules seem at first glance.

Examples of such rules include Judge Learned Hand's famous formula that he hoped would act as an infallible guide in negligence cases. Hand's formula is charmingly simplistic. In his equation, if the probability (P) of the defendant's harm multiplied by the loss (L) exceeded the burden (B) on the defendant, he had a duty to take precautions to prevent the harm. The equation is represented: $P \times L > B =$ duty. If, on the other hand, the burden on the defendant to prevent the harm was greater than the probability, there was no duty, or $P \times L < B =$ no duty.

The problem with using this equation to reach decisions in real cases is apparent almost immediately. For one thing, it is often difficult to quantify the probability of the defendant's harm. What numbers would you use to represent the likelihood of Jamal running a red light and how this action would affect the probabilities for other drivers? Rather than continue to negotiate the tricky math of such formulas, we instead concentrate on the more pragmatic approaches adopted by most court systems.

C. DUTY DOES NOT DEPEND ON VICTIM'S IDENTITY

Returning to our example of Jamal running a red light and crashing into Rick's car, notice that our discussion did not focus on Jamal's duty to Rick as a specific individual. In fact, there is no requirement that Jamal know who his eventual victim may be. The law of duty rests on the defendant and will be imposed to protect any eventual victim.[3] Jamal's duty to drive safely is a duty he owes to everyone on the road, not just Rick. Jamal has no legal defense by claiming that he did not know that Rick was coming in the opposite direction.[4] He had a duty and he violated it. Anyone who was hurt by his actions could have brought suit; it just happened to be Rick.

D. DUTY AS A LEGAL OBLIGATION

The law of duty in civil injuries has some interesting twists and turns. First of all, for a particular person to have a duty, he must have some legal obligation. Jamal, as a driver, has a legal obligation to other drivers and pedestrians to drive responsibly. However, let's change the facts. Consider the following scenario.

Jamal is walking by a lake and sees Rick, a stranger, apparently drowning in a deep part of the lake. Rick, thrashing at the surface, yells out, "Help! I'm drowning!" Jamal, watching from the shore, does nothing to save Rick. Does Rick (or his heirs) have an action against Jamal? Or, put another way, does Jamal have a duty to save Rick?

Answer: No.

Why is the answer no? In our first scenario, Jamal was driving a car and he failed to drive in a safe manner. Rick was injured by Jamal's negligence. Because Jamal had a duty to all other drivers and pedestrians, Rick can prove the first element of a negligence case against Jamal: duty. He can also prove a violation of that duty.

But what about our second scenario? Remember, when you consider a civil injuries case, you must take each step in sequence. The natural tendency with such a factual situation is moral outrage at Jamal's inaction. But this skips over the question of duty. Does Jamal have a duty to save Rick? Does a stranger have a legal duty to save another person from certain death? No. The law does not impose that duty on strangers. We could certainly argue that Jamal had an ethical or a moral duty to try to save Rick, but that is a different question. The law of civil injuries is not a mirror image of society's morality. There are many moral obligations that cannot be enforced by law. If you think it through for a moment, you will realize that using the court system to enforce moral rules could never work. Under such a scenario, you could sue a friend for "not being a good person." The court system would have to spend time and energy trying to discern exactly what a good person is. Instead, courts stay away from the moral issues in most cases. They focus on the facts.

Does a stranger have a legal obligation to save another stranger from certain death? The answer is no. Notice that we keep saying "stranger." The situation can change dramatically if the relationship between Jamal and Rick in our scenario changes. We discuss duty arising from relationship later in this chapter.

E. DUTY DOES NOT ARISE FROM HABIT OR CUSTOM

The question of the defendant's duty to the plaintiff comes from the circumstances of the case — the relationship, if any, between the defendant and the plaintiff and the defendant's actions. It does not arise simply because there is a custom or a tradition.

Example: Most people would agree that holding the door for a person is polite. One day, Mary is carrying a large parcel and as she approaches the door to the lobby of her apartment building, a man precedes her inside. He does not hold the door for her, even though he sees that she has a large package and that it would be nearly impossible for her to open the door for herself. He simply walks inside, letting the door close behind him. Mary slips on the wet pavement when she tries to open the door for herself. Does she have a cause of action against the man?

No. Just because holding the door for someone else is considered to be a polite action, there is no legal obligation (and no duty) for the man to hold the door for Mary. Without a duty, there is no action in negligence.

However, the rules change when the practice is deemed to be a behavior that all reasonable and prudent people would follow. For instance, in a later chapter, we discuss **custom** in regard to medical procedures. In those situations, if a majority of practitioners customarily perform the same action, such as taking a medical history from a new patient, that procedure can be seen as the baseline standard of care and the failure to follow that custom can establish a breach of duty. The important distinction here is that in our first example, of the man not holding the door for Mary, there are several reasons why reasonable and prudent people would not hold the door for her. For one thing, the man simply might not have seen her. The man might have assumed that Mary would be offended by his assumption that she needed help. Using custom to establish duty is normally a procedure reserved for specific circumstances such as medical treatment, safety procedures in creating products, etc. Failing to hold the door does not qualify.

Is there a way to change the facts to create a duty? Suppose, for instance, that the man is the doorman at a hotel. Although nothing in his job description states that he must open doors for people carrying large packages, it is a

Custom
A practice that has acquired a legal status over time such that failing to follow the practice would result in liability

custom followed by every doorman in the city. In this scenario, his failure to act might be considered a breach of duty. If Mary were to sue the hotel, how would Mary prove that this custom existed? She could simply present testimony from other doormen that they follow this practice. This might be enough to establish a custom and generate a duty.

F. DUTY ARISING FROM PROFESSIONAL STATUS

Non-professionals, or laypeople, do not have a duty that arises simply because of their education or training. However, there are many professionals who have a duty imposed on them by law because of their advanced training. Police officers, for instance, have a duty to assist people who are in trouble. Firefighters have the same duty. A firefighter could not, for instance, decide that today he doesn't feel like putting out fires. Stopping fires is his job and because of this, he has a legally imposed duty to act. A bystander might not be under any legal duty to save someone from a burning building, but a firefighter is (which of course does not make the action any less heroic).

Professionals have a higher duty, or standard of care, simply because they are professionals and have more education and training than a layperson.

Medical professionals also have a duty to act. When a patient appears at the hospital with injuries, doctors and nurses are under a legal duty to act to treat him.

1. DIFFERENT LEVELS OF DUTY FOR SOME PROFESSIONALS

Sidebar
How does the plaintiff prove that an expert's standard of care was inadequate? The plaintiff puts another expert on the stand and has her testify that the actions taken by the defendant failed to meet the standard of care for the profession. This means that the plaintiff has to locate an expert willing to testify to those facts. We talk more about locating expert witnesses in a later chapter.

As we discuss in the malpractice section, some professionals have a different standard of care, or a different duty. Medical doctors have one type of duty to a patient, while a specialist, someone like a heart surgeon, has a higher duty, often referred to as a higher standard of care.

2. WHAT IS THE STANDARD OF CARE FOR A PROFESSIONAL?

By way of an example, when a doctor treats a patient, what is his precise legal duty to that patient? Most jurisdictions define the legal duty as the reasonable degree of skill, knowledge, and training that other doctors under similar circumstances in the professional community would exercise. If the doctor fails to live up to that standard, then he has violated the standard of care and therefore has breached the legal duty owed to the patient.

FIGURE 5-2

- Accident reconstruction experts
- Accountants
- Architects
- Attorneys
- Physicians
- Police officers
- Real estate agents
- Stockbrokers
- Surveyors

FIGURE 5-2

Partial List of Professionals Who Are Required to Meet a Higher Legal Duty to Others

3. SPECIALISTS

Some professionals have received intensive training in a very narrow field. This makes them **specialists.** With that greater training and specialization comes a greater legal duty to a patient or a client. The legal duty imposed on a specialist is what would be expected of a specialist with similar training under similar circumstances. Unlike the standard for a professional, the standard for a specialist is not tied to the geographic region where the specialist practices. A specialist is held to the highest standard and this standard is nationwide (some would argue that it is worldwide).[6] We address the duty of medical (and legal) professionals in Chapter 12.

Specialist
One who has become an expert in a particular field through education, training, or both

G. DUTY ARISING OUT OF OTHER FACTORS

When a person creates a dangerous condition, the law imposes a duty on him to take reasonable actions to prevent others from being injured by it. In this situation, it is social policy that determines the duty. After all, the dangerous condition would not exist but for the defendant's actions, so it would seem reasonable to impose a duty on him to safeguard the condition or face the consequences.

HOW THE COURTS DETERMINE DUTY

Courts have been presented with a wide variety of negligence cases, and from these cases they have established some basic ground rules for determining whether a duty exists. This determination is usually a balancing act between the interests of society and the interests of the injured plaintiff. To determine duty, courts might look to factors such as how difficult it would have been for the defendant to avoid injuring the plaintiff, the economics of the situation, and whether imposing such a duty would open up the possibility of a whole host of new lawsuits. See Figure 5-3 for a summary of the various factors used by courts to determine duty.

| **FIGURE 5-3**

Factors That the Courts Use to Establish Duty | ■ Morality of the conduct as viewed by society
■ Whether the courts should be involved in a particular relationship
■ Social utility of the conduct
■ How difficult it would be for the defendant to prevent the injury
■ Can reasonable people agree on the practical means to prevent the injury? | ■ Proximate cause between defendant's actions and the harm to plaintiff
■ Economic considerations
■ Foreseeability
■ Will allowing this case to go forward cause a flood of similar litigation?
■ Will it encourage false claims or claims that are hard to establish?
■ Will it prevent future harm?* |

Valdez v. J. D. Diffenbaugh Co., 51 Cal. App. 3d 494, 124 Cal. Rptr. 467 (1975).

As you can see from Figure 5-3, duty is difficult to quantify and in many ways is a hodgepodge of many different factors, all weighted differently depending on the facts in a particular case. Duty is often difficult to establish, and in some cases, it is almost impossible. Is this a case, as a U.S. Supreme Court justice once said about a different topic, of "I know it when I see it"?

Example: Jamal loves to play golf, but he isn't very good. He tees up his golf ball and hits it. Unfortunately, it doesn't stay in the fairway. It veers well away from where he was aiming and into the adjacent fairway. Jamal yells "fore!" The ball hits Matt in the head. Matt wants to sue Jamal. Can he prove that Jamal had a duty to him?

Answer: Probably not. You could argue that Matt had assumed the risk of getting hit with a golf ball (more about assumption of the risk in the next chapter), but there is another argument. At least one court has ruled that when a golfer yells "fore!" he has satisfied his duty to other golfers.[7]

   **No duty = no negligence.**

Example: Jamal and Carl are camping. Jamal falls asleep in front of the fire. During the night, Carl's sleeping bag catches on fire. Carl wants to bring a suit against Jamal for the damages to his sleeping bag. Can he prove duty?

Answer: Probably not. To have a duty, you must at least be aware of what is occurring. Because Jamal was asleep, Carl is going to have a hard time proving that Jamal acted negligently or failed to act, resulting in the damages to Carl's sleeping bag. Beyond that, Carl may have a hard time proving that Jamal had any duty, whether asleep or not.

A. RELATIONSHIP CAN DETERMINE DUTY

When we use the term *relationship,* we generally think of friends, family, or lovers. Relationship is not used in that context in civil injuries. Instead, relationship refers to the interaction between the parties. You may not know the other drivers on the road, but you have a relationship with them. In this case, it is the relationship of one driver with another. You owe a duty to other drivers to drive in a reasonable manner and exercise ordinary care, even if you don't know them.

B. SPECIAL RELATIONSHIPS

There are certain relationships that by their very nature impose an obligation on one person to the benefit of another. The prime example of this special relationship is parent to child. A parent owes a child a duty to protect her from foreseeable injury and to provide a safe environment. In this situation, the failure of a parent to act to safeguard a child is the violation of a duty. Unlike a previous example in which Jamal owed no duty to Rick, who was drowning in a lake, if we change the scenario and make it a child drowning in a lake, there is no question that the parent has a duty to act to save the child. However, this duty is not absolute. Like any relationship, the legal duty that one person owes to another changes over time. For instance, once the child grows up, does the parent still have the same level of duty to the child that he or she has when the child is a toddler? Obviously, the situation has changed. As the child grows up, most of us would agree that the parent's duty to the child decreases.

The parent-child duty is a direct result of the personal relationship between the parties. The parent is under no greater obligation to someone else's child than to any stranger. Generally, these special relationships only involve two people. See Figure 5-4 for more examples.

Whether a special relationship exists is a question of law. As such, the judge, not the jury, determines it.

ISSUE AT A GLANCE

Example: Martha had a child out of wedlock and decided to give the boy up for adoption. The adoption agency ran routine medical check-ups on the

---

- ■ Employer and employee
- ■ Hotel/motel and guest
- ■ Landlord and tenant*
- ■ Carrier and passenger
- ■ Student and teacher

- ■ Parent and child
- ■ Spouse and spouse
- ■ Day care and child
- ■ Person who created a danger and potential victim

FIGURE 5-4

Special Relationships Giving Rise to Duty

Ventura v. Picicci, 227 Ill. App. 3d 865, 169 Ill. Dec. 881, 592 N.E.2d 368 (1992).

baby boy and discovered that he had an inherited disease. Martha is a carrier of this disease and will definitely pass it on to any male child she has in the future. The adoption agency doesn't tell Martha about the disease. Later, Martha has another boy and he dies because of this disease. Martha discovers that the adoption agency knew about the disease and failed to notify her. She brings suit against the adoption agency, claiming that the agency had a duty to tell her about the disease. Does the agency have such a duty?

Answer: When you evaluate a case like this, you must confine yourself to the facts and try to ignore the emotions. Most people's immediate reaction is outrage that the adoption agency failed to inform Martha. But does the agency have a legal duty? Is there a special relationship between Martha and the adoption agency? No. (See Figure 5-4.) Is there some other legally recognized obligation between Martha and the adoption agency that would make the agency liable? No. The result in this case is clear: Martha's suit against the adoption agency should be dismissed, because she has failed to prove the first element of a negligence case — duty.[8]

DUTY FROM A SOCIAL RELATIONSHIP

A. ARE FRIENDS A SPECIAL RELATIONSHIP?

Do friends fall into the category of special relationships? Under most circumstances, the answer is no.

Example: Jamal is at a party with his friend, Terry. Jamal has too much to drink and Terry begins to worry that Jamal will drive home. Terry asks Jamal if Jamal will permit Terry to drive him home. Jamal refuses and gets behind the wheel of his car and speeds off. Later, Jamal runs a red light and severely injures himself and Tiffany, who is in another car. Tiffany brings suit against Terry, alleging that Terry had a duty to keep Jamal from driving and that Terry did not work hard enough to keep Jamal from driving. Who will win this suit?

Answer: Terry. Under the facts as presented, Terry has no duty to Jamal and they are not in any special relationship; therefore Terry has no duty to keep Jamal from driving. Jamal is responsible for his own drunken driving and Tiffany cannot win a suit against Terry.

Let's change the facts of this case. This time, Jamal is at a party in Terry's home. Terry realizes that Jamal has had too much to drink, but continues to ply him with liquor. Jamal leaves the party driving his own car, has an accident, and injures Tiffany. Does she now have a cause of action against Terry?

In many jurisdictions, the answer to this question is yes. Terry is liable under the theory of social host liability.

B. SOCIAL HOST LIABILITY

In some jurisdictions, a social host can be liable under the facts presented above. Tiffany is suing Terry, alleging that Terry had a duty to stop serving liquor to Jamal when a reasonable host would have realized that Jamal was impaired. When courts created the doctrine of social host liability, they were creating a duty where one had not previously existed. Prior to the creation of this doctrine, a host could claim that he had no duty, and therefore could not be liable for serving drinks to an obviously intoxicated guest. With the adoption of this doctrine in many jurisdictions, the social policy of discouraging drunken driving by imposing legal liability on hosts has contributed to fewer situations such as we find in the hypothetical case.

However, many jurisdictions refuse to impose this duty on a host, unless the host was acting in clearly unreasonable or careless manner. The problem with social host liability is that it sets a bad precedent. How far will a social host's liability go? Consider the following example.

Ted is a diabetic and attends a dinner party at Tom's house. Tom is famous for his desserts and serves up a multi-layered chocolate confection that everyone, including Ted, finds irresistible. On the way home, Ted's blood sugar becomes elevated to the point that he loses consciousness. He crashes into another car and injures the occupants. Do the occupants have a cause of action against Tom?

Answer: Probably not. At some point, Ted's responsibility for his own actions will supersede Tom's carelessness in offering a sugary dessert to a diabetic. This example illustrates the difficulty that many jurisdictions have in imposing any form of social host liability.

PREMISES LIABILITY

Lawsuits involving injuries on land, such as "slip and fall" cases, have increased dramatically over the past few decades. People who sue under the theory of premises liability usually bring this case as a negligence suit. In fact, this area of law has increased so much that premises liability cases justify their own branch of negligence law.

People who possess land have a special duty to the people who visit their property. This duty arises out of the peculiar nature of land itself. Because it is

---

■ A complete description of the legal duty owed by the defendant to this plaintiff, setting out specific facts and allegations
■ A complete description of how the defendant's actions (or failure to act) breached this duty to the plaintiff or a description of the defendant's gross negligence, willful misconduct, or reckless disregard for the safety of others

FIGURE 5-5

What the Complaint Should Say About Duty

fixed and immovable, a dangerous condition could exist on land and a visitor wouldn't necessarily know about it.

A. DUTY IS ON POSSESSOR, NOT OWNER

According to the Restatement of Torts, any person who takes control over the premises, whether as tenant, manager, or any other position, also takes on the duty to keep the premises safe. It is not a defense for this person to claim that he had no responsibility because he was not the actual owner.[9]

Notice that we use the term *possessor* of land when discussing premises liability. These duties are imposed by law on the person who is in possession of the land, not necessarily the owner. The reason the law imposes this duty on the current possessor is because this person is in the best position to know about potential problems and can take action to protect others from them. Consider the following scenario.

Jamal has lived in an apartment for four years. One day, Nancy pays him a visit and slips on a large pile of garbage that Jamal has allowed to accumulate inside his front door. Jamal claims that because he is not the owner of the property, he should not be liable for Nancy's injuries. The landlord claims that he should not be liable to Nancy because he had no way of knowing that Jamal would allow garbage to pile up inside his apartment. With each pointing the finger at the other, Nancy will be unable to get either to pay for her injuries.

Whose responsibility is it to keep the premises safe? In the scenario we have outlined above, it is Jamal's duty. After all, the apartment is his residence. If the harmful condition had arisen outside his apartment, Jamal might have a good argument that the landlord is at fault.

B. CLASSIFYING VISITORS

People who come to the property fit into one of three possible categories: trespasser, licensee, and invitee. In examining the type of duty owed to each, we start with trespassers because their legal status is fairly straightforward.

ISSUE AT A GLANCE

When a person is injured on someone's property, the first task is to classify the person. Is he a trespasser, a licensee, or an invitee? The classification determines the duty.

1. TRESPASSERS

Trespassers
A person who is on the property of another without permission

The rule under the common law is that there is no duty to **trespassers.** Possessors of land have no obligation to make their property safe, or to take reasonable action to ensure the safety of people who trespass on the land.

Example: Jamal's duty to Nancy might be different if she were in a different category of visitor. For instance, suppose that Nancy had not been invited to Jamal's apartment, but had instead broken in to burglarize it. She slips in Jamal's garbage and injures her knee. We have all heard about cases where burglars have sued homeowners because of the injuries they sustained in breaking in, but the news stories generally neglect to report the resolution of such cases. In this situation, Nancy is a trespasser. Possessors of land, like

Jamal, have no duty to trespassers. Nancy's status as a trespasser will have a huge impact on her lawsuit.

A trespasser is someone who is on the property without permission. She does not have to be a burglar; she can simply be uninvited. If she injures herself while she is on the premises without permission, she will be unable to prove the first element of a negligence case. (Without duty, she cannot proceed to breach of duty.)

2. EXCEPTIONS TO THE GENERAL RULE OF NO DUTY TO TRESPASSERS

Over time, the rather harsh rule that a land possessor owed no duty to a trespasser was gradually modified. One of the biggest problems with the rule involved children. Under the law, children always receive special protection. Their inexperience with the world and their lack of maturity require adults to look after them. When a child trespasses on property and is injured, should the same "no duty" rule apply? What if the land possessor had good reason to know that children would attempt to trespass? What if the land possessor has a swimming pool or a junkyard or a closed playground? Shouldn't he be forced to take some precautions to protect children, even if he is under no obligation to protect adult trespassers?

a. The Attractive Nuisance Doctrine

The so-called attractive nuisance doctrine was developed as a direct response to trespassing children. Courts developed this doctrine to specifically address dangerous conditions in areas that children would naturally find enticing. When the doctrine was originally developed, railroads were still the predominant mode of travel in the United States. Switching stations and railroad yards were often irresistible to young children, who were as fascinated by big machines then as they are now. When a child wandered into a railroad yard that had no fences or other protective devices, the child lacked any redress when he was injured. The courts felt that this was too drastic an outcome and carved out the attractive nuisance doctrine, which is really an exception to the rule that there is no duty to trespassers. When a plaintiff brings a suit and alleges the attractive nuisance doctrine to show that there was a duty to the injured child, the plaintiff must meet all the elements of the doctrine before the courts will impose a duty on the possessor.

Elements of the Attractive Nuisance Doctrine

To prove his case, a plaintiff who relies on the attractive nuisance doctrine must show:

- That the defendant has reason to know that there is a dangerous condition on his land (such as a railroad yard) and that children are likely to trespass there
- That the defendant knows that this dangerous condition poses an unreasonable risk of injury to a child

- That a young child, because of her lack of maturity and experience, would not realize how dangerous the condition actually was
- That the financial burden of making the condition safer is slight in comparison with the danger posed to a child
- That the defendant failed to take reasonable precautions to prevent a trespassing child from being injured

If the plaintiff can prove each of these elements, he can show that the defendant did owe a duty to the trespassing child, despite the general rule that no duty exists to trespassers.

b. Rescue Doctrine

Another exception to the general rule of no duty to trespassers involves rescuers. Like children, rescuers also receive special protection under the law.

Example: Timmy is playing and falls down a well on Rhonda's property. Rhonda has failed to properly cover the well. Rick is walking home and hears Timmy cry out. Rick rushes onto Rhonda's property to rescue Timmy and in so doing, he is injured by the shards of metal that protrude from the top of the well. Can Rick bring an action against Rhonda?

Answer: Yes. Although Rick is technically a trespasser (he did not have permission to be on Rhonda's property), and Rhonda has no duty to trespassers, this case falls into an exception. Courts want to promote (and protect) people who seek to rescue others. We have already seen that when a person creates a dangerous condition, he must take steps to protect others from it. Here, we apply this idea to the possessor of real estate and impose a duty.

The courts created the rescue doctrine to address a public policy concern. The courts realized that not allowing a rescuer to be protected under the law might discourage people from rescuing one another.

C. CLASSIFYING VISITORS: LICENSEES

When someone is invited onto the property, that person is not a trespasser. In many jurisdictions, this invited person can fall into one of two categories: licensee or invitee. The defendant's duty to a licensee is different from his duty to an invitee.

Licensee
A person who enters another person's premises for convenience, curiosity, or entertainment

The term **licensee** refers to a guest. This is a person who has come to the premises for personal or social reasons, not business. The duty of a possessor to a licensee is simply to warn of a dangerous condition.

Duty to licensee: warn of dangerous condition.

D. CLASSIFYING VISITORS: INVITEES

An **invitee** is a customer or a client. This person has come to the premises for some business purpose and is not paying a social call. The possessor owes the highest duty to this person. He must not only warn of dangerous conditions, but also take reasonable actions to make the premises safe.

Invitee
A person who has a business purpose in coming onto the property

---

Duty to invitee: warn of dangerous condition and make premises safe.

ISSUE AT A GLANCE

---

1. "ECONOMIC BENEFIT" TEST

Sometimes the distinction between a licensee and an invitee is difficult to determine. Consider the following scenario.

Jamal and Rick have been friends since college. Jamal became a successful businessman and Rick became an accountant. Rick has been handling all of Jamal's financial statements, accounts payable, and taxes since Jamal started out in business. They usually have lunch together every Friday, when they discuss business and also catch up on old college acquaintances. One day, when Jamal shows up at Rick's office to pick him up for their weekly lunch, he steps out on a balcony that Rick is in the process of remodeling. Rick tells Jamal to watch his step, since the balcony is not finished. While Jamal is standing on the balcony, it collapses. Jamal is severely injured. How do we classify Jamal—invitee or licensee?

Answer: ?

One way of addressing this complicated situation is to apply a doctrine courts have developed in recent years, called the "economic benefit" test. Under this test, courts will consider a person to be an invitee if the primary reason for his presence is business with the defendant. Under that situation, Rick would not only be required to warn Jamal of the dangerous condition, but to take reasonable actions to make the dangerous condition safe. If, on the other hand, Jamal's primary reason for being there is for non-business reasons, the economic benefit test would dictate that Jamal must be classified as a licensee. Under that category, Rick must simply warn of a dangerous condition.

Under this test, is Jamal a licensee or an invitee? If the primary reason for the regular Friday luncheons is friendship and catching up, Jamal is a licensee and Rick would have satisfied his duty to Jamal when he warned him about the balcony.

2. ABNORMALLY DANGEROUS OR ULTRA-HAZARDOUS CONDITIONS

A defendant may be liable to all three categories of visitors when she has an abnormally dangerous condition on her premises. An abnormally dangerous

Sidebar
One of the fastest-growing areas of premises liability involves lawsuits based on criminal acts of others. Tenants, customers, and employees are bringing suits against owners and possessors based on the fact that they knew of a potential danger of criminal activity and failed to take action to prevent it. One example would be a poorly lit parking lot where a tenant is assaulted. In such an example, the property owner may be liable to the tenant for maintaining an unsafe condition that allowed a third party to commit a crime.

condition would be keeping wild animals, storing dynamite or other explosives, or any other condition that is extremely dangerous. The term *ultrahazardous* refers to situations that are very difficult to make safe and that pose an extreme risk to anyone nearby. The manufacture of radioactive materials is one such example. When an abnormally dangerous condition exists, the defendant must take precautions to protect all three classifications of visitors. Many of these dangerous conditions are often re-classified as *strict liability* torts, meaning that any injury to a person will result in the defendant's liability, regardless of the safety procedures used. We discuss strict liability torts in a later chapter.

ISSUE AT A GLANCE

When dealing with dangerous conditions, the precautions must be equal to the danger.

FIGURE 5-6

Questions That Should Be Answered in a Premises Liability Lawsuit

Details of the incident:

- How and when did it occur? (Pin down the date as precisely as possible for statute of limitations problems.)
- Describe the location. What condition was the location in? Excellent? Good? Poor? Dangerous?
- Are there any photographs of the location showing the dangerous condition?
- What were the lighting conditions?
- Were there any witnesses to the incident? Get full names, addresses, telephone numbers (including cell and beepers), and e-mail addresses.
- Who was in charge of the premises? Is this person the owner of the property, or is someone else?
- What were the dangerous circumstances that should have put the possessor on notice?
- Were there any warning signs posted?
- Have there been similar incidents on the premises before?

Plaintiff's actions/health:

- Was the plaintiff at fault in any way?
- Did the plaintiff have permission to be on the premises?
- Was the plaintiff an invitee? A licensee? A trespasser? Was the plaintiff in an area where he did not have permission to be?
- Does the plaintiff suffer from vision problems? Does he wear glasses or corrective contact lenses?
- Does the plaintiff have any other prostheses, such as hearing aids, cane, etc.
- Did the plaintiff have any pre-existing medical or physical problems that the incident aggravated?
- If so, give precise dates, complaints, and the names of the doctors who saw the plaintiff.
- What injuries did the plaintiff suffer as a result of this incident? Names of all medical professionals that plaintiff saw as a result of this incident.

- Defendant's residence (this helps to establish the court's jurisdiction)
- Venue
- Plaintiff's cause of action:
    - Defendant was the owner/possessor of the premises
    - Plaintiff had a right to be on the premises as a (licensee) (invitee)
- Defendant had a legal duty to the plaintiff
- Defendant acted in a negligent way, or failed to take reasonable care by the following: (list specific acts or omissions)
- Defendant had actual (or constructive) knowledge of the danger or the danger was foreseeable
- The date, time, and circumstances of the incident that resulted in plaintiff's injuries
- The facts that show the plaintiff did not contribute to his own injuries (in states where contributory negligence is a defense)
- The nature of the plaintiff's injuries
- How the defendant's action, or failure to act, was the proximate cause of the plaintiff's injuries
- The extent of the plaintiff's damages
- The plaintiff's request for relief from the court (the money it will take to compensate the plaintiff)

FIGURE 5-7

**Basic
Contents of
Any Premises
Liability
Complaint**

E. ABOLISHING THE CATEGORIES (AND DISTINCTIONS) BETWEEN INVITEES AND LICENSEES

The problems with deciding who is, and who is not, an invitee and the harsh results that this classification sometimes entails have prompted several jurisdictions to revisit the entire scheme. Illinois and North Carolina are two jurisdictions that have abolished the distinction between invitees and licensees. In those jurisdictions, the occupant owes both the same duty, that of reasonable care under all the circumstances.

Sidebar

Many jurisdictions have questioned the need for a continued distinction between invitee and licensee. Most have rejected the idea of changing the distinction and continue to recognize these common law distinctions.

F. GUEST STATUTES

In some jurisdictions, an opposite approach has been taken — narrowing the definition of invitees and licensees. In these jurisdictions so-called guest statutes have been passed that limit the duty of a possessor when the person is a social guest or a trespasser. In these jurisdictions, the categories of invitee and licensee continue to exist, but a statute limits the type of action, or the amount of damages, that an injured social guest can bring against the host.

Sidebar

In almost all jurisdictions the plaintiff's status as an invitee or a licensee is a question for the jury.

DUTY TO THIRD PARTIES

The general rule about duty to third parties is that a person does not owe a third party any duty. The reason for this rule is that unlike other situations, there is no direct contact between the defendant and a third party and therefore no special relationship. When we say "third party" in this discussion, we are referring to someone other than the plaintiff. For instance, in a typical car wreck case we often see a negligent driver and an injured plaintiff. There is a direct connection between the defendant's negligence and the plaintiff's injuries. We would say that there is proximate cause between the defendant's actions and the resultant damages to the plaintiff. (We discuss proximate cause in greater depth in Chapter 7.) However, in this scenario, a third party would be someone who was neither present in the automobiles nor injured by the collision. Consider the following scenario.

Ted is walking down the sidewalk when a car crash occurs nearby. He is not injured, but the wreck upsets him. He wishes to bring an action against the negligent driver for causing him to be upset. He believes that he has a solid case of intentional infliction of emotional distress. Does he have a cause of action?

Answer: Barring any other facts, no. Ted has no physical injuries and his mental upset at witnessing an accident does not provide a cause of action. If it did, car crash witnesses all over the nation would clog the court system with similar lawsuits. Ted is a third party, that is, someone who is not directly affected by the incident between the defendant and the plaintiff. In this situation, the defendant driver has no duty to Ted.

We could reach the same conclusion about Ted's third party status by using the principle of foreseeability. Is it foreseeable that a pedestrian would suffer from intentional infliction of emotional distress because of the defendant's actions? In the pragmatic world of the law, the answer is no. If Ted could allege some special circumstance, such as the fact that the plaintiff was his child, he might then have a cause of action. But under these facts, he has none.

The general rule that there is no duty to third parties is slowly changing in many jurisdictions to a duty to third parties under certain, specific circumstances.

What about a situation in which the defendant has reason to believe that the third party is in danger from someone? Consider the following scenario.

Dr. M. diagnoses his patient, Danny, with a rare blood disease. The disease is not contagious, but will substantially shorten Danny's life. Dr. M. knows that Danny has recently married. Danny has no plans to tell his new wife about his condition. Does Dr. M. owe any duty to Danny's wife to tell her about Danny's condition?

Answer: No. Why? For one thing, Dr. M.'s duty is to his patient, Danny, and Danny's wife is not Dr. M.'s patient. Dr. M. also has an obligation of confidentiality about his patient's medical treatment. Dr. M. has no obligation to Danny's new wife.

The rule seems very simple and straightforward. A person owes a duty to specific people, not *all* people. But this general statement begins to break down when we change some of the facts.

Example: Danny has been diagnosed with an extremely contagious disease. If Danny has any prolonged contact with anyone, that person will almost certainly become infected with the disease and will probably die. Dr. M. knows that Danny is married. Does he now have a duty to inform Danny's wife about the disease?

Answer: Yes. In our example, the doctor may have not only an ethical duty to tell Danny's wife, he may have a legal duty. Because this scenario deals with a highly infectious disease, this may be enough to shift the focus from the doctor's duty to Danny to the doctor's duty to the general public. We can agree that there are situations in which a doctor's duty of confidentiality to his patient becomes secondary to the doctor's duty to the general public, or third parties. Having said that, however, many other professionals continue to have no legal duty to third parties for dangers that many people would consider to be obvious and serious.

Many jurisdictions have modified the general rule of no duty to third parties to address dangerous situations. In those jurisdictions, the courts have said that a person does have a duty to third parties when the danger is clear, the third party can easily be identified, and warning the third party would not cause any hardship. Once you have opened this door of duty to a third party, how far does it go? Consider the following scenario.

Dr. T. is a psychologist with many clients. Fred is one of them. Fred has a history of violence, including some physical assaults. Dr. T. has been counseling Fred for some time. In the past few months, Fred has been talking regularly about hurting Fred's ex-wife. Fred has described exactly how he plans on abducting his ex-wife, how he will kill her, and how he plans on disposing of her body. Fred has even set a date for this killing: next Tuesday. Does Dr. T. have a legal duty to warn Fred's ex-wife?

Answer: Although most of us would agree that Dr. M. seems to have a moral duty to warn Fred's ex-wife, the situation for Dr. T. is actually very difficult. Dr. T. is bound by law to keep her patient's conversations confidential. Fred may also simply be "blowing off steam" by talking about the murder as a way of fantasizing about something he would never do. Do the specifics of Fred's plan give some guidance? After all, it's one thing to say, "I'm going to kill that person," as opposed to "I'm going to kidnap her next Tuesday when she gets off at work at 3 P.M., kill her with a knife, and dump her body in a secluded area." The specifics of the threat really go to the question of foreseeability. If an action is foreseeable, the situation may impose a duty on Dr. T.

A. FORESEEABILITY OF INJURY TO THIRD PARTY

Perhaps the most famous case dealing with an obligation to third parties and how this rule can (and perhaps should) be modified is *Tarasoff v. Regents of University of California.*[10]

TARASOFF v. REGENTS OF UNIVERSITY OF CALIFORNIA
17 Cal. 3d 425, 551 P.2d 334, 131 Cal. Rptr. 14 (1976)

On October 27, 1969, Prosenjit Poddar killed Tatiana Tarasoff. Plaintiffs, Tatiana's parents, allege that two months earlier Poddar confided his intention to kill Tatiana to Dr. Lawrence Moore, a psychologist employed by the Cowell Memorial Hospital at the University of California at Berkeley. They allege that on Moore's request, the campus police briefly detained Poddar, but released him when he appeared rational. They further claim that Dr. Harvey Powelson, Moore's superior, then directed that no further action be taken to detain Poddar. No one warned plaintiffs of Tatiana's peril.

Plaintiffs' complaints predicate liability on . . . defendants' failure to warn plaintiffs of the impending danger. Defendants, in turn, assert that they owed no duty of reasonable care to Tatiana and that they are immune from suit under the California Tort Claims Act of 1963 (Gov. Code, 810ff).

We shall explain that defendant therapists cannot escape liability merely because Tatiana herself was not their patient. When a therapist determines, or pursuant to the standards of his profession should determine, that his patient presents a serious danger of violence to another, he incurs an obligation to use reasonable care to protect the intended victim against such danger. The discharge of this duty may require the therapist to take one or more of various steps, depending upon the nature of the case. Thus it may call for him to warn the intended victim or others likely to apprise the victim of the danger, to notify the police, or to take whatever other steps are reasonably necessary under the circumstances. In the case at bar, plaintiffs admit that defendant therapists notified the police, but argue on appeal that the therapists failed to exercise reasonable care to protect Tatiana in that they did not confine Poddar and did not warn Tatiana or others likely to apprise her of the danger. Defendant therapists, however, are public employees. Consequently, to the extent that plaintiffs seek to predicate liability upon the therapists' failure to bring about Poddar's confinement, the therapists can claim immunity under Government Code section 856.

No specific statutory provision, however, shields them from liability based upon failure to warn Tatiana or others likely to apprise her of the danger, and Government Code section 820.2 does not protect such failure as an exercise of discretion. "The assertion that liability must . . . be denied because defendant bears no 'duty' to plaintiff begs the essential question — whether the plaintiff's interests are entitled to legal protection against the defendant's conduct. . . . (Duty) is not sacrosanct in itself, but only an expression of the sum total of those considerations of policy which lead the law to say that the particular plaintiff is entitled to protection." (Prosser, Law of Torts (3d ed. 1964)). Liability should be imposed for an injury occasioned to another by his want of ordinary care or skill. Whenever one person is by circumstances placed in such a position with regard to another . . . that if he did not use ordinary care and skill in his own conduct . . . he would cause danger of injury to the person or property of the other, a duty arises to use ordinary care and skill to avoid such danger.

We depart from "this fundamental principle" only upon the "balancing of a number of considerations"; major ones "are the foreseeability of harm to the plaintiff, the degree of certainty that the plaintiff suffered injury, the closeness of the connection between the defendant's conduct and the injury suffered, the moral blame attached to the defendant's conduct, the policy of preventing future harm, the extent of the burden to the defendant and consequences to the community of imposing a duty to exercise care with resulting liability for breach, and the availability, cost and prevalence of insurance for the risk involved."

The most important of these considerations in establishing duty is foreseeability. As a general principle, a "defendant owes a duty of care to all persons who are foreseeably endangered by his conduct, with respect to all risks which make the conduct unreasonably dangerous." As we shall explain, however, when the avoidance of foreseeable harm requires a defendant to control the conduct of another person, or to warn of such conduct, the common law has traditionally imposed liability only if the defendant bears some special relationship to the dangerous person or to the potential victim. Since the relationship between a therapist and his patient satisfies this requirement, we need not here decide whether foreseeability alone is sufficient to create a duty to exercise reasonable care to protect a potential victim of another's conduct. Although, as we have stated above, under the common law, as a general rule, one person owed no duty to control the conduct of another, nor to warn those endangered by such conduct, the courts have carved out an exception to this rule in cases in which the defendant stands in some special relationship to either the person whose conduct needs to be controlled or in a relationship to the foreseeable victim of that conduct. Applying this exception to the present case, we note that a relationship of defendant therapists to either Tatiana or Poddar will suffice to establish a duty of care; as explained in section 315 of the Restatement Second of Torts, a duty of care may arise from either "(a) a special relation . . . between the actor and the third person which imposes a duty upon the actor to control the third person's conduct, or (b) a special relation . . . between the actor and the other which gives to the other a right of protection."

Although plaintiffs' pleadings assert no special relation between Tatiana and defendant therapists, they establish as between Poddar and defendant therapists the special relation that arises between a patient and his doctor or psychotherapist. Such a relationship may support affirmative duties for the benefit of third persons. Thus, for example, a hospital must exercise reasonable care to control the behavior of a patient which may endanger other persons. A doctor must also warn a patient if the patient's condition or medication renders certain conduct, such as driving a car, dangerous to others.

Although the California decisions that recognize this duty have involved cases in which the defendant stood in a special relationship both to the victim and to the person whose conduct created the danger, we do not think that the duty should logically be constricted to such situations. Decisions of other jurisdictions hold that the single relationship of a doctor to his patient is sufficient to support the duty to exercise reasonable care to protect others against dangers emanating from the patient's illness. The courts hold that a doctor is liable to persons infected by his patient if he negligently fails to diagnose a contagious disease or, having diagnosed the illness, fails to warn members of the patient's family.

Defendants contend, however, that imposition of a duty to exercise reasonable care to protect third persons is unworkable because therapists cannot accurately predict whether or not a patient will resort to violence. In support of this argument amicus representing the American Psychiatric Association and other professional societies cites numerous articles which indicate that therapists, in the present state of the art, are unable reliably to predict violent acts; their forecasts, amicus claims, tend consistently to over-predict violence, and indeed are more often wrong than right. Since predictions of violence are often erroneous, amicus concludes, the courts should not render rulings that predicate the liability of therapists upon the validity of such predictions.

The role of the psychiatrist, who is indeed a practitioner of medicine, and that of the psychologist who performs an allied function, are like that of the physician who must conform to the standards of the profession and who must often make diagnoses and predictions based upon such evaluations. Thus the judgment of the therapist in diagnosing emotional disorders and in predicting whether a patient presents a serious danger of violence is comparable to the judgment which doctors and professionals must regularly render under accepted rules of responsibility.

We recognize the difficulty that a therapist encounters in attempting to forecast whether a patient presents a serious danger of violence. Obviously we do not require that the therapist, in making that determination, render a perfect performance; the therapist need only exercise "that reasonable degree of skill, knowledge, and care ordinarily possessed and exercised by members of (that professional specialty) under similar circumstances." Within the broad range of reasonable practice and treatment in which professional opinion and judgment may differ, the therapist is free to exercise his or her own best judgment without liability; proof, aided by hindsight, that he or she judged wrongly is insufficient to establish negligence.

In the instant case, however, the pleadings do not raise any question as to failure of defendant therapists to predict that Poddar presented a serious danger of violence. On the contrary, the present complaints allege that defendant therapists did in fact predict that Poddar would kill, but were negligent in failing to warn. In each instance the adequacy of the therapist's conduct must be measured against the traditional negligence standard of the rendition of reasonable care under the circumstances. In sum, the therapist owes a legal duty not only to his patient, but also to his patient's would-be victim and is subject in both respects to scrutiny by judge and jury.

Our current crowded and computerized society compels the interdependence of its members. In this risk-infested society we can hardly tolerate the further exposure to danger that would result from a concealed knowledge of the therapist that his patient was lethal. If the exercise of reasonable care to protect the threatened victim requires the therapist to warn the endangered party or those who can reasonably be expected to notify him, we see no sufficient societal interest that would protect and justify concealment. The containment of such risks lies in the public interest. For the foregoing reasons, we find that plaintiffs' complaints can be amended to state a cause of action against defendants for breach of a duty to exercise reasonable care to protect Tatiana. We conclude that defendant therapists in the present case are not immune from liability for their failure to warn of Tatiana's peril. We conclude, therefore, that the therapist defendants' failure to warn Tatiana or those who reasonably could have been expected to notify her of her peril does not fall within the absolute protection afforded by section 820.2 of the Government Code.

The judgment of the superior court in favor of defendants is reversed, and the cause remanded for further proceedings consistent with the views expressed herein.

Questions about the case:

1. What is the plaintiff's theory about the liability of Dr. Moore?
2. Are therapists always free from liability when the person who is injured is not their patient?
3. What test does the court create to determine when a therapist should be liable to a third party?
4. What balancing of principles does the court engage in to determine liability in these cases?
5. How does the court explain foreseeability in this case?

FIGURE 5-8		All tort trials		Type of trial		
Tort Cases Disposed of by Trial in State Courts in the Nation's 75 Largest Counties, 2001	Case type	Number	Percent	Jury	Bench	Other*
	All tort trials	7,948	100.0%	90.8%	7.3%	1.9%
	Automobile	4,235	53.3%	92.6%	5.9%	1.5%
	Premises liability	1,268	16.0	91.4	6.2	2.4
	Product liability	158	2.0	91.8	3.2	5.1
	Asbestos	31	0.4	96.8	—	3.2
	Other	126	1.6	90.5	6.3	3.2
	Intentional tort	375	4.7	76.3	20.3	3.5
	Medical malpractice	1,156	14.5	96.2	2.9	0.9
	Professional malpractice	102	1.3	66.3	32.7	1.0
	Slander/libel	95	1.2	78.9	18.9	2.1
	Animal attack	99	1.2	86.9	13.1	—
	Conversion	27	0.3	46.4	46.4	7.1
	False arrest, imprisonment	45	0.6	75.6	20.0	4.4
	Other or unknown tort	390	4.9	82.6	12.1	5.4

Note: Data for case and disposition type were available for 100.0% of the 7,948 tort trials. Detail may not sum to total because of rounding.

—No cases recorded.
*Other trial cases include trials with a directed verdict, judgments notwithstanding the verdict, and jury trials for defaulted defendants. Although these cases are typically placed in a separate category, they are a form of jury trial.

Tort Trials and Verdicts in Large Counties, 2001, Bureau of Justice Statistics, U.S. Department of Justice.

B. CAN A DEFENDANT WAIVE HIS DUTY?

Under certain circumstances, a defendant can legally waive his duty to another. A waiver usually takes the form of a written contract between the defendant and some other party. It often includes language to the effect that the plaintiff, by engaging in some dangerous practice, is waiving all rights to sue the defendant for negligence. However, these contracts are subject to strict interpretation because they often encourage a lax attitude toward the standard of care for another. This means that when there is any ambiguity in the contract, it will be held against the defendant.

Waivers are not legally valid in some situations, such as the duty arising from a special relationship. Many jurisdictions have also said that it is not legal to attempt to contract against your own negligence. Waivers will also not be enforced when they run counter to public policy.

Example: John is suffering from severe chest pain and drives himself to the local emergency room. At the front triage desk, he tells the nurse on duty about his symptoms. The nurse hands him a form and tells him that he cannot be seen by a doctor until he signs the form. John sees a paragraph at the bottom of the form that states, "Patient, by receiving treatment, hereby waives any claim against the attending physician, nurse, or nurse practitioner that may arise due to medical malpractice." John signs the form. Doctors discover that he needs emergency surgery and during the surgery one of the surgeons forgets to remove a sponge. It remains inside John's chest cavity, where it causes a severe infection. Can John sue the doctor for malpractice, even though he waived his right when he came to the hospital?

Answer: Yes. Most jurisdictions would label such a clause a violation of public policy and refuse to enforce it. There is also the issue that John signed the waiver under duress, because he was suffering from severe chest pain and was in dire need of medical treatment.

SKILLS YOU NEED IN THE REAL WORLD

Beginning Your Legal Research

When you get your first research assignment, your impulse will be to grab a book (or click on an Internet site) and get started. That's not where you should begin. Before you tackle any legal research assignment, think it through. Thinking about your assignment doesn't sound like as much fun as doing something, but it can save you lots of time (and anxiety). Let's take a legal research assignment and break it down into steps.

Step One — Key Words

Before you begin your research, take a long, hard look at your question and then begin writing down key words. Here's an example:

Attorney: We've got a case involving a collision at a railroad intersection. Shortly after the accident, the railroad company went out to the site and cut off all the tree limbs that were blocking the view. This sounds like subsequent remedial measures. Normally, that evidence is not admissible in the trial. See if you can find some way to make it admissible.

Paralegal: No problem. When do you need this?

Attorney: Oh, no rush. Before lunch will do.

Before you rush off to the statutes trying to find something dealing with subsequent remedial measures, think about your assignment. What is the issue here? If you don't know what the term *subsequent remedial measures* means, look it up in a legal dictionary. You'll see that it refers to the basic idea that anything done after the accident to make the premises safer can't be used in the trial to show that the premises were unsafe before the accident. (Otherwise, people would be discouraged from repairing dangerous conditions.) Right away, we can jot down some key words: repair, subsequent remedial measures. If you think about it, you will realize that this is an evidentiary question dealing with what kinds of evidence can, and cannot, be admitted at trial.

Step Two — Research from the General to the Specific

In a perfect world, you can turn to the correct answer every time. That occasionally does happen, but most of the time you have to move from the general to the specific. Where should you begin? Start with the most general term on your list and see where that takes you. The most general term on the list is . . . *evidence.* That's about as general as you can get. Start with any good book, digest, or treatise and see where that takes you.

Step Three — Use Your Common Sense

Paralegals sometimes make the mistake of not using their common sense. Let's say that you have researched your topic to the point that you have discovered that evidence of subsequent remedial measures can be admissible to show ownership of the premises in question, under certain conditions. Are you done? What's the most obvious question that follows this result? "What do they mean by 'certain conditions'?" If you anticipate some of the more obvious questions that your research raises, you will be far more effective.

Step Four — Use Free Internet Legal Research Sites

Finally, you should take advantage of the many different free legal research sites currently available online. Not all of these sites have the same depth of coverage, but they can help get you started, especially if the research topic is one with which you are unfamiliar. Any Internet search engine will return numerous hits with the search string "free legal research sites."

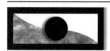 ## THE LIFE OF A PARALEGAL

Getting and Maintaining Complete Information on a Client

When a client comes in, we'll have them fill out an information sheet. It asks a lot of questions about their addresses and telephone numbers. You'd be surprised how many clients don't want to completely fill it out. They'll quibble and say this part doesn't apply, or say that they don't want to fill in the complete form. Sometimes, they're not certain about some information. They don't understand, until I explain it to them, that all of this information comes in handy later on when we're trying to contact them about interrogatories or trial or even settlement. Once I have this information, I'll enter it into our database. We have a commercial database that was specifically designed for law offices. It keeps track of clients' names, addresses, adverse parties, opposing attorneys, you name it. A lot of times while I'm creating a computer file on the client, I'm also creating a physical file, too. I'll generate a client number and paste it on a manila file folder while I'm also entering all of this information on the computer. You have to be able to juggle several different jobs at the same time. A lot of times, I'm entering computer information, putting together a physical file, and answering phone calls all at the same time.

Christina Lynn, Paralegal

ETHICAL ISSUES FOR THE PARALEGAL: KEEPING UP WITH DEVELOPMENTS IN THE LAW

One of the most important things you can do as a legal professional is to keep up with the law on a particular topic. Suppose that your firm handles a lot of personal injury cases. It makes sense for you to stay current on the law in this area. You can do this by reading legal newspapers and legal magazines, but the best way is to read the most recent decisions of the courts in your jurisdiction. There is nothing more embarrassing, and a better justification for a claim of legal malpractice, than relying on a case that has been overruled by a higher court. Your knowledge about recent trends in the law can be extremely valuable to an attorney who might not have taken the time to stay as current on the law as she should have. Those kinds of little reminders of your helpfulness will only make you that much more indispensable to the firm.

Chapter Summary

The first element in a negligence action is duty. A plaintiff must clearly establish that the defendant owed a duty before the plaintiff can present further evidence of how and when the defendant breached that duty, and how that breach was a legal cause of the plaintiff's subsequent injuries. Duty can arise out of specific situations, such as a motorist's duty to the other drivers on the road. Duty can also be established by the special relationship existing between the parties. The defendant's status as a professional, or specialist, subjects him to a higher duty than someone who is considered to be a layperson. Duty may also be established by the fact that the defendant was in possession of the premises and was in a better position to know about potential dangers than anyone else. Finally, some plaintiffs receive a higher level of protection under the law. Children, for instance, are protected in situations in which adults might not receive similar treatment under the law.

Web Sites

■ **Hieros Gamos Law**
http://www.hg.org/torts.html

■ **FindLaw**
http://www.findlaw.com/01topics/22tort/index.html

- ■ **West Net — Negligence Law**
  http://www.west.net/~smith/negligence.htm

- ■ **Wikipedia — Duty of Care**
  http://en.wikipedia.org/wiki/Duty_of_care

Forms and Court Documents

This form is a typical motion to dismiss the plaintiff's claim, filed by the defendant on the grounds of "failure to state a claim on which relief may be granted." Such a motion might be filed when the defendant wishes to dismiss the plaintiff's claim for failure to prove duty.

IN THE SUPERIOR COURT OF GANNETT COUNTY
STATE OF PLACID

John Jones, Plaintiff	) CASE NO. 8790CR)))
vs.	))
Mary Wilson, Defendant	)

Motion to Dismiss

Defendant, by counsel, pursuant to Placid State Rules of Civil Procedure 12(b), moves the court to enter its order of dismissal of this action on the grounds that the plaintiff's complaint fails to state a claim on which relief can be granted, warranting dismissal pursuant to P.S.R.C.P 12(b)(6).

 (a) Plaintiff fails to state a legally cognizable cause of action, which is a prerequisite to the relief he requests.

This the _____ day of July 2002.

Respectfully submitted,

By: _____
Attorney for Defendant

Certificate of Service

This is to certify that the undersigned has this date served this document in the above-captioned action on all other parties to this cause by depositing a copy hereof, postage prepaid, in the United States Mail, properly addressed to the attorney for each party as follows:

This the _____ day of July 2002.

Respectfully submitted,

By: _____
Attorney for Defendant

Key Terms

Custom	Licensee	Standard of care
Duty	Specialist	Trespasser
Invitee		

Review Questions

1 What is a legal duty?
2 How would you describe the relationship between the terms *duty* and *foreseeability?*
3 What duty is owed by one stranger to another?
4 X Company has adopted the custom of always double-checking its packaging before sending out its patented fruitcakes. One day, an inspector fails to notice that a piece of sharp metal has fallen into a fruitcake. Does X Company have a duty to inspect its product simply because it adopted the custom of always doing so?
5 List at least five professions that have a higher standard of care or duty than that of a layperson. Now explain why these professions have a higher duty.
6 How is the legal duty of a professional different from that of a specialist?
7 Explain what is meant by a "special relationship" under negligence law. How do special relationships affect duty?
8 What is the duty owed by the possessor of premises to a trespasser? Are there any exceptions to this rule?
9 What is the attractive nuisance doctrine? Why was this doctrine created?
10 What is the difference between an invitee and a licensee? Give an example of both.
11 What is an "abnormally dangerous" or "ultra-hazardous" condition and how does this affect the analysis of the defendant's duty?
12 Why was the court in the *Tarasoff* case willing to extend the doctor's liability to a third party?
13 Can a defendant waive her duty to a plaintiff? If so, under what circumstances would a waiver be valid? Under what circumstances would a waiver be considered invalid?
14 What is a "12(b)(6) motion"?

Applying What
You Have Learned

1   "True to Our Word" Burglar Alarm Company installed a state-of-the-art burglar system in High Art Galleries last year. Two nights ago, a burglar broke into the gallery by climbing through a skylight. He stole 20 paintings valued at over $100,000. The skylight was not wired to the burglar alarm system. The gallery owners have found a safety expert who will testify that any professional would have wired the skylight and that failure to do so is a breach of the standard of care. Is this enough to show that the alarm company had a duty?

2   Same facts as above, but with one slight change. When the alarm company installed the system, they had the gallery sign a contract that stated that they would not be liable for any break-ins or thefts that occurred because of unprotected "windows, doors, or skylights." Is this a valid waiver of their duty? If the gallery owners signed this contract, are they now barred from suing the alarm company?

3   ABC Sign Company is in the business of designing billboards. They do not make the actual signs; they simply design what will go on them. They also do not install the signs. A different company is responsible for that. Sandy is a nurse at the local hospital and one evening, when she is leaving work, a large sign falls on her and breaks both of her legs. Sandy sues ABC Sign Company for negligence, specifically alleging that ABC failed to inspect its sign. If the company had inspected the sign, they would have seen that several of the supporting bolts had rusted through. Sandy must establish that ABC had a duty to her. Can she prove it?

4   Does your state recognize the doctrine of social host liability? If so, what are the elements?

5   Has your state abolished the distinction between licensee and invitee, or is it still in use? Does your state's definition of licensee and/or invitee differ in some ways from the definition provided in the text? If so, how?

6   What are some of the factors the court considered in finding the psychiatrist owed a duty to third parties in *Tarasoff v. Regents of University of California?*

Endnotes

[1] *Becker v. Schwartz,* 46 N.Y.2d 401, 413 N.Y.S.2d 895, 386 N.E.2d 807 (1978).
[2] *Ortiz v. Chicago,* 79 Ill. App. 3d 902, 398 N.E.2d 1007 (1979).
[3] *Rockweit by Donohue v. Senecal,* 187 Wis. 2d 170, 522 N.W.2d 575 (1994).
[4] *Hertelendy v. Agway Ins. Co.,* 177 Wis. 2d 329, 501 N.W.2d 903 (1993).
[5] *Tubbs v. Argus,* 140 Ind. App. 695, 225 N.E.2d 841 (1967).
[6] *Pesantes v. United States,* 621 F.2d 175 (5th Cir. 1980).
[7] *Cavin v. Kasser,* 820 S.W.2d 647 (1991).
[8] *Olson v. Children's Home Society,* 204 Cal. App. 3d 1362, 252 Cal. Rptr. 11 (1988).
[9] Restatement (Second) of Torts, §360.
[10] *Tarasoff v. Regents of University of California,* 17 Cal. 3d 425, 551 P.2d 334, 131 Cal. Rptr. 14 (1976).

Breach of
Duty Under
Negligence Law

Chapter Objectives

■ Determine when a breach of duty has occurred

■ Describe how a defendant's actions (or failure to act) violate the standard of reasonableness under tort law

■ Be able to explain the difference between the objective and subjective standards of care

■ Define *res ipsa loquitur* and negligence per se

■ Describe how to locate expert witnesses

 **INTRODUCTION**

In this chapter, we address the concept of breach of duty. This is the second element of the four (duty, breach, causation, and damages) that must be proved in any negligence case. We assume as we discuss the various topics related to breach that the existence of the duty has already been proved. Now that we have made that determination, we must next explore whether the defendant's actions (or his failure to act) is a breach of duty under negligence law.

WHO BREACHED A DUTY IN THE CHUMLEY CASE?

As we continue to explore the details of the Chumley case, we must answer the question of who, if anyone, breached a duty to Mr. and Mrs. Chumley. If we have established that someone had a duty to maintain the intersection in a safe manner, our next question must be, whose duty was it? There are two obvious choices. If our theory is that the railroad tracks are owned and operated by the railroad company and these tracks are dangerous, it would seem to be a straightforward proposition to say that the railroad company breached its duty. However, we could just as easily make the same claim against the town government. After all, it is responsible for maintaining all the roads inside the town limits. If the intersection was unsafe, the town's employees must shoulder some responsibility. Rather than choose between these two possible defendants, most plaintiffs would opt to sue them both. Just to be on the safe side, the plaintiff in the Chumley case will also list the railroad engineer as a defendant, under the theory that he may have also acted in a negligent manner. (Suppose, for instance, that he could have stopped his train in time to avoid the collision if he had been paying attention.)

Now that we have some idea about who will be sued, we must also address the question of how to prove negligence. The plaintiff's attorney (like the defendants' attorneys) will focus on proof throughout the lawsuit. How will the plaintiff prove that the intersection was dangerous? Put another way, how will the plaintiff prove that the three defendants breached their legal duty?

The plaintiff's team will present evidence and witness testimony that attempts to conclusively show that the intersection was not safe at the time that Mr. Chumley drove across it and was hit by the locomotive. One way of presenting this evidence is to have the plaintiff testify about the conditions that day. However, we do not have that option in this case. Mr. Chumley had traumatic head wounds and suffers from amnesia. He can't remember anything about the collision. Is there some other way of presenting this evidence? One method that many plaintiffs' attorneys use is expert testimony. The plaintiff in this case could hire a safety expert and ask him or her to evaluate the intersection and give an expert opinion about the conditions. We discuss expert testimony later in this chapter.

BREACH OF DUTY

Simply because the plaintiff was injured does not establish that the defendant violated a duty. To satisfy a cause of action for negligence, the plaintiff must show not only that he was injured, but also that the injury was directly tied to the defendant's breach of a duty to him.[1] One of the ways of answering that question is to determine whether the defendant failed to use reasonable care in his actions. Here is an example: Joe is driving his car and fails to stop for a stop sign. When he runs the stop sign, he causes a car accident with Barbara. Does Joe owe a duty to Barbara? Yes. Joe owes a duty to all other motorists, and because Barbara is a motorist, he owes a duty to her. Has Joe breached his duty? If the standard that we use is whether Joe caused an unreasonable risk of harm, the answer to that question must be yes. (However, a defendant is not required to exercise greater care than what the plaintiff is required to exercise for her own safety.)[2]

The plaintiff must prove not only that the defendant breached a duty, but also that this breach was closely connected to her injuries.

ISSUE
AT A
GLANCE

In this example, determining a breach of duty is rather simple. However, there are many other situations in which determining a breach can be quite difficult. Courts have created various doctrines and tests to help determine when a breach of duty has occurred. One such test is the **reasonable person standard.** To determine if a breach of duty has occurred, courts will often ask the question, what would a reasonable person have done under the same circumstances? If this hypothetical reasonable person would not have acted the way the defendant did, the court can feel justified in its determination that the defendant has breached a duty.

Obviously, the court is basing its decision on the fact that a hypothetical reasonable person would not take any action that would cause an unreasonable risk of harm to other people. However, there have been many situations in which the hypothetical reasonable person standard has been difficult if not impossible to apply. In novel situations, for example, the hypothetical standard may not be the best approach. In the last chapter, we discussed another method used to evaluate the defendant's duty: economic benefit analysis. The idea of using a cost-benefit analysis to determine breach of duty has great appeal, as we see in the discussion of product liability cases. However, cost-benefit analysis will not work in every situation either. We must therefore examine breach of duty at its most basic level and build up an understanding of the ramifications as we go.

Reasonable person standard
The standard used by the court as a yardstick by which it can evaluate the defendant's actions in a particular case

Sidebar
Once a legally recognized duty has been established, the next point, the breach of that duty, must be clearly shown. To determine a breach of duty, the parameters of that duty must be determined. Precisely what actions create the standard of care? Only when the standard of care has been determined can the defendant's actions be evaluated to see if he has violated it. Under most situations, the standard of care is what a reasonably prudent person would have done under the same circumstances as the defendant.[3]

One way of determining breach of duty is to first determine the standard of care and then determine if the defendant's actions failed to meet that standard.

ISSUE
AT A
GLANCE

A. THE OBJECTIVE STANDARD

Sidebar

Some commentators have suggested that the reasonable person standard is one that can—and should— take into account the fact that people are fallible and should therefore include a consideration for those potential faults.[5]

Every person is required by law to use a basic level of common sense and care in his actions.[4] Having said that, however, it is usually up to the jury, not the individuals involved, to determine just what that common sense and caring action should have been. When evaluating the defendant's actions, we do not look at them from his viewpoint. A defendant could justify his actions subjectively on almost any grounds. We look instead at what objectively occurred. We are permitted to take into account unusual or stressful events that occurred around the actions, but we only take those into account as they might have affected a reasonable person. We do not take into account, in most situations, the subjective characteristics of the defendant. For instance, if one driver does not drive with the same level of proficiency as another driver, we do not give this first driver any special advantage. To do so would open up a world of problems in every civil case. A defendant would claim that he should receive special treatment because of a mental or physical characteristic that is somehow different from the population at large. Instead, we generally hold all defendants to the same standard of care. This means that people with special characteristics, whether they are emotional or mental, are treated the same as people who do not have such characteristics. (Later we discuss how this rule has some limited exceptions when dealing with certain physical characteristics.)

Example: Ron has a low IQ. While he is driving to work one day, he sees a new sign that he does not understand and as a result he crashes into a highway crew who are working on the road. Ron claims that because of his low IQ, he should not be held to the same standard of care as people with a higher IQ. The court will not allow a special standard of care for Ron. People with lower intelligence or people who suffer from certain forms of mental problems are held to the same standard as people who have normal intelligence and normal mental processes. The defendant's actions are not judged by whether he carried out a specific act, but whether he exercised that degree of care that a reasonable person would have exercised under the facts of the case.[6]

When evaluating the reasonableness of the defendant's actions, the jury compares the defendant's actions with those of a hypothetical reasonable person. The jury must answer the question: What would this person have done under similar circumstances?

Sidebar

The standard of care depends on the facts of the case. There is no set formula that will determine the standard of care in every situation. Courts look at the peculiar features of each case and base a decision on standard of care on what a hypothetical reasonable person would have done in the same circumstances.[7]

This principle of holding defendants to the same standard also applies to people who are intoxicated. When persons are acting under the influence of alcohol or some other drug, they cannot claim a special privilege under the law when they cause an unreasonable risk of harm to other people. They are held to the standard of what a reasonable, sober person would do. Put another way, intoxication does not create a special category under the law.

The same rule applies to people who are legally insane. When we have a situation involving a person who is claiming that at the time of the incident he was legally insane, his conduct will be judged by the standard of what a sane person would have done under the same circumstances. An insane person is held to the same standard as a sane person.[8]

FIGURE 6-1

Plaintiff
Winners with
Awards
Reduced

Plaintiff winners with awards reduced in tort trials due to contributory or comparative negligence in state courts in the nation's 75 largest counties, 2001

Case type	Number of tort trials with a plaintiff winner[a]	Tort trials with awards reduced		
		Percent	Number	Mean percent reduction
All tort trials[b]	4,045	14.4%	584	37.5%
Automobile	2,553	12.7%	324	36.8%
Premises liability	518	33.4	173	41.5
Product liability	68	13.7	9	27.6
Asbestos	19	—	—	—
Other	49	19.0	9	27.6
Intentional tort	214	8.5	18	27.2
Medical malpractice	307	6.6	20	30.5
Professional malpractice	51	13.7	7	31.6
Slander/libel	39	2.5	1	40.0*
Animal attack	65	6.3	4	43.3
Conversion	13	—	—	—
False arrest, imprisonment	19	—	—	—
Other or unknown tort	199	13.8	27	37.4

Note: Data on whether awards were reduced for contributory or comparative negligence were available for 99.0% of sampled trials with a plaintiff winner and a known initial award amount. Detail may not sum to total because of rounding.
*Not mean but actual reduction amount. No cases recorded.
[a]Only includes plaintiffs who won an intitial monetary damage award.
[b]Includes bench and jury trials, trials with a directed verdict, judgments notwithstanding the verdict, and jury trials for defaulted defendants.

Tort Trials and Verdicts in Large Counties, 2001, Bureau of Justice Statistics, U.S. Department of Justice.

B. THE JURY DETERMINES THE STANDARD OF CARE

Ultimately, the people who determine the standard of care are the jurors. Who better to determine the standard of care than these representatives of the community? With their varied backgrounds and experiences, jurors can bring a sense of what the community at large considers to be reasonable actions. Most jurisdictions agree and make the question of violation of the standard of care a fact question and therefore one that the jury must resolve in deliberations.[9] However, when the jury clearly ignores the applicable laws or makes an unreasonable determination, the trial judge is authorized to overturn that verdict.[10] In evaluating the defendant's actions in a case calling for a basic standard of care, the jury must consider what an average person would do, not what someone with special abilities could do. There have been instances of people taking amazingly difficult or brave actions. Simply because someone, somewhere was able to perform an amazing act (such as wrenching

Sidebar

How is the evaluation of standard of care affected when the defendant is confronted with two equally unpleasant alternatives? For instance, suppose the defendant is attempting to flee from a fire and can either jump through a window or knock over another person to get to an open door? Either alternative is unappealing. Suppose that the defendant chooses to knock over the plaintiff instead of jumping through the window and receiving numerous cuts and bruises? In this case, the jury is called upon to evaluate the situation and to answer the question: Did the defendant choose a reasonable course of action? There are times when the defendant's actions in injuring someone else might actually be reasonable under the circumstances.[11]

a car door off its hinges in an act of desperation), this singular act does not raise the standard for everyone else. Those acts of superhuman strength occupy a place of their own and are not factored into the jury's consideration of what an average person's standard of care should be.[12]

C. PHYSICAL CHARACTERISTICS

We have said that a defendant cannot claim a special privilege or a different standard under the law because of certain characteristics. However, there is an exception to this rule. There are times when a defendant can claim a different standard when a physical characteristic is involved. Let's take the defendant's age as an example. Children are not held to the same standard as adults. We do not expect the same level of maturity and judgment to be exercised by a child as by an adult. Therefore, if a child is involved in a negligence action, the duty will change. The standard becomes what a child of the same age and background would do when placed in a similar situation. If age is one such physical characteristic that will result in a shift in the standard of care, are there other physical characteristics that will do the same? In fact, there are. A physically handicapped person is not held to the same standard as a fully able person. For instance, a person who is paralyzed from the waist down is held to the standard of a hypothetical reasonable and similarly paralyzed person. The law does not expect that a paralyzed person can respond in the same way as a person who isn't paralyzed. Another example would be handicaps such as blindness.

Notice that mental characteristics such as intelligence or emotional disturbance usually do not affect the defendant's standard of care while physical characteristics do. Tort law seems to have a bias toward characteristics that are more easily defined. It is easy to tell if a person is paralyzed or not. It is much harder to determine if someone is suffering from an emotional or psychological problem. Mental characteristics are much harder to determine and in such cases courts usually opt for a uniform standard. However, when a characteristic is easily defined, such as the fact that the defendant is a child, courts will usually take that characteristic as the basis to modify the defendant's standard of care.

As a general rule, the defendant's physical characteristics, such as handicaps, can be taken into account when evaluating his actions. As a general rule, his mental characteristics will not.

D. OTHER SITUATIONS IN WHICH THE STANDARD OF CARE IS MODIFIED: EMERGENCIES

There are other circumstances that can affect the defendant's standard of care and thus the determination of whether she has breached a duty to the plaintiff. Emergencies are a prime example. In an emergency situation people are not expected to act with the same level of care and consideration as they would in a more relaxed setting. Courts have consistently recognized that emergency situations change the nature of one person's duty to another. What would be a breach under a normal situation might not be considered a breach in an emergency.

Example: Rhonda is a firefighter who responds to a call at a burning apartment building. During her frantic efforts to free two children who are trapped on the fourth floor of the apartment building, she breaks the window, reaches through, and seizes both children. She inadvertently breaks one child's wrist. Under a normal situation, her actions would probably be considered a breach of duty. However, because of the fire and imminent threat, most jurisdictions would rule that she has not breached a duty.

E. CUSTOM OR TRADITION TO ESTABLISH BREACH OF DUTY?

Can we establish a standard of care based on custom or tradition? For instance, in certain parts of the country it is a custom of motorists who are driving in the right lane on interstate highways to move over to the left lane to allow motorists on the entrance ramp some room to get on the road. There is no law that requires this lane change to accommodate a driver entering the highway. One day, Jean is attempting to get onto a highway from an entrance ramp. As she begins to merge into the right lane, she is cut off by a man driving in the right lane who has refused to move over to the left lane. Jean runs off the roadway and her car is damaged. She sues the other driver, claiming that he violated a standard of care. She claims that the custom of changing lanes has essentially become the standard of care that a hypothetical reasonable person would follow under similar circumstances. However, courts have been very reluctant to use traditions or customs in this way. In this situation, Jean will most likely lose her suit. Consider the opposite side of this argument. If a custom or tradition established a standard of care, anyone who followed the custom would be immune from suit, even if the custom were faulty. Plaintiffs would be unable to bring a suit against anyone who claimed that he was following a local custom or tradition. When we discuss product liability cases, we consider a modification of this rule, but for general purposes, tradition will not establish a duty (or a subsequent breach).

 **PROFESSIONALS HAVE A HIGHER STANDARD OF CARE**

Professional
Someone who either through education, training, or a combination of both, possesses skills that an average person does not

In the last chapter, we explained the duty owed by someone who is a **professional.** A professional has a higher standard of care than a non-professional. Doctors and lawyers, among others, have a higher standard of

The standard of care for a doctor is the degree of care, skill, and proficiency that would be exercised by a similar physician faced with the same or similar circumstances.[13]

care to their patients and clients than someone who does not hold that designation. The reason for a higher standard of care should be obvious. Professionals have received extensive training in their chosen fields (and charge higher fees) because of their expertise. Along with that higher status comes a higher standard of care that is often stated as what another professional, in good standing, would do under similar circumstances.

Professionals are entitled to greater financial rewards for attaining their positions. However, they also must shoulder a higher standard of care.

Specialist
A professional who has achieved the highest level of training and expertise in a given field

There are some professionals who are classified as **specialists.** A specialist is someone who has an intensive educational background and expertise in a very specific area. A specialist is held to an even higher standard than is a professional. The standard for a specialist is what any other specialist with similar training and background would have done under similar circumstances.

COURT DOCTRINES THAT HELP TO DETERMINE BREACH OF DUTY

In some cases, the standard of care has been fixed by statute or some other enactment. For instance, the standard of care for possessors of land is usually set out in a statute. In medical malpractice cases, the standard has been set by case law. In other cases, such as when a defendant is handling particularly dangerous materials, the standard may be set by a combination of statutes and case law. Later, we discuss safety statutes and how they play a crucial role in setting the standard of care for motorists.

Just as we have seen with duty, courts have created several different doctrines to help determine when a breach of duty has occurred. Two of the best-known examples of these doctrines are *res ipsa loquitur* and negligence per se.

A. *RES IPSA LOQUITUR*

As we have already seen in the previous chapter, courts have created doctrines over the centuries to address specific problems in negligence cases. We know that in any negligence case, there must be proof of the four elements: duty, breach of that duty, causation linked to the breach, and damages. In some instances, court doctrines have been developed to deal with inadequacies in one or more of these elements.

Res ipsa loquitur literally means, "The thing speaks for itself." It was created to assist plaintiffs in helping to prove the element of breach of duty in certain kinds of cases.

Example: Ron is caught in traffic one day on a bridge just outside Washington, D.C. He hears a loud roar and turns just in time to see a 747 jetliner screaming toward the bridge. The plane hits the bridge and Ron's car. Ron is severely injured. The plane's fuselage breaks into thousands of pieces and a large portion of the plane ends up in the river. Can Ron sue the airline company for negligence?

Consider the elements of a negligence case. Can Ron prove duty? Do the airline company and the pilot have a duty to Ron? We can establish that element without too much effort. Airlines certainly must have a duty to passengers and others to protect them from air disasters. Has the company and/or pilot breached that duty? Now we have a slight problem. One of the elements that Ron would have to prove in a traditional negligence case is *how* the breach occurred. Ron is no expert on airplane crashes and when he approaches people who are considered experts, they tell him that there could be several reasons why the plane crashed and that no one will ever know for sure which reason is the right one. The plane itself has broken into thousands of fragments and piecing together exactly what happened might well be impossible.

If Ron pursues a traditional negligence action, he will not be able to prove his case against the airline company. What evidence can he present to show that the airline company or the pilot was negligent? He does not know what happened on the airplane; he can't prove specific acts of negligence. Here is where the doctrine of *res ipsa loquitur* comes to his rescue.

Under *res ipsa,* a defendant is presumed to have acted negligently (or breached his duty) when certain actions occur. To take advantage of *res ipsa,* the plaintiff must show:

- That the event is one that ordinarily would not occur without someone acting negligently
- That the event was caused by some instrumentality exclusively in the defendant's control
- That the event was not caused, even in part, by the plaintiff's actions or failure to act

When Ron brings his lawsuit against the airline company, can he prove each of these elements? Was the event one that ordinarily would not occur without someone acting negligently? Airplanes do not normally fall out of the sky; so the answer to this question is yes. Was the instrumentality that caused the event exclusively in the defendant's control? The airline company owned and operated the airplane; it was serviced, maintained, and operated by airline personnel, so this step is also proved. Did Ron contribute to his own injuries? Remember that Ron was simply caught in traffic on a bridge. He did not contribute to his own injuries and therefore he has satisfied every element of a *res ipsa* claim. That being the case, Ron can now bring his lawsuit and will probably win, as well.

Res ipsa loquitur
"The thing speaks for itself" (Latin); the principle that under certain circumstances, such as the type of accident that would not ordinarily occur without some form of negligence, the defendant's negligence can be presumed

ISSUE AT A GLANCE

Res ipsa loquitur claims allow a plaintiff to bring an action even when he cannot prove what precisely happened to cause his injury.

1. THE COMMONSENSE ELEMENT OF *RES IPSA LOQUITUR*

Almost all jurisdictions follow some form of *res ipsa* doctrine. (The exceptions are Michigan, Pennsylvania, and South Carolina.) *Res ipsa* is sometimes referred to as the "commonsense" negligence claim. It is often used in cases like airplane crashes and other catastrophes in which the plaintiff has no ability to determine what the defendant did wrong, except to say, "There just had to be negligence." This sounds more like common sense than any intensive legal analysis. The plaintiff is not even required to prove that the only explanation for the incident is negligence; he simply has to show that this kind of incident normally does not happen without negligence. In many ways, a negligence claim based on *res ipsa* makes the plaintiff's jobs at trial much easier than they ordinarily would be.

2. DEFENSES TO A *RES IPSA* CLAIM

Sometimes the only way to pin down exactly what happened in a particular case is to present expert testimony to explain the sequence of events, and the technicalities involved, to the jury.

Although we examine defenses to negligence cases in a later chapter, a word about defenses to *res ipsa* claims is included here. A defendant's best defense against such a claim is to attack the individual elements of the *res ipsa loquitur* doctrine. A defendant could show, for instance, that he was not in the exclusive control of the instrumentality or that the plaintiff in some way contributed to his own injuries. Attacking the first element of *res ipsa* (the event is one that ordinarily does not occur without negligence) is hard to do. How does a defendant prove a negative? Given that the first element relies almost completely on common sense, a defendant would have better luck attacking the second and third elements instead. *Res ipsa* claims are also subject to the contributory negligence defenses in states that still recognize that concept. (See Chapter 9, Defenses to Negligence.)

3. PLEADING *RES IPSA LOQUITUR:* WHAT THE COMPLAINT SHOULD ALLEGE

When pleading *res ipsa,* the complaint should use language that invokes the doctrine in your jurisdiction. At a minimum, a *res ipsa loquitur* complaint should contain language that states:

- That the instrumentality that caused the plaintiff's injury was under the exclusive control of the defendant
- That the event that occurred is one that would not normally occur without negligence
- That the plaintiff was not responsible for and in fact did not exercise any control over the instrumentality

FIGURE 6-2

Excerpts from Real Complaints Alleging *Res Ipsa Loquitur*

- (Unattended railroad car rolls down track, strikes plaintiff) "[T]he collision would not have occurred, and defendant's train car would not have struck the plaintiff if the defendant had exercised due care in controlling, maintaining and using said railroad car, the details of such control being exclusively within the knowledge of the defendant and not within the knowledge of the plaintiff."
- (Construction crane suddenly swings out of control, strikes plaintiffs while they are walking through parking lot) "[T]he operation and control of the construction crane was wholly and exclusively within the control of the defendant, and the plaintiffs having no control or responsibility for said crane, were struck by said crane, an event that would not normally occur without negligence on the part of the defendant."

FIGURE 6-3

Incidents in Which *Res Ipsa Loquitur* Has Been Used Successfully

- Plane crashes
- Railroad derailments
- "Exploding" soda bottles
- Building collapses

B. NEGLIGENCE PER SE

Another court-created doctrine that is useful to plaintiffs is **negligence per se**. Here, the plaintiff can prove a breach of duty by showing that the defendant violated a statute. As far as the law is concerned, violation of certain types of statutes equates to violation of the duty of care. Negligence per se means "negligence by itself." This is a doctrine that states that the court can infer (or even presume) breach of duty when the defendant violated a statute at the time that he injured the plaintiff. To take advantage of negligence per se, the plaintiff must show:

> **Negligence per se**
> Negligence in and of itself; the principle that the violation of a safety statute establishes a presumption of breach of duty in a negligence action

- That the statute was, in fact, violated
- That the statute was designed with safety in mind
- That the defendant's violation of the statute was a major factor in the plaintiff's injuries
- That the plaintiff was in a "class" of people the statute was intended to protect

In negligence per se, reasonable conduct is dictated by statute, not the reasonable person standard.

ISSUE AT A GLANCE

Example: Rick is driving at 90 mph and loses control of his car. He runs off the road and crashes into Joan's car. At the time, Joan was at the wheel of her

FIGURE 6-4

Evaluating the Defendant's Breach

- The defendant knew or should have known that his action/inaction would cause a potential hazard.
- The defendant knew or should have known that an injury to someone was foreseeable.
- The defendant's action/inaction was a proximate cause of the plaintiff's injury.

FIGURE 6-5

The Most Common Acts of Negligence

- Failure to drive safely
- Excessive speed
- Failure to keep a proper lookout
- Following too closely
- Driving under the influence of alcohol or some other drug

- Failure to warn of dangerous conditions
- Unsafe work conditions
- Unsafe premises
- Failure to maintain equipment

car, waiting for a light to turn green. Joan brings a suit against Rick, basing her claim on negligence per se. Can she prove the elements?

Let's take each element of negligence per se and apply it to the facts of this scenario. The first element is proof that the statute was violated. Proving that the statute was in fact violated is usually quite simple. Testimony from a police officer that he issued a ticket to Rick for driving too fast would be enough evidence to prove this element.

What about the second element—that the statute was designed with safety in mind? Before we answer this question, perhaps we should take a moment to address why this element is required. Suppose that instead of being charged with speeding and reckless driving, Rick instead had crashed into Joan's car at a normal speed. When the police arrive, they discover that Rick's license is expired. Can Joan use this as evidence of negligence per se? No. The doctrine was created as a way of helping plaintiffs prove breach of duty. Rick's driver's license status, at least under these facts, has nothing to do with Joan's injuries. Put another way, could Rick reasonably foresee that having an expired driver's license would put other drivers at risk? Probably not. Could Rick reasonably foresee that driving at excessive speed would put other drivers at risk? Absolutely. So the answer to why the statute involves safety goes back to our prior analysis of foreseeability. In fact, throughout negligence law, we rarely stray from the issue of foreseeability. Joan can prove the second element of her claim because speeding statutes were designed primarily as a safety precaution.

What about the third element? Many jurisdictions have inserted this element (a causal link between the statute violation and the plaintiff's injuries) for the same reason given in the previous paragraph. Presuming

Sidebar

Some jurisdictions require that the plaintiff present a theory of negligence that at least suggests the negligence of the defendant in a negligence per se case. If there are several possible theories, the plaintiff must present some evidence to eliminate the other non-negligence theories.

Leading Causes of Unintentional Injury Deaths, United States, 1998.		Figure 6-6
Motor Vehicle	43,501	Leading Causes of Unintentional Deaths by Injury in the United States*
Falls	16,274	
Poisoning**	10,255	
Drowning	4,406	
Choking	3,515	
**Includes solid and liquid poisoning only.		

*National Safety Council, 1998.

negligence in a case where the statutory violation had nothing to do with the accident seems a bit unfair. However, we do not have that problem in Joan's suit. She can easily prove that Rick's excessive speed had a direct link to her injuries.

Finally, we reach the fourth element. Was Joan in a "class" of persons designed to be protected by the statute? Why was this statute created in the first place? Speed limit statutes are created to punish people who drive at excessive speeds, because those people often pose a threat to other motorists. Again we come back to the issue of foreseeability. Was it foreseeable that another motorist could be hurt by Rick's negligent driving? Yes. Joan is a motorist, therefore she falls into the class of people that the statute was designed to protect.

Joan has now proved all four elements of her negligence per se allegation, which means that she has also proved breach of duty. Assuming that she can also prove causation and damages, she should be successful in her action against Rick.

1. WHAT THE COMPLAINT SHOULD SAY ABOUT NEGLIGENCE PER SE

Most authorities agree that some or all of the following language should be used when drafting a complaint based on negligence per se.

- There was a safety statute in effect at the time of the plaintiff's injury.
- The defendant violated that safety statute in the following, specific ways: (list each way that the defendant violated the safety statute).
- The defendant's violation of the statute was a proximate cause of the plaintiff's injuries.
- The statute was specifically designed with safety in mind.
- The plaintiff was clearly in the class of persons for whom the statute was created.

2. EXPLORING A *RES IPSA LOQUITUR* CLAIM

PERKINS v. AAA CLEANING
30 A.D.3d 790, 816 N.Y.S.2d 600

ROSE, J.

Appeal from an order of the Supreme Court (Mulvey, J.), entered June 3, 2005 in Tompkins County, which granted defendant's motion for summary judgment dismissing the complaint.

Allegedly because of her exposure to a disinfecting solution while cleaning an ambulance in April 1999, plaintiff Kathleen Perkins (hereinafter plaintiff) developed asthma and reactive airway syndrome that thereafter made her hyperreactive to environmental irritants. On December 7, 1999, plaintiff experienced respiratory distress while working as a clerk at the offices of the Town of Dryden in Tompkins County. Alleging that this episode was triggered by vapors released from the solutions that defendant had used to clean the carpets at her workplace, and that defendant had failed to properly apply the solutions, ventilate the offices or warn her of the danger of inhaling the vapors, plaintiff and her husband commenced this negligence action against defendant. When defendant moved for summary dismissal of the complaint, Supreme Court granted the motion, finding no evidence that defendant either could have foreseen the risk of respiratory injury to plaintiff or acted negligently in applying the cleaning solutions and ventilating the offices. Plaintiffs appeal.

Initially, plaintiffs contend that Supreme Court erred in extending defendant's time to move for summary judgment beyond the 60-day time period provided by the rules of the Sixth Judicial District (see CPLR 3212[a]). Under the circumstances here, however, we are not persuaded that the court abused its discretion in accepting as good cause defendant's reasonable explanation that its delay was due to difficulties in obtaining deposition transcripts and a written opinion from its expert (see CPLR 3212[a]; *Brill v. City of New York*, 2 N.Y.3d 648, 652 [2004]; *La Duke v. Albany Motel Enters.*, 282 A.D.2d 974, 974 [2001]).

Turning to the merits, it is axiomatic that conduct is not considered negligent and no liability results where the type of injury sustained is not one of the foreseeable hazards that are normally associated with such conduct (see *Di Ponzio v. Riordan*, 89 N.Y.2d 578, 583-584 [1997]; *Kemper v. Arnow*, 18 A.D.3d 939, 940-941 [2005], *lv denied*, 5 N.Y.3d 708 [2005]). Here, defendant met its initial burden of showing that the condition which allegedly caused plaintiff's injury was not a foreseeable risk of its conduct. The only evidence in the record of the known health risks of the chemicals used in the cleaning solutions are the advisories in the applicable Material Safety Data Sheets. They give no indication that an adverse respiratory condition may result from inhalation of the solutions' vapors. While the sheet for the undiluted preconditioning agent warns that inhalation of its vapors may cause dizziness, headaches or unconsciousness and it should be used with adequate ventilation, this sheet pertains to the vapors of the concentrated chemical rather than the diluted solution actually applied to the carpet and it gives no warning that the vapors may cause respiratory distress such as that experienced by plaintiff. In addition, defendant presented the opinion of a forensic chemist that the vapors released by the diluted solutions actually applied in the cleaning of the carpets would have had concentrations of chemicals below the minimums recognized as being harmful to humans. Thus, defendant presented evidence that the risk of harm alleged by plaintiffs was not a known risk of its cleaning of the carpets (see *Di Ponzio v. Riordan, supra* at 584, 657 N.Y.S.2d 377, 679 N.E.2d 616).

This evidence shifted the burden to plaintiffs to raise a question of fact as to the foreseeability of the risk of harm to plaintiff. They attempted to carry their burden by offering the report of one of plaintiff's treating physicians, Michael Lax. Although Lax opines that plaintiff's exposure to certain components of defendant's cleaning solutions irritated her hyperreactive airways, he does not state that any of the chemicals in those solutions are generally known by either experts or laypersons to be respiratory irritants. Nor does Lax address the opinion of defendant's chemist that the amount of chemicals in the vapors released would ordinarily be harmless (*cf. Cazsador v. Greene Cent. School*, 220 A.D.2d 862, 863-864 [1995] [finding the risk foreseeable where the subject chemical was known to be an irritant]). Finally, even if they were not harmless, there is no evidence that defendant had any way of knowing of plaintiff's hypersensitivity (*cf. Holmes v. Grumman Allied Indus.*, 103 A.D.2d 909, 910 [1984] [finding a duty to warn may exist, even though only a small percentage of users may suffer an allergic reaction, if the defendant had knowledge or constructive notice of the danger]). In light of this, plaintiffs failed to raise a question of fact. Accordingly, we agree with Supreme Court's conclusion that the risk of respiratory injury to plaintiff was not a foreseeable consequence of defendant's carpet cleaning and, thus, defendant owed no duty to her concerning that particular risk.

ORDERED that the order is affirmed, with costs.

CARDONA, P.J., CREW III, CARPINELLO AND MUGGLIN, JJ., CONCUR.

Questions about the case:

1. What are the plaintiff's contentions in this suit?
2. How does the court describe breach of duty in the context of foreseeability?
3. How did expert evidence contribute to the end result in this case?
4. What role, if any, did the plaintiff's hypersensitivity play in the final result in this case?

EXPERT EVIDENCE AND BREACH OF DUTY

Many times the only way to establish that the defendant breached his duty to the plaintiff is through the presentation of expert testimony. Was the defendant speeding at the time of the collision? Naturally enough, the defendant claims that he was not. The plaintiff believes that he was. Is there any way to settle this issue? One way is to locate an expert in accident reconstruction. This expert can calculate the defendant's speed based on the conditions: the skid marks, the impact point, the spread pattern of broken glass, etc.

An expert witness is someone who, either through training or education, has acquired specialized knowledge that most people don't have. Because of this specialized knowledge, an expert witness is permitted to do the one thing that no other witness is allowed to do: testify about a conclusion in the case. Lay witnesses are not allowed to offer any opinion about what happened in the case or who was at fault. Expert witnesses can. Because this opinion can have a big impact on the jury, there are several requirements the attorney must meet before the witness will be allowed to offer this opinion. The attorney will have

FIGURE 6-7

Case Processing Time and Days in Trial, by Case and Trial Type, 2005

Case type	Mean days in trial		Mean months from filing to disposition*	
	Jury	Bench	Jury	Bench
All cases	3.9	1.7	26.1	20.3
Tort cases	3.7	1.5	26.0	20.6
Contract cases	4.8	1.7	26.2	20.6
Real property cases	2.9	1.6	30.4	18.8

Note: Data on the number of days in trial were available for 94% of jury trials and 96% of bench trails. Data on the number of months from complaint filing to case disposition were available for 99.9% of jury trials and 99.5% of bench trials.
*Disposition refers to the date the verdict was rendered for jury trials and the date the decision was announced for bench trials.

Civil Bench and Jury Trials in State Courts, 2005, Bureau of Statistics, U.S. Department of Justice.

FIGURE 6-8

Expert Checklist

Name, address, fax, beeper, cell phone and telephone numbers, and e-mail address
What's the best and fastest way to contact this person?
Training and background (be thorough)
    Academics
    Degrees

Schools attended
Publications
Honors, awards
Association memberships, positions held
Testified as an expert witness before? How often? Primarily for one side or the other?

to establish the qualifications of the expert, and show how this person has specialized knowledge about an area and how this testimony would assist the jury in reaching a verdict.

SKILLS YOU NEED IN THE REAL WORLD

Locating Expert Witnesses

How do you locate an expert witness? In the old days, the process was hit or miss. But in these days of advanced technology and a new openness among the professions, finding an expert is much easier. Need an expert who will testify that excessive sugar intake causes blackouts? You can probably find one in the legal classifieds. Experts realized years ago that being in the business of testifying is lucrative. Some experts even advertise on the Internet.

Here are some methods for finding an expert witness:

- Word of mouth
- The pro who beat you last time
- Listings maintained by the bar
- Other prominent cases
- Associations
- Advertisements
- Internet

Word of Mouth

One of the best ways to find an expert is by talking with other firms and other paralegals that have used experts in the past. This kind of personal experience with a witness is invaluable. For instance, the other paralegal may tell you that although this witness has an impressive resume (the term *curriculum vitae* is often used with experts), he is arrogant and difficult to work with. If you're going through the trouble of hiring an expert to work on a case, you need to find someone you can work with. It doesn't matter how impressive a person's credentials are if he doesn't return phone calls or, even worse, makes a bad impression on the jury.

The Pro Who Beat You Last Time

Surprisingly enough, many attorneys will hire the expert who beat them last time. Keep a list of all of the expert witnesses who have testified for the other side in prior cases and complete the checklist (Figure 6-9) on each one. Is this a person you'd rather have working with you than against you? If the answer is yes, retain this expert on your next big case.

Listings Maintained by the Bar

Local and state bar associations often have lists of people who are qualified to testify as expert witnesses on a wide variety of topics. Although this will help you get started, once you locate a likely candidate, you should always try to find people

FIGURE 6-9

The Pro from Last Time Scoring Sheet

Expert witness name: _____
Case testified in: _____
Overall ranking (on a scale of five): _____

Testimony on the witness stand

Very Good		Not much impact			Terrible
5	4	3	2	1	0

Personality: impact with the jury

Very Good		Not much impact			Terrible
5	4	3	2	1	0

Ability to explain complex issues

Very Good		Not much impact			Terrible
5	4	3	2	1	0

Use of charts, diagrams, and other aids

Very Good		Not much impact			Terrible
5	4	3	2	1	0

How well did the witness do on cross-examination?

Very Good		Not much impact			Terrible
5	4	3	2	1	0

How much did he or she contribute to the other side's win?

Very Good		Not much			Not at all
5	4	3	2	1	0

Notes:

who have worked with this person in the past. Ask the expert for references, such as other firms who have used her in the past. If she refuses this reasonable request, that alone has told you plenty about her and means you should move on to the next person on your list.

Other Prominent Cases

Many paralegals maintain files of prominent cases and the names of the expert witnesses who testified in those cases. This file not only is helpful in locating experts for future cases, but may also provide the basis for cross-examination of the other side's expert. For instance, if you can show that in the past five years this witness has only testified for the defense, this could show a possible bias against plaintiffs.

Associations

Some professional associations maintain lists of people who have testified or could testify about particular topics. Your next case might involve the American Numismatist Association (coin experts). Contact the association and find out if they have a list of qualified experts.

Advertisements and the Internet

The least successful techniques for finding good experts are advertisements and the Internet. Both of these media have the same problem: inability to double-check facts. Just because someone advertises in the back of a legal magazine or has a nice Web page does not make her an expert witness. What makes a person an expert witness is training and education, not a nice ad. However, if you can't locate a witness any other way, start with the Web page or back page ad and then thoroughly interview this person. Ask for references. Double-check the resume or curriculum vitae. Talk to other people who've worked with her. Remember, this person could make or break your case, so the more you know about her the better.

There are some Internet sites that can provide you with valuable information. TASA is one such site (Technical Advice for Attorneys, www.tasanet.com). At this site, you can search for a dizzying variety of expert witnesses, arbitrators, mediators, and other consultants.

THE LIFE OF A PARALEGAL

"Red Flagging" Records

As the case gets closer to trial, I help get the file organized and prepare trial notebooks. I go through the entire file and red flag anything that could be of concern. I look at the client's prior medical histories, whether they've had previous personal injury cases, what their work history has been like, anything that the other side might focus on. You look at every aspect of the clients themselves. Are they a credible witness? You try to get a feel for and screen the client to see if they are a good person to take to trial. Some clients, you can tell right away that they wouldn't make a good witness, either because they're anxious or crying all the time or for some other reason. You go through different documents, seeing if anything conflicts. You compare dates and make sure that they all match up. If they don't, you red flag them. This check-through is real helpful. You don't ever want to take even the simplest things for granted. In one case that I was involved with, in looking over the accident report and the photos of the car that were provided, I realized that the car in the photos wasn't the same vehicle that was listed in the accident report. The insurance carrier had taken a picture of the wrong car, one that was involved in another accident not related to our case. No one else had caught it and we used it to our advantage. You should always check the basic information to make sure that you've got your facts right. You don't want to assume anything. I go through the case step by step and look at everything. When you're putting a trial notebook together, or just reviewing records, as a rule, more information is always better. The attorney might not ever use it, but it's there if they do.

Gwyn Huffman, Paralegal

ETHICAL ISSUES FOR THE PARALEGAL: CONFIDENTIALITY

A client's communications with his attorney are as confidential as those made to a doctor or a pastor. Unless it falls into a narrow exception, an attorney cannot be compelled to testify about what the client has told him. Although paralegals are not protected by this same evidentiary privilege, they should always act as though they are. Revealing sensitive or even mundane information about a client can have disastrous consequences. When a paralegal reveals confidential information about a client, the client may decide to take action. This action could be as simple as firing the lawyer, bringing a complaint before the bar, or even a legal malpractice claim naming not only the lawyer but also the paralegal as defendants. Confidentiality extends not only to the facts and issues of the client's case, but could even extend to the client's identity. There are times when the client does not wish anyone else to know that he is represented by an attorney. Any questions about this or any other potentially confidential manner should be handled with the blanket statement, "I'm not allowed to discuss the firm's business." By taking that simple precaution, you keep the client's trust and avoid a potential legal entanglement later on.

Chapter Summary

Once the legal duty of the defendant has been established, the plaintiff must then prove that the defendant breached this duty. Proving breach of duty involves not only evidence and testimony, but also an analysis of the law. Court doctrines have been created over time to assist with this analysis. *Res ipsa loquitur* is a doctrine that courts created to assist plaintiffs in proving negligence when a more traditional legal analysis left them without a possibility of recovery. To prove a *res ipsa* claim, the plaintiff must show several factors, including that the instrument that caused the plaintiff's injury was under the control of the defendant; the injury that occurred was something that does not normally occur unless negligence is present; the plaintiff did not contribute to her own injuries; and that of the two parties, the defendant is in a better position to explain what happened than the plaintiff. Another doctrine that was created to help establish breach of duty is negligence per se. Under negligence per se, if the plaintiff can show that the defendant was violating a safety statute at the time of the plaintiff's injuries, that the plaintiff was in a class of persons designed to be protected by the safety statute, and the defendant's violation of this statute was a proximate cause of the plaintiff's injuries, the court is allowed to infer that the defendant did, in fact, breach his duty.

Web Sites

▨ *Jensen v. White Star Line*
   http://www.andersonkill.com/titanic/negl.htm

▨ **University of Washington Law School, tort law PowerPoint presentation**
   http://www.law.washington.edu/Streetlaw/lessons/Torts_Negligence_Pres.ppt

▨ **Essortment — Defining Breach of Duty**
   http://ar.essortment.com/breachoffidu_rkwv.htm

Forms and Court Documents

In this section, we examine an excerpt from the complaint in the Chumley case. This excerpt focuses on the allegations of the various defendants' breach of duty.

STATE OF PLACID   IN THE SUPERIOR COURT OF HALEY COUNTY
                   SUPERIOR COURT DIVISION
COUNTY OF HALEY   FILE NUMBER: _____

CHARLES CHUMLEY,	)	
	)	
Plaintiff	)	
	)	
vs.	)	COMPLAINT
	)	JURY TRIAL DEMANDED
	)	
NATIONAL RAILWAY COMPANY,	)	
TOWN OF CLING,	)	
and STANLEY W. BLUE	)	
	)	
Defendant	)	
	)	
	)	

Paragraphs 1-15 are omitted for this discussion. Please see the appendix for the entire Chumley Complaint.

16.

The Town breached this duty of due care by the following acts of negligence:

a. it failed to close the crossing pursuant to state law, when it knew, or in the exercise of due care should have known, that the crossing constituted an unreasonable hazard to vehicular or pedestrian traffic;

b. it failed to require the installation, construction, erection, or improvement, of warning signs, gates, lights, stop bars, or such other safety devices when it knew or should have known in the exercise of reasonable care that such devices were necessary;

c. it allowed the crossing to remain in use with absolutely no safety devices with total, wanton, and reckless disregard for the safety of vehicular and pedestrian traffic;

d. it allowed the vegetation and trees adjacent to the tracks to obstruct the view by motorists of the tracks and approaching trains when it knew, or in the exercise of due care should have known, that such vegetation and trees constituted an unreasonable hazard to vehicular and pedestrian traffic;

e. it failed to keep the public street free from unnecessary obstructions in violation of State law.

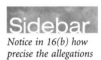

Sidebar

Notice in 16(b) how precise the allegations are.

Sidebar

Although the strongest part of the case would seem to be an allegation of vegetation growing along the track that obscured the oncoming train [16(d)], this is not the only allegation brought in the complaint. Why? One answer is that by making several allegations, the plaintiff is improving his chances of a recovery if the jury decides against him on the vegetation issue.

Key Terms

Negligence per se   *Res ipsa loquitur*
Professional   Specialist
Reasonable person standard

Review Questions

1 Can we use *res ipsa* or negligence per se doctrines in the Chumley case? Explain why or why not.
2 In any given situation, once you have determined that a duty was owed, how do you determine if a breach of that duty has occurred?
3 What is the reasonable person standard and how does it help determine breach of duty?
4 How does "standard of care" apply to breach of duty?
5 In determining a breach of duty, you must look at the facts objectively. Why?
6 Mental characteristics of tortfeasors are not taken into account, but physical characteristics, such as blindness, often are. Why does the law make this distinction?
7 Should a judge determine the standard of care instead of a jury? Why or why not?
8 Can custom establish a breach of duty? Why or why not?
9 A professional is held to a higher standard of care than a layperson. What is that standard? How is that standard different for specialists?
10 When we hold a specialist to a higher standard of care, does that mean that proving a negligence case against a specialist is easier than proving one against a professional? Why or why not?
11 Explain *res ipsa loquitur.* Why was this doctrine created?
12 What are some of the defenses available to a claim of *res ipsa loquitur?*
13 What is the doctrine of negligence per se? Why was this doctrine created?
14 How is *res ipsa loquitur* different from negligence per se?

Applying What You Have Learned

1 Using the following facts, draft a complaint alleging *res ipsa loquitur:*
    Our firm represents the estate of a passenger who was killed in a plane crash. The plane crashed into the sea and very little evidence has been recovered, especially in regard to what caused the crash.
2 Using the following facts, draft a complaint alleging negligence per se:
    In the Chumley case, assume that the train engineer was exceeding the posted speed limits for trains by traveling 30 mph when 25 mph was the restricted speed limit.

3 Tom is home one afternoon and notices that the local telephone company is replacing a telephone pole on the corner of Tom's lot. Two hours after the workers complete the installation of the new telephone pole, it falls, crushing Tom's roof and injuring Tom. Does Tom have a negligence per se claim? Go through each element of negligence per se and prove or disprove the elements.

4 How does your state define negligence per se?

5 Does your state follow the doctrine of *res ipsa loquitur*? If so, does your state's approach differ from the general one presented in the text?

Endnotes

[1] *Fields v. Napa Milling Co.,* 164 Cal. App. 2d 442, 330 P.2d 459 (1958).

[2] *Handley v. Halladay,* 92 N.M. 76, 582 P.2d 1289 (1978).

[3] *Denver & R.G.R. Co. v. Norgate,* 141 F. 247 (8th Cir.), *cert. denied,* 202 U.S. 616, 50 L. Ed. 1172, 24 S. Ct. 764 (1905).

[4] *Estate of Mullis by Dixon v. Monroe Oil Co.,* 349 N.C. 196, 505 S.E.2d 131 (1998).

[5] Restatement (Second) of Torts §283, comment b.

[6] *Gould v. American Family Mut. Ins. Co.,* 198 Wis. 2d 450, 543 N.W.2d 282 (1996).

[7] *Gould v. American Family Mut. Ins. Co.,* 198 Wis. 2d 450, 543 N.W.2d 282 (1996).

[8] *Garafola v. Rosecliff Realty Co.,* 24 N.J. Super. 28, 93 A.2d 608 (1953).

[9] *Palombizio v. Murphy,* 146 Conn. 352, 150 A.2d 825 (1959).

[10] Restatement (Second) of Torts §285, comment f.

[11] Restatement (Second) of Torts §295.

[12] Restatement (Second) of Torts §298, comment d.

[13] *Vergara v. Doan,* 593 N.E.2d 185 (1992).

Proximate
Cause

Chapter
Objectives

- Determine when a defendant's actions (or omissions) are the proximate cause of a plaintiff's injuries

- Explain the various court tests used to establish the existence of proximate cause

- Explain the concept of foreseeability

- Describe the significance of *Palsgraf v. New York*

- Apply your knowledge of proximate cause in preparing pleadings

- Define the concepts of intervening and superseding causes

 ## PROXIMATE CAUSE IN
THE CHUMLEY CASE

Mr. Chumley was severely injured and Mrs. Chumley was killed when their car was struck broadside by a locomotive. In earlier chapters, we examined how Mr. Chumley's attorney would have to prove duty and breach of duty in order to bring a negligence claim against the railroad company. In this chapter, we explore the concept of causation or the degree of the defendants' responsibility for the injuries to Mr. and Mrs. Chumley. In the Chumley case, the analysis for proximate cause is relatively straightforward. If the railroad company's employees were at fault, there can be no question of the direct responsibility of those employees for the injuries to the plaintiffs. However, suppose that after the collision, Mr. Chumley received substandard care at the hospital. Or suppose that Mr. Chumley had pre-existing injuries. Should the railroad company also be liable for those injuries? We address these issues in addition to exploring the concepts of intervening and superseding causes as they apply to the issue of proximate causation.

INTRODUCTION

Proximate causation
The facts that show the defendant's legal responsibility for the injuries to the plaintiff, also known as legal cause

In this chapter, we explore the third element of a negligence claim: **proximate causation.** Before a plaintiff can succeed in a negligence action, she must prove that there was a direct link between the defendant's breach of duty and the resulting injuries to her.

A. PROVING PROXIMATE CAUSE

*Duty → Breach →
Causation →
Damages*

Proof of proximate cause actually involves a two-step analysis: There must be a determination that (1) the defendant breached the duty of care, and (2) the breach was the cause of the injury.

1. BREACH OF DUTY OF CARE

We discussed breach of duty in the previous chapter. That element must be satisfied before any analysis of causation can begin. It is important to reiterate that the basic elements of a negligence case are sequential. A plaintiff must prove each of the elements, beginning with duty and concluding with damages. The plaintiff is not permitted to skip over any element. This concept is crucial to an understanding of negligence in general and proximate cause in particular.

2. BREACH WAS THE CAUSE

The second element of proof for proximate cause is that the breach of duty was the proximate cause of the injury. Without this proof, the element of causation is not proved and the plaintiff's negligence case collapses. We spend the remainder of this chapter addressing the question of how the plaintiff proves causation and the various court-created tests and doctrines that have developed over the centuries to address this issue.

B. THE LAW ON PROXIMATE CAUSE TENDS TO BE VAGUE

Although it is the third specified element of a negligence claim, the issue of proximate cause is not as clear or as settled as any of the other elements of negligence. Experts have been arguing over the term since it was created. What is and is not proximate cause often depends on the facts of a particular case. Another problem with proximate cause has to do with public policy. This element of negligence is the one most easily assailed by public policy concerns. Just how far should a defendant's liability to the plaintiff extend? That sounds more like a philosophical question than a strictly factual one. Consider the following scenario.

John drives negligently and crashes his car into another car driven by Tara. Tara, a professional athlete, breaks her leg in the wreck. She sues John for her injuries. When Tara is taken to the hospital, she receives substandard care from the physician on duty. The doctor does a poor job of treating her broken leg. As a result, an infection sets in. Tara becomes very ill and eventually the infection in her leg becomes so bad that her leg must be amputated. Is John liable for all of Tara's injuries or just some of her injuries? If he is liable for some of the injuries, which ones are they?

Some would argue that John should be liable for everything that happened after he acted negligently. Although this argument has a certain appeal, there are some obvious problems in applying it. Because of Tara's injury, she is cut from the college track team, where she had been a major competitor. She then loses her scholarship. Should Tara be allowed to recover the cost of her remaining education from John? Tara also had plans of trying out for the U.S. Olympic team and believed that she was a solid contender to make that team. Should Tara be allowed to sue John for the millions of dollars she would have made in endorsements after becoming a medal winner in the next Olympics? Should Tara's future children be allowed to bring suit against John because their mother was an amputee for the rest of her life and was not able to provide the same level of interaction with them that other mothers provided?

As you can see, the argument for the defendant's continued responsibility for his negligence could be spun out to ridiculous lengths. The further removed from the defendant's actual negligence, the more tenuous the connection (and the more difficult it becomes to prove). A different argument suggests that John should only be liable for the injuries that are closely connected with his negligence. Any other negligence (such as the malpractice by the doctor) should be assessed against that person. Creating a theory of causation that makes a defendant liable only for those actions closely and obviously resulting from his negligence is certainly easier to prove in a courtroom than the never-ending and far-reaching causation theory proposed earlier. However, this theory also means that there will be times when a plaintiff will not be satisfied with the amount of her recovery, or the scope of the defendant's responsibility. Faced with these two conflicting theories, the courts have opted for the second. They have chosen, time and again, a more limited scope of the defendant's responsibility.

There is a benefit to society in eventually terminating defendants' responsibilities in cases. Even negligent people need to know when all possible claims against them are exhausted. More than simply letting negligent people off the hook, however, a more limited theory of causation and responsibility allows the rest of society some assurance that a particular case can and will end. The various witnesses and others involved can be secure in the knowledge that, regardless of the particular parties' level of satisfaction, no additional claims will be forthcoming from a specific incident of negligence. We have seen other examples of this desire to close off the claims in particular cases. Statutes of limitation are a good example. Those statutes provide a time limit in which a claim must be brought or it is barred forever. The concept of proximate cause was created as a way for courts to determine the parameters of a defendant's responsibility.

DEVELOPING THE CONCEPT OF PROXIMATE CAUSE

Sidebar

Proximate causation involves proof of responsibility.

Proximate cause analysis varies depending on the nature of the civil injury. For instance, the analysis is often very different between negligence cases and intentional tort cases. A defendant who acts with intent or in wanton, willful, or reckless disregard for the safety of others may be legally responsible for all the ramifications of his actions, however remote. Many jurisdictions also follow this rule when the defendant's actions are criminal in nature. However, when the claim is based on negligence, different rules apply. Most jurisdictions apply the proximate cause rule to negligence cases. These jurisdictions make a defendant liable only for the logical or foreseeable results of his actions.[1]

A. HISTORICAL DEVELOPMENT OF PROXIMATE CAUSE

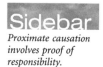

Sidebar

The term proximate cause *was first suggested by an English jurist, Lord Bacon, who wrote, "in jure non remota causa, sed proxima, spectatur" (in law, not the remote cause, but the proximate cause is sought).*[2]

The concept of proximate cause has been a bone of contention in jurisprudence for centuries. Different societies have applied different standards to how far the defendant's liability should extend. The English standard, which eventually found its way to the United States, has a stated preference for factually closer connections to the plaintiff's injuries than more remote causes.

B. PROBLEMS DEFINING PROXIMATE CAUSE

Sidebar

Regarding proximate cause "there is perhaps nothing in the entire field of law which has called forth more disagreement, or upon which the opinions are in such a welter of confusion."[3]

No jurisdiction has come up with a test for proximate cause that works in all cases. The very concept is often difficult to define. There may be a subtle purpose here. Some experts believe that this vagueness is actually helpful. It gives the court a more fluid approach to the issue, unlike the other elements of negligence, which only allow for a fairly straightforward analysis.

Proximate cause has long been recognized as a confusing concept because the term makes it sound as if the defendant's negligence has to be closest in time to the plaintiff's injury. However, that is not true. A plaintiff can be injured by Defendant *A*, then subsequently injured by Defendant *B*, and Defendant *A* may still be liable to the plaintiff. Because nearness in time is not the primary consideration when deciding proximate cause, courts have developed various tests to help them determine proximate cause. The working definition for proximate cause used by many jurisdictions is one that states, "a cause without which the accident could not have happened."[6] It has also been described as the "primary moving cause," or the "predominating cause" of the plaintiff's injuries.[7] With so many definitions of proximate cause, we need a working definition of proximate cause to frame the rest of our discussion.

C. WORKING DEFINITION OF PROXIMATE CAUSE

The most widely accepted definition of proximate cause (and the one we use for the remainder of the chapter) involves the following:

1 Proof of an injury caused by the defendant
2 That occurred in a natural, unbroken, and continuous sequence
3 That was uninterrupted by any intervening causes
4 That produced the plaintiff's injury
5 Without which the result would not have occurred.[8]

1. ELEMENTS OF THE WORKING DEFINITION

In the next few paragraphs, we expand on the concepts raised in the working definition.

a. Proof of an Injury Caused by the Defendant

The first element of the working definition of proximate cause is the plaintiff's proof that the injuries were caused by the defendant. Without that proof, there can be no case against the defendant and the remainder of the working definition, indeed of the entire case, would be useless.

b. In a Natural, Unbroken, and Continuous Sequence

This element of the working definition requires that the series of events beginning with the defendant's negligence and ending with the plaintiff's injuries all involved a natural sequence. There were no intervening actions; it was an unbroken chain of events. If there is a disruption in the sequence between the defendant's actions and the ultimate injuries, it could well be that the defendant was not the cause of the injuries.

Sidebar

Other commentators have gone even further in denouncing the term proximate cause. Prosser, for instance, in his well-known treatise, Prosser and Keeton on the Law of Torts,[4] states: "The term 'proximate cause' is applied by the courts to those more or less undefined considerations which limit liability even where the fact of causation is clearly established. The word 'proximate' is a legacy of Lord Chancellor Bacon, who in his time committed other sins. The word means nothing more than near or immediate; and when it was first taken up by the courts it had connotations of proximity in time and space which have long since disappeared. It is an unfortunate word, which places an entirely wrong emphasis upon the factor of physical or mechanical closeness. For this reason 'legal cause' or perhaps even 'responsible cause' would be a more appropriate term."[5]

Sidebar

Lord Bacon was also responsible for a few other legal maxims that are somewhat confusing. Consider: "[I]t were infinite for the law to judge causes of causes, and their impulsions one of another; therefore it contenteth itself that the immediate cause, and judgeth of acts by that, without looking to any further degree."[9]

c. Uninterrupted by Any Intervening Causes

We discuss intervening and superseding causes later in this chapter. A word about them here, however, helps to establish the reason for this requirement in the working definition. If some other defendant, or some other force of nature, intervened between the original defendant's negligence and the plaintiff's ultimate injuries, the original defendant my be released from liability. (Consider the scenario discussed earlier, concerning Tara's injuries and the malpractice by her attending physician.)

d. Produced the Plaintiff's Injuries

Although it sounds like a basic point, it must be established that the defendant's actions actually did cause the plaintiff's injuries. Example: John runs a red light and causes a minor collision with Barbara's car. Fortunately, Barbara is not hurt. There is no question of John's negligence, but Barbara has not received any physical injuries. Later, at work, a colleague bumps into Barbara and she falls, injuring her knee. John is not the cause of Barbara's knee injury, despite the fact that she was in an accident earlier that day.

e. Without Which the Result Would Not Have Occurred

Proximate cause is sometimes defined as the natural, foreseeable, and probable consequence of an act of negligence.

This is often the pivotal issue in any negligence case. Most jurisdictions have some form of this test as part of their working definitions of proximate cause. The defendant's actions must be such that had it not been for his negligence, the result (the plaintiff's injuries) would not have occurred. Later, we discuss the various court-created "tests" or doctrines used to determine this particular point, including the substantial factor test and the "but for" test.

2. RESTATEMENT'S POSITION ON DEFINING PROXIMATE CAUSE

The Restatement of Torts takes a slightly different approach to defining proximate cause. According to the Restatement, under proximate cause a defendant may be liable for the harm to the plaintiff from his conduct, as long as he is the legal cause of the harm.[10] The Restatement's position on "legal cause" is very similar to the elements we have set out above.

D. PROXIMATE CAUSE REQUIRES A CLOSE CONNECTION BETWEEN THE DEFENDANT'S ACTIONS AND THE PLAINTIFF'S INJURIES

Under proximate cause theory it is easier to decide which events are too remote in time to be considered the direct cause of the plaintiff's injuries than it is to determine which events are close enough. Generally, the more tenuous the connection between the defendant's actions and the plaintiff's

FIGURE 7-1

**Arguments
in Support of
Proximate
Cause**

■ Protracted defendant responsibility
   would be difficult, if not impossible,
   to enforce. For instance, when
   would the defendant's liability be
   cut off? Surely his liability must
   terminate at some point.

■ By making the defendant liable only
   for his actions closely connected to

his negligence, there is a deterrent
effect on negligent conduct.

■ The legal system would eventually
   bog down under the litigation
   involved in making a defendant
   liable for all remote consequences
   of his negligence.

injuries, the less likely that proximate cause will be found. This is often
referred to as "remoteness." However, the reverse situation is often confusing.
Given the facts of the Chumley case, for instance, can we say with any degree of
certainty what the proximate cause is?

We know that Mr. Chumley was driving his car south on Morgan Street
and that he crossed the railroad tracks. We also know that his car was struck
on the driver's side by the locomotive owned and operated by National Railway Company. Those facts are not in dispute. Can we, from this simple factual
scenario, determine that the defendant railway company was the proximate
cause of his injuries?

Actually, we cannot. The first problem with the factual outline is that it
fails to establish the first two elements of a negligence case: duty and the breach
of a duty. For the sake of argument, we will assume that these questions have
been answered. Defendant railway company had a duty to Mr. Chumley and
subsequently breached it, either by some action taken shortly before the collision, or by failing to maintain the tracks in such a way that motorists could
see an oncoming train. If those two elements are satisfied, can we then determine proximate cause? Actually, we still need some additional information.
What, for instance, were Mr. Chumley's injuries? (For a complete overview of
the Chumley case, see the appendix.) We know that Mr. Chumley was
severely injured and that Mrs. Chumley died in the collision. His injuries
seem to be closely connected both in time and sequential events to the collision with the train. Is that enough? Do we need to know about his medical
treatment? Do we need to know if his car was struck by another car shortly
after the accident? Do we need to know, in fact, everything that happened both
immediately before and immediately after the collision? The answer to all
these questions is yes. In later chapters, we discuss how a paralegal can
learn all this information (and a great deal more) through discovery. We
still need some additional information before we can complete our analysis
of proximate cause in the Chumley case. For instance, we need to know what
the law considers to be a remote cause.

1. REMOTE CAUSES ARE LESS LIKELY TO BE CONSIDERED PROXIMATE CAUSE

In the pragmatic world of civil lawsuits, a plaintiff who can show a direct
factual connection between his injuries and the defendant's negligence has a

much greater chance of prevailing at trial than a plaintiff who can only show a remote connection. Direct factual connections (proximate causes) lend themselves to greater precision and easier methods of proof at trial. In a courtroom, if the plaintiff's proof is uncertain, this will almost always accrue to the defendant's favor.

2. REMOTE CAUSES ARE HARDER TO PROVE

Sidebar

The plaintiff must show not only a negligent act, but that this act was the legal cause of his injuries. Some jurisdictions simplify this analysis by requiring a "reasonably close" connection between the defendant's actions and the plaintiff's injuries.[11]

The more remote the cause of the plaintiff's injuries, the more difficult it is for the plaintiff to prove who actually caused the harm. Remember that the plaintiff must prove her case to the satisfaction of the jury and to a preponderance of the evidence. If the jurors are not convinced of a factual connection between the defendant's actions and the plaintiff's injuries, the jury will not find the defendant liable.

When dealing with remote events, it is also more likely that some other event either contributed to or even superseded defendant's negligence in causing the plaintiff's injuries.

Finally, although it is hardly the predominant factor, it is ultimately unfair to a defendant to find him liable for actions that are remote in time and fact from the plaintiff's injuries.

Sidebar

Some jurisdictions define probable cause as that first act that produces an injury immediately, or sets other events in motion.

3. PROXIMATE CAUSE DEPENDS ON THE FACTS IN THE CASE

Determining proximate cause involves following a chain of events back, like a detective, to uncover the original event that brought about the plaintiff's injuries and then to decide if that event should be ascribed to the defendant.[12] Because determining probable cause depends so much on the facts of the case, a paralegal must know these facts as well as anyone else involved in the case. What was the sequence of events that ended with the plaintiff's injuries? Who, precisely, was involved and what part did this person play? Later, we discuss investigative methods that can be used to determine these facts, but there is no substitute for having a solid understanding of the facts of a case.

Sidebar

The term legal cause *was created in part to deal with the confusion surrounding the term proximate cause. "Legal cause," "direct cause," "efficient cause," and "proximate cause" all refer to the same doctrine.*

4. EVALUATING A CASE FOR PROXIMATE CAUSE

John is driving his car one afternoon and fails to stop for a stop sign. John's car crashes into the side of Barbara's car and Barbara is severely injured. John is also injured in the collision. These are the facts of a simple—and all too common—car collision case. How can we analyze this case for proximate cause?

Under a factual analysis of this case, Barbara's injuries appear to be a direct result of the collision with John's car. John appears to be the sole and proximate cause for Barbara's injuries. On the other hand, John was also injured. John's injuries are a result of the collision with Barbara's car.

For a defendant to be found liable for the plaintiff's injuries, the plaintiff must prove that (1) the defendant acted in a negligent way and (2) this negligence is the legal cause of the plaintiff's injuries.*

*Restatement (Second) of Torts §430.

Strictly speaking, each has been injured by the other's car. If we were to approach this case from a purely factual scenario, free from any determination of wrongdoing, our analysis would end here. Each has been injured by contact with the other's car. However, proximate cause is concerned with more than the basic facts. Proximate cause addresses how the facts ultimately determine liability.

When Barbara later brings a suit against John for negligent driving, she must prove that John was the proximate cause of her injuries. In this case, she should not have any trouble doing so. Notice that the analysis in this case focuses on John's negligence, not simply on the series of events that ended with Barbara's injuries. Proximate causation involves the proof of John's actions, or failure to act, and how those actions were a direct cause of Barbara's injuries. However, in many cases, proving proximate causation is not as clear-cut as this example. Consider this next scenario.

John has borrowed a car from his friend, Ted. Ted has not maintained the car very well and has noticed recently that the brakes do not seem to be working well. He does not tell John about the brake problem. As John is approaching the stop sign, he applies the brakes and nothing happens. John fails to stop at the stop sign and crashes into Barbara's car. Does this scenario change the analysis for proximate causation?

In the first example, John was the proximate cause of Barbara's injuries. Looking at the case from a factual viewpoint, John is still the driver of a car that injures Barbara, but is it John's negligence that causes the collision? Many juries would likely assign the negligence not to John, but to Ted. At what point does the negligence of one party overcome the responsibility of another party? Suppose in the most recent example that Ted had informed John about the brake problem, but John decided to drive the car anyway. Who is the proximate cause of Barbara's injuries now? As you can see, proximate cause often involves a balancing of the various factors and responsibilities of the parties involved.

E. PROXIMATE CAUSE MUST SHOW THAT THE DEFENDANT IS RESPONSIBLE

As part of this element of proving causation, the facts must point to the defendant's responsibility for the actions that ultimately led to the plaintiff's injuries. Put another way, the defendant is responsible for all consequences

FIGURE 7-3

**Civil Justice
Survey of
State Courts**

Major findings from the 2005 Civil Justice Survey of State Courts include —

- A jury decided almost 70% of the approximately 26,950 general civil trials disposed of in 2005.
- About 60% of the general civil trials included in the survey involved a tort claim and about a third involved contractual issues.
- Plaintiffs won in almost 60% of trials overall.
- The median damage award for plaintiffs who won monetary damages in general civil trials was $28,000.
- Punitive damages were awarded to 5% of plaintiff winners in general civil trials in 2005.
- In the nation's 75 most populous counties, the number of general civil cases disposed of by jury or bench trial declined by about 50% from 1992 to 2005.

Civil Bench and Jury Trials in State Courts, 2005, Bureau of Justice Statistics, U.S. Department of Justice.

that are reasonably foreseeable based on his conduct. In the example above, in which John is driving Ted's car unaware that the brakes are faulty, he may well avoid any liability for Barbara's injuries. In such a case, liability would most likely shift to Ted.

F. FORESEEABILITY

Foreseeability
The extent to which the defendant should have anticipated that her actions could cause possible injuries to another

Courts in this country have wrestled with the concept of proximate cause for decades. In the famous *Palsgraf* case, the concept of **foreseeability** was brought into greater prominence as a method to determine when a defendant's actions were the legal cause of the plaintiff's injuries. The concept of foreseeability encompasses the view that a defendant should only be liable for a plaintiff's injuries when the defendant's actions (or failure to act) would likely result in the kind of injuries that the plaintiff sustained. Using foreseeability as the test for proximate cause provided at least a workable test that courts could apply to various suits and provided some measure of predictability from case to case.

The jury must determine if it was foreseeable that the defendant's conduct created a risk of harm to the plaintiff and whether the result was foreseeable.

Pay particular attention to the concise wording used by Justice Cardozo as he lays out the basic facts of the Palsgraf case.

1. THE *PALSGRAF* CASE

The *Palsgraf* case was one of the first — and some would argue the best — court-created doctrine to examine and analyze foreseeability in proximate cause. The *Palsgraf* case continues to be taught in law schools around the country, even though it is over 70 years old.

PALSGRAF v. LONG ISLAND R.R. CO.
162 N.E. 99 (1928)

HELEN PALSGRAF, Respondent,

v.

THE LONG ISLAND RAILROAD COMPANY, Appellant.

Cardozo, C.J.

Plaintiff was standing on a platform of defendant's railroad after buying a ticket to go to Rockaway Beach. A train stopped at the station, bound for another place. Two men ran forward to catch it. One of the men reached the platform of the car without mishap, though the train was already moving. The other man, carrying a package, jumped aboard the car, but seemed unsteady as if about to fall. A guard on the car, who had held the door open, reached forward to help him in, and another guard on the platform pushed him from behind. In this act, the package was dislodged, and fell upon the rails. It was a package of small size, about fifteen inches long, and was covered by a newspaper. In fact it contained fireworks, but there was nothing in its appearance to give notice of its contents. The fireworks when they fell exploded. The shock of the explosion threw down some scales at the other end of the platform, many feet away. The scales struck the plaintiff, causing injuries for which she sues. The conduct of the defendant's guard, if a wrong in its relation to the holder of the package, was not a wrong in its relation to the plaintiff, standing far away. Relatively to her it was not negligence at all. Nothing in the situation gave notice that the falling package had in it the potency of peril to persons thus removed. Negligence is not actionable unless it involves the invasion of a legally protected interest, the violation of a right. "Proof of negligence in the air, so to speak, will not do." (Pollock, Torts). "Negligence is the absence of care, according to the circumstances." 1 Beven, Negligence (4th ed.) The plaintiff as she stood upon the platform of the station might claim to be protected against intentional invasion of her bodily security. Such invasion is not charged. She might claim to be protected against unintentional invasion by conduct involving in the thought of reasonable men an unreasonable hazard that such invasion would ensue. These, from the point of view of the law, were the bounds of her immunity, with perhaps some rare exceptions, survivals for the most part of ancient forms of liability, where conduct is held to be at the peril of the actor. If no hazard was apparent to the eye of ordinary vigilance, an act innocent and harmless, at least to outward seeming, with reference to her, did not take to itself the quality of a tort because it happened to be a wrong, though apparently not one involving the risk of bodily insecurity, with reference to some one else. In every instance, before negligence can be predicated of a given act, back of the act must be sought and found a duty to the individual complaining, the observance of which would have averted or avoided the injury. The ideas of negligence and duty are strictly correlative. The plaintiff sues in her own right for a wrong personal to her, and not as the vicarious beneficiary of a breach of duty to another. A different conclusion will involve us, and swiftly too, in a maze of contradictions. A guard stumbles over a package which has been left upon a platform. It seems to be a bundle of newspapers. It turns out to be a can of dynamite. To the eye of ordinary vigilance, the bundle is abandoned waste, which may be kicked or trod on with impunity. Is a passenger at the other end of the platform protected by the law against the unsuspected hazard concealed beneath the waste? If not, is the result to be any different, so far as the distant passenger is concerned, when the guard stumbles over a valise which a truck man or a porter has left upon the walk? The passenger far away, if the victim of a wrong at all, has a cause of action, not derivative, but original and primary. His claim to be protected against invasion of his bodily security is neither greater nor less because the act resulting in the invasion is a wrong to another far removed. In this case, the rights that are said to have been violated, the interests said to have been invaded, are not even of the same order. The man was not injured in his person nor even put in danger. The purpose of the act, as well as its effect, was to make his person safe. If there was a wrong to him at all, which may very well be doubted, it was a wrong to a property interest only, the safety of his package. Out of this wrong to property, which threatened injury to nothing else, there has passed, we are told, to the plaintiff by derivation or succession a right of action for the invasion of an interest of another order, the right to bodily security. The diversity of interests emphasizes the futility of the effort to build the plaintiff's right upon the basis of a wrong to some one else. The gain is one of emphasis, for a like result would follow if the interests were the same. Even then, the orbit of the danger as disclosed to the eye of reasonable vigilance would be the orbit of the duty. One who jostles one's neighbor in a crowd does not invade the rights of others standing at the outer fringe when the unintended contact casts a bomb upon the ground. The wrongdoer as to them is the man who carries the bomb, not the one who explodes it without suspicion of the danger. Life will have to be made over, and human nature transformed, before prevision so extravagant can be accepted as the norm of conduct, the customary standard to which behavior must conform. The argument for the plaintiff is built upon the shifting meanings of such words as "wrong" and "wrongful," and shares their instability. What the plaintiff must show is "a wrong" to herself, i.e., a violation of her own right, and not merely a wrong to some one else, nor conduct "wrongful" because unsocial, but not "a wrong" to any one. We are told that one who drives at reckless speed through a crowded city street is guilty of a negligent act and, therefore, of a wrongful one irrespective of the consequences. Negligent the act is, and wrongful in the sense that it is unsocial, but wrongful and unsocial in relation to other travelers, only because the eye of vigilance perceives the risk of damage. If the same act were to be committed on a speedway or a racecourse, it would lose its wrongful quality. The risk reasonably to be perceived defines the duty to be obeyed, and risk imports relation; it is risk to another or to others within the range of apprehension. This does not mean, of course, that one who launches a destructive force is always relieved of liability if the force, though known to be destructive, pursues an unexpected path. It was not necessary that the defendant should have had notice of the particular method in which an accident would occur, if the possibility of an accident was clear to the ordinarily prudent eye. Some acts, such as shooting, are so imminently dangerous to any one who may come within reach of the missile, however unexpectedly, as to impose a duty of prevision not far from that of an insurer. Even today, and much oftener in earlier stages of the law, one acts sometimes at one's peril. Under this head, it may be, fall certain cases of what is known as transferred intent, an act willfully dangerous to A resulting by misadventure in injury to B. These cases aside, wrong is defined in terms of the natural or probable, at least when unintentional. The range of reasonable apprehension is at times a question for the court, and at times, if varying inferences are possible, a question for the jury. Here, by concession, there was nothing in the situation to suggest to the most cautious mind that the parcel wrapped in newspaper would spread wreckage through the station. If the guard had thrown it down knowingly and willfully, he would not have threatened the plaintiff's safety, so far as appearances could warn him. His conduct would not have involved, even then, an unreasonable probability of invasion of her bodily security. Liability can be no greater where the act is inadvertent. Negligence, like risk, is thus a term of relation. Negligence in the abstract, apart from things related, is surely not a tort, if indeed it is understandable at all. Negligence is not a tort unless it results in the commission of a wrong, and the commission of a wrong imports the violation of a right, in this case, we are told, the right to be protected against interference with one's bodily security. But bodily security is protected, not against all forms of interference or aggression, but only against some. One who seeks redress at law does not make out a cause of action by showing without more that there has been damage to his person. If the harm was not willful, he must show that the act as to him had possibilities of danger so many and apparent as to entitle him to be protected against the doing of it though the harm was unintended. Affront to personality is still the keynote of the wrong. Confirmation of this view will be found in the history and development of the action on the case. Negligence as a basis of civil liability was unknown to mediaeval law. For damage to the person, the sole remedy was trespass, and trespass did not lie in the absence of aggression, and that direct and personal. Liability for other damage, as where a servant without orders from the master does or omits something to the damage of another, is a plant of later growth. When it emerged out of the legal soil, it was thought of as a variant of trespass, an offshoot of the parent stock. This appears in the form of action, which was known as trespass on the case. The victim does not sue derivatively, or by right of subrogation, to vindicate an interest invaded in the person of another. Thus to view his cause of action is to ignore the fundamental difference between tort and crime. He sues for breach of a duty owing to himself. The law of causation, remote or proximate, is thus foreign to the case before us. The question of liability is always anterior to the question of the measure of the consequences that go with liability. If there is no tort to be redressed, there is no occasion to consider what damage might be recovered if there were a finding of a tort. We may assume, without deciding, that negligence, not at large or in the abstract, but in relation to the plaintiff, would entail liability for any and all consequences, however novel or extraordinary. There is room for argument that a distinction is to be drawn according to the diversity of interests invaded by the act, as where conduct negligent in that it threatens an insignificant invasion of an interest in property results in an unforeseeable invasion of an interest of another order, as, e.g., one of bodily security. Perhaps other distinctions may be necessary. We do not go into the question now. The consequences to be followed must first be rooted in a wrong. The judgment of the Appellate Division and that of the Trial Term should be reversed, and the complaint dismissed, with costs in all courts.

Judgment reversed.

2. AN ANALYSIS OF *PALSGRAF:* "ORBIT OF THE RISK" DOCTRINE (FORESEEABILITY)

What makes the *Palsgraf* case so important, decades after it was decided? First, the case stands as a model of a well-written and well-reasoned legal decision. Second, it clearly establishes a legal principle that has proved to be important ever since: foreseeability. Finally, the case has often served as an example of how courts can create other new legal concepts.

The "zone of foreseeability" (also known as the "orbit of risk" doctrine) developed by Chief Justice Cardozo in the *Palsgraf* case holds that a person is only liable to others when his actions could foreseeably result in injuries to others. Essentially, a defendant is only liable when the plaintiff falls inside the "orbit of risk" of his actions. If his actions result in an injury that is clearly not foreseeable (such as someone helping another onto a train and triggering an explosion that causes scales to fall and injure the plaintiff), there is no proximate cause and therefore no liability.

Under the foreseeability doctrine, harms can be categorized by those that could reasonably be expected to occur and those that could not. This provides the court with a workable model to assess liability. If the jury determines that the defendant's action could foreseeably have injured the plaintiff, the court can find the defendant liable. On the other hand, if the jury finds that the actions were not foreseeable, the verdict would go in the defendant's favor. However, in practice, this neat theory tends to break down on the issue of defining exactly what foreseeability is.

3. DEFINING FORESEEABILITY AFTER *PALSGRAF*

Foreseeability can be defined as:

1. A natural and continuous sequence, unbroken by any new and independent cause, that produces plaintiff's injury;
2. Without which the injury would not have occurred; and
3. From which a person of ordinary prudence could have reasonably foreseen that such a result, or some similar result, was likely or even probable under the facts as they existed at that time.[13]

Put another way, the "foreseeability" element of proximate cause is satisfied at law when the defendant could have anticipated the danger that his negligence would create for others.[14] There is no requirement that the defendant must anticipate the precise nature of the threat, or even to whom the danger is posed, as long as a reasonably prudent person would have foreseen the possibility.[15] Using the reasonable person standard as a way of determining foreseeability would seem to be a positive solution to the quandary of defining the term, but in the practical world of civil injury litigation, this standard often becomes vague and highly dependent on the facts of the particular case.

COURT-CREATED TESTS FOR PROXIMATE CAUSE

Courts have wrestled with the definition of proximate cause almost from the instant that the term was first used. Over time, at least two major court doctrines have been created as a way of assessing proximate cause and thus the defendant's liability. The two most popular tests are the "but for" test and the "substantial factor" test.

Under the "but for" test, a defendant's actions will be the proximate cause when the plaintiff's injuries would not have occurred but for the defendant's negligence.

ISSUE AT A GLANCE

A. "BUT FOR" TEST

The "but for" test states that but for someone's negligence, the plaintiff would not have been injured. This test applies a very rigid standard to the facts of a case. The jury must reach a conclusion that but for the defendant's actions, the plaintiff would not have suffered the injuries in the case. Although the test sounds simple to apply, jurors often find themselves caught in a dilemma in how to apply the test. Essentially, this test requires that the plaintiff prove that had it not been for the defendant's actions, the plaintiff would not have been injured. In the often uncertain actions surrounding car crashes, slip and fall cases, and the myriad other negligence actions, this simple cause and effect is often hard to prove.

In the Chumley case, for instance, can we say that but for the defendant railway's actions, the plaintiff would not have been injured? We have one obvious problem with that question. What if the plaintiff himself was negligent? What if Mr. Chumley failed to stop at the intersection as he is required to do by law? His failure to exercise due care would mean that Mr. Chumley cannot conclusively say that, but for the defendant railway's failure to maintain a safe intersection, he would not have been injured. (We discuss defenses to negligence in Chapter 9.) The rigidity of this test has forced some jurisdictions to adopt a different approach: the substantial factor test.

Under the substantial factor test, a defendant is the proximate cause of the plaintiff's injuries when he is the predominant, major, or substantial factor in causing those injuries.

B. "SUBSTANTIAL FACTOR" TEST

Another test that is used in many jurisdictions is the "substantial factor" test. This test mandates that a defendant will be liable to the plaintiff if the defendant's actions were a primary factor in the plaintiff's injuries.[17] This is the test advocated by the Restatement of Torts. Many argue that the substantial factor test is more forgiving than the but for test, because the substantial factor test only requires that the defendant play a significant role in injuring the plaintiff, while the but for test requires that the defendant play a predominant role. Some jurisdictions use both tests; some use one or the other. The important feature to keep in mind about these tests is that they are designed as guides for the courts and juries. They do not take the place of the fact-finder. There is nothing foolproof about either test. Each case must be taken on its own merits.

To better explain the difference between the substantial factor test and the but for test, let's examine the facts of an actual case.

DOUBROVINSKAYA v. DEMBITZER
20 Misc. 3d 440, 452, 858 N.Y.S.2d 874, 884 (N.Y. Sup. 2008)

JACK M. BATTAGLIA, J.

On the morning of January 24, 2006, Plaintiff and Defendant were each proceeding northbound in the right lane for moving traffic on Ocean Avenue in Brooklyn. Plaintiff was riding a bicycle; defendant was driving his car; Plaintiff was ahead of Defendant. At the intersection of Ocean Avenue and Avenue P, the roadway had been opened, and the right lane and part of the left lane of Ocean Avenue as they traversed the intersection were covered by metal plates; construction equipment and material at the right curb precluded circumventing the plates on the right.

As Plaintiff approached the intersection, she moved from the right lane into the portion of the left lane that was not covered by the plates. Defendant proceeded through the intersection in the right lane. Behind Plaintiff in the left lane was another car, and that driver sounded its horn. Plaintiff then moved her bicycle from the left lane into the right lane, where it struck the driver's side of Defendant's car.

There is no dispute that Plaintiff did not signal by hand that she was changing lanes, as she was required to do by law. Nor is there any dispute that Defendant failed to sound his horn, as he was required to do by law "when necessary." Defendant testified that he was aware that Plaintiff had moved from the right lane to the left in order to avoid the metal plates, but his testimony was somewhat inconsistent as to whether he was aware that she would be moving back to the right lane from the left once she passed the metal plates.

The Court instructed the jury in accordance with the Pattern Jury Instructions as to negligence and foreseeability generally; as to the general duty owed by a motorist to a bicyclist, and by a bicyclist for her own safety and as to the statutory standard of care that Defendant owed Plaintiff under Vehicle and Traffic Law 1146, and that Plaintiff owed Defendant under Vehicle and Traffic Law 1128, 1163, and 1237. The Court also instructed the jury as to burden of proof, comparative fault, and proximate cause.

The jury verdict sheet also followed that found in the Pattern Jury Instructions. The instructions and verdict sheet required that the jury first answer as to whether Defendant was negligent, and, if so, whether his negligence was a substantial factor in bringing about the accident. If both questions were answered in the affirmative, the jury was then required to answer as to whether Plaintiff was negligent, and, if so, whether her negligence was a substantial factor in bringing about the accident. Only if the jury answered both questions in the affirmative would an allocation of fault be made as between Plaintiff and Defendant.

The Court notes that the instructions and verdict sheet found in the Pattern Jury Instructions do not expressly recognize the possibility that a plaintiff's negligence might be the sole proximate cause of an accident; indeed, the jury does not consider the plaintiff's negligence until after it has determined whether the defendant's negligence was a proximate cause. Further complication is added by the instruction that a plaintiff bears the burden of proving by a preponderance of the evidence that the defendant's negligence was a substantial factor in bring about the accident, but that the defendant bears the burden of proving by a preponderance of the evidence that the plaintiff's negligence was a substantial factor in bringing about the accident. (See PJI 1:60.)

In what may be the only opinion to address this anomaly, the Second Department held that, notwithstanding that the trial court "submitted written interrogatories to the jury separately inquiring as to negligence and proximate cause with regard to the defendant and the injured plaintiff," the appellate court could "properly consider the injured plaintiff's actions, not on the issue of comparative negligence, but on the totality of the proof in the jury's evaluation of the issue of proximate cause," and determine that "the jury could reasonably have concluded that . . . the sole proximate cause of this accident was the conduct of the injured plaintiff."

In finding that Defendant was negligent, the jury must have found that he was aware or should have been aware that Plaintiff would be moving back into the right lane of traffic after she passed the metal plates while traveling in the left lane, and that he failed to use due care by proceeding past her in the right lane, or by failing to sound his horn, or both. Despite Defendant's contention now that it was not foreseeable that Plaintiff would return to the right lane after passing the plates, the jury obviously disagreed, and that finding was clearly supported by the evidence and the weight of the evidence.

In finding that Defendant's negligence was not a substantial factor in bringing about the accident, the jury must have found that Plaintiff's negligence was, in effect, the sole proximate cause of the accident — that is, that the Plaintiff's negligence was the only substantial factor in bringing about the accident. And so Defendant contends on this motion. It is important to note that neither party argued to the jury that the sounding of the horn by the second motorist, preceding Plaintiff's moving from the left lane to the right, was either negligent or a substantial factor in bringing about the accident. Again, on the question whether Plaintiff's negligence was a substantial factor in bringing about the accident, and necessarily whether it was the only substantial factor, Defendant bore the burden of persuasion.

"A jury verdict should not be set aside as against the weight of the evidence unless the jury could not have reached the verdict by any fair interpretation of the evidence. A jury's finding that a party was at fault but that such fault was not a proximate cause of the accident is inconsistent and against the weight of the evidence only when the issues are so inextricably interwoven as to make it logically impossible to find negligence without also finding proximate cause. When the verdict can be reconciled with a reasonable view of the evidence, the successful party is entitled to the presumption that the jury adopted that view."

Violation of a provision of the Vehicle and Traffic Law "constitutes negligence per se . . . but does not necessarily lead to the conclusion that the defendant's action was a proximate cause of the accident; the defendant may be totally at fault, not at all at fault, or partially at fault."

Nonetheless, appellate courts have held that a jury's finding of negligence without a finding of proximate cause is inconsistent and against the weight of the evidence when the negligence inheres in conduct that violates the Vehicle and Traffic Law.

The opinions do not articulate any test or methodology for determining when the questions of negligence and proximate cause are "inextricably interwoven," but the condition must exist where the two concepts overlap, and that is at foreseeability. "The risk reasonably to be perceived defines the duty to be obeyed." *Palsgraf v. Long Island R.R. Co.*, 248 N.Y. 339, 344, 162 N.E. 99 (1928). The scope of the duty of care varies with the foreseeability of the possible harm. Foreseeability determines the scope of the duty once a duty is found to exist. Although the precise manner in which the harm occurred need not be foreseeable, liability does not attach unless the harm is within the reasonably foreseeable hazards that the duty exists to prevent.

Foreseeability is also a lynchpin of proximate cause, particularly where it is alleged that the act of someone other than the defendant severs the causal connection between the defendant's negligence and the harm suffered by the plaintiff. Liability turns on whether the intervening act is a normal or foreseeable consequence of the situation created by the defendant's negligence. An intervening act may not serve as a superseding cause, and relieve an actor of responsibility, where the risk of the intervening act occurring is the very same risk which renders the act negligent.

These principles apply when it is the plaintiff's own conduct that is alleged to be the sole or superseding cause of the harm suffered. What reasonable care requires may both be determined by and determinative of the question as to whether the activity of an injured person was an intervening cause of an accident; foreseeability bears on both issues.

As already noted, the jury here must have found that Defendant failed to use due care by proceeding to pass Plaintiff, or failing to sound his horn, or both, even though he was aware or should have been aware that she would be moving back into his lane after she passed the obstacle in the roadway. The Vehicle and Traffic Law provides that "every driver of a vehicle shall exercise due care to avoid colliding with any bicyclist, . . . and shall give warning by sounding the horn when necessary." (See Vehicle and Traffic Law 1146.) Not every driver who comes upon a bicyclist must sound a horn; whether it is negligent to fail to employ a warning via a horn must be considered in the light of the relevant circumstances. Moreover, the failure of a motorist to sound the horn, even if negligent, may not be the proximate cause of a collision with a bicyclist."

The reason for sounding a horn (or, rather, the legitimate reason) is to make one's presence known, in this case, to the bicyclist, and the risk addressed by the statutory requirement that the horn be sounded "when necessary" is that the bicyclist might enter the motorist's path of travel. That is exactly what happened here, and might have been avoided, had Defendant sounded his horn, which he admittedly did not. He argues that, "in the split second in which this accident occurred, it would have made no difference if he had sounded his horn." (Affirmation in Opposition, ¶17.) But that would only be so if he had waited until he was upon Plaintiff before sounding his horn. If, as the jury may have found, he should have sounded his horn, he should have sounded it sooner than that.

Similarly, if the jury's finding of negligence was based on Defendant's proceeding past Plaintiff, it must have been because he was aware or should have been aware that she would be moving back into his path of travel in the right lane. It was clearly foreseeable under these circumstances that Plaintiff would collide with Defendant in the right lane, as she did. Defendant's contention that "Plaintiff simply struck defendant's vehicle with her bicycle wheel and the actions of the two parties are totally separable" (id., ¶31) does not comport with the jury's assessment of Defendant's conduct.

It may be that enough has been said to require that Plaintiff's motion be granted. But consideration of Plaintiff's conduct is at least appropriate, given that the evidence establishes her own clear negligence. Again, it was Defendant's burden to show that Plaintiff's negligence was the sole proximate cause of the accident. Plaintiff failed to signal by hand before changing lanes, although she was required to signal by the Vehicle and Traffic Law (see VTL 1163, 1164), and she gave no explanation other than that she did not know that she was so required. The risk addressed by the statutory requirement that a signal be given is that of a collision with a motorist, bicyclist, or pedestrian in the other lane. That is exactly what happened here, and might have been avoided, if Plaintiff had given the signal, which she admittedly did not. A jury could find, therefore, that her conduct was a substantial factor in bringing about the accident.

Finally, it might well be that a jury could conclude on the evidence presented that Plaintiff was negligent in not looking more carefully before changing lanes, and that her negligence in this respect was a substantial factor in bringing about the accident. Unlike the failure to signal, however, which would require a finding of negligence and proximate cause, we cannot know from the verdict sheet whether the jury reached any conclusion as to Plaintiff's care in seeing what there was to be seen.

In any event, given the jury's finding of Defendant's negligence, and the risk created and foreseeable consequences, a finding that Plaintiff's negligence in failing to look carefully was the sole proximate cause of the collision would also be against the weight of the evidence. The protection for bicyclists that is mandated by the statutory requirement that a motorist sound the horn is protection given as well, if not particularly, to the bicyclist who does not look carefully. Likewise, if Defendant was deemed negligent because he passed Plaintiff before she moved back into the right lane, it was foreseeable that she might move into the lane without awareness of his presence.

Plaintiff's motion for a new trial is granted. The parties shall appear for jury selection in the Jury Coordinating Part on June 30, 2008, or on such other date on which they might agree in a signed stipulation "so ordered" by the court.

Questions about the case:

1. What are the basic facts that resulted in the plaintiff's injuries in this case?
2. What were the jury instructions regarding the defendant's negligence and whether he was a substantial factor in the plaintiff's injuries?
3. How did the jury decide the issue of proximate cause for the plaintiff's injuries?
4. What is the court discussing when it refers to the issues of proximate cause and negligence as being "inextricably interwoven"?
5. Why does the court refer to foreseeability as the "lynchpin of proximate cause"?

PLEADING PROXIMATE CAUSE

On a practical level, attorneys have long since realized that the more tenuous the connection between the plaintiff's injuries and the defendant's actions, the more the plaintiff should focus on the facts of the case to establish proximate cause. After all, failure to prove this element negates the rest of the case. Another complicating factor is that, in many ways, proximate cause is determined on a case-by-case basis. Given the almost infinite variety of ways that negligent actions (or inactions) can result in injuries to others, each case must be considered on its merits and the theories and court tests applied to the specific facts of the pending case.

As such, when pleading proximate cause, the best practice is to break the facts of the case down into the smallest discernible units possible to explain each phase of the case and to help relate the defendant's actions to the plaintiff's injuries. (For an example of how to phrase proximate cause language, see Forms and Court Documents at the end of this chapter.)

The plaintiff must always prove that the defendant was the legal cause of the plaintiff's injuries. The plaintiff will lose the case on a directed verdict for the defendant if the plaintiff fails to prove causation.

ISSUE AT A GLANCE

A. IS PROXIMATE CAUSE A DEFENSE?

A defendant does not have to raise the failure to prove proximate cause as a defense. Proximate cause is an essential element of the plaintiff's case, and failure to prove it demands a verdict for the defendant.[18] A general denial is sufficient to attack the issue of proximate cause.

B. IN THE END, PROXIMATE CAUSE IS A JURY QUESTION

Some commentators suggest that proximate cause is both a factual question (which the jury determines) and a question of law (which the judge decides).

Whether the defendant's actions rise to the level of proximate cause of the plaintiff's injuries is a question for the jury. The underlying principle behind proximate cause is a question of public policy, that is, how far the law will extend the defendant's responsibility for negligent conduct.[19]

Proximate cause is a jury question

ISSUE AT A GLANCE

Because the plaintiff will present evidence attempting to prove that the defendant was the proximate cause of the plaintiff's injuries, the jurors must receive some direction about how they make this decision. The judge can, and often does, give the jurors a jury charge (often called a jury instruction) that explains what proximate cause is. The jurors will actually receive numerous jury charges before they retire to consider their verdict, and in a negligence case the issue of proximate cause is likely to be an important one.

According to the Restatement of Torts, the jury's function is to determine: (1) if the defendant's breach of duty was a substantial factor in causing the plaintiff's injuries and (2) how to apportion responsibility (and damages) if there are two or more defendants.[20]

Practical suggestion: For sample jury instructions on proximate cause, see 18A Am. Jur. Pleading and Practice Forms (rev.), Negligence, Form 223, 224. This would make a good addition to the jury instructions subfile in one of your pending cases.

FIGURE 7-4

Sample Jury Instruction on Proximate Cause

Ladies and gentlemen of the jury, I charge you that the plaintiff bears the burden of proving proximate cause in this case. I hereby charge you that a proximate cause of an injury is a cause which, in natural and continuous sequence, produces the injury, and without which the injury would not have occurred.

Bolen v. Woo, 96 Cal. App. 3d 944, 158 Cal. Rptr. 454 (1979).

1. HOW MUCH EVIDENCE DOES THE PLAINTIFF HAVE TO PRODUCE TO MAKE PROXIMATE CAUSE A JURY QUESTION?

Plaintiffs are not required to prove proximate cause to an absolute certainty. As long as the plaintiff presents substantial evidence tending to show proximate cause, it then becomes the jury's function to decide if it exists. In some jurisdictions, even if the plaintiff presents a "scintilla" of proof of proximate cause, it must be presented to the jury for a determination.

2. ON APPEAL, COURTS WILL LEAVE THE JURY'S DETERMINATION INTACT, UNLESS CLEARLY WRONG

Appellate courts are bound by the jury's determination of proximate cause (because it is largely a factual determination) except where the jury's conclusion is clearly wrong.[21] When the jury clearly disregards the facts of a case and decides that proximate cause exists when there are no supporting facts, an appellate court could overturn the verdict and find for the defendant.

MULTIPLE DEFENDANTS AND PROXIMATE CAUSE

Our discussion so far has focused on the actions of one defendant. What happens to the analysis when more than one defendant is involved? We have already seen that liability for two negligent defendants will usually be apportioned between them according to their degree of negligence. However, suppose the facts clearly show that only *one* defendant could have been negligent?

Example: Tara is sitting in her backyard, which borders on a wooded section. Two hunters, one on each side of Tara's property, fire their rifles at the same time, mistakenly believing that Tara is a deer. Tara is hit by one bullet but it is impossible to tell which hunter fired the shot. How does the court decide proximate cause?

When the plaintiff is injured by the negligence of Defendant *A* and then receives additional injuries because of Defendant *B*'s negligence, Defendant *A* is not absolved of liability. In such a case, both defendants may be liable to the plaintiff, each for the injuries his negligence proximately caused.

	Jury	Bench
How many civil trials were decided by a jury or judge?	18,404	8,543*
Who were the litigants?[a]		
Individual vs. individual	45.5%	33.7%*
Individual vs. business	30.4	22.2*
Business vs. individual	1.8	17.9*
Business vs. business	6.4	16.8*
Who won?[b]		
Plaintiffs overall	54.5%	68.0%*
Plaintiffs in torts	52.8	60.8
Plaintiffs in contracts	61.6	70.1*
What was the median final award?[c]		
In all cases	$30,500	$24,000
In tort cases	24,300	21,100
In contract cases	74,000	25,000*
What percent of prevailing plaintiffs were awarded $1 million or more?		
In all cases	6.3%	1.6%*
In tort cases	5.7	3.7
In contract cases	8.7	1.0*
What percent of plaintiff winners seeking punitive damages were awarded punitive damages?[d]	34.0%	19.6%
What percent of cases were terminated within two years?[e]	56.9%	76.0%*

FIGURE 7-5

Bench and Jury Trials in State Courts, by Selected Characteristics, 2005

*Jury-bench difference is significant at the 95% confidence level.
[a]Data on litigant pairings were available for 99.8% of jury and 99.7% of bench trials. Bench and jury percentages do not add to 100% due to the exclusion of hospital and government litigants.
[b]Data on plaintiff winners were not applicable to real property trials. Data were available for 99.7% of tort and contract jury trials and 99.4% of tort and contract bench trials.
[c]There were 9,376 jury and 4,794 bench trials in which the plaintiff won an award. Median award amounts were calculated for plaintiff winners in tort and contract cases.
[d]Includes only the 1,824 plaintiff winners who sought punitive damages. Data were available for 96.6% of trials.
[e]Case processing data were available for 99.9% of jury and 99.5% of bench trials.

Civil Bench and Jury Trials in State Courts, 2005, Bureau of Justice Statistics, U.S. Department of Justice.

When liability cannot be determined between two negligent defendants, both are held liable, despite the fact that only one could have actually caused the injuries. The reasoning behind this apparent exception to assessing responsibility against the negligent party is a public policy concern. Presented with this problem, the court is faced with either finding both defendants liable, or finding neither liable. The second option leaves an innocent plaintiff without any possibility of recovery. Because both defendants were acting negligently, both will pay, even if only one could have proximately caused the plaintiff's injuries.

INTERVENING CAUSES

Intervening cause
Any event that occurs after the initial plaintiff's injury that contributes to or aggravates those injuries

Superseding cause
Any event that occurs after the initial plaintiff's injury that replaces one act of negligence with another

An **intervening cause** contributes to the plaintiff's injuries. When two or more defendants act negligently, both can be liable to the plaintiff. Only when the intervening cause rises to the level of creating an independent proximate cause is it classified as a **superseding cause.** A superseding cause relieves the original defendant's liability by substituting the negligence of the next defendant.

What makes a negligent act an intervening cause or a superseding cause? This is usually a factual question that must be determined by the jury (or, in a bench trial, the judge). Classifying causes as intervening and superseding often becomes very confusing, especially because so many jurisdictions have different rules about these terms. In some jurisdictions, for example, the original defendant remains liable for any foreseeable negligence by another party. In other jurisdictions, the original defendant is not liable for intervening negligence by another that could not have been reasonably foreseen.

An intervening cause can expand the pool of defendants from the original defendant to the one who caused the additional injuries to the plaintiff. Some jurisdictions follow a rule that is easier to implement: A superseding cause must come from some source not associated with the original defendant. If the source of the additional injuries is somehow associated with the original defendant, the original defendant remains liable.[22]

According to the Restatement (Second) of Torts, an intervening force is one that operates to produce harm to the plaintiff after the original defendant's negligent act or omission has occurred.

When two or more defendants combine to injure the plaintiff, each may be considered intervening causes and all will be liable to the plaintiff.

A. SUPERSEDING CAUSES

Not all jurisdictions draw a clear distinction between intervening and superseding causes. Some jurisdictions follow the rule that the original defendant is responsible for the plaintiff's injuries, even when some new force contributes or cooperates in the plaintiff's injuries, whether this new force was foreseeable or not.[24]

A superseding cause eliminates the original defendant's negligence by replacing it with the negligence of another. To be classified as a superseding cause, the new negligent act must be one that exceeds the original defendant's negligence to such an extent as to render it nearly meaningless. Put another way, a superseding cause is one that takes precedence over the original negligent act and makes that original negligent act legally "remote."[23]

Example: Tom is driving his car on the freeway during rush hour and in a moment of distraction, he allows his front bumper to tap the back bumper of the car in front of him. He puts on his warning flashers and climbs out. Elizabeth, the other driver, also gets out of her car. While they are inspecting the minor damage, Ron, who is speeding and driving recklessly in the breakdown lane, crashes into both cars, pinning Elizabeth between both cars and severely injuring her. Ron's liability for Elizabeth's injuries will likely be considered a superseding act to Tom's original negligence in bumping into Elizabeth's car.

Some jurisdictions have done away with the distinctions between intervening and superseding causes, considering them unworkable. Instead, they have substituted a foreseeability analysis. Those jurisdictions ask the question: Was the injury to the plaintiff foreseeable, no matter what the source? If the answer is yes, the defendant is liable.[25]

The basic policy behind superseding causation is that there are times when it is unreasonable or unjust to make the original defendant liable for negligence that was so obviously exceeded by the actions of a second defendant.[26]

Example: Ted and Marsha were invited to a wedding held at a friend's house. The invitations included the following language: "The ceremony will take place beside the family pool (weather permitting); please arrange for child care as seating is limited and we cannot provide supervision for children." Ted and Marsha decide to bring their three-year-old daughter, Tiffany, to the ceremony. During the nuptials, neither parent supervises Tiffany, who is playing in the backyard near the unfenced pool. Tiffany falls into the pool and suffers brain damage when she nearly drowns. Ted and Marsha sue the friend for failing to properly fence the pool. The court rules that Ted and Marsha's negligence in failing to properly supervise Tiffany supersedes any negligence of the homeowner in failing to fence off the pool.[27]

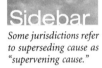

Defendants *A* and *B* are both negligent, but Defendant *B*'s negligence clearly outweighs Defendant *A*'s. Defendant *B* is a superseding cause and only she will be liable to the plaintiff.

B. ACTS OF GOD OR ACTS OF NATURE

Finally, there is a category of events that fall outside the classifications of proximate cause, intervening cause, or even superseding cause. These are "acts of God," also sometimes referred to as "acts of nature." Plaintiffs are barred from bringing suit against individual defendants for natural catastrophes. For example, when the plaintiff is injured in a tornado or earthquake, the plaintiff cannot sue any specific person for his injuries. In effect, acts of nature fall outside the realm of tort law.

However, there are some exceptions to this general rule. A plaintiff may be permitted to bring an action against a defendant who failed to follow routine and normal precautions against expected natural forces, such as building a retaining wall to hold in dirt from a recent excavation in an area where rainfall is often heavy or sudden. In such a case, the defendant's actions have increased the likelihood of injury from an act of nature and therefore he can be liable.

 SKILLS YOU NEED IN THE REAL WORLD

Internet Legal Research

The days of curling up in a law library to spend hours poring over books on arcane legal topics are long over. These days, you need fast answers and even faster research methods. In the past few years, the Internet resources available to legal researchers have increased dramatically. With this huge increase there has been a growing misconception about Internet legal resources. One of the biggest problems with Internet legal research is that many of these sites limit their coverage. If the legal database only covers cases from the past ten years, any valuable case that is more than a decade old will not be listed, even if it is the most important case for your research. Having stated that caveat, however, there are some valuable legal research sites available on the Internet, and they can dramatically lessen your research time.

Strategies for Online Legal Research

Before you begin researching any topic on the Internet, you must decide what you want to know and what you do *not* want to know. Some sites will cycle you through endless links until you have lost the thread of your research. You should come up with a list of key words and terms before you begin researching. After that, you should confirm what sources you need. For instance, are you researching federal law or state law? This will help you focus on Web sites that concentrate on those areas.

All Web Sites Are Not Created Equal

As you conduct your research, you should concentrate on the pedigree of the site, which refers to the URL address. If you are researching U.S. Supreme Court cases, for instance, and you have a choice between *http://www.Ronniehatesthe Supremecourt.org* and *http://www.supremecourtus.gov/* (which is the actual link to the Supreme Court of the United States), you would probably have more success at the second site than the first. Besides getting to your primary sources more quickly, the first site sounds like a site that would not provide the same depth of coverage or accuracy in sources that could be found at the second. As you visit legal research sites, evaluate the URL address to determine where this information is coming from. For legal research purposes, you are safest with government, law school, and university Web sites.

Free Sites

Rather than provide a list of the available free legal research Web sites here (that would probably have expired or become inactive by the time you read this section), I have provided a list of Internet search engines. Your best bet to find free legal research sites is to visit a major Internet search engine and enter a search term such as "legal research sites." General Internet search engines include:
http://www.yahoo.com
http://www.excite.com

http://www.dogpile.com
http://www.google.com

Pay Sites

Just about everyone has either heard of or worked with Westlaw (*http://www.westlaw.com*). However, there are other sites, such as Lexis-Nexis (*http://www.lexis-nexis.com*) that also provide in-depth coverage. Free sites cannot compete with the pay sites in terms of scope, timeliness, and comprehensiveness. Pay sites provide access to all state and federal court decisions, state and federal codes, and other sources too numerous to list. Lexis-Nexis also provides access to the invaluable Shepard's service, so that you can "shepardize" your cases on line.

THE LIFE OF A PARALEGAL

Balancing Work and School

When I decided to get a paralegal degree, I was already working full time. I knew that I'd have to do some of my homework during lunch breaks, so the first thing I did was run it by my boss. Both of the bosses that I've had while I've been in the paralegal program have been totally supportive. Their approach was, "Well, this will only make you better at what you're doing."

I take Internet courses through a local community college. During lunch, I'll log on to my course Web site to take care of an assignment. If I have to do a paper or a project, I'll stay at work late to type it up, or to use our library for research. Our library has statutes and other books, and that's very helpful. I also asked an attorney across the street if I could borrow his library. He was very kind and told me that I could come over any time that I needed to. One semester, I spent nearly every lunch hour over there, reading and researching. It's amazing how friendly most people will be, if you explain your situation to them. They have just opened up their resources to me. It makes you realize how nice most of the people in the legal community are.

I've always been interested in the law. When I worked for the city's legal department the city attorney asked me if I was interested in going back to school. The city had a tuition reimbursement policy. I really hadn't given it that much thought until he mentioned it to me. I thought, "I'd be stupid not to do it. Now is my chance." I thought that at least I'd try it and if I couldn't do it, I'd stop. So far, it's worked out really well.

My advice to anyone trying to balance school and work: don't put anything off until the last minute because everything will go wrong. Try to stay ahead of the game; try to get your assignments done ahead of time. When I have a doctor's appointment or a dentist's appointment, I take my books with me. As I'm sitting in the waiting room for an hour, I read. Use every spare minute of your time to stay ahead. After a while, you get in the habit of doing that. Then it's a relief when you've got something due and you've already done it.

Pamela Tallent, Paralegal

ETHICAL ISSUES FOR THE PARALEGAL: ATTORNEY-CLIENT PRIVILEGE

Often considered to be one of the most sacred tenets of law, the attorney-client privilege protects communications between clients and attorneys from being revealed to others. An attorney who is called to the stand and asked to testify about a conversation with a client can legally refuse to answer these questions. The attorney cannot be held in contempt or otherwise penalized for failure to answer such questions. Is a paralegal protected by a similar privilege? No. There are some jurisdictions that have held that the presence of the paralegal during an attorney-client discussion may actually waive or eliminate the privilege. That being true, a paralegal cannot refuse to answer questions about conversations with a client. However, the paralegal should ensure that the attorney-client privilege is not waived under other circumstances. Because the conversations between the attorney and the client are supposed to be private, the paralegal should make sure that they remain so. The best way to do this is not to discuss any client business away from the office. Unless given permission to do so, it is a good idea to refuse to state that a particular person is even represented by the attorney.

Chapter Summary

Courts have been wrestling with the concept of proximate cause since its origins in the early 1600s. As the third element of a negligence action, the plaintiff must prove that the defendant's action (or inaction) brought about the plaintiff's injuries. However, proving that connection is often difficult, given the vague way that proximate cause is often defined by courts. An early attempt to bring more consistency to the application of proximate cause analysis is the famous *Palsgraf* case, which held that a defendant would not be the proximate cause (and thus not liable) for the plaintiff's injuries when it was not foreseeable that the defendant's negligent act would result in the plaintiff's injuries. However, the test of foreseeability continues to be a difficult test to apply in some cases. Additional court doctrines have been created to deal with the proof required in proximate cause cases. For instance, some jurisdictions have adopted the "but for" test, meaning that the defendant will only be liable when the plaintiff would not have been injured but for the defendant's actions. Other jurisdictions have opted for the "substantial factor" test. Under that test, a defendant will be considered the proximate cause of the plaintiff's injuries when he is the predominant or major cause of those injuries. Finally, courts must also apportion blame when more than one defendant is involved. In some cases, two or more defendants will be negligent and this liability must be divided among them. In other cases, such as superseding negligence, one defendant's negligence will so outweigh another defendant's negligence as to remove all of the other defendant's liability to the plaintiff.

Web Sites

- **Wikipedia — Proximate Cause**
  http://en.wikipedia.org/wiki/Proximate_cause

- **Law.com — Proximate Cause**
  http://www.law.com (click in search box for proximate cause issues)

- **Free Legal Dictionary**
  http://legal-dictionary.thefreedictionary.com (click in search box for articles about proximate cause)

Forms and Court Documents

Here is an excerpt from a complaint filed in a real case (although the names of the parties have been changed). Notice how the language in paragraph 9 sets out proximate cause.

STATE OF PLACID		IN THE SUPERIOR COURT
COUNTY OF BARNES		FILE NUMBER: _____

Jane Smith,	)	ANSWER
Plaintiff	)	
	)	
vs.	)	
	)	
John Doe,	)	
Martha Doe,		
Defendants		

The plaintiff, Jane Smith, complaining of the defendants, alleges and says the following:

1.

That plaintiff Jane Smith is a citizen and resident of Barnes County, Placid.

2.

That, upon information and belief, defendant Martha Doe (hereinafter "defendant driver") is a citizen and resident of Barnes County, Placid.

3.

That, upon information and belief, defendant John Doe (hereinafter "defendant owner") is a citizen and resident of Barnes County, Placid.

a. Further, upon information and belief, defendant owner was the registered owner of the vehicle involved in the collision at issue in this case, said vehicle being a 1999 Ford, license plate number FAB 9925.

b. That, at all times mentioned herein and upon information and belief, defendant driver was operating and using the aforementioned vehicle with the authority, consent, permission, and knowledge of defendant owner, and defendant's driver's operation and use of the vehicle was under the direction and control of defendant owner.

c. Furthermore, at all times mentioned herein and upon information and belief, defendant driver was a member of the family or household of defendant owner and was living in such person's home; that the vehicle driven by defendant driver was owned, provided, and maintained for the general use, pleasure, and convenience of the family; and that the vehicle was being so used with the express or implied consent of defendant owner.

Therefore, any negligence on the part of defendant driver in causing plaintiff's injuries should be imputed to defendant owner under the family purpose doctrine.

4.

That, on or about the 19th day of October, 2000, at approximately 9:40 A.M., plaintiff was operating a motor vehicle traveling North on Union Street in Rock Pleasant, Barnes County, Placid.

5.

That, at the same time and place, defendant driver was operating the aforementioned 1999 Ford motor vehicle and was traveling South on Brown Drive in Barnes County, Placid.

6.

That defendant driver entered plaintiff's lane of travel, thereby causing a collision with plaintiff's vehicle.

7.

That defendant driver admitted at the scene that she did not see plaintiff's vehicle before pulling out into the intersection.

8.

That defendant driver was negligent in that she:

a. While operating a motor vehicle on the public streets and highways, failed to keep a reasonable and proper outlook in plaintiff's direction of travel.

b. Failed to maintain the vehicle that she was operating and drove the vehicle in such a manner so as to deprive the defendant of such control over the vehicle as a reasonable and prudent person would maintain under all the circumstances then existing.

c. Drove a motor vehicle upon the public streets and highways at a speed greater than was reasonable and prudent under the conditions then existing in violation of P.G.S. 20-141 (a).

d. Drove her vehicle at a speed greater than that which was posted for the particular street or highway upon which said automobile was being operated in violation of P.G.S. 20-141 (b).

e. Failed to yield the right of way to the plaintiff's automobile, which was lawfully proceeding in a straight line of travel.

9.

That, as a direct and proximate cause of the negligent conduct of the defendant driver, plaintiff was seriously injured, causing her great pain and suffering, medical expenses, lost wages, physical and mental anguish, and permanent injuries.

10.

That, as a direct and proximate result of the aforementioned negligence of defendant driver, plaintiff has sustained damage to her person in an amount in excess of Ten Thousand Dollars ($10,000.00), representing damage to plaintiff's person, medical bills, pain and suffering, lost wages, mental anguish, and permanent injuries.

WHEREFORE, plaintiff demands judgment against the defendants as follows:
1. That plaintiff have and recover of defendants, jointly and severally, a sum in excess of Ten Thousand Dollars ($10,000.00) for compensatory damages, plus interest as allowed by law, including prejudgment interest.
2. That a jury trial be had on all issues of fact.
3. That the costs of this action be taxed against the defendants, including a reasonable attorney's fee for plaintiffs' attorneys as provided by P.G.S. 6-21.1.
4. For such other, further, and different relief as the Court deems just, reasonable and proper.

This the _____ day of _____, 200_____

_____
Attorney for Plaintiff

Key Terms

Foreseeability   Proximate causation
Intervening cause   Superseding cause

Review Questions

1   What is proximate cause?
2   How does proximate cause differ from the proof of the series of events in the case?
3   Some commentators suggest that the law on proximate cause is deliberately vague. Why would this be so?
4   What are three arguments in support of proximate cause?
5   Why should a defendant's liability be limited only to proximate causes?

6   Some authors refuse to use the term *proximate cause,* and prefer to use the terms *legal cause* or *responsible cause.* Are these labels more descriptive? Why or why not?

7   Why would one of the requirements of a working definition of proximate cause involve the proof of a "natural, unbroken, and continuous sequence" of events?

8   Explain foreseeability.

9   Why is the *Palsgraf* case considered to be so important?

10 Explain the "orbit of the risk" doctrine from *Palsgraf.*

11 Would the analysis of the *Palsgraf* case have been different if the man attempting to board the train had carried a box labeled "Dangerous Explosives: Do Not Drop"? Explain.

12 Explain the difference between the "but for" test and the "substantial factor" test.

13 Describe how the defendants in the Chumley case are the proximate cause of the plaintiff's injuries by detailing the precise facts that give rise to their liability.

14 Is there a justification for altering the rules of proximate cause to limit them to the immediate injuries caused by the defendant? If so, justify this position based on the concepts in this chapter.

15 How is the Restatement's position on proximate cause different from the approach used in some jurisdictions?

16 Explain proximate cause analysis when two or more defendants are implicated, but only one could have been negligent.

17 Explain intervening causes.

18 How is an intervening cause different from a superseding cause?

19 How does an act of nature affect the proximate cause analysis?

20 Explain the attorney-client privilege.

Applying What
You Have Learned

1   Assuming that we can prove that Mr. Chumley stopped at the railroad crossing, looked, but could not see the oncoming train because of obscuring vegetation, draft a paragraph explaining how the railway company is the proximate cause of his injuries.

2   June is driving home on January 10th of this year and comes to a stop at a red light at an intersection in the Town of Lucy, Barnes County, State of Placid. She is on State Street. The intersecting road is called Dellinger Boulevard. As she waits for the light to turn green, a 2002 Ford Explorer SUV driven by Randy Reckless approaches from the east on Dellinger Boulevard and runs the red light. June, who sees that the light in her direction has turned green, begins to accelerate and reaches the intersection just as Randy Reckless runs the red light. Randy's vehicle slams into June's car on the driver's side. June is pinned inside the car and it takes over two hours to get her out. When the local fire department finally frees

her, they discover that June has numerous broken bones and internal injuries. Police cite Randy for failing to stop at the red light, failure to yield, and reckless driving.

Draft a complaint based on these facts and pay particular attention to your allegation of proximate cause. How do you allege proximate cause under these facts?

3 How does your state define foreseeability?

4 Does your state follow the basic holding in *Palsgraf,* or has it developed a different definition of proximate cause?

Endnotes

[1] *Oklahoma Gas & Electric Co. v. Hofrichter,* 196 Ark. 1, 116 S.W.2d 599 (1938); *Hunter v. Horton,* 80 Idaho 475, 333 P.2d 459 (1958).

[2] *Hentschel v. Baby Bathinette Corp.,* 215 F.2d 102 (2d Cir. 1954).

[3] *Chism v. White Oak Feed Co.,* 612 S.W.2d 873 (1981).

[4] Prosser and Keeton on the Law of Torts, 5th ed., West Wadsworth (1984).

[5] Quoted in *Beilke v. Coryell,* 524 N.W.2d 607 (1994).

[6] *Malo v. Willis,* 126 Cal. App. 3d 543, 178 Cal. Rptr. 774 (1981).

[7] *Maryland Steel Co. v. Marney,* 88 Md. 482 (1898).

[8] *Collins v. American Optometric Assn.,* 693 F.2d 636 (7th Cir. 1982); *Sosa v. Coleman,* 646 F.2d 991 (5th Cir. 1981).

[9] *Hentschel v. Baby Bathinette Corp.,* 215 F.2d 102 (2d Cir. 1954).

[10] Restatement (Second) of Torts §430, comment d.

[11] *Livingston v. Gribetz,* 549 F. Supp. 238 (D.C.N.Y. 1982).

[12] *Bole v. Pittsburgh Athletic Co.,* 205 F. 468 (3d Cir. 1913).

[13] *Goode v. Harrison,* 45 N.C. App. 547, 263 S.E.2d 33 (1980).

[14] *Coleman v. Equitable Real Estate Investment Management, Inc.,* 971 S.W.2d 611 (1998).

[15] Id.

[16] Prosser and Keeton on the Law of Torts, 5th ed., West Wadsworth (1984) §48.

[17] *Coleman v. Equitable Real Estate Investment Management, Inc.,* 971 S.W.2d 611 (1998).

[18] *Clement v. Rousselle Corp.,* 372 So. 2d 1156, *cert. denied,* 383 So. 2d 1191 (1979).

[19] *Bell v. Irace,* 619 A.2d 365 (1993).

[20] Restatement (Second) of Torts §434.

[21] *Stahl v. Metropolitan Dade County,* 438 So. 2d 14 (1983).

[22] *Chambers v. Bunker,* 598 S.W.2d 204 (1980).

[23] *Crull v. Platt,* 471 N.E.2d 1211 (1984).

[24] *Northwest Mall, Inc. v. Lubri-Lon International, Inc.,* 681 S.W.2d 797 (1984).

[25] *Becker v. Barbur Blvd. Equipment Rentals, Inc.,* 81 Or. App. 648, 726 P.2d 967 (1986).

[26] *Rockweit by Donohue v. Senecal,* 187 Wis. 2d 170, 522 N.W.2d 575 (1994).

[27] *Perotta v. Tri-State Ins. Co.,* 317 So. 2d 104, *cert. denied,* (Fla.) 330 So. 2d 20 (1976).

Damages

Chapter Objectives

- Describe the basic differences between compensatory, punitive, and nominal damages
- Explain the difference between general and special damages
- Explain how a plaintiff proves damages at trial
- Describe the basic steps involved in an asset search
- Explain the difference between a loss of consortium claim and a pain and suffering claim

 **DAMAGES IN THE CHUMLEY CASE**

Mr. Chumley's health, prior to the crash, was excellent, with only occasional ulcer trouble, and some infrequent thyroid problems. In the five years before the crash, he had missed only three days from work. However, after the collision, his health took a drastic turn for the worse. The injuries he received have had a dramatic impact on his life. In addition to his physical injuries, there are also out-of-pocket expenses and the pain and suffering he has endured.

FIGURE 8-1

Charles Chumley: Medical Bill Summary

EMS	$ 365.50
Bolstridge Memorial Hospital	$219,380.01
Haley County Hospital	$ 2,677.94
Morningside Surgical Residence Associates	$ 12,935.00
Springfield Radiological Associates	$ 4,561.00
Carr-Headley Rehabilitation	$ 83,494.41
Turlow Bone and Joint: Sean Turlow & Carla Moyers, M.D.	$ 6,151.20
Morrisville Associates	$ 760.00
Option Care Infusion Therapy	$ 11,875.00
Home Health Visits	$ 2,354.00
Total	$344,554.06

In this chapter, we address the fourth and final element of a negligence case: damages. Just as we have seen with the other three elements of a negligence claim, proof of damages involves its own set of problems.

The plaintiff's legal team must calculate the total financial loss suffered by the plaintiff. This calculation must include not only the plaintiff's medical bills, but also any other financial loss directly attributable to the collision. In addition to these damages, the plaintiff must also put a dollar amount on such intangibles as pain and suffering. In this chapter, we discuss how these damages are calculated, and how this fourth and final element of a negligence case is proved. (For a sample of the medical records involved in the Chumley case, please see the appendix.)

Mr. Chumley's injuries included a closed head injury; fractured left tibia; internal hemorrhaging; hemo-pneumothorax (blood-filled, collapsed lung); and severe abdominal trauma. In addition, he had five broken ribs and a left hip fracture. Mr. Chumley has had extensive surgery on several occasions, and suffered from severe infections. For three months following the collision, Mr. Chumley languished in a coma, his breathing controlled by a ventilator. When he finally revived, doctors noted that Mr. Chumley suffered from short-term memory loss. For example, he cannot remember anything about the collision. Several months later, he was diagnosed with diabetes mellitus. Significantly, there is no family history of diabetes. Mr. Chumley's doctors have determined that the severe trauma he received to his head and abdomen, and the resultant injuries to both his brain and his pancreas, are the most likely cause of the diabetes mellitus.

The outlook for Mr. Chumley is bleak. He has suffered extensive brain damage and internal injuries and is now suffering from severe diabetes. His doctors believe that he may only have one or two years of life left. Before the wreck occurred, Mr. Chumley had a good chance of living well into his 70s.

We have contacted an expert in economic analysis and asked him to take a look at the long-term financial impact of Mr. Chumley's injuries and the medical bills associated with Mr. Chumley's recovery and maintenance. The medical bills alone are $344,554.06. However, the expert points out that Mr. Chumley also has lost time from work and has a decreased life span, pain and suffering, and future medical needs. The figure the expert has come up with is $1,230,119.00. (For a complete copy of this report, see Appendix A.)

 **INTRODUCTION TO DAMAGES**

The final step in our analysis of negligence actions involves the element of damages. Damages refer to the monetary, property, or personal losses suffered by the plaintiff. The point of an award of damages is to restore the plaintiff to the condition he was in prior to the injury, if that is possible. A second consideration is to punish the defendant for his negligence and send a message to others that similar negligent actions will result in monetary losses.

Paying the victim for his injuries is not a new concept. Early Hebrew law provided that a person who injured another must pay a set fee for an injured hand, an injured eye, etc. This idea of apportioning a strict monetary amount for parts of the body was later revived in the schedule seen in worker's compensation statutes.[1]

Damages come in at least three broad categories, although some jurisdictions break them down in other ways. These broad categories include:

- Compensatory damages
- Punitive damages
- Nominal damages

A. COMPENSATORY DAMAGES

Compensatory damages are designed to do exactly what their title suggests: to compensate the victim for losses caused by the defendant's negligent conduct. The stated purpose of compensatory damages is to place the plaintiff in the condition she was in prior to the injury. Of course, that is often impossible. In situations where it is impossible to return the plaintiff to her original condition, compensatory damages are designed to compensate her for the change in her condition. Some jurisdictions define compensatory damages as the monetary assessments paid by the defendant to "make the plaintiff whole" again. These assessments usually take the form of monetary payments made by the defendant to the plaintiff to compensate the plaintiff for injury and property and other losses. Compensatory damages are usually divided into two separate categories: general and special damages.

When the plaintiff's injuries are financial, the jury's award of money is designed to put the plaintiff back in the situation he was in before the defendant's negligence. When the plaintiff's injuries are physical, money is seen as a form of compensation for aggravation, pain, and suffering, even though these conditions do not lend themselves to monetary calculation. The plaintiff can recover for all harm past, present, and future.

There are two types of compensatory damages: general (nonspecific) and special (specific).

ISSUE AT A GLANCE

1. GENERAL DAMAGES

General damages
Those awards that
are closely tied to
the defendant's
negligence[4]

General damages are those payments by the defendant to the plaintiff that are most closely associated with the defendant's negligent act. One example of a general damage is pain and suffering. General damages are usually harder to quantify. For instance, how much is pain and suffering actually worth? The jurors must often rely on their own feelings and life experiences to come up with a figure that they believe will compensate the plaintiff for his disfigurement, paralysis, or constant pain. The result is often unpredictable. The jury awards in two very similar cases can have wildly different amounts of general damages. In most jurisdictions, the plaintiff is not required to state a specific amount that he is seeking to recover in general damages; the plaintiff usually leaves this determination to the jury.

The Restatement uses a slightly different definition of general damages. According to the Restatement, general damages are those injuries that result so frequently from most negligence and other tort actions that their existence can be assumed and their amount can be proved at trial.

a. Pain and Suffering

How much should a jury award for the plaintiff's "pain and suffering"? The jury might turn to the judge for an instruction on this point. Unfortunately, the law here is vague. The jury is allowed to award an amount that a "reasonable person" would believe was just compensation for the plaintiff's injury. This standard allows a great deal of freedom to juries to determine what is reasonable in any particular case.

b. Presenting an Argument to the Jury for Pain and Suffering and Other General Damages

Per diem
By the day or daily

Because general damages are often difficult to quantify, an attorney will often resort to practical arguments in asking the jury to award money to his client. For instance, an attorney might present a **per diem** argument by asking the jury if it is "worth" $2 a day not to have the pain that his client suffers. The attorney might then point out that experts believe that his client will live another 20 years at a minimum. Two dollars a day, 365 days a year, for 20 years amounts to $14,600. When the plaintiff's pain is severe, or when the plaintiff has a disfiguring scar, this daily amount could easily climb to $50 a day, or even $100. These simple equations give the jury solid figures to work with. On the other hand, the defendant's attorney might argue that any large amount of money is simply a windfall to a plaintiff who is either exaggerating his pain or actively deceiving the jury.

There is no mandated mathematical formula that a jury must follow when determining general damages.

Lost earnings are usually classified as special damages, lost future earning capacity as general damages. If a complaint alleges both losses, each must be proved separately.

The following are some of the factors that an expert will use to determine lost future income:

■ What is the highest and best career the plaintiff could possibly have had?
■ How many more productive years was the plaintiff likely to have?
■ What is the plaintiff's life expectancy based on actuarial tables?
■ How does the plaintiff's current disability affect his possibility for future employment?
■ What are the plaintiff's future costs for medical treatments, rehabilitation, etc.?
■ Will the plaintiff require retraining or reeducation?
■ What is the best possible income the plaintiff can anticipate following this injury?
■ What is the total amount of all of these calculations?
■ What is the "present value" of this amount?

FIGURE 8-2

Calculating Lost Future Income

A plaintiff can recover for past and future damages if they fall into one of the following categories:

■ Bodily harm
■ Loss of or reduction in earning capacity
■ Medical expenses
■ Damage to personal property
■ Emotional distress

FIGURE 8-3

Past and Future Damages

| ■ Bodily harm
■ Pain and suffering | ■ Emotional distress |

FIGURE 8-4

General, Compensatory Damages That the Jury May Award Without Proof of Financial Loss by the Plaintiff

---

The plaintiff is entitled to request reimbursement for past losses and any future losses tied to the defendant's negligent conduct.

ISSUE AT A GLANCE

2. SPECIAL DAMAGES

Special damages are those damages that are usually easier to quantify because they have specific amounts. Examples of special damages are items such as the plaintiff's total medical bill for the injuries sustained in the accident, or the total time lost from work. Similarly, the plaintiff is also entitled to recover for payments to doctors and other medical providers for treatment received as a direct result of the defendant's actions. The plaintiff must present proof of the amount of his special damages and, in most jurisdictions, he must state an exact amount of special damages he is seeking to recover.

Special damages
Those damages, such as medical bills, closely tied to the plaintiff's injuries and for which a specific amount can usually be calculated

a. Lost Wages

To prove the plaintiff's lost wages, something more than testimony is required. A bald assertion such as "I would have made over $100,000 this year if it hadn't been for the accident" is not legally sufficient. How does the plaintiff prove actual lost wages? She must present tax returns, pay stubs, affidavits from employers or clients, IRS 1099 forms, and similar items. The paralegal is often the person directly responsible for gathering, storing, and organizing this information for trial.

b. Medical Bills

Plaintiffs are often anxious about paying their medical bills. They have received the treatment and have been billed for this service long before the case ever comes to trial. The hospital may have even attempted collection actions against the client. Usually, the plaintiff's attorney will intercede with the medical providers and at least inform them that the plaintiff's case is in litigation. However, the plaintiff often remains concerned about the payment of what are often enormous medical bills. Certainly, these bills should be summarized and pleaded in the complaint as special damages, payable by the defendant because of his negligence. The plaintiff is entitled to recovery for all medical treatments tied to the injuries she received from the defendant.

 **Special damages can usually be determined to a reasonable certainty.**

c. Future Losses

A plaintiff is permitted to seek recovery for future medical services that are reasonably certain to be required. The award is supposed to take into account all reasonable expenses relating to medical care, including charges for doctors, nurses, therapists, and medical supplies. The plaintiff is also entitled to compensation for having to hire someone else to perform her job while she is incapacitated. However, a plaintiff is not legally entitled to compensation for lost "time," that is, the time lost from leisure activities while recuperating from the injuries.

Measuring Future Lost Income

At the end of the trial, the jurors will be instructed that before they can determine an amount of future lost income, they must determine the difference between what the plaintiff's future income would have been before he was injured and what it will be now that he has been injured. Proving lost future income usually involves expert testimony. The expert will calculate future lost income, based on complicated formulas involving the plaintiff's past income, his education, his likelihood of promotion, and a wide range of other factors. (For an example of such a calculation, see Appendix A.)

		FIGURE 8-5
■ Prescription costs	■ Travel expenses (to and from	**Examples**
■ Special equipment	medical appointments)	**of Special**
■ Damage to automobile	■ Costs of doctor, psychiatrist,	**Damages**
■ Professional nursing daycare	chiropractor, etc.	

3. PROVING DAMAGES

What is the standard that the plaintiff must meet in proving his damages? Generally, the plaintiff must meet the same standard with regard to damages as he had to meet for proving the other elements of his action. In most jurisdictions, this standard is preponderance of the evidence. There is no relaxation of proof for this final element. The nature and extent of the damages and the defendant's responsibility for them must all be proved at trial before the jury is authorized to award any amount to the plaintiff. Having said this, however, there is a recognized practical limitation on this theory. If the jury is convinced of the defendant's liability for the first three elements of the negligence claim, it is impractical to think that the jurors will require the same level of proof for the plaintiff's medical and other bills.

Courts require a certain level of certainty in calculating damages. Although no court has ever developed a precise mathematical formula for doing so, most jurisdictions are in agreement that the amount of damages must be based on testimony and evidence, not mere conjecture or the emotions of the jurors.[5]

a. Why Is the Distinction Between General and Special Damages Important?

First of all, how damages are classified in a particular case is important to the plaintiff when it comes to presenting proof. General damages are often harder to prove than special damages. General damages involve intangibles such as pain and suffering and loss of emotional support. Proving these damages often involves testimony from the plaintiff's friends and family about the effect that the accident has had on her. This testimony is, by its very nature, purely subjective. On the other hand, special damages involve presentations of bills and other hard evidence. They are not subjective and they present the jury with a straightforward proposition. If the jurors believe that the defendant is responsible for the plaintiff's damages, they will usually award special damages with little demur. Another reason why the classification is important is that if the case should go up on appeal, general damages are easier for the defendant to appeal than special damages.

b. Day-in-the-Life Video

One method of proving damages in a dramatic fashion is the "day-in-the-life" video. This presentation has become almost routine in cases involving severe injuries. For instance, when a plaintiff has been left permanently disabled, the plaintiff's attorney may hire a video producer to videotape the plaintiff going through normal daily activities. These videos can be extremely effective when the jurors see just how difficult it is for a crippled plaintiff to get out of bed in the morning, or to make breakfast. The video will also show the plaintiff interacting with others, such as home health care nurses. As a visual aid, they are unsurpassed for giving the jury an accurate, and often unforgettable, peek into the plaintiff's life. The extra expense is often justified by larger jury awards for crippled plaintiffs.

c. Proving Property Losses

Different types of evidence are required to prove the existence of different types of damages. Property losses, for example, are handled differently than the evidence presented to prove pain and suffering.

Fair market value
The amount that a willing buyer would pay for an item that a willing seller would accept

When the plaintiff claims damage to or reduction in value for his property, he must present some evidence showing what the value of the property was before the defendant's actions and what the value of the property is after the defendant's negligence. This often involves calculations of the **fair market value** of the property. Fair market value is usually determined by an appraiser — someone who is an expert in the field and can give an accurate estimate of the property's value.

d. Collateral Source Rule

Collateral source rule
An evidentiary rule that prohibits the jury from being told about the plaintiff's other sources of compensation, such as insurance, worker's compensation, etc.

When a jurisdiction has a **collateral source rule,** it means that the jury cannot be told that the plaintiff has received compensation from other sources. Most people have insurance of some form, and after a person is injured, several different insurance policies will reimburse the plaintiff for medical treatment or property damage. In jurisdictions that follow the collateral source rule, the jury cannot be informed that the plaintiff has already received compensation for some of the injuries claimed in the complaint. The reasoning behind the collateral source rule is that if the jury were permitted to hear about the plaintiff's other sources of compensation, they might be inclined to lower the amount awarded to the plaintiff at the conclusion of the trial. In essence, this would penalize persons who did the right thing: obtained insurance coverage for medical treatment and property damage. A plaintiff who has fully insured himself against potential losses will end up with a smaller award than a plaintiff who failed to take such reasonable precautions. Thus, the collateral source rule prohibits the defense from introducing evidence showing that the plaintiff had other insurance coverage that has already been paid out for some of the plaintiff's injuries.

Although the jury will not be informed of the plaintiff's other sources of compensation during their deliberations, the jury's final award will be reduced by the judge to reflect the amounts that the plaintiff has already received. A jurisdiction that follows the collateral source rule does not allow a plaintiff to receive awards for injuries that have already been compensated. In the end, the judge will review the jury's award and make appropriate reductions for medical bills that have already been paid on the plaintiff's behalf.

▪ disability income ▪ worker's compensation	▪ public assistance

FIGURE 8-6

Other Compensatory Sources That the Jury May Be Told About in Jurisdictions That Follow the Collateral Source Disclosure Rule

e. Mitigation of Damages

A plaintiff is obligated to **mitigate** or lessen her damages whenever reasonably possible. This means that the plaintiff is not permitted to refuse medical treatment for the injuries caused by the defendant's negligence and then later bring an action when the injuries worsen.

For instance, in the Chumley case, Mr. Chumley's obligation to mitigate could have arisen if he had chosen not to undergo certain medical procedures, or if he failed to follow up medical attention. Certainly, a failure to take his insulin medication would raise a mitigation of damages issue.

Example: John is an independent contractor who installs roofs. One day as he is climbing up some scaffolding that has been improperly placed by Dave Defendant, he falls and injures his shoulder. John's doctor recommends that John receive immediate surgery to tighten John's shoulder muscles. John refuses. Later, John suffers from frequent subluxations, that is, his shoulder pops out of joint. The pain from this is excruciating. John brings suit against Dave for the expensive procedure involved to build up John's shoulder joint. The court rules against John, stating that John had a responsibility to mitigate his damages when doing so was reasonable.[6]

4. EMOTIONAL DISTRESS

In many jurisdictions, a plaintiff is not allowed to recover for injuries that are psychological only. In those jurisdictions, the emotional impact must be coupled with some physical impact. For instance, in these jurisdictions, a plaintiff cannot request damages when the defendant's actions cause the plaintiff to lose sleep or to feel anxious, but there is no other physical injury. In many other jurisdictions, this requirement of physical trauma has either slowly eroded or been replaced entirely with actions allowing recovery for purely emotional or psychological injuries.[8]

5. LOSS OF CONSORTIUM

Another type of damage that falls into a special category is a **loss of consortium** claim. This is a claim raised not by the injured plaintiff, but by his or her spouse. This claim states that when the plaintiff was injured, the marital relations between the plaintiff and spouse were also injured. In all jurisdictions, the spouse is entitled to file some form of loss of consortium claim. The spouse is entitled to damages for the loss of companionship, affection, sexual

Mitigation of damages
The responsibility of the plaintiff to lessen her potential injuries or losses by taking reasonable actions to seek medical treatment or take other precautions when a reasonable person in the same situation would have done so

Sidebar
Mitigation of damages is often seen in contract disputes as well. A vendor has an obligation to sell perishable merchandise to another when the original customer refuses to purchase it. The vendor can then sue the original purchaser for the difference between what he would have received on the sale and what he actually received from another purchaser.[7]

Sidebar
An award of damages for emotional distress, or mental anguish, can include not only the plaintiff's sufferings in the past, but also any mental distress the plaintiff is likely to endure in the future.[9]

Loss of consortium
A claim filed by the spouse of an injured party for the loss of companionship in the marriage caused by the injuries

relations, and other losses that frequently occur when one spouse has been injured. At trial, the plaintiff's legal team must present additional testimony and evidence to prove this claim. Often, the affected spouse will take the stand and give testimony about the marital relationship prior to the plaintiff's injuries and how that relationship has been affected since the accident.

6. PRIOR INJURIES

One of the best attacks that the defendant's attorney can mount against the plaintiff is a claim that the plaintiff was actually injured in a prior accident and this prior accident is what caused his pain, not the collision he had with the defendant. A paralegal should always ask the plaintiff about any prior medical problems, including prior accidents or collisions. Any prior injury that is even vaguely like the current injury should be closely documented. At trial, the plaintiff's attorney will have to address this issue of prior injuries, to make sure that the jury understands that this prior injury has nothing to do with the

FIGURE 8-7

Median Compensatory and Punitive Final Awards for Plaintiff Winners in Select Trial Cases

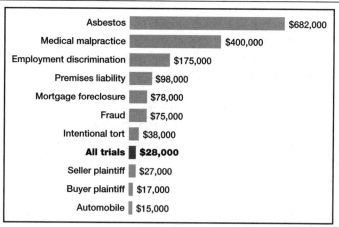

Civil Bench and Jury Trials in State Courts, 2005, Bureau of Statistics, U.S. Department of Justice.

FIGURE 8-8

Learning About Prior Injuries: Three Proven Methods

1 *Ask the client.* The best way to learn about prior injuries and accidents is to simply ask the client. Most clients will be honest and forthright about prior injuries, but there are always some who try to conceal these facts.

2 *Review the medical records carefully.* You should always carefully review the medical records provided by the client and returned by medical offices through discovery. Occasionally, you will see a reference to a "prior complaint." This, or similar language, indicates that the client has been injured before.

3 *Review prior lawsuits.* Even if the client claims that she has never been involved in a prior lawsuit, a quick check of the local docket is always a good idea. Sometimes clients genuinely forget prior suits. Other times, a client may be actively deceiving his legal team. Better to know this before the defense attorney produces it — with a dramatic flourish — in the middle of the trial.

■ Claim has no basis in fact or law	■ Attorney or party harasses opposition	**FIGURE 8-9**
■ Suit involves a matter that is clearly frivolous	■ Attorney or party engages in unnecessary delaying tactics	**Actions That Could Justify a Claim of Bad Faith**
■ Attorney makes threats against opposition witnesses		

current claim and to deflate any attempt by the defense to make a dramatic presentation during its case.

7. BAD FAITH DAMAGES

Often confused with punitive damages (discussed later), bad faith damages generally do not involve the facts of the case but involve instead a party's conduct during the litigation. For instance, if a plaintiff brings a lawsuit solely for the purpose of harassing the defendant, the plaintiff may be subject to bad faith damages. In such a situation, the court might order that the plaintiff pay the costs of the action and the defendant's attorney's fee. Normally, the losing party in a suit is not required to pay the fees of the opposing attorney. However, when a party files frivolous claims or has engaged in unethical or unfair tactics, a judge is authorized to make such an award.[10]

TEXAS MOTO-PLEX, INC. v. PHELPS
2006 WL 246520 (Tex. App.-Eastland 2006)

MEMORANDUM OPINION

Terry McCall, Justice.
This case involved an accident at a motocross facility when a rider, John Phelps, struck a tractor performing track maintenance behind a jump. The other rider, Bryce Hawk, missed the tractor but was also injured. Phelps and Hawk sued Texas Moto-Plex, Inc. and obtained a judgment for actual and punitive damages. Texas Moto-Plex appeals, contending that plaintiffs' claims were barred by a pre-accident release; plaintiffs' expert was improperly allowed to testify about James Teague's (a co-owner of the track) subjective awareness of an extreme degree of risk to the riders; the evidence was legally and factually insufficient to show gross negligence; the riders were contributorily negligent; the punitive damages awarded to Hawk were excessive; and the trial court applied the wrong prejudgment and postjudgment interest rate. We find the punitive damages awarded to Hawk are excessive but, otherwise, affirm.

Background Facts
Phelps and Hawk traveled to Texas Moto-Plex, a new motocross track in Fort Bend County, to practice riding. Texas Moto-Plex charged riders an

entrance fee and required them to sign a release. Phelps went to the registration shed to pay the fees and sign the release. A Texas Moto-Plex employee told Phelps that two tractors and a bulldozer were grooming the back section of the track. Phelps walked outside, saw the equipment, and then paid for both. With Hawk's permission, Phelps signed the release for both. Phelps told Hawk about the track maintenance. Hawk looked toward the track and observed the bulldozer working.

Phelps and Hawk finished unloading their bikes and putting on their riding gear. They entered the track from the designated starting gate and slowly rolled the track on their motorcycles to check its condition. They saw the tractors and bulldozer working on the back portion of the track and were able to avoid them using a detour created by previous riders.

Phelps and Hawk rode for approximately two hours, during which time they took two breaks. They refueled one of the motorcycles during the brief second break. When they reentered the track, they did so at the second turn rather than the starting gate. Also during this break, Lindsay Wadsworth moved the tractor he was operating from the back side of the track to the area between the first jump and third turn.

Phelps and Hawk were unaware that Wadsworth had moved the tractor. They did not do another slow roll but proceeded to ride at normal speed. They did not see the tractor until they were airborne coming off of the first jump. Hawk was able to avoid the tractor by jumping off of his motorcycle. He sustained only minor injuries and did not require medical assistance. Phelps, however, struck the tractor and broke his leg. Phelps ultimately required two surgeries.

Phelps and Hawk sued Texas Moto-Plex for negligence and gross negligence. Texas Moto-Plex admitted its negligence but denied that it was grossly negligent and contended that Phelps and Hawk were at least partly to blame for their own injuries. The case was tried to a jury which found Texas Moto-Plex solely responsible for the injuries and awarded Phelps actual damages of $191,931 and Hawk actual damages of $1,000. The jury also found that their injuries resulted from Texas Moto-Plex's gross negligence and awarded each plaintiff exemplary damages of $75,000.

Did the Trial Court Err by Allowing Appellees' Expert to Testify Regarding Texas Moto-Plex's Knowledge?

Phelps and Hawk were required to obtain a malice finding to recover punitive damages. The statute in effect at the time for this case, Tex. Civ. Prac. & Rem. Code §41.001(7)(B) (1997), defined "malice" as either a specific intent to cause substantial injury (which was not alleged) or an act or omission:

> (i) which when viewed objectively from the standpoint of the actor at the time of its occurrence involves an extreme degree of risk, considering the probability and magnitude of the potential harm to others; and
> (ii) of which the actor has actual, subjective awareness of the risk involved, but nevertheless proceeds in conscious indifference to the rights, safety, or welfare of others.

The current statute defines "malice" as a specific intent to cause substantial injury or harm, and the former alternative definition of "malice" is now the definition for "gross negligence." In this opinion, we use the terms "malice" and "gross negligence" as synonyms.

Texas Moto-Plex argues that the trial court erroneously allowed appellees' expert, Randall Alan Nelson, to testify that Texas Moto-Plex had actual, subjective awareness of an extreme degree of risk. Texas Moto-Plex does not dispute that Nelson was a motocross expert, and the record supports that proposition. Nelson had ridden and raced motorcycles since the 1950s and had served as a referee and technical director for two national motorcycle associations.

The trial court's decision to admit Nelson's testimony is subject to an abuse of discretion review, *Nat'l Liab. & Fire Ins. Co. v. Allen*, 15 S.W.3d 525, 527-28 (Tex. 2000), and a harmful error analysis. *Horizon/CMS Healthcare Corp. v. Auld*, 34 S.W.3d 887, 906 (Tex. 2000).

There are significant limits on the ability of a person to testify about another's state of mind and to offer expert opinions. Texas Moto-Plex correctly notes that under Tex. R. Evid. 702 expert testimony must be based upon "scientific, technical, or other specialized knowledge" as to which a witness could be qualified as an expert by "knowledge, skill, experience, training, or education" and that it must "assist the trier of fact to understand the evidence or to determine a fact in issue."

Texas Moto-Plex, however, overstates the extent of Nelson's testimony. Nelson's testimony was not an unsupported, conclusory opinion on Texas Moto-Plex's state of mind but, rather, was more fairly described as a recitation of largely undisputed facts. This is best shown by the following testimony:

> Q. Please explain what acts or omissions of the owners of Texas Moto-Plex, when viewed from their standpoint at the time of the occurrence, involved an extreme degree of risk considering the probability of the potential harm to others and of which were — they were aware of the risk involved, but nevertheless proceeded with conscious indifference.
>
> A. I think that they had an understanding that these motorcycles are traveling at significant speeds, certainly 40 to 60 miles an hour, maybe greater speeds. And I certainly believe that they would have an understanding that if one of these motorcycles ran point-blank into a piece of earthmoving equipment, that it would be catastrophic for the operator. I think they also knew that motorcycles are circuiting this course when they put this piece of equipment there, and they put that piece of equipment there giving instructions to a sixteen-year-old person for operating it. So I — I just believe they had to understand that what an impact between a motorcycle and one of these vehicles could do to an operator, could kill them easily, and certainly that they're moving these pieces of equipment without — certainly we understand they had some notice that they were on the back side at some point in time, but with no additional notice they're moving them around the track in a hide-and-go-seek kind of a situation where the — it could be devastating, and in fact was devastating in this case.

The record establishes that these facts were undisputed and were known to Texas Moto-Plex. The senior Texas Moto-Plex official present at the time of the accident was Teague. He was a co-owner of the track and was driving one of the tractors. Texas Moto-Plex's employee, Joe Salinas, testified that riders usually hit the first jump traveling more than forty miles an hour with the more aggressive riders doing fifty to sixty miles an hour. Clearly, if a motorcycle traveling at that speed hit a tractor or bulldozer, one could expect serious injuries to result. Teague admitted that the track was open while the equipment was performing its maintenance activities. The tractor behind the first jump was being driven by Lindsey Wadsworth, who was seventeen years old at the time. Teague is the one who told Wadsworth to go work the area between the first jump and third turn. Phelps and Hawk were warned about the equipment when they arrived but received no notice that Wadsworth's tractor was being moved.

Does the Record Support the Jury's Malice Finding?

The jury found that the injuries of Phelps and Hawk resulted from Texas Moto-Plex's malice which Phelps and Hawk were required to prove by clear and convincing evidence. Tex. Civ. Prac. & Rem. Code Ann. §41.003 (Vernon 1997). Texas Moto-Plex challenges these findings on legally and factually insufficient evidence grounds.

When the burden of proof is by clear and convincing evidence, evidence is legally insufficient when no reasonable fact-finder could form a firm belief or conviction that the matter to be proven is true. *In re J.F.C.*, 96 S.W.3d 256, 264-65 (Tex. 2002). For this review, we must consider all the evidence and not just the evidence favoring the verdict. *City of Keller v. Wilson*, 168 S.W.3d 802, 817 (Tex. 2005). For factual sufficiency challenges, the question is whether the evidence is such that a fact-finder could reasonably form a firm belief or conviction that the defendant is guilty of malice. *In re C.H.*, 89 S.W.3d 17, 18-19, 25 (Tex. 2002).

Section 41.001(7)(B)'s definition of malice mirrors the Texas Supreme Court's definition of gross negligence in *Transp. Ins. Co. v. Moriel*, 879 S.W.2d 10, 23 (Tex. 1994). A review of case law discussing gross negligence findings is, therefore, helpful in addressing this issue.

Malice or gross negligence requires much more than ordinary negligence. Rather, a plaintiff must prove the presence of both an objective element (extreme risk) and a subjective element (actual awareness). See *Mobil Oil Corp. v. Ellender*, 968 S.W.2d 917, 921 (Tex. 1998). Extreme risk requires more than the remote possibility of injury or a high probability of minor harm but instead requires proof that serious injury to the plaintiff was likely. *Universal Servs. Co. v. Ung*, 904 S.W.2d 638, 641 (Tex. 1995). Actual awareness requires proof that the defendant knew about the peril but that its acts or omissions demonstrate that it did not care. See *Wal-Mart Stores, Inc. v. Alexander*, 868 S.W.2d 322, 326 (Tex. 1993).

A. Extreme Risk

It is undisputed that maintenance work was being performed by a bulldozer and two tractors when Phelps and Hawk arrived at the track, that they were advised of this, and that they did in fact see the equipment before entering the track. It is also undisputed that Phelps and Hawk took a slow lap when they entered the track, that they saw the equipment, and that they noted a detour path made by previous riders. Phelps and Hawk rode on the track for approximately two hours during which time the equipment remained in the same location. While taking a break, one of the tractors moved from the back to an area between the first jump and third turn.

Phelps and Hawk received no express warning that the tractor had been moved. No track employee told them about the movement; and no flags, signs, or other warning devices were employed. Texas Moto-Plex contends that Phelps and Hawk failed to enter the track at the starting gate and that, if they had done so, they would have seen the tractor. Texas Moto-Plex also argues that, if they had taken a slow lap before resuming their ride, they would have seen the tractor. Those assertions, however, are not relevant to the question of whether moving the equipment so that it was behind a ramp without providing appellees an express warning created an extreme risk.

The jury's finding is adequately supported even without reference to the disputed expert testimony. It is common knowledge that motocross riding involves high speeds and jumping. In fact, tracks are designed to facilitate that with the use of dirt ramps and banked turns. Having tractors engaged in maintenance activities on the track at the same time as it is being used by motocross riders creates the very risk manifested here: collisions between riders and equipment.

B. Subjective Awareness

This was a new track. Teague, a co-owner, was on-site and performing track maintenance at the time of the accident. Wadsworth, a young motocross rider, was performing volunteer maintenance work using one of the track's two tractors. They were working on the back of the track when appellees arrived. Eventually, Teague instructed Wadsworth to move to the area around turn three. Teague testified that he did not expect Wadsworth to work on any other area besides turn three and that he never saw him more than one-half way between the turn and the first jump. Wadsworth testified that Teague instructed him to work the area between the back end of the third turn and the bottom of the first jump.

Motocross is an individual sport involving both skill and strategy. Motocross tracks are designed with this in mind. Teague acknowledged, for example, that every rider is different and that different people would hit the first jump differently. Teague testified that he would travel approximately ten feet on the first jump, while others might travel as far as seventy-five feet. Riders will travel at considerably different speeds due both to different levels of skill and at different parts of the track. It is not unusual for them to travel between forty to sixty mph.

There was considerable dispute about how much a careful rider might see beyond the first jump as he approached it and where one should start riding on the track. For example, Teague testified that he always rode looking two turns ahead. Phelps and Hawk, on the other hand, testified that they were required to pay attention to the track in front of them and that it was impossible for them to see what was on the back side of the first jump. Texas

Moto-Plex contended that Phelps and Hawk should have begun at the starting gate. Phelps and Hawk testified that everyone who was not practicing their racing starts started where they did and that it was safer to do so.

Although Salinas testified that he told Phelps that the equipment might move, Phelps was adamant in his testimony that Salinas had not said that. Phelps testified that his impression from what Salinas said that day was that the tractors would only be working in the area where he first saw them.

Teague disputed the need for flaggers or other express warning devices contending that he did not realize Wadsworth was so close to the bottom of the first jump and that the accident would have been avoided if appellees had been more careful by taking a slow lap or entering the track at the starting gate. Teague also contended it was common practice for machinery to operate on the track during practice sessions. Nelson, on the other hand, testified that track maintenance should not be going on while riders are on the track. Nelson also testified that, in sending Wadsworth to work between the third turn and first jump, Teague had to realize that he created a hazard that posed a high degree of risk to the riders.

It was the jury's role to resolve this conflicting testimony. *Golden Eagle Archery, Inc. v. Jackson,* 116 S.W.3d 757, 761 (Tex. 2003) (jurors are the sole judges of the credibility of the witnesses and the weight to be given their testimony). We believe that testimony in the record is both legally and factually sufficient to establish:

(1) Teague was aware heavy equipment and motorcycle riders were on the track at the same time;

(2) Teague opted to do this for economic reasons rather than close the track or utilize an express warning system;

(3) Teague asked Wadsworth to move his tractor from the back side of the track to work the area between the third turn and first jump;

(4) Teague was aware Wadsworth's tractor was operating between the third turn and first jump;

(5) Riders approaching the first jump would have at least reduced ability to see equipment on the jump's back side;

(6) If a motorcycle rider struck a tractor or bulldozer it could cause considerable injury; and

(7) Teague did not advise the riders on the track that the equipment was being moved to a different location.

There was legally and factually sufficient evidence that Teague and thus Texas Moto-Plex created an extreme risk and was subjectively aware of that risk but chose to proceed nonetheless with conscious indifference to the safety of Phelps and Hawk. Texas Moto-Plex's legal and factual sufficiency challenges to the jury's malice findings are overruled.

Punitive Damages

The jury awarded Phelps compensatory damages of $191,931 and punitive damages of $75,000. The jury awarded Hawk compensatory damages of $1,000 and punitive damages of $75,000. Texas Moto-Plex challenges the award to Hawk contending it is based upon factually insufficient evidence or, alternatively, it is constitutionally excessive.

A. The Test for Factual Sufficiency

Exemplary damage awards must be reasonable in amount and rational in light of their purpose to punish malicious conduct and deter its repetition. *Lubbock County v. Strube*, 953 S.W.2d 847 (Tex. App.-Austin 1997, *pet. denied*). We may reverse an exemplary damage award or suggest a remittitur only if we determine that the evidence supporting the award is so factually insufficient or the verdict is so against the great weight and preponderance of the evidence as to be manifestly unjust. Id. The Texas Supreme Court has adopted five factors, commonly referred to as the "*Kraus*" factors, for our analysis. They are:

(1) the nature of the wrong;
(2) the character of the conduct involved;
(3) the degree of culpability of the wrongdoer;
(4) the situation and sensibilities of the parties concerned; and
(5) the extent to which such conduct offends a public sense of justice and propriety.

Alamo Nat'l Bank v. Kraus, 616 S.W.2d 908, 910 (Tex. 1981).

The relevant evidence, without reference to the challenged expert testimony, has been discussed above in our review of the sufficiency of the jury's malice finding and will not be repeated here. We believe that the evidence is factually sufficient to support a punitive damage award. The amount of that award is, in our opinion, controlled more by recent constitutional authority rather than the application of the *Kraus* factors; and, therefore, we will turn to constitutional principles to review the propriety of the jury's award.

B. The Test for Constitutional Due Process

Courts have long struggled to ascertain the constitutional limits on punitive damage awards. The U.S. Supreme Court recently revisited this issue in *State Farm Mut. Auto. Ins. Co. v. Campbell*, 538 U.S. 408, 123 S. Ct. 1513, 155 L. Ed. 2d 585 (2003). The Court recognized that states possess discretion over the imposition of punitive damages but that this discretion is limited by the Due Process Clause of the Fourteenth Amendment which prohibits the imposition of grossly excessive or arbitrary punishments. Id. at 416.

The Supreme Court in *Campbell* reaffirmed *BMW of N. Am., Inc. v. Gore*, 517 U.S. 559, 116 S. Ct. 1589, 134 L. Ed. 2d 809 (1996), and its three-part analysis for reviewing punitive damage awards. *Campbell*, 538 U.S. at 418. Courts are required to consider three guideposts: (1) the degree of reprehensibility of the defendant's misconduct; (2) the disparity between the actual or potential harm suffered by the plaintiff and the punitive damages award; and (3) the difference between the punitive damages awarded by the jury and the civil penalties authorized or imposed in comparable cases. *Gore*, 517 U.S. at 575. The Supreme Court, however, indicated that, while applying the second guidepost, "in practice, few awards exceeding a single-digit ratio between punitive and compensatory damages, to a significant degree, will satisfy due process." *Campbell,* 538 U.S. at 425.

The jury's punitive damage award was seventy-five times Hawk's compensatory award. On its face, this would suggest the award is constitutionally excessive. Hawk, however, correctly notes that *Gore* allows consideration of not only the actual damages but also the potential for harm a defendant's conduct caused. One need look only at Phelps's injuries to appreciate that Hawk was fortunate and could easily have been more severely injured. Hawk asks us to not give Texas Moto-Plex "credit for the fortuitous outcome of this accident in Hawk's case."

The Supreme Court has held that "the most important indicium of the reasonableness of a punitive damages award is the degree of reprehensibility of the defendant's conduct." *Gore,* 517 U.S. at 575. Teague was guilty of poor judgment; but his conduct involved no intentional act, ill-will, spite, evil motive or the purposeful injury of another. Teague was not in a position of trust, such as a fiduciary. Nor was any evidence introduced indicating any pattern of misconduct by Teague or any other Texas Moto-Plex agent or employee.

Phelps testified that he did not believe that anyone should be punished. Nelson, the expert, agreed that Teague did not strike him as being cruel or criminal or as being a bad man. But, rather, Teague seemed to be someone who made a mistake.

We believe that Hawk's punitive damage award violates the Due Process Clause of the Fourteenth Amendment. Texas Moto-Plex has requested a remittitur to reduce the award of $75,000 to $9,000 which would be nine times Hawk's actual damage award. Under the facts of this case, that request is appropriate.

Conclusion

The trial court's judgment is affirmed except for the award of excessive punitive damages to Hawk. Texas Moto-Plex's request for a remittitur is granted. Pursuant to Tex. R. App. P. 46.3, if within fifteen days of the date of this opinion Hawk files a remittitur of his punitive damage award from $75,000 to $9,000, then the judgment will be reformed to reflect the remittitur and, as reformed, affirmed. If the remittitur is not timely filed, then the trial court's judgment as to Hawk will be reversed; and his claim remanded to the trial court for a new trial.

Questions about the case:

1. What activities led to the plaintiffs' injuries in this case?
2. Why was it significant that the defendants moved the tractor during a break?
3. Why was it necessary that the jury find malice on the part of the defendants before punitive or exemplary damages could be awarded?
4. According to the court, what is "extreme risk"?
5. What factors must a court consider in order to find that an award of punitive damages is reasonable?

B. PUNITIVE DAMAGES

An award of punitive damages against a defendant is the jury's way of punishing the defendant for particular actions. Punitive damages are awarded in addition to compensatory damages. When the jury awards punitive damages, the jurors are essentially sending a message to the defendant that his conduct was particularly reprehensible and deserves to be punished. The jury in a civil case is not empowered to request jail time for the defendant, so the only real punitive action the jury can take is financial.

1. TORT REFORM AND PUNITIVE DAMAGES

Many jurisdictions have passed statutes that limit the jury's total amount of punitive damages in any case to an amount that is three times the total amount of compensatory damages. These statutes were passed out of a perception of runaway juries awarding millions of dollars to plaintiffs in punitive damages for relatively minor lawsuits. Whether this perception is true is a matter of some debate.

1930s	Researchers begin to link smoking with health problems.	**FIGURE 8-10**
1940s	Major movie stars smoke cigarettes in their movies; cigarettes seen as "cool."	**The Changing Social and Legal Attitudes Toward Nicotine**
1964	U.S. Surgeon General links smoking with lung cancer.	
1964+	Lawsuits based partly on the Surgeon General's report are almost all unsuccessful. Courts rule that smokers do not have a cause of action when they voluntarily take up the smoking habit.	
1966	New federal statute requires health warnings on all cigarette packages.	
1971	All cigarette advertisements on television and radio are banned.	
1973	Arizona becomes the first state to restrict smoking in public buildings. Over the next few years, most states follow suit.	
1988	Surgeon General C. Everett Koop states that tobacco is as addictive as cocaine or heroin.	
1994	Top cigarette executives testify before Congress that cigarettes are not addictive.	
1994	Minnesota and Mississippi bring the first successful lawsuit against the tobacco industry, under the theory of being reimbursed for their payments to Medicaid for medical bills of people who had died from smoking-induced health problems. Other states quickly follow suit.	
1995	FDA places tighter advertising restrictions on tobacco products, especially those aimed at underage smokers.	
1995	FDA makes the controversial ruling that nicotine can be regulated like any other drug; tobacco companies sue, and eventually that determination is overturned.	
1996	Former tobacco executive admits that his company knew that nicotine was addictive, and had studies confirming that fact going back to the 1950s.	
1998	Tobacco industry settles lawsuits with 46 states for $206 billion, making it the largest civil settlement in U.S. history.	

Punitive damages are relatively rare in negligence actions because, by the very nature of the claim, the plaintiff's injuries were caused by inattention, not out of malice. However, punitive damages can be awarded in negligence cases where the defendant's actions reveal a wanton disregard for the safety of others. Punitive damages can be awarded against a corporation or an employer.[11]

In some jurisdictions, punitive damages are not permitted against a deceased defendant. Because punitive damages are designed to punish, the fact of the defendant's death precludes this application. In many jurisdictions, a person who has been declared legally insane cannot be forced to pay punitive damages.

Punitive damages are designed to punish the defendant for his actions; they can be tailored to his actions and his income.

---

2. TOBACCO COMPANIES AND PUNITIVE DAMAGES

In 2001, a Florida jury awarded a staggering $144 billion in punitive damages against the tobacco industry. After deliberating only four hours, the jury announced its verdict, which easily surpassed the largest punitive damages award ever assessed in that state. The case involved a class action lawsuit against several tobacco companies, including Philip Morris U.S.A. Inc.

C. NOMINAL DAMAGES

A brief word should be said here about nominal damages. A nominal damage is the jury's award of a small amount of money to the plaintiff. In some cases, the plaintiff may have received a legal injury, but the jury does not believe that a large payment is either warranted or justified. In such a case, the jury may award the plaintiff the amount of $1, to show that although the plaintiff presented a technically proficient case, as far as the jury is concerned, the plaintiff's actual injuries are non-existent. Generally, nominal damages are not seen in typical negligence cases because the plaintiff must prove loss as part of his case.

D. EQUITABLE REMEDIES

There are times when a plaintiff's demand cannot be satisfied by monetary damages. For example, suppose that Gail has a large, 300-year-old oak tree in front of her home. One day, the local telephone company informs her that they are planning to cut the tree down to make room for a new telephone pole. Gail brings suit to stop the telephone company. In this case, she is not seeking monetary damages for the removal of the tree; she is asking the court to order the telephone company not to cut the tree down. Her suit invokes the court's equity powers. **Equity** refers to a court's power to enforce justice.

When a plaintiff brings suit requesting an **injunction,** as Gail is doing in this case, the plaintiff is asking the court for an order specifically directing someone to stop performing a specific action. In this case, the court could order that the telephone company cease and desist in its plans to cut down the tree. Simply because Gail has requested an injunction doesn't mean that the court will grant it. In fact, the court will have a hearing in which the judge decides whether to grant the injunction. Once the court enters an order, if a person ignores the order the court can punish the party through its contempt powers.

A court's equity power can be exercised alongside its normal powers. For example, it is common for the parties in a personal injury suit to seek a **declaratory judgment** about a particular issue in the case. An insurance company might file such an action to determine if it is legally bound to provide (and pay for) a legal defense in a situation in which their insured is sued. (For further discussion about these issues, see Chapter 13.)

Another example of an equitable remedy is a temporary restraining order. This order specifically directs a person to stop performing a specific action and sets a date for a full-court hearing on the plaintiff's request. Temporary restraining orders are usually seen in situations where immediate action is required and there is no time to set a later court date. Gail might file for a temporary restraining order if the telephone company employees show up and begin preparing to cut down the tree. Temporary restraining orders are often seen in cases of domestic violence as well.

Equity
The court's authority to order individuals and corporations to do (or not do) certain activities because they are unjust

Injunction
A court order that demands a certain action, or that prohibits a certain action

Declaratory judgment
A court order that specifies the duties and obligations of a party

 ## EVALUATING A CASE FOR POTENTIAL DAMAGES

One of the first questions that a plaintiff usually asks her attorney once the lawsuit is underway is, "How much money am I going to get from this case?" The defendant might ask, "How much am I likely to lose?" Unfortunately, there is no reference book that can provide the answer to either question. Each case is unique, and any experienced lawyer will probably answer both questions the same way: "It depends." The final verdict in any lawsuit depends on many different factors: the nature of the claim, the type of injuries, the quality of the opposing counsel, the judge's rulings, and the ultimate makeup of the jury. Whether you are affiliated with the plaintiff or the defense, it makes sense to understand some of the factors that go into evaluating a case.

A. EVALUATING A CASE

Case evaluations are not an exact science. They rely on both objective facts and an intuitive understanding of judges and juries. The most important starting point for any case evaluation involves an objective and hard-nosed review of the facts.

B. REVIEWING THE FACTS OF A CASE

Even before you review the plaintiff's injuries, careful attention must first be paid to the defendant's liability. Here is where a firm understanding of the four elements of a negligence action is absolutely essential. Once you have gone through the four-step analysis of duty, breach of duty, causation, and damages that we have outlined in the past four chapters, there is one other consideration that usually goes into any case evaluation: the likelihood of recovery.

There are times when the case against the defendant is easy to prove, but he has no assets. Pursuing such a claim would only be an exercise in futility. No matter how good the case against the defendant, if he has no financial

FIGURE 8-11

Reasons for Conducting an Asset Search

- To determine if a lawsuit will result in a likely recovery
- To collect on a judgment
- To locate hidden assets
- To locate assets in a probate matter

FIGURE 8-12

Some of the More Famous (or Infamous) Jury Verdict Awards

Hot coffee:
In 1992, a woman in New Mexico was awarded $3 million in punitive damages when she was scalded by a cup of hot coffee. However, she never received that amount. In a settlement after trial, she was awarded a much smaller (and confidential) amount to avoid a lengthy appeals process.

O.J. Simpson:
In 1997, a civil jury awarded the families of Ronald Goldman and Nicole Brown Simpson $8.5 million in compensatory damages and $12.5 million in punitive damages against former football star O.J. Simpson in a wrongful death action.

Exxon Valdez:
In 2002, the U.S. Supreme Court refused to overturn a jury award of $5 billion against Exxon Oil Company for the Exxon *Valdez* oil spill off the coast of Alaska in 1989 — still the worst oil spill in U.S. history.

FIGURE 8-13

Verdict Form

We the jury find, as to Count One of the Complaint

For the Plaintiff
For the Defendant

(Only when the jury has found for the Plaintiff) we further find that defendant is liable to the plaintiff in the amount of $_____.

resources it is ultimately going to be a waste of time to bring a lawsuit against him. These are the brutal lessons of legal finances. Moral victories may vindicate the soul, but they do not pay salaries.

C. ASSET SEARCHES

In many situations, the law firm may conduct an asset search of a defendant before deciding to accept a case. It is always important to assess the defendant's ability to pay damages long before the actual complaint is filed. If the defendant is covered by an insurance policy, knowing the policy limits is an important consideration (if they can be learned prior to filing the complaint).

In the practical world that attorneys must inhabit, a great case might become one to pass up for the simple reason that the defendant is "judgment proof." Such a defendant has no assets, no insurance coverage, and no other way of paying any damages assessed against him by the jury. In such a case, an asset search prior to filing would be an excellent precaution.

Sidebar

In most jurisdictions, the judge is authorized to overturn the jury's award of damages, even to overturn the jury's verdict, if the judge believes that the jury's award does not conform to the facts of the case. If the defendant loses the trial, he will often request that the judge take just such an action. This motion is called a JNOV (judgment non obstante veredicto: a judgment "notwithstanding the verdict").

D. JURY'S FUNCTION IS ASSESSING DAMAGES

When a party seeks damages, it is usually up to the jury to decide what amount, if any, should be awarded. In cases in which the case is tried before a judge without a jury, the judge assumes that role. Once the jury has heard all of the evidence and the judge has instructed the jury on the law of damages, it is up to the jury to determine the final amount. In complex cases, the jury will often be given a verdict form to help in deciding the issues.

E. JURY INSTRUCTIONS

Before the jurors retire to consider the verdict, the judge will inform them about the law in the case. This is called a jury charge, or jury instruction. In a jury charge, the judge reads the applicable law to the jurors to help guide them in their deliberations. For instance, in a case involving punitive damages, the judge might read the following jury charge:

> Ladies and gentlemen of the jury, I hereby instruct you that you may award punitive damages only if you find by a preponderance of the evidence that the conduct of the defendant in this case was malicious or taken in reckless disregard of plaintiffs' rights.

When the jurors retire to consider the facts of the case and how they should finally decide the case, they are supposed to be guided by the jury instructions. The jury charge in a negligence case could easily run to dozens of pages. In these days of copy machines and computers, many judges give a written copy of the charge to the jurors to aid them in their deliberations.

FIGURE 8-14

Types of Civil Cases Receiving Punitive Damages

- In 2001, 6%, or 356, of the 6,504 civil trials with plaintiff winners in state courts in the nation's 75 largest counties resulted in punitive damage awards.

- The types of tort cases in which plaintiff winners were most likely to receive punitive damages included slander/libel (58%), intentional torts (36%), and false arrest/imprisonment (26%) cases.

Punitive Damages Awards in Large Counties, 2001, Bureau of Justice Statistics, U.S. Department of Justice.

FIGURE 8-15

Final Awards for Plaintiff Winners

Over 60% of plaintiff winners were granted final awards of $50,000 or less

Plaintiff winners in civil bench and jury trials were awarded an estimated sum of $6 billion in compensatory and punitive damages in 2005. Among the 14,000 plaintiffs awarded monetary damages, the median final award amount was $28,000. Contract cases in general had higher median awards ($35,000) than tort cases ($24,000).

Almost two-thirds (62%) of all plaintiff award winners were awarded $50,000 or less. A small percentage (about 4%) of all plaintiff award winners were awarded $1 million or more. Plaintiff winners in asbestos cases tended to win the highest award amounts. The median final award in asbestos cases was almost $700,000. More than three-quarters of all award amounts in asbestos cases were greater than $250,000.

Cases with median final awards over $150,000 included other product liability ($500,000), medical malpractice ($400,000), false arrest or imprisonment ($259,000), employment discrimination ($175,000), and tortious interference ($169,000).

Motor vehicle accident cases accounted for more than 40% of all plaintiff award winners in 2005. The median award in motor vehicle accident cases was $15,000. Forty percent of plaintiff winners in motor vehicle accident trials were awarded $10,000 or less.

Civil Bench and Jury Trials in State Courts, 2005, Bureau of Justice Statistics, U.S. Department of Justice.

 SKILLS YOU NEED IN THE REAL WORLD

Keeping Track of Medical Records

It is surprising how many clients fail to keep an accurate record of their medical bills. The paralegal must often work with the client for days or even weeks to get copies of all the different medical bills. Clients often forget about treatments they have received, who gave them, and when they received them. In addition to the doctors' bills, the client should be reminded to keep track of receipts for items such as:

- Prosthetic devices: walkers, canes, crutches, etc.
- Over-the-counter medication purchases: aspirin, etc.
- Comfort aids such as special head rests, cushions, or mattresses

Once all the medical providers have been documented, a complete and accurate list should be developed for the amounts owed. Thoroughness is absolutely essential at this stage. If the plaintiff fails to request sufficient special damages before the case is resolved, she cannot go back and request additional compensation from the defendant. When the case is resolved, the defendant is only obligated to pay the amount in the jury verdict or the agreed-upon settlement. Any undiscovered charges become the plaintiff's responsibility.

THE LIFE OF A PARALEGAL

Paperwork and Phones

My biggest surprise about working for a lawyer is that there is nothing magical about paperwork. For instance, when you need to file a motion, you type it up, have the attorney sign it and take it over to the courthouse or call a courier to take it for you. It's no big deal. That absolutely shocked me. I had visions of every court document requiring triple signatures and service guys who had to formally accept it from you. It's like that with certificates of service. You prove that you served a document by saying that you did it. That's it. I almost had a heart attack the first time that I had to file a motion at the courthouse. When I handed it to the clerk, she didn't even look at it. She just stamped it and that was it. I always thought that this stuff was very formal and required all kinds of technicalities.

The hardest part of my job is juggling all of the different tasks. You are doing all of this work and you still have to answer the telephone. The phone has to be the top priority because that's how clients contact you, and you have to be available. When a judge calls, you have to drop everything and give it your total attention. In between phone calls, you are trying to figure out what priority to give to other tasks. I don't guess; I ask the attorney for some direction. I make her prioritize. I'll say, "Which of these is the most important to you?" It isn't always what I think. Sometimes it's more important that a letter get mailed than a motion get filed. I wouldn't have thought that before I started working here. I would have thought that a court document always gets higher priority than a letter, but it all depends on what's going on in a particular case.

Celeste Jenks, Paralegal

ETHICAL ISSUES FOR THE PARALEGAL: NATIONAL PARALEGAL ASSOCIATIONS

There are two major national paralegal associations, the National Federation of Paralegal Associations (NFPA) and the National Association of Legal Assistants. Practicing paralegals and paralegal students are eligible to join either or both of these organizations. Benefits of membership include newsletters, annual conventions, and a ready-made network of friendly professionals who can often assist a paralegal with difficult or unusual legal matters. Both organizations have created model rules of ethical behavior for paralegals. The Web sites for both are provided below.

In addition to these national organizations, almost all states have some form of local paralegal association. These smaller chapters meet regularly to discuss important issues and practice concerns. You can often locate a local paralegal association by contacting the bar association or by asking practicing paralegals.

Chapter Summary

The final element in a negligence case is the plaintiff's proof of loss, or damages. A plaintiff's request for damages can fall into three broad categories: compensatory, punitive, and nominal damages. Compensatory damages are the plaintiff's out-of-pocket losses and losses for pain and suffering. Compensatory damages can be divided into general damages and special damages. General damages consist of the plaintiff's losses that are difficult to quantify. How much is it worth to the plaintiff to endure the pain associated with his injuries? This question is answered by the jury in its award of damage amounts. Special damages refer to those damages that can be stated with specificity, for example, medical bills and lost wages. Punitive damages are those jury awards that are designed to punish the defendant for his actions. They are often called exemplary damages. A jury awards punitive damages as a way of discouraging others from committing the same actions as the defendant. Nominal damages refer to minor awards that have little significance. To prove this fourth and final element of a negligence action, the plaintiff must present evidence of his losses.

Web Sites

▨ **National Association of Legal Assistants**
http://www.nala.org

▨ **National Federation of Paralegal Associations**
http://www.paralegals.org

▨ **'Lectric Law Library**
http://www.lectlaw.com (click on the search box for damage issues)

▨ **Gonzaga Law Review — Calculating Tort Damages for Future Lost Earnings**
http://classweb.gmu.edu/mkrauss/damages-income.html

▨ **Cornell Law School — Damages (Wex)**
http://www.law.cornell.edu/wex/index.php/Damages

▨ **Wikipedia — Tort Reform**
http://en.wikipedia.org/wiki/Tort_reform

Forms and Court Documents

Notice the loss of consortium claim alleged in paragraph 9.

STATE OF PLACID	IN THE SUPERIOR COURT
COUNTY OF BARNES	FILE NUMBER: _____

Joseph Josephson and)
Marie Josephson,)
Plaintiffs)
)
vs.)
)
Darryl Dangerous,)
Defendant

Complaint

Now comes the plaintiffs in the above-styled action and complaining of the defendant do hereby allege:

1.

Plaintiffs are both citizens and residents of Barnes County, State of Placid.

2.

Defendant is a citizen and resident of Barnes County, State of Placid.

3.

On December 20, 2002, plaintiff Joseph Josephson was driving a 2001 Honda Viper, northbound on Starnes Cove Road in the City of Bevanston, State of Placid.

4.

Defendant, Darryl Dangerous, was driving his car, a 1976 Mercury Impala, on the same road, driving in a southbound direction.

5.

As the two cars approached one another on Starnes Cove Road, Defendant Dangerous crossed the centerline of the road and entered the plaintiff's lane of traffic, striking the plaintiff's car in a head-on collision. At all times prior to the collision, plaintiff was operating within his lane of traffic and did not depart from his lane until his automobile was struck by the defendant's automobile.

6.

Defendant was negligent in that defendant:
a. Failed to maintain a proper lookout
b. Failed to keep his car within his own lane of traffic

c. Drove at excessive and dangerous speeds

d. Failed to keep his vehicle under proper control

7.

As a result of the collision, plaintiff received serious and painful bodily injuries causing medical and other expenses, lost earnings, and other damages, in an amount in excess of $10,000.

8.

Plaintiffs incorporate each and every allegation as set forth hereinabove and repeat and re-allege each such averment hereinafter with the same force and effect.

9.

As a direct and proximate result of the injuries sustained by Plaintiff Joseph Josephson, the husband of Plaintiff Marie Josephson, resulting from the collision herein complained of and by the Defendant's negligence as alleged, Plaintiff Marie Josephson has been caused to be deprived of love, companionship, society, relations, and normally expected and rendered household duties and chores performed and rendered by Plaintiff Joseph Josephson prior to the collision herein complained of. Plaintiff Marie Josephson's spouse, Joseph, was able to and in fact did perform and render such services prior to the collision complained of herein and such loss of consortium is a direct and proximate result of the negligence of the Defendant and the resulting injuries to Plaintiff's spouse.

WHEREFORE, the Plaintiffs pray that the Court as follows:

1. That the Plaintiffs have and recover a judgment against the Defendant in an amount in excess of $10,000.00 for personal injuries.
2. That the Defendant be assessed with punitive damages as permitted by law.
3. That prejudgment interest be awarded as provided by law.
4. That the costs of this action be taxed against the Defendant.
5. That all issues raised be tried before a jury.
6. For such other and further relief as the Court may deem just and proper.

This the _____ day of June 2003.

_____

Clarence D. Arrow
Attorney for Plaintiffs
State Bar No. 000-998

Certificate of Service

This is to certify that the undersigned has this date served this document in the above-captioned action on all other parties to this cause by depositing a copy hereof, postage prepaid, in the United States Mail, properly addressed to the attorney for each party as follows:

This the _____ day of June 2003.

Respectfully submitted,
By: _____
Attorney for Plaintiffs

Key Terms

Collateral source rule	Equity	Loss of consortium
Compensatory damages	Fair market value	Mitigation of damages
	General damages	Per diem
Declaratory judgment	Injunction	Special damages

Review Questions

1 What are the three categories of damages?
2 Why do courts make a distinction between general and special damages?
3 Describe how the plaintiff would go about proving property losses.
4 Explain fair market value.
5 What is the collateral source rule and what significance does it have for the plaintiff?
6 Why is a plaintiff required to mitigate his damages, when possible?
7 Explain loss of consortium claims.
8 Why should you ask about prior existing injuries?
9 Under what circumstances would a claim of bad faith be justified?
10 When and under what circumstances is a plaintiff entitled to receive punitive damages?
11 How has tort reform affected the award of punitive damages in many jurisdictions?
12 What are nominal damages?
13 What are three important factors to consider when evaluating a case for damages?
14 Why would a plaintiff conduct an asset search of a defendant prior to bringing suit?
15 What is a verdict form? When is it used?

Applying What You Have Learned

1 Larry's wife of 47 years died last year and was sent to a local crematorium for processing. After the body was purportedly cremated, Larry received a

decorative jar that was supposed to contain his wife's ashes. Several months later, Larry saw news reports that the crematorium in question had been seized by the local authorities and dozens of corpses had been recovered that had been scheduled to be cremated, but had never actually been processed. Instead, the bodies were simply left outside or stacked in a shed. Larry decides to sue the crematorium. What kind of damages, if any, can Larry seek?[12]

2   Linda is involved in a car collision. The driver of the other car ran a red light and struck Linda's car on the driver's side. Linda was severely bruised. She was taken to the hospital and discharged the next day. Her hospital bill was $2,456. Because she was in terrible pain, she lost almost eight days from work. When she returned, she found that she had trouble concentrating. She kept reliving the collision in her mind. Her work suffered and her employer eventually fired her. She worked as advertising salesperson, which means that she spent most of her day driving from one client to another. Because of the accident, she suffers from terrible anxiety whenever she gets behind the wheel of a car. What type of damages can Linda seek against the other driver and how would you classify these damages: compensatory-general, compensatory-special, punitive, or nominal?

3   Draft an answer to the complaint in the Forms and Documents section. How should the defendant respond to the loss of consortium complaint?

4   What types of compensatory damages are permissible in your state? Can a plaintiff recover for a "psychic" injury, or must the injury be tied to a physical injury?

Endnotes

[1]Origin and History of Hebrew Law, John M.P. Smith, Hyperion Press, 1990.
[2]Leviticus, 24:17-20.
[3]Restatement (Second) of Torts, §902.
[4]Restatement (Second) of Torts, §621 (1977).
[5]*Walston v. Greene*, 246 N.C. 617, 99 S.E.2d 805 (1957).
[6]*Fuches v. S.E.S. Co.*, 459 N.W.2d 642 (1990).
[7]*International Correspondence School, Inc. v. Crabtree*, 162 Tenn. 70, 34 S.W.2d 447 (1931).
[8]*Tancredi v. Dive Makai Charters*, 823 F. Supp. 778 (D.C. Haw. 1993).
[9]*Davis v. Green*, 188 F. Supp. 808 (W.D. Ark. 1960).
[10]*Edwards-Warren Tire Co. v. Coble*, 102 Ga. App. 106, 115 S.E.2d 852 (1960).
[11]Restatement (Second) of Torts, §909.
[12]*Gray Brown-Service Mortuary, Inc. v. Lloyd*, 729 So. 2d 280 (1999).

Defenses to Negligence

- **Explain the difference between contributory negligence and comparative negligence**

- **List and explain some of the exceptions to contributory negligence such as the last clear chance doctrine and the rescuer doctrine**

- **Describe the various types of comparative negligence systems in place in the United States**

- **Be able to draft a comparative negligence defense in an answer**

- **Explain the continued significance of contributory negligence law in the United States**

 ## THE RAILROAD'S DEFENSE
IN THE CHUMLEY CASE

This chapter focuses on defenses peculiar to negligence actions. One of the more important questions to be answered in the Chumley case is which model of negligence does the jurisdiction follow? If the Chumley case is tried in a jurisdiction that follows the contributory negligence model, the analysis of the case will be very different than it would be in a comparative negligence juris-diction. If the case is tried in one of the few remaining contributory negligence jurisdictions, the outcome for Mr. Chumley is in doubt. The reason for this is that there is no evidence, and Mr. Chumley cannot provide any, that he stopped at the railroad crossing (as required by law) before proceeding across the tracks and colliding with the train. In a contributory negligence state, Mr. Chumley's failure to stop could remove any possibility of recovery in this case. However, if the Chumley case is filed in a comparative negligence jurisdiction, Mr. Chumley's possible negligence is only one of many factors to consider and probably will not cause any major problems for the legal team representing him. Before we can further analyze the legal implications of Mr. Chumley's case, we must first discuss exactly what contributory and comparative negligence are.

INTRODUCTION TO CONTRIBUTORY NEGLIGENCE

Contributory negligence
A defense available in only a few jurisdictions that provides that a plaintiff who is even partially at fault is barred from any recovery

The doctrine of **contributory negligence** was once followed in almost all juris-dictions. Contributory negligence is a court-created doctrine that prevents any award to plaintiffs when they contribute to their own injuries. Under the most draconian application of contributory negligence, a defendant who is 99 percent at fault will not pay any damages to a plaintiff who is 1 percent at fault in the accident. In the last few decades of the twentieth century, many jurisdictions abandoned contributory negligence in favor of a more flexible — and some would argue more just — system called comparative negligence. Under that system, the plaintiff's negligence is measured against the defendant's negligence and the plaintiff's ultimate recovery is reduced by the percentage of his fault.

Most other countries that have a legal system similar to that in the United States have long since abandoned contributory negligence. For instance, all of the following countries follow some form of comparative negligence scheme:

The doctrine of con-tributory negligence has been called one of the harshest doctrines in law.[2]

- All European Union countries, including Great Britain
- Canada
- New Zealand
- Australia[1]

A. HISTORICAL REASONS FOR THE DEVELOPMENT OF CONTRIBUTORY NEGLIGENCE

Why would such a harsh rule ever be developed? Over the decades, several justifications have been offered. Some commentators have suggested that contributory negligence is actually a component of proximate cause analysis.

Alabama	**Contributory Negligence**
Alaska	Comparative Negligence: adopted by legislature in 1986
Arizona	Comparative Negligence: adopted 1984
Arkansas	Comparative Negligence: adopted "pure" comparative negligence in 1954; later amended to plaintiff's negligence must be less than defendant's
California	Comparative Negligence
Colorado	Comparative Negligence: statute passed in 1971; plaintiff's negligence must be less than 50%
Connecticut	Comparative Negligence: statute passed in 1973, amended in 1986; plaintiff who is 50% at fault can still recover
Delaware	**Contributory Negligence**
Florida	Comparative Negligence: first state to judicially adopt comparative negligence
Georgia	Comparative Negligence: plaintiff must be less than 50% at fault to recover
Hawaii	Comparative Negligence: adopted in 1969
Idaho	Comparative Negligence: adopted the Georgia plan of comparative negligence in 1971. It requires that plaintiff's negligence be less than 50%
Illinois	Comparative Negligence: adopted in 1986
Indiana	Comparative Negligence: adopted in 1983; plaintiff who is 50% negligent may still recover
Iowa	Comparative Negligence: adopted in 1984; plaintiff is denied recovery when more than 50% at fault
Kansas	Comparative Negligence: adopted in 1974; plaintiff can recover only when less than 50% at fault
Kentucky	Comparative Negligence: adopted in 1984; "pure" comparative fault
Louisiana	Comparative Negligence: adopted in 1979; "pure" comparative fault
Maine	Comparative Negligence: adopted in 1965
Maryland	**Contributory Negligence**
Massachusetts	Comparative Negligence: plaintiff must be less than 50% at fault to recover
Michigan	Comparative Negligence: adopted in 1979; "pure" comparative fault
Minnesota	Comparative Negligence: adopted in 1969; plaintiff must be less than 50% at fault to recover
Mississippi	Comparative Negligence: adopted in 1910
Missouri	Comparative Negligence: adopted in 1983; "pure" comparative fault
Montana	Comparative Negligence: adopted in 1975
Nebraska	Comparative Negligence: adopted in 1913
Nevada	Comparative Negligence: plaintiff can be up to 50% at fault
New Hampshire	Comparative Negligence: plaintiff who is 50% at fault can still recover
New Jersey	Comparative Negligence: adopted in 1973; plaintiff can be up to 50% at fault and still recover
New Mexico	Comparative Negligence: adopted in 1980; "pure" comparative fault
New York	Comparative Negligence: "pure" comparative negligence

(continued)

FIGURE 9-1

A State-by-State Breakdown Showing Contributory Negligence States and Comparative Negligence States

FIGURE 9-1 **(continued)**	
North Carolina	**Contributory Negligence**
North Dakota	Comparative Negligence: adopted in 1973; plaintiff's negligence must be less than defendant's
Ohio	Comparative Negligence: plaintiff may be up to 50% at fault and still recover
Oklahoma	Comparative Negligence: adopted in 1979; plaintiff may be up to 50% at fault and still recover
Oregon	Comparative Negligence: plaintiff may be up to 50% at fault and still recover
Pennsylvania	Comparative Negligence: adopted by statute in 1976; plaintiff may be up to 50% at fault and still recover
Rhode Island	Comparative Negligence: "pure" comparative negligence
South Carolina	**Contributory Negligence**
South Dakota	Comparative Negligence: plaintiff's negligence must be "slight"
Tennessee	Comparative Negligence: modified comparative negligence; remote contributory negligence will mitigate damages, not bar recovery
Texas	Comparative Negligence: follows New Hampshire plan
Utah	Comparative Negligence: defendant's negligence must exceed plaintiff's
Vermont	Comparative Negligence: plaintiff can be up to 50% negligent and still recover
Virginia	**Contributory Negligence**
Washington	Comparative Negligence: adopted in 1981; "pure" comparative negligence
West Virginia	Comparative Negligence: modified system of comparative negligence
Wisconsin	Comparative Negligence: plaintiff may be up to 50% at fault and still recover
Wyoming	Comparative Negligence: legislature adopted in 1973; plaintiff may be up to 50% at fault and still recover

That argument runs something like this: To prove that the defendant is liable to the plaintiff, the plaintiff must prove that the defendant had a duty, that he violated that duty, and that the violation of that duty was the proximate cause of the injuries to the plaintiff. When the plaintiff has actually contributed in some way to his own injuries, the causal connection between the defendant's actions and the resulting harm is disrupted and should therefore absolve the defendant of any liability. However, this argument fails to take into account many of the other doctrines that have developed over time that have modified proximate cause analysis.

Another justification for contributory negligence is that a plaintiff should enter the court with *clean hands*. This term is usually reserved for actions by plaintiffs who seek injunctive relief from the courts. In injunctive relief, the plaintiff requests a court order preventing the defendant from taking some action, such as bulldozing a tree or selling corporate bonds. The court is permitted to deny the request when it is obvious that the plaintiff has been acting improperly. Similarly, supporters of contributory negligence claim that this rule should apply in negligence actions. If the plaintiff can be shown to be at least partially at fault for his own injuries, the clean hands doctrine should operate to bar his recovery. However, the doctrine of clean hands in injunctive cases is not a complete bar to a plaintiff's request; it is simply a factor that the court can consider in deciding what action, if any, to take.[3] Another argument against the clean hands doctrine is "last clear chance," discussed later in this chapter.

A more cynical reason for contributory negligence can be found in its historical roots. The doctrine of contributory negligence arrived on the legal scene at the same time as the Industrial Revolution was sweeping through the United States and Great Britain. This newfound wealth and the prosperity that it generated were considered vital to our national interest. Anything that might slow, or even disrupt, this development was seen as bad. Contributory negligence was a doctrine ready-made for the industrial mishaps, maimings, and deaths that occurred through industrial accidents. By eliminating recovery against a major railroad or other corporation when the plaintiff was in some way at fault for his own injuries, these business sectors were protected from a deluge of lawsuits, which allowed these industries to prosper and develop.[4]

Sidebar

Contributory negligence is also an excellent way for a judge to keep control of "runaway juries," that is, juries that might be swayed by the facts of a case to award large damages to a sympathetic plaintiff against a huge corporation.

B. DEFINING CONTRIBUTORY NEGLIGENCE

According to the Restatement of Torts, contributory negligence is defined as the plaintiff's failure to take reasonable care for his own safety.[5] Put another way, contributory negligence is the plaintiff's lack of ordinary care that merges with the defendant's negligence to bring about the plaintiff's injuries. Under the theory of contributory negligence, the plaintiff is held to a standard of care for his own actions at the same time that the defendant is held to a standard of care for his actions toward the plaintiff.[6] In practice, this standard of care is often different for the two parties. Many jurisdictions apply a more rigid standard of care toward the defendant in a contributory negligence action than is applied to the plaintiff. The reason for this is that by holding the plaintiff to a lower standard, there is less chance of the harsh result that sometimes results in contributory negligence cases.[7]

Sidebar

One commentator has referred to contributory negligence as the "all-or-nothing lottery."[8]

If a plaintiff is found to be contributorily negligent, she will receive nothing, no matter how severe her damages.

ISSUE
AT A
GLANCE

Negligence and contributory negligence are not flip sides of the same coin. In a negligence action, the defendant can be liable to the plaintiff for breaching a duty to the plaintiff that results in the plaintiff's injuries. In contributory negligence, we do not see the reverse, that is, that the plaintiff breached a duty to the defendant. Instead, contributory negligence is a theory that states that the plaintiff breached a duty of care to herself and this breach merged with the negligence of the defendant to bring about the plaintiff's injuries.

Sidebar

Some commentators have suggested that a better name for contributory negligence would be "contributory fault" or "contributory misconduct."[9]

The basic premise behind contributory negligence is that a plaintiff should not be permitted to recover damages from someone else's negligence when she failed to exercise reasonable care herself. To take advantage of contributory negligence, there is no requirement that the defendant knew about the plaintiff's negligence prior to the incident.

Although this theory sounds practical enough, in practice it often has drastic results. In states where contributory negligence is still the law of the land, a defendant who is clearly at fault can be absolved of all liability by a showing that the plaintiff was at fault in a minor way. Dissatisfaction with the sometimes unjust results in these cases has led many jurisdictions to abandon the concept entirely and opt for a more reasonable and judicious approach: comparative negligence (discussed later in this chapter).

A defense of contributory negligence presumes negligence on the part of the defendant.

Contributory negligence is a complete bar to recovery; comparative negligence will lessen the plaintiff's recovery in proportion to his own negligence in bringing about his injuries.

1. WHY STUDY CONTRIBUTORY NEGLIGENCE?

Unless you live in one of the few states that continues to follow contributory negligence, why should you bother to study the concept at all? The reason is simple: Even in states that have adopted some form of comparative negligence, contributory negligence continues to have an important impact. Because most jurisdictions once followed contributory negligence theories, the case law that developed under those theories provides an important underpinning to current cases. In addition, comparative negligence developed as a direct response to contributory negligence and it is difficult to understand comparative negligence principles without referring to the doctrine of contributory negligence.

2. WHY DOES THE DOCTRINE CONTINUE TO EXIST?

Sidebar

Contributory negligence is based on the premise that justice is served best when the courts stay out of the business of apportioning degrees of fault among the parties.[10]

Although only a handful of states still follow contributory negligence, the question arises: Why would any state continue to apply a doctrine that almost all legal commentators consider to be overly harsh and sometimes unjust? There are several possible reasons. These states may continue to follow more conservative legal views on a wide variety of topics that include an adherence to contributory negligence. In states in which contributory negligence has been eliminated, the judiciary has often taken the lead by abolishing the doctrine. Later, the state legislature makes the change official by enacting a

A plaintiff is considered to be contributorily negligent if:

1 he breaches the duty imposed upon him by law to protect himself from injury;

2 his actions concur and cooperate with actionable negligence of the defendant; and

3 his actions contribute to the injuries as a proximate cause.*

FIGURE 9-2

The Elements of Contributory Negligence

*Steinauer v. Sarpy County, 217 Neb. 830, 353 N.W.2d 715 (1984).

statute that changes the law from contributory negligence to comparative negligence. In many states, such as Delaware, the judiciary has taken the time-honored position that the courts do not have the power to create law, only to interpret it. In these states, the judiciary may favor a move from contributory negligence to comparative negligence, but feels obligated to leave this decision to the state legislature. Another reason could be simple inertia. Society changes rapidly; the legal community does not. In the states in which contributory negligence continues to remain in effect, there may be a simple reluctance to abandon a century or more of legal precedents for the dramatically different concept of comparative negligence.

Sidebar

"Plaintiff may be contributorily negligent if his conduct ignores unreasonable risks or dangers which would have been apparent to a prudent person exercising ordinary care for his own safety."[11]

C. THE DOCTRINE OF "AVOIDABLE CONSEQUENCES"

Although sometimes confused with contributory negligence, the doctrine of avoidable consequences is actually a completely separate doctrine. It focuses on what happened after the accident, not the plaintiff's actions before the accident. Under this doctrine, the plaintiff must take reasonable steps to obtain proper medical treatment for his injuries or to protect damaged property. Under the doctrine of avoidable consequences, the plaintiff is not entitled to recover damages from his failure to take these steps. Example: Carl is injured in a collision. He refuses medical treatment, and as a result his minor injury becomes aggravated to the point that he requires major surgery and prolonged rehabilitation. Carl sues the driver who caused the collision. The jury awards damages to Carl, but only for the medical treatments and expenses that he would have required after the wreck, not for his exacerbated injuries due to his own failure to look after himself.[12] It is similar to the principle of mitigation of damages discussed in Chapter 8.

D. HOW MUCH AT FAULT MUST PLAINTIFF BE?

Different states follow different rules on this point. Under the basic theory of contributory negligence, a plaintiff can be barred from recovery for any amount of negligence, no matter how slight. However, some states have modified that approach, requiring that the defendant prove the plaintiff's contributory negligence was more than a small amount.[13]

The basic issue in contributory negligence is whether the plaintiff knew of the danger he was in, whether he failed to exercise ordinary care to protect himself, and whether his failure to exercise such care contributed in some way to his own injuries.[14]

Example: Tom visits Claire at her family farm. She offers to give Tom a ride on the family tractor. She admits that she has had very little experience driving the tractor, but Tom climbs on the back anyway. While they are traveling to the pond, Claire loses control of the tractor and Tom falls off, severely injuring his back. This occurred in a contributory negligence state. Will Tom be prevented from recovering under the theory of contributory negligence?

Answer: Yes.[15]

E. IS THERE SUCH A THING AS "CONTRIBUTORY NEGLIGENCE PER SE"?

Sidebar

In some jurisdictions, the defendant's violation of a safety statute (negligence per se) bars the use of contributory negligence as a defense.[16]

What if the plaintiff is violating a safety statute at the time of the accident? Under contributory negligence, would this mean that she has committed "contributory negligence per se"? (See negligence per se in Chapter 6.) Most jurisdictions do not follow such a hard-and-fast rule. If the plaintiff is violating some statute at the time of her injuries, her violation is one more element that the defendant may use to show contributory negligence. However, the plaintiff's violation must be a proximate cause of her own injuries. For example, Marsha is driving a car that has a broken taillight. As she proceeds through a green light, Ted's car broadsides her. Ted has failed to stop at the red light. At trial, Ted raises the defense of contributory negligence by claiming that at the time of the accident, Marsha was driving in violation of a safety equipment statute (that is, non-functioning taillight). This fact alone will not justify a defense of contributory negligence because there is no causal connection between the broken taillight and the subsequent collision.

F. THE "ALL OR NOTHING" ELEMENT OF CONTRIBUTORY NEGLIGENCE

Much of the criticism about contributory negligence has to do with its "all or nothing" approach to a negligence action. If the plaintiff has not contributed in any way to her own injuries, she is permitted to recover all the damages the jury has awarded. However, if she has contributed, even in a minor way, to her own injuries, she is not entitled to any of the jury's award. In this modern era, many question the continued wisdom of such a system.

G. IS CONTRIBUTORY NEGLIGENCE DOOMED?

Some commentators argue that the doctrine of contributory negligence will eventually disappear from the U.S. legal system. In support, they point to the many jurisdictions that have abandoned the concept over the past 30 years.[17] However, there are many legal concepts that have been modified or eliminated in some jurisdictions that continue to have full legal effect in others. Whether contributory negligence will eventually disappear as a civil injuries doctrine is still an open question.

H. EXCEPTIONS TO CONTRIBUTORY NEGLIGENCE

Almost as soon as the concept of contributory negligence was developed, courts began carving out exceptions by stipulating certain types of cases, or certain factual scenarios, that would preclude the use of contributory negligence. Among the most famous, and certainly the most discussed, is the last clear chance doctrine.

1. LAST CLEAR CHANCE

Under the **last clear chance doctrine,** a plaintiff's contributory negligence will be excused if the defendant had the last opportunity of avoiding the accident and failed to do so.

The application of the last clear chance doctrine is highly dependent on the facts of the case. As such, it is often considered a malleable doctrine, that is, one that can fit many different situations.[19] It was developed as a way of allowing a partially negligent plaintiff to avoid the strict and often harsh application of contributory negligence. If contributory negligence is a doctrine that helps a negligent defendant avoid liability, last clear chance is a doctrine that helps a negligent plaintiff avoid a finding of contributory negligence.[20]

a. Proving Last Clear Chance

In many jurisdictions, the plaintiff is allowed to raise the issue of last clear chance as a routine matter when the defendant raises the defense of contributory negligence. Just as the burden of proving contributory negligence is on the defendant, the burden of proving last clear chance is on the plaintiff. Ultimately, it is the jury's decision whether the doctrine applies to the facts of a particular case.

b. Pleading Last Clear Chance

Depending on the jurisdiction, the plaintiff may be able to raise evidence of last clear chance at trial, or may be required to raise it as a contention in her

Last clear chance
A claim by a plaintiff in a contributory negligence allegation that the defendant was the person who had the last opportunity to avoid the event that caused the plaintiff's injuries and therefore the defendant should remain liable for the injuries, despite any negligence by the plaintiff

Sidebar

Last clear chance is also known as the doctrine of discovered peril, the doctrine of supervening negligence, the humanitarian doctrine, the doctrine of gross negligence, and the doctrine of subsequent negligence.[18]

Sidebar

In jurisdictions that have adopted comparative negligence, last clear chance has generally been abolished along with contributory negligence, because it is so closely tied to that doctrine.

FIGURE 9-3	The plaintiff must present evidence showing:	■ That the defendant had the ability to avoid the accident
Proving Last Clear Chance	■ That he or she was in a dangerous position	■ That the defendant failed to exercise ordinary care to prevent the injuries to the plaintiff
	■ That he or she was unable to escape the danger through ordinary care	■ That there was proximate cause between the defendant's failure to act and the resultant injuries to the plaintiff
	■ That the defendant either knew or should have known that the plaintiff was in danger	

FIGURE 9-4	■ There is competent or compelling evidence that a sudden emergency existed.	■ The emergency was caused by the defendant.
Factors to Consider When Determining If Sudden Emergency Applies	■ The plaintiff's apprehension must be a response to what a reasonable person would consider to be a life-threatening situation.	■ The plaintiff was the person in danger. (If the plaintiff was rescuing another person, this doctrine does not apply; instead the rescuer doctrine applies.)*
	■ That danger could not have been anticipated.	

*Katcher v. Heidenwirth, 254 Iowa 454, 118 N.W.2d 52 (1962).

Sidebar

The doctrine of last clear chance has been almost as contentious and controversial as that of proximate cause or even contributory negligence itself.

complaint. Check the applicable case law to be sure of the procedure in your state. The elements of last clear chance are set out in Figure 9-3.

 ISSUE AT A GLANCE

Last clear chance is usually only available to plaintiffs in contributory negligence actions. It is invoked by the person who is injured as a way of refuting a claim of contributory negligence.[21]

2. SUDDEN EMERGENCY

Sudden emergency
A doctrine that relieves a person of the normal standard of care because of a swiftly developing and dangerous event

Another exception to contributory negligence is the **sudden emergency** doctrine. Under this doctrine, when a plaintiff is confronted with a sudden emergency, something that requires a quick response, he will not be held to the same standard as would a plaintiff who had more time to consider his actions. This situation is also seen in traditional negligence analysis. In an emergency, a person is not expected to exercise the same standard of care, whether the person is a defendant in a negligence action or a plaintiff in a contributory negligence counterclaim.[22] This doctrine was originally created to avoid some of the difficult situations that can develop under contributory negligence. Holding the plaintiff to a lower standard of care in an emergency makes it easier for the plaintiff to avoid a claim of contributory negligence.[23]

3. ASSUMPTION OF THE RISK

We have discussed assumption of the risk in regard to intentional torts, but it is also an important defense in negligence cases. Essentially, a defense of assumption of the risk is the defendant's assertion that the plaintiff should be barred from recovering any damages because the plaintiff knowingly placed himself in a dangerous situation (a defense that admittedly sounds a great deal like contributory negligence). Despite the similarity to contributory negligence, many jurisdictions continue to apply the defense of assumption of the risk to comparative negligence cases as well. Other comparative negligence jurisdictions have abolished the defense. The assumption of the risk defense is based on the idea that the plaintiff knew the danger he was getting into and voluntarily assumed the risk. In such a situation, the plaintiff waives the right to sue for damages. Whenever a defendant raises a claim of the assumption of the risk, the defendant must prove that the plaintiff knew a particular action was dangerous and voluntarily engaged in it. Without that proof, the jury cannot find that the plaintiff knowingly undertook a risky action.

> **Sidebar**
>
> *A prudent person, in the face of a life-threatening danger, may not always exercise the same degree of judgment that a hypothetical reasonable person would.*[24]

Example: Ron likes to ride "mechanical bulls." One evening, he hears about a new club that has opened in town and has a brand new mechanical bull that the owners claim is more powerful than any other in the state. Ron goes to the club and waits his turn to ride the bull. A club employee hands Ron a waiver form that reads, in part, "By agreeing to ride the mechanical bull, you acknowledge that you are engaging in a dangerous activity that can cause serious injury or even death. You agree that you assume the risk of this activity and absolve this club for any negligence in the operation of this bull." Ron signs and gets on the bull, but unfortunately for him, the bull has not been properly maintained and three seconds into his ride the main drive pulley breaks and throws Ron 20 feet. Ron is severely injured and wants to bring suit against the club. The club owners counter with the defense of assumption of the risk. Who will win?

Answer: Ron may lose. Although there are several other potential issues raised here, assumption of the risk is a good defense for the club owners. After all, if they can prove that Ron knew the danger involved and voluntarily assumed the risk, he may lose at trial. However, this issue may be complicated by the fact that Ron did not knowingly and voluntarily assume the risk of the club's negligence, only the dangers associated with riding a properly functioning mechanical bull.

4. OTHER EXCEPTIONS TO CONTRIBUTORY NEGLIGENCE

a. Plaintiff's Age and Physical Factors

We have already discussed the reasonable person standard in other contexts related to negligence, so it should not be any surprise that it also factors into exceptions to the rule of contributory negligence. For instance, what standard applies to a claim of contributory negligence involving a child or a visually

impaired person? The general rule is that a child is held to the standard of a
similarly situated child and an impaired person is held to the standard of a
hypothetical reasonable person with the same disability.[25]

However, the same limitations of the reasonable person standard in other
contexts also apply here. For instance, although a plaintiff can claim age or
some other physical factor as justification for a lower standard of care, she is
not allowed to plead intoxication or mental deficiency as a means of lowering
the standard of care in contributory negligence. When a contributory negligence claim involves intoxication, for example, the plaintiff's inebriation does
not lessen her standard of care any more in a contributory negligence action
than it does for the defendant's standard of care in the main negligence action.

Under contributory negligence, a plaintiff is required to use her senses in a
normal way to "maintain a lookout" and to take whatever other steps a reasonable person would to keep herself safe.[26]

b. Mental Incompetence

In almost all jurisdictions, a legally insane person cannot be liable under contributory negligence.[27] The reasoning behind this exception is the same as that
for not finding legally incompetent people liable in other contexts. Such people
are incapable of assessing their responsibilities or conforming their conduct
to society's standards and deserve special protection under the law.

5. THE RESCUER DOCTRINE

When a person is attempting to save the life of another the doctrine of contributory negligence does not apply.[28] Of course, this assumes that the rescuer
did not put the person in jeopardy in the first place. This doctrine has been
applied when people engage in actions that would otherwise be considered
contributory negligence, such as running into a fiery building to save another
person or jumping into icy water to save a drowning man. The reasons for this
doctrine are obvious: Society does not wish to penalize people who rescue
others. This doctrine applies even when the rescuer takes desperate and
extremely dangerous chances in rescuing another.[29]

I. SITUATIONS IN WHICH CONTRIBUTORY NEGLIGENCE DOES NOT APPLY

There are many types of situations in which the defense of contributory
negligence does not apply, even in jurisdictions that continue to follow the
doctrine. See Figure 9-5.

ISSUE AT A GLANCE

The defendant must prove the plaintiff's contributory negligence.
It is usually raised in the context of an affirmative defense in the
defendant's answer.[31]

FIGURE 9-5

Types of Cases in Which Contributory Negligence Is Not a Factor

Contributory negligence is not a defense to

- Breach of contract[i]
- Intentional torts[ii]
- Willful, wanton, or reckless conduct[iii]
- Strict liability (in some jurisdictions)

- Ultra-hazardous activities[iv]
- Product liability[v] (in some jurisdictions)

[i]*Brown v. Chapman,* 304 F.2d 149 (9th Cir. 1962).
[ii]*Reynolds v. Guthrie,* 145 Kan. 315, 65 P.2d 272 (1937).
[iii]*Mahoney v. Corralejo,* 36 Cal. App. 3d 966, 112 Cal. Rptr. 61 (1974).
[iv]*Carlson v. Glanville,* 170 Cal. App. 2d 246, 338 P.2d 580 (1959).
[v]*Davenport v. Walker,* 280 S.C. 588, 313 S.E.2d 354 (1984).

J. CONTRIBUTORY NEGLIGENCE IS A JURY QUESTION

All jurisdictions provide that the determination of contributory negligence is a question for the jury.[32] The defense must present sufficient evidence to convince the jury that the plaintiff contributed to his own injuries and that the jurors must follow the law in awarding no damages. The court can intercede on the defendant's behalf only in rare cases. For instance, one jurisdiction allows directed verdicts of contributory negligence against the plaintiff only when the facts are "very clear" that the plaintiff was at fault.[33]

In jurisdictions where contributory negligence is followed, the jury is often instructed that the plaintiff must take reasonable actions to protect himself, and the jury must decide if he failed to do so. Along these lines, the court might instruct the jury as follows:

Ladies and Gentlemen of the jury, I charge you that the plaintiff's risk must be unreasonable at the time that he took it.[34] I further charge you that is not contributory negligence if the plaintiff was placed in the position of being forced to take a risky action by the negligence of the defendant.[35]

COMPARATIVE NEGLIGENCE

The doctrine of **comparative negligence** was developed as a way of circumventing the frequently harsh rulings in contributory negligence cases. Whether adopted by state legislatures or by judicial decree, comparative negligence has swept away contributory negligence in all but a handful of states.

The underlying principles of the various comparative negligence theories may be different, but the general approach is the same. Instead of forfeiting any recovery, a plaintiff who is negligent will have his ultimate recovery reduced by the proportion of his negligence.

Comparative negligence
An approach to negligence cases that balances the negligence of the defendant against the negligence of the plaintiff and permits a reduced recovery for the plaintiff in proportion to the plaintiff's negligence

The ghost of contributory negligence still haunts many of the comparative negligence jurisdictions, either because the common law principles that developed under that theory still form an important part of the new law, or because the comparative negligence statutes are simply a form of modified contributory negligence.[36]

A. HISTORICAL DEVELOPMENT OF COMPARATIVE NEGLIGENCE

The concept of comparative negligence is as old as Roman law and has been adopted by most countries that follow the Roman model. In the U.S. law system, contributory negligence was the model adopted by almost all jurisdictions and comparative negligence is a relatively recent phenomenon. That is not to say that comparative negligence was not considered by various states, even as early as the nineteenth century. Georgia, for example, experimented with the concept in the mid-1800s. However, most states began adopting comparative negligence statutes and case law in the mid- to late twentieth century. In fact, the latter part of the twentieth century saw a growing momentum of states turning away from contributory negligence in favor of comparative negligence.[37]

States that have adopted comparative negligence through judicial action have generally opted for the "pure" form, while states that have adopted the concept through legislation have usually opted for the modified form. This difference could be explained by the prominence of the insurance industry lobby. The modified form of comparative negligence is much more insurance-friendly than the pure form. From 1969 onwards, several states have adopted some form of modified comparative negligence scheme. The different schemes are shown in Figure 9-1.

Under comparative negligence, a plaintiff is not barred from recovery if he is negligent; however, his ultimate award will be reduced in proportion to his negligence.

B. THE UNIFORM COMPARATIVE FAULT ACT

The Uniform Comparative Fault Act was proposed as a way of creating a more uniform approach to comparative negligence in the various states. However, it has never been enacted in its entirety in any jurisdiction. Instead, portions of the act have been incorporated into statutes or comparative negligence schemes. Some states use the act as a guideline for judicial interpretations.[38]

C. THE THREE MODELS OF COMPARATIVE NEGLIGENCE

Different types of comparative negligence approaches are taken by different jurisdictions. Some have adopted the pure form of comparative negligence, while the vast majority of others have adopted a modified form. Tennessee may be the only state to adopt the "slight-gross" model of comparative negligence.

There are three different forms of comparative negligence:

▦ **Pure**   ▦ **Slight-Gross**

▦ **Modified**

ISSUE
AT A
GLANCE

---

1. PURE COMPARATIVE NEGLIGENCE

Under pure comparative negligence schemes, a plaintiff is entitled to receive an award of damages no matter how great her fault, assuming that the defendant is also found to be at fault. In pure comparative negligence states, a determination that the plaintiff is 75 percent at fault and the defendant is 25 percent at fault would have the following result: The plaintiff would be entitled to receive only 25 percent of her total damages.

Under the "New Hampshire" plan, a plaintiff can recover if she is 50 percent negligent or less. If she is more than 50 percent negligent, she is barred from recovery, echoing the provisions of contributory negligence.

Under the "Georgia" plan, a plaintiff must be less than 50 percent negligent before she can recover.

> **Sidebar**
>
> *Pure comparative negligence has been adopted in three of the most populous states: New York, California, and Florida. As a consequence, more litigants are involved with pure comparative negligence than any other form.*[39]

2. MODIFIED COMPARATIVE NEGLIGENCE

Under the modified comparative negligence rules, a plaintiff's recovery could be limited in at least two ways. In some jurisdictions, a plaintiff's negligence must be less than 50 percent. In those states, like Georgia, if the plaintiff's negligence is greater than 50 percent, or greater than the defendant's negligence, she will receive no recovery, mirroring the result in a contributory negligence jurisdiction. In other states that follow a form of modified comparative negligence, the plaintiff's negligence can be equal to the defendant's negligence. In those states, the plaintiff's recovery will be reduced by the amount of her percentage of fault. If the plaintiff is 50 percent at fault, she will receive only half of her damages. However, even in these states, a plaintiff is not entitled to any recovery if her negligence exceeds the defendant's.

> **Sidebar**
>
> *Modified comparative negligence is sometimes referred to as the "50 percent rule."*

3. SLIGHT-GROSS COMPARATIVE NEGLIGENCE

This rule is followed in only a small percentage of jurisdictions. Under the "slight-gross" comparative negligence scheme, a plaintiff is entitled to recover if her negligence is slight and the defendant's negligence is great. However, if

FIGURE 9-6

Types of Cases in Which Comparative Negligence Would Apply

- General negligence claim involving damage to persons or property
- Nuisance actions
- Malpractice actions (discussed in Chapter 12)[i]
- Negligent misrepresentation
- Negligence of common carrier[ii]

[i]*Newell v. Corres*, 125 Ill. App. 3d 1087 (1984).
[ii]*Floyd v. Albany*, 105 Ga. App. 31, 123 S.E.2d 446 (1961); *Roberts v. Yellow Cab Co.*, 240 A.2d 733 (1968).

the plaintiff's negligence is more than what a jury would consider to be slight, she is not entitled to any recovery. Tennessee, for example, allows a plaintiff to recover when her negligence is a "remote" cause, but not when her negligence is a proximate cause.

4. COMBINATIONS OF APPROACHES

In some jurisdictions, different forms of comparative negligence are followed depending on the issues in the case. For instance, a state could follow modified comparative negligence in personal injury cases and pure comparative negligence in product liability cases.

The New Hampshire plan is the most popular form of comparative negligence, having been adopted in more states than any other comparative negligence scheme (18 in all). Most jurisdictions have enacted some form of statute officially making comparative negligence the law of the land. The Georgia plan is the next most popular. Under the Georgia rule, a plaintiff must be less negligent than the defendant before he will be allowed to recover.

Sidebar

Review your state's statutes on contributory negligence or comparative negligence to verify the rules governing negligence actions.

D. TYPES OF CASES IN WHICH COMPARATIVE NEGLIGENCE APPLIES

Comparative negligence generally applies only to actions involving physical or property damage. In many jurisdictions, actions based on other torts (intentional torts, product liability torts, strict liability torts, etc.) will often follow entirely different rules.

In states that follow a modified form of comparative negligence, the judge is permitted to rule that the plaintiff is not entitled to any recovery when his negligence "clearly exceeds" that of the defendant. In such a situation, the case will not be submitted to the jury and the judge will enter a judgment in favor of the defendant.

E. COMPARATIVE NEGLIGENCE AND PUNITIVE DAMAGES

Generally, the adoption of comparative negligence doctrines does not affect a plaintiff's right to seek punitive damages. However, on a practical level, if a plaintiff is negligent in a case in which he claims negligence by the defendant, his own fault may weigh against the award of punitive damages.[40]

F. HOW COMPARATIVE NEGLIGENCE AFFECTS PROXIMATE CAUSE ANALYSIS

Generally, the principles of proximate cause (discussed in Chapter 7) are not affected by a jurisdiction's switch from contributory negligence to comparative negligence. However, there are some important points to raise about proximate cause analysis under comparative negligence. Some jurisdictions have adopted a rule commonly referred to as the "sole proximate cause" rule. Under this rule, if the plaintiff is the sole proximate cause of his injuries, he is not entitled to recover any damages from a negligent defendant. This ruling, which sounds like a revival of contributory negligence, has more to do with proximate causation. A plaintiff who cannot prove that the defendant was the proximate cause of his injuries, even in a comparative negligence state, has failed to establish the third element of a negligence action (causation) and therefore his claim must fail.[41] The jury is responsible for making the determination of sole proximate cause.

G. DEFENSES TO COMPARATIVE NEGLIGENCE

As a general rule, the defenses available under contributory negligence are not available under comparative negligence. The simple reason for this is that defenses such as assumption of the risk, last clear chance, and others are not needed when the jury is permitted to weigh the actions of both parties and award damages even if both are negligent. However, this approach is not followed in all jurisdictions. Some states adhere to the view that assumption of the risk is a defense that is independent of comparative negligence, while others have abolished the defense as inconsistent with comparative negligence. Similarly, some jurisdictions have also abolished the "sudden emergency" or "sudden peril" doctrines because they tend to confuse the issues involved in a comparative negligence case.[42]

Sidebar

At least two states that follow comparative negligence models (Oregon and Connecticut) have abolished the doctrine of last clear chance.[43]

1. THE RESCUER DOCTRINE

Many jurisdictions have retained this defense only to the extent that the rescuer's behavior can factor into comparative negligence when the rescuer acts recklessly.[44]

2. MENTALLY INCOMPETENT PERSONS

Under comparative negligence, a mentally ill person's actions are evaluated in much the same way that they were evaluated under contributory negligence.

*When evaluating a
comparative negligence
case, the legal team
must investigate the
claim thoroughly,
paying particular
attention to the actions
of all the parties, not
just the defendant.
What standard of care
applies to the plaintiff
in the case? Was the
plaintiff at fault? If so,
to what degree? These
questions must be
answered before the
complaint is filed to
ensure that the client is
properly represented at
trial and that no sur-
prises occur during
trial.*

If the mentally ill person has enough mental capacity to recognize that his actions are negligent, his ultimate recovery can be reduced by his percentage of fault. However, when a person is held to be mentally incompetent, his degree of fault often will not be a consideration in trial.

H. PLEADING COMPARATIVE NEGLIGENCE

We have previously seen that contributory negligence is an affirmative defense that must usually be raised in the defendant's answer before he will be allowed to take advantage of it. When a jurisdiction follows a comparative negligence model, does that same rule apply? Jurisdictions seem to be split on this issue. Most attorneys opt for the safe course and make some allegation in the complaint that the plaintiff's negligence "equaled or exceeded" any negligence of the defendant. That way, even if their jurisdictions do not require an affirmative statement in the answer alleging comparative negligence, the attorney has raised the issue anyway. (See the Contributory Negligence and Comparative Negligence Answers at the end of this chapter.)

I. SETTLEMENT ISSUES IN COMPARATIVE NEGLIGENCE CASES

In comparative negligence jurisdictions, a claims adjuster no longer has the option of refusing to settle a case when the plaintiff could be found negligent. Obviously the settlement discussions in a comparative negligence state will be more involved and more complicated than in a state that follows contributory negligence. For example, the insurance company knows that the plaintiff may receive some form of recovery, even when she is at fault. Under this scenario, it may make more sense to settle such a case prior to trial. On the other hand, in a contributory negligence state, this pressure to settle a close case may often be considerably less.

J. MULTIPLE DEFENDANTS AND COMPARATIVE NEGLIGENCE

Although some commentators claim that multiple defendants in comparative negligence jurisdictions are more antagonistic than multiple defendants in contributory negligence states, the truth is probably that co-defendants are just as adversarial in all states. It is common practice for co-defendants to file cross-claims against one another, whether they are in contributory negligence states or comparative negligence states. In either event, they will seek to prove that the plaintiff was negligent and that some other co-defendant was primarily responsible for the injuries.

If you find that the plaintiff was negligent in this case, state the percentage of the plaintiff's overall fault. If you find that the defendant was negligent in this case, state the percentage of the defendant's overall fault.	**FIGURE 9-7** **A Jury Interrogatory Form in a Comparative Negligence Case**

K. MOTIONS FOR DIRECTED VERDICT IN COMPARATIVE NEGLIGENCE CASES

We have seen in Chapter 1 that a motion for directed verdict is a common occurrence in a contributory negligence case, and it is not uncommon for such a motion to be granted. However, in comparative negligence jurisdictions, a directed verdict for the defendant would be rare, because the jury must determine the percentage of fault of both parties. Some states provide that a judge can only grant such a motion when the evidence of the plaintiff's negligence is clear and convincing and is greater than 50 percent.[45]

L. THE JURY'S VERDICT

In some jurisdictions, the jury is asked a series of questions to help determine the percentage of fault of all parties. The jury might, for instance, be sent back to deliberate with a set of interrogatories, asking them specific questions. (See Figure 9-7.) On appeal, an appellate court will normally leave the jury's finding of percentages intact and will only alter the findings when they are obviously against the weight of the evidence.[46]

BLOCK v. MORA

_____ S.W.3d _____, 2009 WL 35421 (Tex. App.-Amarillo)

OPINION

PATRICK A. PIRTLE, Justice.

Appellant, David Block, appeals from a judgment rendered in favor of Appellee, Kimberly Mora, following a jury trial of his personal injury cause of action arising out of a collision between the vehicle being driven by Mora and Block's pickup truck.

Factual Background

Block's petition alleged he was driving westbound on Olton Road near an intersection with Wal-Mart's parking lot in Plainview, Texas, when Mora's vehicle collided with his pickup truck after she exited the parking lot onto Olton Road. In response, Mora filed a general denial and asserted two affirmative defenses — contributory negligence and, alternatively, unavoidable accident.

Block's claim was tried in a two-day, jury trial. The testimony at trial indicated that, before leaving his house for work the day of the accident, Block placed a spare tire atop four, five gallon buckets of hydraulic oil in the bed of his pickup truck. He did not secure the tire. Later that day, while returning home from work via Olton Road, Block was driving approximately forty-five miles per hour. As he approached the intersection of Olton Road and the Wal-Mart parking lot, Mora pulled her vehicle in front of him, causing her vehicle to collide with the front end of his pickup truck. On impact, the spare tire flew forward, knocking out the pickup truck's rear window and striking Block in the back of the neck and shoulder while pushing him against the steering wheel. Block, his wife, and an expert damages witness testified as to the nature and extent of his injuries.

Mora testified that, when the accident occurred, she was driving her mother's vehicle without permission and had not obtained a driver's license. She admitted that the accident was her fault. After Block rested his case-in-chief, Mora put on a single witness to rebut Block's damages evidence and rested.

At the jury charge conference, the trial court proposed submission of the Texas Pattern Jury Charges standard broad form, joint submission of negligence and proximate cause as Question No. 1, and proportionate responsibility as Question No. 2. Furthermore, the trial court proposed the use of the term injury in both questions. Block's counsel objected to the submission of the two questions, asserting that Mora had admitted fault and there was no evidence that he was contributorily negligent in causing the accident. In lieu thereof, Block proposed an instruction that stated: "Kimberly Mora has admitted that her negligence proximately caused the occurrence in question." Alternatively, Block requested that the term occurrence be substituted for the term injury in Question No. 1.

The trial court overruled his objections, denied the alternative instruction, and charged the jury, in pertinent part, as follows:

JURY QUESTION NO. 1
Did the negligence, if any, of those named below proximately cause the injuries, if any, to David Block?
Answer "Yes" or "No" for each of the following:
a. Kimberly Mora _____
b. David Block _____

Because, in answering Question No. 1, the jury answered "no" to subpart "a" and "yes" to subpart "b," the jury was not required to answer Question No. 2. When asked in Question No. 3, "what sum of money, if paid in cash, would fairly and reasonably compensate David Block for his injuries, if any, that resulted from the collision," the jury awarded no damages. Thereafter, the trial court entered a judgment that Block take nothing by his suit and awarded costs to Mora. In Block's subsequent motion for judgment notwithstanding the verdict, he re-urged his objections made during the jury charge conference. The trial court denied his motion and this appeal followed.

Discussion

Block asserts that the evidence at trial supported judgment in his favor because Mora's negligence was established as a matter of law, and there was no evidence indicating he was contributory negligent and/or proximately caused the accident or his injuries. As such, he asserts the trial court erred in giving comparative fault instructions to the jury and/or denying his motion for judgment notwithstanding the verdict.

Comparative Fault

Because comparative responsibility involves measuring the parties' comparative fault in causing plaintiff's injuries, it necessitates a preliminary finding that the plaintiff was in fact contributorily negligent. Contributory negligence contemplates an injured person's failure to use ordinary care in regard to his or her own safety, and requires proof that the plaintiff was negligent and that the negligence was the proximate cause of his or her injuries. The standards and tests for determining contributory negligence are the same as those for determining negligence and the rules of law applicable to the former are applicable to the latter.

Submission to the jury of a comparative fault question is not allowed "without sufficient evidence to support the submission." There is no question that the evidence was sufficient to support the submission of Mora's negligence. The question is, was there sufficient evidence to support the submission of Block's negligence? To determine whether legally sufficient evidence supported the submission of Block's negligence to the jury in a comparative fault question, we must first examine the record for evidence supporting his negligence and ignore all evidence to the contrary.

Block's Negligence and Proximate Cause

Mora contends Block was negligent in placing his spare tire atop the hydraulic oil cans in the bed of his pickup truck and that such negligence proximately caused his injuries when the spare tire struck him during the collision. In support, she cites Block's testimony that he failed to secure the tire on the truck bed when he left home for work the day of the accident. As a result, she contends that, while Block may not have caused the collision, he was contributorily negligent in causing his injuries. At trial, the defendant bears the burden of proving that the plaintiff was contributorily negligent by a preponderance of the evidence.

Mora failed to meet that burden by failing to establish that, by placing the unsecured spare tire in the back of his truck, Block committed an intrinsically harmful act or breached a legal duty to Mora or to the public at large. Block's omission cannot constitute contributory negligence in the absence of a breach of some legal duty. Furthermore, there was no evidence that Block was cited for any traffic violation due to the collision, nor did Mora cite any traffic law violated by Block. The uncontroverted testimony at trial indicated Block had driven his pickup truck with the fifteen pound spare tire in its bed to and from work at forty-five miles per hour without incident until Mora collided with his pickup truck. Under these circumstances, it cannot be said that Block engaged in a negligent act by placing the spare tire in the bed of his pickup truck.

Furthermore, proximate cause is comprised of two elements — cause in fact and foreseeability. A "negligent act or omission is not a cause in fact unless 'but for the conduct the accident would not have happened.'" If the accident would have occurred even if the injured party had taken the required precautions, his failure to do so cannot be a substantial factor in bringing about the accident. Cause in fact is established when the act or omission was a substantial factor in bringing about the occurrence, and without it, the event would not have occurred.

Block's failure to secure the spare tire did not cause the vehicular collision; nor did it cause the spare tire to suddenly fly forward and crash into the cab of his pickup truck. The unsecured spare tire merely provided a scenario in which Block's injuries were potentially enhanced or increased. Mora failed to produce any evidence that but for Block's conduct the accident would not have happened. Having failed to establish that Block's conduct was a cause in fact, Mora failed to establish proximate cause.

Here, regardless of whether Block secured the spare tire, the accident would have occurred. Having failed to preliminarily establish that Block was contributorily negligent in causing the accident, Mora was not entitled to the submission of a comparative negligence question. Accordingly, the trial court erred in submitting Question Nos. 1 and 2.

Enhanced or Increased Injuries

Mora contends the trial court did not err in submitting Question Nos. 1 and 2 because Block's conduct caused his injuries to be enhanced or increased. Whether Block's failure to secure the tire in the pickup truck's bed enhanced or increased his injuries suffered in the accident is of no moment as to the issue of comparative negligence. Under Texas law, the concept of comparative negligence has "no application to a plaintiff's actions which antedate the defendant's negligence."

In Kerby, 503 S.W.2d at 527, a linen truck driver appealed a jury verdict wherein he was found to be thirty-five percent at fault for his injuries because, on impact with a school bus, he was thrown through an open sliding door of the truck and, then, the truck toppled over him. Reversing the trial court and court of appeals, the Supreme Court held that the truck driver's conduct of driving with the door open did not constitute contributory negligence because it did not contribute to the accident; rather, it only provided a scenario in which the injuries suffered in the accident were enhanced or increased.

Block met his burden of proof establishing Mora was negligent in causing the collision. The evidence at trial established she had a duty to yield the right of way to Block, failed to do so and, as a result, collided with Block's pickup truck. At trial, Mora admitted she was at fault. Thereafter, it was incumbent upon Mora to establish her affirmative defense, i.e., that Block was contributorily negligent. She failed to do so. As such, Mora is liable to Block for any injuries he may have sustained resulting from her failure to yield the right of way.

Conclusion

We reverse the judgment of the trial court and remand the cause for further proceedings in conformance with this opinion.

Questions about the case:

1. Explain the basic facts of this case. How was the plaintiff injured?
2. How do the issues of comparative and contributory negligence figure in this case?
3. How does the court maintain that Mora failed to meet her burden of showing that Block was contributorily negligent?
4. Did Block meet his burden of proof? If so, how?
5. Why did the court rule the way that it did?

SMITH v. CIANELLI
2006 WL 697479, *5 (Conn. Super. 2006)

MARK H. TAYLOR, Judge.

I. Background

These actions were commenced by Gregory Smith, who was the unfortunate victim of two automobile accidents during the same month; the first on April 9, 1999, and the second on April 29, 1999. These matters were consolidated for trial on June 13, 2002 (Gilardi, J.). John Barboza, now deceased, is represented in these proceedings by the administrator of his estate, Norman Fishbein. General liability and damages are not contested in either of these combined files, except to the extent that they should be apportioned between the parties.

II. Facts

The first accident occurred on Interstate 91 in New Haven, and there is no dispute as to the following facts. At or about 7:42 A.M. on the morning of April 9, 1999, three automobiles were heading in a northerly direction in three contiguous lanes near Exit 3. The plaintiff, Gregory Smith was in the right lane. The defendant, Julie Cianelli, was in the center lane, and an unknown driver and automobile were in the left-hand lane. Cianelli's automobile collided with the left-rear side of Smith's automobile causing him to lose control, spin 180 degrees around across the road and hit the barrier on the left-hand side of the highway causing approximately $4,000.00 in damages to his 1993 Volvo sedan. Smith testified that he was driving in the right lane at a speed of 55-60 miles per hour. Immediately prior to the collision, Smith heard the squeal of wheels and saw Cianelli's vehicle lose control. He then saw her strike the back of his vehicle. He has no recollection of seeing the third unknown vehicle.

Cianelli testified that as she was driving in the center lane at approximately 55 miles per hour, she noticed that the unknown vehicle had a "dealer plate" and that the driver was conversing on his cellular telephone. She also testified that she took some interest, along with her husband who was also in the car, in identifying the individual driving the unknown vehicle because her husband is an automobile dealer. At or about the time she was discussing these matters with her husband, Cianelli testified that the unknown driver suddenly and without warning changed lanes from the left lane to the center lane. At the time of this sudden and unanticipated lane change, her automobile was positioned in a manner that some portion of the front left side of her vehicle was in close proximity to some portion of the back right side of the unknown vehicle. She testified that this required her to immediately apply her brakes to avoid a collision. She also testified that she shut her eyes, panicked and lost control of her vehicle. Her husband similarly testified that she panicked.

Immediately after this incident, Smith sought medical treatment from the following medical providers: Dr. Arthur Siegel, neurologist, Dr. Anthony Lavorgna, chiropractor, and Dr. Donald Austria, a general practitioner.

The second accident occurred approximately three weeks later on April 29 at 8:02 A.M., when Smith was traveling in a southerly direction on Hemingway Avenue in East Haven. There is no dispute between the parties that as Smith approached Tyler Street at approximately 40 miles per hour, John Barboza negligently made a left-hand turn in front of Smith's on-coming vehicle. Smith applied his brakes but was unable to stop before colliding head-on with the side of Barboza's vehicle, causing approximately $900 in damage to Smith's 1984 Audi sedan.

On the same day and thereafter, Smith continued to seek regularly scheduled treatment from the same medical providers that he had seen in connection with the first accident. As the result of either or both of these accidents, Smith suffered injuries to the lumbar, dorsal and cervical areas of his spine. In the opinions of various medical professionals, he has sustained permanent partial impairment to each of these areas. In a report of April 28, 2000, Dr. Siegel ascribes a 5% permanency to the dorsal spine attributable to injuries caused by the second accident with Barboza. In the same report, Dr. Siegel also ascribes a 2.5% permanency to Smith's cervical spine and 7.5% permanency to his lumbar spine, both attributable to injuries caused by the first accident with Cianelli. He also reported an injury to his left knee.

However, Dr. Siegel's medical records are inconsistent with regard to the cause of the injury to Smith's cervical spine. In a report dated April 16, 1999, Dr. Siegel indicates that Smith's neck is "asymptomatic." Yet on April 30, 1999, Dr. Siegel discusses "persistence of symptoms" and refers to neck discomfort among others in this category. He then goes on to discuss the April 29 accident as the cause of injury to Smith's dorsal spine.

To add further confusion to the issue of the permanent partial injuries to various portions of Smith's spine, Dr. Lavorgna's notes and reports are entirely inconsistent. Dr. Lavorgna's notes do not seem to discuss injuries to Smith's dorsal or cervical spine. In fact, his notes from the date of the second accident April 29, 1999, specifically state "there have been no significant events since the last report." The notes then consistently refer to the treatment of L5 and S1 areas of the lumbar region. In a report from Dr. Lavorgna to Dr. Siegel dated April 11, 2000, Lavorgna ascribes a 7% permanent partial injury to Smith's lumbar spine attributable to the first accident and makes no other findings. Yet in a letter to Attorney Michael F. O'Connor dated May 6, 2004, Lavorgna states that Smith's cervical and dorsal ailments are attributable to the second accident on April 29, 1999. This is thoroughly inconsistent with his notes and his previous report to Dr. Siegel.

Several years thereafter, Smith sought treatment from Doctors Mangieri, an orthopedic surgeon, and Opalak, a neurosurgeon. This medical treatment was for continued significant neck pain and for knee pain that has received no permanency rating, but which appears to have some foundation in the medical record for attribution to the first accident. Despite the more significant disability ratings for Smith's lumbar and dorsal areas, Doctors Mangieri and Opalak have focused their efforts on a significant problem with Smith's cervical spine, which is considered significant enough to seriously consider surgical treatment.

The parties have submitted two issues for consideration to the court. The first issue is to determine the degree of fault between Cianelli and the "unknown driver" in the first accident. The second issue is for the court to determine the relative causes of Smith's injuries attributable to the first compared with the second accident.

III. Discussion

A. Cianelli Vis-à-Vis the "Unknown Driver"

The court will first address the degree of fault attributable to the "unknown driver" in the first accident that occurred on April 9, 1999. At the hearing in this matter, it was suggested that the court consider two legal principles; first, the assumption that others will obey the law, and second, the principle of sudden emergency.

As driver of an automobile in Connecticut, Ms. Cianelli was entitled to assume that other drivers would obey the law. Therefore, Cianelli had the right to assume that the "unknown driver" would obey all statutes governing the operation of motor vehicles in this state and that he would use the care that a reasonably prudent person would use in the same circumstances. Cianelli was allowed to make this assumption until she knew or in the exercise of reasonable care should have known that the assumption has become unwarranted. See *Turbert v. Mather Motors, Inc.*, 165 Conn. 422, 429, 334 A.2d 903 (1973). Based upon a preponderance of credible evidence, the "unknown driver" changed lanes suddenly and without sufficient warning. Therefore, the court finds that the "unknown driver" committed an act of statutory negligence, in violation of General Statutes §14-236(1), by moving from one lane to another on a multiple lane highway without ascertaining whether the lane change could be accomplished with reasonable safety.

Ms. Cianelli urges the court to consider the existence of a sudden emergency in the court's evaluation of whether she acted as a reasonable person under the circumstances. "The sudden emergency doctrine applies only in cases in which the operator is suddenly confronted by a situation not of his own making and has the opportunity of deciding rapidly between alternative courses of action." *Mei v. Alterman Transport Lines, Inc.*, 159 Conn. 307, 312, 268 A.2d 639 (1970). However, a person choosing a course of action in an emergency is nonetheless required to exercise the care of an ordinarily prudent person acting in such an emergency.

The court finds that Cianelli was, indeed, faced with an emergency situation. The court further finds, however, that she failed to exercise the care of an ordinary prudent person acting in such an emergency. There are two factors that the court takes into consideration in this regard. First, there was testimony from Cianelli that she panicked, applied the brakes and shut her eyes. Second, she also testified that her attention was focused on the dealer plate and the identity of the "unknown driver," instead of keeping a proper lookout. A driver is required to keep a reasonable lookout for any persons and traffic likely to encounter. She is chargeable with notice of dangers or conditions that she could become aware through a reasonable exercise of her faculties. *McDonald v. Connecticut Co.,* 151 Conn. 14, 17, 193 A.2d 490 (1963).

Had Cianelli been more focused on the location of Smith's car in advance of the sudden emergency, and had she kept her eyes open throughout the emergency situation, she would have had the opportunity to keep her vehicle in proper control. Nonetheless, the court finds the negligence of the "unknown driver" to be the primary and more significant cause of the accident. As Cianelli approached the right-rear side of his automobile, the "unknown driver" failed to keep a proper lookout for her vehicle, which set in motion the chain of events that caused the accident. The court therefore assigns liability as follows: seventy-five percent to the "unknown driver" and twenty-five percent to Cianelli.

B. The Cause of Smith's Injuries

As the parties acknowledge and the court also finds, the medical records are less than perfectly clear and consistent concerning the cause of Smith's injuries to his lumbar, dorsal and cervical spine. Dr. Siegel's opinions appear to be far more consistent than Dr. Lavorgna's opinions, and they also appear to relate to and be based upon more contemporaneous observations of Mr. Smith's conditions. Despite the inconsistencies in these reports, the court sees no reason to dramatically depart from Dr. Siegel's opinion that the lumbar and cervical injuries occurred as the result of the first accident on April 9, 1999. It is also relatively clear from the record that Smith's knee injury was due to the first accident as well.

The plaintiff cites the case of *Card v. State,* 57 Conn. App. 134, 747 A.2d 32 (2000) to support an apportionment of the vast majority of damages to the first accident. In *Card,* the Appellate Court approved the apportionment instructions of the trial court, wherein there were three different defendants, each of whom was involved in different automobile accidents with the same plaintiff within a relatively short period of time. In *Card,* the plaintiff was unable to differentiate the extent to which each accident caused her damages within reasonable medical certainty. The court therefore approved an instruction that allowed the jury to equally apportion damages among the three defendants.

In *Card,* the Appellate Court reasoned that "the trier of fact's responsibility in cases involving injuries sustained in successive accidents is to apportion the damages among the parties whose negligence caused the plaintiff's injuries. We hold that the trial court should instruct the jury that if it is unable to determine how much of the plaintiff's damages is attributable to each tortfeasor, the jury may make a rough apportionment. The absence of conclusive evidence concerning allocation of damages will not preclude apportionment by the jury, but will necessarily result in a less precise allocation than that afforded by a clearer record." (Internal quotation marks omitted.) Id., at 145, 747 A.2d 32.

Given the lack of clarity in the expert opinions of the medical professionals involved in the treatment of Smith, the court will apply the rule in *Card* to apportion some of his cervical injuries to the second accident. There is some indication, based upon Dr. Siegel's records, that Smith's injury to his cervical spine from the first accident was aggravated by the second accident as it became symptomatic, or more symptomatic after the accident that occurred on April 29, 1999.

IV. Conclusion

The injuries to Smith's dorsal spine related to the second accident were relatively minor compared with the long-lasting treatment of his lumbar spine and the continuing treatment of his cervical spine and knee. In fact, there was very little treatment for Smith's dorsal spine, if any at all. Therefore, the court apportions damages as follows: 90% attributable to the first accident and 10% to the second.

The court has previously concluded that the "unknown driver" was responsible for three-quarters of the first accident, compared with Cianelli's responsibility for one-quarter of Smith's injuries. Accordingly, in the case of *Smith v. Barboza*, the defendant is liable for $4,500.00 of the stipulated damages of $45,000.00 for both cases. In the case of *Smith v. Cianelli*, the defendant is liable for damages in the amount of $10,125.00 of the remaining $40,500.00. The "unknown driver" is responsible for the remaining $30,375.00 in damages.

Questions about the case:

1. How was the plaintiff involved in two separate accidents?
2. Why did the court find that Cianelli was 25% liable for the plaintiff's injuries?
3. What role did the "unknown driver" play in the first accident?
4. How does the court resolve the issues concerning the confusing medical notes and treatment received by the plaintiff?

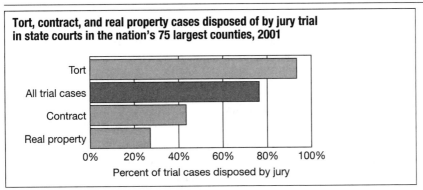

Tort, contract, and real property cases disposed of by jury trial in state courts in the nation's 75 largest counties, 2001

FIGURE 9-8

Tort, Contract, and Real Property Cases Decided by Jury Trials in State Courts

Civil Trial Cases and Verdicts in Large Counties, 2001, Bureau of Justice Statistics, U.S. Department of Justice.

 SKILLS YOU NEED IN THE REAL WORLD

Preparing a Trial Notebook

A trial notebook is a handy reference guide that is filled with all the legal topics and questions that an attorney will need at trial. We use the term *notebook* broadly here. Some attorneys use a system of file folders containing all the information that they will need for trial, while others actually use a three-ring binder. The benefit of a binder is that the pages can be securely fastened inside the cover, while folders have a tendency to disappear, usually at the most inopportune moment. Trial notebooks are used by attorneys to help them stay organized during the course of a trial. A good trial notebook should contain:

> Voir dire questions
> Motions in limine
> Trial briefs
> Notes for opening statements
> Witness list
> Direct or cross-examination points to be raised with specific witnesses
> Evidence to be admitted during the direct examination of specific witnesses
> Any foundation questions required for specific evidence
> Evidence list
> Exhibit list
> Foundation questions for specific types of evidence
> Relevant pleadings including the complaint, answer, counterclaim, cross-claim
> Witness deposition excerpts and summaries
> Medical summaries and crucial medical records
> Relevant case law: usually about issues that the attorney anticipates will arise during trial

Many attorneys have a standard format for a trial notebook. This format may be unique to the particular attorney, so you should learn his or her system.

It is usually helpful to have all the items contained in a single notebook. Large documents, such as lengthy depositions, can be held in separate files. The crucial points of a deposition transcript can be copied off as single pages and placed under the heading for that witness.

Paralegal Trial Notebook

In addition to the attorney notebook, a paralegal should have a trial notebook as well. What types of information should you have in your trial notebook? If you are attending the trial with the attorney, your focus will be slightly different from the attorney's. You are there to support the attorney and to anticipate problems. Trying a case is a stressful event and it often brings out the worst (and sometimes the best) in an attorney. Anything that you can do to eliminate complications helps alleviate that stress (and makes you that much more valuable to the attorney).

A paralegal trial notebook is built on the premise of avoiding problems at trial or being able to handle them as expeditiously as possible. Your notebook should contain:

Basic information about the case: case file number, important filing dates, copies of the complaint and answer (unmarked) as well as your own highlighted copy of both documents

Evidence checklist, cross-referenced by witness and foundation questions

Jury charts, juror questions, and a section listing improper questions that may be asked by the opposing counsel with the cases that clearly state such questions are improper

Order of witnesses who will testify and the evidence that should be admitted during each witness's testimony

Contact information: witness telephone, cell phone, and beeper numbers (for those occasions when you must contact that witness immediately)

Telephone, beeper, and cell phone numbers and e-mail addresses of
- Opposing counsel
- Opposing counsel's paralegal/legal assistant/legal secretary (they usually know how to get in contact with the attorney better than anyone else)
- Name of the judge's secretary, law clerk, and other staff and their direct dial numbers (Sometimes it is easier to contact these people with a cell phone call in the courthouse hallway than to try to talk to them personally.)
- Client's work, home, cell, beeper, and any other telephone number where he or she can be reached, including e-mail address and contact numbers for friends and relatives (You never know whom you may have to speak with to track down a missing client.)

Home telephone numbers of all trial team members, including attorneys, paralegals, runners, and anyone else who might be useful

Names, addresses, and telephone numbers for special witnesses, such as expert witnesses, investigators, etc.

Names and contact information for any support personnel, such as FedEx, UPS, court reporters, computer technicians, network administrator, even the attorney's laptop manufacturer (Remember Murphy's Law: Anything that can go wrong will go wrong, and at the worst possible moment.)

Complete list of all equipment needed for the trial, as well as a checklist showing that each piece of equipment has been tested and confirmed working. Back-up lightbulbs for projectors; dark-colored duct tape (for emergency patches and to hold down pesky wires and electrical cords)

Diagram of the courthouse, showing the location of bathrooms, vending machines, and water fountains (and designated smoking areas for clients who smoke)

A paralegal notebook with all this information will make trial work a much smoother and less stressful experience.

THE LIFE OF A PARALEGAL

Working with Insurance Adjusters

We do a lot of plaintiff work and that means working with insurance adjusters. Adjusters are odd creatures. We have them from all ends of the spectrum. Some of them are very nice and pleasant people, but others will go out of their way to make your life miserable — and they can really succeed in doing that. Overall, I think we have a good rapport with most of the ones that we deal with. Some insurance companies are just harder to deal with. I don't know if they've been trained to be that way, or not, but there are some companies that when you get the case, you just know that you are going to have a harder time because it's X Insurance Company. You can prove that their insured was at fault a hundred times over, and they still don't want to pay. We settle most of our cases, just like everybody else, but there are some companies that force you to go to the limit before they will settle.

We will contact the adjuster pretty early on in the case. Usually, by the time the client comes to us, they have already had contact with the adjuster themselves. The first thing that we do is send the adjuster a letter of representation telling them that we represent the client now and that the adjuster should deal with our firm from now on. The attorney will also tell the client not to speak with the adjuster anymore. We communicate with adjusters through faxes, phone, mail, you name it. What's interesting is that I've never actually met a single adjuster in person.

Elizabeth Adams, Paralegal

ETHICAL ISSUES FOR THE PARALEGAL: PARALEGALS WHO CAN APPEAR IN COURT

As we have seen in previous chapters, a paralegal must avoid the unauthorized practice of law. This not only includes avoiding giving legal advice but also appearing in court to represent a client. However, it is important to note that a paralegal can appear in court to represent clients in some hearings. For instance, there are proceedings involving Social Security benefits and other administrative hearings in which a paralegal can represent another person. A paralegal may accompany the attorney to court and may often act as an indispensable assistant to the attorney, but the paralegal is not allowed to conduct direct or cross-examination during the trial, or to perform any of the other duties normally associated with attorneys.

Chapter Summary

Contributory negligence is a defense to negligence actions in only a handful of jurisdictions, yet this principle remains an important doctrine in tort law. Under contributory negligence, a plaintiff who is partially at fault is barred from any recovery. This rather drastic finding was originally justified under the theory that the plaintiff's own negligence affected the proximate cause analysis. However, over time several important exceptions developed to contributory negligence to help soften its application. Among these exceptions, the doctrine of last clear chance has proven to be the most widely used, and the most controversial. Under last clear chance, a negligent plaintiff will not be barred from recovery when the defendant had the last opportunity of avoiding the accident and failed to do so. Other exceptions to the contributory negligence defense include the sudden emergency doctrine and the rescuer doctrine.

A growing dissatisfaction with contributory negligence encouraged many jurisdictions to adopt a new system: comparative negligence. Under comparative negligence a plaintiff's negligence will not bar his recovery but will simply reduce the amount of his award. Over time, at least three different approaches to comparative negligence have developed. Under pure comparative negligence, a plaintiff's negligence is compared to the defendant's, no matter how negligent the plaintiff's actions were. A plaintiff who is 99 percent at fault can still recover from a defendant who is 1 percent at fault. However, his award will be reduced by the amount of his negligence. Modified comparative negligence is the system adopted by most jurisdictions. There are two approaches to modified comparative negligence. Under one plan, a plaintiff can recover when he is up 50 percent at fault. If at greater than 50 percent at fault, he cannot recover. Under the other plan, the plaintiff's negligence must always be less than the defendant's. The third approach to comparative negligence is the "slight-gross" model in which the plaintiff can recover only when his negligence is slight in comparison with the defendant's.

Comparative negligence is the predominant form of defense to negligence actions, having been adopted in one form or another in all but a few states.

Web Sites

▨ **Law.com Definition of Contributory Negligence**
http://dictionary.law.com/definition2.asp?selected=341

▨ **Washington Law School**
http://www.washlaw.edu/subject/torts.html

▨ **Wikipedia — Contributory Negligence**
http://en.wikipedia.org/wiki/Contributory_negligence

▨ **'Lectric Law Library — Comparative Negligence**
http://www.lectlaw.com/def/c076.htm

Forms and Court Documents

Excerpt from defendant's answer in a contributory negligence jurisdiction

STATE OF PLACID   IN THE SUPERIOR COURT
COUNTY OF BARNES   FILE NUMBER: _____

JOHN SMITH,   )   ANSWER
Plaintiff   )
)
vs.   )
)
JANE DOE,   )
Defendant   )

Defendant denies the allegations contained in paragraph 3 of the plaintiff's complaint and further alleges that the sole and proximate cause of the collision between the defendant's automobile and the plaintiff's automobile was the negligence of the plaintiff in

- failing to maintain a proper lookout
- failing to stop at a posted stop sign as required by statute
- driving at excessive speeds

WHEREFORE, defendant, having fully answered the complaint of the plaintiff, prays as follows:

1. That this action be dismissed as to this Defendant
2. That Plaintiff have and recover nothing of this Defendant
3. That there be a trial by jury
4. That the Defendant recover his costs, including reasonable attorney's fees, as provided by law; and
5. That this Defendant have and recover such other and further relief as this Court may deem appropriate.

Respectfully submitted, this the _____ day of _____, 200__.

_____

Clarence D. Arrow
Attorney for the Defendant

Answer excerpt in a state that follows a modified comparative negligence model

STATE OF PLACID	IN THE SUPERIOR COURT
COUNTY OF BARNES	FILE NUMBER: _____

JANE SMITH,	)	ANSWER
Plaintiff	)	
	)	
vs.	)	
	)	
JOHN DOE,	)	
MARTHA DOE	)	
Defendants		

Defendants deny the allegations contained in paragraph 3 of the plaintiff's complaint and further allege that the sole and proximate cause of the collision between the defendants' automobile and the plaintiff's automobile was the negligence of the plaintiff in

- failing to maintain a proper lookout
- failing to stop at a posted stop sign as required by statute
- driving at excessive speeds

As a result of the above negligence, plaintiff's negligence equaled or exceeded that of the defendants and consequently the plaintiff should take nothing by his complaint.

WHEREFORE, Defendants, having fully answered the Complaint of the Plaintiff, pray as follows:

6. That this action be dismissed as to these Defendants
7. That Plaintiff have and recover nothing of these Defendants
8. That there be a trial by jury
9. That the Defendants recover their costs, including reasonable attorney's fees, as provided by law; and
10. That these Defendants have and recover such other and further relief as this Court may deem appropriate.

Respectfully submitted, this the _____ day of _____, 200__.

_____

Clarence D. Arrow
Attorney for the Defendants

Key Terms

Comparative negligence   Last clear chance
Contributory negligence   Sudden emergency

Review Questions

1   Most of the states that have adopted "pure" comparative negligence did it
    through judicial action; most of the states that enacted comparative
    negligence through legislation opted for a more limited form of
    comparative negligence. What is the reason for this discrepancy?
2   Why would such a harsh concept as contributory negligence be devel-
    oped in the first place?
3   It is said that comparative negligence developed as a reaction to contrib-
    utory negligence. In what way?
4   Is comparative negligence an improvement over contributory negli-
    gence? If so, how?
5   In recent years, there have been claims of runaway juries and huge awards
    in personal injury cases brought to plaintiffs with purportedly marginal
    cases. Does this situation call for the reinstitution of contributory neg-
    ligence? Why or why not?
6   What are the three elements of a contributory negligence claim that a
    defendant must prove?
7   Explain the last clear chance doctrine. When does it apply? When is this
    defense not available in a negligence action?
8   What is a "sudden emergency," and what effect does it have on a con-
    tributory negligence case?
9   Why is contributory negligence not a defense to intentional torts?
10 Explain the difference between the various types of comparative
    negligence.
11 How is "pure" comparative negligence different from "modified"
    comparative negligence?
12 Some commentators have suggested that comparative negligence is
    inconsistent with traditional proximate cause analysis. Draft an argu-
    ment in support of this view.

Applying What You Have Learned

1   Joe is driving his motorcycle in a state in which helmet use is required by
    statute. Joe is not wearing his helmet because it flattens his hair and he
    thinks he looks sexy without it. As Joe is driving down the highway, a car
    driven by Amanda pulls out directly in front of Joe. Joe runs into Aman-
    da's car and receives severe head injuries. Joe sues Amanda in a state that
    follows the "Georgia" plan on comparative negligence. You are on the jury
    in Joe's case. What is your verdict?

2   If Mr. Chumley's case is filed in a state that still follows contributory negligence, is he likely to lose? Why or why not?

3   John buys a ticket for a Ferris wheel ride at a traveling carnival. The back of the ticket has language that states, "Ferris wheels are a dangerous form of entertainment. The purchaser assumes all risks in the operation and function of the Ferris wheel and waives any claims against the Carnival Company for any negligence that might occur in the operation of said Ferris wheel or for any damages or injuries he may receive as a result of this ride." While John is sitting in one of the seats, the operator wanders away from his post and doesn't see that several bolts attaching the seat to the wheel have come loose. John's seat falls and he is injured. Can he sue the carnival company? If your answer is yes, what defenses are available to the carnival company? Does your answer change if the entire incident occurred in a contributory negligence state?

4   It's the annual office picnic and Steve has arrived late. He is supposed to be running one of the large grills. He rushes to the grill and spills in an immense amount of lighter fluid, thinking that it will get the grill hot in a short period of time. He doesn't realize that the can of lighter fluid has several leaks and when he lights the grill, fire shoots from the grill and catches Steve's clothing on fire, causing severe burns. Draft a complaint based on these facts and then an answer using contributory negligence as a defense. What key points must you raise in your answer?

5   John was injured in a crash with another car driven by Martha. At the end of the trial, the jury determines that John and Martha are both 50 percent at fault in the accident. This states follows the "New Hampshire" rule. What is the result in this case?

6   Using the same facts as the previous question, evaluate the case under the "Georgia" rule. Is the result in the case different? If so, how?

Endnotes

[1] *Maki v. Frelk*, 85 Ill. App. 2d 439, 229 N.E.2d 284 (1967).

[2] Turk, Comparative Negligence on the March, 28 Chi.-Kent L. Rev. 189 (1950).

[3] The Law of Torts §22.1; Prosser, Torts (4th ed.).

[4] *Sun Oil Co. v. Seamon*, 349 Mich. 387, 84 N.W.2d 840 (1957).

[5] Restatement (Second) of Torts §463.

[6] *O'Connor v. G.R. Packing Co.*, 74 App. Div. 2d 37, 426 N.Y.S.2d 557, *aff'd*, 53 N.Y.2d 278, 440 N.Y.S.2d 920, 423 N.E.2d 397 (1980).

[7] Restatement (Second) of Torts §468, comment c.

[8] Using Comparative Fault to Replace the All-or-Nothing Lottery Imposed Intentional Torts, 46 Vand. L. Rev. 121 (1993).

[9] *Hoelter v. Mohawk Service, Inc.*, 170 Conn. 495, 365 A.2d 1064 (1975).

[10] *Commercial Union Assur. Cos. v. Western Farm Bureau Ins. Cos.*, 93 N.M. 507, 601 P.2d 1203 (1979) (*Scott v. Rizzo*, 96 N.M. 682, 634 P.2d 1234 (1981)).

[11] *Smith v. Fiber Controls Corp.*, 300 N.C. 669, 673, 268 S.E.2d 504, 507 (1980).

[12] Restatement (Second) of Torts §918 (1); *Bailey v. J. L. Roebuck Co.*, 135 Okla. 216, 275 P. 329 (1929).

[13] *Benton v. Hillcrest Foods, Inc.*, 524 S.E.2d 53 (1999).

[14] *Willis v. Stauffer Chemical Co.*, 348 So. 2d 158, *on reh'g*, 349 So. 2d 1390, *cert. denied*, 352 So. 2d 1047 (1977).

[15] *Willis v. Stauffer Chemical Co.*, 348 So. 2d 158, *on reh'g*, 349 So. 2d 1390, *cert. denied*, 352 So. 2d 1047 (1977).

[16] *Byrne v. Kansas City, Ft. S. & M. R. Co.*, 61 F. 605 (6th Cir. 1894).

[17] Malone, Some Ruminations on Contributory Negligence, 65 Utah L. Rev. 91 (1981).

[18] *Kirby v. Larson*, 400 Mich. 585, 256 N.W.2d 400 (1977).

[19] *Exum v. Boyles*, 272 N.C. 567, 158 S.E.2d 845 (1968).

[20] *Sanders v. State Farm Ins. Cos.*, 354 So. 2d 663, *cert. denied*, 356 So. 2d 436 (1977).

[21] *Maricle v. Spiegel*, 213 Neb. 223, 329 N.W.2d 80 (1983).

[22] *Hrivnak v. Perrone*, 472 Pa. 348, 372 A.2d 730 (1977).

[23] *Bruggeman v. Illinois C. R. Co.*, 147 Iowa 187, 123 N.W. 1007 (1909).

[24] *Ruffo v. Schwegmann Bros. Giant Supermarkets, Inc.*, 424 So. 2d 470 (1982).

[25] *Andre v. Allynn*, 84 Cal. App. 2d 347 (1948).

[26] *Safeco Ins. Co. v. Watertown*, 529 F. Supp. 1220 (1981).

[27] *Noel v. McCaig*, 174 Kan. 677 (1953).

[28] *Norris v. Atlantic C. L. R. Co.*, 152 N.C. 505, 67 S.E. 1017 (1910).

[29] *Wilford v. Salvucci*, 117 Vt. 495, 95 A.2d 37 (1953).

[30] *Jacobs v. General Accident Fire Life Assur. Corp.*, 14 Wis. 2d 1, 109 N.W.2d 462 (1961).

[31] *Holiday Inns, Inc. v. Drew*, 276 Ark. 390, 635 S.W.2d 252 (1982).

[32] *Lindenberg v. Needles*, 203 Md. 8, 97 A.2d 901 (1953).

[33] *Jaworski v. Great Scott Supermarkets*, 71 Mich. App. 235, 247 N.W.2d 363 (1976).

[34] *Papagni v. Purdue*, 74 Nev. 32, 321 P.2d 252 (1958).

[35] Restatement (Second) of Torts §473.

[36] Am. Jur. 2d, Negligence §1160.

[37] Prosser, Comparative Negligence, 51 Mich. L. Rev. 465 (1953).

[38] Miller, Adoption of the Uniform Comparative Fault Act, 14 Pac. L.J. 835 (1983).

[39] Am. Jur. Negligence §1140 (2003).

[40] *Pedernales Electric Cooperative, Inc. v. Schulz*, 583 S.W.2d 882 (1979).

[41] *Finninger v. Johnson*, 692 S.W.2d 390 (1985).

[42] *Knapp v. Stanford*, 392 So. 2d 196 (1980).

[43] Conn. Gen. Stat. Ann. §52-572h(m); Or. Rev. Stats. §8.475.

[44] *Ouellette v. Carde*, 612 A.2d 687 (1992).

[45] *Lillemoen v. Gregorich*, 256 N.W.2d 628 (1977).

[46] *Martin v. Bussert*, 292 Minn. 29, 193 N.W.2d 134 (1971).

Strict Liability and Products Liability

Chapter Objectives

- Explain the difference between strict liability and other negligence actions

- Define the basic characteristics of a products liability lawsuit

- Explain how the case law of strict liability shifted from pro-business to pro-consumer

- Explain the three theories on which a products liability case can be based

- Describe the significance of cases such as *Rylands v. Fletcher* and *MacPherson v. Buick Co.*

 **INTRODUCTION**

Although we usually begin each chapter with a discussion of the Chumley case, because that case did not involve a claim of strict liability or products liability, we examine the facts of a different case here.

A PRODUCTS LIABILITY CASE: TIRE BLOWOUT

Susan is driving her car one day when the left front tire suddenly blows out. Susan's car overturns and she is seriously injured. During her hospital stay, Susan learns that her model of car and the type of tires that she had on her car have been involved in numerous lawsuits across the country. Apparently, this brand of tires has a history of blowouts. Many people across the United States have been injured or killed when these tires blew out at high speeds. Susan, who has severe injuries and huge medical bills, is strongly considering bringing a products liability lawsuit against the tire manufacturer. Does Susan have a case? As we explore the issues in this chapter, we analyze the facts of her case and decide if she can actually bring a products liability lawsuit.

We begin by addressing the issue of strict liability, then move to the issue directly involved in Susan's case: product liability.

STRICT LIABILITY

Strict liability
A finding of liability regardless of fault

The theory behind **strict liability** is that there are some activities that are so dangerous that a person is liable for any harm caused by them, whether or not he was negligent. This theory runs counter to the theory of negligence we have explored in previous chapters. Under the traditional analysis, a defendant first must have a duty to the plaintiff, he must breach that duty, the breach must be the proximate cause of the plaintiff's injuries, and the plaintiff must have sustained legally recognizable damages. However, in strict liability the courts short-circuit the first two elements. Instead of requiring proof of the defendant's breach, the court now assumes that the defendant's actions were the cause of the plaintiff's injuries. This assumption was a substantial departure from previous negligence law and created a stir in the legal community when it was first created.

Before a defendant can be held liable under strict liability, he must be engaged in some activity that the court deems to be "ultra-hazardous," or "abnormally dangerous." These activities are usually limited to the manufacture of explosives, poisons, or firearms and similar high-risk activities.[1]

A. ULTRA-HAZARDOUS ACTIVITY

Ultra-hazardous
A condition of special or unusual dangerousness

Under the theory of strict liability, the defendant is liable for all the injuries that result when he engages in **ultra-hazardous** or abnormally dangerous activity. This is true even if the defendant was not at fault, and even though he exercised all the normal precautions that should have been taken. Suppose that the defendant is in the business of manufacturing dynamite. During the manufacturing process, the dynamite explodes and injures the plaintiff. The

---

FIGURE 10-1

Examples of Ultra-hazardous Activities

---

dynamite company would be liable for the plaintiff's injuries, even though the company followed all the safety precautions that were required by law, and even if it could not have anticipated that the dynamite would explode under those conditions. Many other types of activities have been labeled as ultra-hazardous (see Figure 10-1).

Under strict liability a defendant is liable for the injuries caused by his activities whether or not he was negligent.

ISSUE AT A GLANCE

B. A SHORT HISTORY OF STRICT LIABILITY

1. BACKGROUND

Prior to the late 1800s, a plaintiff who was injured by a defendant who was engaged in dangerous activity had no recourse if he could not prove that the defendant was negligent. Although proof of negligence was seemingly a reasonable requirement, in practice it often produced harsh results. For one thing, in cases of industrial accidents, the plaintiff was often in no position to prove how the defendant corporation was negligent. Often, the evidence was destroyed along with everything else. When a dynamite factory explodes and injures nearby villagers, how can they prove that the company was negligent? Another problem with applying traditional negligence theory to such cases is that the courts often required a rigorous standard on the question of duty. In the early 1800s, there was virtually no industry and consumers dealt directly with craftspeople. Consumers ordered specific products and had definitive contractual relationships with the producers. However, by the 1860s, this model, although still a feature of case law, was no longer the economic reality. Consumers no longer dealt directly with producers. Instead, they dealt with retailers, such as Sears and Roebuck, or local general stores that provided a wide range of products on store shelves. However, as it often is, the

Sidebar

In ruling that natural gas is an ultra-hazardous instrumentality, a Wyoming federal court stated, "Because of the dangerous characteristics and properties of natural gas, a utility engaged in the business of transmitting and distributing natural gas has a duty to the public of exercising the high degree of care and diligence proportionate to the danger presented that was known or should have been known by the utility in building, emplacing and maintaining its gas mains and service lines."[2]

legal community was slow to grasp this change in society. Instead, it clung to the outmoded belief that the parties could negotiate risks and costs directly with one another, and cases involving defective products were still considered more a contract case than a torts case.

When plaintiffs brought suit against a defendant engaged in dangerous activities, more often than not they were turned away with no compensation. The courts began to realize that their approach was causing widespread injustice and they began casting about for some other legal theory. Fortunately, a new case holding appeared to clear a path out of this morass.

No discussion of the concept of strict liability would be complete without reference to the case of *Rylands v. Fletcher*. Decided in England in 1868, this was one of the first cases to establish the principle of strict liability for abnormally dangerous situations. The ruling in *Rylands* was that if a person maintained an abnormally dangerous condition on his property, he would be liable for any damages that resulted from that condition whether he was negligent or not. This case was applied to situations in which people kept dangerous animals, carried out dangerous manufacturing processes, and a wide range of other inherently dangerous activities. Later, this principle was embodied in the Restatement of Torts. (See Figure 10-2.)

Although the decision in *Rylands* seems modest by today's standards, it was the equivalent of a legal earthquake. All across Britain and the United States, commentators were swift to condemn or hail the decision. Some judges applied the decision in their own cases; many others refused to ever follow such a radical notion.

2. DEVELOPING STRICT LIABILITY IN THE UNITED STATES

The *Rylands* principle was adopted slowly in the United States. The courts in this country were very generous toward businesses in the 1800s. Throughout the century, courts consistently ruled in favor of large corporations, such as railroads, and against consumers and others injured by these corporations. The rationale behind these rulings was that any decision that would have a negative impact on the company might have a corresponding negative impact on the developing economy. The Industrial Revolution had only recently begun and jurists were often of the opinion that these companies should be given as much freedom as possible.

Sidebar

Strict liability is also known as absolute liability.

Sidebar

The Rylands *case involved an action by the owners of a mine against a mill owner. The mill owner had a large pond built above a working mine. The contractor who built the reservoir failed to properly support it and the pond collapsed and flooded the mine.*

Sidebar

"The principle of the [Rylands] case, somewhat fuzzy to be sure, was that a person who sets in motion some extraordinary or dangerous process must take the consequences; it would be no excuse to show that he was as careful as he could be, or as careful as the reasonable man."[3]

FIGURE 10-2

Justifying a Ruling of Strict Liability Under the Restatement of Torts*

There are six different conditions that will lead to a ruling of strict liability:

1 The existence of a high degree of risk to some person or to property
2 The likelihood that some harm will result from this condition is great
3 The inability of the owner to eliminate the risk by reasonable care
4 The extent to which the activity is uncommon
5 The activity is inappropriate in the place where it is carried out
6 The value of the activity is outweighed by the risk in carrying it out

*Restatement (Second) of Torts, §520.

However, over time the principle in *Rylands* was slowly applied to one situation after another. Blasting was ruled an ultra-hazardous activity, if for no other reason than to encourage railroads and road builders to be extremely careful in this very dangerous activity. Later, poison manufacturing was added to the list. Keeping wild animals was also ruled to be an ultra-hazardous activity. Since the 1860s, the list has grown considerably.

C. STRICT LIABILITY FOR ANIMAL BEHAVIOR

Strict liability lawsuits can be based not only on abnormally dangerous conditions, but also on other situations. For instance, when a person keeps a wild animal on his premises, such as a lion or a tiger, and that animal injures the plaintiff, the animal's owner can be sued on the basis of strict liability in tort. If the animal is wild, the owner is considered to be on notice that the animal is dangerous and that he will therefore be responsible for any injuries that the animal causes. The rule changes slightly when we discuss domestic animals. Normally, a pet owner will not be strictly liable when his dog bites another person, unless the owner had reason to believe that the dog was dangerous. Under the law, the owner is put on notice that his animal is dangerous when the pet has acted aggressively in the past. Many states have a rule that essentially gives every dog one free bite. What that rule means is that an owner is not put on notice that the dog is aggressive until it has actually bitten someone. After that point, the owner will then be liable if the dog attacks anyone else. Many states have modified that rule. For instance, some states have adopted a rule that creates a presumption of dangerousness in certain breeds of dog. Pit bulls, for example, have been ruled to be dangerous dogs in some jurisdictions, even when individual dogs have not demonstrated any aggressive behavior before their first attack.

D. STRICT LIABILITY HAS NOT BEEN ADOPTED IN ALL JURISDICTIONS

The concept of strict liability for ultra-hazardous activities has not been adopted in all jurisdictions. In the jurisdictions in which it has not been made the law of the land, other theories, such as modified negligence theory, have been put into service.

E. STATUTE OF LIMITATIONS CONCERNS IN STRICT LIABILITY LAWSUITS

Whenever a strict liability lawsuit is contemplated, it is important to note the applicable statutes of limitations. As we have discussed in prior chapters, a statute of limitations is a time limit placed on a lawsuit that sets a deadline by which a plaintiff must bring a case or the case is waived. Other statutes may also cause concern in these cases.

Some states, such as North Carolina, have complicated products liability statutes. Under these statutes, it is very difficult for a person to prove that a defective product injured her. Not only is the standard of proof higher in these states, but in many situations the statute of limitations is shorter.

INTRODUCTION TO PRODUCTS LIABILITY

Products liability
Also known as "product liability," the liability assessed against a manufacturer, seller, wholesaler, etc., for placing a dangerous or defective product on the market that causes injury or damage

When we discuss **products liability** we're talking about a relatively recent legal innovation. A lawyer from the early 1900s would not have been familiar with the term. Only in the last few decades has the law progressed to such an extent as to allow consumers to bring lawsuits against manufacturers who create defective products. Prior to the creation of products liability as a separate category of tort law, these types of cases, if they were permitted at all, were generally handled under the broad umbrella of negligence cases.

The typical products liability case involves a defective product purchased by the plaintiff who was subsequently injured by the product. The injury is generally the result of a defective design or a product that has been manufactured in a dangerous way. Products liability cases are firmly rooted in public policy concerns. In situations in which a consumer is injured by the negligence of a multinational corporation, the law has begun to favor the consumer with her limited resources over the corporation with its vast resources.

The public policy behind products liability theory is based on the idea that by discouraging corporations from producing faulty products, the law can provide financial incentive to corporations to create safer products.

ISSUE AT A GLANCE  **We use the term *products liability* to refer to almost any type of case that involves an action against a manufacturer or seller of a product that subsequently injures an individual.**

A. PRODUCTS LIABILITY IN THE UNITED STATES

In the 1800s, if a consumer was injured by a defective product, she had very little legal recourse. These suits, if allowed at all, had the requirement of **privity.**

Privity
A direct financial relationship between the parties. For example, when a home seller signs a contract for the sale of his home to a buyer, the parties are in privity with one another

1. PRIVITY OF CONTRACT REQUIREMENT

Under nineteenth-century analysis, if there was no privity of contract between the consumer and the manufacturer, there could be no cause of action for negligence. This was the rule of law in this country for decades even though modern business transactions usually involve a consumer purchasing products from a middleman (i.e., a retailer) rather than the manufacturer.

This limited view was first espoused in *Winterbottom v. Wright*, an 1842 English case that was enthusiastically adopted in the United States as a means of preventing strict liability and products liability actions by consumers injured by defective products.

Exceptions to the harsh results of the *Winterbottom* rule were created within a few years of its adoption in the United States. For instance, one court created an exception when the product was "inherently dangerous," such as a handgun or an explosive. This exception sounds very much like what other courts had done in creating strict liability in the first place.

2. THE THEORY UNDERLYING THE PRIVITY REQUIREMENT

The idea behind the privity requirement, although not directly expressed in the case law, is that both parties had certain expectations in a contract and each had some power over the other to affect the appearance and safety of the ultimate product. There were at least three problems with this approach:

1   It gave no relief to third parties, people not in privity, for injuries sustained by a dangerous product.

2   It failed to recognize an important change in society, that is, a move away from direct contact between manufacturer and consumer by the creation of intermediaries such as retailers in the chain of commerce from raw materials and production through the retail and the resale of products.

3   It also permitted corporations to be, if not careless about safety, at least to put it as a secondary consideration.

The original judicial approach had favored the corporation under the theory that fledgling manufacturers needed time and resources to develop their products. The theory was that this "breathing space" would help the United States develop economically and this increase in overall economic health would essentially work its way down to every member of society.

In practice, exactly the opposite occurred. The manufacturers and corporations, like spoiled children, indulged themselves and failed to apply their profits toward improved safety and better design of products. In an environment in which profits are the only yardstick, all other considerations, even those concerning injuries to consumers, take a back seat.

B. A NEW JUDICIAL APPROACH

The problems with the judicial approach to product liability cases became obvious even to the most conservative and pro-business members of the judiciary. The corporations were clearly not going to take action to protect consumers unless forced to do so. Legislatures around the country, with some important exceptions, were reluctant to enact any laws that might be

Sidebar

In creating the rule that privity must exist between the injured consumer and the manufacturer, the judge ruled, "I am clearly of the opinion that the defendant is entitled to our judgment. We ought not to permit a doubt to rest upon this subject, for our doing so might be the means of letting in upon us an infinity of actions. . . . There is no privity of contract between these parties; and if the plaintiff can sue, every passenger, or even any person passing along the road, who was injured by the upsetting of the coach, might bring a similar action. Unless we confine the operation of such contracts as this to the parties who entered into them, the most absurd and outrageous consequences, to which I can see no limit, would ensue." Winterbottom v. Wright, 10 M. & W. 109, 152 Eng. Rep. 402 (Ex. 1842).

restrictive of business. Events seemed bogged down in a stalemate primarily of the courts' creation.

Then a new judicial interpretation changed the status quo. New York Appellate Justice Benjamin Cardozo, in a case that would eventually have national importance, wrote a decision about a faulty automobile tire and opened up an entirely new branch of law.

1. THE *MACPHERSON* CASE AND A CHANGE IN JUDICIAL ATTITUDES

The *MacPherson* case is significant because it signaled the beginning of the end of the pro-business court rulings in strict liability and products liability cases.

MACPHERSON v. BUICK MOTOR CO.
217 N.Y. 382, 111 N.E. 1050, 1055 (1916)

CARDOZO, J.

The defendant is a manufacturer of automobiles. It sold an automobile to a retail dealer. The retail dealer resold to the plaintiff. While the plaintiff was in the car, it suddenly collapsed. He was thrown out and injured. One of the wheels was made of defective wood, and its spokes crumbled into fragments. The wheel was not made by the defendant; it was bought from another manufacturer. There is evidence, however, that its defects could have been discovered by reasonable inspection, and that inspection was omitted. There is no claim that the defendant knew of the defect and willfully concealed it. The charge is one, not of fraud, but of negligence. The question to be determined is whether the defendant owed a duty of care and vigilance to any one but the immediate purchaser.

The foundations of this branch of the law, at least in this state, were laid in *Thomas v. Winchester*. A poison was falsely labeled. The sale was made to a druggist, who in turn sold to a customer. The customer recovered damages from the seller who affixed the label. "The defendant's negligence," it was said, "put human life in imminent danger." A poison falsely labeled is likely to injure any one who gets it. Because the danger is to be foreseen, there is a duty to avoid the injury. Cases were cited by way of illustration in which manufacturers were not subject to any duty irrespective of contract. The distinction was said to be that their conduct, though negligent, was not likely to result in injury to any one except the purchaser. We are not required to say whether the chance of injury was always as remote as the distinction assumes. Some of the illustrations might be rejected today. The principle of the distinction is for present purposes the important thing.

The defendant argues that things imminently dangerous to life are poisons, explosives, deadly weapons — things whose normal function it is to injure or destroy. We find in the opinion of Brett, M. R., afterwards Lord Esher (p. 510), the same conception of a duty, irrespective of contract, imposed upon the manufacturer by the law itself: "Whenever one person supplies goods, or machinery, or the like, for the purpose of their being used by another person under such circumstances that every one of ordinary sense would, if he thought, recognize at once that unless he used ordinary care and skill with regard to the condition of the thing supplied or the mode of supplying it, there will be danger of injury to the person or property of him for whose use the thing is supplied, and who is to use it, a duty arises to use ordinary care and skill as the condition or manner of supplying such thing."

We hold, then, that the principle of *Thomas v. Winchester* is not limited to poisons, explosives, and things of like nature, to things which in their normal operation are implements of destruction. If the nature of a thing is such that it is reasonably certain to place and limb in peril when negligently made, it is then a thing of danger. Its nature gives warning of the consequences to be expected. If to the element of danger there is added knowledge that the thing will be used by persons other than the purchaser, and used without new tests then, irrespective of contract, the manufacturer of this thing of danger is under a duty to make it carefully. That is as far as we are required to go for the decision of this case. There must be knowledge of a danger, not merely possible, but probable. It is possible to use almost anything in a way that will make it dangerous if defective. That is not enough to charge the manufacturer with a duty independent of his contract. Whether a given thing is dangerous may be sometimes a question for the court and sometimes a question for the jury. There must also be knowledge that in the usual course of events the danger will be shared by others than the buyer. Such knowledge may often be inferred from the nature of the transaction. But it is possible that even knowledge of the danger and of the use will not always be enough. The proximity or remoteness of the relation is a factor to be considered. We are dealing now with the liability of the manufacturer of the finished product, who puts it on the market to be used without inspection by his customers. If he is negligent, where danger is to be foreseen, a liability will follow. We are not required at this time to say that it is legitimate to go back to the manufacturer of the finished products and hold the manufacturers of the component parts. To make their negligence a cause of imminent danger, an independent cause must often intervene; the manufacturer of the finished products must also fail in his duty of inspection.

This automobile was designed to go fifty miles an hour. Unless its wheels were sound and strong, injury was almost certain. It was as much a thing of danger as a defective engine for a railroad. The defendant knew the danger. It knew also that the car would be used by persons other than the buyer. This was apparent from its size; there were seats for three persons. It was apparent also from the fact that the buyer was a dealer in cars, who bought to resell. The maker of this car supplied it for the use of purchasers from the dealer.

We think the defendant was not absolved from a duty of inspection because it bought the wheels from a reputable manufacturer. It was not merely a dealer in automobiles. It was a manufacturer of automobiles. It was responsible for the finished product. It was not at liberty to put the finished products on the market without subjecting the component parts to ordinary and simple tests.

The obligation to inspect must vary with the nature of the thing to be inspected. The more probable the danger, the greater the need of caution.

Other rulings complained of have been considered, but no error has been found on them.

The judgment should be affirmed.

2. THE SIGNIFICANCE OF THE *MacPHERSON* CASE

Because the *MacPherson* case was such a departure from previous court rulings, it was slow to catch on in other jurisdictions. But by the 1950s, nearly every state had adopted the *MacPherson* approach. It is interesting to note that Justice Cardozo himself seemed uncomfortable with the consequences of his own reasoning. In 1931, he pulled back from the trend that he had helped to set in motion. In one case,[4] he stated, "[T]he hazards of a business conducted on these terms are so extreme as to enkindle doubt whether a flaw may not exist in the implication of a duty that exposes to these consequences."

ISSUE AT A GLANCE

The "MacPherson rule" has been extended far beyond the original issues involved in that case. It was eventually applied to situations involving third parties, companies that were not in the business of manufacturing, and even to bystanders.

C. THE BASIC ELEMENTS OF A PRODUCTS LIABILITY CASE

With the holding in the *MacPherson* case, the era of products liability suits had begun. We now examine the details of these claims and the basic requirements. The first, and most obvious, requirement is that the plaintiff must sustain some form of personal injury. No matter how defective the product, if it fails to injure the plaintiff, there is no cause of action. The loss suffered in a products liability case can also include property damage. Another requirement is that the injury originate either from a defective design or a dangerous application of the product.

Products liability cases are really a hybrid between lawsuits on the basis of a contractual relationship between the parties and losses based on personal injuries incurred by one of the parties.

FIGURE 10-3 **The Reasoning Behind Creating Products Liability Theory**	A consumer who is injured by a faulty product ought to have the right to seek compensation from the manufacturer who created the defective product. Traditionally, such a case would fall under negligence law. However, at that time, such actions required privity. Plaintiffs found it difficult, if not impossible, to establish privity. Result: Abolish privity as a requirement.

D. PRODUCTS LIABILITY CASES DO NOT INVOLVE CONSUMER DISSATISFACTION

Products liability lawsuits do not involve cases in which a product fails to live up to consumers' expectations. When the consumer is dissatisfied with the product's performance, he can bring a different type of civil action, but he is not permitted to bring a products liability claim. Products liability cases have as one of their most important ingredients an injury to the plaintiff. This injury can be physical, financial, psychological, or property-based.

For instance, when the consumer is sold a defective item — one that does not work properly — such a suit is usually handled as a contractual dispute. Products liability litigation focuses on dangerous and harmful products.

In states in which strict liability in tort had already been accepted, the courts fixed on this as the principle to use in products liability cases. First, they removed the requirement of privity of contract, then they made the manufacturer liable for any injuries from a defective product, under the theory that allowed others to be held liable for defective or dangerous conditions in ultrahazardous situations. In strict liability, people who kept wild animals or companies that manufactured poisons or explosives were liable for any injuries that occurred whether the plaintiff could prove that they were negligent or not.

This theory would now be applied to consumer products. Cases in which a manufacturer created a product that eventually injured a person were analogous to a company that manufactured dynamite; the company had put a dangerous product into the stream of commerce and the responsibility for the eventual injury would be laid at the feet of the manufacturer in strict liability.

In states that had never adopted strict liability in tort, there was a different approach. Privity of contract was also removed as a requirement of recovery, but these states based suits on a different theory. Strict liability was not an option, so these jurisdictions opted for a variation of contractual law. Although privity had been removed, the courts continued to impose other contractual obligations as though the end-consumer and the manufacturer were still contractual parties. Specifically, courts imposed warranties on the manufacturers and allowed plaintiffs to recover for breaches of those warranties.

In permitting such suits, courts relied on express warranties, that is, those promises stated by the manufacturer and other parties in the stream of commerce. End-users were given the benefit of these express warranties even though they technically may not have been contractual parties, at least not with the original manufacturer.

Products liability cases can be based on negligence, strict liability, or breach of warranty.

ISSUE
AT A
GLANCE

Courts also created "implied" warranties, that is, promises and conditions that any reasonable person would assume that a manufacturer gives when it creates a product.

E. WARRANTIES

Warranty
A pledge, assurance, or guarantee that a particular fact is true

One of the most important areas of products liability lawsuits deals with express and implied **warranties.** There are several warranties that are now either presumed under the law or required for manufacturers and suppliers when they sell products.

1. WARRANTY OF MERCHANTABILITY

Some states have never completely adopted the theory of strict liability in tort, or have not recognized it in the context of products liability cases. Those states are Delaware, Massachusetts, Michigan, North Carolina, and Virginia. In those states, a products liability case must be based on some alternative theory, such as breach of warranty.[6]

The warranty of merchantability is the implied promise that the product will perform normally and safely. When a product is actually dangerous, it violates this warranty and this can provide the basis for an action against the manufacturer.

2. WARRANTY OF FITNESS FOR PURPOSE

Like the warranty of merchantability, the warranty of fitness for particular purpose is an implied promise that the product will perform the duty for which it has been advertised. The seller is essentially promising the buyer that the product will satisfy the buyer's needs. Although implied, it often has a factual basis in statements and representations made by the seller. The implied warranty of fitness for purpose is different from the implied warranty of merchantability in the following critical way: The implied warranty of fitness for purpose is based on the representations, statements, and negotiations between the buyer and seller and is therefore highly dependent on the type of proof that can be had about these representations.

Proof of a breach of warranty requires no showing of fault and is therefore a "strict liability" tort.[7]

Example: David goes to his local computer supplier and asks for a single computer that will handle two different, and usually incompatible, computer systems. After a few minutes' thought, the salesman takes him to the model

---

FIGURE 10-4

U.C.C. Position on Implied Warranties

U.C.C. §2-314. Implied Warranty: Merchantability; Usage of Trade

(1) Unless excluded or modified (Section 2-316), a warranty that the goods shall be merchantable is implied in a contract for their sale if the seller is a merchant with respect to goods of that kind. Under this section the serving for value of food or drink to be consumed either on the premises or elsewhere is a sale.

(2) Goods to be merchantable must be at least such as

(a) pass without objection in the trade under the contract description; and

(b) in the case of fungible goods, are of fair average quality within the description; and

(c) are fit for the ordinary purposes for which such goods are used; and

(d) run, within the variations permitted by the agreement, of even kind, quality and quantity within each unit and among all units involved; and

(e) are adequately contained, packaged, and labeled as the agreement may require; and

(f) conform to the promises or affirmations of fact made on the container or label if any.

(3) Unless excluded or modified (Section 2-316), other implied warranties may arise from course of dealing or usage of trade.

1 An express warranty was given.
2 The product failed to conform to the warranty.
3 The plaintiff suffered damages because of this failure.
4 The plaintiff notified the manufacturer of the breach.

A Plaintiff Must Prove the Following Elements Under an Express Warranty Theory

Odyssey Compu-3000 and says, "This is the one for you." David pays for the computer and takes it home. When he starts the computer, he discovers that the computer is not configured to run either computer operating system. Does he have an action against the computer store for breach of an implied warranty of fitness for purpose?

Answer: Yes. When the salesman directed David to that particular computer, he was essentially saying that this computer is the one that can meet David's needs. Although he didn't specifically make that statement, it is certainly a reasonable interpretation of his actions and an implied promise that the computer would fit David's needs.

3. EXPRESS WARRANTIES

In addition to implied warranties, any warranties actually stated by the manufacturer will also be applied. So-called express warranties could cover a wide range of activities, such as guarantees about how and under what conditions the product will perform, statements about safety and inspection, or even health hazards associated with use.

F. LIABILITY WITHOUT FAULT UNDER PRODUCTS LIABILITY

Just as we saw in our discussions on strict liability cases, products liability lawsuits do not focus on the intent of the parties. A plaintiff is not required to show that the manufacturer deliberately set out to create a defective design. Such proof would be almost impossible. Instead, products liability cases are firmly rooted in strict liability theory or warranty theories. However, products liability cases go one step further than most strict liability suits. In a negligence action, one of the primary elements that the plaintiff must prove is that the defendant was at fault. In states that follow a comparative negligence model, the plaintiff is not required to prove that the defendant was completely at fault, but proof of fault is still a requirement. This is not true of strict liability cases in general and products liability cases specifically. A plaintiff can bring a successful products liability lawsuit against a manufacturer without proving that the manufacturer was at fault. In fact, it is not a defense in a products liability lawsuit that the manufacturer followed all the safety requirements.

Sidebar

Although most products liability cases seem firmly rooted in tort law applications, there is a side branch of these cases that actually bases the plaintiff's case in breach of warranty. Some have argued that this smaller offshoot of warranty-based products liability arose because some states (such as Delaware, Massachusetts, Michigan, and Virginia) never adopted the concept of strict liability in tort for defective products. Basing a products liability case on a broken promise involves proof of contractual relationship between the parties. Cases in this vein often rely on the Uniform Commercial Code for both the types of warranties given for a product and the types of damages that can be recovered. Because most states have adopted the U.C.C. in virtually identical language, this does create more uniformity across court decisions.

FIGURE 10-6

Express
Warranties
Under the
Uniform
Commercial
Code

U.C.C. §2-313?? Express Warranties by Affirmation, Promise, Description, Sample
(1) Express warranties by the seller are created as follows:

(a) Any affirmation of fact or promise made by the seller to the buyer which relates to the goods and becomes part of the basis of the bargain creates an express warranty that the goods shall conform to the affirmation or promise.

(b) Any description of the goods which is made part of the basis of the bargain creates an express warranty that the goods shall conform to the description.

(c) Any sample or model which is made part of the basis of the bargain creates an express warranty that the whole of the goods shall conform to the sample or model.

(2) It is not necessary to the creation of an express warranty that the seller use formal words such as "warrant" or "guarantee" or that he have a specific intention to make a warranty, but an affirmation merely of the value of the goods or a statement purporting to be merely the seller's opinion or commendation of the goods does not create a warranty.

FIGURE 10-7

Defective
Products in
Product
Liability Trials

Defective products in product liability trials in the 75 largest counties, 2001

- Of the 144 product liability trials for which the type of defective product was known, 28% dealt with asbestos or other toxic substances.
- Cases involving defective vehicles such as automobiles, trucks, or airplanes accounted for about 12% of the 144 product liability trials.
- Defective construction, electrical, or manufacturing equipment was involved in about 19% of the 144 product liability trials disposed of in the nation's 75 largest counties during 2001.
- Punitive damages were awarded to plaintiff winners in 3 of 144 product liability trials (not shown in table).
- There was 1 tobacco product liability trial in the nation's 75 largest counties in 2001. This was a jury trial involving 1 plaintiff against 4 business defendants. The jury ruled in favor of the defendants.

Type of defective product	Product liability trials[a]	
	Number	Percent
Total	144	100.0%
Toxic substances	40	27.9%
Asbestos	31	21.8
Other substances	9	6.1
Equipment[b]	27	18.7
Home appliances and items[c]	24	17.0
Other product[d]	21	14.6
Vehicle[e]	18	12.4
Medical[f]	8	5.5
Food[g]	6	4.0

Note: Type of defective product was known for 144 of the 158 product liability trials. Detail may not sum to total because of rounding.
[a]Trials include bench and jury trials, trials with a directed verdict, judgments notwithstanding the verdict, and jury trials for defaulted defendants.
[b]Includes construction, electrical, and manufacturing equipment.
[c]Includes home furniture, small appliances, workshop tools, yard equipment, TV/stereo/VCR appliances, and sporting goods.
[d]Includes natural gas, tobacco, and other products.
[e]Includes automobiles, trucks, and other forms of transport (airplanes).
[f]Includes nonprescription and prescription drugs, cosmetics, breast and other internal implants, and other medical equipment and devices.
[g]Includes food in restaurants and grocery stores.

Tort Trials and Verdicts in Large Counties, 2001, Bureau of Justice Statistics, U.S. Department of Justice.

G. THE STANDARD OF CARE IN PRODUCTS LIABILITY CASES

Given that a products liability case can be brought under several different types of theories, when the case is based on negligence, an important issue arises: What is the standard of care? Is the standard of care that a manufacturer must follow different from what a retailer must follow? Unfortunately, courts have been vague in spelling out the standard of care in products liability cases. Instead of using precise terms, they often simply state that the manufacturer's duty is "reasonable care." Usually this is interpreted in the same way that the standard of care is applied in any negligence case: The standard of care is what a reasonable person, under the same circumstances, would have used. Because the conduct in question is that of a manufacturer instead of an actual human being, the courts create a hypothetical "reasonable manufacturer" and ask a similar question: What would this hypothetical reasonable manufacturer have done under similar circumstances? If this hypothetical manufacturer would have tested and inspected its products before shipping them out to consumers, the failure of the defendant company to do the same is a breach of the standard of care. Of course, determining what is reasonable under the circumstances is often a hotly contested issue.

1. MANUFACTURER'S DUTY TO TEST AND INSPECT PRODUCTS

The law places a burden on the manufacturer to both test and inspect its products to ensure that they are not dangerous.[8] How far does this obligation extend? A manufacturer is required to test and inspect during the manufacturing process and to test the finished product, but is not required to have detected a latent defect that would not appear in normal testing or inspection.[9] When a manufacturer creates a product, it has a duty to test that product for defects and flaws. The more complicated and dangerous a product is, the more likely it will require greater testing, inspection, and design analysis to ensure the product does not injure consumers.

Obviously, machines with more moving parts will require a greater degree of testing and review than would a simple object. This view is echoed in the Restatement of Torts, which suggests that the standard to be used should be an amount of care commensurate with the dangerousness of the object.

The plaintiff must present proof that:
1 The manufacturer owed the plaintiff a duty
2 The manufacturer subsequently breached that duty
3 The manufacturer's breach was the proximate cause of the plaintiff's injury
4 The plaintiff has legally compensable injuries

FIGURE 10-8

Proving Products Liability Under a Negligence Theory

a. Food

The degree of care required in food is higher than is found in many other products (for obvious reasons). For many years, there was a split between "natural" contaminants in food and "unnatural (or foreign)" contaminants. A consumer who was injured by biting into a fish bone while eating canned fish would, under most situations, have no cause of action against the company, but if the same fish contained a piece of metal, the consumer would have a cause of action. This distinction has gradually faded over the years. Courts have come to realize that natural substances can be just as damaging as foreign ones, so they have instead focused on what a reasonable person would expect from the food. If bones or any other contaminants would not reasonably be expected in the food, the person injured would have a cause of action.[10]

b. Compliance with Safety and/or Health Regulations

Suppose that the manufacturer can show that it followed all applicable safety and health regulations? How will this compliance affect the manufacturer's liability? Some courts have held that such compliance is at least a rebuttable presumption of proper testing and inspection; some have ruled that it is conclusive proof of proper testing and inspection.[11]

H. PRODUCTS LIABILITY PER SE?

If a products liability case is based on negligence, does this also mean that other negligence principles, such as negligence per se, will operate in this area as well?

Example: Furry Foods put out a food product called furry beef jerky. Consumers who ate this modified beef jerky became seriously ill. Upon investigation, it turned out that part of the "furry" texture of the beef jerky came from the presence of mold, which had caused the consumers to become ill. Several plaintiffs have filed suit against Furry Foods and as part of their allegations have shown that Furry failed to have the new jerky inspected by the state food and drug agency. This is a clear violation of an existing statute. As we have already seen, violation of a safety statute in a negligence case can justify the use of negligence per se (a rebuttable presumption that the defendant has committed negligence). Can the same theory be used here?

Answer: In most jurisdictions, yes. So long as the plaintiffs can meet the requirements of a negligence per se action (the purpose of the statute was designed to protect a class of persons; the plaintiff was a member of the class to be protected, etc.), the plaintiffs are entitled to use negligence per se theory against Furry Foods.

I. PUBLIC POLICY ARGUMENTS FOR PRODUCTS LIABILITY CASES

Products liability litigation is based on the premise that of the two parties involved, the individual consumer and the company that created the product, the company is in a better position to remedy the danger than is the consumer. The theory underpinning these cases is that if a company is sued successfully for a dangerous product, the company will have a financial incentive to change the product to make it safer. Over time, this natural tendency toward creating better products will ultimately result in most products being made better, stronger, and safer. One could certainly argue that with the extent of products liability lawsuits brought in the United States, this reasoning has shown to be correct. After all, the United States has one of the world's strongest economies while at the same time creating products that are generally far safer than products produced 50 or 100 years ago. Although detractors would point out that products liability suits have damaged the U.S. economy, America is the world's remaining superpower, with an enormously strong and vibrant economy, even in the face of products liability verdicts that far exceed amounts seen in most other countries. In the United States, products are continually refined and made safer and more effective for the consumer. Many argue that this is a direct result of products liability litigation placing the burden on the manufacturers to create safer products. Others might argue that safer products are the result of other forces and that the U.S. economy perseveres despite huge jury awards. This issue is hotly debated.

J. PROVING A PRODUCTS LIABILITY CASE

To prove a products liability case, the plaintiff must show that the product was defective in some way. Under the law of products liability, there are three categories of defects. These include design defects, manufacturing defects, and defects in marketing.

1. DESIGN DEFECTS

A design defect is an inherent problem with the product. Something in the manufacturing or design has created a product that can cause damage. This damage could come in the form of personal injury or property damage. A design defect includes objects that, although designed to suit a particular use, can be unreasonably dangerous in that use.

An example of a design defect would be a game called lawn dart. In this game, players throw one-foot-long steel-tipped oversized darts at a target laid on the ground. The steel-tipped arrows were sharp enough to pierce through skin, and it was not uncommon during play for one of the darts to strike one of the players. Although lawn darts were manufactured correctly, in their use their design was potentially dangerous.

2. MANUFACTURING DEFECTS

A manufacturing defect is a defect in the product that is caused by faulty manufacturing processes or through the use of inadequate base materials. Relatively few lawsuits are based on manufacturing defects.

Example: Tom is shopping at a local grocery store and picks up a bottle of soda. As soon as his hand touches it, the bottle explodes. Tom's hand is injured, and he brings a products liability lawsuit against the soda manufacturer. Does he have a products liability case?

In this example, the products liability lawsuit would probably be based on a manufacturing design defect. Normally, soda bottles do not explode on contact. Tom's lawsuit will be based on a manufacturing defect, alleging that something in the manufacturing process caused the bottle to be unnaturally prone to explode. This could be caused by the fact that the bottle material was too thin to support the pressurized liquid inside it, or it could be because of some other manufacturing defect. What is important is that Tom can base his products liability lawsuit on the fact that a manufacturing process has resulted in a dangerous product.

3. DEFECTS IN MARKETING

When a products liability lawsuit is based on a marketing defect, this usually means that the lawsuit is based on faulty instructions or the company's failure to warn the consumer of a potential danger of the product. For example, manufacturers of upright refrigerators and freezers now routinely include warnings about the dangers of children playing inside unattended refrigerators. This is because children, once inside the closed refrigerator, do not have sufficient strength to open the door. When the door is sealed, they quickly run out of oxygen. Manufacturers of large plastic bags include similar warnings on their products about the dangers of smothering.

4. PLEADING PRODUCTS LIABILITY CASES

When we say that a products liability suit is a strict liability action, what we are really saying is that a products liability suit can be brought even when the defendant can demonstrate a high degree of caution and strict adherence to safety rules and regulations. A strict liability offense, such as a products liability suit, is not dependent on fault. The plaintiff must simply show that the product was defective in some way and that the defect caused an injury. The plaintiff is not required to show that the manufacturer was at fault.

What is interesting about these theories of recovery is that they are not mutually exclusive. A plaintiff is allowed to plead these theories in the alternative in his complaint. This means, on a practical level, that the plaintiff is allowed to sue for breach of warranty, sue on the basis of a contractual relationship, sue on the basis of negligence, and sue on the basis of a products liability claim, even though some of the elements of each of these claims are

(a) One engaged in the business of selling used products who sells a used product in a defective condition is, with the exceptions set forth in Subsection (c), subject to liability for harm to persons or property caused by the product's defect.

(b) A used product is defective for the purposes of this Section if, at the time of commercial sale, it contains a manufacturing defect, is defective in design, or is defective because of inadequate instructions or warnings, as defined in §2.

(c) Used products sellers are not subject to liability under this Section if:

(1) the sale of the used products is accompanied by clear and conspicuous language informing the buyer in writing that the seller disclaims all legal responsibility for products defects that might cause harm, provided that the seller makes no material representations or warranties with regard to products safety or performance relating to the time period, or component part of the products that caused harm, to which the disclaimer purports to apply; or

(2) the circumstances surrounding the sale, including the age and condition of the product, would have caused a reasonable person in the buyer's position to expect the products to be accompanied by the risk that caused the plaintiff's harm.

FIGURE 10-9

Restatement Position on Products Liability— Liability for the Sale or Distribution of Defective Products

contrary to one another. For example, a suit alleging negligence must involve proof that the defendant acted in an unreasonable way. On the other hand, a products liability case has no requirement of negligence whatsoever. Regardless of these seeming contradictions, a plaintiff in a products liability lawsuit is entitled to plead all the theories that are available. The plaintiff is not required to choose the theory on which he bases his case. The jurors are permitted to make up their own minds about which theory is the most likely. If this seems to you as though a products liability suit would be much easier to prove, your observation would be correct. However, this does not necessarily mean that everyone who sues a manufacturer for defective products will win. Winning a products liability lawsuit is still a difficult proposition, and is often based on the facts of the particular case.

K. MODEL UNIFORM PRODUCTS LIABILITY ACT

Although the United States Department of Commerce created the Model Uniform Products Liability Act as a guideline for the various states, there is no federal products liability law. Many states have created their own products liability statutes, based in whole or in part on the Model Uniform Products Liability Act.

L. DISCOVERY IN PRODUCTS LIABILITY CASES

Frequently, products liability cases are brought in the context of class action lawsuits. In such cases, the discovery can be enormous. Documents and other materials produced through discovery requests can fill entire rooms. In such huge cases, it is common for the lawyers involved to use special software to help them sift through the huge quantity of material. Often the attorneys will scan every document and then save these digital documents on a computer hard drive or a CD. Once saved, the software can be used to cross-reference the documents with pleadings, deposition transcripts, and other discovery materials.

The idea behind products liability is that a manufacturer can be liable for producing a defective product even though the manufacturer followed all the safety precautions and manufacturing processes that were customary at the time the product was created. Courts reason that the cost and burden of improving the product is more sensibly placed on the shoulders of the manufacturer than on the consumer.

Can a product liability case be based on a product that does not appear to be dangerous at all, until it is misused and turned into a bomb?

ONTIVEROS v. 24 HOUR FITNESS CORP.
2008 WL 5265208, 7 (Cal. App. 2 Dist. 2008) _____ Cal. Rptr. 3d _____, 08 Cal. Daily Op. Serv. 15,344, 2008 Daily Journal D.A.R. 18,581

Mosk, J.

Introduction

Plaintiff and appellant Susana Ontiveros (plaintiff) sustained personal injuries while exercising on a stair step machine at a fitness center owned and operated by defendant and respondent 24 Hour Fitness USA, Inc. (defendant). She sued defendant, asserting, inter alia, a claim for strict product liability. The trial court granted defendant's summary judgment motion as to that claim on the grounds that plaintiff acknowledged in her membership agreement that defendant could not be held liable for defective exercise equipment and that defendant provided "recreational services."

On appeal, plaintiff contends that there are triable issues of fact concerning whether the dominant purpose of plaintiff's transaction with defendant was for the use of defendant's exercise machines or for the provision of fitness services. We hold that the undisputed evidence shows that the dominant purpose of plaintiff's membership agreement with defendant was for the provision of fitness services and that as a result, defendant is not strictly liable to plaintiff under a product liability theory of recovery. We therefore affirm the judgment.

Factual Background

A. Defendant's Facts

At the premises where plaintiff was injured, defendant operated a fitness center at which members could utilize various exercise equipment and participate in aerobic exercise classes, among other activities, pursuant to the terms of a membership agreement between defendant and the member. According to defendant's risk management analyst, each of defendant's exercise facilities offered the following equipment, services, and amenities: free weights; cardio-vascular conditioning machines and other specialized fitness equipment; group exercises such as aerobics, dance classes, and yoga; testing centers to record certain physical characteristics such as blood pressure and weight; an optional introductory membership program that included three sessions with staff trainers; and locker rooms. For additional fees, a member could obtain personal training and nutritional counseling.

Plaintiff entered into a membership agreement with defendant, which was thereafter modified to provide an upgraded membership. Both her original agreement and upgraded agreement contained liability release provisions that included the following language: "You understand and acknowledge that [defendant] is providing recreational services and may not be held liable for defective products. By signing below, you acknowledge and agree that you have read the foregoing and know of the nature of the activities at [defendant's facilities] and you agree to all the terms of the front and back pages of this agreement and acknowledge you have received a copy of it and the membership policies."

The upgraded membership agreement entitled plaintiff to use defendant's facilities, described as "Active," "Express," and "Sport." An "Active" facility referred to a facility that is less than 25,000 square feet, offering fitness amenities such as group exercise classes, weight training, cardiovascular equipment, and locker rooms. A "Sport" facility referred to a facility generally 25,000 to 50,000 square feet, offering the same amenities as the other facilities, as well as further amenities.

As to the incident in question, defendant referred to plaintiff's allegations that she was injured while exercising on stair step equipment at defendant's facility in Panorama City. According to plaintiff's allegations, due to the failure of a component part, both "steps" of the machine lost all resistance as she was using it, causing plaintiff to fall backwards off the machine onto the floor.

B. Plaintiff's Evidence

Plaintiff did not dispute defendant's facts set forth above or argue that there were conflicting inferences that could be drawn from those facts. Instead, she provided the additional facts set forth in this section.

Plaintiff purchased a membership with defendant because she wanted to lose weight and believed that exercising using defendant's exercise equipment would help her achieve that goal. Plaintiff could not afford to purchase exercise equipment on her own and believed that using defendant's equipment would be the most cost effective means of obtaining the exercise she wanted.

Because plaintiff was familiar with exercise machines, which she described as simple to use, she did not need instruction, training, or assistance from defendant concerning the use of its exercise machines, and no such instruction, training, or assistance was provided to her by defendant. Although all of defendant's trainers were certified, defendant's staff members that worked in the area where members used exercise equipment were not certified trainers.

Plaintiff could have purchased from defendant, at an additional cost, the services of a trainer and nutritional counseling, but she chose not to do so. Plaintiff did not become a member of defendant to take aerobic classes, to check her blood pressure, to determine her body fat, or to use the sauna and steam room. She purchased her membership with defendant for the sole purpose of using exercise equipment.

Procedural Background

Plaintiff sued defendant, asserting causes of action for premises liability and strict product liability. The trial court heard and granted defendant's summary adjudication motion on the premises liability cause of action, a ruling that plaintiff does not challenge on appeal. Defendant then filed a motion for summary judgment as to the remaining strict product liability cause of action on the ground that the claim "was not actionable against defendant as defendant was not in the chain of distribution of the allegedly defective exercise equipment which caused her injury." Defendant also relied on the waiver or release language in plaintiff's agreement acknowledging that defendant was providing "recreational services" and could not be held liable for a defective product.

Plaintiff opposed the motion on the ground that defendant was in the chain of distribution; plaintiff's product liability claim could not be waived; and the dominant purpose of plaintiff's membership agreement with defendant was the use of defendant's exercise machines, not the performance of fitness services.

After hearing argument, the trial court granted defendant's motion and entered judgment. According to the trial court, "Defendant's motion is granted because there exist no triable issues of material fact, and moving party is entitled to judgment as a matter of law. Plaintiff has acknowledged in the Club Membership Agreement that Defendant 'does not manufacture fitness or other equipment' and that it provides 'recreational services.'"

Plaintiff filed a timely appeal from the judgment of dismissal following the order granting defendant's motion for summary judgment.

Discussion

Strict Product Liability Claim

Plaintiff acknowledges that if the dominant purpose of her agreement was to provide fitness services, and not just the use of exercise equipment, she cannot prevail on her strict product liability claim because defendant would not be in the chain of distribution of the equipment. She contends, however, that there are triable issues of fact concerning the dominant purpose of her transaction with defendant, citing to *Murphy v. E.R. Squibb & Sons, Inc.* (1985) 40 Cal.3d 672, 221 Cal.Rptr. 447, 710 P.2d 247 (*Murphy*). According to plaintiff, her evidence shows that she purchased her membership with defendant for the sole purpose of using the exercise equipment that defendant made available at its fitness facility. She claims she did not need any of the fitness services available to her under the agreement, and defendant did not provide any such services to her. Thus, under plaintiff's view of the evidence, defendant is strictly liable for defects in its equipment.

Defendant agrees that for purposes of the product liability analysis, the key distinction is whether defendant provided a service, in which case it would not be strictly liable for defective equipment, or whether defendant just made equipment available for use, in which case defendant would be strictly liable for defective equipment because defendant would, in effect, be in the chain of distribution. According to defendant, the dominant purpose of its transaction with plaintiff was to provide the various fitness services that were available to plaintiff under her agreement.

The general principles of California's product liability law have been summarized in *Bay Summit Community Assn. v. Shell Oil Co.* (1996) 51 Cal.App.4th 762, 772-773, 59 Cal.Rptr.2d 322 (*Bay Summit*).

> Our high court first adopted the strict liability doctrine in *Greenman v. Yuba Power Products, Inc.* (1963) 59 Cal.2d 57, 62 [27 Cal.Rptr. 697, 377 P.2d 897, 13 A.L.R.3d 1049], holding "a manufacturer is strictly liable to consumers when an article it places on the market, knowing that it is to be used without inspection for defects, proves to have a defect that causes injury to a human being." *Greenman* reasoned the doctrine would "insure that the costs of injuries resulting from defective products are borne by the manufacturers that put such products on the market rather than by the injured persons who are powerless to protect themselves." The court recognized imposing strict liability would discourage the marketing of unsafe products and was necessary to "protect consumers in an increasingly complex and mechanized society." One year later, the court extended the strict liability doctrine to retailers because retailers "are an integral part of the overall producing and marketing enterprise that should bear the cost of injuries resulting from defective products." (*Vandermark v. Ford Motor Co.* (1964) 61 Cal.2d 256, 262 [37 Cal.Rptr. 896, 391 P.2d 168].) *Vandermark* explained that holding retailers strictly liable would (1) enhance product safety since retailers are in a position to exert pressure on manufacturers; (2) increase the opportunity for an injured consumer to recover since the retailer may be the only entity "reasonably available" to the consumer; and (3) ensure fair apportionment of risk since retailers may "adjust the costs of such protection between them in the course of their continuing business relationship."
>
> The courts have since applied the doctrine to others similarly involved in the vertical distribution of consumer goods, including lessors of personal property, developers of mass-produced homes, wholesale and retail distributors. Although these defendants were not necessarily involved in the manufacture or design of the final product, each was responsible for passing the product down the line to the consumer. Thus, the parties were "able to bear the cost of compensating for injuries" and "played a substantial part in insuring that the product was safe or were in a position to exert pressure on the manufacturer to that end."

Plaintiff relies on the decision in *Murphy, supra,* 40 Cal.3d 672, 221 Cal.Rptr. 447, 710 P.2d 247. In that case, the plaintiff filed a personal injury claim against a retail pharmacy and a drug manufacturer alleging injuries from her mother's use of the prescription drug DES during pregnancy. As to the plaintiff's products liability claim, the court held that the trial court had correctly granted the pharmacy's motion for judgment on the pleadings. In doing so, the Court of Appeal observed, "It is critical to the issue posed to determine if the dominant role of a pharmacist in supplying a prescription drug should be characterized as the performance of a service or the sale of a product." Quoting with approval from the Court of Appeal decision in *Carmichael v. Reitz* (1971) 17 Cal.App.3d 958, 978, 95 Cal.Rptr. 381, the court in *Murphy* stated that the distinction for purposes of the products liability analysis was "'between a transaction where the primary objective is the acquisition of ownership or use of a product and one where the dominant purpose is to obtain services.'" The court in *Murphy* also quoted with approval from the decision in *Magrine v. Krasnica* (1967) 94 N.J.Super. 228, 227 A.2d 539, 544, stating, "'the *essence* of the transaction between the retail seller and the consumer relates to the *article sold*. The seller is *in the business* of supplying the product to the consumer. It is that, and that alone, for which he is paid. A dentist or physician offers, and is paid for, his professional services and skill. That is the *essence* of the relationship between him and his patient.'" Based on its analysis of the role of a pharmacist, the court in *Murphy* held that a pharmacy in dispensing prescription drugs is performing a service and therefore is not strictly liable for an inherent defect in a drug.

Although the decision in *Murphy, supra,* 40 Cal.3d 672, 221 Cal.Rptr. 447, 710 P.2d 247 is instructive as to the distinction under the strict liability doctrine between providing a product for use by a consumer and providing a service, it is factually different from this case because *Murphy* involved an actual sale of a product by a professionally licensed defendant. Here, there was no sale and no evidence of services by a licensed professional.

This case is more analogous to the decision relied upon by defendant, *Ferrari v. Grand Canyon Dories* (1995) 32 Cal.App.4th 248, 38 Cal.Rptr.2d 65 (*Ferrari*). In that case, the plaintiff was a customer injured on a whitewater rafting trip sponsored and conducted by the defendant. She sued the defendant under, inter alia, a product liability theory of recovery. The trial court granted summary judgment on the plaintiff's product liability claim and the Court of Appeal affirmed that ruling.

In determining whether the defendant's river rafting company was strictly liable for the injuries plaintiff suffered as a result of an allegedly defective raft, the court in *Ferrari, supra,* 32 Cal.App.4th 248, 38 Cal.Rptr.2d 65 analyzed the application of the product liability doctrine in cases where the transaction involved both a product and a service.

> Plaintiff contends the raft is a product as contemplated by the doctrine of strict product liability, and defendants are therefore subject to strict liability as licensors of the raft. In a given transaction involving both products and services, liability will often depend upon the defendant's role. For example, an airline passenger injured because of a defect in the craft would have a strict liability claim against the manufacturer. The manufacturer's role is that of a provider of a product, the airplane. On the other hand, the airline operating the plane would be primarily involved in providing a service, i.e., transportation. The airline is itself the end user of the product and imposition of strict liability would be inappropriate.

Although the facts in the instant case concerning the provision of services are not as compelling as those at issue in *Ferrari, supra,* 32 Cal.App.4th 248, 38 Cal.Rptr.2d 65, they do support the conclusion that the dominant purpose of plaintiff's membership agreement was to provide fitness services. In addition to entitling her to use exercise equipment, plaintiff's agreement entitled her to engage in aerobics, dance classes, and yoga, among others activities. It also allowed her to take advantage of testing centers where she could check her blood pressure and weight. Thus, unlike in *Garcia, supra,* 3 Cal.App.3d 319, 82 Cal.Rptr. 420, in which the defendant laundromat owner provided washers and dryers for use by customers, and apparently nothing more, there is undisputed evidence here that defendant provided more to members than just the use of exercise machines. That evidence shows that defendant was in the business of providing fitness services and made exercise machines available to members as an incident to those services. Thus, the law of strict product liability does not apply to defendant under the facts of this case, and defendant was therefore entitled to summary judgment on the product liability claim.

That plaintiff chose not to avail herself of the services provided under her membership agreement does not change the essential nature and purpose of that agreement because it is the terms of her agreement, rather than her subjective intentions, that define the dominant purpose of her transaction with defendant. There is no evidence that plaintiff ever explained to defendant that she only wanted to use its exercise machines, not its services, or that the mutual intention of the parties was to exclude such services. Her uncommunicated subjective intent in that regard is therefore irrelevant. From the language of her agreement and defendant's uncontradicted evidence, we conclude that the dominant purpose of plaintiff's membership agreement was to make available fitness services; accordingly, plaintiff has no valid claim under the strict product liability doctrine.

Disposition

The judgment of the trial court is affirmed. Defendant is awarded its costs on appeal.

We concur: TURNER, P.J., and ARMSTRONG, J.

Questions about the case:

1. Did the waiver that the plaintiff signed when she joined the gym prevent her from bringing the lawsuit in this case? Why or why not?
2. How was the plaintiff injured in this case?
3. What is the plaintiff's argument that the defendant's fitness center is strictly liable for her injuries?
4. What was the purpose in creating California's strict liability approach to manufacturers?
5. Explain the court's reasoning in preventing the plaintiff from bringing her product liability case.

M. RETAILERS AND "MERE CONDUITS"

When the plaintiff brings an action against a retailer, the plaintiff must show that the product was dangerous and that the retailer had reason to know that the product was dangerous. When the retailer acts as a mere conduit, that is, someone who forwards products from one location to another, the plaintiff will have a more difficult time proving his products liability suit.

When a retailer acts in some capacity that is greater than a mere conduit, the retailer's obligations include a requirement to test and inspect. Some jurisdictions require that a retailer who assembles parts or takes any other proactive role in the distribution of the project has a correspondingly greater role in testing and inspecting the products for defects.

Example: Haphazard Company buys and resells all types of merchandise at wholesale prices. When Haphazard makes out a receipt to a customer, the following information appears at the bottom: "By purchasing this product, you and reseller, purchaser or other person who later comes into possession of this product in the stream of commerce, disclaims and waives any action in products liability or negligence against Haphazard Co., Inc., for any failure to properly inspect, test or examine any products sold by us."

Toby purchases a safety harness from Haphazard. Later, the harness, which was made from poor-quality materials, breaks while Toby is using it to climb a tree to cut off a limb. Toby falls and is severely injured. Can he bring a suit against Haphazard Co.? Put another way, did Toby waive any possible lawsuit against the company by accepting the receipt?

Answer: Toby did not waive his rights to sue. Sidestepping the question of whether the "waiver" was validly created between Toby and Haphazard Co., there is a more basic question involved here. Can a company disclaim its own negligence? Courts have ruled that when a retailer, seller, or manufacturer places a defective product into the "stream of commerce," it cannot disclaim liability from its own negligence.[12]

N. INHERENTLY DANGEROUS OBJECTS

There are some objects that have been specifically designed to be dangerous. These objects, such as handguns, are considered to be inherently dangerous. In fact, their dangerousness forms the basis of their function. There is no way to make a handgun safe without essentially destroying its function. For instance, if you remove the trigger to prevent the gun from firing, the gun ceases to function. Because a consumer purchases a handgun desiring it to function, there is very little that a manufacturer can do to minimize the danger inherent in the design.

FIGURE 10-10

**Class Action
Lawsuits**

A class action lawsuit requires that (1) the number of persons be so numerous that it would be impractical to bring them all before the court, (2) the named representatives can fairly represent all of the members of the class, and (3) the class members have a well defined common interest in the questions of law or fact to be resolved (*Black's Law Dictionary*).

Of the 11,908 civil trials litigated in 2001, only 1 could be classified as a class action. This lawsuit, "Bell v. Farmers Insurance Exchange," resulted from the decision of Farmers Insurance Exchange to classify their claims' representatives as administrative personnel, which exempted the insurance company from having to pay overtime. The suit was certified as a class action because it involved over 2,400 California claims adjustors. The jury trial took place in Oakland, California, and a finding was entered for the plaintiffs. The award totaled $124.5 million of which $90 million was for uncompensated overtime, $1.2 million for double time, and $34.5 million for prejudgment interest. The case took almost 5 years from filing to verdict to litigate.

Source for additional case details: *The National Law Journal* (February 2002) Vol. 24, No. 22 (Col. 3).

Civil Trial Cases and Verdicts in Large Counties, 2001, Bureau of Justice Statistics, U.S. Department of Justice.

O. DEFENSES TO PRODUCTS LIABILITY ACTIONS

Defendants have many of the same defenses to a products liability case that they have in other tort actions. These include:

- Contributory negligence/comparative negligence
- Assumption of the risk
- Obvious hazard (a manufacturer will not be liable for failure to warn about an open and obvious danger or one that is a matter of common knowledge)

 **THE TIRE BLOWOUT HYPOTHETICAL**

Now that you have reviewed this chapter, we return to Susan's tire blowout case. Can she bring a products liability action against the tire manufacturer? In most jurisdictions, the answer would be an unequivocal yes. Whether Susan proceeds on a negligence theory or a breach of warranty theory, she should have no trouble in making out a case of products liability. Whether she convinces the jury to award her damages is another matter entirely, but she should certainly survive a pretrial motion to dismiss the case.

SKILLS YOU NEED IN THE REAL WORLD

Maintaining the Chain of Custody for Evidence

Evidence is important in all cases, but it is often critical in products liability cases. In one case, a client reported that when she handled a sealed can of cat food, the can exploded, severely injuring her hand. Her hand became infected with some rare form of bacteria and required several operations. The client eventually lost some of the use of her hand. What started out as a clear-cut case of products liability swiftly became no case at all when the client reported that she threw away the can of cat food. Without that crucial piece of evidence, there was really no solid case. After all, how could the attorney prove that the can was defective if he could not produce the actual can?

Securing and storing evidence is an important skill for any paralegal. However, simply obtaining the evidence is not enough. In many cases, the chain of custody is also important. The chain of custody refers to all the people who come into contact with the evidence. Whoever handles the evidence should be recorded, by name, in case there is any question later about tampering. In the best situation, the evidence should be handled by as few persons as possible. If you obtain evidence from the client, note the date and time that you received it. Note the appearance of the evidence. Put it in a secure place and leave it there. On television shows, detectives always put evidence in sealed plastic bags. They don't do this to preserve finger-prints; they do it to keep anyone from tampering with the evidence. In a criminal case, the prosecution must present testimony from everyone who handled the evidence in order to prove the chain. You should adopt the same standards in a civil case. The less contact with the evidence, the better. If features of the evidence are important, such as expiration dates, warranty notices, or other information, photograph the evidence and work from the photographs. When you work with evidence that is perishable, such as the contents of an exploded cat food can, wrap it in plastic and store it in a freezer. Later, if tests are required, the contents can be thawed and examined. If they are left out to spoil, valuable evidence, such as the presence of harmful bacteria, will be lost.

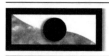

THE LIFE OF A PARALEGAL

Becoming a Paralegal

I had been thinking about taking paralegal courses for some time. After speaking with a friend of mine who works as a paralegal, I decided to start taking some classes. Almost as soon as I started my classes, my friend called me and said that the attorney that she was working with needed an office manager. I interviewed for the job and was hired. Although I was hired as an office manager, the attorney began giving me more and more paralegal work to do. He also encouraged me to continue my courses at the Community College. At first, I was preparing motions and other basic legal work. However, before long, I was handling very complicated civil cases.

One of the things that surprised me the most about the law was how nice the attorneys were. The attorneys that I work with, and even the opposing attorneys, were always very polite to one another. I thought that they would argue and fight with each other at every opportunity. In fact, it was just the opposite. Most attorneys are very nice people and very ethical. I think that movies and television have given attorneys a bad name. Most of the ones that I know are good and decent people.

When I started working for the firm, the attorney that I worked with did have a computer on his desk, but he never touched it. He had me draft all of the complaints and answers on my own computer and then give them to him for proofing. I learned a lot about drafting legal documents that way.

Before long, I was drafting discovery documents, preparing settlement packages, helping to interview clients and helping prepare the case for trial. It is fascinating work.

Renae Elam, Legal Assistant

ETHICAL ISSUES FOR THE PARALEGAL: FRIVOLOUS LAWSUITS

In situations involving strict liability lawsuits in general and products liability law-suits in particular, there is a certain temptation to bend or break the rules. After all, most of these suits are brought against large corporations that are considered to be wealthy and faceless. Some frivolous lawsuits have been brought against manufacturers simply on the premise that the company will probably be more likely to pay to settle the case rather than risk negative media coverage. With this potential for fraudulent claims, the paralegal and the attorney should always be on the lookout for a client who appears to be manufacturing a claim just to make some money. Indications that a claim is fraudulent can come from a variety of sources.

For instance, the client's story does not stand up under close scrutiny. The client gives conflicting versions of how he was injured. There is no direct connection between the plaintiff's reported injuries and the supposed design defect of the product. Another indication of a fraudulent claim comes when you investigate the client's background and discover that he has brought other frivolous claims against other manufacturers. You should always be on the lookout for any indication that the client is not being truthful with you. A frivolous lawsuit can be the basis of a bad faith claim later in the litigation. A groundless lawsuit will also reflect badly on the law firm itself. Firms, and attorneys, have been sanctioned for bringing frivolous lawsuits. If a paralegal discovers any information that would tend to indicate that the claim is fraudulent, she should bring this to the attorney's attention immediately.

Chapter Summary

In this chapter, we learned that there are some classes of injuries that fall into the category of strict liability. When the plaintiff is injured by a defective product, or by actions that the court considers to be abnormally dangerous, the defendant's proof of adherence to safety rules and regulations, and his testimony about how careful he was carrying out the procedures, are considered irrelevant. Strict liability is liability without regard to the defendant's fault. Therefore, a strict liability case can be successfully brought against the defendant even when he is not technically negligent or at fault. A form of strict liability lawsuit is a products liability action. Under a products liability action, a person who has been injured by a defective product is permitted to sue the manufacturer or the seller of the product, even though she is not able to prove exactly how the defect came about. In most cases, the mere fact that the product was defective and dangerous and that it injured someone is enough to sustain the minimal requirements of a products liability lawsuit.

Web Sites

■ **Product liability law**
http://www.productliability-lawyers.com/

■ **Overview of product liability**
http://www.law.cornell.edu/ (click "search sitewide" and enter "product liability" and/or "strict liability")

■ **Consumer product warranties — Magnuson-Moss Act (United States Code)**
http://www4.law.cornell.edu/uscode/15/ch50.html

■ **Model Punitive Damages Act — Products Liability Cases**
http://www.law.upenn.edu/bll/archives/ulc/mpda/MPDAFNAL.htm

■ **U.S. Consumer Product Safety Commission**
http://www.cpsc.gov

Forms and Court Documents

This is a complaint form, based on the factual scenario presented at the beginning of the chapter.

STATE OF PLACID		IN THE SUPERIOR COURT
COUNTY OF BARNES		FILE NUMBER: _____

Susan Wilson,	)	Complaint
Plaintiff	)	
	)	
vs.	)	
	)	
Haley Tire Company	)	
Defendant		

Product Liability Complaint

1.

Defendant Haley Tire Company (hereafter "Defendant") is a corporation organized under the laws of the State of Placid and is actively engaged in the manufacture and distribution of automobile tires commonly used on passenger automobiles.

2.

Defendant manufactured tires under the "Wild One," "One for the Road," and "Beast" brand names from 1999 through 2002 in the State of Placid.

3.

Defendant distributed the tires it manufactured through various wholesale and retail outlets, including Sam's Tahoe Dealership, located in Springfield, Placid.

4.

On May 15, 2000, the plaintiff purchased a 2001 model Orion Sports Utility Vehicle from Sam's Tahoe Dealership.

5.

This vehicle was equipped with "Beast" brand tires as standard equipment.

6.

On June 1, 2002, the plaintiff was operating her 2001 Orion Sports Utility Vehicle in a safe and reasonable manner, when the driver's side front tire suffered an explosive decompression, commonly called a "blowout."

7.

The tire blowout caused the plaintiff to lose control of her automobile and crash. She suffered extensive physical and emotional injuries.

8.

At the time of plaintiff's injuries, she was using the tires manufactured by the defendant in the manner and method anticipated by the defendant. Plaintiff was not aware of any defect in the tires, nor had the plaintiff been informed that the "Beast" brand tires on her automobile had been the subject of a nationwide recall commencing on May 28, 2002.

9.

When the plaintiff sustained her injuries more fully alleged below, the automobile tires were in a defective condition that caused them to be unreasonably dangerous to the plaintiff in that the tires had a pre-existing design defect that caused them to explosively decompress at high speeds.

10.

Plaintiff was not aware, and could not have become aware by reasonable inspection of said tires, that the tires were defective and dangerous.

11.

Defendants owed the plaintiff a duty to provide said automobile tires in a fit condition for use and tires that were free of defects. Defendant breached this duty to the plaintiff.

12.

The Defendant's breach was the sole and proximate cause of the plaintiff's injuries.

13.

As a result of the defendant's breach, plaintiff has sustained the following injuries, to wit. . . .

WHEREFORE, the plaintiff prays that she have and recover of the defendant:
1. General compensatory damages in excess of $10,000.00.
2. Special damages in the amount of $305,712.00.
3. Such other relief as the court may deem just and equitable.

Respectfully submitted, this the _____ day of _____, 200____.

_____

Clarence D. Arrow
Attorney for the Plaintiff

Key Terms

Privity	Ultra-hazardous
Products liability	Warranty
Strict liability	

Review Questions

1   How is a strict liability action different from a negligence action?
2   Why does the law consider the defendant's care and correct procedures in a negligence case, but ignore them in a strict liability lawsuit?
3   How is a strict liability lawsuit different from an intentional tort?
4   How would you define the term *abnormally dangerous activity*?
5   Explain the history of strict liability in the United States.
6   How have judicial rulings changed in strict liability cases from the mid-1800s through the 1900s?
7   What is the significance of the *Rylands* case?
8   Prior to the 1960s, if a person wished to sue a manufacturer of a defective or dangerous product, what series of recovery was available to him?
9   What is the significance of the *MacPherson* case?
10 What are the three theories of products liability lawsuits?
11 What are some of the alternative theories of recovery in products liability lawsuits?
12 How is the law of product liability applied to retailers?
13 What are examples of "inherently dangerous" objects?
14 Why is it important to preserve evidence?
15 What is the "chain of custody" for evidence?

Applying What You Have Learned

1   Ajax Company has come up with a new toy. This toy is a spaceship that when activated flies through the room in a great sweeping circle, spilling out candy. The spaceship is designed with sharp angles and points on the wings and nose. The first time it was used, the spaceship, while flying around the room, struck Toby in the face. He has been severely scarred. Does Toby have a products liability cause of action? If so, on what theories should he base his products liability lawsuit?
2   Does it matter in our products liability case against the tire manufacturer that Susan did not keep the tire? Would the tire be helpful in the lawsuit? If so, how?
3   ABC Computer Company has produced a new laptop computer that it says is "the most user-friendly computer in the world." Gene purchases the computer and the first time he turns it on he receives a severe electric shock. Draft a products liability complaint on these facts using breach of warranty and strict liability theories.

Endnotes

[1] *Doundoulakis v. Hempstead,* 42 N.Y.2d 440, 398 N.Y.S.2d 401, 368 N.E.2d 24 (1977).

[2] *Hynes v. Energy West, Inc.,* 211 F.3d 1193 (Wyo. 2000).

[3] Lawrence Friedman, A History of American Law, Murray Printing Co., Forge Village, Mass., 1973, p. 425.

[4] *Ultramares Corp. v. Touche,* 255 N.Y. 170, 174 N.E. 441 (1931).

[5] Lawrence Friedman, A History of American Law, Murray Printing Co., Forge Village, Mass., 1973, p. 589.

[6] Miller & Lovell, Products Liability 7 (1977).

[7] *McCarty v. E. J. Korvette, Inc.,* 28 Md. App. 421, 347 A.2d 253, 264 (1975).

[8] Restatement (Second) of Torts §395, comment f.

[9] *Hoemke v. New York Blood Center,* 912 F.2d 550 (2d Cir. 1990).

[10] *Flagstar Enterprises, Inc. v. Davis,* 709 So. 2d 1132 (1997).

[11] *Zaccone v. American Red Cross,* 872 F. Supp. 457 (N.D. Ohio 1994).

[12] *Ruzzo v. LaRose Enterprises,* 748 A.2d 261 (2000).

[13] *Suter v. San Angelo Foundry & Mach. Co.,* 406 A.2d 140 (1979).

Defamation

Chapter Objectives

- Define defamation and apply it to factual situations
- Distinguish between libel and slander
- Explain slander per se
- Explain how damages are assessed in libel and slander cases
- Define the importance of "publication" in defamation cases

 **INTRODUCTION**

Although we usually begin each chapter with a discussion of the Chumley case, this chapter, like the prior chapter, does not involve any of the legal issues raised in that case. Instead, we examine the facts of a different case here.

Susan is a college student and, like many students, she shops at stores close to the college campus. Susan writes checks to pay for her goods at these various stores and she has always been scrupulous about keeping track of her money. One day, she walks into a local grocery store and sees a large sign by the main entrance. The sign reads: "These deadbeats have robbed us of money by passing bad checks at this establishment. If you see any of these people, tell them what you think about them — after all, because they violate the law, they raise your prices." Just below this statement, which is written in black, bold letters at least five inches tall, Susan sees her own name, among five others. She is immediately embarrassed and humiliated, all the more so because she knows that she has never written a bad check at this or any other store. She immediately approaches the store manager and tells him that there has been some error. The manager, in front of a large group of shoppers, says, "So, you're one of the deadbeats. Man, you people are all the same. Always making excuses. I should call the police on you right now. Get out of my store and don't come back until you pay off your bad checks!"

Susan has come to our firm for a consultation. She wants to know if she has a cause of action against the store for presenting false information about her to the public. We assess her case after addressing the topic of defamation.

DEFAMATION

Defamation is a rather strange tort. It is one of the few torts that provide a cause of action for injuring another person's reputation. Historically, defamation was one of a number of strict liability torts. Under the common law, for example, it was no defense to defamation that the statement was made innocently, that the plaintiff was a public figure, or that the statement was made on a matter of public concern by a media affiliate. The law of defamation has changed considerably in the past few decades.

Defamation
A false attack on the reputation or character of another

A. WHAT IS DEFAMATION?

When a person falsely injures another person's reputation, or exposes that person to public humiliation or degradation, the person injured is permitted to bring suit against the other. A defamatory statement tends to harm the person's reputation in the community or cause others to stop associating with her.[1] Essentially, when a person is defamed, it injures her ability to deal with others in society.

The theory behind making defamatory statements actionable is that individuals should be free to enjoy their reputations and good names without the stigma of false statements. Allowing a plaintiff to bring suit for defamation is one way for an individual to protect her status in society.[2] Defamation is different from other torts in that the focus of the action is not the injury to the plaintiff's physical, financial, or emotional status, but the damage done to her reputation.

FIGURE 11-1

Restatement Position on Defamation

According to the Restatement of Torts, defamation consists of:

■ A false and defamatory statement concerning the plaintiff;

■ An unprivileged publication to a third party;

■ Fault amounting to at least negligence on the part of the publisher; and

■ Legal recognized cause of action for the statement or proof of special harm.*

*Restatement (Second) of Torts §558.

To defame someone is to make or write a statement that is false and that injures the plaintiff's character or reputation. Defamation requires that this statement be heard or seen by someone else.

ISSUE AT A GLANCE

B. DEFAMATION COMES IN TWO FORMS

Slander
Spoken defamation

Defamation can occur in two ways. When a person makes a defamatory statement verbally, this is referred to as **slander.** When a person makes a defamatory statement in writing, this is referred to as **libel.**

Libel
Written defamation

Defamation comes in two forms: written defamation and verbal defamation. When someone defames another person in writing, that is libel. When someone defames another person verbally, that is slander.

ISSUE AT A GLANCE

Because the elements for libel and slander are similar, we address the general elements of defamation and then discuss issues peculiar to each.

Sidebar

Libel and slander are generally considered to be different forms of defamation, with slightly different elements and different types of damages assessed. However, these differences are not as pronounced as other types of torts, such as the differences between the torts of assault and battery.

C. ELEMENTS OF DEFAMATION

In the following sections, we examine each of the elements of a defamation action. In defamation cases, most jurisdictions follow the requirement that proof of the plaintiff's allegations must be **clear and convincing.** This is also the standard recommended by the Restatement of Torts.[3]

1. DEFAMATORY LANGUAGE

a. Definition

The first and most important element of any defamation action is that the words used actually defame the plaintiff. Defamatory language is any statement that subjects the plaintiff to public ridicule, hatred, or contempt. There are many types of vicious and unsavory statements that are not considered to be defamatory. Insults, for example, are generally not classified as defamation.

Clear and convincing
A measure of proof that is higher than preponderance of the evidence, but less than beyond a reasonable doubt; clear and convincing proof is evidence that is likely to be true under the facts

FIGURE 11-2

**The Elements
of Defamation**

In most jurisdictions, defamation consists of:

■ Unprivileged   ■ Of false statements
■ Publication   ■ That are the proximate cause of injury to another.*

*Barry College v. Hull, 353 So. 2d 575 (1977).

Statements that injure the plaintiff's feelings are also not defamatory. To be defamatory, the statement must injure the plaintiff's reputation or hold the plaintiff up to public ridicule, embarrassment, or humiliation. Insults do not meet this standard.

b. Opinions

Is an opinion defamation? Example: John asks Ted what he thinks about Carl. John says, "I think he's dishonest." Is this a defamatory statement?

Answer: It depends. In most jurisdictions, a pure opinion is not actionable as defamation. However, this rule does have certain exceptions. For example, a statement that is otherwise an opinion may cross the line into defamation if we add some additional facts. For instance, suppose that John says, "I happen to know that Carl is dishonest." Although this statement sounds very similar to the first, under defamation law, it is quite different. The second statement sounds as if it is based on some particular instance or on a fact that John has not yet stated. In such a situation, the closer the opinion comes to a factual statement, the more likely it is considered defamatory.

2. FALSE STATEMENTS

In addition to the language causing the plaintiff embarrassment or financial loss, the statement must also be false. One of the main defenses to a defamation action is that the statement is true. If the statement is true, it is not defamatory and therefore cannot form the basis of either a slander or libel action. We discuss this defense in greater detail later in this chapter.

3. THE STATEMENT REFERS TO THE PLAINTIFF

a. Burden of Proof

Although it sounds rather obvious, the plaintiff must prove that the defamatory statement was made about him. Sometimes this is difficult for the plaintiff to prove. Suppose that the defendant makes a statement such as, "He's a child molester." That statement certainly sounds as though it qualifies as defamation. However, before the jury could be allowed to reach that conclusion, the plaintiff would have to prove that the statement was made about him. If the defendant is pointing to a group of people that includes the plaintiff, how can anyone be sure that the defendant is referring to the plaintiff? These determinations depend on the unique facts of each case. If the defendant singles out the plaintiff in some way so that it becomes clear to others that the defendant is talking about him, the plaintiff will probably prove his case. If not, then the plaintiff's case may fail. It is not a requirement that the defendant specifically name the plaintiff, as long as it is clear to others that the defendant is referring to the plaintiff.

A defamatory statement does not actually have to name the plaintiff. In most jurisdictions, if a statement can reasonably be interpreted as referring to the plaintiff, the courts will rule that the defendant has defamed the plaintiff even though the defendant never referred to the plaintiff by name.[4]

ISSUE
AT A
GLANCE

What if the link to the plaintiff is tenuous? Is it enough that someone might have connected the plaintiff to the defamatory statement? Courts have consistently held that the statement must clearly refer to the plaintiff. A statement so vague that it may or may not have referred to the plaintiff is not actionable as defamation.[5]

b. Is It Possible to Defame a Group?

Suppose that Darrell Defendant makes the following statement: "It is well known that white males are incapable of telling the truth." John is a white male and doesn't like Darrell's statement. Can he bring a defamation action against Darrell?

Answer: No. To bring an action, John must prove that he, as an individual, was defamed. John has no cause of action simply because he belongs to a group that has been maligned.[6]

However, the rule changes when the group is small and readily identifiable. Suppose that Darrell's statement refers to a family. Darrell says, "That X family is full of liars and thieves." Can any member of that family bring suit against Darrell? In most jurisdictions, the answer is yes, because the statement was made about a clearly ascertainable plaintiff, that is, one of the members of that particular family.

4. PUBLICATION

In all jurisdictions, publication or communication of the defamatory statement is an essential requirement. Courts use the terms *publication* and *communication* interchangeably; we use the term *publication* for the remainder of the chapter. When a person publishes a defamatory statement, she communicates that statement to someone other than the plaintiff. When the defamation is slander, it must be heard and understood by someone other than the plaintiff. When the defamation is libel, or written, it must be read and understood by someone other than the plaintiff. If a writing is not intended to be published, and is accidentally read by a third person, most jurisdictions will hold that no publication occurred, and therefore there has been no defamation.

Example: Tina writes in her diary: "I know that Ted is a thief and a liar." Tina's mother, while cleaning her room, finds Tina's diary and reads this sentence. Ted files an action for libel. Can he prove publication?

Answer: No. Tina's diary was not intended for publication — in fact, one could argue that it was never intended to be read by anyone but Tina — so the accidental reading by Tina's mother will most likely not satisfy the publication requirement.

It is not enough that the plaintiff prove a mere possibility that someone might have heard or read the statement. The plaintiff must actually establish that the statement was communicated to someone other than herself.

In addition to the requirement that the statement be communicated to a third party, it is also essential that the third person realize the significance of the statement. Because of this requirement, a defamatory statement made in a language that no one but the defendant and the plaintiff can understand is not actionable.

 **Publication refers to expressing a statement in writing or speaking it aloud.**

---

5. INJURY TO THE PLAINTIFF'S REPUTATION

In addition to the other elements, the plaintiff must also prove that her reputation was damaged by the defendant's statement. As we see later, in libel and slander per se, damages are presumed. When the case involves "simple" slander or libel, the plaintiff must prove special damages. Damages and the methods used to assess them are discussed later in this chapter.

Are there plaintiffs who already have such bad reputations that they cannot be defamed? The answer seems to be yes. We'll use an extreme example here. Suppose that Adolf Hitler or Joseph Stalin were still alive. Is there anything that someone could say about them that would hurt their reputations?

On a more realistic level, suppose that John *X* is an admitted child molester. A local newspaper refers to him as an evil monster. Does John *X* have provable damages? In most cases, the answer would have to be no. Society clearly considers child molesters to be some of the lowest and most despicable criminals. Calling Mr. *X* a "monster" surely would not hold him up to any greater public humiliation than his self-confessed activities with children.[7]

D. SIMPLE LIBEL

The term *simple libel* is used in many jurisdictions to distinguish from other, and usually more complex, forms of libel, such as libel per quod and

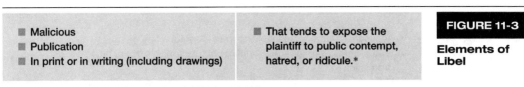

FIGURE 11-3

Elements of Libel

■ Malicious
■ Publication
■ In print or in writing (including drawings)

■ That tends to expose the plaintiff to public contempt, hatred, or ridicule.*

*Ajouelo v. Auto-Soler Co., 61 Ga. App. 216, 6 S.E.2d 415 (1939).

■ Cartoons*
■ Movies**

■ Signs
■ Effigies

*Russell v. McMillen, 685 P.2d 255 (1984).
**Brown v. Paramount Publix Corp., 270 N.Y.S. 544 (1934).

libel per se. When we speak of simple libel, we are referring to a defamatory writing. However, before we can examine the complexities of libel law, the issue we must address first is how the law defines *writing*.

1. WHAT IS A WRITING?

In libel, the definition of a *writing* is often called into question. Courts have interpreted writing to include: drawings, pictures, printed material, photographs, newspaper columns, books, and magazines, among others.[8] The significance of a writing is that it is usually considered to be a more permanent medium of expression than oral statements. A printed statement can reach many more people and for a longer period of time than a spoken statement.

2. LIBEL PER QUOD

When a statement must be interpreted before it is considered defamatory, many jurisdictions refer to it as *libel per quod*. Libel per quod is a statement that may appear innocuous standing by itself, but becomes clearly defamatory when other facts are considered.

Example: A local newspaper prints the following announcement: "Mary Jones of 112 Elm Street announces the birth of a healthy, 7-pound baby boy on May 2."

Although this announcement does not appear to be defamatory, Mary Jones is a Catholic nun who has taken a vow of celibacy. This announcement, when understood in the context of other facts, creates a defamatory statement.

When libel per quod is alleged, the jury is called upon to evaluate the statement and determine if it was defamatory. The plaintiff must prove that the third party — in this case, the newspaper's readers — knew the extrinsic facts and could therefore connect the statement and the facts and create a defamatory conclusion.[9]

FIGURE 11-5	■ Accusations of a crime involving moral turpitude
Examples of Libel Per Se	■ Statements regarding the plaintiff's unfitness for his trade, business, or profession
	■ Statements that the plaintiff has a communicable, sexual disease

3. LIBEL PER SE

Libel per se is any writing (including a drawing) about a specific category of defamatory statements that is considered to be so serious that an injury to the plaintiff's reputation may be presumed. For example, when the defendant accuses the plaintiff of being a convicted felon or of having a sexually transmitted disease, these statements would be considered libel per se.

When the plaintiff presents proof of libel per se, she is entitled to a presumption that the defendant acted with malice and a presumption of recoverable damages that can be assessed by the jury. To satisfy the test of libel per se, the words used must be unambiguous and interpreted in a natural and reasonable way. See Figure 11-5 for examples of statements that are libel per se.

ISSUE AT A GLANCE

"A libel per se is a malicious publication expressed in writing, printing, pictures, caricatures, signs, or other devices which upon its face and without aid of extrinsic proof is injurious and defamatory. . . . In its most general and comprehensive sense it may be said that any publication that is injurious to the reputation of another is a libel."[10]

E. SLANDER

When a person is defamed verbally, this is slander. Generally, a slanderous statement must be stated loud enough for someone other than the plaintiff to hear it. The statement must be one that calls the plaintiff's character or reputation into question. Insults and cutting remarks are not slander. A slanderous statement must injure the plaintiff's reputation. Many courts hold slander to a higher burden of proof than libel. After all, a libelous statement can be produced on demand in a courtroom. The writing can be viewed by the jury and considered on its own merits. A verbal statement necessarily involves testimony from others about what they heard. The witnesses may remember the statement differently or differ about the context in which it was made. A libelous statement is permanent; a slanderous statement is, by its very nature, ephemeral.

1. DEFINING SLANDER

Slander refers to oral statements, or, as some jurisdictions put it, a defamatory statement made in some way other than in writing. Slander includes not only

■ The speaking of ■ Defamatory words	■ That tends to expose the plaintiff to public contempt, hatred, or ridicule or interferes with the plaintiff's ability to earn a living in his business.*	**FIGURE 11-6** **The Elements of Slander**

*Axelrod v. Califano, 357 So. 2d 1048 (1978).

■ Defendant spoke defamatory words that tended to injure the plaintiff's reputation, trade, or livelihood.	■ The statement was false. ■ The statement was published or communicated to a third person.*	**FIGURE 11-7** **Proving Slander Per Se**

*Presnell v. Pell, 298 N.C. 715, 260 S.E.2d 611 (1979).

statements but gestures, sign language, or any other form of non-written communication.

2. SLANDER PER SE

Slander per se is very similar to libel per se. When the defendant accuses the plaintiff of committing a crime involving theft or dishonesty, or of having a communicable sexual disease, slander per se is triggered and the plaintiff is entitled to special damages. Special damages are those damages that are beyond mere humiliation or embarrassment. When a statement is classified as slander per se, malice and injury to reputation are presumed.

3. SPECIAL DAMAGES

In slander, the plaintiff must show some form of special injury or that the statement falls into a category of legally recognized injurious statement before the plaintiff will be entitled to an award of damages.[11] For instance, the plaintiff would have to prove that her reputation was damaged or that her business suffered because of the slanderous statement. These damages must be tied to the defendant's slanderous statement.

4. IS LIBEL MORE SERIOUS THAN SLANDER?

There is an interesting disparity between the application of written defamation and spoken defamation. Libel is considered to be more injurious to the plaintiff because the written word is more permanent. Writings can last for centuries and permanently ruin the plaintiff's reputation and good name in a way that slander is incapable of doing. Most jurisdictions consider libel to be more serious because writing is a process that takes time and thought. A person can blurt out something that she has not fully considered, but writing is a deliberate, drawn-out process that usually involves review by others and more than sufficient time for the author to modify a defamatory statement. When the

FIGURE 11-8

Defenses
Available in
Defamation
Actions

■ The statement is not defamatory.
 ■ The person defamed is
   deceased.
	■ The defendant is protected by a
	   privilege.
	 ■ The statement is the truth.

author publishes a defamatory statement, it shows her clear intent to offer an injurious statement in a way that a slanderous statement usually cannot.

F. DEFENSES TO DEFAMATION

As we have seen in other chapters, some unique torts trigger unique defenses. Defamation is perhaps the best example of that axiom. There are defenses available in defamation actions that are rarely, if ever, seen in other causes of action. These defenses are summarized in Figure 11-8.

1. THE STATEMENT IS NOT DEFAMATORY

The most obvious defense to a suit for slander or libel is that the statement is not defamatory. As we have already seen, insulting, provocative, or annoying statements do not fall into the category of defamatory statements. If the defendant can establish that the statement does not qualify as defamatory, the court must dismiss the action.

2. THE DEFAMED PERSON IS DECEASED

In most situations, a person who has died cannot be defamed. Although this rule has certain specific exceptions, in general it means that the heirs and friends of a deceased individual do not have a cause of action for a defamatory statement made about the deceased. In a certain sense, deceased persons are fair game for nearly any statement.

3. PRIVILEGES

Certain individuals are protected under the law from defamation actions. The law recognizes that there are times when individuals should be allowed to speak freely, offer their opinions, and even make allegations without fear of being sued. When a person is protected from being sued, it is commonly called a privilege or immunity. This privilege can be raised as a defense and, if proved, will result in a dismissal of the action.

In most jurisdictions, the issue of privilege is an integral part of a defamation action. Whether a statement is privileged is contingent on several key features. First of all, the conditions under which the statement was made must be examined. If the defendant can show that the statement was made in a

FIGURE 11-9

Statements made by:
- Judges in judicial proceedings
- Witnesses while testifying at trial
- Witnesses and experts in mental competency or commitment hearings
- Pleadings in civil cases
- Members of Congress while engaged in official duties

Examples of Absolute Privileges

privileged circumstance, for example, a statement she made to her attorney or a member of the clergy, she has a defense to the defamatory statement. In such a situation, even though the defamatory statement was relayed to a third person, this person is bound by an oath of confidentiality. The law of privileges has a practical element here as well. If a plaintiff could allege slander by a statement that a person makes to her attorney, the entire conversation between the attorney and the defendant would be open to examination. This would have a chilling effect on the relationship and the free flow of information between attorneys and clients. The same rationale holds true for the other types of privileges recognized under defamation law.

Members of Congress and state legislators are protected by a privilege against defamation for any comments that they make while the legislature is in session. This means that a senator can make a statement that would otherwise be deemed to be slander, but cannot be sued for making that statement on the floor of the Senate. Politicians are not completely protected by this privilege. When Congress is not in session, or the politician is not meeting on government business, he or she has no greater protection than any other person.

a. Absolute Privileges

Some privileges are absolute, meaning that any defamatory statement made under specified circumstances can never be the basis of a defamation action. An example would be the private communication between a client and an attorney.

b. Qualified Privileges

Other privileges are considered to be qualified. A qualified privilege is one that protects the defendant from a defamation action as long as the defendant does not use the privilege as a ruse, or abuse the privilege as a way of making defamatory statements without paying the consequences. In some jurisdictions, for instance, an attorney's closing argument in a trial enjoys a qualified privilege. An attorney's slanderous statement about a person may be protected, as long as it is made for purposes associated with the trial, not simply as a way for the attorney to slander an individual.

Qualified privileges come up in other contexts. Employers, for example, enjoy a qualified privilege for certain types of statements. For instance, if the employer is legally obligated to make a statement, such as in an accident report in which the employer states that the plaintiff was responsible for the accident,

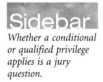

Whether a conditional or qualified privilege applies is a jury question.

FIGURE 11-10

Qualified Privileges

- Statements in which both parties have a business interest
- Statements criticizing employee work performance

- Statements regarding the factual reasons for an employee's dismissal
- Statements to law enforcement made on a good faith belief that a crime has been committed or is about to occur

an action in defamation will not be permitted. Other situations that would trigger a qualified privilege are listed in Figure 11-10.

4. THE STATEMENT IS TRUE

It is a classic defense in a defamation action that the defendant's statement was true. If the statement is true, the defendant has a complete defense and the plaintiff's action should be dismissed.

ISSUE AT A GLANCE

Truth is a complete defense to a claim of defamation, even when the statement was made with malice.

When truth is raised as a defense, it does not matter that the defendant acted with malice, ill will, or hatred in making the statement. Truth is an absolute bar to a defamation action. However, many jurisdictions provide that the statement must be true at the time that it is made, not one that becomes true later on.

Example: Paula Publisher accuses Ted of being a thief and an embezzler in an editorial she writes called "Local Scoundrels." Local grand jurors read the article and launch an investigation of Ted. Ted loses his job when his employer sees that he is being investigated. Ted then steals from his former employer because he can no longer pay his bills and is arrested on theft charges. Ted sues Paula for defamation. Paula counters that her statement was true. In support of her contention, she shows that Ted was arrested for theft. Ted shows that the statement was not true at the time that Paula made her statement, and therefore he is entitled to sue her for defamation. She files a motion for summary judgment. The court rules in Ted's favor. (Under this scenario, Ted's suit will not be dismissed, but his likelihood of being awarded a large amount of damages is low; after all, Ted actually is a thief.)

5. "GOOD FAITH" STATUTES

Some jurisdictions have so-called good faith statutes that have been specifically passed to insulate the press from defamation lawsuits for reporting on various issues of public concern. Under these statutes, if a reporter can show that she acted in good faith, a defamation action will not be permitted. In cases

> - The nature of the statement itself
> - The number of people to whom the statement was published
> - The effect of the statement on the plaintiff's reputation
> - The plaintiff's mental anguish, humiliation, and embarrassment
>
> In cases where special damages must be proved:
>
> - The financial and property losses directly linked to the defendant's defamatory statement

FIGURE 11-11

Types of Evidence a Jury or Judge Can Consider in Awarding Damages in Defamation Cases

where the press reports something incorrectly, some jurisdictions require that the press print a retraction before the good faith statute will protect the media from a defamation action.

G. DAMAGES IN DEFAMATION CASES

As we have already seen with libel per se and slander per se, harm may be presumed from certain types of defamatory statements. This harm may be limited to the damages for emotional distress, but the plaintiff is still permitted to recover.[14]

When the court awards damages to a plaintiff who has been libeled, the court takes into account the wider reach of a libelous statement compared to a slanderous statement. After all, a slanderous statement is often overhead by only a few people, while printed material can reach thousands. In the era of the Internet, libelous material could reach millions of people. Assessing damages for libel must take into account the fact that the defamatory statement will be read or seen by a much greater audience, with the result that the plaintiff will be injured far more severely than in most typical slander cases.

In making its decision about the amount of damages to award a plaintiff who has proved a defamation case, the jury is allowed to consider several different factors: the nature of the statement, that is, just how defamatory was the statement; how many people heard it or read it; what was the plaintiff's character and reputation before the incident and how has it been affected since; and to what extent has the plaintiff suffered mental anguish, humiliation, or embarrassment because of the defamatory statement.

When the statement is slander the plaintiff must prove special damages. Special damages are the financial and other losses suffered by the plaintiff that are directly tied to the defendant's actions.

H. CONSTITUTIONAL LIMITS ON DEFAMATION ACTIONS

Defamation actions give plaintiffs the right to sue people who make statements about them. The First Amendment to the United States Constitution guarantees freedom of speech. Where is the dividing line between this right

FIGURE 11-12	Is the plaintiff:

Analyzing Constitutional Defenses to Defamation Actions	A public figure or a private figure?
	 Is the defendant:
	     Media or non-media?
	 Is the statement:
	     A matter of public or private concern?

and the prohibition against defamatory statements? There is an immediate and obvious tension between defamation actions and the First Amendment. The right of freedom of speech was seen as vital by the framers of the Constitution; it was so important that it is embodied in the First Amendment, preceding even the right to jury trial and the presumption of innocence in criminal proceedings (Fifth Amendment). In evaluating any supposedly defamatory statement, the question often arises as to how the court balances the protections of the First Amendment against an individual's right to protect her reputation.

1. ANALYZING A DEFAMATION CASE FOR CONSTITUTIONAL IMPLICATIONS

The guarantees of the First Amendment are propounded in the U.S. Constitution, which is a federal document. Defamation actions are almost always brought in state courts, applying individual state laws. When a constitutional defense is raised, judges are faced with a multi-layered analysis. They often follow this analysis:

"Under the First Amendment, there is no such thing as a false idea. But there is no constitutional value in false statements of fact. . . . Our decisions recognize that a rule of strict liability that compels a publisher or broadcaster to guarantee the accuracy of his factual assertions may lead to intolerable self-censorship."[15]

1. Has the plaintiff proved defamation according to state law?
2. Is the plaintiff entitled to recover under state law?
3. If the answer to both questions 1 and 2 is yes, does the First Amendment protect the defendant's otherwise defamatory statement?

If the answer to question 3 is yes, the judge must dismiss the case against the defendant.

2. THE *NEW YORK TIMES* RULE

The Supreme Court was faced with the issue of balancing the constitutional guarantees against state-based defamation actions in *New York Times Co. v. Sullivan*.[16] The decision in that case brought about dramatic changes in how defamation actions are brought and also affected the standard of proof in such cases.

One of the biggest changes wrought by the *New York Times* case was that, to a certain extent, state law concerning defamation was "usurped" by a holding that essentially changed the rules. The U.S. Supreme Court held that when the plaintiff is a public person and the statement involves a matter of public concern, the standard of proof that the plaintiff must meet to prove a defamation case is much higher than when the case involves a private individual and a statement that does not involve a matter of public debate. In the first instance, public figures can "recover for injury to reputation only on clear and convincing proof that the defamatory falsehood was made with knowledge of its falsity or with reckless disregard for the truth."[17] In essence, the court ruled that a public figure could only recover when he could show that the statement was made with "actual malice." The court recognized that applying this high standard might mean that plaintiffs with legitimate concerns would be barred from bringing suits for defamation, but considered that public figures would have to pay the price to balance out the need for constitutional protections. However, the balance between individual concerns and constitutional protections shifts when the plaintiff is a private individual. Individual states are allowed to set their own standards for proof in such cases.

The actual malice test — sometimes called the *New York Times* Rule — held that when a public figure, such as a public official, raises a claim of defamation, she will not be entitled to damages unless she can present clear and convincing evidence that the statement was made with "actual malice."[18]

a. Malice

In the context of defamation, **malice** refers to the defendant's hatred, ill will, or bad feelings toward the plaintiff. Malice has a fluid definition, however, depending on the nature of the communication. For a statement under the protection of the First Amendment, malice means the defendant's reckless or intentional statement of a false fact.

Malice
Reckless or false statements. Legal malice is a court-created doctrine that supplies the element by assuming that certain phrases could only have been motivated by ill-will. Examples would include falsely accusing someone of a crime or other despicable act

Although the plaintiff must normally prove malice, there are some statements that are considered under the law to be motivated by malice without the need of further proof. We have seen a similar approach adopted in libel per se and slander per se. Examples of these statements where malice would be inferred include:

- Implicating the defendant in a crime (in most jurisdictions there is no requirement that the crime be a felony)
- Making statements designed to show that the defendant is not legally entitled to practice her profession (e.g., that a lawyer has been disbarred or that a doctor has been stripped of her license to practice medicine, etc.)
- Accusing the plaintiff of having a communicable sexual disease (e.g., syphilis, AIDS, etc.)

When such statements are made, and they are false, the court will presume malice. In addition to presuming malice, courts will also presume some type of harm to the plaintiff. Under other situations, the plaintiff would have to show that the defamatory statement injured her reputation. However, when the statement falls into one of the categories above, injury is presumed and the plaintiff is entitled to some amount of damages to be determined by the jury.

FIGURE 11-13	Actual malice has been found in all of the following situations:
Examples of Actual Malice	■ A newspaper uses inflammatory headlines but then backtracks in the body of the article
	■ A person accuses a public official of perjury when he knows the definition of perjury and also knows that the plaintiff did not commit that act
	■ News media accuse the plaintiff of being the "prime suspect" in a heinous crime when they already have information that the police no longer classify the plaintiff as a suspect

FIGURE 11-14	■ Private attorneys (not attorneys affiliated with city, county, or state government)	■ Part-time deputies or "honorary" deputies
Examples of People Who Have Been Ruled *Not* to Be Public Figures		■ A person contesting a defamatory statement

If malice sounds like a slippery concept, no less a person than Justice Oliver Wendell Holmes would agree. In his famous book, *The Common Law,* Holmes addresses the issue of malice in slander cases:

> Malice must exist, but . . . it is presumed from the mere speaking of the words; that again you may rebut this presumption of malice by showing that the words were spoken under circumstances which made the communication privileged, — as for instance, by a lawyer in the necessary course of his argument — it is said that the plaintiff may meet this defence [sic] in some cases by showing that the words were spoken with actual malice.[19]

b. Malice and Negligent Investigation

There is no actual malice when the defendant did a poor job of investigating the claim against the plaintiff prior to publishing the statement. Malice requires some awareness that the statement is false or reckless disregard of the truth.

3. THE SHIFTING STANDARD DEPENDING ON THE PLAINTIFF'S NOTORIETY

When the plaintiff in a defamation case is a private individual, the plaintiff need only show simple fault or negligence on the part of the defendant. However, the rule changes when the plaintiff is famous. Celebrities, politicians, and other famous people have placed themselves in the public eye and enjoy less protection than private individuals. Public figures must show actual malice before they will be allowed to recover against the person making the defamatory statement.

- Judges, including superior, state, district, probate judge, etc.[i]
- Law enforcement officers (although some jurisdictions will consider this on a case-by-case basis)[ii]
- Corrections officers[iii]

[i]*Times Pub. Co. v. Huffstetler*, 409 So. 2d 112 (1982).
[ii]*McCusker v. Valley News*, 121 N.H. 258, 428 A.2d 493 (1981).
[iii]*Sweeney v. Prisoners' Legal Servs.*, 146 App. Div. 2d 1, 538 N.Y.S.2d 370 (1989).

Example: Freddie Famous is a noted public figure. He is the governor of a large state. Reggie Reporter works for a national news agency. On the evening news, Reggie reports that Governor Famous has been squandering public funds on a secret love nest that he has built to share with one of his female staff workers, despite the fact that the governor has been married to Mrs. Famous for over 30 years. After Reggie files his report, the governor brings a defamation action against him. If the Governor can show that Reggie was slipshod in his research and relied on untrustworthy sources for his information, will the governor win his defamation suit? In most cases, the answer is no. Simply showing that Reggie may have been negligent in his reporting may not be enough for the governor to recover against Reggie. The reason for this is that the facts of this case fall clearly into the arena of constitutional protections. First of all, the plaintiff is a public figure. Second, the defendant is a member of the media, and third, the report concerns a matter of public concern — improper use of government funds. Reggie will benefit from a finding that he had no actual malice in filing his report.[21]

The problem with the actual malice standard is that in everyday practice it often becomes confusing to apply. For instance, the Court in *New York Times v. Sullivan* did not provide any clear guidance about the basic ground rules for determining actual malice or even who should be considered a public figure or public official. Subsequent cases have sought to clear up these deficiencies, but this is an area of law that is bound to undergo more changes in the coming years.

When the question of the plaintiff's status as a public figure or public official surfaces in a defamation case, the judge must rule whether the plaintiff falls into that category.

I. DEFAMATION IN CYBERSPACE

The World Wide Web has created new and novel issues in defamation law. When a person is defamed on the Internet, what jurisdiction is empowered to hear the case? More specifically, where does the plaintiff file her suit? The Internet is truly a global phenomenon. A writer in Kiev can defame a person in New York City. Cyberspace raises a myriad of issues regarding jurisdiction and the lack of uniformity of laws among the states and throughout the international community.

Some states have taken the initiative in addressing these issues. Michigan and Alaska have expanded the definition of defamation and their criminal statutes on stalking to include harassment over the Internet. When a person uses the Internet to harass another it is often referred to as *cyber-stalking*.

RIEMERS v. MAHAR
748 N.W.2d 714, 716-722 (N.D. 2008)

CROTHERS, Justice.

Roland Riemers appeals from a summary judgment dismissing his defamation action against Rick Mahar. We conclude Riemers failed to raise genuine issues of material fact about his claim, and we affirm the summary judgment.

I

The Shared Parenting Initiative was an initiative on the state ballot in the November 2006 general election, which proposed changes to child custody and child support laws. The Family Law Reform Initiative proposed changes to child custody, divorce, domestic violence, and child support laws, but it did not receive enough signatures to be placed on the state ballot for the November 2006 general election. Riemers helped draft the Family Law Reform Initiative and was a proponent of both initiatives.

Riemers sued Mahar for defamation after Mahar wrote an article published in the *Walsh County Record*, on September 20, 2006, criticizing the Shared Parenting Initiative and the Family Law Reform Initiative. Mahar's article also included statements about Riemers and his support of the initiatives:

> I have been following with considerable interest the progress of the Shared Parenting Initiative (SPI) and the Family Law Reform Initiative authored by Mitchell Sanderson and Roland Riemers respectively. Voters may recall that Messrs. Riemers and Sanderson ran for North Dakota Governor/Lt. Governor on the Libertarian ticket in the 2004 election. Mr. Riemers, who ran for Governor, and Mr. Sanderson, who ran for Lt. Governor, lost that one having received a paltry one percent of the votes.
>
> I have spent hours and hours on the Internet, reading blogs, reading newspaper articles, listening to radio talk shows, reading the initiatives, etc. I've even heard Mr. Sanderson present at the Walsh County Commission meeting on two occasions. The conclusion that I have reached is that neither Mr. Riemers nor Mr. Sanderson have any interest whatsoever in children or families. They are self-absorbed zealots who will stop at nothing to avenge what they perceive to be their ill-treatment by a court system who didn't happen to see things their way. These initiatives are about power, control, and winning at any cost. They are not about families and children.
>
> The reader can learn all about Mr. Riemers' motives by simply going online, Googling "Roland Riemers Court Case" and then follow the links to the N.D. 2001 Supreme Court ruling and the 2004 N.D. (*Riemers v. Peters-Riemers*) Supreme Court ruling. . . . If one reads, for example, the 2004 Supreme Court decision on his appeals and then the Family Law Reform Initiative one will no longer wonder what might have inspired the Initiative. His success at the Supreme Court was similar to his level of success in his bid for Governor. His attitude seems to be "if I do something and it is against the law then the answer is simple — change the law." Again, this is opinion.

Rick Mahar, "Kissing the High Ground Goodbye," *Walsh County Record,* Sept. 20, 2006.

Mahar also criticized both initiatives, argued they would hurt families and the state and said, "Perhaps the system needs to be tweaked a little. It does not, however, need to be demolished. These initiatives are not the answer. They are the products of rage and vengeance and are truly the fruit of the poison tree." The article was submitted to the Associated Press and appeared in various other newspapers throughout the state.

Riemers publicly supported both initiatives. Riemers wrote an article in support of the Family Law Reform Initiative, published in the *Grand Forks Herald* on May 17, 2006. He was interviewed for an article about the two initiatives, which was published in the *Grand Forks Herald* on July 24, 2006. Riemers responded to Mahar's article in a letter published in the *Walsh County Record* on October 4, 2006, in which he promoted the Shared Parenting Initiative and addressed Mahar's arguments and criticism. Riemers was also a candidate for the United States Senate in 2006 and wrote about his support for the two initiatives in an article about his candidacy, which was published in the *Cavalier County Republican* on October 30, 2006.

Mahar moved for summary judgment, arguing his article does not contain defamatory statements about Riemers, the statements in the article are privileged political speech protected from defamation actions by the federal and state constitutions, and Riemers is a public figure who must show the alleged defamatory statements were made with malice. In support of his motion, Mahar submitted an affidavit explaining his position, a copy of his article, copies of newspaper articles Riemers authored, copies of the two initiatives, answers to interrogatories from both Riemers and Mahar, and other evidence.

Riemers opposed the motion for summary judgment. He argued Mahar's motion was lacking in substance, summary judgment is not appropriate in defamation cases, Mahar's article was not privileged communication, Riemers is not a public figure, and Mahar's statements in the article were defamatory and not merely hyperbole. Riemers did not submit any evidence in support of his argument.

The district court granted Mahar's motion for summary judgment and dismissed the suit. The court considered each statement Riemers claimed was defamatory and concluded the statements either were true or were Mahar's opinion. The court concluded even if Mahar's statements could be considered false, the statements are privileged political speech, Riemers is a public figure and was required to provide evidence the defamatory statements were made with actual malice, Riemers failed to present any evidence of malice, and Mahar did not abuse the privilege extended to his statements. The court also noted that Riemers did not present any evidence Mahar's article caused him to experience hatred, contempt, ridicule or obloquy, that he was shunned or avoided, or that he was injured in his occupation.

Riemers argues the district court erred in concluding that he is a public figure and that he had to prove Mahar's statements were made with malice because Mahar's article never identified Riemers as a political candidate or sponsor of the initiatives and because Mahar was not attacking him as a public figure, and therefore the public figure defamation standard does not apply. He argues the court did not apply North Dakota statutory defamation laws, because North Dakota statutes do not restrict defamation suits against public figures, and if the court had correctly applied the statutory defamation provisions, Riemers met the requirements. He claims the court erred in ruling that it was important Riemers did not present any evidence establishing any facts in dispute, because the only evidence that was necessary was Mahar's article. Riemers contends the district court erred in making findings of fact about the truthfulness of Mahar's statements because it made credibility determinations and weighed evidence not appropriate in summary judgment and because whether the statements were made with malice is a question for the jury.

"Every person may freely write, speak and publish his opinions on all subjects, being responsible for the abuse of that privilege." N.D. Const. Art. I, §4. However, "every person, subject to the qualifications and restrictions provided by law, has the right of protection from bodily restraint or harm, from personal insult, from defamation, and from injury to the person's personal relations." N.D.C.C. §14-02-01. Under N.D.C.C. §14-02-02, defamation includes libel or slander. "Libel is a false and unprivileged publication by writing, printing, picture, effigy, or other fixed representation to the eye, which exposes any person to hatred, contempt, ridicule, or obloquy, or which causes the person to be shunned or avoided, or which has a tendency to injure the person in the person's occupation." N.D.C.C. §14-02-03. Slander is a false and unprivileged publication, other than libel, which:

1. Charges any person with crime, or with having been indicted, convicted, or punished for crime;
2. Imputes to the person the present existence of an infectious, contagious, or loathsome disease;
3. Tends directly to injure the person in respect to the person's office, profession, trade, or business, either by imputing to the person general disqualifications in those respects which the office or other occupation peculiarly requires, or by imputing something with reference to the person's office, profession, trade, or business that has a natural tendency to lessen its profits;
4. Imputes to the person impotence or want of chastity; or
5. By natural consequence causes actual damage.

N.D.C.C. §14-02-04.

A publication is not defamatory unless it is false. *Bertsch v. Duemeland,* 2002 ND 32, ¶11, 639 N.W.2d 455. There is no liability for privileged communications because "'some communications are so socially important that the full and unrestricted exchange of information requires some latitude for mistake.'" *Riemers,* 2004 ND 192, ¶5, 688 N.W.2d 167 (quoting *Fish,* 2003 ND 185, ¶10, 671 N.W.2d 819). A privileged communication is a communication made:

1. In the proper discharge of an official duty;
2. In any legislative or judicial proceeding or in any other proceeding authorized by law;

3. In a communication, without malice, to a person interested therein by one who also is interested, or by one who stands in such relation to the person interested as to afford a reasonable ground for supposing the motive for the communication innocent, or who is requested by the person interested to give the information; and

4. By a fair and true report, without malice, of a judicial, legislative, or other public official proceeding, or of anything said in the course thereof.

N.D.C.C. §14-02-05.

Riemers is correct that there are no special restrictions on defamation actions involving public figures in the North Dakota statutory defamation provisions; however, we can not read our statutes in isolation. The United States Supreme Court has held the First and Fourteenth Amendments of the United States Constitution limit state defamation law in several respects, including defamation actions for statements made about public figures. *See Masson v. New Yorker Magazine, Inc.*, 501 U.S. 496, 510, 111 S.Ct. 2419, 115 L.Ed.2d 447 (1991); *Milkovich v. Lorain Journal Co.*, 497 U.S. 1, 14-15, 110 S.Ct. 2695, 111 L.Ed.2d 1 (1990).

The limits on defamation actions for statements made about public figures exist because of concerns for free speech. False statements are bound to be made in the course of vigorous public debate. One of the prerogatives of American citizenship is the right to criticize public men and measures. Such criticism, inevitably, will not always be reasoned or moderate; public figures will be subject to "vehement, caustic, and sometimes unpleasantly sharp attacks." *Hustler Magazine v. Falwell*, 485 U.S. 46, 51, 108 S.Ct. 876, 99 L.Ed.2d 41 (1988). While false assertions have little value, imposing liability for all false statements relating to public figures would have a chilling effect on speech about public figures, and freedoms of expression require breathing room. Without limitations on defamation actions, destructive self-censorship would occur limiting free speech. Given the importance of the free and open exchange of ideas, a public figure is prohibited from recovering damages for defamatory criticism unless there is clear and convincing evidence the defamatory statement was made with actual malice. *Gertz v. Robert Welch, Inc.*, 418 U.S. 323, 342, 94 S.Ct. 2997, 41 L.Ed.2d 789 (1974). Whether someone is a private or a public figure is a question of law. *Lundell Mfg. Co. v. American Broadcasting Companies, Inc.*, 98 F.3d 351, 362 (8th Cir.1996) ("determination of plaintiff's status is a question of law governed by federal constitutional law").

Public figures include nonpublic persons who are "'intimately involved in the resolution of important public questions or, by reason of their fame, shape events in areas of concern to society at large.'" *Gertz*, 418 U.S. at 337, 94 S.Ct. 2997 (quoting *Curtis Pub. Co. v. Butts*, 388 U.S. 130, 162, 87 S.Ct. 1975, 18 L.Ed.2d 1094 (1967)). Public figures generally "enjoy significantly greater access to the channels of effective communication and hence have a more realistic opportunity to counteract false statements than private individuals normally enjoy"; therefore the state's interest in protecting private individuals is greater because they lack effective opportunities for rebuttal and are more vulnerable to injury. *Gertz,* at 344, 94 S.Ct. 2997. Public figures often have assumed roles of special prominence in society's affairs. *Id.* at 345, 94 S.Ct. 2997. Some are public figures for all purposes because they occupy positions of such persuasive power and influence. *Id.* More commonly they have "thrust themselves to the forefront of particular public controversies in order to influence the resolution of the issues involved." *Id.* In either case they invite attention and comment. *Id.* Because they inject themselves in public controversies, "public figures have voluntarily exposed themselves to increased risk of injury for defamatory statements." *Id.*

There are two types of public figures: an individual who has achieved such "fame or notoriety that he is a public figure for all purposes and in all contexts," and an individual who "voluntarily injects himself or is drawn into a particular public controversy and thereby becomes a public figure for a limited range of issues." *Gertz,* 418 U.S. at 351, 94 S.Ct. 2997. An individual should not be deemed a public figure for all purposes unless there is clear evidence of general fame or notoriety in the community and pervasive involvement in society's affairs. *Id.* at 352, 94 S.Ct. 2997. To determine an individual's public figure status we look at the nature and extent of the individual's participation in the controversy giving rise to the alleged defamation. *Id.*

In this case, Riemers is at least a limited purpose public figure. While Riemers may not have sponsored either initiative, he drafted the Family Law Reform Initiative and was one of its main proponents. He voluntarily assumed a role of special prominence in the controversy and sought to influence its outcome. Riemers also had access to channels of effective communication. After Mahar's article was published, Riemers published an article rebutting Mahar's allegations and criticism. Riemers also wrote and published various other newspaper articles and gave interviews about the Family Law Reform Initiative and the Shared Parenting Initiative before and after Mahar's article was published. The controversy existed prior to Mahar's article and continued to exist at the time the article was published. Mahar's article was limited to discussing the controversy and Riemers' role in the controversy. We conclude Riemers was, as a matter of law, a limited purpose public figure.

Because Riemers was a public figure, he was required to present clear and convincing evidence Mahar's statements were false and were made with actual malice. Actual malice is knowledge that the statements are false or that the statements were made with reckless disregard for whether they were false. *Gertz,* 418 U.S. at 334, 94 S.Ct. 2997. The plaintiff must demonstrate the author had serious doubts about the truth of his publication or had "a high degree of awareness of the probable falsity." *Masson,* 501 U.S. at 510, 111 S.Ct. 2419. The standard for actual malice "should not be confused with the concept of malice as an evil intent or a motive arising from ill will." There is no genuine issue and the court must grant summary judgment "if the evidence presented . . . is of insufficient caliber and quantity to allow a rational finder of fact to find actual malice by clear and convincing evidence." The question whether the evidence in the record in a public figure defamation case is sufficient to support a finding of actual malice is a question of law because in cases raising First Amendment issues, the appellate court has an obligation to examine the whole record and to ensure the judgment does not constitute a forbidden intrusion on free expression.

We conclude Riemers was a limited purpose public figure and was required to present evidence raising a genuine issue of fact about actual malice. Riemers failed to meet his burden. We affirm the district court's summary judgment dismissing Riemers' defamation action against Mahar.

Questions about the case:

1. What does Riemers allege that Mahar wrote that was defamatory?
2. Were Mahar's comments privileged communications and would such a classification have a bearing in a defamation case?
3. How did the trial court classify Mahar's statements?
4. What is the basis of Riemers's claim that he was not a public figure?
5. Does North Dakota recognize exceptions for public figures? If not, why then does Mahar win this case?

 ## ANALYZING A CASE
OF DEFAMATION

Now that we have reviewed the laws of defamation, let's return to the hypothetical case we addressed at the beginning of this chapter. To review the pertinent facts of Susan's case: First of all, her name has appeared on a sign in a store. The sign names her, among others, as a "deadbeat" and at the very least accuses her of committing a crime. Does she have a libel case against the store?

Taking the elements of defamation one by one, has the store manager published a defamatory statement? The sign can be, and certainly has been, read by other store customers. The statement is false, because Susan has never passed a bad check at the store. The statement is defamatory, because it accuses her of a crime, and her reputation has been injured, because this is a grocery store where she and many of her college friends routinely shop. The libel case seems fairly strong. Is there also a case for slander? Remember that when Susan approached the store manager, he accused her of being a deadbeat again, suggested that he would call the police to have her arrested, and banished her from the store while shouting that she had pending bad checks. This scenario would seem to qualify as a slander case. Susan has two potential claims against the store, one for libel and the other for slander. She will have to prove her damages to the jury, but the elements for both seem to be satisfied.

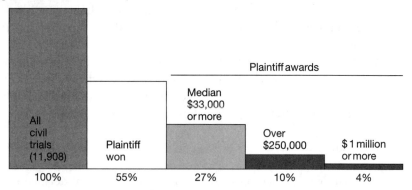

FIGURE 11-16

Civil Trial Cases and Verdicts in Large Counties, 2001

In 2001 plaintiffs in the 75 largest counties won just over half the 12,000 general civil cases at trial, with 442 or 4% awarded $1 million or more

Plaintiff awards

All civil trials (11,908)	Plaintiff won	Median $33,000 or more	Over $250,000	$1 million or more
100%	55%	27%	10%	4%

- During 2001 a jury decided almost 75% of the 12,000 tort, contract, and real property trials in the nation's 75 largest counties. Judges adjudicated the remaining 24%. Tort cases (93%) were more likely than contract cases (43%) to be disposed of by jury trial.
- The 11,908 civil trials disposed of in 2001 represents a 47% decline from the 22,451 civil trials in these counties in 1992.
- In jury trials, the median award decreased from $65,000 in 1992 to $37,000 in 2001 in these counties.
- Two-thirds of disposed trials in 2001 involved tort claims, and about a third involved contractual issues.
- Overall, plaintiffs won in 55% of trials. Plaintiffs won more often in bench trials (65%) than in jury trials (53%), and in contract trials (65%) more often than in tort (52%) or real property trials (38%).
- An estimated $4 billion in compensatory and punitive damages was awarded to plaintiff winners in civil trials. Juries awarded $3.9 billion to plaintiff winners while judges awarded $368 million. The median total award for plaintiff winners in tort trials was $27,000 and in contract trials $45,000.
- Punitive damages, estimated at $1.2 billion, were awarded to 6% of plaintiff winners in trials. The median punitive damage award was $50,000.
- Plaintiffs prevailed in about a fourth (27%) of medical malpractice trials. Half of the 311 plaintiffs who successfully litigated a medical malpractice claim won at least $422,000, and in nearly a third of these cases, the award was $1 million or more.

Civil Trial Cases and Verdicts in Large Counties, 2001, Bureau of Justice Statistics, U.S. Department of Justice.

 SKILLS YOU NEED IN THE REAL WORLD

Balancing School and Work

If you are like most paralegal students, you are trying to balance a job, a family, and a school career, all at the same time. When you walk such a tightrope, it is easy to fall off. One way to achieve balance is to do some studying during lunch or to work on class assignments after you are "off duty" at work.

Before you rush headlong into doing your studies and assignments at work, there are some important issues to consider. The most obvious is that you should not use the time your boss is paying you to work on your studies. You should remember that the firm is paying you for your efforts, so never, ever work on school assignments while you are being paid to work for the firm. In addition to that basic ground rule, there are some other important considerations for anyone trying to balance school and work.

Let's look at five simple rules that you should follow to achieve a greater balance between work and school and that will hopefully help you be better at both.

Rule #1. Get the Boss Involved

If you are going to do schoolwork at your job, get your boss involved. Explain to him or her that you will only be working on your schoolwork during your lunch break or after hours. You might be surprised how understanding most employers will be.

Explain the situation to your boss and emphasize that you will not work on schoolwork while you're being paid to work for the firm, but that during times when you are technically off the clock, you'd like to spend some time studying and working on school material.

Rule #2. Prioritize

Everyone has heard about prioritizing. Prioritizing is going through your in basket until everything is put in the out basket, right? Wrong. Prioritizing is putting first things first. Prioritizing takes discipline and time; that's why most people don't like to do it. Although there are as many rules for prioritizing as there are people, we'll focus on only one. We'll call this crisis prioritizing. Create a category labeled "top priority," or "absolute to do," or anything else you'd like to call it and put only those tasks there that actually qualify. Look at it this way: Here is a list of items that you must take care of immediately or face real trouble. Only those items should be listed there. Force yourself to keep this particular category to a minimum.

Once you've established the crisis category, create a list of things that should be done soon. For a busy person, these are the only categories that you need. You could create a long-range to-do list, but chances are that you will never have time to look at it. For a busy student and full-time worker, you have two levels: crisis and soon-to-be crisis.

One secret of prioritizing is to schedule your work and studying around your own metabolism. If you are a morning person, do your studying before you go to work. If you are a night owl, schedule schoolwork then.

Rule #3. Delegate

If your response to delegation is "Hey, I'm low person on the totem pole; I don't have anyone to delegate to!" you may very well be wrong. You may not have anyone at work that you can delegate to, but you do have other people in your life. Get your kids involved in your studies. Have family members help you. Recruit friends, children, spouses, significant others, and anyone else you can find to help you.

Rule #4. It's Time to Get Organized

Organization actually takes time and effort, but it pays huge dividends. If your idea of organization is keeping a big stack of stuff on your living room table, you really aren't organized. Get some books on organization. Visit some of the Web sites mentioned at the end of this chapter. Get help and suggestions from others about how to get more organized — and how to stay that way.

One method used by many people to get organized is to create a master calendar. You could even go so far as to color-code various entries, but if that's a little over the top for you, a simple entry showing school assignments, test dates, and work assignments will be enough to give you an idea of what you're facing. The nice thing about writing this material down is that it lessens that two o'clock in the morning anxiety attack that all busy people have. You know the feeling: You suddenly bolt up in bed, convinced that you forgot to file an important pleading, or submit an important assignment, or any of the hundred other things that could have slipped by you. If you have a master calendar, you can climb out of bed and reassure yourself that the deadline isn't until next week, heave a sigh of relief, and go back to sleep.

Rule #5. Get Those Creative Juices Flowing

The real secret to getting a lot of things done isn't rigid schedules and unending work — it's getting creative. One paralegal has dictation software loaded on her laptop. On her 20-minute drive to work every morning, she dictates letters and other materials that she can print at work. Another paralegal carries a mini tape recorder with her wherever she goes. When she gets an idea, she dictates it to herself. Later, she plays the tape back and writes down any good ideas.

Many paralegals also get creative with their use of time. Pam Tallent studies whenever she has a chance. For instance, some paralegals study while they are waiting for the bus or when they are sitting in a doctor's waiting room.

If you follow these rules and use your own ingenuity, you'll find that it is easier to balance your school and work loads and free up some time to relax.

 THE LIFE OF A PARALEGAL

The Life of a Brand New Paralegal

Christina Truitt has only been a paralegal for about three months. Coming from a secretarial background, she was surprised by how different working at a law office can be from a traditional office.

"When I showed up, no one even knew that I'd been hired. They were all surprised when they found out that I was there to replace a lady who'd put in her notice two days before. She trained me on her position, but I could tell that her heart really wasn't in it. I was on my own right from the start. I realized pretty quickly that if I were going to figure all of this stuff out, I'd have to get organized.

"I took home copies of a lot of the basic forms that we used every day and I made notes on them. I'd write on the margins what the different terms meant and why we would use this form in this particular case. Later, I started making up my own forms to help me keep track of things. The hardest part, at least at first, was learning the terminology. The legal terms were flying at me from day one, and I had to ask a lot of questions to get things clarified. I was doing all of this while having a lot of client contact. The phone rings all the time and I'm talking to clients in between doing all of this other stuff. I am also a full-time student, so learning how to balance my time was crucial. I'm taking some classes during the day, one evening class, and an Internet class. While I'm learning my new job, I'm also trying to stay on top of my classes. It makes you a lot better at organization. I study for my classes on my lunch breaks and do a lot of schoolwork in the evenings.

"I really enjoy the legal field. You are constantly getting new challenges and meeting people with new problems. It's a good feeling when you can help them out."

Christina Truitt, Paralegal

ETHICAL ISSUES FOR THE PARALEGAL: CONFLICTS OF INTEREST

One of the most important ethical issues for both attorneys and paralegals is avoiding a conflict of interest. At its simplest, a conflict of interest is any issue that arises between the client and the attorney in which the client's interest may be subordinated to some other concern. For instance, when an attorney represents both the plaintiff and the defendant in a lawsuit, there is a definite and obvious conflict of interest. After all, if the attorney represents both, whose interest is she safeguarding? Similar problems arise when an attorney is the business partner of the client. The lawyer's legal advice may be tainted by considerations of how the client's actions might affect their business relationship.

Ethical rules for both attorneys and paralegals emphasize avoiding even the appearance of a conflict of interest. Paralegals are often called upon to review the roster of clients to make sure that any newly acquired client does not have an interest that runs counter to that of a previous client. The prime example would be representing the husband in a divorce action and then the wife in a child custody dispute. Such representation would be considered a conflict of interest and would justify the firm refusing to represent the wife on the subsequent suit, especially because it was based in some part on the prior divorce action. Conflicts of interest can also come up in personal injury cases. If the potential plaintiff has met with the firm and discussed the possibility of representation in his personal injury suit against a particular defendant, the firm cannot then meet with the defendant, who is also seeking legal representation, even if the plaintiff did not actually hire the firm to represent him.

One method of avoiding potential conflicts of interest is by performing a "conflicts" check. Paralegals, attorneys, and secretaries routinely review new files to make sure that no potential conflicts are involved. There is even legal software available to help with this process.

Chapter Summary

An action for defamation can be brought when a plaintiff believes that a statement has injured his reputation. Such an action is one of the few ways that a person can seek to protect his reputation from false allegations. To prove defamation, the plaintiff must show that a defamatory statement was made, that the statement was false, that it referred to the plaintiff, and that it injured the plaintiff's reputation. Defamation comes in two forms: libel and slander. Libel is written defamation, which can include books, cartoons, signs, and other objects. Slander is oral or spoken defamation and is usually limited to speech. The plaintiff's injury and awardable damages are presumed in specific situations, such as when the statement involves the false accusation of a crime, of an infectious disease, or of the legal inability to engage in the plaintiff's chosen trade. Traditional analysis of defamation actions changed significantly after the U.S. Supreme Court's decision in *New York Times v. Sullivan*. In that case, the Court ruled that the standard of proof in defamation actions depended on the classification of the plaintiff as a public or private figure. If classified as a public figure, the plaintiff could only recover if she could show actual malice on the defendant's part. If classified as a private individual, actual malice is not required. These rules reflect the fact that some individuals, such as celebrities, who deliberately seek fame and notoriety, must put up with more comments and discussions as compared to private individuals, who are entitled to greater protection.

Web Sites

■ **Online defamation**
   http://legal.web.aol.com/decisions/dldefam/

■ **Find Law articles about defamation**
   http://www.findlaw.com (click on "search findlaw" for defamation, slander, etc.)

■ **Legal search engines**
   Using any search engine, type in "legal search engines," and then save the results for a search involving any of the issues raised in this chapter.

■ **Timeslips (time and billing software for law offices)**
   http://www.timeslips.com/

Forms and Court Documents

A complaint alleging libel

STATE OF PLACID		IN THE SUPERIOR COURT
COUNTY OF BARNES		FILE NUMBER: _____

Lawrence Lookgood,	)	Complaint
Plaintiff	)	
	)	
vs.	)	
	)	
Placid News, Inc.,	)	
Defendant	)	

Complaint for Libel

COMES NOW the plaintiff and complaining of the Defendant Placid News, Inc., alleges the following:

1.

Defendant Placid News, Inc. (hereinafter "Defendant") is a corporation incorporated under the laws of this State. Defendant's principal office is located at 1001 Burke Avenue, Barnes County, Pacific City, Placid.

2.

Defendant is the owner and principal publisher of the Placid News Herald. This is a newspaper, published daily and distributed statewide.

3.

On August 19, 2002, agents employed by the Defendant wrote an article about the plaintiff. This article contained false and defamatory statements about the plaintiff in that the article stated that the Plaintiff had fathered several children with his secretary, Lisa Doe. This statement was published in conjunction with another in which the Plaintiff was quoted as saying that he and his wife, Mrs. Julia Lookgood, had always enjoyed a happy and monogamous marriage. The clear implication of the article is that the Plaintiff engaged in an extramarital affair with his secretary and fathered children with her while he was married to Julia Lookgood.

4.

The defamatory article was distributed by the Defendant's agents to its distributors throughout the state. The defamatory article was read by thousands of individuals, including the Plaintiff's wife, children, and co-workers.

5.

The defamatory matter injured the Plaintiff's reputation, held him up to public ridicule and humiliation, and affected his ability to interact with his clients. The defamatory statement was intended to cause, and did cause, injury to the plaintiff's reputation.

6.

Plaintiff is not a public figure and defendant's agents knew that the statement was false, or acted with reckless disregard of the truth of the statement contained in said article.

WHEREFORE, Plaintiff prays that the Court award the following damages:

a. General damages in the amount of _____;
b. Special damages in the amount of _____; and
c. Punitive damages in an amount to be determined by the court.
d. Plaintiff also requests costs of suit; and
e. Such other and further relief as the court may deem just and proper.

Respectfully submitted, this the _____ day of _____, 200_____.

_____

Clarence D. Arrow
Attorney for the Plaintiff

Key Terms

Clear and convincing proof	Malice
Defamation	Slander
Libel	

Review Questions

1 What is the difference between libel and slander?
2 How is libel per se different from slander per se?
3 Can a cartoon be considered defamatory? If so, what type of defamation is it?
4 How is the Restatement's definition of defamation (Figure 11-1) different from the general definition of defamation (Figure 11-2)?
5 Can a family be defamed? Why or why not?
6 Explain the term *publication.*
7 Why is it necessary that the plaintiff prove publication to be successful in her defamation action?
8 Mailing a letter to the plaintiff is usually not considered to be publication. Why?
9 How can the plaintiff prove that her reputation was damaged?
10 What is libel per quod?
11 In libel per se, malice is often presumed. Why?
12 Is libel potentially more damaging to the plaintiff than slander? If so, how?
13 It is often said that truth is an absolute defense to defamation. Explain.
14 Other than truth, what types of defense are available in a defamation action?
15 Explain the difference between an absolute privilege and a qualified privilege.
16 Why does a celebrity receive less protection under defamation law than a private person?
17 How do courts balance the First Amendment right of freedom of speech against a person's right to bring a defamation action?
18 What is the *New York Times* Rule?
19 What is actual malice?

Applying What You Have Learned

1 One evening, Ted, the news anchor on a local television show, reads the following from his prepared TV script: "In the news today, John Doe has been arrested and charged with child molestation." Ted pauses, and then, ad-libbing, says, "Man, that guy is always getting into trouble. Someone should teach that pedophile a lesson."

In fact, John Doe has not been arrested or charged with any crime and has never been in trouble with the law before. Does John have a cause of action for defamation against Ted? If so, what type of action can he bring? Explain your answer.

2 Draft an answer to the complaint in the Forms and Court Documents section. What constitutional issues may also be involved in this case?

3 Draft a complaint based on the Case for Defamation. What are the possible defenses that a defendant might use in an answer?

4 Has your state expanded the definition of slander per se or libel per se? If so, what category of statements is covered?

5 What types of privileges and immunities are recognized in your state in regard to defamation actions? Are they more extensive than what the text suggests, or less so?

Endnotes

[1] *Swenson-Davis v. Martel,* 354 N.W.2d 288, 135 Mich. App. 632 (1984).

[2] *Berg v. Consolidated Freightways, Inc.,* 280 Pa. Super. 495, 421 A.2d 831 (1980).

[3] Restatement (Second) of Torts §580A, comment f.

[4] *Cosgrove Studio & Camera Shop, Inc. v. Pane,* 408 Pa. 314, 182 A.2d 751 (1962).

[5] *Weinstein v. Bullick,* 827 F. Supp. 1193 (E.D. Pa. 1993).

[6] *Cox Enters. v. Bakin,* 206 Ga. App. 813, 426 S.E.2d 651 (1992).

[7] *Wynberg v. National Enquirer, Inc.,* 564 F. Supp. 924 (D.C. Cal. 1982).

[8] *Ostrowe v. Lee,* 175 N.E. 505, 256 N.Y. 36 (1931).

[9] *Linebaugh v. Sheraton Mich. Corp.,* 198 Mich. App. 335, 497 N.W.2d 585 (1993).

[10] *Renwick v. News and Observer Pub. Co.,* 304 S.E.2d 593 (1983).

[11] *Reiman v. Pacific Development Soc.,* 284 P. 575, 132 Or. 82 (1930).

[12] *Miller v. Lear Siegler, Inc.,* 525 F. Supp. 46 (D.C. Kan. 1981).

[13] *Gonzalez v. Avon Products, Inc.,* 609 F. Supp. 1555 (D.C. Del. 1985).

[14] *Hearst Corp. v. Hughes,* 466 A.2d 486, 297 Md. 112 (1983).

[15] *Gertz v. Robert Welch, Inc.,* 418 U.S. 323 (1974).

[16] 376 U.S. 254, 11 L. Ed. 2d 686, 84 S. Ct. 710.

[17] *Gertz v. Robert Welch, Inc.,* 418 U.S. 323 (1974).

[18] *New York Times Co. v. Sullivan,* 376 U.S. 254, 11 L. Ed. 2d 686, 84 S. Ct. 710 (1964).

[19] Oliver Wendell Holmes, The Common Law, Little, Brown and Company, Boston (M. Howe ed., 1963).

[20] *Buendorf v. National Pub. Radio, Inc.,* 822 F. Supp. 6 (D.D.C. 1993).

[21] *Triangle Publications, Inc. v. Chumley,* 253 Ga. 179, 317 S.E.2d 534 (1984).

Malpractice

 **CHUMLEY AND MALPRACTICE**

When Mr. Chumley was airlifted from the crash scene to a local hospital, the attending physician failed to diagnose some of his internal injuries. Mr. Chumley suffered blunt trauma to his abdomen, but the physician failed to notice a potentially fatal spleen puncture. In fact, on the nurse's note that the firm has received through discovery, the message in Figure 12-1 appears.

The first hurdle is learning how to decipher this medical language. Unfortunately, that topic is too broad for a chapter that focuses on medical

FIGURE 12-1

Nurse's Note

malpractice. The note actually says, "Patient complains of severe left upper quadrant pain upon palpation. Dr. Smith notified. — DB"

Now that we know what the nurse's note says, do we have a case for medical malpractice against the attending physician? We answer that question over the course of this chapter.

INTRODUCTION TO PROFESSIONAL MALPRACTICE

When professionals fail to live up to the standards of their profession, their clients may have a cause of action against them. In this chapter, we address the issue of malpractice cases. After defining what a malpractice case is, we then proceed to specific examples showing how such cases are proved. Although malpractice cases are brought against a wide variety of professions, the two most common are medical malpractice and legal malpractice.

WHAT IS MALPRACTICE?

Malpractice
The failure of a professional to exercise an adequate degree of skill, expertise, and knowledge for the benefit of the client or patient; otherwise known as professional negligence

In a suit for **malpractice,** the plaintiff is alleging that the defendant, who is a professional, injured the plaintiff while performing his profession. Although we proceed in the discussion as though malpractice is an entirely separate form of tort action, in fact it is not. Malpractice cases are usually based solidly in negligence theory, but because these cases raise so many unique issues, the topic of malpractice deserves a chapter to itself.

The basis of a malpractice action is that a person who claims to have special knowledge and skill causes personal injury or wrongful death to the plaintiff during the execution of that skill. The typical example of a malpractice action is when a doctor negligently injures his patient while treating him for some injury. The doctor's negligence in the treatment gives the plaintiff a cause of action against him.

Notice that malpractice actions are based on the negligent performance of the professional's duties. An essential part of any malpractice claim is that the injury occurred during, and as a direct result of, the professional's actions

Litigants	Number of total trials[a]
All trials	**26,984**
Individual versus—	
Individual	11,224
Business	7,472
Hospital	1,546
Government	1,383
Business versus—	
Individual	1,852
Business	2,604
Hospital	9
Government	198
Hospital versus[b]—	
Individual	13
Business	16
Hospital	7
Government versus[b]—	
Individual	384
Business	151
Government	22

FIGURE 12-2

Civil Trials in State Courts, by Litigation Pairings, 2005

[a] Litigant data were available for 99.7% of trials.
[b] There were no reported cases in which a hospital/medical company filed against the government or in which the government filed against a hospital/medical company.

Civil Bench and Jury Trials in State Courts, 2005, Bureau of Justice Statistics, U.S. Department of Justice.

while performing his particular area of expertise. When the defendant is not acting in his professional capacity and causes injury, there is no cause of action for medical malpractice. Instead, that case would simply be treated as any other negligence action.

Example: Doctor Ted is driving home from work and fails to stop for a red light. He hits Frank's car. Frank brings a medical malpractice action against Doctor Ted. Doctor Ted files a motion to dismiss for failure to state a valid cause of action. How does the judge rule?

Answer: The judge will dismiss the case. Doctor Ted was not acting in his professional capacity at the time of the accident, so a malpractice case is not authorized.

In malpractice cases, the defendant is held to a higher standard than what is seen in typical negligence cases. Recall that the standard of care in most negligence cases is the "reasonable person standard." Under that standard, the plaintiff must show that the defendant failed to act as a reasonable person

Sidebar

From the first medical malpractice case in the United States: "Action of the case declaring that on the 10th of October 1791, the plaintiff's wife had a scrofulous tumor in one of her breasts, which required amputation; that the defendant, who then was, and for many years before had been a practicing physician, and professed to be well skilled in surgery, and in the amputation of limbs, applied to the plaintiff and affirmed to him that he had competent skill and knowledge to cut off his wife's breast, and to make a cure of it, and that he could and would for a reasonable reward, perform said operation, with skill and safety to his said wife; and the plaintiff relying upon the de-fendant's declara-tions aforesaid, con-sented to his perform-ing said operation, and agreed to pay him therefor [sic] whatever should be a reasonable compensation; and the defendant in consider-ation thereof undertook and promised to per-form said operation with skill and safety to the wife of the plaintiff; and that on the 10th of October aforesaid, the defendant did cut off the breast of his said wife, and performed said operation in the most unskillful, igno-rant and cruel manner, contrary to all the well-known rules and prin-ciples of practice in such cases; and that after said operation, the plaintiff's wife lan-guished for about three hours and then died of the wound given by the hand of the defendant; and that the defendant
(continued)

would have done under similar circumstances and that this failure was a proximate cause of the plaintiff's injuries. This is not the standard used in malpractice cases. In malpractice cases, we use a variation of the reasonable person standard. Malpractice cases are also unique among negligence cases because the plaintiff must prove that there was a relationship between him and the professional. In fact, proof of a doctor-patient relationship is absolutely critical in proving medical malpractice. It is this relationship that gives rise to the special obligations that the defendant-doctor has toward the patient.

Medical malpractice cases have received a great deal of attention in the past couple of decades because of several large jury verdicts awarded to plain-tiffs. Some of these awards have been enormous, stretching into hundreds of millions of dollars. As a result, the field has undergone dramatic changes. State legislatures have enacted new statutes to modify the statutes of limitation or to limit the size of verdicts that plaintiffs may receive in such cases. Many com-mentators have spoken of a "medical malpractice crisis" in which "runaway juries" constantly award huge verdicts to plaintiffs, which results in greater malpractice insurance premiums for doctors and may even drive some phy-sicians out of the profession entirely. We address these issues as well, but first, we take a look at the history of medical malpractice actions.

A. A BRIEF HISTORY OF MEDICAL MALPRACTICE

Although medical malpractice cases seem like a relatively recent phenomenon, they have been around for hundreds of years. The first medical malpractice case in the United States was filed in 1794. However, these cases were few and far between. There has been a dramatic rise in these cases beginning after World War II and rising steadily ever since.

The medical profession has not always been held in high esteem. In the 1800s, physicians were often poorly trained and unlicensed.[2] Medical treat-ments were rudimentary and, by modern standards, lacking in proper hygiene and follow-up care. According to one commentator, "The notoriously low quality of medical training aggravated the profession's declining status."[3] There was a dramatic increase in medical malpractice cases in the 1840s and 1850s and these cases brought about some important changes in the medical field, most notably licensing of physicians.

B. DEFINING MEDICAL MALPRACTICE

For our purposes, we use the following working definition of medical mal-practice: when the physician's deviation from the accepted standard of care is a proximate cause of the patient's injury.

Malpractice cases can be based on any of several different theories. For instance, when a physician operates on the plaintiff without the plaintiff's consent, this is technically a battery. The doctor-patient relationship also has a contractual basis. One could argue that when the doctor violates the standard of care, she is essentially breaching a contractual term. However, the vast majority of malpractice cases are based on negligence theory and its concomitant requirement of proving duty to the plaintiff, breach of that duty, proximate causation, and resultant damages.

Medical malpractice cases are often brought not only against physicians, but also nurses and other medical providers. For the sake of brevity, we simply refer to the "defendant-doctor" with the understanding that all of these medical providers may be named defendants in medical malpractice cases.

C. WHAT IS THE BASIS FOR A MEDICAL MALPRACTICE CASE?

As we noted above, a medical malpractice case can be based on any of several different theories. For instance, a medical malpractice case could be based in intentional tort theory.

1. BATTERY

When a patient alleges intentional contact of a harmful or offensive nature against a medical provider during the course of his treatment, the patient is essentially raising a battery claim. Almost all medical treatments involve some form of physical contact between the doctor and patient. If this is true, are all medical procedures batteries? If we analyze the elements of battery, we see that a medical procedure, such as invasive surgery, seems to satisfy all the elements of battery — except one. True, cutting open the plaintiff's body is a "harmful or offensive contact," but there is one important element missing. In most medical procedures, the doctor obtains consent from the patient before carrying out the procedure. In such a case, there is no battery, because the plaintiff has given the doctor permission to carry out the contact.

What happens in situations where the doctor does not obtain permission or when the doctor exceeds the scope of the permission?

Example: While Tom is waiting for the bus, he suddenly faints. Doctor Ted happens to be driving by, and when he sees Tom faint, he stops to lend a hand. Tom is obviously not in any immediate danger, so bystanders call for an ambulance. While they are waiting, Doctor Ted sees a cyst on Tom's hand and expertly cuts it off with a scalpel he happens to have with him. Has Doctor Ted battered Tom?

Answer: Yes. Tom did not give Doctor Ted consent to touch him, or to operate on him.

An important caution about the hypothetical above: Had Tom's injury been life-threatening, the rules about consent would change. We explore this important exception surrounding medical emergencies later in this chapter.

When a battery does not occur within the scope of the physician's treatment, such as when a doctor happens to get involved in a fist-fight with another man at a local grocery store, the other man cannot bring a malpractice

Sidebar

had wholly broken and violated his undertaking and promise to the plaintiff to perform said operation skillfully and with safety to his wife; whereby the plaintiff had been put to great cost and expense and been deprived of the service, company and consortship [sic] of his said wife — damages in the amount of £1,000."[1]

Sidebar

The Code of Hammurabi (1750 B.C.) provided what is perhaps the earliest known proscription against medical malpractice: "If a physician make a large incision with the operating knife, and kill him . . . his hands shall be cut off."

action. Malpractice claims based on battery are limited to the arena of medical treatment.[4]

Similarly, when the doctor's contact with the patient exceeds the scope of the treatment, it may also provide the basis for a malpractice claim.

Example: While he is treating a young child, a doctor strikes the child in an effort to make her stop crying. Even when the doctor has a valid consent to perform the procedure, he does not have consent to strike the child.[5]

2. CONTRACT

Recovery in a medical malpractice case can also be premised on a contract theory. In most medical situations, a contract is either express or implied between the parties. The doctor provides professional medical services and skills in exchange for payment from the patient. Although some jurisdictions allow contractual relationship as one theory of recovery in medical malpractice cases, no jurisdiction limits such actions exclusively to this area of law. If a medical malpractice case were based solely on a contractual basis, this would dramatically limit the patient's ability to sue for negligent actions. It would also ignore some of the public considerations that are an important basis of medical practice.[6]

However, there is one element in a medical malpractice case that does resonate with contractual theory. As we see later in this chapter, the plaintiff must prove that there was a doctor-patient relationship between the two parties in the malpractice case.

3. NEGLIGENCE

The majority of medical malpractice cases are based on the theory of negligence. As such, these cases are based on a familiar formula:

1 Duty of the doctor to the plaintiff-patient
2 Breach of that duty
3 Proximate cause
4 Damages suffered by plaintiff

In a malpractice case, we could add one additional component to Element 1: proof of a doctor-patient relationship between the parties. We discuss each of these negligence elements in the next section.

THE BASIC ELEMENTS OF A MEDICAL MALPRACTICE CLAIM

Although previous chapters have addressed the basic elements of any negligence claim, medical malpractice negligence cases involve special issues unique to these claims.

A. DUTY

When we discuss duty in the context of a medical malpractice case, we are talking about using a different standard to evaluate the defendant's actions. The duty imposed on a physician is to use reasonable skill, care, and expertise to ensure the safety and well-being of the patient.[7] This duty arises as a direct consequence of the **physician-patient relationship.** When a doctor takes on a patient, the doctor is required to use her skills in the best interests of the patient.

When does a physician's duty to a patient begin? Courts have been called upon to decide this issue many times and, over the decades, some basic factors have emerged to establish this relationship: the nature of the services that the physician will perform, the circumstances surrounding the plaintiff's request for medical assistance, and whether the physician takes a medical history from the patient.[8]

Among the duties that a physician owes a patient is the duty to diagnose the plaintiff's injury or sickness. Doctors must use reasonable skill and care in making this diagnosis, because it will determine the future course of the patient's treatment. A misdiagnosis could be as devastating to the patient as gross negligence in performing a procedure.

Physician-patient relationship
The legally recognized relationship between a physician and patient in which the physician brings her skill to bear in the care and treatment of the patient; this relationship also triggers the evidentiary physician-patient privilege that protects the patient's communications with the physician from compulsory revelation

B. BREACH

The second element of a medical malpractice case is proof that the defendant-doctor breached the duty she owed to the patient. Unlike typical negligence cases that will often revolve around proof of causation or damages, medical malpractice cases often hinge on this single issue. In fact, our discussion of breach must encompass many different concepts and involve issues that are usually not seen in a typical negligence case.

When a plaintiff brings a medical malpractice case, the central issue frequently is whether the defendant-doctor breached her duty to the plaintiff. This proof of the breach of duty boils down to whether the defendant-doctor violated the standard of care. If she did, she has breached the duty; if she did not, then no breach occurred and she may be entitled to a verdict in her favor. Some commentators have said that the standard of care is the "threshold question" that must be determined in any malpractice case.[9]

■ Duty to fully inform the patient about procedures, tests, etc. ■ Duty to notify the patient about results of tests and procedures	■ Duty to notify patient about the need for alternate treatment ■ Duty to refer patient to another physician	**FIGURE 12-3** **Other Duties That Doctors Owe Patients**

1. DEFINING THE STANDARD OF CARE

Standard of care
The standard used
by the law to deter-
mine negligence; the
standard that dictates
that the defendant
must act in the same
manner as a reason-
able, prudent
professional

The **standard of care** is an important issue in medical malpractice cases; here we define what this standard is and how it is applied. If the plaintiff can show that the defendant-doctor failed to exercise the same degree of skill, knowledge, and care as other doctors in the professional community, the plaintiff can establish that the doctor failed to use the appropriate standard of care in his case. However, medical treatment involves highly complex issues that the average person on a jury would find difficult, if not impossible, to understand. Diagnosis, treatment, and care of a patient, and the standard of care that prevails in the medical community at the time, are not matters of common knowledge. How then can a jury member decide if the defendant-doctor's behavior in a case violated the standard of care? The plaintiff must present expert testimony to explain the procedures, the course of treatment, the standard of care that should have been applied, and how the defendant-doctor's actions fell below that standard.[10]

 **One of the essential elements of a claim for medical negligence is that the defendant breached the applicable standard of medical care owed to the plaintiff.[11]**

2. MODERN APPROACHES TO STANDARD OF CARE

The standard of care applied in most jurisdictions relies heavily on testimony about particular procedures, the state of medical education and knowledge, and an examination of the techniques used by a physician to treat the plaintiff. In some jurisdictions, this standard of care is imposed by reference to the state of the medical field at the time of the treatment. We examine specific elements of this standard of care by reviewing the law applicable to the physician's experience level and the local and national standards, and by reference to statutory law.

a. Level of Experience

The applicable standard of care does not shift depending on the experience level of the practitioner. Newly licensed doctors do not enjoy a lower standard of care than seasoned veterans. All are held to the same standard.

b. National Versus Local Standards

Does the standard of care vary by location? For instance, is the standard of care for a rural doctor lower than the standard of care for an urban doctor? Historically, the answer was yes. Under the "locality rule," courts allowed a lower standard of care for rural doctors under the theory that they had less access to recent developments in medicine, had fewer opportunities for continuing medical education, and because communication to rural areas was difficult.

FIGURE 12-4

**Standard of
Care by
Statute**

In a malpractice action, the claimant shall have the burden of proving by evidence as provided by subsection (b):

(1) The recognized standard of acceptable professional practice in the profession and the specialty thereof, if any, that the defendant practices in the community in which the defendant practices or in a similar community at the time the alleged injury or wrongful action occurred;

(2) That the defendant acted with less than or failed to act with ordinary and reasonable care in accordance with such standard; and

(3) As a proximate result of the defendant's negligent act or omission, the plaintiff suffered injuries which would not otherwise have occurred.*

*Tenn. Code Ann. §§29-26-115 to -118 (2000).

However, in recent years, this rule has come under increasing attack. Many have argued that although this rule might have had some relevance in the nineteenth and early twentieth centuries, in an age of telephones, the Internet, mandatory licensure, and required continuing education, such a rule makes little sense. In fact, many states that formerly followed the locality rule have begun to phase it out.

In the modern era, most jurisdictions follow the rule that requires a physician to treat the plaintiff with the same degree of reasonable, ordinary care and skill as any other physician in good standing in the same area of practice, whether that area encompasses rural or urban areas or both. There has been a gradual movement away from geographic limits on the standard of care, in response to nationally standardized education at medical schools.

c. Establishing Standard of Care by Statute

Although there has been a growing trend to "nationalize" the standard of care through case law decisions, there are states that have codified the standard of care. In these states, the standard of care is determined by statutes that not only establish the basic duty to the patient, but also enact other provisions that limit the application of the statute of limitations, provide greater procedural requirements, and limit the amount of damages that can be awarded in a particular case. A statute that codifies the standard of care is shown in Figure 12-4. We address some of the other legislative initiatives later in this chapter.

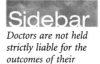

Doctors are not held strictly liable for the outcomes of their treatments.

d. Elements to Consider in Establishing the Standard of Care

In any medical malpractice case, the plaintiff's theory of negligence must eventually come down to proof. Specifically, how does the plaintiff prove that the physician violated the standard of care? One way is to present testimony from another expert witness, typically another physician, who will state that the defendant violated the standard of care. Some of the typical scenarios seen in medical malpractice cases are highlighted in Figure 12-5.

An expert witness's testimony can be challenged on the basis that the expert lacks detailed knowledge about the plaintiff's current medical problems or the plaintiff's medical history.[12]

FIGURE 12-5

**Violation of the
Standard of
Care**

The standard of care is violated when the physician fails to

■ recognize the extent of the plaintiff's injuries or his illness
■ properly diagnose the plaintiff's illness
■ order additional diagnostic procedures that would have revealed the plaintiff's
condition

Sidebar

*Before an expert is
allowed to state his
opinion to the jury, the
attorney who called the
expert to the stand
must establish the
expert's credentials.
This is done by asking
the expert about his
education, credentials,
membership in pro-
fessional organizations,
publications, and clin-
ical experience. Once
that information is
brought out, the attor-
ney is then allowed to
submit the witness as
an expert. This is called
qualifying the witness.
If the judge accepts the
witness as an expert,
then, and only then,
may the attorney ask
about the specific
medical issues involved
in the plaintiff's case. A
paralegal should learn
the expert's credentials
as early in the litigation
process as possible to
assist the attorney in
qualifying the witness.*

3. EXPERT TESTIMONY IN MEDICAL MALPRACTICE CASES

In many jurisdictions it is not only a good idea to present expert testimony
about the defendant's violation of the standard of care, it is actually a
requirement. For instance, some states require that a medical malpractice
complaint be accompanied by a sworn affidavit from an expert witness
testifying to the defendant's negligence before the suit will be allowed to
proceed. When an expert testifies at trial, the expert must present testimony
showing what the standard of care was and how the defendant-doctor's
treatment failed to live up to that standard, and establish a causal relationship between that failure and the injuries suffered by the plaintiff.[13] In many
states, the rules of civil procedure require that the expert be actively involved
in the practice of medicine.

There are specific limitations about what an expert can say. Because
medical treatment is a highly specialized area, beyond the everyday experience
of most jurors, the expert is allowed to testify about the treatment that the
plaintiff should have received. The expert is also allowed to give an opinion
that the defendant-doctor's treatment clearly violated that standard. However,
an expert witness is not allowed to make any statements about who should
prevail in the suit or to urge the jury to award specific types of damages. The
expert's testimony is limited to the medical issues. The jury has the final say
about the verdict and the award, if any.[14]

4. SPECIALISTS

Specialist
A person with exper-
tise that exceeds
that of a regular
practitioner

When a medical malpractice case involves someone who is considered to be a
specialist in a particular field, the standard of care the specialist must follow
is higher than that of a general practitioner. Specialists are required to
exercise the same degree of skill and care as other practicing specialists.
Specialists are also required to know and apply the most recent advances
in their specialties.[15] In many jurisdictions the implicit geographical limitations on the standard of care for general practitioners are removed
for specialists. A specialist must essentially meet the standard followed by
similar specialists throughout the nation.[16] When a doctor is considered to
be a specialist, she must not only exercise the same degree of skill and
knowledge as a general practitioner, but also meet the standard for specialists
in the same area.[17]

C. PROXIMATE CAUSE IN MEDICAL MALPRACTICE CASES

Just as we have seen with any other negligence case, a medical malpractice action must also establish a causal connection between the defendant-doctor's negligence and the resultant injuries to the plaintiff. Whether the plaintiff has actually presented sufficient proof on this point is an issue for the jury. In this context, proximate cause is defined in much the same way that it is in any negligence case. The plaintiff must show that the defendant is liable for the natural and probable consequences of his negligent act.

In a malpractice action, the plaintiff must prove that the defendant failed to follow the standard of care and that this failure was a proximate cause of his injuries.

ISSUE
AT A
GLANCE

D. DAMAGES

Just as we saw in negligence cases, the medical malpractice plaintiff must prove not only the first three elements of duty, breach of duty, and causation, but also that the defendant's actions resulted in legally recognizable damages. However, damages in medical malpractice cases often involve issues not seen in most other types of negligence cases. For one thing, the defendant is never liable for the plaintiff's original injury, that is, the injury that made the plaintiff seek medical treatment in the first place. In medical malpractice cases, the defendant is only liable for negligently treating the plaintiff. If the plaintiff suffers pain and discomfort during treatment that meets the standard of care, that pain and suffering are not recoverable. After all, the plaintiff would have suffered that pain anyway. The defendant-doctor is only liable for the pain and discomfort that flow directly from his negligence. As you can imagine, separating out the pain that the plaintiff would have suffered even under the best care from the additional pain that the plaintiff endured because of negligence is often a difficult task. To further complicate the issue of damages, the defendant-doctor is also not liable for a failed treatment, as long as this treatment was not below the applicable standard of care. Sometimes even the best medical care does not cure the patient. A doctor is not liable for failing to save the plaintiff; he is only liable for negligent care of the plaintiff.

In addition to these restrictions on damages, many states have enacted statutes that specifically insulate medical providers for good faith efforts or "honest mistakes."

Having specified what the plaintiff is not allowed to recover, we now address the issue of what types of damages the plaintiff can recover. As we have already stated, the plaintiff is allowed to recover for any pain and suffering directly attributable to the defendant's negligence. The plaintiff can also recover for any mental suffering tied to this same negligence.

FIGURE 12-6	The jury can consider any or all of the following in assessing the plaintiff's damages:
Assessing Damages	■ Permanency of injury ■ Disfigurement ■ Loss of earning capacity ■ Shortened life expectancy ■ Chances of further medical complications	■ Loss of consortium (loss of companionship and services to a spouse) ■ Estimate of costs of future medical care, in-home nursing, etc.

If the plaintiff suffers any permanent injury, such as a scar or a loss of bodily function, he can recover for such losses. Suppose that the plaintiff can no longer carry on his previous employment? He would be permitted to sue for damages for the loss of his earning capacity. In addition to these damages, the jury is also allowed to consider the plaintiff's diminished life expectancy, the increased chances of diseases or infections, or permanent disfigurement.

How does the jury put a monetary value on these types of damages? It is up to the plaintiff's attorney to present some yardstick for the jury to use in assessing damages. Obviously, the attorney will present testimony about the plaintiff's prior earning capacity or his favorite hobbies (which he can no longer enjoy). The attorney will often suggest a monetary amount for each of these items: pain and suffering, loss of earning capacity, etc. (Loss of earning capacity will involve expert testimony.) The final amount, if any, the plaintiff will receive is up to the jury. Other factors to consider in assessing damages are found in Figure 12-6.

1. SPECIFIC TYPES OF INJURIES

In medical malpractice cases there are often injuries that are not seen in other types of negligence cases. Examples of these unique injuries are "wrongful birth" and "wrongful death" cases, among others.

a. Wrongful Birth

When a plaintiff brings a wrongful birth (sometimes called a "wrongful pregnancy" case), the plaintiff is alleging that a physician was negligent when he performed a sterilization procedure on the plaintiff. Often these cases are brought when patients seek to be sterilized because they have an increased chance of giving birth to a child with birth defects. They wish to avoid the pain of bringing a deformed child into existence by having themselves sterilized either through a tubal ligation (woman) or a vasectomy (man). In such a case, the parents may be entitled to general damages for the pregnancy, pain, and suffering for giving birth to a deformed child, and other out-of-pocket costs. However, many jurisdictions have been unwilling to assess the total cost of raising such a child against the doctor who performed the negligent sterilization procedure.

b. Wrongful Adoption

A wrongful adoption case is based on the premise that when an adoption agency conceals material facts about an adopted child's physical or mental condition, it is misrepresenting the facts to the adopting parents. This misrepresentation is especially important in the case of adopted children because the new parents have no way of knowing whether the child requires additional treatment that, if not given, could aggravate a pre-existing condition.

The elements of a wrongful adoption action include:

- False statements of material fact, such as the child's health history
- Made intentionally or with reckless disregard of the truth
- Provided to the adopting parents
- To induce them to adopt the child
- Parents relied on this information
- Parents adopted the child

c. Wrongful Death

Sidebar

Some jurisdictions permit the plaintiff to recover for other types of damages, such as "loss of chance." In loss of chance, the defendant's failure to properly diagnose the plaintiff's condition resulted in a delay that prevented him from obtaining the correct treatment in time to make a difference.

Wrongful death actions raise a whole host of legal issues and could easily justify an entire chapter by themselves. The basis of a wrongful death claim is that the defendant caused the death of another through his negligence. In a medical malpractice claim, this death is caused by the negligent treatment the deceased received. Usually, a cause of action in wrongful death is limited to those individuals who are the survivors of the deceased and dependent on him for support. When the decedent's survivors bring suit, they are allowed to sue for loss of companionship, mental pain and suffering, general compensatory damages for the loss of income that the deceased would have produced for the family, and medical and funeral expenses.

2. PUNITIVE DAMAGES

Sidebar

Some courts have ruled that punitive damages are permissible in cases in which the defendant was reckless and "consciously indifferent" to the consequences suffered by the plaintiff.[20]

Punitive damages are allowed in medical malpractice cases. Usually, they are only awarded in cases in which the physician was grossly negligent or acted in bad faith. Some states limit the award of punitive damages to cases in which the jury finds "actual malice" on the part of the defendant-doctor.[18] Examples of actual malice include deliberately falsifying, destroying, or altering medical records or encouraging staff members to commit perjury.[19]

States have followed different paths in their attempts to limit damage awards in medical malpractice cases. Their options include some or all of the following:

- Limiting the size of the total award for non-economic damages, such as pain and suffering
- Modifying or eliminating the concept of joint and several liability
- Limiting the amount of punitive damages
- Modifying how the jury is permitted to assess punitive damages

FIGURE 12-7

Statutory Limitations on Awards in Medical Malpractice Cases

FIGURE 12-8

Plaintiff Winners Who Sought and Were Awarded Punitive Damages in Civil Trials, by Selected Case Types, 2005

Case type	Number of plaintiffs who sought punitive damages[a]	Punitive damages awarded[b]		Number of cases with punitive damages	
		Number	Median amount	Over $250,000	$1 million or more
All cases	**1,823**	**700**	**$64,000**	**191**	**93**
Tort cases[c]	**822**	**254**	**$55,000**	**59**	**43**
Medical malpractice	56	6	2,835,000	5	5
Intentional tort	141	126	81,000	13	4
Conversion	31	12	50,000	5	2
Slander/libel	38	24	13,000	9	6
Motor vehicle	417	67	7,500	9	8
Animal attack	23	0	/	/	/
Contract cases[c]	**1,001**	**446**	**$69,000**	**132**	**50**
Tortious interference	42	18	6,888,000	12	11
Employment discrimination	84	10	115,000	1	1
Fraud	259	151	100,000	67	7
Seller plaintiff	88	14	86,000	2	0
Buyer plaintiff	372	138	53,000	20	3
Other employment disputes	93	86	10,000	12	10

/No cases reported.
[a]Data on punitive damages sought are available for 99.9% of total trial cases with a plaintiff winner.
[b]Data on punitive damages awarded are available for 97.5% of total trial cases with a plaintiff winner. Median amounts are reported prior to adjustments, post-trial activity, or appeals and are rounded to the nearest thousand.
[c]Specific case types will not sum to tort and contract totals because not all case types are shown in the table.

Civil Bench and Jury Trials in State Courts, 2005, Bureau of Justice Statistics, U.S. Department of Justice.

3. PUNITIVE DAMAGES AND TORT REFORM

The growing perception of runaway juries awarding millions of dollars to plaintiffs who have suffered relatively minor injuries has encouraged legislatures across the country to enact tort reform legislation. Almost every statute focuses on punitive damages awards in some capacity. Although the actual statistics might not support the perception of frivolous lawsuits and mega-verdicts, there is no question that affordable malpractice insurance for physicians and other health care providers is becoming harder and harder to come by.

When physicians are sued for medical malpractice, and they have a malpractice insurance policy, the insurance company must provide legal counsel. Although the insurance company pays the attorney's fee, the attorney's responsibility is to protect the interests of the insured doctor. We discuss insurance issues in much greater depth in the next chapter; however, it is important to understand the role of malpractice insurance and the limitations placed on the medical profession because of it. If medical malpractice insurance premiums become too high, doctors are forced to choose between two unpleasant choices. On the one hand, they can simply leave the practice of medicine for some other profession in which insurance premiums are not so high, or they can pass the premium increases on to their patients in the form of higher fees for medical treatment. Doctors are often reluctant to do either, but usually choose the latter.

In the 1980s, legislatures across the nation began enacting tort reform legislation as a way of limiting the number of malpractice cases and the amount of awards that insurance companies must pay, especially in the form of punitive damages. The most popular of these reforms is to limit the total amount of punitive damages that a jury can award. In many states, for example, plaintiffs are limited to specific amounts for punitive damages, no matter what the facts of a particular case may be. In other jurisdictions, punitive damages are capped as a multiple of the total compensatory damages. For instance, the State of Placid has a statute that limits punitive damages to three times the amount of compensatory damages. In this state, if John's damages are $10,000, but the doctor has acted in bad faith or with actual malice, the most that the jury could award John would be $30,000.[21] Whether these statutory limitations have actually cut down on the number of malpractice cases is a question open for debate.

 ## INFORMED CONSENT

The general rule is that before a medical procedure can be performed, the doctor must obtain consent from the patient. This consent acts to insulate the doctor from any claim of battery, but it also serves another important function: It may prevent a medical malpractice claim. A patient is entitled to bring an action based on inadequate **informed consent.** The basis of this claim is that the patient was never made aware of the risks involved in the procedure or was never told about treatment alternatives so that she could make an informed decision about whether to risk the procedure in the first place. For a plaintiff to succeed on a claim of inadequate informed consent, she must prove the following:

Informed consent
An agreement by a person to allow some type of action after having been fully informed and after making a knowing and intelligent decision to allow the action

1 The defendant-doctor failed to adequately describe the procedure to the patient, especially the treatment alternatives and the foreseeable risks involved.

2 A reasonable and prudent person would not have undergone the procedure if she had been adequately informed.

3 The lack of informed consent is a proximate cause of the plaintiff's injuries.[22]

Sidebar

Under the requirement of informed consent, a physician who performs a medical procedure on a patient without consent has committed a battery. One exception to this rule is emergency situations.

Informed consent must be based on adequate information and the patient's understanding of what the procedure entails and what the risks of the procedure are. Whether informed consent was given in any particular case is a question for the jury. Part of what the jury will be called upon to evaluate is the manner of the interchange between the doctor and the patient, the patient's ability to ask questions, and the degree of explanation offered by the doctor. The jurors are often instructed that the test they should apply is what information a reasonable, prudent patient should have been given, not what the doctor, in his judgment, decided that the patient should know.

A. STATUTORY REQUIREMENTS IN INFORMED CONSENT

Many states have codified the informed consent requirement. See Figure 12-9 for Pennsylvania's informed consent statute.

B. EMERGENCIES

Sidebar

When dealing with minors or others who are legally incapable of giving consent, the physician must obtain consent from a parent or guardian.

One of the few exceptions to the requirement of informed consent is an emergency situation. When the patient is in a life-threatening situation, the physician is not required to seek informed consent from the patient or anyone else.[23] The reason for this rule is obvious. If a medical provider had to wait until she obtained valid consent from the patient, or a family member, the patient might well die.[24] In such cases, the court will imply consent to the treatment because most people would have consented to a life-saving procedure had they been able to.

FIGURE 12-9

Pennsylvania Statute on Informed Consent

Informed consent

    (a) Duty of physicians — Except in emergencies, a physician owes a duty to a patient to obtain the informed consent of the patient or the patient's authorized representative prior to conducting the following procedures:

        (1) Performing surgery, including the related administration of anesthesia.

        (2) Administering radiation or chemotherapy.

        (3) Administering a blood transfusion.

        (4) Inserting a surgical device or appliance.

        (5) Administering an experimental medication, using an experimental device or using an approved medication or device in an experimental manner.

    (b) Description of procedure — Consent is informed if the patient has been given a description of a procedure set forth in subsection (a) and the risks and alternatives that a reasonably prudent patient would require to make an informed decision as to that procedure. The physician shall be entitled to present evidence of the description of that procedure and those risks and alternatives that a physician acting in accordance with accepted medical standards of medical practice would provide.

    (c) Expert testimony — Expert testimony is required to determine whether the procedure constituted the type of procedure set forth in subsection (a) and to identify the risks of that procedure, the alternatives to that procedure and the risks of these alternatives.

    (d) Liability —

        (1) A physician is liable for failure to obtain the informed consent only if the patient proves that receiving such information would have been a substantial factor in the patient's decision whether to undergo a procedure set forth in subsection (a).

        (2) A physician may be held liable for failure to seek a patient's informed consent if the physician knowingly misrepresents to the patient his or her professional credentials, training or experience.*

*Pa. Stat. §1303.504.

C. SCOPE OF INFORMED CONSENT

A validly obtained informed consent gives the physician permission to perform the procedure and essentially eliminates a medical malpractice claim on this ground. However, a question often arises in informed consent as to the scope of the consent. Just how far does this consent extend? For instance, can a physician claim that the patient consented to all types of actions, including negligent actions? Consider the following scenario.

Dr. *X* obtains a valid consent from Paula Patient to operate on her right kidney. However, he negligently operates on her left kidney. When Paula brings a medical malpractice claim, Dr. *X* claims that Paula consented to the procedure. How does the judge rule?

Answer: The judge will rule in Paula's favor. Paula's consent does not relieve the doctor of liability for his own negligence. On a practical level, nowhere in the informed consent did the doctor suggest that he would operate on the wrong kidney.

Would the answer to this question change if the surgeon exceeds the scope of the informed consent? Suppose that while the physician is operating on Paula, he discovers a lesion on her leg that he removes. The site of this surgery later becomes infected and causes Paula significant problems. Can she bring a medical malpractice action under this situation? Absolutely. Again, the physician did not mention anything about operating on Paula's leg in the context of a surgery on her kidney. Dr. X has exceeded the scope of the informed consent and he is liable to Paula for the resultant infection.[25]

Informed consent does not apply to negligent actions by the physician.

PLEADINGS IN MEDICAL MALPRACTICE CASES

Pleadings in medical malpractice cases raise a host of issues not normally seen in other types of negligence actions. For one thing, many states require that a complaint be accompanied by a sworn affidavit from a medical expert detailing how the defendant violated the standard of care in the plaintiff's case. Another important point to consider is identifying the correct defendant. You should confirm that the right doctor is being sued. These days, many doctors can be involved in a patient's treatment. Identifying the actual negligent doctor may take a little extra time and digging, but will save time, effort, and an allegation of bad faith later on in the case.

Plaintiffs' attorneys often consider other elements of medical malpractice cases before deciding to accept them. These include:

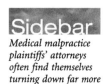

Medical malpractice plaintiffs' attorneys often find themselves turning down far more cases than they accept.

- Is the case worth the time and effort it will take to complete it? Some commentators claim that a medical malpractice should be worth at least $30,000 before an attorney accepts it. After all, while the case is pending, the plaintiff's attorney must continue to pay his staff as well as rent and utilities.
- Does the attorney have enough time to devote to the case? The average medical malpractice case can take up to 100 hours of preparation. This time can increase dramatically if the attorney has never handled a medical malpractice case and must educate himself on the procedures.
- Is the plaintiff a sympathetic witness? If not, the jury may not like him and may be less inclined to award damages.
- How clear is the liability in the case? For instance, if the defendant-doctor is obviously at fault, that may be a factor weighing heavily toward accepting a case that would have been marginal for other reasons.
- How extensive are the damages? If the defendant-doctor was clearly negligent, but the plaintiff suffered few actual damages, it may not be worth the firm's time to accept the case.

1	Check the applicable rules of civil procedure.	
2	Has the correct defendant(s) been identified?	
3	Notice pleading should raise all applicable issues and facts to back up the claims.	
4	Has the investigative responsibility (Rule 11 under the Federal Rules of Civil Procedure) been satisfied?	
5	Is each paragraph worded clearly and concisely?	
6	What is the jurisdiction and venue?	
7	What is the prayer for relief?	
8	Is it signed by plaintiff's attorney?	
9	Attachments, including the expert's affidavit, included?	
10	Certificate of service included?	

FIGURE 12-10

Rules for Drafting a Medical Malpractice Complaint

 DISCOVERY ISSUES IN MALPRACTICE CASES

Once the pleadings have been filed and served on opposing sides, the discovery phase begins. In many ways, discovery in medical malpractice cases is very similar to other types of personal injury cases. Discovery takes place through oral depositions, requests for production of documents, and interrogatories. However, medical malpractice cases also involve some unique discovery issues. For one thing, anyone reviewing the medical records must be proficient in the terminology and wording used in medical records to describe various symptoms and the procedures used to deal with them. For instance, can you decipher the nurse's note in Figure 12-11?

FIGURE 12-11

Nurse's Note in Medical Record

Translation of the nurse's note:
Gutter splint to left arm. Circulation okay. Tylenol number 3 times 1 by mouth for complaint of pain. Verbalized understanding of discharge instructions and splint care. Knows to follow up with the orthopedic doctor November 28, 2002. Discharged from the department ambulatory in no acute distress. DB

1. State in detail the medical history you obtained from the plaintiff on the first occasion that you met with plaintiff.
2. State in detail the plaintiff's medical history as it was relayed to you by plaintiff.
3. State in detail the symptoms that the plaintiff complained of.
4. Please state the following: the plaintiff's chief complaint, family history, personal history, and psychiatric history as you learned it from the plaintiff.

VIII DEFENSES TO MEDICAL MALPRACTICE CLAIMS

A paralegal should keep up with all recent legislative changes in medical malpractice statutes. This is an area that undergoes constant change.

An act of negligence that is not discovered until some time after it has been committed is often referred to as "latent negligence."

Sidebar

When reviewing medical malpractice cases, it is extremely helpful to have a medical encyclopedia on hand to help you decipher the terms and procedures. Helpful print versions include Physician's Desk Reference, Tabor's Cyclopedic Medical Dictionary, American Medical Association Complete Medical Encyclopedia, and Gray's Anatomy. Online sources include:

■ **National Library of Medicine**
http://www.nlm.nih .gov/medlineplus/
■ **Mayo Clinic**
http://www .mayoclinic.com/
■ **WebMD**
http://my.webmd .com/webmd_today/ home/default

Just as we have seen with the other elements of a medical malpractice claim, the defenses applicable to such a case often raise unique issues. A defense of statute of limitations is common enough in any negligence action, but when applied to a medical malpractice case a new issue arises: exactly *when* does negligence occur?

A. STATUTE OF LIMITATIONS

In many jurisdictions the statute of limitations for a malpractice action is three to four years. But medical malpractice cases raise some interesting and unique issues when it comes to the cause of action. For instance, when does the cause of action begin? Does the plaintiff's cause of action, for calculating the statute of limitations, begin when the negligence occurs or when the patient discovers it? Unlike car wrecks, a patient may not know about a doctor's negligence for some time. For example, if a surgeon leaves a medical sponge inside the patient's body, the patient may not find out about it for weeks or even months. Does the statute begin running on the date of the surgery or when the patient discovers the negligence? Jurisdictions have been wrestling with this issue for years. A general consensus has emerged. Many states follow the example set out in Figure 12-13. Under that construction, the statute of limitations begins running at the time of the negligent procedure and runs for three years, or it begins running when the patient discovers the negligent procedure and runs for one year after that point. The statute gives the patient the benefit of the doubt by explaining that the plaintiff's cause of action terminates on the expiration of whichever term is the longest.

B. CONTRIBUTORY NEGLIGENCE OF THE PATIENT

We have addressed the issue of contributory negligence in other contexts. Interestingly enough, this defense is often a factor in medical malpractice cases as well. Although called by different names in different states, the theory is simple enough. A defendant-doctor is permitted to raise a defense that the

FIGURE 12-13

Wisconsin
Statute of
Limitations
on Medical
Malpractice
Cases

(1) Except as provided by subs. (2) and (3), an action to recover damages for injury arising from any treatment or operation performed by, or from any omission by, a person who is a health care provider, regardless of the theory on which the action is based, shall be commenced within the later of:

(a) Three years from the date of the injury, or

(b) One year from the date the injury was discovered or, in the exercise of reasonable diligence should have been discovered, except that an action may not be commenced under this paragraph more than 5 years from the date of the act or omission.

(2) If a health care provider conceals from a patient a prior act or omission of the provider which has resulted in injury to the patient, an action shall be commenced within one year from the date the patient discovers the concealment or, in the exercise of reasonable diligence, should have discovered the concealment or within the time limitation provided by sub. (1), whichever is later.

(3) When a foreign object which has no therapeutic or diagnostic purpose or effect has been left in a patient's body, an action shall be commenced within one year after the patient is aware or, in the exercise of reasonable care, should have been aware of the presence of the object or within the time limitation provided by sub. (1), whichever is later.*

*Wis. Stat. Ann. §893.55.

FIGURE 12-14

Common Jury
Instructions in
Malpractice
Cases

"It is the duty of a patient to follow the reasonable instructions and submit to the reasonable treatment prescribed by his physician or surgeon."*

"If you decide that the defendant was negligent and that his negligence was a proximate cause of injury to the plaintiff, it is not a defense that something else may also have been a cause of the injury. However, if you decide that the sole proximate cause of injury to the plaintiff was something other than the conduct of the defendant, then your verdict should be for the defendant."**

*Merrill v. Odiorne, 113 Me. 424, 94 A. 753 (1915).
**Illinois Pattern Jury Instruction, Civil, No. 12.05 (3d ed. 1995).

plaintiff's injuries were aggravated by the plaintiff's own failure to seek proper medical care or to follow medical procedures. Essentially, the defendant is stating that the plaintiff has caused his own aggravated symptoms and the defendant should be relieved of liability because of it.

Is the following case excerpt a contract case or a torts case?

GONZALEZ v. KALU
43 Cal. Rptr. 3d 866 (2006), (Cal. App. 2 Dist. 2006)

CROSKEY, J.

Gabriela Gonzalez appeals a summary judgment in a legal malpractice action based on the statute of limitations, Code of Civil Procedure section 340.6. After filing an administrative complaint against her employer with the

Department of Fair Employment and Housing (DFEH) and telling Gonzalez that the case would take a very long time and that he would call her or send her a letter, Emelike I. Kalu had no contact with Gonzalez for almost three years. Gonzalez contends the limitations period was tolled or did not commence during the time Kalu failed to communicate with her. We conclude that there are triable issues of fact as to whether Kalu continued to represent Gonzalez during that time, which would toll the limitations period, and whether such "continuing representation" was for a period sufficient to make her action timely. We therefore will reverse the summary judgment.

Factual and Procedural Background

1. Factual Background

Gonzalez worked for a building maintenance company as a cleaner in a food court. She hired Kalu on June 2, 2000, to represent her in a claim against her employer in connection with allegations of sexual harassment by a fellow employee. Kalu sent a letter to the employer on June 6, 2000, stating that the employer was legally responsible for the alleged harassment. The letter demanded a settlement and stated that if the employer failed to settle the matter, Gonzalez would file claims with the appropriate federal and state administrative agencies and proceed to litigation. The letter warned the employer not to retaliate by terminating Gonzalez's employment. By the end of the month, Gonzalez told Kalu that she had been fired.

Kalu filed an administrative complaint with the DFEH on July 31, 2000, alleging sexual harassment only. He sent a letter to Gonzalez's former employer that same day stating that her discharge was an act of retaliation, that he had requested a right-to-sue letter, and that upon receipt of a right-to-sue letter he would sue the employer for sexual harassment and wrongful termination. According to Gonzalez, Kalu or someone in his office told her that same day "that the case was going to take very long, and they were going to call me or send me a letter."

Gonzalez maintains that she did not hear from Kalu and did not attempt to contact him from July 31, 2000, until June 2003, when she visited his office to pick up her file for purposes of separate litigation against her former employer and first learned that Kalu was not prosecuting her case. She maintains that Kalu never informed her before June 2003 that he would not prosecute the matter further. According to Kalu, he orally informed Gonzalez at some time that he would not file a lawsuit on her behalf. Kalu maintains that Gonzalez agreed to drop the case if no settlement was forthcoming and that his last conversation with her before she picked up the file in June 2003 was in December 2000. Although Kalu's usual practice was to advise a client in writing upon his withdrawal from representation, there is no evidence of such a writing in this case.

2. Trial Court Proceedings

Gonzalez filed a complaint against Kalu in the superior court on January 23, 2004. She alleges in the complaint that she retained Kalu to represent her in an action for sexual harassment, that Kalu failed to adequately investigate and prosecute the case, and that he failed to commence a civil action within the one-year limitations period. She alleges counts for legal malpractice, breach of fiduciary duty, and breach of contract.

Kalu moved for summary judgment based on Code of Civil Procedure section 340.6 in December 2004. The sole ground for the motion was that Gonzalez in the exercise of reasonable diligence should have discovered more than one year before she filed her complaint that Kalu had failed to timely file a complaint for sexual harassment in the superior court. Kalu argued that his failure to communicate with Gonzalez after July 31, 2000, despite his purported promise to call her or send her a letter, should have alerted Gonzalez that he had not prosecuted her case and should have caused her to discover before January 23, 2003, that he had not commenced a civil action.

Gonzalez argued in opposition that reasonable minds could differ as to when she reasonably should have discovered Kalu's failure to file a complaint in the superior court. She also argued that in light of Kalu's statement on July 31, 2000, that the case would take "very long" and that he would call her or send her a letter, and his failure to inform her that he was withdrawing from representation and would not commence a civil action, he continued to represent her for purposes of tolling the *869 limitations period under Code of Civil Procedure section 340.6, subdivision (a)(2).

The court granted the motion. The order granting the motion stated in pertinent part, "plaintiff contends that she had retained defendant Emelike I. Kalu, an attorney, to file a complaint against her employer; that he had failed to do so within the applicable one-year period; and that her last contact with defendant Emelike I. Kalu was in July 2000 when she was told that she would be receiving a call or letter from him[.] . . . [R]easonable persons cannot differ: the one-year period in which plaintiff could have filed suit against defendant Emelike I. Kalu had expired by the time plaintiff commenced this action on January 23, 2004." Gonzalez moved for a new trial arguing that the limitations period was tolled during the time she reasonably believed that Kalu continued to represent her, and that her failure to discover before June 2003 that Kalu had not commenced a civil action was reasonable. The court denied the motion stating, "it is unreasonable that after almost three years of noncommunication, the plaintiff would believe that her case was still being pursued despite a total lack of communication from the defendant," and stating that Gonzalez could have simply called Kalu's office to inquire whether her case was still active.

Contentions

Gonzalez contends her complaint was timely because (1) the limitations period was tolled during the time she reasonably believed that Kalu continued to represent her; and (2) her failure to discover before June 2003 that Kalu had not commenced a civil action was reasonable.

Discussion

Code of Civil Procedure Section 340.6 and Continuous Representation
Code of Civil Procedure section 340.6 states that an action against an attorney

for professional malpractice, other than actual fraud, must be commenced within one year after the plaintiff actually discovered or reasonably should have discovered the facts constituting the wrongful act or omission, or within four years after the wrongful act or omission, whichever is earlier. (Id., subd. (a).) The limitations period is tolled, however, if any of the statutory bases for tolling applies.

The limitations period is tolled while the attorney continues to represent the plaintiff regarding the same specific subject matter. (Code Civ. Proc., §340.6, subd. (a)(2).) The period is tolled even if the client is aware of the attorney's negligence. Quoting the legislative history, the California Supreme Court in *Laird v. Blacker* (1992) 2 Cal. 4th 606, 618, 7 Cal. Rptr. 2d 550, 828 P.2d 691 stated that the purposes of tolling based on continuous representation are "to 'avoid the disruption of an attorney-client relationship by a lawsuit while enabling the attorney to correct or minimize an apparent error, and to prevent an attorney from defeating a malpractice cause of action by continuing to represent the client until the statutory period has expired.'" The latter purpose reflects the understanding that a client who relies on an attorney ordinarily is not able to evaluate the attorney's professional services and should be entitled to rely on the attorney's competence and good faith while the representation continues.

Code of Civil Procedure section 340.6 does not expressly state a standard to determine when an attorney's representation of a client regarding a specific subject matter continues or when the representation ends, and the legislative history does not explicitly address this question. An attorney's representation of a client ordinarily ends when the client discharges the attorney or consents to a withdrawal, the court consents to the attorney's withdrawal, or upon completion of the tasks for which the client retained the attorney. Some authorities state that the representation also ends if the attorney withdraws unilaterally without the consent of either the client or a court, despite any breach of duty, if the client actually has or reasonably should have no expectation of further services.

"Of course, even when further representation concerning the specific subject matter in which the attorney allegedly committed the complained of malpractice is needed and contemplated by the client, the continuous representation toll would nonetheless end once the client is informed or otherwise put on notice of the attorney's withdrawal from representation." (*Shumsky v. Eisenstein, supra,* 726 N.Y.S.2d at pp. 370-371, 750 N.E.2d 67.)

Some California courts have endorsed the purported "New York rule" that for purposes of the continuing representation rule, an attorney-client relationship exists only as long as "'there are clear indicia of an ongoing, continuous, developing and dependent relationship between the client and the attorney'" and the relationship "'is marked with trust and confidence.'" Other California courts have rejected that purported rule because those requirements are not stated in Code of Civil Procedure section 340.6. We agree with *Worthington* and *O'Neill* that section 340.6, subdivision (a)(2) neither states nor implies that an attorney's representation of a client continues only as long as those conditions are present.

Some California courts have stated, "Continuity of representation ultimately depends, not on the client's subjective beliefs, but rather on evidence of an ongoing mutual relationship and of activities in furtherance of the relationship." (*Worthington v. Rusconi, supra,* 29 Cal. App. 4th at p. 1498, 35 Cal. Rptr. 2d 169; accord, *Lockley v. Law Office of Cantrell, Green, Pekich, Cruz & McCort, supra,* 91 Cal. App. 4th at p. 887, 110 Cal. Rptr. 2d 877.) In both *Worthington* and *Lockley,* however, there were continuing contacts between the attorney and client regarding the specific subject matter of the representation. *Worthington* and *Lockley* held that those contacts established continuing representation and did not rule on the question whether an attorney's representation of a client can continue when there are no contacts. (*Worthington, supra,* at p. 1498, 35 Cal. Rptr. 2d 169; *Lockley, supra,* at pp. 889-891, 110 Cal. Rptr. 2d 877.)

Kalu contends the representation ended when the limitations period on the sexual harassment claim expired because the loss became irremediable at that time. He argues that when a loss is irremediable, an attorney cannot correct or minimize the alleged error, so tolling would not serve the purposes of the continuous representation rule. We do not construe Code of Civil Procedure section 340.6, subdivision (a)(2) so restrictively. Subdivision (a)(2) does not state that the limitations period is tolled only as long as the injury is remediable, but that the period is tolled during the time "the attorney continues to represent the plaintiff regarding the specific subject matter in which the alleged wrongful act or omission occurred." Although one of the purposes of the continuous representation rule is "to 'avoid the disruption of an attorney-client relationship by a lawsuit while enabling the attorney to correct or minimize an apparent error,'" another purpose is "'to prevent an attorney from defeating a malpractice cause of action by continuing to represent the client until the statutory period has expired.'" The latter purpose would not be served if tolling ended when the client's loss arguably became irremediable and the attorney, by continuing to represent the client until the limitations period for a malpractice action had expired, could then exploit the client's reliance and escape malpractice liability. Absent a statutory standard to determine when an attorney's representation of a client regarding a specific subject matter ends, and consistent with the purposes of the continuing representation rule, we conclude that for purposes of Code of Civil Procedure section 340.6, subdivision (a)(2), in the event of an attorney's unilateral withdrawal or abandonment of the client, the representation ends when the client actually has or reasonably should have no expectation that the attorney will provide further legal services. (See 1 Mallen & Smith, Legal Malpractice, *supra,* Theory of Liability — Common Law, §8.2, p. 948; *Shumsky v. Eisenstein, supra,* 726 N.Y.S.2d at pp. 370-371, 750 N.E.2d 67.) That may occur upon the attorney's express notification to the client that the attorney will perform no further services, or, if the attorney remains silent, may be inferred from the circumstances. Absent actual notice to the client that the attorney will perform no further legal services or circumstances that reasonably should cause the client to so conclude, a client should be entitled to rely on an attorney to perform the agreed services and should not be required to interrupt the attorney-client relationship by filing a malpractice complaint. After a client has no reasonable expectation that the attorney will provide further legal services, however, the client is no longer hindered by a potential disruption of the attorney-client relationship and no longer relies on the attorney's continuing representation, so the tolling should end. To this extent and for these reasons, we conclude that continuous representation should be viewed objectively from the client's perspective and reject the dicta in *Worthington v. Rusconi* to the contrary.

Thus, the rule that we have stated allows the client, consistent with the purposes of the continuing representation rule, to avoid the disruption of an attorney-client relationship that would result from the filing of a malpractice action, but only as long as the client actually and reasonably believes that the representation is continuing. Whether the client actually and reasonably believed that the attorney would provide further legal services regarding a specific subject matter is predominantly a question of fact for the trier of fact, but can be decided as a question of law if the undisputed facts can support only one conclusion. (Cf. *Jordache Enterprises, Inc. v. Brobeck, Phleger & Harrison* (1998) 18 Cal. 4th 739, 751, 76 Cal. Rptr. 2d 749, 958 P.2d 1062.)

3. Whether Gonzalez Believed or Reasonably Should Have Believed More Than One Year Before Filing Suit That Kalu Had Withdrawn from Representation Is a Triable Issue of Fact

Gonzalez hired Kalu on June 2, 2000, to represent her in connection with her allegations of sexual harassment. The retainer agreement signed by Gonzalez stated that she authorized Kalu to take all steps that he deemed necessary to prosecute the claim against her employer, including "to institute appropriate legal proceedings." Kalu sent a letter to the employer on June 6, 2000, demanding settlement and threatening to file administrative claims and proceed to litigation. Kalu filed an administrative complaint verified by Gonzalez with the DFEH on July 31, 2000, and sent another letter to the employer the same day stating that he had filed an administrative complaint and would file a lawsuit after receiving a right-to-sue letter. According to Gonzalez, Kalu or someone from his office told her on July 31, 2000, "that the case was going to take very long, and they were going to call me or send me a letter." Gonzalez testified in her deposition that Kalu never informed her that he was withdrawing from her representation and that she never told him not to proceed. She testified that she did not contact Kalu because she was waiting for him to contact her. There is no evidence that Kalu informed Gonzalez, or that she knew, that the administrative complaint was likely to lead to the relatively prompt issuance of a right-to-sue letter as opposed to a lengthy period of administrative review, that a civil action under the Fair and Employment and Housing Act (Gov. Code, §12900 et seq.) must be filed within one year after receiving a right-to-sue letter (Gov. Code, §12965, subd. (b)), or that he provided any information concerning the timing of litigation apart from "that the case was going to take very long." Moreover, there is no evidence that Kalu explained to Gonzalez the significance of a civil action as distinguished from an administrative complaint or stated that he would contact her when he filed a lawsuit. Viewing the evidence in the light most favorable to Gonzalez as the party opposing summary judgment, we must assume that Kalu never informed Gonzalez that he would not continue to prosecute her case. The evidence presented supports the conclusion that Gonzalez reasonably believed that by filing an administrative complaint Kalu had commenced the prosecution of her claim, that he would continue to take all measures reasonably necessary to prosecute the claim, that the matter would not be resolved for a "very long" time, and that he would contact her at the appropriate time. Because reasonable minds could differ, in these circumstances we cannot conclude as a matter of law that the absence of communication for almost two years and six months (from July 31, 2000, until January 23, 2003, one year before Gonzalez filed her malpractice complaint) after filing an administrative complaint should have caused Gonzalez to believe that Kalu had withdrawn or abandoned her or should have caused her to inquire so as to learn before January 23, 2003, that he no longer represented her.

Viewing the evidence in the light most favorable to Gonzalez as the party opposing summary judgment, we conclude that reasonable minds could differ as to whether Gonzalez reasonably should have believed more than one year before filing suit that Kalu had withdrawn from representation or abandoned her. There are triable issues of fact as to whether the limitations period was tolled based on continuing representation, and, if so, whether it was tolled for a period sufficient to make Gonzalez's action timely.

Disposition
The judgment is reversed. The matter is remanded for further proceedings consistent with the views expressed herein. Gonzalez is entitled to recover her costs on appeal.

KLEIN, P.J., AND KITCHING, J., CONCUR.

Questions about the case:

1. How much time elapsed between Gonzalez hiring her attorney and her next communication with him?
2. What circumstances might toll the statute of limitations in this case?
3. What are the issues surrounding whether or not the attorney represented Gonzalez?
4. Did Kalu ever notify Gonzalez that he was not going to represent her in the case?
5. What are Gonzalez's allegations of legal malpractice against Kalu?

THE CHUMLEY CASE: FOLLOW-UP ON MEDICAL MALPRACTICE ISSUE

Now that we have examined the many issues involved in a medical malpractice case, we return to the question that began this chapter: Does Mr. Chumley, in addition to his other claims, also have a claim for medical malpractice against the attending physician? Yes, he does. The doctor's failure to examine and diagnose Mr. Chumley's spleen problem is clearly malpractice.

LEGAL MALPRACTICE

In addition to medical malpractice claims, other professionals are increasingly becoming the targets of malpractice litigation. In the past decade, for instance, **legal malpractice** claims have risen dramatically. A legal malpractice claim is similar in some ways to a medical malpractice claim. When a plaintiff brings a legal malpractice claim, she is alleging that the attorney failed to perform his professional duties and that this failure resulted in an identifiable loss to the client. Legal malpractice, like medical malpractice, is a question of fact and must be determined by the jury (or judge, in a bench trial).

Legal malpractice
Professional negligence committed by an attorney during the course of his representation of a client

A. THE ATTORNEY'S DUTY

A legal malpractice claim is not authorized when one person wishes to sue another person who happens to be an attorney. For instance, if an attorney and a non-attorney go into business together, the non-attorney is not allowed to bring a legal malpractice claim against the lawyer for some claim arising from the business. A legal malpractice claim must be based on the attorney-client relationship. It is this relationship, like the doctor-patient relationship, that gives rise to the special duty owed by the attorney to the client, the breach of which gives the client a legal remedy.

B. BREACH OF DUTY

An attorney must exercise the same level of skill, legal knowledge, and ability for the client as is found in other members of the bar.[26] However, this standard does not require an attorney to live up to the same level of diligence and devotion seen by the most extraordinary attorneys in the area. Essentially, the law looks at an attorney's skill and knowledge and how it compares to an average cross-section of the bar. If the attorney's actions fall below this general average, he can be said to have violated the standard of care. Generally, when an attorney acts with honesty and good faith, this will often negate many claims of legal malpractice.

1. ADDITIONAL PROOF OF BREACH REQUIRED

Legal malpractice actions are interesting in that many jurisdictions require that the plaintiff prove that, but for the attorney's negligence, she would have won the underlying suit, or achieved a particular result. Often, the plaintiff has difficulty proving this element. Not all legal mistakes rise to the level of legal malpractice. How, for instance, would a client prove that but for the attorney's negligence, he would have won a jury trial? Absent obvious or gross negligence, an attorney could truthfully claim that no one ever knows for sure what a jury will do and the chances of the jury finding for the client were just as likely as the jury finding for the other party. However, not all legal malpractice cases involve jury trials. In a non-jury situation, the proof of negligence often becomes easier.

Is there a cause of action for negligence per se when an attorney violates an ethical rule? In most jurisdictions, the answer is no. Ethical rules are qualitatively different from the safety rules that form the basis for the traditional negligence per se claim.

2. EXPERT TESTIMONY

Just as we saw in medical malpractice cases, expert testimony is also permissible, and sometimes mandatory, in establishing the standard of care that an attorney should have met in a particular case. For instance, some jurisdictions require expert testimony in malpractice cases in which the attorney is a certified specialist in a particular area of law.[27]

Sidebar

In some legal malpractice cases, the judge is called upon to determine the standard of care. After all, the judge is also an attorney.

Example: Al Attorney has been retained to represent Sid. The case involves a simple and straightforward car crash. Sid, while stopped at a red light, was rear-ended by Terry. Sid retains Al to sue Terry for the damages to Sid's car and Sid's medical expenses. At the time that Al becomes Sid's attorney, there is over a year before the statute of limitations runs. Al fails to investigate the claim and waits too long to file Sid's complaint. The statute of limitations runs and Sid's claim is barred. Sid brings a legal malpractice action against Al. Does he have a prima facie case against Al?

Answer: Absolutely. Sid can establish that there was an attorney-client relationship between himself and Al; he can also prove that Al failed to file a complaint prior to the expiration of the statute of limitations, despite the fact that Al had over a year to do so. Sid can prove the first two elements of his legal malpractice claim: Al's duty to him, and Al's breach of that duty. What about the third and fourth elements? Is there proximate cause between Al's breach

---

When proving a legal malpractice case, the client must allege:

- The attorney owed a duty to the client.
- The attorney breached that duty and the client would have been successful in the underlying legal action had it not been for the breach.
- The breach was the proximate cause of the client's loss.
- The client has provable damages for this breach.

FIGURE 12-15

Proving Legal Malpractice

and Sid's damages? Again the answer is yes. Sid would have been entitled to monetary damages if he had won his suit. Now he must pay those bills himself. His payments are directly caused by Al's breach of duty in failing to file a complaint.

C. PROVING DAMAGES

In legal malpractice, the client is permitted to recover for the loss of his claim, or, put another way, the amount of money he would have received if the attorney had not committed legal malpractice. What if the damages in the first case are not clearly established? In that case, the client must prove not only that the attorney's negligence cost him the damages he would have received in the underlying suit, but he must also prove what those damages would have been. The result is almost two trials in one: In the first, the client is proving the attorney's negligence; in the second, the client is proving the damages he would have received in the underlying case.

D. DEFENSES IN LEGAL MALPRACTICE CASES

Because legal malpractice resembles medical malpractice in so many ways, it should not be any surprise to learn that many of the same defenses are permissible in both types of cases. For instance, an attorney is permitted to raise the contributory negligence of the client as a defense to legal malpractice. How can a client be contributorily negligent? Suppose that the attorney asks the client to produce a specific document without which the attorney is unable to proceed and the client never produces it. In such a case, the attorney's ineffectiveness was abetted by the client's refusal to cooperate. Other defenses available to the attorney include use of the attorney's best judgment. When a client hires an attorney, he is not hiring someone to simply speak for him, he is hiring a professional with a wealth of knowledge, experience, and skill. The client not only is relying on this skill, he must also understand that the

FIGURE 12-16

Ten Ways to Avoid Legal Malpractice Claims

1   The firm should avoid marginal or questionable cases in the first place.
2   When turning down a case, explain to the person that the case is weak, why it is weak, and explain this in writing.
3   Always remind the person of the date the statute of limitations runs.
4   Keep track of all details by writing them down and putting them in the file.
5   Never promise the client that the case is a "winner," or that there is no doubt about the case.
6   Document everything, including contacts with the client.
7   Follow up with letters.
8   Keep track of client meetings, appointments, etc. (some malpractice insurers require a record system or time management software).
9   Avoid "crisis management."
10 Anticipate problems and deal with them before they become crises.

Abandonment of the case	Failure to comply with court rules	**FIGURE 12-17**
Inadequate preparation	Absconding with funds	**Examples of Legal Malpractice**
Inadequate representation	Conflicts of interest	
Failure to keep client informed		

Plaintiff winners in state courts in the nation's 75 largest counties, 2001

FIGURE 12-18

Plaintiff Winners in State Courts

Case type	All trial cases	
	Number	Plaintiff winners[b]
All trial cases[a]	11,681	55.4%
Tort cases	7,798	51.6%
Automobile	4,121	61.2
Premises liability	1,260	42.0
Product liability	154	44.2
Asbestos	30	60.0
Other	124	40.3
Intentional tort	366	56.8
Medical malpractice	1,149	26.8
Professional malpractice	99	52.5
Slander/libel	94	41.5
Animal attack	99	66.7
Conversion	28	46.4
False arrest, imprisonment	45	42.2
Other or unknown tort	383	50.9
Contract cases	3,625	64.8%
Fraud	602	58.3
Seller plaintiff	1,196	76.8
Buyer plaintiff	779	61.5
Mortgage foreclosure	22	72.7
Employment discrimination	160	43.8
Other employment dispute	282	55.7
Rental/lease	276	64.9
Tortious interference	133	57.9
Partnership dispute	41	46.3
Subrogation	61	67.2
Other or unknown contract	73	56.2
Real property cases	258	37.6%
Eminent domain	49	40.8
Other real property[c]	209	36.8

Note: Data on plaintiff winners were available for 99.9% of trials. Detail may not sum to total because of rounding.
[a]Trial cases include bench and jury trials, trials with a directed verdict, judgments notwithstanding the verdict, and jury trials for defaulted defendants.
[b]Excludes bifurcated trials where the plaintiff litigated only the damage claim. There were 216 trials where only the damage claim was litigated.
[c]Includes title disputes, boundary disputes, and other real property cases.

Civil Trial Cases and Verdicts in Large Counties, 2001, Bureau of Justice Statistics, U.S. Department of Justice.

attorney is prohibited from doing certain things because of it. What if the client wishes the attorney to fabricate court documents or suborn perjury and the attorney refuses to do so? Such a failure is not legal malpractice.

OTHER TYPES OF PROFESSIONAL MALPRACTICE

In recent years, other professionals have been targeted with malpractice claims. For instance, claims have been made against accountants for failing to properly document tax returns or account for funds. In some jurisdictions, counselors and even educators have been hit with malpractice claims. Whether malpractice claims will expand into other areas is a question that will be answered in the next few years.

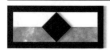

SKILLS YOU NEED IN THE REAL WORLD

Reviewing and Summarizing Medical Records

When summarizing medical records, it is important to remember the purpose of the summary. Why summarize medical records at all? The first and most obvious answer is so that the attorney can have a handy reference. A reference should be short, concise, and helpful. It does not make any sense to prepare a medical records summary that is nearly as long and comprehensive as the records themselves. However, brevity is a skill and one not easily acquired. How do you know what to say — and what not to say?

Many paralegals, when faced with the prospect of summarizing a two-foot-high pile of medical documents, will take a deep breath and then begin to organize. One of the best organizational schemes, at least from a legal standpoint, is putting all medical records in chronological order. This makes them easier to understand, and often will help with discovery questions dealing with the plaintiff's prior, unrelated medical claims and pre-existing injuries. At this point, the paralegal is not evaluating the actual treatment the plaintiff received. It is best not to attempt too many tasks at the same time. Getting the medical records in chronological order is sufficient at this stage.

Once the records are organized by date, what then? Now it is time to summarize. There are two generally accepted methods for summarizing medical records: narratives and page reference. The narrative summary consists of an overall description of the treatment that the plaintiff received, when he received it, and by whom. A page-reference summary provides page-by-page, and often line-by-line, summaries of what exactly happened in each record. Although these two approaches have different merits, many firms opt for a blended approach. They will prepare narrative summaries of the medical records overall, and then have the paralegal focus on particular entries to produce a page-by-page summary.

Here is an example of a narrative medical record summary in the Chumley case:

"The collision between Mr. Chumley's car and the locomotive occurred on August 23 of last year at 4:30 P.M. in the town of Cling, State of Placid.

"First responder was City of Cling EMT. They assisted firefighters in cutting Mr. Chumley out of the car. He was placed on a backboard and given the extensive nature of his injuries, Cling EMT called for Emergency Air Lift.

"EAL arrived at 4:49 P.M. and airlifted Mr. Chumley to Mission Hospital, which is three minutes away. In Mission Emergency Room, Mr. Chumley's medical condition was summarized as follows:

"Closed head injury; fractured left tibia; internal hemorrhaging; hemo-pneumothorax (air and blood in the pleural cavity); five broken ribs, all on his left side; left hip fracture and severe abdominal trauma. Mr. Chumley was unconscious at the time.

"On August 30, Mr. Chumley had a tracheotomy performed. Infection set in almost immediately. On August 31, attending physician Dr. Grubb, decided to . . . ."

A page-by-page reference is provided in the appendix, along with extensive information about the Chumley case.

THE LIFE OF A PARALEGAL

Screening and Evaluating Medical Malpractice Cases

Our firm handles strictly plaintiff work in medical malpractice cases. Normally, a potential client will call the office and I or one of the other legal assistants will take the call. There are a multitude of calls that are going to be received. Many of them complain about something that a doctor did or did not do. A large percentage of those complaints are things that are either not actionable as a medical malpractice claim or should be addressed by one of the many licensing boards, or at the least questionable as to whether it is feasible to pursue, factoring in the potential expenses associated with bringing an action versus any potential recovery. Statistics in this state show that only a small percentage of the medical malpractice cases that are brought are successful.

When we are screening calls, especially one with merit, we present it to one or all of the partners in the firm. Normally we will also have a weekly meeting where we go over all of the pending cases, their status and any potential statute of limitations issues. We also have time to present cases that have been phone screened in order for the attorneys to decide as a firm whether it is a matter which they wish to meet with the potential client and discuss in specific detail all aspects of the claim and investigate further. If it is a case, we make a follow-up call to the person and arrange a time to meet with one of the attorneys and a legal assistant to gather more information. During the interview with the client, we review all of the questionable medical treatment and subsequent treatment that they may have had. We also give an overview of what a medical malpractice action is, explain what is required of a plaintiff in order to substantiate or prove the case (burden of proof), the costs associated, the need for experts who are willing to offer opinions and potentially testify regarding the care provided by the potential defendant and basically the pros and cons of a medical malpractice case. If the client understands all these issues and risks, have their questions addressed and are willing to proceed, understanding the risks, we then proceed and have the person execute medical authorization release forms and some form of agreement with the firm, either to investigate the matter or a contract to represent.

Our investigation of the matter begins by obtaining a list of all physicians that the client has seen subsequent to the physician or care that is the reason that they have sought our firm out. Following that meeting, I or another legal assistant will proceed in obtaining copies of all medical records, including X-rays, pathology report, diagnostic reports, lab reports, MRIs, CT-scans and any other documents that will ultimately be needed to review the claim of malpractice by the attorneys and experts and organize them.

John Purvis, Legal Assistant

ETHICAL ISSUES FOR THE PARALEGAL: FEE SPLITTING OR SHARING

When dealing with malpractice cases, one particular area of ethical concern often surfaces. Suppose that the plaintiff's attorney has a standing agreement with a local physician or chiropractor that they will not only recommend the other's services to their clients, but they will also share the fees they receive on shared cases? Although it is not uncommon for attorneys to share fees with one another, such as when one attorney refers a client to another, sharing fees with non-lawyers is an area full of ethical minefields. For instance, when an attorney splits a fee with a physician, there is at least the appearance that an unethical relationship exists. Looking at the arrangement from the outside, it can appear that the physician is directing a patient to a particular lawyer simply to obtain the fee, and the lawyer could be directing the client to a particular doctor for the same reason. Although this might sound innocuous enough, just how far does this relationship go? For instance, does the physician have any say over which case the attorney accepts? Does the attorney have the right to influence the physician's diagnosis? As you can see, fee sharing with non-lawyers is fraught with difficulties. Non-lawyers also include legal assistants. Fee splitting between lawyers and legal assistants is considered to be unethical under the American Bar Association Ethics rules. Consider ABA Model Guideline 9:

> A lawyer must not split legal fees with a legal assistant nor pay a legal assistant for the referral of legal business.[28]

Chapter Summary

Medical malpractice claims are a variation of a traditional negligence claim. In alleging malpractice, the plaintiff must prove that the defendant owed him a duty, that the physician violated that duty by failing to follow the established standard of care, and that this failure was a proximate cause of his injuries.

The physician's duty arises from the doctor-patient relationship. The physician must use the same level of skill, knowledge, and expertise as other physicians. Although medical malpractice claims appear to be a relatively recent phenomenon, actually they have been occurring for centuries. There has been an increase in medical malpractice claims in the last few decades, however. Whether this increase in claims has actually resulted in a dramatic increase in jury awards against doctors is a matter of some controversy. Medical malpractice cases almost always involve testimony by some expert, usually another physician, that establishes that the defendant's conduct in the case either was, or was not, in accord with the applicable standard of care. However, this testimony is not conclusive on the issue. It is up to the jury to decide if the defendant violated the standard of care. In recent years, legislatures across the country have enacted tort reform statutes that impose limits on a physician's liability or impose a cap on the amount of damages that a plaintiff can receive in a medical malpractice case.

Malpractice claims are not limited to medicine. Legal malpractice cases are becoming increasingly common as well. In a legal malpractice case, the plaintiff alleges that the attorney owed him a duty to act in conformity with the expertise, skill, and knowledge of other attorneys and breached this duty in a specific way. Usually, the plaintiff in a legal malpractice case must prove that absent the attorney's negligence, he would have succeeded in the underlying legal action that he claims the attorney mishandled.

Web Sites

- *Washington Post* article: **Medical Malpractice and the American Jury**
  http://www.washingtonpost.com/wp-srv/style/longterm/books/chap1/ medical.htm

- **Consumer Action and Information Center of Hawaii**
  http://www.consumerlaw.com/medical.html

- **Insurance Information Institute**
  http://www.iii.org/

- **Legal Malpractice**
  http://www.consumerlaw.com/legalmal.html

- **ABA Standing Committee on Legal Assistants**
  http://www.abanet.org/legalservices/paralegals/

Forms and Court Documents

Medical malpractice complaint

STATE OF PLACID   IN THE SUPERIOR COURT
COUNTY OF BARNES   FILE NUMBER: _____

Charles Chumley,   )
Plaintiff   )
)
vs.   )
)
Joseph C. Doe, M.D.   )
Doe & Roe Medical Associates, P.A.,
Defendants

Complaint

COMES NOW, Charles Chumley, Plaintiff in the above-styled action and makes the following allegations:

1.

At all times pertinent to this action, Defendant Joseph C. Doe, M.D. (hereafter referred to as Defendant Doe) was a licensed medical doctor in the State of Placid.

2.

In Defendant Doe's capacity as a medical doctor he was a managing partner in the firm of Doe & Roe Medical Associates, P.A. (hereafter referred to as Defendant Doe & Roe, P.A.), a registered Professional Association in the State of Placid.

3.

Both Dr. Doe and Doe & Roe, P.A. were engaged in the practice of medicine through their office located at 212 Alameda Canyon Road, City of Barnes, State of Placid.

4.

At all material and pertinent times to this complaint, Defendants Doe and Doe & Roe, P.A. had a physician-patient relationship with the plaintiff.

5.

On August 23, last year, the plaintiff was involved in an automobile-train collision that caused the plaintiff severe and life-threatening injuries.

6.

On August 23, last year, the plaintiff was transported to Mission Hospital and admitted into the Mission Emergency Room.

7.

Defendant Doe, in his capacity as plaintiff's physician, visited him at the Mission-Barnes Emergency Room and examined the plaintiff.

8.

On August 23 and for all times afterward, Defendant Doe and Defendant Doe & Roe, owed a duty of reasonable care to plaintiff to use that knowledge, skill, and care that is generally used in similar cases and circumstances by physicians in communities having similar medical standards and available facilities, which duty these defendants breached by the following: Defendant Doe failed to diagnose plaintiff's severe abdominal injuries, including plaintiff's splenic injury.

9.

As a direct and proximate cause of Defendant Doe's failure to diagnose the plaintiff's medical injuries, he was not treated for his abdominal injuries for 28 hours following his admission to Mission-Barnes Hospital.

10.

As a direct and proximate cause of Defendant Doe's failure to diagnose and treat the plaintiff's injuries, plaintiff suffered from peritonitis. Plaintiff's spleen was removed on August 30, last year.

11.

As a direct and proximate cause of Defendant Doe's breach of the duty that he owed the plaintiff, plaintiff incurred economic, physical, and mental damages in addition to and in aggravation of, the injuries that he received as a result of the automobile-train collision that occurred on August 23, last year.

12.

As a direct and proximate result of Defendants' negligence, plaintiff suffered disability, disfigurement, mental anguish, loss of capacity for the enjoyment of life, expensive hospitalization, medical and nursing care and treatment, loss of earnings, loss of ability to earn money and aggravation of a previously existing condition, to wit, his injuries from the automobile-train collision occurring on August 23, last year. These losses are permanent in nature. Plaintiff will suffer continued losses and impairments in the future.

WHEREFORE, the plaintiff requests judgment for damages against defendants, individually and jointly and severally, as follows:

Plaintiff prays that the Court award the following damages:

a. General damages in the amount of _____ ;

b. Special damages in the amount of _____ ; and

c. Punitive damages in an amount to be determined by the court;

d. Plaintiff also requests costs of suit; and

e. Such other and further relief as the court may deem just and proper;

f. Plaintiff also requests a trial by jury on the issues raised in this Complaint.

Respectfully submitted, this the _____ day of _____, 200 __.

_____

Clarence D. Arrow
Attorney for the Plaintiff

Key Terms

Informed consent   Malpractice   Specialist
Legal malpractice   Physician-patient relationship Standard of care

Review Questions

1 If the first U.S. medical malpractice case was filed in 1794, why are medical malpractice cases considered to be such a pressing and immediate problem?

2 How has the medical profession's standard of care changed in the past two centuries? How has this standard of care and the treatment of patients affected the societal standing of physicians?

3 Medical malpractice cases can be based on one of at least three different theories. What are they?

4 Why are the courts reluctant to frame all medical malpractice cases in terms of contract theory? Is there some public consideration that puts the physician-patient relationship outside the framework of a simple contractual relationship?

5 What are the basic elements of a medical malpractice claim?

6 What are some examples of the ways in which a physician can breach her standard of care to the patient?

7 Why is expert testimony needed to prove the basic elements of the plaintiff's case?

8 Why would many states or jurisdictions require an expert's affidavit before the plaintiff's complaint can be filed? Is there some public policy behind this requirement?

9 Under the law of medical malpractice, a recent graduate of medical school and a seasoned physician are held to the same standard of care. Does this make sense? Why or why not?

10 Many jurisdictions have moved away from local definitions of the standard of care. Why?

11   A specialist is held to a different standard of care. What is it? Why should a specialist be held to a different standard of care than a general practitioner?

12   How have various tort reforms affected the way that a medical malpractice case is brought or how damages are assessed in such cases?

13   Why have many state legislatures enacted caps or limits on punitive damages awards?

14   Should punitive damages awards be limited in medical malpractice cases? Why or why not?

15   What is informed consent? What elements must be established to show that the plaintiff gave informed consent?

16   What is an exception to the requirement that informed consent must be obtained prior to carrying out any procedure?

17   Explain what the scope of informed consent is.

18   Some law firms employ legal nurse consultants or nurse paralegals to assist with medical malpractice cases. How could such individuals be helpful?

19   What are some of the defenses available in medical malpractice cases?

20   How is legal malpractice defined?

21   What is the attorney's duty to the client?

22   Is expert testimony ever used in legal malpractice cases? If so, how?

23   What are some ways that a paralegal can help a firm avoid a claim of legal malpractice?

24   Explain the difference between a narrative medical summary and a page-by-page medical summary.

Applying What
You Have Learned

1   Nancy has decided to undergo a radical new therapy to cure her cancer. There is only one doctor in the country who practices this procedure. When Nancy meets with the physician, he takes great pains to point out to her what the risks of this procedure are. After listening to everything that the doctor has to say, Nancy decides to go ahead with the procedure. During the treatment, an unexpected complication develops. Nancy's doctor realizes that another procedure must be used. Should the doctor obtain a new informed consent from Nancy?

2   Drew, who suffers from obesity, decides that he wants to undergo an operation that will reduce the size of his stomach, commonly referred to as "stomach stapling." Drew will be physically unable to eat as much food as he was before the procedure and therefore should lose weight. When the doctor appears in Drew's hospital room to tell him all about the procedure and obtain Drew's informed consent, Drew says, "I don't want to know the details. It grosses me out. I'll get sick if you tell me anything. I trust you. Just do it." Is this a valid informed consent? Is there anything that the doctor can do to prevent, or at least minimize, any medical

malpractice claim that Drew may have later because of lack of informed consent?

3 Draft a complaint based on the facts in the case excerpt. How would you allege a breach of the standard of care in that case?

4 Locate your state's statute of limitations on medical malpractice cases. What does it provide about a patient's cause of action?

Endnotes

[1] *Cross v. Guthery*, 1 Am. Dec. 61 (1794).

[2] 69 Tenn. L. Rev. 385 (2002).

[3] 69 Tenn. L. Rev. 385 (2002).

[4] *Jure v. Raviotta*, 612 So. 2d 225, *cert. denied*, 614 So. 2d 1257 (1992).

[5] *Burton v. Leftwich*, 123 So. 2d 766 (1960).

[6] *Norton v. Hamilton*, 92 Ga. App. 727, 89 S.E.2d 809 (1955).

[7] *Hill v. Stewart*, 209 So. 2d 809 (1968).

[8] *Martinez v. Lewis*, 969 P.2d 213 (1998).

[9] 43 Baylor L. Rev. 1 Legal Malpractice in Texas, Beck (1991).

[10] *Jacoves v. United Merchandising Corp.*, 9 Cal. App. 4th 88, 11 Cal. Rptr. 2d 468 (1992).

[11] *Goins v. Puleo*, 350 N.C. 277, 512 S.E.2d 748 (1999).

[12] 43 Baylor L. Rev. 1 Legal Malpractice in Texas, Beck (1991).

[13] *Sayer v. Williams*, 962 P.2d 165 (1998).

[14] *Clark v. Sporre*, 777 N.E.2d 1166 (2002).

[15] *Heinrich v. Sweet*, 308 F.3d 48 (1st Cir. 2002).

[16] *Naccarato v. Grob*, 180 N.W.2d 788 (1970).

[17] *Vergara by Vergara v. Doan*, 593 N.E.2d 185 (1992).

[18] 43 Baylor L. Rev. 1 Legal Malpractice in Texas, Beck (1991). *Moskovitz v. Mt. Sinai Medical Ctr.*, 69 Ohio St. 3d 638, 635 N.E.2d 331 (1994), *cert. denied*, 130 L. Ed. 2d 602, 115 S. Ct. 668, ___ U.S. ___ (1994).

[19] Id.

[20] *Ditto v. McCurdy*, 86 Haw. 84, 947 P.2d 952 (1997).

[21] 13 Okla. City U. L. Rev. 135, Arancibia (1988).

[22] *Spano v. Bertocci*, 299 A.D.2d 335 (2002).

[23] *Hawkins v. Rosenbloom*, 17 S.W.3d 116 (1999).

[24] *Shine v. Vega*, 429 Mass. 456 (1999).

[25] *Davis v. Hoffman*, 972 F. Supp. 308 (E.D. Pa. 1997).

[26] *Babbitt v. Bumpus*, 73 Mich. 331 (1889).

[27] *Fidler v. Sullivan*, 93 App. Div. 2d 964, 463 N.Y.S.2d 279 (1983).

[28] ABA Model Guidelines for the Utilization of Legal Assistant Services, Guideline 9.

Insurance

Chapter Objectives

- Explain the role of insurance coverage in personal injury cases
- Describe how insurance policy limits affect settlement negotiations
- Define an insurance company's duty to defend its insured and when this obligation is triggered
- Explain "no-fault" insurance
- Describe and explain the basic components of an insurance policy

 **MR. CHUMLEY AND THE INSURANCE COMPANY**

Mr. Chumley has a standard automobile insurance policy. This policy covers monetary losses from personal injuries, medical payments, and collision damage, among other things. As we have already seen, Mr. Chumley was severely injured in the collision with the train. He was rushed to the hospital shortly after the collision, where he began incurring huge medical bills. His car was also completely destroyed. His wife was killed and there are funeral costs to pay. He cannot return to his job, so his income has been affected. Which of these losses is covered by his insurance? If the insurance company pays these claims, what effect does this have on his lawsuit against the railroad company? After all, if he is compensated for his medical bills, how can he sue the railroad company for recovery of bills that have already been paid? We examine all these issues in this chapter and provide a general framework for how law firms on both sides of a lawsuit deal with insurance companies. First, we discuss the general history and concepts of insurance.

INTRODUCTION

Although there are dozens of different forms of insurance ranging from flood insurance to crop insurance, there are only a few types of insurance that figure prominently enough in tort law to justify a separate discussion. Broadly speaking, automobile insurance and homeowner's insurance are the two most important areas of insurance law, at least as they apply to personal injury cases and the other topics we cover in this chapter. An understanding of insurance law is crucial for anyone planning on entering the field of personal injury law. Even more important than understanding the underlying principles of the insurance industry is an understanding of how the individuals involved, from insurance agents to claims adjusters to insurance defense attorneys, function in the day-to-day world of slip-and-fall, car wreck, and personal injury lawsuits.

THE IMPACT OF INSURANCE ON CIVIL SUITS

Insurance coverage has an enormous impact on the course of a civil suit. When deciding whether to take a case, the plaintiff's attorney must consider the likelihood of recovering damages. If the defendant has no insurance and no assets, the potential recovery is almost non-existent. In the pragmatic world of personal injury lawyers, no matter how good a case the plaintiff may have, if there is no possibility of recovery, the attorney will probably refuse to take the case. Plaintiffs' attorneys are almost always paid on a contingency fee, typically one-third of the total recovery. A case with clear defendant liability but no possibility of judgment means that the plaintiff's attorney has no financial incentive to take the case. Even if the attorney would like to take the case, just on "general principles," he has staff, rent, and other overhead costs to consider. When attorneys take on too many such cases, they lose money and jeopardize their ability to pay the costs of running a law office.

When the defendant has insurance coverage, the possibility of a recovery suddenly becomes greater. After all, the defendant's insurance coverage is specifically designed to pay out liability claims. A typical automobile insurance policy also provides an attorney to represent the defendant, under the "duty to defend" provision. This means that the plaintiff's attorney will be dealing with an attorney on the other side of the litigation and that makes the entire process more predictable, although not necessarily any easier.

Determining whether the defendant has insurance coverage is usually very simple. In most car collisions, the police have been called and an accident report has been filled out. Part of that report will include some basic information about the defendant's coverage. However, discovering how much coverage the defendant has (the policy limits) has traditionally been more difficult.

We explore a typical insurance policy in depth and focus on automobile insurance policies, but first we briefly address the development of insurance.

 ## HISTORY OF INSURANCE

The basic scheme behind insurance is deceptively simple: Individuals (policyholders) make payments (premiums) to the insurance company, which pools the money and uses this pool of money to pay out any claims made by a policyholder. This arrangement spreads the risk of loss over a wide group so that no one individual must bear the brunt of a large financial loss. Insurance companies are often seen as an important element of the economy because they guarantee that businesses and individuals will be able to recover from devastating losses, such as fires or automobile collisions. Without insurance, business owners would have no way of reestablishing themselves after a catastrophe. Given this crucial economic importance, and the fact that insurance companies have a great deal of leverage when dealing with the individual policyholder, all states have passed legislation restricting and regulating insurance companies.

Without insurance, there are only three possible methods to compensate an individual for a loss: (1) the individual bears the total burden, (2) the individual who caused the loss pays for it, or (3) a statute provides that some other agency, such as worker's compensation, pays the loss.

Insurance companies have existed for centuries. Lloyd's of London, the world's most famous insurance company, has existed since 1688. Lloyd's originally started out as a coffee house for merchant sailors and eventually branched out from coffee to insuring merchant fleets that undertook dangerous ocean voyages to secure spices, precious minerals, and, oddly enough, coffee.

Dislike or outright hatred of insurance companies is not a recent phenomenon. In many ways, this industry could qualify as the business most people love to hate. Statutes governing the insurance industry have existed since the 1800s, but the second half of the twentieth century saw the largest growth in insurance legislation. Much of the early insurance regulation was a direct response to outright corruption on the part of some insurance companies. For instance, a company might collect life insurance premium payments from an insured for years and then refuse to pay when she died, leaving her spouse and children in financial straits.[1] Part of this resentment of insurance companies was based on the perception that these large, faceless corporations cared more for profits than their responsibilities to their insured customers. One could argue that this sentiment is still prevalent.

Before 1944, the U.S. Supreme Court had consistently ruled that insurance was not *commerce* as that word is defined under the Commerce Clause of the United States Constitution. As such, Congress was prevented from enacting legislation to regulate the industry nationwide. However, after the decision in *United States v. South-Eastern Underwriters Association*,[2] the Supreme Court's view changed. Reversing its earlier position, the Court ruled that insurance was commerce and therefore could be regulated. Congress quickly took up the Supreme Court's suggestion by creating the first of many federal statutes regulating the insurance industry. The McCarran-Ferguson Act established that in most questions regarding insurance law, state law would apply, except where insurance touched on national issues such as anti-trust, federal taxation, and the jurisdiction of the Federal Trade Commission. In those situations, insurance companies come under the jurisdiction of federal statutes.

Sidebar

When researching insurance law, go to state law for insurance-related issues, such as policy provisions, exclusions, and duty to defend. Look to federal law when researching issues such as an insurance company's obligation to pay federal taxes, compliance with securities regulation, and labor issues.

V   WHAT IS INSURANCE?

Premium
The insured's payment to the insurance company

Indemnify
To compensate a person who has suffered a loss

Insurance coverage is a type of contract between an individual (the insured) and an entity (the insurance company). The insured pays a **premium** (often a specific, monthly amount) in exchange for the insurance company's promise to pay (or **indemnify**) for the insured's property loss, medical bills, funeral expenses, liability, etc., up to a specified total amount.

Almost anything can be insured. Any potential loss is insurable, so long as it does not violate public policy, or stem from the insured's intentional conduct or fraud. For example, some celebrities insure their faces against loss. If they are singers, they may insure their voices. A drug dealer, on the other hand, could not insure her consignment of cocaine, because such an insurance agreement would run counter to public policy (if not an actual criminal statute).

VI   THE INSURANCE CONTRACT

Policy
A written insurance contract

The insurance **policy** is actually a form of contract. As such, it has many of the same elements that are seen in any contract. However, unlike many other types of contracts, insurance policies are tightly regulated by state statutes. In fact, an insurance policy must conform to the applicable state statute or it is void.

FIGURE 13-1

Civil Trials
Disposed of in
State Courts

Number of civil trials disposed of in state courts in the nation's 75 largest counties, 2001		
Case type	**Number of trials**[a]	**Percent**
All	11,908	100.0%
Tort cases	7,948	66.7%
Automobile	4,235	35.6
Premises liability	1,268	10.6
Product liability	158	1.3
Asbestos	31	0.3
Other	126	1.1
Intentional tort	375	3.1
Medical malpractice	1,156	9.7
Professional malpractice	102	0.9
Slander/libel	95	0.8
Animal attack	99	0.8
Conversion	27	0.2
False arrest, imprisonment	45	0.4
Other or unknown tort	390	3.3
Contract cases	3,698	31.1%
Fraud	625	5.2
Seller plaintiff	1,208	10.1
Buyer plaintiff	793	6.7
Mortgage foreclosure	22	0.2
Employment discrimination	166	1.4
Other employment dispute	287	2.4
Rental/lease	276	2.3
Tortious interference	138	1.2
Partnership dispute	40	0.3
Subrogation	69	0.6
Other or unknown contract	73	0.6
Real property cases	262	2.2%
Eminent domain	52	0.4
Other real property[b]	210	1.8

Note: Data for case types were available for 100% of the 11,908 trial cases. Detail may not sum to total because of rounding.
[a]Trials include bench and jury trials, trials with a directed verdict, judgments notwithstanding the verdict, and jury trials for defaulted defendants.
[b]Includes title disputes, boundary disputes, and other real property cases.
See *Methodology* section for case type definitions.

Civil Trial Cases and Verdicts in Large Counties, 2001, Bureau of Justice Statistics, U.S. Department of Justice.

Within the restrictions of state rules and regulations, an insurance policy, because it is a contract, gives the parties wide latitude about particular points. The parties are free to negotiate all of the terms, except those specifically required by law or public policy.[3]

A. THE INSURANCE POLICY

If the insurance policy is a contract, what is the insured receiving in exchange for her premium payments? Actually, the insured receives three benefits:

1   The insurance company agrees to compensate the insured for specific losses covered by the policy.

Fiduciary
A relationship in which one person, or entity, is obligated to act in a trustworthy relationship to the other. A fiduciary has the duty to act in the best interests of the other. A common example of a fiduciary relationship is the attorney-client relationship

2   The insurance company agrees to provide an attorney to the insured should the insured be sued for any actions covered by the policy.

3   The insurance company agrees to act as a **fiduciary** in handling the insured's policy matters (one bound by legal and ethical duties to act in the best interests of another).[4]

Should the insurance company breach any of these promises, it has violated the terms of a contract, and the insured is entitled to bring suit to enforce the contract provisions. The insurance contract is normally referred to as a policy, and we use that terminology for the rest of this chapter.

The terms *contract* and *policy* are used interchangeably by most legal authorities.

The typical insurance policy has several component parts. These include the declarations page, the insurance agreement, a definitions section, and exclusions. The policy often includes a section detailing the duties of the insured after an accident or loss and information about how to file a claim. There are usually general provisions in the policy that deal with issues such as bankruptcy of the insured and subrogation rights of the insurance company. Each of these provisions is explored in greater depth as we discuss automobile insurance. However, before moving to automobile insurance, we address common state laws applicable to insurance.

B. STATE LAWS REGARDING INSURANCE POLICIES

Insurance has been heavily regulated by the states for decades. These regulations affect everything from creating an office of state insurance commissioner (or similar title) to the size of the type font used in policies. In fact, many states have statutes that specify not only the size of the type used in the policy, but also require the use of boldface lettering for certain terms. These initiatives are all designed to make the policy easier to read and to avoid the old adage that "large print giveth and small print taketh away." In the past, small print, buried in the policy, has been used to disguise policy limitations and other restrictions on the policyholder's rights.

§58-38-20. Format requirements

(a) All insurance policies and contracts covered by G.S. 58-38-35 must be printed in a typeface at least as large as 10 point modern type, one point leaded, be written in a logical and clear order and form, and contain the following items:

(1) On the cover, first, or insert page of the policy a statement that the policy is a legal contract between the policy owner and the insurer and the statement, printed in larger or other contrasting type or color, "Read your policy carefully";

(2) An index of the major provisions of the policy, which may include the following items:

a. The person or persons insured by the policy;

b. The applicable events, occurrences, conditions, losses, or damages covered by the policy;

c. The limitations or conditions on the coverage of the policy;

d. Definitional sections of the policy;

e. Provisions governing the procedure for filing a claim under the policy;

f. Provisions governing cancellation, renewal, or amendment of the policy by either the insurer or the policyholder;

g. Any options under the policy; and

h. Provisions governing the insurer's duties and powers in the event that suit is filed against the insured.

(b) In determining whether or not a policy is written in a logical and clear order and form the Commissioner must consider the following factors:

(1) The extent to which sections or provisions are set off and clearly identified by titles, headings, or margin notations;

(2) The use of a more readable format, such as narrative or outline forms;

(3) Margin size and the amount and use of space to separate sections of the policy; and

(4) Contrast and legibility of the colors of the ink and paper and the use of contrasting titles or headings for sections.

FIGURE 13-2

North Carolina "Readable Insurance Policy" Act

In addition to requirements about what font size can be used in policies, some states go so far as to mandate the basic provisions of an insurance policy or to demand that an insurance policy's language be simplified so that policyholders can understand it. These "readable" insurance policies require that the language and terms used in the policy avoid legal and/or technical terms. See Figure 13-2 for an example of such a statute.

In addition to format requirements, there is one other important area of state law that factors prominently in civil suits: All states require that motorists possess minimum amounts of insurance coverage as a condition of receiving a valid driver's license from the state.

Sidebar

States that have statutes setting out minimum print sizes and boldface requirements include California, Wisconsin, North Carolina, Idaho, Missouri, Louisiana, Oregon, Alabama, and New York, among many others.

AUTOMOBILE INSURANCE

Lawsuits involving car crashes are the most common form of personal injury case. That fact alone would justify an extensive review of automobile

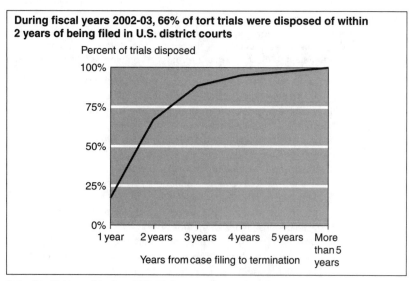

FIGURE 13-3

Length of Time Between Filing and Termination of Tort Cases

During fiscal years 2002-03, 66% of tort trials were disposed of within 2 years of being filed in U.S. district courts

Federal Tort Trials and Verdicts, 2002-03, Bureau of Justice Statistics, U.S. Department of Justice.

insurance law. However, there is another element that makes a close study of automobile insurance law even more pertinent: Automobile insurance is required by law.

A. STATUTORY MINIMUM LIABILITY COVERAGE

All states have enacted statutes that dictate the minimum amount of insurance coverage that a car driver must have. Typically, the coverage falls into these categories:

- Liability coverage:
  - Bodily injury
  - Property damage
- Medical payments
- Uninsured motorist/underinsured motorist

B. LIABILITY COVERAGE

When the insured has liability coverage, it means that if he causes injuries to another person or damages property, the insurance company will compensate the injured party, up to the stated limit of the policy. Typically, this provision covers the injured person's medical and funeral expenses, lost wages, disability, pain and suffering, and legal fees, among others. Because this is a statutory requirement, liability coverage is usually broken down into two component parts: bodily injury and property damage.

§16451. Owner's policy
An owner's policy of motor vehicle liability insurance shall insure the named insured and any other person using any motor vehicle registered to the named insured with the express or implied permission of the named insured, against loss from the liability imposed by law for damages arising out of ownership, maintenance, or use of the motor vehicle within the continental limits of the United States to the extent and aggregate amount, exclusive of interest and costs, with respect to each motor vehicle, of fifteen thousand dollars ($15,000) for bodily injury to or death of each person as a result of any one accident and, subject to the limit as to one person, the amount of thirty thousand dollars ($30,000) for bodily injury to or death of all persons as a result of any one accident and the amount of five thousand dollars ($5,000) for damage to property of others as a result of any one accident.*

*Cal. Stat. §16451.

C. BODILY INJURY

When an insurance policy insures against bodily injury, it usually refers to any injury, disease, wound, or sickness caused by the insured. This provision also covers the death of the injured party. The policy limits are usually stated as a total award per person injured or per accident. For instance, if a driver has policy limits of $300,000/$300,000, this means that the insured has a maximum policy limit of $300,000 for each person injured by her or $300,000 total payout for an accident, even if the actual proof of loss exceeds that amount. Most such policies contain language expressly limiting the extent of liability. For instance, the policy might contain a provision that reads:

> The limit of liability shown on the Declarations Pages for each person is the insurance company's maximum limit of liability for damages for bodily injury. These damages include damages for care of the injured person, loss of services or death that is the legal responsibility of the insured.

D. PROPERTY DAMAGE

When the insurance policy provides for property damage, this is usually construed to mean any type of property injury, loss, or destruction for which the insured is legally responsible. As we have seen in the previous example, policy limits of $300,000 means that the total payout for property damage is limited to that amount, even if the actual damages are higher.

E. MEDICAL PAYMENTS (MP)

The typical medical payments clause often states:

> The insurance company agrees to pay reasonable expenses incurred for necessary medical and funeral services because of bodily injury, as that term is defined in the Definitions section of this policy.

Although state law requires automobile insurance coverage, most drivers are unaware of the basic provisions of their insurance policies.

According to one study, "The current system of paying for auto injuries suffers from two fundamental problems: premiums are too high and victims with serious injuries rarely receive full compensation."[5]

FIGURE 13-5

**Parts of a
Typical
Automobile
Insurance
Policy**

■ Declarations Page:
  ■ Lists the name of the insured, the automobiles covered, the policy limits, and any drivers who are covered by the policy
■ Definitions
■ Coverage for Damage to Your Auto (Collision/Comprehensive Coverage)

■ Liability Coverage (Bodily Injury/Property Damage)
■ Medical Payments
■ Uninsured Motorist Coverage
■ Underinsured Motorist Coverage
■ Insured's Duties After Accident
■ General Provisions

This provision means that the insurance company will pay for medical (and often funeral) expenses incurred by the insured or anyone else covered by the policy. Most such policy provisions have specific limitations that do not apply medical payments to experimental procedures or treatments that are not commonly and customarily recognized throughout the medical profession. This exclusion often limits medical payments for **thermography,** acupuncture, or other nontraditional assessments and treatments.

Thermography
An assessment tool that can monitor temperature changes in the skin; often used by plaintiffs' attorneys as a way of showing that there is greater blood flow in an injured area, and is therefore a "picture of the pain"

F. UNINSURED MOTORIST COVERAGE

Uninsured motorist coverage was created as a way of protecting motorists from other drivers who do not have insurance. Although it is a legal requirement to have automobile insurance, that does not stop some drivers from operating cars without it. In situations in which these uninsured drivers cause accidents, the injured party would have no way to receive compensation. The injured party could attempt to sue the uninsured driver, but a person who cannot afford to pay her car insurance premiums usually has no other assets.

The standard uninsured motorist coverage clause usually provides:

The insurance company agrees to pay compensatory damages which the insured is legally entitled to recover from the owner or operator of an uninsured motor vehicle when:

■ The insured incurs bodily injury caused by an accident and
■ Property damage is incurred due to an accident.
■ The owner/operator's liability for damages must arise out of the ownership, use, or maintenance of an uninsured motor vehicle.

Before a plaintiff can take advantage of the UM coverage provision in her policy, there are certain procedural steps that must be followed. In many states, for instance, the plaintiff/insured must give the insurance company 30 days' notice that she will request the full amount of the UM policy limits. Other common procedural steps include additional requirements if the potential claim is greater than the coverage. Before proceeding on a UM claim in any state, a paralegal should spend some time getting familiar with the procedural requirements.

G. UNDERINSURED MOTORIST COVERAGE

A standard underinsured motorist (UIM) coverage clause provides:

> The insurance company agrees to pay compensatory damages that the insured is legally entitled to recover from the owner or operator of an underinsured motor vehicle when:
>
> - The insured incurs bodily injury caused by an accident.
> - The owner/operator's liability for damages must arise out of the ownership, use, or maintenance of an underinsured motor vehicle. The insurance company will only pay such damages when the limits of liability under any applicable insurance policy have been exhausted.

H. IMPORTANT PROVISIONS IN TYPICAL AUTOMOBILE POLICIES

Although an insurance policy can run to dozens of pages and contain language dealing with a wealth of issues, for a paralegal working at either a plaintiffs' firm or a defense firm, there are only a handful of provisions that are critically important. Among these are the insurance company's duty to defend the insured, the insurance company's right of subrogation, and the topic of "stacking."

1. DUTY TO DEFEND

One of the main duties that an insurance company has under its policy is to provide a legal defense for an insured when she is sued by someone and the suit is covered by the policy. In a typical example, the insured is involved in a car wreck and the other party sues her for negligence. Under this scenario, the insurance company has an obligation to provide a defense for the insured.

How does the insurance company meet this obligation? Usually, the insurance company hires an attorney to represent the insured in the lawsuit. This attorney represents the insured, but is paid by the insurance company. The attorney who represents the insured owes her duty to the insured, even though the insurance company is paying for her services. This duty to defend has spawned a whole class of attorneys who specialize in insurance defense work. We discuss insurance defense firms (and plaintiffs' firms) later in this chapter.

Suppose, for example, that the insurance company wrongfully denies the insured paid legal counsel. What options does the insured have? The insured can bring suit against the insurance company seeking a court order declaring that the insurance company has a legal obligation to provide (and pay for) the insured's defense. This means that there would actually be two lawsuits pending: a negligence action, in which the insured is the defendant and the plaintiff is the person injured in the accident, and a second action based on breach of contract, in which the insured is the plaintiff and the insurance company is the defendant. This second action is usually in the form of an action for declaratory judgment. (An example of a declaratory judgment on this issue is provided at the end of this chapter, under Forms and Court Documents.)

2. SUBROGATION

Subrogation
In claiming a legal right or a debt, the substitution of one person for another

The term **subrogation** refers to the insurance company's right to sue the tortfeasor in its own right to recover the money it has paid out to the insured. In essence, subrogation works this way: The insured files a claim for injuries caused by a negligent driver. The insurance company pays the claim and the insured is satisfied. However, the insurance company is now out the money it has paid on the claim. If the insurance policy contains a subrogation claim, it permits the insurance company to file suit in its own right against the negligent driver to recover for the damages that she caused, and that the insurance company subsequently paid out to its insured. Usually, this right to "stand in the shoes" of the insured is set out in the policy. Part of this right of subrogation may also include the insurance company's ability to call the insured to testify at trial. In fact, most insurance policies contain provisions in which the insured promises not to hinder the insurance company's subrogation action against another.

One insurance company can file a subrogation claim against another insurance company. Suppose that Insurance Company *A* has paid more than its share of damages to an insured. It can seek reimbursement for the excess payment from Insurance Company *B*.

3. "STACKING" OF POLICIES

a. Introduction

Stacking
The policy limits of one policy are added to the policy limits of one or more other policies, increasing the available funds to the sum of all policies

In situations in which the insured's policy limits are not enough to cover her medical payments, is there a way of increasing the available pool of funds? Is there a way, for instance, to add the policy limits of the insured's policy to that of another policy? The short answer is yes, with certain limitations. **Stacking** insurance policies means that two (or more) policies are combined, thus increasing the overall policy limits.

FIGURE 13-6

Typical Subrogation Clause

This Company may require from the insured an assignment of all right of recovery against any party for loss to the extent that payment therefore is made by this Company.

Example: Ted has been injured in a car accident. His policy limit for medical payments is $15,000. Ted's friend, John, was actually driving Ted's car at the time of the collision. John's medical payment policy limit is $50,000. Under certain circumstances, Ted can increase his overall policy limit to $65,000 by combining, or stacking, his insurance policy with John's policy.

b. Limit of Liability Provisions and Stacking

Insurance companies attempt to limit stacking by inserting language in the "limits of liability" clause of the policy that is usually some variation of the following:

> The insurance company's "limit of liability" shown on the Declarations Page of this policy is the maximum "limit of liability" for each person injured in any one accident, regardless of the number of:
>
> 1 Claims made
> 2 Vehicles or premiums shown on the Declarations Page
> 3 Vehicles involved in the accident

When the policy does not specifically exclude stacking, policies can be combined in a variety of ways:

- For injury to the insured
- For injury to the insured's relative (while occupying a car covered by the policy)
- For an injury to the insured while occupying a car owned by the insured but not covered by the insured's policy
- For an injury to the insured while occupying another person's insured automobile
- For an injury to the insured when she was not occupying an automobile, but was injured by an insured driver in another vehicle

The rules regarding stacking vary considerably from state to state. When considering the applicability of stacking to the facts of a particular case, research stacking under your state's laws.

I. "NO-FAULT" INSURANCE

In the traditional approach to a personal injury case, the judge or jury ultimately determines who was at fault and then forces that person to pay the damages. There are at least two flaws in this system: It can take months, if not years, for a claim to be settled, and juries can sometimes be capricious in their awards. The concept of **no-fault insurance** was created to deal with both of these shortcomings.

Under a no-fault system, the insurance company pays for the insured's damages, whether the insured was at fault in the accident or not. Obviously,

Sidebar

Stacking is commonly seen in cases involving underinsured (UIM) and uninsured motorist (UM) cases.

Sidebar

Among the states that have adopted no-fault insurance are Massachusetts, New Jersey, New York, Pennsylvania, Colorado, Florida, Hawaii, Kansas, Michigan, Minnesota, Utah, North Dakota, and Kentucky.

No-fault insurance Insurance that requires an insurance company to pay for the insured's damages regardless of who was at fault in causing the damage

FIGURE 13-7	Advantages	Disadvantages
Advantages and Disadvantages of No-Fault Insurance	▩ Faster payment of claims ▩ Less litigation ▩ Lower insurance rates (in theory) ▩ Fewer large jury verdicts	▩ Pain and suffering awards are not permitted ▩ Negligent drivers are "protected" from their bad driving ▩ Higher insurance rates (in practice) ▩ Does not pay for property damage (usually covered by some other part of the policy)

people who are insured under a no-fault system receive immediate compensation for damages, because there is no need for a trial to determine fault. But there is a quid pro quo. In a no-fault system, the insured is limited in the types of actions and damages she can receive from the other driver. For instance, in no-fault states, the injured party may not be entitled to pain and suffering awards.

If no-fault insurance sounds like a radical concept, it is interesting to note that all states have at least an element of no-fault in their automobile insurance policies. For instance, under most policies, medical payments and property damage are paid to the insured without regard to fault.

In some states, no-fault coverage is referred to as "personal injury protection" or PIP.

J. EXCLUSIONS

An insurance policy does not apply in all situations. For example, one evening, Ted has too much to drink at a local bar and decides to drive home. En route, he runs off the road and damages his car. He calls a tow truck and while the tow truck driver is pulling his car out of a ditch, a police officer drives up and begins questioning Ted. He smells alcohol on Ted's breath and eventually charges him with driving under the influence of alcohol. Later, when Ted files a claim for property damage to his car, the insurance company refuses to pay. The company cites its **exclusion** for damages caused by the insured while under the influence of alcohol. As proof that the exclusion applies, they point out that Ted was cited for DUI shortly after damaging his car.

Exclusion
The persons, types of losses, or damages not covered by an insurance policy

"Vehicle" has been defined to include not only automobiles and motorcycles, but also other conveyances that would not, at first glance, appear to fall into the category, such as horse-drawn carts, rowboats, and speed boats. Tractors and trailers, on the other hand, do not.[6]

1. INTENTIONAL INJURIES

Almost all insurance policies contain an exclusion for the intentional actions of the insured. A typical example would read:

> The insurance policy does not provide any coverage for an insured who intentionally causes bodily injury and/or property damage.

FIGURE 13-8

Determining If an Object Is a "Vehicle"

When a question arises about whether a particular mode of transportation is covered by an insurance policy, the courts will look to the following:

- How the vehicle was used
- How it was constructed
- Whether it was licensed by the state
- How risky it is to operate

This provision prevents an insured from deliberately injuring another or damaging property and then being able to circumvent responsibility for her actions by requiring her insurance company to pay for her intentional violence.

Accident policies are often written with numerous exclusions that limit the insurance company's liability. When a specific incident falls within an exclusion, the insurance company will refuse to pay.

ISSUE AT A GLANCE

---

2. OTHER EXCLUSIONS

Among the other types of exclusions are provisions that limit payment to situations when the insured is in a vehicle. This often triggers some interesting litigation. For example, see Figure 13-8 for various tests to determine if a conveyance is a "vehicle" that is covered by the policy.

HOW INSURANCE COVERAGE AFFECTS SETTLEMENT

Because insurance is such an important issue in the lawsuit, the plaintiff's attorney wants to know, as early as possible, what amount of coverage the defendant has. If the defendant has only the minimum coverage required by law and the plaintiff's damages are extensive, this will affect how the attorney proceeds on the case or even her decision whether to accept the case.

A. DISCOVERY ISSUES WITH INSURANCE

For many years, the issue of revealing the defendant's policy limits was hotly contested. Defendants, and insurance companies, were usually reluctant to provide this information to the plaintiff, often in the belief that it would affect the way the suit was prosecuted. The issue was finally settled on the federal level by the passage of Rule 26 of the Federal Rules of Evidence. That rule is set out in Figure 13-9. Many states have followed the federal rule. With that change, learning the defendant's policy limits was made considerably easier.

How is the word accident *defined? Is there a legal definition of this term that supplants the generally accepted definition? The answer is no. Accident and accidental have never been given an all-inclusive legal definition. Most jurisdictions simply require that this word, when found in an insurance policy, be construed in its common and ordinary way.*[7]

FIGURE 13-9	(a)(1) Except to the extent otherwise stipulated or directed by order or local rule, a party shall, without awaiting a discovery request, provide to other parties:
Rule 26, Federal Rules of Evidence. General Provisions Governing Discovery; Duty of Disclosure	(D) for inspection and copying as under Rule 34 any insurance agreement under which any person carrying on an insurance business may be liable to satisfy part or all of a judgment which may be entered in the action or to indemnify or reimburse for payments made to satisfy the judgment.

Once the case is underway, the next consideration is settlement. Obviously, the plaintiff's attorney wishes to settle the case as early in the process as possible, while there may be several reasons why the defendant's attorney is in no particular hurry to settle. In situations in which the insurance company tenders the policy limits (i.e., they simply volunteer to pay the full amount of the insured's coverage) the pressure on the plaintiff to settle becomes intense. After all, the plaintiff will actually receive the policy limits, while she may not receive any additional money from the defendant individually, even if the jury awards her a large verdict.

Settlement negotiations involve the plaintiff's attorney and the defendant's attorney. Before finishing our discussion of settlement, we take a slight side journey into the world of both of these legal teams, so that we can understand the different types of pressures brought to bear on these attorneys and how they handle these pressures.

B. SPECIALIZATION AMONG PERSONAL INJURY ATTORNEYS

Attorneys who handle personal injury cases tend to specialize as either plaintiffs' attorneys or insurance defense attorneys. There are several reasons for this specialization. One reason is simple preference. Some attorneys enjoy representing plaintiffs and occasionally "taking on Goliath" to see if they can win. Other attorneys might find it more rewarding, both financially and emotionally, to represent defendants. Other reasons for this split are more practical. Once an attorney handles a number of plaintiffs' cases, he is better versed in that approach and might find changing sides a difficult adjustment. An insurance defense attorney, on the other hand, might find switching to the plaintiff's side not only impractical but also difficult because of conflict-of-interest claims. Consider an attorney who has worked with ABC Insurance Company for the past ten years, representing their policyholders in court, who then decides to take a plaintiff's case against the same company. This would raise a whole host of ethical problems. As a result, most attorneys spend their legal careers on one side or the other.

1. PLAINTIFFS' FIRMS

We discussed plaintiffs' firms in Chapter 4, but an additional word about them here is warranted. The attorney who represents the plaintiff in a personal injury case almost always does so under a contingency fee agreement. Under this agreement, the attorney is entitled to a percentage of the final award. The typical arrangement is for the attorney to receive 33 percent of the final recovery. If the jury awards a $3 million verdict, $1 million goes to the plaintiff's firm. However, if the plaintiff receives nothing at the end of the case, the attorney also receives nothing. This arrangement, although it induces an attorney to work hard to get the highest possible amount for the client, also puts a great deal of financial pressure on the plaintiff's attorney. Until the case is settled, there is essentially no money coming in. For a plaintiffs' attorney to remain in practice, he must have cases settling or reaching final verdict on a regular basis.

2. INSURANCE DEFENSE FIRMS

Attorneys and paralegals who work for insurance defense firms often have a standing agreement with one or more insurance companies that they will provide a legal defense to the insurance company's policyholders who are sued. Usually, insurance defense firms bill by the hour. It is virtually unheard of for an insurance defense attorney to work on a contingency basis for an insurance company. The insurance policy provides that the company will pay for the insured's legal defense. This means that the defendant's attorney represents the defendant but is actually paid by the insurance company. Any possible ethical complexities arising from this arrangement were settled decades ago by consistent court decisions that mandated that the defense attorney's responsibility is to the defendant, not the insurance company.

Insurance defense firms concentrate a great deal of energy on billing their clients. Usually, these firms bill insurance companies on a monthly basis. These bills are itemized so that the insurance companies can see exactly what the firm has done in the past four weeks. This system, although more financially stable than the plaintiffs' firm, brings its own pressures. For instance, some insurance defense firms have been known to overbill insurance companies, or even charge for work that was not done. The financial temptation to bill for every possible legal activity sometimes becomes too great. Ethical insurance defense firms do not engage in such practices, but they often put great pressure on attorneys and paralegals to keep a strict accounting of the time they spend on individual cases to make sure that the firm is paid for the work that is actually done.

These are the two sides that are brought together in a personal injury suit. The plaintiff is represented by a capable attorney who will not earn her fee until the case ends successfully. The insurance defense attorney, on the other hand, makes the same amount of money per hour whether the case settles or not. Why then would the defendant's attorney ever seek to settle a case? Shouldn't all defense attorneys stand fast and never bargain in good faith? Certainly, the longer they work on the case, the more hours they can bill. But there are other considerations for insurance defense attorneys. For one thing, there are the ethical rules. If the defendant wishes to settle the case and reaching a settlement would be in the best interests of the client, the insurance company, and ultimately the overburdened court system, a lawyer will try to work out a settlement. There are other, more pragmatic concerns for the insurance defense attorney as well. If the attorney never seeks to settle cases and consistently loses cases at trial, the insurance company is likely to seek other counsel.

C. SETTLEMENT

When both sides to a suit seek to settle a case, they are actually engaging in a form of contract. One side promises to do something in exchange for a promise (or a payment) from the other side. We take an example from the Chumley case.

After extensively investigating the case, Mr. Chumley's attorney filed suit against the railroad company alleging negligence. Now, in an effort to bring the case to a conclusion, the plaintiff's attorney serves a settlement demand letter on the attorneys who represent the railroad company. The letter is set out in Figure 13-10.

For additional materials on the Chumley case, please see the appendix.

FIGURE 13-10	I. M. Lawyer, P.A.
Settlement Letter in the Chumley Case	444 Eaton Street

I. M. Lawyer, P.A.
444 Eaton Street
Beauty Spring, PL 28655
Phone: (828)439-4476
Fax: (828)439-4995 E-mail: lawyer@juno.com

April 24, 2003

Allnation Insurance Company
300 Dollar Street
Capitol City, PL 28888

Re: Claimant: Charles Chumley
     Insured: Charles Chumley
     Date of Loss: August 23, 2002
     Claim No.:   66563

Dear Sir or Madam:

I have been retained by Charles Chumley with respect to recovery of damages due to personal injuries suffered by Mr. Chumley in a train collision which occurred on August 23, 2002, and which involved your insured, National Railroad Company, Inc.

I have been directed to do everything that is necessary to present, settle, and collect this claim for damages.

I have evaluated this claim for settlement purposes. This letter and the enclosures are presented to you for the purpose of attempting to settle this claim.

FIGURE 13-10

(continued)

I. Liability

National Railroad Company owns and maintains a section of railroad tracks passing through the Town of Cling, Placid, at an intersection with Morgan Street in that town (Railroad Crossing # 2156E). There are no railroad crossing arms or warning devices at that intersection. This intersection had vegetation and trees obstructing and/or severely restricting the view of Morgan Street. National Railroad Company failed to maintain the vegetation and trees growing at this intersection right-of-way. The railroad company owed a duty of care to reasonably and safely maintain the tracks and the right-of-way surrounding the tracks at this intersection.

On August 23, 2002, at approximately 4:30 P.M., the Railroad's train struck Mr. Chumley's autombile as his automobile attempted to cross the tracks at Morgan Street. The train knocked Mr. Chumley's automobile off the road and pushed the car approximately 100 yards down the tracks from the point of impact. Mr. Chumley was severely injured and his wife, Julia, was killed.

II. General Damages

As a result of the incident, Mr. Chumley has suffered a number of injuries, endured medical examinations, and suffered short-term and long-term health conse-quences. Injuries resulting from the collision include a closed-head injury, fractured left tibia, internal hemorrhaging, hemo-pneumothorax, and severe abdominal trauma. In addition, he had five broken ribs and a left hip fracture. Seven days after the collision, Mr. Chumley had a tracheostomy placed. Infection set in there-after, causing acute and chronic bronchitis.

For several weeks after the collision, Mr. Chumley remained in a coma, with his breathing controlled by mechanical ventilation. It took several weeks after coming out of the coma for Mr. Chumley to reorient himself to his surroundings. Doctors noted that Mr. Chumley suffered from short-term memory loss.

In October 2002, Mr. Chumley was diagnosed with diabetes mellitus. He has no family history of this disease, but Mr. Chumley's doctors have determined that the severe trauma he received from the collision, to his head and abdomen, and the resulting injuries to both his brain and pancreas are the most likely cause of the diabetes mellitus.

III. Loss of Consortium

As a result of the collision, Mrs. Julia Chumley, Mr. Chumley's wife of many years, was killed. Because of her death, Mr. Chumley has lost his spousal relationship and her assistance in their family home. He and their children have lost her compan-ionship and affection forever.

IV. Enclosures

Enclosed are the following records and reports for your review:

1. Emergency Room Record, Mission Hospital
2. Operative Report, Mission Hospital
3. Medical Report from Dr. Dexter Cleckner, M.D., Barnes County Hospital
4. Medical Report from Dr. Melissa Walker, M.D., Thorne Rehabilitative Hospital

V. Settlement

If this case can be resolved within 30 days and without the expense of litigation, I would recommend settlement in the amount of $3,000,000.00.

Very truly yours,

_____

I. M. Lawyer
Placid State Bar # 006640

D. RELEASES

Release
To surrender or give up a legal right to sue another; the document or court filing in which this right is surrendered

Once a case is settled, the parties release one another from the claims in the lawsuit. A **release** is an official relinquishment of the plaintiff's claim against the defendant, in exchange for the money payment through the settlement. When a party signs a release, she is foregoing all possible actions she may have against the other. The end result of the settlement is a complete dismissal of the complaint, often in the form of a dismissal with prejudice (although it may be called by another name in some jurisdictions).

STATE FARM MUT. AUTO. INS. CO. v. SWARTZ
2006 WL 1118924, *6 (Ohio App. 5 Dist. 2006)

EDWARDS, J.
Defendant-appellant Melvin R. Swartz appeals from the June 7, 2005, Judgment Entry of the Richland County Court of Common Pleas which entered judgment in favor of plaintiff-appellee State Farm Mutual Automobile Insurance Company against appellant in the amount of $30,000.00.

Statement of the Facts and Case
This case arises from a motor vehicle accident which occurred on March 25, 2002, in Mansfield, Ohio. The accident involved three motor vehicles. One of the vehicles was driven by Billy J. Stamper. Stamper had an automobile insurance policy with State Farm Mutual Automobile Insurance Company [hereinafter appellee]. Appellant was driving one of the other vehicles. Appellant failed to stop his vehicle at a stop sign at an intersection and attempted to make a right-hand turn onto another street. Appellant's vehicle was struck from behind by a southbound vehicle (the third vehicle involved) operated by Paul E. Temple, II, a non-party. After the impact, appellant's vehicle went left of center and struck, head on, the motor vehicle operated by Stamper. According to appellee and Stamper, Stamper incurred serious bodily injury as a direct and proximate result of the impact. Stamper submitted a claim to State Farm. State Farm paid $30,000.00 to/and on behalf of Mr. Stamper for personal injuries.

On May 24, 2004, appellee filed a complaint in the Richland County Court of Common Pleas. Appellee sought payment from appellant for the sum paid to Stamper claiming a right to subrogation. Subsequently, appellant filed a motion to dismiss alleging that appellee had failed to join an indispensable party, namely, Temple. The trial court overruled appellant's motion by a Judgment Entry filed June 2, 2004.

The case proceeded to trial on May 31, 2005. During the trial, appellant filed a motion for directed verdict. In that motion, appellant contended that appellee failed to prove it had a right to subrogation because it failed to present Stamper's insurance policy or otherwise prove a right to subrogation of Stamper's claim. The trial court granted the motion for directed verdict on the issues of statutory and contractual subrogation. However, the trial court overruled the motion for directed verdict on the issue of equitable subrogation. Ultimately, the jury returned a verdict in favor of appellee in the amount of $30,000.00. The Judgment Entry on Jury Verdict was filed on June 7, 2005.

It is from the June 7, 2005, Judgment Entry that appellant appeals, raising the following assignments of error:

The Trial Court Erred in Not Directing the Verdict for the Defendant and Allowing This Case to Procedd [sic] to Jury Decision as the Plaintiff Produced No Evidence of a Contract or any Obligation on the Plaintiff's Part to Pay the Damages and Allowing Equitable Subrogation and the Plaintiff to Recover on That Inappropriate Claim.

In the third assignment of error, appellant argues that the trial court should have directed a verdict in favor of appellant because appellee failed to produce evidence of a contract or obligation on appellant's part to pay the damages suffered by Stamper and that appellee was not entitled to equitable subrogation. In other words, appellant contends that appellee failed to produce sufficient evidence to entitle appellee to a right of subrogation. We disagree.

As stated in assignment of error II, the standard of review for the grant or denial of a motion for directed verdict is as follows: whether there was probative evidence which, if believed, would permit reasonable minds to come to different conclusions as to the essential elements of the case, construing the evidence most strongly in favor of the non-movant. *Sanek v. Duracote Corp.* (1989), 43 Ohio St. 3d 169, 172, 539 N.E.2d 1114. This is a question of law, not one of fact. *Hargrove v. Tanner* (1990), 66 Ohio App. 3d 693, 695, 586 N.E.2d 141; *Vosgerichian v. Mancini Shah & Associates, et al.* (Feb. 29, 1996), Cuyahoga App. Nos. 68931 and 68943, 1996 WL 86684.

There are three distinct kinds of subrogation: legal (equitable), statutory and conventional (contractural). *Blue Cross & Blue Shield Mut. of Ohio v. Hrenko,* 72 Ohio St. 3d 120, 1995-Ohio-306, 647 N.E.2d 1358. The trial court sustained appellant's motion for directed verdict as to conventional (or contractual) subrogation and statutory subrogation. Specifically, the trial court found that appellee failed to provide proof that the contract of insurance between appellee and Stamper contained a subrogation clause and there was no applicable statutory right of subrogation. The trial court found that only an equitable (or legal) subrogation claim survived. Accordingly, the trial court's award of damages was premised upon an equitable subrogation claim.

Legal or equitable subrogation is a doctrine "under which, as a result of the payment of a debt by a person other than the principal debtor, there is a substitution of the former in the place of the creditor to whose rights he succeeds in relation to the obligation of the debtor, to the end that the burden of obligation be ultimately placed upon those to whom it primarily belongs, although in the recognition of the rights of others it may have been, for a time, borne by those who are only secondarily liable for the debt." *Maryland Cas. Co. v. Gough* (1946), 146 Ohio St. 305, 315, 65 N.E.2d 858. Equitable subrogation entitles an insurer to all the rights and remedies of the insured against a third party if: (1) the insurer indemnifies the insured for a loss occasioned by the third party; and (2) the loss is covered by the insurance policy.

Medical payment subrogation has been enforced under the doctrine of equitable subrogation. In *Allstate Ins. Co. v. LaCivita* (Aug. 9, 1996), Portage App. No. 94-P-0118, 1996 WL 494800, the court adopted the rationale that "the equitable right of subrogation is the legal effect of payment, and inures to the insurer without any formal assignment or any express stipulation to that effect in the policy." Id. at 6 (citing *State Farm Mut. Auto. Ins. Co. v. Scott* (Dec. 20, 1993), Clinton App. No. CA93-05-013); In accord, *Travelers Indemnity Co. v. Brooks* (1977), 60 Ohio App. 2d 37, 38-39, 395 N.E.2d 494. In *LaCivita,* the court held that because the insurer proved, through the testimony of the insured that it was her insurance company, that she made a claim for damages to the automobile, and that it paid the amount of damages to the vehicle, the doctrine of equitable subrogation was applicable.

We agree with the above cited decisions. Accordingly, we turn to the evidence to determine if appellee demonstrated an equitable claim. In this case, appellee presented testimony that Stamper had an automobile insurance policy from appellee, that Stamper made a claim for injuries sustained in the accident and that appellee paid for the damages arising from that injury. We find that appellee met its burden to prove an equitable subrogation claim.

For the foregoing reasons, appellant's third assignment of error is overruled.

The judgment of the Richland County Court of Appeals is affirmed.

GWIN, P.J. and FARMER, J. concur.

Judgment Entry

For the reasons stated in our accompanying Memorandum-Opinion on file, the judgment of the Richland County Court of Common Pleas is affirmed. Costs assessed to appellant.

Questions about the case:

1. What was the basis of the insurance company's action against Swartz?
2. What are the three distinct kinds of subrogation?
3. What is legal or equitable subrogation?
4. Where does the equitable right of subrogation come from?
5. Did the insurance company present enough evidence to justify receiving payment from Swartz for the medical payments it made on behalf of its insured? Explain.

SKILLS YOU NEED IN THE REAL WORLD

Deciphering Insurance Policies

Many times during your legal career, you will find yourself reading insurance policies. Insurance policies are hard to read because they are lengthy documents filled with obscure terms and often include confusing sub-parts and references. When reviewing an insurance policy, here is a five-step process to help you master the details.

1. Start with the Declarations Page

The declarations page is a separate sheet that contains basic information about the policy. Some of the information that you will find on this page includes:

- The insurance policy number (critical for any correspondence with the insurance company)
- The date the policy became effective
- The named insured
- The vehicles covered

2. Next, Review the Coverage

Once you have looked over and noted the basic identifying information, your next stop should be the information provided about coverage. A sample is provided in Figure 13-11.

3. Read Through the Definitions

Most insurance policies contain a section entitled "definitions." This section specifically defines any important term used in the policy. If you wish to see how the insurance company defines "business purpose," you can find their definition

Coverage	Limits	
Liability Bodily Injury Each Person/Each Accident	$300,000/$300,000	**FIGURE 13-11** **Coverage Provisions from a Sample Declarations Page**
Property Damage Each Accident	$100,000	
Medical Payments Each Person	$1,000	
Combined UM/UIM Coverage Bodily Injury Liability Each Person/Each Accident	$300,000/$300,000	
Combined UM/UIM Coverage Property Damage	$100,000	

here. Definitions can become crucial in any litigation with an insurance policy. Remember that most jurisdictions construe any ambiguities in the policy against the insurance company, so if there is a problem with a definition, better to know about it sooner rather than later.

4. Review the Limits of Liability

This important provision is where the insurance company spells out the conditions under which it will not be required to pay out damages. Review this section carefully to make sure that the accident or the people involved in your cases are not excluded under the terms of the policy. You should also confirm that there are no actions taken by the parties involved in the case that put them outside the insurance policy's coverage. A common example is the use of alcohol or drugs that caused the collision. Such behavior is frequently excluded from coverage in most insurance policies.

5. Confirm What Is Covered

Finally, go through the section marked "Insuring Agreement" or "Policy Agreement" and note exactly what the insurance policy does cover. For instance, under the Medical Payments Coverage section, does the company pay for acupuncture, chiropractic, or other categories of medical treatment? How does the insurance company limit or define medical fees? All of these points are critical in applying the insurance policy to the particular case.

 THE LIFE OF A PARALEGAL

I worked as a computer programs analyst for years before getting laid off and deciding to go back to school to become a paralegal. I went to work for a small firm almost as soon as I started my classes. I was surprised at how different a law office is from other types of offices. My biggest problem was that my "secretarial skills"—for want of a better term—weren't what they could have been. I had to learn some of the basics, like the right way to take a phone message. When I first started answering the phone, I'd just jot down the person's name and telephone number. When I handed it to the attorney, he'd say, "What's this about?" After that, I learned that you had to get more information. I had to learn how to type up letters and motions from a tape machine. The attorney I worked with just used a tape recorder. He'd dictate everything and I'd have to type it up from the tapes.

The firm I work for handles just about everything, although we concentrate on personal injury cases. My particular specialty—learned through a lot of trial and error—is getting medical records. Contacts are everything when you're trying to get records. I think I was lucky when I first started doing it because I was honest with people. I'd call them up and say, "Hey, I don't know what I'm doing. I'm new, so forgive me if I mess up." Once I got a name, like someone at the hospital records department, whenever I called back, I'd always ask for that person. I still do that. If I'm not sure about exactly what I'm doing when I call someone up, I'll just tell them. Most people are really friendly to you. Once I get the records ordered, I keep track of them. I get them all organized and filed so that the attorney can go through them later and get what he needs out of them. I'll sift through them all and find out exactly what insurance paid and what the client paid. I'll summarize all of this information for ease of reference and make sure that the attorney sees it.

The way I see the role of the paralegal, I'm here to free up some of the attorney's time so that he can make more money. The more money he makes, the better it is for all of us. That's how I approach everything I do, from answering the phones to organizing medical records. What can I do that will make this easier on the attorney, and free him up to get some more clients so that he can keep paying me?

Leah Laidley, Paralegal

ETHICAL ISSUES FOR THE PARALEGAL: INSURANCE FRAUD

Studies have shown that one out of three automobile insurance claims involves some type of fraud.[8] Fraudulent insurance claims account for 10-20 percent of the average premium. Insurance fraud arrests have also increased dramatically over the past three years and cost the economy over $80 billion a year.[9] All of these factors point to a disturbing reality: If you work for a personal injury firm for any length of time, some of your clients will engage in insurance fraud.

Defrauding an insurance company appears to be one of the so-called victimless crimes. After all, who is going to feel sorry for a large corporation? Policyholders may sometimes feel that they are entitled to some return on the premiums they have been paying for years. Financial pressures may also figure prominently in the policyholder's decision to commit fraud. How can you, as a paralegal, avoid becoming involved in insurance fraud? Here are some telltale signs:

- The client continually inflates, exaggerates, or overstates her losses
- The amount of loss seems to be out of line with the visual damages
- The client has had numerous other claims with other insurance companies

The good news for a paralegal is that the one thing you can do to avoid having the firm implicated in an insurance fraud case is the one thing you should be doing already: documenting the file. You should insist on proper documentation of every claim. No matter what loss the client claims he has suffered, you must have documentation of the extent of the loss and out-of-pocket expenses. You will need this information when you prepare for settlement anyway; getting it will also avoid any claim that you or your firm is involved in an insurance scam.

If you suspect that one of your clients is attempting to defraud the insurance company, report your suspicions to the attorney immediately. This may be a client that the firm would be better off not representing.

Chapter Summary

Insurance is a complicated topic and involves many aspects of law. Insurance policies themselves are actually contracts between the insurance company and the insured in which the insurance company promises to indemnify or reimburse the insured for losses covered by the policy in exchange for the insured's premium payments. Insurance coverage is a crucial issue in personal injury cases for several reasons. For one, the insurance policy's monetary limits often determine the size of the plaintiff's ultimate award in a case. For another, the insurance company has, among its other obligations, the duty to provide a legal defense to an insured who is being sued.

Interpreting how insurance law applies to a given factual situation is often difficult. For instance, in some cases, individual insurance polices can be combined, or "stacked," to provide additional coverage to a person who has suffered injury. In other situations, "no-fault" insurance may be state law. Under no-fault, the insurance company pays a claim without first determining who was the cause of the injury. Automobile insurance is further complicated by the fact that all states have statutes requiring that motorists possess at least a minimum amount of coverage before they are allowed to drive. These statutes not only regulate drivers; they also regulate insurance companies. The insurance industry is one of the most heavily regulated industries in the country, and this regulation applies not only to how individual policies are drafted, but also to the type of exclusions that an insurance company, is allowed to make. An exclusion is a listed reason why the insurance company will not pay a claim. Typical exclusions include intentional destructive acts by the insured and alcohol or other drug use.

Finally, this chapter also explored the world of plaintiffs' and insurance defense law firms. These firms have very different approaches to cases that are not only the product of the different ways that they are compensated, but stem from different demands placed on them by their clients. Insurance defense firms, for instance, are hired by insurance companies to defend policyholders who have been sued. They are, therefore, paid by the insurance company, but owe their legal duty to the insured.

Web Sites

■ **ABA Tort, Trial and Insurance Practice Section**
http://www.abanet.org/tips/home.html

■ **New York State Department of Insurance**
http://www.ins.state.ny.us/puborder.htm

■ **Lloyd's of London**
http://www.lloyds.com

■ **Findlaw.com**
http://www.findlaw.com (click on search box and enter "insurance,"
"declarations page," or "uninsured motorist coverage")

■ **Business Journal — World Insurance News**
http://www.businessjournal.com/s/insurance/

Forms and Court Documents

Complaint form — insured sues insurance company for failure to defend
under insurance policy.

In this pleading, Stanley Blue, the engineer of the train that struck Charles
Chumley, is seeking a declaratory judgment from the court establishing that
the insurance company is required, by the terms of the insurance, to provide a
legal defense to him.

STATE OF PLACID	IN THE SUPERIOR COURT
COUNTY OF BARNES	FILE NUMBER: _____

Stanley Blue,	)
Petitioner	)
	)
vs.	)
	)
Bay Rock Insurance Company, Inc.,	)
Defendant	)

Petition for Declaratory Judgment

1.

At all times mentioned, Petitioner Stanley Blue (hereafter "Petitioner") was a
resident of Barnes County, Placid, and an employee of Railroad Company.

2.

Defendant Bay Rock Insurance Company, Inc. (hereafter "Defendant") is and
at all times mentioned was a corporation organized, existing, and doing business under and by virtue of the laws of this state.

3.

On May 5, last year, Defendant issued to Railroad Company an accident and
liability policy (hereafter "the insurance policy") that insured the Railroad
Company and "all of its employees" against liability or loss resulting from
bodily injury or death caused by any person and resulting from the use of the
Railroad's equipment.

4.

The accident and liability policy was issued and became effective on May 5, last year, and remained in effect until midnight, May 4, this year.

5.

The insurance policy, a copy of which is attached to this Complaint as Petitioner's Exhibit "A," provided that the Defendant would defend in the name and on behalf of Petitioner any suits which might at any time be brought against the company or its employees on account of personal injuries or death resulting from the operation or use of railroad equipment, including train locomotives such as the one Petitioner was operating. The policy states the Defendant's obligation to defend, at its own cost, all suits brought against the Railroad Company or its employees, on account of injuries or death resulting from the use of railroad equipment. The policy further provided that the Defendant had exclusive control of the defense of any suit brought against the Railroad Company or its employees for injuries specified in the policy.

6.

On August 23, last year, Petitioner was acting as engineer and operator of a locomotive engine and three cars (hereafter "the train"), two of which were carrying cargo, the remaining car being empty. As the train approached the intersection of the railroad track and Morgan Street, Town of Cling, State of Placid, Charles Chumley was driving his car south, towards the intersection of the railroad line with Morgan Street. As the train entered the intersection, it struck the car driven by Charles Chumley. As a result of the collision, Charles Chumley received severe personal injuries and the other occupant of the vehicle, Mrs. Julia Chumley, was killed.

7.

Charles Chumley eventually brought suit against the Railroad Company alleging negligence on the part of the Railroad Company in maintaining the intersection and in the operation of the train on the day of the incident. Petitioner Stanley Blue was named as a defendant in this action as well. A copy of Chumley v. National Railroad Company, et al., is provided as Petitioner's Exhibit "B" to this Complaint.

8.

Petitioner gave proper notice of the collision to his employer and proper notice to Defendant Insurance Company, as required under the terms of the insurance policy.

9.

On April 1 of this year, Defendant Insurance Company retained the services of Sterling and Silver, Attorneys at Law, to represent the Railroad Company in the action filed by Charles Chumley. However, Defendant Insurance did not provide legal counsel for Petitioner. In a letter dated April 4 of this year, Defendant Insurance Company notified Petitioner that it had no obligation to the Petitioner and would therefore provide no legal representation for the Petitioner in the action filed by Charles Chumley.

10.

Defendant's failure to provide legal counsel violated the insurance policy's duty to defend the Petitioner.

WHEREFORE, Petitioner respectfully requests that the court enter judgment declaring that:

1. The insurance policy issued to Railroad Company provides coverage for the Petitioner in this action, and
2. The Defendant, by the terms of said insurance policy, is obligated to provide a legal counsel and services per the insurance agreement, to represent the Petitioner in the underlying action, to wit: Chumley v. National Railroad Company, Stanley Blue, and Town of Cling.

Respectfully submitted,

This the _____ day of _____, 2003

_____

Susan Vengeance
Attorney for Petitioner, Stanley Blue
State Bar No. 12345

Key Terms

Exclusion	Policy	Stacking
Fiduciary	Premium	Subrogation
Indemnify	Release	Thermography
No-fault insurance		

Review Questions

1 How did the insurance industry develop over time? What impact does this history have on modern cases?
2 List and discuss the parties to an insurance policy. What responsibilities does each of these parties have?
3 How does insurance affect a civil suit?
4 What is an insurance premium?
5 How does an insurance company owe fiduciary duty to an insured?
6 How do states regulate the insurance industry?
7 Why do states require minimum automobile liability coverage for motorists?
8 Periodically, states enact new statutes requiring that insurance policies be readable or understandable. Why are such statutes necessary? Why don't insurance companies take the initiative and make their policies understandable without such statutes?

9   Explain the two components of liability coverage.
10 Explain the basic features of an automobile insurance policy.
11 What types of coverage are common in automobile insurance policies?
12 What is uninsured motorist coverage?
13 Compare and contrast uninsured motorist coverage with underinsured motorist coverage.
14 Explain the insurance company's "duty to defend."
15 List and explain the various parts of a typical insurance policy.
16 Explain subrogation.
17 Explain stacking insurance policies.
18 How does no-fault insurance differ from regular auto insurance?
19 What are the advantages of no-fault insurance?
20 What are some of the typical exclusions found in insurance policies?
21 Why are exclusions allowed in policies?
22 How does insurance coverage affect settlement?
23 When can a plaintiff use the discovery process to find out the limits of a defendant's policy?
24 How do plaintiffs' firms differ from insurance defense firms?
25 How are plaintiffs' firms and insurance defense firms compensated?
26 What is a settlement letter?
27 What is a release?
28 What steps should you follow when reviewing an insurance policy?

Applying What You Have Learned

1   According to one source, almost 15 percent of the average insured's premium is spent on bodily injury claims that are frivolous or fraudulent. Why is this so? Is there some way to correct the system to eliminate such claims?
2   Ted has been injured in an automobile collision. Another driver, Clark Collision, rear-ended Ted's car while Ted was stopped at a red light. The accident occurred on May 15 of this year. Ted's car was totaled. The car has a Blue Book value of $8,000. Ted's medical injuries were relatively minor: $3,000. He had arthroscopic surgery performed on his knee. Here is a summary of his medical bills:

Doctors' medical service	$1,500
Civil Rehabilitation Services	$1,500

Based on this information, prepare a settlement letter patterned on Figure 13-10, the Settlement Letter in the Chumley Case.

3   Does your state use the no-fault insurance system? What is the mandatory minimum coverage permissible in your state?

Endnotes

[1]Lawrence Friedman, A History of American Law, New York, Simon & Schuster, 1978, p. 476.

[2]322 U.S. 533 (1944).

[3]*Trinity Universal Ins. Co. v. Willrich,* 13 Wash. 2d 263, 124 P.2d 950 (1942).

[4]*Birth Center v. St. Paul Companies, Inc.,* 567 Pa. 386, 787 A.2d 376 (2001).

[5]Joint Economic Committee, Auto-Choice; Executive Summary (1998).

[6]Am. Jur. Insurance §633.

[7]Insurance §559, Am. Jur. 2d.

[8]Insurance Research Council, 1996.

[9]Insurance Research Council, 2001.

Fraud, Misrepresentation, and Business Torts

Chapter Objectives

- Explain how a civil action for fraud is brought

- Define negligent misrepresentation

- Detail the elements required to prove a negligent misrepresentation suit

- Explain the tort of interference with contract

- Define the concepts of dram shop liability and worker's compensation

 **THE SHAREHOLDER'S SUIT**

In the 1990s and early 2000s, the End-Run Corporation was a high flyer. Its stock price, which had remained around $20 per share in the 1980s, rose to over $100 per share in the last few years. End-Run posted huge profits and proclaimed a rosy future. End-Run executives received huge, and apparently well-earned, seven-figure salaries and a host of perquisites. Then a reporter for the local newspaper broke a story claiming that the "huge profits" of End-Run were actually part of a corporate scheme to fool stockholders and the public. In fact, End-Run was seriously in debt, but had disguised the fact by clever (and illegal) accounting practices. Tom, who owns 1,000 End-Run shares, has just walked into our office. He wants to sue End-Run for what he says is outright fraud. Does he have a case? If so, what type of action can our firm file against End-Run? Before we can analyze his case, we need a solid understanding of the law of fraud, deceit, and negligent misrepresentation.

 ## INTRODUCTION

In this chapter we explore the various actions associated with fraud, deceit, and misrepresentation. We also examine the types of torts associated with business transactions, such as consumer actions and interference with contract rights.

Everyone knows that lying is something to be avoided. However, when does a lie, or a knowing misrepresentation, become actionable in tort law? Obviously not everyone who has told a lie has been sued. In fact, most lies are not actionable at all. However, under certain circumstances, a falsehood does give a person a cause of action against another person.

An outright lie can give rise to several possible actions. For instance, if the lie is in the context of a contractual agreement, this can provide the basis for a breach of contract suit. If the lie is unintentional, or made without concern for the actual truth, the plaintiff can sue for negligent misrepresentation. However, when and under what circumstances does a statement, or an action, become a misrepresentation? We begin with the simpler issue of fraud before moving into the more complex world of negligent misrepresentation.

 ## FRAUD

The problem with words such as "fraud" and "deceit" is that they have been overused; their precise, legal meanings have been diluted over time to the point that they are almost incapable of an exact definition.

Fraud is a word that lends itself to many possible definitions. People have been lying, cheating, and scamming each other forever. A basic definition of fraud could be a deceitful action against another to gain some form of advantage. Fraud includes outright lying, deceit, surprise, trickery, false claims, and the whole panoply of treachery practiced by human beings. While it may be difficult to define what fraud is, we can certainly say what fraud is not. Fraud is an intentional action. There is no negligent fraud. Fraud is an affirmative action and requires knowledge on the part of the person carrying it out that he is defrauding another. Later we discuss the tort of negligent misrepresentation, but for fraud, the plaintiff must show the defendant's intent. Fraud can occur when a person knowingly makes a false statement or when a person conceals or withholds a fact.

Example: One afternoon, Mary goes out shopping for antiques. She approaches John, who is standing beside a lovely nineteenth-century armoire with a "for sale" sign taped to it. Mary asks, "How much?" John responds, "How much are you offering?" She looks the armoire over again and offers $300. John says, "Okay." Mary has a friend help her load the armoire into her truck. Just as she is about to pull away, an irate man runs up to her and accuses her of theft. Mary explains that she bought the armoire from John, who has now disappeared. The irate man says that he is the rightful owner and that he did not intend to sell the armoire. Later, when Mary catches up with John and asks for her money back, John says, "I never told that you that I didn't own it." Can Mary sue John for fraud?

Answer: Yes. Although John did not make an actual statement claiming that he had the right to sell the armoire, he did withhold the fact that he did not have that right. Under these facts, withholding a fact is equivalent to making a false statement. Both are actionable.

Sidebar

"Fraud, actual and constructive, is so multiform as to admit of no rules or definitions. 'It is, indeed, a part of equity doctrine not to define it,' says Lord Hardwicke, lest the craft of men should find a way of committing fraud which might escape such a rule or definition."[1]

Fraud involves any act (or omission) that conceals the breach of a legal duty or material fact. This act must cause injury to the plaintiff or give the defendant an unjustified or unconscionable advantage.

ISSUE AT A GLANCE

A. PROVING FRAUD

To prove fraud, the plaintiff must show the following:

1. The defendant made a representation of a material fact or concealed a fact
2. The representation was false
3. The defendant knew the representation was false
4. The defendant made the representation with the intent that the plaintiff would rely on it
5. The plaintiff's reliance on the representation was reasonable under the circumstances
6. The plaintiff suffered injury from his reliance on the representation.

One of the key elements involved in proof of fraud is that the representation involved a **material fact.** This is a fact that is crucial to the parties' understanding of the transaction or a key point of negotiation. In the example provided above, John's lack of ownership of the armoire was a material fact. It was a central point of the negotiations and an assumption that Mary made based on John's behavior. Many states have enacted statutes spelling out exactly what is a material fact. In fact, many refer to a misrepresentation of a "material past or present fact." A material past fact is simply a statement about a past fact, such as a statement detailing exactly where the armoire was manufactured and how it has been treated by previous owners. A material present fact refers to John's ownership of the armoire.

Material fact
A fact that is basic to a contract, one that the parties consider to be an essential ingredient of the negotiations

FIGURE 14-1

Civil Bench and Jury Trials in State Courts

Seventy percent of civil trials involved individuals suing other individuals or businesses; 40% of trials involved one plaintiff and one defendant

The most common civil trials involved an individual suing either another individual (42%) or a business (28%). Businesses sued other businesses in about 10% of all civil trials. In 2% of all civil trials, a government entity initiated the lawsuit.

Excluding class action lawsuits, almost 86,000 litigants were involved in general civil trials in 2005. Forty percent (10,800) of all civil trials disposed of in state courts in 2005 involved one plaintiff and one defendant. Almost half (47%) of all civil bench and jury trials in 2005 had multiple defendants, and more than a quarter (29%) had multiple plaintiffs.

Plaintiffs won in the majority of tort and contract trials

Plaintiffs won in more than half (56%) of all general civil trials concluded in state courts. In 2005, a higher percentage of plaintiffs won in contract (66%) than in tort (52%) cases.

Among tort trials, plaintiffs were most likely to win in cases involving an animal attack (75%), followed by motor vehicle accident (64%), asbestos (55%), and intentional tort (52%) cases. Plaintiffs had the lowest percentage of wins in medical malpractice trials (23%), product liability trials that did not involve asbestos (20%), and false arrest or imprisonment trials (16%), compared to plaintiffs in other tort cases.

In contract cases, plaintiffs won in the majority of trials for all case types except subrogation (28%), which involves an insurance company seeking to recover the amount paid on behalf of a client. Mortgage foreclosure cases, in which the plaintiff was either a mortgage company or other financial lending institution, had the highest percentage of plaintiff winners (89%) of all tort and contract cases in 2005.

Judges hear business litigation more often than juries

Civil cases tried before juries and judges in state courts differed in terms of the litigants, plaintiff win rates, damage awards, and case processing times. Bench trials (57%) had a higher percentage of business litigants than jury trials (39%) and were likely to be decided in less time than jury trials. Judges were more likely than juries to find for plaintiffs. Plaintiffs won in 68% of bench trials, compared to about 54% of jury trials.

The median damage awards in 2005 were statistically similar for both jury and bench trials overall. Contract cases tried before a jury ($74,000), however, had significantly higher median final awards than contract cases decided by a judge ($25,000).

Individuals accounted for the majority of plaintiffs in tort trials; businesses were more heavily represented as plaintiffs in contract disputes

In 2005, individuals accounted for the largest percentage of plaintiffs (81%) and defendants (50%) in civil trials. This held true in both tort and real property trials. For contract trials, the majority of defendants were businesses (58%). Also in contract trials, a larger percentage of plaintiffs were businesses (43%) than in tort (4%) or real property (9%) cases.

Real property cases involved the highest percentage of government plaintiffs (26%) and defendants (11%). A hospital or medical company was the plaintiff in less than 1% and the defendant in less than 6% of all civil bench and jury trials in 2005.

Civil Bench and Jury Trials in State Courts, 2005, Bureau of Justice Statistics, U.S. Department of Justice.

■ Any false statement that is reasonable and one upon which the plaintiff relies	**FIGURE 14-2**
■ A willful, intentional misstatement that gives the defendant an unfair advantage over the plaintiff	**Activities That Are Classified as Fraud**

■ Failing to fulfill a promise that was made in good faith	■ Exaggerations or "puffing" ■ Opinions (in most situations)	**FIGURE 14-3**
		Activities That Are Not Classified as Fraud

It is not fraud to make the types of statements we commonly associate with selling techniques. For instance, it is not a material misrepresentation to claim that a car is "the best car in the world." On the other hand, it is a material misrepresentation to claim that the car has never been in an accident when it actually has been. "Puffing" and other exaggerations are par for the course in a transaction and most buyers do not take such claims seriously.

It is difficult to come up with a solid definition of a material fact that will work in all situations. Suffice to say that a material fact is one of those facts that would make or break the deal between the parties.

Example: John and Ted have decided to open a craft store together. They have extensively negotiated the partnership deal between them. For instance, the partnership takes effect on January 1 of next year and each man will contribute $20,000 to the business. Both will work a minimum of 40 hours per week at the business. John prefers to work on Tuesdays and Thursday evenings, but he is flexible about other times. Ted is a morning person and plans on being at the store every morning at 8 A.M. Which of these facts is a material fact and which is not?

Answer: All of the contractual details concerning monetary contribution, the date that the partnership takes effect, and how many hours each man must work at the business. The non-material facts include each man's stated preference about when he will actually work. Their preferences are not essential components to the contract and therefore they are not material facts.

Sidebar

Deceit is considered to be a lesser form of fraud. It can be any false representation that misleads another person and is often used in the same context as fraud.

B. ALLEGING FRAUD IN THE COMPLAINT

When a complaint alleges fraud, the plaintiff must present enough detail in the complaint to show material facts, how these facts were untrue, and specific instances (times, places, and contents) of false representations.[2] Simply stating that the plaintiff was defrauded will not satisfy the requirements of notice pleading in most states.[3]

In most jurisdictions, fraud must be proven by **clear and convincing evidence.** This essentially means that someone alleging fraud has a higher standard to meet than allegations made in other types of civil cases (in which preponderance of the evidence is usually enough).

Clear and convincing evidence
A level of proof higher than mere preponderance of the evidence. In most civil trials preponderance of the evidence is sufficient.

C. LIMITATIONS ON FRAUD ACTIONS

In some jurisdictions, omission of a material fact will not support a claim for fraud unless the defendant had a legal obligation to disclose it. Usually, the obligation to disclose a fact is limited to those with fiduciary responsibilities. As we have already seen, a fiduciary is a person or corporation that has a legal and ethical duty to act in the best interests of another. When a fiduciary fails to disclose a material fact, this failure can be the basis of a fraud claim. It can also be the basis for other actions as well, including negligent misrepresentation.[4]

D. FRAUD AND CRIMINAL LAW

Civil actions for fraud are complicated by the fact that what makes a particular situation actionable under civil law also makes it punishable under criminal law. Fraud is a form of theft under criminal law. As a form of theft, fraud involves proof by the prosecution that the defendant used trickery, deceit, or deliberate falsehood to deprive the victim of his property. There is a reason that these elements sound similar to the elements of a civil action for fraud. The common law crime of fraud and the tort of fraud developed from the same legal source. In fact, several centuries ago, there was no clear distinction between civil and criminal actions. Fraud was fraud. Nowadays, that same confusion between civil and criminal actions still haunts any allegation of fraud. For instance, in the scenario we used to open the discussion of fraud — Mary's purchase of furniture she wrongfully believed was owned by John — are John's actions criminal or civil? Actually, they are both. Mary has a civil action against John for her monetary loss — the money she paid him believing that he was the owner — and the state also has an action against John for defrauding Mary of her property, namely, her money.

As we saw in Chapter 1, civil actions and criminal actions can be based on the same facts, but the litigation in each case proceeds independently of one another. The same witnesses may testify about the same events, but the end result of the two cases will be different. In the criminal case, John faces jail time and a fine. In the civil case, he faces a court order forcing him to repay Mary for her out-of-pocket expenses (and any other damages the court deems proper).

Although the topic of fraud has a great deal of potential for both civil and criminal actions, negligent misrepresentation does not. That action is usually a civil action only.

 **NEGLIGENT MISREPRESENTATION**

In many ways, negligent misrepresentation resembles an action for fraud, with one important difference. In fraud, the plaintiff must show that the defendant's false statement was made knowingly. In negligent misrepresentation, the plaintiff may simply show that the defendant was reckless or negligent in representing the truth to the plaintiff.[5] The important distinction between negligent misrepresentation and fraud is that a person may be liable for a statement made in good faith, but with careless disregard for its truth, under negligent misrepresentation, but will not be liable for the same statement under fraud. In many ways, this tort allows a cause of action for a simple misstatement. As such, most courts impose a higher standard of proof in such cases. This higher standard places more emphasis on the plaintiff's allegations.

Although most negligence cases do not require any relationship between the parties, negligent misrepresentation cases often do. After all, the plaintiff must prove that he relied on a statement by the defendant and that this reliance was reasonable under the circumstances. Often this proof of reasonable reliance springs from the fact that the plaintiff and defendant knew one another, that they did business together, or that there was some other relationship between them that made the plaintiff's actions understandable.

A. THE RESTATEMENT POSITION ON NEGLIGENT MISREPRESENTATION

The Restatement of Torts provides valuable guidance on the question of negligent misrepresentation. The Restatement position covers situations in which a person gives false information in the course of his business, profession, or employment. See Figure 14-4.

The Restatement makes it clear that when a person's only loss is monetary, the court should adopt a more "restricted rule of liability" than the standard used in fraud cases.[6] Many states have adopted the Restatement's position on negligent misrepresentation.

(1) One who, in the course of his business, profession, or employment, or in any other transaction in which he has a pecuniary interest, supplies false information for the guidance of others in their business transactions, is subject to liability for pecuniary loss caused to them by their justifiable reliance upon the information, if he fails to exercise reasonable care or competence in obtaining or communicating the information.
 	
 (2) Except as stated in Subsection (3), the liability stated in Subsection (1) is limited to loss suffered
    (a) by the person or one of a limited group of persons for whose benefit and guidance he intends to supply the information or knows that the recipient intends to supply it; and
    (b) through reliance upon it in a transaction that he intends the information to influence or knows that the recipient so intends or in a substantially similar transaction.
 	
 (3) The liability of one who is under a public duty to give the information extends to loss suffered by any of the class of persons for whose benefit the duty is created, in any of the transactions in which it is intended to protect them.*

FIGURE 14-4

Negligent Misrepresentation Under the Restatement of Torts

*Restatement (Second) of Torts §552.

FIGURE 14-5

Punitive Damages in Civil Trials, 2005

Punitive damages were awarded to 5% of plaintiff winners in general civil trials in 2005

Punitive damages are awarded to punish and deter the defendant. Punitive damages were sought in 13% of the approximately 14,000 general civil trials with plaintiff winners in 2005. Plaintiffs were awarded punitive damages in 700 of the 14,000 trials (5%).

The median overall punitive damage amount awarded to plaintiff winners was $64,000. About a quarter (27%) of the punitive damage awards in 2005 were over $250,000 and 13% were $1 million or more. Of the approximately 450 contract cases in which punitive damages were awarded, plaintiffs were awarded punitive amounts of $250,000 or more in 40% of the trials.

Tortious interference ($6,900,000) and medical malpractice ($2,800,000) cases had among the highest median punitive damage awards for specific contract and tort case types. During 2005, there were less than 20 of each case type in which punitive damages were awarded. Among the case types in which punitive damages were awarded most frequently — intentional torts, fraud, and buyer plaintiff cases — the median punitive damage awards were $100,000 or less.

Civil Bench and Jury Trials in State Courts, 2005, Bureau of Justice Statistics, U.S. Department of Justice.

B. ELEMENTS OF NEGLIGENT MISREPRESENTATION

Negligent misrepresentation consists of the following elements:

1   The defendant, in the course of his business or profession, makes a false statement
2   Believing that the statement is true
3   But without reasonable grounds for his belief or in reckless disregard of the truth
4   The plaintiff suffered a financial loss because of his reasonable reliance on this false statement

C. TRADITIONAL TORT ANALYSIS FOR NEGLIGENT MISREPRESENTATION

Negligent misrepresentation is a type of negligence, so the traditional tort analysis applies. In the next sections, we address the issues of the four-part test for negligence cases: duty, breach, causation, and damages.

1. DUTY AND BREACH OF DUTY

Privity
The direct relationship between the parties to a contract that arises from their involvement in creating the contract

Duty in the context of negligent misrepresentation usually arises out of a relationship between the parties. Unlike other types of negligence, negligent misrepresentation resembles contractual actions more than personal injury cases. In contract cases, the right of the parties to sue one another is based on their contractual relationship. In order to sue, the parties must be in **privity** with one another. Because of this, actions for negligent misrepresentation are much closer to contract actions than they are to personal injury cases.

An exception to this general rule of privity between the parties is for businesses that supply information as their product. Businesses such as accounting or research firms owe a duty to exercise reasonable care and diligence in the way that they obtain their information and pass it along to others, even when these others are not in a direct, contractual relationship with them. As a corollary to this approach, however, most courts construe those who would reasonably rely on such a report to a small group, that is, the clients and those others who would foreseeably rely on the information provided.

The standard of care imposed on defendants in negligent misrepresentation cases is to use reasonable care in making statements. When a defendant has a business relationship with another person and supplies him with false information, either through incompetence or disregard of the truth, the defendant has violated his duty to the plaintiff. However, when the information is provided to another person with whom there is no business relationship, such as a favor to a friend, there is no duty to use reasonable care.

2. CAUSATION

The plaintiff's reliance on the information provided by the defendant must be reasonable for the element of causation to be satisfied. If the plaintiff's actions are unreasonable, the defendant can claim that the plaintiff contributed to his own damages. Contributory or comparative negligence is as much of a defense to the tort of negligent misrepresentation as it is for other types of negligence.

However, as we have seen in other torts, the defendant takes the plaintiff as he finds him. Therefore, a plaintiff with slow mental abilities or one who is suffering from a particular handicap is held to the standard of a similarly situated plaintiff. This standard is imposed to protect the more vulnerable elements of society from others who would prey on their disabilities.[8]

3. DAMAGES

Payment of damages for negligent misrepresentation raises several interesting questions. For example, in our discussion of typical automobile negligence cases, the plaintiff was entitled to compensatory damages, such as pain and suffering, and special damages, such as medical bills. In those cases, the plaintiff was also entitled to punitive damages. In many ways, the damages available for negligent misrepresentation are more limited. According to the Restatement of Torts, the following types of damages are available in negligent misrepresentation cases:

> Compensatory damages for monetary losses calculated as:
> The difference between the purchase price of what the plaintiff received and the loss suffered from his reliance on the faulty information provided by the defendant.

In most jurisdictions, the plaintiff is entitled to any or all of the following types of damages:

- Fees associated with applications, licenses, permits, etc.
- Commission fees paid to real estate brokers, agents, or others who are paid on a commission basis
- Monetary difference between a loan that the plaintiff thought he was going to receive and the loan he finally received
- Out-of-pocket expenses associated with finding, obtaining, and receiving a new service
- In some cases, punitive damages, if the plaintiff can show malice on the part of the defendant
- Attorney's fees for bringing an action against the defendant (when defendant acts with malice)

D. OPINIONS AND NEGLIGENT MISREPRESENTATION

Under negligent misrepresentation, an opinion may be grounds for a cause of action, but only when the opinion is presented as based on some fact. For instance, many jurisdictions apply the rule that a statement from a loan officer that the loan can be obtained is a mere opinion and does not provide a basis for a cause of action in negligent misrepresentation.

Example: Ted has applied for a loan at the local bank. Jack, the loan officer, looks over his paperwork and then tells Ted that the bank's underwriters must approve the loan. Ted asks, "How does it look?" Jack responds, "I think it looks pretty good."

Ted goes on a buying spree, believing that he will soon have the loan proceeds to pay for the items. Jack calls him later in the week with some bad news. "I'm afraid your loan application was turned down." Ted is furious and wants to sue the bank, and Jack, for negligent misrepresentation. Does he have a case?

Answer: No. Jack's statement to Ted was an opinion and was not apparently based on any fact. How could we change the scenario to give Ted a cause of action? Jack could make a statement such as, "I can tell you that they are going to approve this application. I've seen a dozen just like it this week and every one of them was approved." When a statement is expressed as though it were a fact, the statement becomes actionable under negligent misrepresentation.[9] (For a similar situation, see the case excerpt.)

Negligent misrepresentation is also authorized in situations in which the speaker has special knowledge or expertise in a certain area, and the speaker makes a statement that a reasonable person would rely on.

Example: Arthur is a certified public accountant and has been asked to review the finances of XYZ Corporation. After several weeks, he issues a report stating that XYZ Corporation is in excellent financial health and poised for a major expansion. Myron, who is one of XYZ's employees and owns a few shares of the company's stock, decides to use his life savings to purchase 1,500 additional shares of XYZ stock as a way of beefing up his retirement holdings.

Unfortunately, two days after Myron purchases the stock, the company announces that it is filing for bankruptcy. Arthur's report is filled with inaccuracies. Myron sues Arthur. Does he have a cause of action?

Answer: Yes. Many jurisdictions are now allowing a cause of action in such a case for anyone who could foreseeably rely on a CPA's report on the financial health of a company. Myron is an employee and a stockholder. He falls into that category.[10]

E. NEGLIGENT MISREPRESENTATION VERSUS MISTAKE

Where do we draw the line between a simple mistake and an action that can be characterized as negligent misrepresentation? In some ways, they are very similar. After all, a party may be relieved of contractual obligations if he can show either negligent misrepresentation or mistake. However, the similarities end there. "Mistake" as a defense is available when both parties have made some error about the contract. When only one party makes a mistake about the contract, the contract continues to have legal effect.[11] Negligent misrepresentation, on the other hand, is made by only one party and, when proved, gives the other party the right to void the contract.

F. PLEADING NEGLIGENT MISREPRESENTATION

On a practical level, proving negligent misrepresentation is easier than proving fraud. Having said that, however, the plaintiff must still set out a clear case of negligence. Often that is quite difficult. The plaintiff must present evidence of the specific false statement or information provided by the defendant, how the plaintiff relied on this information, and that his reliance was reasonable. The plaintiff must also show proximate cause between that reliance and the monetary injury he suffered. Finally, the plaintiff must show a direct connection between a monetary loss and the defendant's actions. Unlike personal injury cases in which certain types of damages are obvious, the damages in negligent misrepresentation cases may be difficult to quantify. See Figure 14-6.

G. DEFENSES TO NEGLIGENT MISREPRESENTATION

The defenses available in negligent misrepresentation cases are similar to the defenses available in most negligence cases. However, there are several other defenses that are more or less unique to this tort. They are:

- Truth
- Opinion

FIGURE 14-6
 	
Pleading Pointers in Negligent Misrepresentation Cases
	■ Point to a specific conversation or communication in which false information was provided
	■ Provide dates, times, and settings for this conversation or communication
	■ Detail how the information was relayed and why, precisely, this information was false
	■ Provide the background information (contract negotiation, buyer-seller transaction, etc.) if the information was provided in the context of a broader communication
	■ Provide direct quotes (or close approximations) of exactly what the defendant stated
	■ Explain the relationship between the plaintiff and defendant (fiduciary, partners, business associates, etc.)
	■ Detail how, precisely, the plaintiff relied on this information
	    ■ Plaintiff purchased certain items because of the defendant's information
	    ■ Plaintiff undertook certain actions because of the defendant's information
	    ■ Plaintiff did/did not . . .
	■ Show how the plaintiff's reliance on the false information was reasonable
	■ Detail how the plaintiff's monetary losses were directly tied to the false information
	■ Show how the plaintiff has suffered a financial loss by detailing exactly what extra money plaintiff has had to pay, or specific amounts lost, by his reliance on the defendant's statement

■ Statement did not concern a material fact
■ No detrimental reliance on the statement
■ No damages
■ Waiver

1. TRUTH

Perhaps the most obvious defense to negligent misrepresentation is that the statement was not false. After all, it is one of the essential elements of the claim that the plaintiff must prove that the statement was false or made in reckless disregard of the truth. If the statement is true, the plaintiff's case is essentially destroyed.

2. OPINION

In most situations, an opinion is not actionable. An opinion is simply the defendant's belief or "feeling" about a particular event and lacks a solid grounding in fact. The exception is when the opinion is offered as though it were a fact. Another exception concerns people who are in the business of giving opinions about specific issues. An attorney, for example, is often called upon to give an opinion about the law. The client is entitled to rely on that opinion.

3. STATEMENT DID NOT CONCERN A MATERIAL FACT

The defendant can also raise the defense that her statement, even if false, was not about a material fact, and therefore cannot be the basis of a negligent misrepresentation claim. Essentially, the defendant is claiming that her statement did not concern any fact that would cause another person to change his behavior or to influence his conduct.

4. NO DETRIMENTAL RELIANCE ON THE STATEMENT

When the plaintiff hears a false statement, but takes no action based on that false statement, he has not relied on it. It is not enough that the plaintiff prove that the defendant's statement was false; the plaintiff must also show that he relied on it in some way. If the plaintiff did not rely on the statement to his detriment, he has failed to prove an essential element of negligent misrepresentation.

5. NO DAMAGES

Similar to the last defense, a defendant is entitled to raise the defense that even if the statement was false and the plaintiff relied on it, the plaintiff suffered no damages because of it. Under the Restatement position, which has been adopted in one form or another by nearly all jurisdictions, pecuniary loss is an essential element of the claim. As far as this tort is concerned, mental pain and anguish are not damages. The plaintiff must show some form of monetary loss or he is not entitled to recover.

> **Sidebar**
> *The plaintiff may be able to recover under some other tort for mental pain and anguish caused by the defendant's statement, such as infliction of emotional distress.*

6. WAIVER

Finally, a defendant can claim that even if all of the elements are met, the plaintiff waived any right to pursue his action. A waiver occurs when the plaintiff signs a document officially relinquishing a legal right, or it can occur through conduct.

Example: During the course of Ted's business, Ted has made a statement that clearly constitutes a negligent misrepresentation. John, the person who received this false statement, acknowledges it and then continues to work with Ted anyway. Ted can now argue that because of John's **ratification,** he has waived any right to sue for the negligent misrepresentation.

> **Ratification**
> The process of confirming and accepting a previous action; a void contract can be ratified after the fact to make it legally enforceable

H. DEFENSES THAT ARE UNAVAILABLE IN NEGLIGENT MISREPRESENTATION

It is not a defense to a claim of negligent misrepresentation that the defendant did not have a particular person in mind when he made his false statement. Anyone who could foreseeably have relied on her false statement has a

- That the defendant had no knowledge of the veracity of the statement
- That there was no privity of contract between the parties
- That the defendant acted in good faith

Defenses Not Available in Negligent Mis- representation Cases

potential claim against her. Other defenses that are not available to defendants in negligent misrepresentation cases are listed in Figure 14-7.

1. NO KNOWLEDGE

Defendants are not permitted to raise the defense that they had no knowledge of the accuracy of their statements at the time that they made them. A negligent misrepresentation case is based on the theory that the defendant failed to use reasonable care and competence in making her statement, so the fact that she failed to verify its accuracy actually helps the plaintiff prove one of his essential elements.[12] In fact, many jurisdictions allow a claim against the defendant precisely because he had no knowledge, at the time that he made the statement to the plaintiff, that it was true.[13]

2. LACK OF PRIVITY

Although we have said that privity of contract is often found in negligent misrepresentation cases, there is no requirement that it exist. Therefore a defense of no privity of contract will not exempt the defendant from the consequences of her false statement. As long as the plaintiff can show that it was foreseeable that he would rely on the defendant's statements, and that his reliance was reasonable, the plaintiff has presented sufficient proof.[14]

3. GOOD FAITH

In many jurisdictions, the defendant's good faith in making the statement is also not a defense.[15] The true test is whether the defendant had reasonable grounds for believing that her statement was true. Without that reasonable belief, her good faith is immaterial.[16]

INTERFERENCE WITH CONTRACT

A. INTRODUCTION

Suppose that the owner of a local stadium has entered into a contract with a famous rock band to perform six shows next month. The owner anticipates that the revenue from this show will be outstanding and he has even installed extra seats, improved lighting, and hired additional security guards after signing the band to perform. Two weeks before the band is to perform, the stadium owner sees an article in the local paper advertising the band's performance, but stating that the band will actually be performing at a local amphitheater, owned and operated by Al Amp. He calls the band's manager and learns that Al Amp contacted the band one day after the band signed with him and lured the band away by promising them more money and the chance to record a live album at the site. The stadium owner is furious and comes to our firm for advice. He knows that he can sue the band for breach of contract, but he wants to go after Al Amp. What kind of suit can he bring against him?

The tort of interference with contract, sometimes called interference with contractual relations, is a civil action that can be brought against a third party who interferes with the business relationship between two other parties. If the stadium owner can satisfy the elements of this tort, he may be able to win at trial.

Sidebar

The scenario presented in this section is very similar to the original English case that first brought the tort of interference with contract into prominence. In that case, a famous opera singer was lured away from performing at one opera house by the owner of another house. Lumley, the opera house owner who had a contract with the singer, sued Lye, who lured her away. He won his case and a place, or at least a footnote, in legal history.[17]

B. ELEMENTS OF INTERFERENCE WITH CONTRACT

Interference with contract consists of the following elements:

1 There was a contract between the plaintiff and a third party.
2 The defendant knew that such a contract existed.
3 The defendant acted intentionally to induce the third party to breach the contract.
4 The defendant's actions were the proximate cause of the breach of contract.
5 The plaintiff suffered damages as a result of the breach of contract.[18]

While several of these elements are self-explanatory, the third element needs some additional clarification. What, for instance, is "intentional" conduct necessary to establish the third element of interference with contract? Is it enough that the defendant simply suggests to the third party that he walk away from a contract, or must the defendant do more before he will be liable? The answer, in most jurisdictions, is that the defendant must do more than simply suggest a contract breach.

Generally, the defendant must make a concerted effort to get the third party to breach his contract. The courts will examine not only what the defendant did, but also his motives for doing it. If the defendant induced the third party to breach the contract and then employed the third party for the same purpose, courts will consider that to be a major factor in determining the defendant's liability. However, the courts will also balance the actions of the defendant against the interests of society as a whole. Is there a good policy reason why the third party should be free to work with others?

All of these factors make a determination of interference with contract difficult.[19]

Compare these two situations: XYZ Company is the largest employer in the area. Among its many interests is software design. The company insists that all employees, prior to hiring, sign a non-compete contract. This contract provides that if an employee leaves the company, for any reason, he or she cannot compete directly or indirectly with any of the company's interests for a period of five years within a 1,000-mile radius of the company's main head-quarters. Steve is an XYZ employee who is approached by a landscape design company. They want to hire Steve to work for them to develop new landscape design software. Steve quits his job and goes to work for the company. XYZ sues the company on the theory of interference with contract because of the non-compete contract. As the basis of this contention, the company claims that it was considering creating landscape and home design software. How will the court rule on this suit?

Answer: In most jurisdictions, XYZ will lose. Although there is a non-compete contract and the landscape company did approach Steve and lure him away from his employment (essentially inducing Steve to breach his employment contract with XYZ), there is a larger, societal issue here. First of all, XYZ's non-compete contract is too broad. By insisting on a five-year, 1,000-mile radius of non-competition, the company is stifling innovation and new businesses. Second, the courts are consistent in ruling that employees have the right to move on to new employment, and this right carries greater weight than a company's right to the employee's services.

Scenario 2: Sal works for Outdoor Advertising, Inc., a firm that markets and installs highway billboards. Sal believes that he can create a new company doing the same thing and make himself rich. When he leaves his old job, he takes the client list with him. He then begins contacting his old clients and asking them to switch to his new company. When several of the clients express concerns that they might have some legal liability for breach of contract, Steve assures them that he will help defray any legal costs if they should be sued. Outdoor Advertising learns what Steve is up to and brings an interference with contract suit against him. How will the court rule?

Answer: Steve is likely to lose. Although Steve has the right to leave the firm, and may even have the right to approach his old customers to see if they wish to change firms, he has certainly acted improperly by offering to pay their legal bills if they are sued. This undoubtedly induced many of Outdoor Advertising's customers to breach their contracts.[20]

In interference with contract, the defendant's actions do not have to be tortious. The tort does not spring from how the defendant interferes but simply by interfering. In such a case, the defendant does not have to engage in threats or battery or any other tortious activity. Simply luring the party away from the plaintiff is enough.[22]

Although we discuss interference with contract as a civil injury, it is important to point out that not all states categorize it this way. New York, for instance, classifies this as a cause of action based on breach of contract, not as a tort.[23]

The tort of interference with contract has a long history. Originally developed in ancient Rome, it was based on the theory that another person should not be allowed to interfere with someone's slave. Later, the concept was expanded to include employees and eventually parties to a contract.[21]

 **DECEPTIVE TRADE PRACTICES**

A. DECEPTIVE TRADE PRACTICES ACT

Most states have some type of statute that prohibits deceptive trade practices. The Uniform Deceptive Trade Practices Act, which has been adopted, although with substantial modifications, by a majority of states, provides that a person engages in deceptive trade practices when, during the course of his business, he

1 Passes off goods or services as his own when they are in fact someone else's
2 Sets out to confuse the origin, certification, or association of goods
3 Sets out to confuse the certification of the goods or their affiliation
4 Uses deceptive advertisements or statements to create the impression that the goods originated from one geographic area when they actually originated from another
5 States that the goods have qualities that they in fact do not have
6 Represents that the goods are new when in fact they are used

The purpose of a deceptive trade practices act is to prevent merchants and others from tricking consumers into buying goods that they otherwise would not want. To bring an action under a state deceptive trade practices act, the plaintiff must show

1 That the defendant took advantage of the plaintiff's lack of knowledge about an item
2 By engaging in one of the proscribed acts[25]

The Uniform Deceptive Trade Practices Act has been adopted, in whole or with modifications, in the following states: Colorado, Delaware, Georgia, Hawaii, Illinois, Maine, Minnesota, Nebraska, New Mexico, Ohio, Oklahoma, and Oregon.[24]

B. PUBLIC AND PRIVATE ENFORCEMENT UNDER DTPA

The interesting thing about an action under the Deceptive Trade Practices Act is that two actions are authorized. The Act permits private enforcement through a civil suit, but it also authorizes government actions. In many ways, a state DTPA resembles a criminal action. As we have seen in other contexts, a private action (battery, for example) can give rise to a civil cause of action and a criminal charge. Deceptive trade practices are similar in that the government and the individual can both bring actions. However, they are different in that the government action will not result in jail time. Instead, the defendant may be ordered to pay a civil judgment.

In states that authorize public and private enforcement of deceptive trade practices, the state attorney general is usually the person authorized to bring the public actions.

FIGURE 14-8

Largest Civil Damage Award, 2005

Largest damage award was $172 million

Of the civil trials sampled in state courts nationwide in 2005, the largest damage award was granted to approximately 116,000 California employees who brought a class action lawsuit against a large retail corporation.

The lawsuit was originally filed in 2001 by several former employees and was expanded to cover California employees working for the retailer between 2001 and 2005. The employees claimed that the retailer had violated a California state law requiring that employees working six hours or more be given a 30-minute, unpaid lunch break. Under the law, if an employee was not permitted the break, the company was required to pay a full hour's wages in compensation. The employees maintained that they were owed more than $66 million plus interest.

After four months of testimony and three days of deliberation, an Alameda County jury awarded the plaintiffs $57 million in general damages and $115 million in punitive damages.

Civil Bench and Jury Trials in State Courts, 2005, Bureau of Justice Statistics, U.S. Department of Justice.

CONSUMER PROTECTION LAWS

In addition to the other types of business torts we have discussed in this chapter, there are also numerous "consumer protection" statutes that exist on the state and federal level. Many of these statutes have tort-like features. These protections include the Federal Truth-in-Lending laws, the Uniform Commercial Code, and state limitations on debt collection practices. If a particular case involves a consumer-protection issue, both state and federal statutes should be reviewed to see if they apply.

SEXUAL HARASSMENT

In recent years, countless companies and several branches of the United States military have faced claims of sexual harassment. These claims are often expensive to resolve and, while pending, can have a debilitating effect on management and work relationships. When harassment occurs in the workplace, employee morale and productivity are often seriously affected. Even more important, the victim's sense of security is violated and companies are often assessed with large verdicts for permitting such activity to occur.

A. SEXUAL HARASSMENT IN THE WORKPLACE

Everyone has the right to work in an environment free from sexual harassment and to be evaluated solely on work performance. Sexual harassment is defined in a variety of ways in different states. We address the basic issues found in such suits, but there is no substitute for reviewing state-specific law on this topic.

B. WHAT IS SEXUAL HARASSMENT?

Sexual harassment covers a wide range of behaviors, from obvious acts such as fondling someone's body to more subtle ones such as making suggestive comments. In general, sexual harassment is any unwelcome behavior in the workplace that:

- Relates to a person's gender or sexuality
- Is intentional and/or repeated
- Is unwanted and not returned, and
- Interferes with a person's ability to do his or her job, or has an effect on working conditions.

There are two types of sexual harassment actions recognized in most jurisdictions, quid pro quo and hostile environment.

1. QUID PRO QUO SEXUAL HARASSMENT

In an action alleging quid pro quo sexual harassment, the plaintiff alleges that the defendant requested sexual acts as a basis for employment. Such cases are often seen in the context of a defendant offering the plaintiff favorable working conditions, promotions, or other incentives in exchange for sex.

2. HOSTILE ENVIRONMENT SEXUAL HARASSMENT

Hostile environment sexual harassment occurs when unwelcome sexual conduct interferes with an individual's job performance or creates a hostile, intimidating, or offensive work environment. Actions based on hostile environment can be brought even though the harassment did not result in tangible or economic job consequences. For example, plaintiffs do not have to allege that they were fired or passed over for a promotion when they refused to engage in sexual activity.

 **DRAM SHOP LIABILITY**

The vast majority of states have some form of dram shop liability. The basic premise behind dram shop liability is that a business (or, in some states, an individual) who furnishes alcohol to an obviously intoxicated person should

FIGURE 14-9

Florida Statute §768.125. Liability for Injury or Damage Resulting from Intoxication

A person who sells or furnishes alcoholic beverages to a person of lawful drinking age shall not thereby become liable for injury or damage caused by or resulting from the intoxication of such person, except that a person who willfully and unlawfully sells or furnishes alcoholic beverages to a person who is not of lawful drinking age or who knowingly serves a person habitually addicted to the use of any or all alcoholic beverages may become liable for injury or damage caused by or resulting from the intoxication of such minor or person.

bear part of the responsibility for the injuries this person later inflicts. Under the common law, there was no such cause of action against someone who furnished alcohol to another. Many states adopted dram shop liability by judicial interpretation of negligence law. Over the years, many state legislatures have codified dram shop liability. An example of a typical statute is found in Figure 14-9.

WORKER'S COMPENSATION

The topic of worker's compensation could easily fill an entire book. Although the basic idea behind worker's compensation statutes is deceptively simple, in practice it can often become quite complicated.

A. THE BASIC PREMISE OF WORKER'S COMPENSATION

Worker's compensation is based on the simple premise that workers who are injured on the job will receive a fixed, monetary award in return for giving up the right to sue their employer. The entire system is designed to short-circuit lengthy litigation by employees against employers for on-the-job injuries. Workers' families are also entitled to an award in situations in which the worker is killed on the job. Employers pay into the system to compensate employees for their injuries. When an employee is injured on the job, he files a claim with the worker's compensation board, seeking reimbursement for medical payments and other financial losses. An employee covered by worker's compensation is prevented, in most cases, from bringing suit against the employer under traditional tort theory. The attraction of worker's compensation is that the employers receive some degree of assurance that they will not be sued by the employees, while the employees receive some amount of assurance that they will receive compensation for their claims without going through the burdensome process of filing a lawsuit.

B. BRINGING A CLAIM UNDER WORKER'S COMPENSATION

When an employee is injured on the job, he will file a claim under worker's compensation. If the injury is job-related, the employee is entitled to payment for medical bills and associated costs. If the employee's injury is permanent in nature, the employee is entitled to a settlement that takes into account the degree of impairment and the effect of this impairment on future earnings. Instead of bringing a claim through the court system, an employee brings a claim through the state worker's compensation board. Although this board can be called many things in many states, the basic structure is the same. Claims are evaluated by administrative law judges, who are empowered to make decisions in such claims. Although they are not judges in the usual sense, they do have the power to render final decisions in claims.

C. THE ISSUES IN WORKER'S COMPENSATION

Although the premise of worker's compensation sounds simple, in practice it can often get bogged down in the details. For instance, suppose that Mary is injured on the job. She injures her right hand while loading some heavy boxes onto a shelf in the back storage room. The injury to her hand is severe. She has suffered some broken bones and what appears to be some permanent nerve damage. Mary is in constant pain. How does her claim proceed through worker's compensation?

When Mary is injured on the job, one of the first things that she is supposed to do is to report her injury to her employer. This report triggers several significant events. For one thing, it puts her employer on notice that she has been injured and that her injury should be cared for. If Mary fails to report her injury, her claim may be delayed or refused under worker's compensation. The reporting of the injury also gives the employer some relevant information upon which to begin an investigation.

D. ASSIGNING MONETARY VALUES TO INJURIES

One of the underlying theories of worker's compensation is that injuries to various parts of the employee's body have a set amount of recovery. This system of assigning monetary value to injuries is very much like the ancient system of tort law in which the loss of a hand justified more compensation for the victim than the loss of a toe. Under worker's compensation, the nature of the victim's injury, coupled with its permanence, will have a profound impact on the final monetary award. However, because the permanence of the worker's injury is often hotly debated, medical testimony is usually required to prove this point.

Sidebar

*In many ways, worker's
compensation claims
resemble abbreviated
lawsuits. There is a
claim raised by the
employee; there is
a response by the
employer. Attorneys
usually represent both
sides. There is an
administrative law
judge whose responsi-
bility involves ruling on
the claim and deciding
issues of law and fact.
However, if you observed
a worker's compensation
hearing, the level of
informality would
probably surprise you.
Worker's compensation
hearings are frequently
conducted in offices and
conference rooms, not
in courtrooms.*

A physician may testify, usually through deposition, about the nature of the worker's injury. Returning to our example of Mary and her injured hand, suppose that a doctor determines that Mary has a permanent, 50 percent loss of use of her right hand. In such a case, the worker's compensation administrative law judge will refer to a schedule to determine how much to award Mary for such a loss. This may sound simple and straightforward, but when it comes down to actual cases, the issues often become quite complicated. Suppose, for example, that Mary disputes the doctor's findings. Is she entitled to an independent doctor's opinion? The answer is usually yes. There are a host of other issues that could surface in a typical worker's compensation case, including an employer's contention that the employee's job duties did not include the activity in the course of which she was injured, the impact on her future employment, and the total amount of her award.

Attorneys and law firms that handle worker's compensation often develop a specialty in this area. Because of the complicated nature of cases, statutes, and rulings, most attorneys believe that they cannot do an adequate job in representing an injured worker or an employer unless they spend a great deal of time specializing in such cases. When a paralegal goes to work for a worker's compensation firm, the paralegal often finds that her duties involve worker's compensation cases exclusively.

PETRIE v. WIDBY
194 S.W.3d 168 7 (Tex. App.-Dallas 2006)

Opinion
Opinion by Justice LANG-MIERS.

In his sole issue in this interlocutory appeal, Richard Petrie contends the trial court erred by overruling his special appearance. His sisters, Joan Widby and Helene McWilliams, sued him for, among other things, misrepresentations about the transfer of ownership of stock owned by their mother, Helen Petrie. For the reasons that follow, we affirm the order of the trial court.

Factual and Procedural Background

Helen Petrie, the parties' mother, owned 4,032 shares of Norfolk Southern Corp. stock valued at approximately $180,000. In 1973, while living in Tennessee, Helen executed her Last Will and Testament in which she devised all of her property to Petrie, Widby, and McWilliams in equal shares. In early 2003, McWilliams asked an attorney whether Helen's will would have to be probated. She told the attorney that all of their mother's assets were in her and her siblings' names except the stock. The attorney advised McWilliams that probate would be unnecessary if Helen added Petrie, Widby, and McWilliams' names to the stock certificates. McWilliams told Petrie about the attorney's advice, and Petrie told his sister he would handle the paperwork necessary to add their names to the stock certificates.

In March 2003, Helen was diagnosed with dementia and possibly early-onset of Alzheimer's disease. Four months later, in July 2003, Helen gave Petrie her power of attorney. She also signed a form transferring ownership of the stock to Petrie and herself as joint tenants with right of survivorship.

Around this same time, Petrie told McWilliams that Norfolk Southern would not add all three of their names to their mother's stock certificates but would only add one name and that he put his name on the stock certificates along with their mother's name. McWilliams testified she trusted her brother and thought when their mother passed away, they would avoid probate and Petrie would split the stock three ways. McWilliams testified that Petrie did not tell her the stock was placed in both his and his mother's names as joint tenants with right of survivorship. A month later, in August 2003, Petrie moved Helen from Tennessee to Texas.

Around March 2004, after the stock had already been transferred to the joint tenancy in Helen's and Petrie's names, Petrie told his sister Widby that he wanted to schedule a meeting in Texas with an attorney to discuss preservation of their mother's assets and that she should attend the meeting. The meeting was held in Dallas, Texas, with a Texas attorney, Charles Bedsole. During the meeting, Petrie and Widby discussed their mother's assets with Bedsole and talked about what they needed to do and what the future expenses would be if Helen was placed in an assisted living facility. Widby testified that Bedsole asked Petrie to list Helen's assets, and he listed the stock. She also testified that Petrie represented to the attorney that the stocks "were mother's." Petrie did not disclose during this meeting that the stock was held in Helen's and his names as joint tenants with right of survivorship.

On May 30, 2004, Helen passed away in Texas. She was buried in Tennessee. In June, the family held a memorial service in Collin County, Texas. Following the service, Petrie told McWilliams that he was concerned about having to pay all of the taxes on the stock. McWilliams told him that once the stock was equally distributed, each of them would pay their share and he would not be responsible for all of the taxes. McWilliams testified that Petrie said, "Well, I don't know, I have to check into that." She testified Petrie did not disclose that he owned the stock with Helen as joint tenants with right of survivorship. Sometime that fall, McWilliams asked Petrie whether he needed her help in getting the stock distributed. She testified Petrie told her he was having to sign "one form after another" and "this is all we can do right now."

At some point, McWilliams and Widby learned their brother had received all of the stock and that he refused to distribute their share to them. They filed this lawsuit, seeking a declaration that the power of attorney their mother gave to Petrie was invalid because Helen was incompetent at the time she signed it. They also alleged negligent misrepresentation, fraud, breach of fiduciary duty, conversion, and sought the imposition of a constructive trust. They contended Petrie negligently and intentionally misrepresented the facts surrounding the transfer of ownership of the stock and remained silent when he had a duty to disclose the facts. Petrie filed a special appearance in which he argued the trial court did not have personal jurisdiction over him because he had no continuous and systematic contacts with Texas and because he did not commit a tort in Texas.

Findings of Fact and Conclusions of Law

After a hearing, the trial court overruled Petrie's special appearance and filed two sets of findings of fact and conclusions of law. On appeal, Petrie challenges the trial court's order denying his special appearance, arguing there is no or insufficient evidence to support several of the trial court's findings of fact and conclusions of law. For purposes of our decision, we quote findings of fact numbers 15 and 21:

> 15. In or around March, 2004, Mr. Petrie and Plaintiff Joan P. Widby, at Mr. Petrie's prompting, retained and met in person with an attorney in Dallas, Texas, Charles Bedsole, to discuss, among other things, the preservation of Ms. Petrie's assets. Defendant made a number of statements during this meeting. Among other statements, Mr. Petrie stated in this meeting, while in the presence of Mr. Bedsole and Plaintiff Joan Widby, that Helen Petrie owned approximately 4,032 shares of stock in Norfolk Southern company and that these shares of Stock belong to Helen Petrie. Defendant made this statement in response to an inquiry from Mr. Bedsole into what assets were owned by Ms. Petrie at the time that would then belong to Ms. Petrie's estate upon her passing. Mr. Bedsole solicited this information so that he could determine how such assets could be protected from creditors, estate taxes and any others. Mr. Petrie, despite knowing about the prior execution of the form ostensibly giving himself a joint ownership with right of survivorship in the Stock, did not inform either Mr. Bedsole or Plaintiff Widby that the Stock, due to the execution of that form, was not an asset that would belong to Mr. Petrie's estate upon her passing. Had Mr. Petrie indicated such, Plaintiffs would then have been able to cause documentation to be executed to either change ownership in the Stock back to Ms. Petrie individually or to have Plaintiffs and Defendant be joint owners in the Stock with right of survivorship. Plaintiffs' claims in substantial part thus arise from and relate to Defendant's attendance at and statements and omissions made during the March 2004 meeting in Dallas, Texas.

> 21. Ms. Petrie passed away on May 31, 2004, in Collin County, Texas. At the time of her death, Ms. Petrie's residence was: 2401 Country View Lane, No. 333, McKinney, Collin County, Texas, 75069. Several days after Ms. Petrie's passing, Mr. Petrie, while in Collin County, Texas, told Plaintiff Helene P. McWilliams that he was concerned that he, individually, would be required to pay significant taxes on the Stock. Plaintiff Helene P. McWilliams responded that he would not and that each of the Parties would pay their own share of the taxes for the Stock after same was distributed to each of them. Mr. Petrie said nothing further on the subject and again failed to say anything about his having made himself a joint owner of the Stock with right of survivorship pursuant to the alleged Power of Attorney. Had Mr. Petrie informed Plaintiffs of such, they would have had the opportunity to cause necessary documents to be executed to either change ownership in the Stock back to Ms. Petrie individually or to have Plaintiffs and Defendant be joint owners in the Stock with right of survivorship.

Petrie also challenges the trial court's conclusion of law that the exercise of personal jurisdiction over him will not offend traditional notions of fair play and substantial justice.

The Parties' Contentions

Petrie contends he is not subject to the trial court's jurisdiction because (1) he does not own a business or conduct business in Texas, (2) all of the transactions related to the transfer of stock from Helen to him were done in Tennessee, (3) the stock certificates remained in Tennessee until Helen's death, and (4) after her death, new stock certificates were issued to him in Kansas. On the other hand, Widby and McWilliams argue the trial court had both specific and general jurisdiction because Petrie purposefully established minimum contacts with Texas. They argue the trial court had specific jurisdiction based on two misrepresentations and omissions Petrie made while in Texas: (1) in the March 2004 meeting with the attorney in Dallas, Petrie misrepresented the ownership of the stock and failed to disclose that he owned the stock with Helen as joint tenants with right of survivorship; and (2) in the June 2004 conversation in Collin County, Texas, following their mother's memorial service, when McWilliams and Petrie were discussing payment of the taxes on the distribution of the stock, Petrie failed to disclose to McWilliams that he owned the stock with Helen as a joint tenant with right of survivorship. They also argue Petrie had sufficient minimum contacts to support the exercise of general jurisdiction.

Standard of Review

In reviewing a trial court's order denying a special appearance, we review the court's factual findings for legal and factual sufficiency and its legal conclusions de novo.

Findings of fact in a case tried to the court have the same force and effect as a jury's verdict on special issues. We review the trial court's findings of fact by the same standards that we apply in reviewing the evidence supporting a jury's answers. *Anderson,* 806 S.W.2d at 794.

In reviewing the legal sufficiency of a finding of fact, we consider only the evidence and inferences that support the challenged finding and disregard all contrary evidence and inferences unless the evidence could not be rejected by the fact finder. We uphold the trial court's finding against a legal sufficiency challenge if there is any probative evidence to support the finding.

In reviewing a factual sufficiency point of error, we consider all of the evidence. A finding will be set aside only if the evidence is so weak or the finding is so against the great weight and preponderance of the evidence that it is wrong and manifestly unjust.

In so doing, we do not pass on the witnesses' credibility or substitute our judgment for that of the trier of fact. In addition, the trial court, as fact finder, is the sole judge of the credibility of the witnesses and may accept or reject all or any part of a witness's testimony.

We review challenges to a trial court's conclusions of law as a matter of law. We independently evaluate the trial court's conclusions of law, and we give limited deference to a trial court's application of law to facts. The trial court abuses its discretion when it misapplies the law.

Analysis

Purposeful Availment

Petrie argues the trial court's findings of fact numbers 15 and 21 are "legally irrelevant" to the determination of the ownership of the stock. But Widby and McWilliams's claims do not only concern the transfer of ownership of the stock. They also claim fraud and negligent misrepresentation arising from statements and omissions Petrie made while he was in Texas. And a nonresident who travels to Texas and makes statements alleged to be fraudulent is subject to specific jurisdiction in Texas. *Deason,* 165 S.W.3d at 415; see *Am. Type Culture Collections, Inc. v. Coleman,* 83 S.W.3d 801, 806-07 (Tex. 2002) (specific jurisdiction exists when defendant's contacts with forum are purposeful and cause of action arises from or relates to those contacts).

At the hearing on the special appearance, Widby testified it was Petrie's idea to have a meeting in Texas with an attorney to discuss the preservation of Helen's assets. At the meeting, Petrie told the attorney the stock was Helen's. When he listed Helen's assets for the attorney, he listed the stock. Widby testified Petrie failed to tell her or the attorney that the stock was actually owned by Helen and Petrie as joint tenants with right of survivorship. Additionally, McWilliams testified that during a discussion after Helen's memorial service in Texas, Petrie expressed concern about having to pay all of the taxes on the stock. When she told him she and Widby would pay their share, he failed to tell her that the stock was in his and Helen's names as joint tenants with right of survivorship. Petrie did not deny that he made these statements and did not deny that he failed to disclose this information. He just claims they are "irrelevant." We disagree.

Petrie purposefully availed himself of the laws of Texas through these purposeful contacts with the State. And Petrie should have realized that the consequences of having made the representations or omissions in Texas could reasonably lead to being haled into court in Texas. *Deason,* 165 S.W.3d at 415. Accordingly, we conclude the evidence is legally and factually sufficient to support the trial court's findings of fact numbers 15 and 21.

Fair Play and Substantial Justice

Petrie also challenges the trial court's conclusion of law that the assumption of jurisdiction over Petrie will not offend traditional notions of fair play and substantial justice. In a special appearance, a defendant bears the burden of presenting "a compelling case that the presence of some consideration would render jurisdiction unreasonable." *Guardian,* 815 S.W.2d at 231 (quoting *Burger King,* 471 U.S. at 477).

Appellant did not make any argument or cite to the record or authority to support this contention in his initial brief. In his reply brief, Petrie attempts to argue the assumption of jurisdiction would offend traditional notions of fair play and substantial justice. He contends this is so because (1) all of his contacts in Texas occurred at least one year and five months before plaintiffs filed suit, (2) the contacts are too attenuated to support jurisdiction, (3) the contacts were random in nature, (4) none of the contacts support the conclusion that Petrie could reasonably anticipate being called into a Texas court, and (5) he was not seeking a benefit, advantage, or profit regarding ownership of the stock when he engaged in these activities. But these are factors to consider in determining whether Petrie purposefully availed himself of the laws of the State of Texas, the first prong of the analysis. See *Michiana,* 168 S.W.3d at 784-85. We have already determined that he did.

Additionally, Petrie does not argue or cite authority for the factors we must consider in making the determination of whether the exercise of jurisdiction over a defendant comports with traditional notions of fair play and substantial justice. See *World-Wide Volkswagen Corp. v. Woodson,* 444 U.S. 286, 292 (1980) (setting out factors to consider). And the allegation that Petrie committed a tort in Texas leads us to conclude that the exercise of specific jurisdiction would not offend traditional notions of fair play and substantial justice. See *Deason,* 165 S.W.3d at 415; *Morris v. Kohl-Yorks,* 164 S.W.3d 686, 694-95 (Tex. App.-Austin 2005, pet. dism'd). As a result, the trial court did not err when it concluded that exercising jurisdiction over Petrie will not offend traditional notions of fair play and substantial justice.

In summary, Widby and McWilliams met their burden of presenting sufficient jurisdictional facts by alleging Petrie committed a tort in Texas and Petrie did not negate all bases for the exercise of jurisdiction. We overrule Petrie's sole issue.

Conclusion

We conclude the evidence is legally and factually sufficient to support the trial court's order denying Petrie's special appearance. Because we conclude the trial court had specific jurisdiction over Petrie, we do not decide whether Petrie's contacts with Texas would also support the assumption of general jurisdiction. Accordingly, we affirm the trial court's order denying Petrie's special appearance.

Questions about the case:

1. Explain why the children of Helen Petrie wished to avoid probate and how they planned to do it.
2. Why is it significant that the stock in question was listed in both the mother's and son's names, but not the daughters'?
3. What are the allegations of the sisters against their brother?
4. Explain Petrie's claim that the trial court's ruling is against "fair play and substantial justice."

FOLLOW-UP ON THE SHAREHOLDER'S SUIT

We began this chapter with a hypothetical situation involving the End-Run Corporation and a shareholder with 1,000 shares who wishes to sue the corporation for its false announcements and statements regarding the company's financial health. Now that we have reviewed the various types of business torts that could be brought in this situation, are any of them appropriate to this situation?

First, let's review the basic facts. Tom, who already owns 1,000 shares of End-Run stock, wants to sue the corporation for making false statements. Can he meet the essential elements of a fraud action? Remember that the elements for fraud consist of the following: (1) The defendant made a representation of a material fact or concealed a fact; (2) the representation was false; (3) the defendant knew the representation was false; (4) the defendant made the representation with the intent that the plaintiff would rely on it; (5) the plaintiff's reliance on the representation was reasonable under the circumstances; and (6) the plaintiff suffered injury from his reliance on the representation.

Assuming that Tom can present some proof to show that the company knew that it was making a false statement at the time it was made, elements 1-3 would seem fairly straightforward. What about the fourth element? There is no requirement that the plaintiff must show that the false statement was made with him in mind. If the plaintiff is in the group of people likely to be affected by the false statement, this element is met. Tom is a shareholder and falls into this category. We begin to run into problems, though, with the fifth element. Tom must show that his reliance on the representation was reasonable. This presupposes that Tom took some action with respect to the false information. We know that Tom already owns 1,000 shares. Unless we can show that Tom purchased more stock as a result, or took some other action, he cannot show any detrimental reliance on the information. We may also have some trouble with the last element. How does Tom show that he suffered economic injury? Surely the fact that he purchased the stock for a much higher price than it is worth now should be enough to prove damages, shouldn't it? In the pragmatic world of the courts, this may not be enough. The fact that Tom's stock was worth a lot more last year than it is worth this year may not be enough to prove an actual economic injury for Tom. There may be ways of dealing with this problem, but it is certainly an issue that the legal team must face.

Overall, Tom may not have a very strong case against End-Run, at least for fraudulent misrepresentation. His case for negligent misrepresentation also suffers from the same drawbacks.

 ## SKILLS YOU NEED IN THE REAL WORLD

Helping to Try a Case

Up to now, we have discussed the preliminary work that goes into preparing for a civil trial. Now it is time to address actually trying a case. Although the paralegal will not be involved in questioning witnesses on the stand or making a closing argument to the jury, a paralegal can have an equally crucial role in the trial. As the paralegal, you will often be the person to act as the resource person: You will find crucial documents at critical times during the trial, you will coordinate witness appearances, you will help set up jury demonstrations, and you will research last-minute legal issues. As such, a good trial paralegal must be prepared to deal with a wide range of problems and be able to handle them efficiently.

We assume that settlement negotiations have broken down and the case is scheduled for trial. Barring any last-minute miracles, this case looks like it will actually go before a jury. The firm has gone into trial mode. The attorneys have locked themselves in their offices to review the file and to prepare. You must also get ready. Here are five things you should do before you begin any trial.

1. Get the Lay of the Land

When it seems likely that a particular case is actually going to go to trial, it's time for you to get into trial mode, too. If you think of a trial as a battle (and, in many ways, it is), you should do what military professionals do: reconnaissance work. Go to the courthouse and find out which courtroom is reserved for your case. If the courtroom is locked, ask courthouse personnel to open it for you. Explain to them that you are there getting ready for trial. Once you are inside, draw a basic diagram of the room. Locate the witness stand, judge's bench, and attorney tables. The plaintiff usually has the table closest to the jury box. Sit in the jury box and look at the room from their perspective. If you have a friend with you, have the friend talk in a normal tone of voice from the witness stand. Can you hear him? If not, is there a microphone? These are the things that you can tell witnesses later.

Next, locate electrical outlets. These days, attorneys and paralegals often bring laptop computers, overhead projectors, and even printers into the courtroom. Are there enough plugs to accommodate all of these devices? If not, will you need a power strip, extension cords, etc.? Will you need to tape the cords down so that people won't trip over them?

If the attorney wants to make notes during an opening or closing argument, is there a chalkboard, whiteboard, or easel? Make sure that you have back-up supplies for whatever is available. Don't rely on the courthouse personnel to supply you with a dry-erase marker when the one in the courtroom goes dry just as the attorney is starting his closing argument.

2. Do a Trial Run with All Equipment

According to Murphy's Law, if it can go wrong, it will, at the worst possible moment. Keep this in mind if your team is going to be using any equipment during the trial, such as an overhead projector. Do a trial run with the device shortly before the trial. If it is a digital projector, does it actually work with the attorney's laptop? Try it and see. Do you have back-up lightbulbs and the right cable connectors? If possible, do a trial run with the equipment in the courtroom. In one case, an attorney had prepared a wonderful closing argument as a PowerPoint presentation. However, when it came time to present it to the jury, he suddenly realized that there was no place to project it. There was no screen and not even a blank wall in the courtroom. You can help avoid little disasters like this by doing a trial run with all equipment.

3. Check the Layout of the Courthouse

As part of your reconnaissance work at the courthouse, don't neglect the layout of the building outside the courtroom. If you are unfamiliar with the building, draw a map of the facility. You are going to have witnesses waiting around to testify. Where are they going to sit? What if they need to go to the bathroom or get a quick snack? If you know where these areas are, you can direct them—and also know where to look if they disappear. Take crucial witnesses to the courthouse and make sure that they know where to go. Take them right into the empty courtroom and show them where the witness stand is. Many witnesses are nervous about testifying, so this trip to the courtroom will give them a big boost of confidence just when they need it most.

4. Master the Trial Notebook or Case Files

By the time the case is actually about to go to trial, you should know the case file as well as the attorney, if not better. Test yourself: Can you find any particular document, transcript, motion, or pleading in less than ten seconds? If you can, you know the file; if you can't, you have more work to do. At some point in the trial, something unexpected will happen and the attorney will need a document that you hadn't anticipated that you would need. Can you find it immediately? There is nothing more frustrating—and nerve-wracking—than floundering in the middle of a cross-examination because a particular document is lost.

5. Get Ready for Stress

If you are good at handling stress, you are in the right business. Unfortunately, most people aren't. Trials are stressful events. They will be stressful for you in ways that are different than the stress the attorneys will feel. You will find yourself constantly trying to anticipate where the case is going so that you can be ready with the right thing at the right time. There are ways that you can reduce stress, such as following the first four tips in this section, but there is no way to reduce all stress.

You know that both you and the attorney will be under a great deal of stress, so prepare ways to deal with it. If you like to exercise, don't neglect it during the trial. At least take a break at the end of the day to take a walk or do something else that you find enjoyable. Unfortunately, too many stressed-out people turn to alcohol or food or some other unhealthy diversion. Over time, these short-term responses will take their toll on you. The longer the trial, the more stress on everyone involved. You need to learn to deal with the stress or it will tear you apart—too often there is no middle ground.

 THE LIFE OF A PARALEGAL

When I start getting ready for trial, I first go through the discovery. I dig through it, pulling out pertinent documents that establish the crucial points in the case and show what the parties did. I put these all together and then make four copies of the whole package. One copy is for my attorney, one is for the judge, one for the opposition, and one is for the witnesses. The reason that I make so many copies is that it helps speed things up and helps everyone stay focused. The judge and opposing attorney can follow along when my attorney is questioning a witness about a particular document. In some places, the court rules dictate that the opposing attorney gets a copy. But we do it even when the rules don't require it. We keep one copy of the package up at the witness box so that the attorney can direct the witness to a particular page. I separate out each exhibit, prepare a table of contents and then put a tab on each specific document so that everyone can find it quickly. I number the documents sequentially, so that when the attorney asks the witness to turn to page 35, everyone else has the same page in front of them.

After I put the exhibits together, the next thing I focus on is the pleadings. I go through them thoroughly. I look for anything that either side has admitted and I list it. Then I list the denials; that's what we will have to prove at trial. I've already gone through prior discovery responses and drafted follow-up questions. Now, I pull all of that information together.

These days, you get papered to death. You have to have a good handle on your file and be able to find your information quickly. That's not only true for trial preparation, but for settlement as well. A lot of times you might have an arbitration hearing and you'll need to access this stuff quickly and efficiently. My rule is: you can't be too organized.

Jane Huffman, Paralegal

ETHICAL ISSUES FOR THE PARALEGAL: COACHING WITNESSES

When we discuss preparing for trial, there is one ethical issue that always rears its head: coaching witnesses. We have already seen that preparation for trial is critical and that is no less true when talking about preparing witnesses to testify. However, when does preparation cross the line into coaching? First of all, what do we mean by "coaching" a witness? When a person coaches a witness, he is telling the witness what he should say when he is on the stand. That is clearly unethical and illegal. It is one thing to tell a witness what he should say; it is another to tell a witness what he is likely to hear. Although this sounds like splitting hairs, in the reality of a legal practice, this line is easy to maintain. You should never tell a witness how he or she should answer a specific question. You should never tell a witness to lie. Your advice to a witness should always be simple and direct. You should always tell the witness to tell the truth, even when the truth doesn't put the witness in a good light. Besides being unethical, a dishonest witness will almost always get caught out. When a witness can be shown to be untruthful about one point in his testimony, the jury will probably discount all of his testimony. When you assist in preparing a witness, it is common for you to tell the witness what he can expect during his time on the stand. You might tell him that he will be sworn and that he will be questioned about specific topics. You should tell a witness that he will be cross-examined and what the purpose of the cross-examination is. If there are unpleasant details in the testimony, you can advise the witness that he will, most likely, be asked about them. However, this preparation does not include rehearsing the witness in how he should answer particular questions. You should not "feed" the witness his lines. His testimony must be his own.

Chapter Summary

In this chapter, we discussed torts that are normally associated with business dealings. When a plaintiff believes that he has been the victim of fraud, he can present a civil case in which he alleges that the defendant made a false statement to him, knowing that it was false, on which the plaintiff relied, and from which the plaintiff suffered some type of monetary damage. When the defendant makes a statement without knowing that it is true, or in reckless disregard of the truth, he can be sued for negligent misrepresentation. The essential elements of an action for negligent misrepresentation include a statement made by the defendant, in the course of the defendant's trade or occupation, upon which statement the plaintiff justifiably relied. Another essential element of a negligent misrepresentation action is that the plaintiff suffered some type of monetary loss as a result of the false statement.

There are several defenses available to a claim for negligent misrepresentation, including the truth of the statement made by the defendant, that the statement was an opinion, that the plaintiff did not actually rely on the statement to his detriment, or that the plaintiff suffered no monetary loss because of the false information.

In addition to actions for fraud and negligent misrepresentation, a plaintiff can also bring other types of business torts including interference with contract and deceptive trade practices. An action for deceptive trade practices can include not only a private action, but a public action brought by the state attorney general.

Web Sites

■ **Internet Fraud (FBI)**
  http://www.fbi.gov (click on search box and enter "Internet fraud")

■ **Federal Trade Commission**
  http://www.ftc.gov/

■ **U.S. Business Advisor**
  http://www.business.gov/

Forms and Court Documents

A Complaint Alleging Misrepresentation

STATE OF PLACID	IN THE SUPERIOR COURT
COUNTY OF BARNES	FILE NUMBER: _____

Bart Bowler,   )
Plaintiff   )
)
vs.   )
)
Rockingham Finance, Inc. and)
Mark Wolf,   )
Defendants

Complaint

COMES NOW, Bart Bowler, Plaintiff in the above-styled action and makes the following allegations:

1.

Plaintiff is and was at all times relevant to the allegations in this Complaint, a citizen of Barnes County, State of Placid.

2.

Defendant Rockingham Finance, Inc., (hereafter "Rockingham Finance") is a corporation organized under the laws of the state of Placid and maintains its headquarters in Barnes County.

3.

Defendant Mark Wolf is an employee of Rockingham Finance Corporation and was employed by Rockingham Finance as a loan officer at all times pertinent to the allegations in this Complaint.

4.

On September 6, 2002, Plaintiff entered into a sales contract with Able Properties to purchase the Fiesta Ball, a bowling alley, and the five acres of land surrounding it for $2 million. The agreement provided that the purchase was contingent upon Plaintiff's obtaining financing by October 10, 2002.

5.

Plaintiff tendered $10,000 earnest money to seller and the same amount was due upon acceptance.

6.

Plaintiff contacted his banker, James Willoughby, at Placid State Bank to obtain financing. Placid State Bank was not interested in financing that large a loan, so Willoughby suggested Plaintiff contact Rockingham Finance.

7.

Willoughby and Plaintiff later met with Mark Wolf, a vice president of Rockingham Finance. The three discussed financing arrangements in general terms; Rockingham Finance was willing to lend 80 percent of the appraised value or the sale price, whichever was lower.

8.

The required appraisal, however, was not scheduled to be completed until after the financing contingency date set forth within Plaintiff's sales agreement.

9.

In early October, the appraiser verbally assured Plaintiff that the appraisal would be for at least $2 million. Plaintiff then called Wolf at Rockingham Finance, explained he was risking $20,000 earnest money and requested assurance that Rockingham Finance would extend the loan. According to Plaintiff, Wolf responded affirmatively.

10.

On October 8, 2002, Plaintiff released the financing contingency in exchange for the seller's agreement to a 30-day extension of the November 1, 2002, closing date.

11.

Two days later, Plaintiff and Wolf discussed a repayment schedule and interest rates.

12.

In mid-November, the appraisal came in at $2.1 million. In late November, Wolf informed Plaintiff that Rockingham Finance National had rejected the loan.

13.

The Fiesta Ball was thereafter sold to another purchaser and Plaintiff forfeited $5,000 earnest money.

14.

As a result of Defendant Wolf's false and misleading statement, Plaintiff incurred monetary losses.

15.

Defendant Wolf's statement concerning Rockingham Finance's approval of the Plaintiff's loan was made in reckless disregard of the truth.

16.

Defendant Wolf's statement was negligent misrepresentation of the actual facts involved in the loan approval process.

WHEREFORE, the plaintiff requests judgment for damages against defendants, individually and jointly and severally, as follows:

a. General damages in the amount of _____;
b. Special damages in the amount of _____; and
c. Punitive damages in an amount to be determined by the court;
d. Plaintiff also requests costs of suit; and
e. Such other and further relief as the court may deem just and proper;
f. Plaintiff also requests a trial by jury on the issues raised in this Complaint.

Respectfully submitted, this the _____ day of _____, 200__.

_____

Clarence D. Arrow
Attorney for the Plaintiff

Key Terms

Clear and convincing evidence
Material fact

Review Questions

1 Are there any factual changes that you could make to our Shareholder's Suit hypothetical that would give Tom a stronger case against End-Run?
2 What is fraud and how does it differ from negligent misrepresentation?
3 What are the elements of fraud?
4 Some have said that fraud is not something that can be done unknowingly. Why?
5 Courts have consistently refused to limit the definition of what acts constitute fraud. Why have they been reluctant to do so?
6 What is a material fact?
7 How do normal salesmanship statements differ from fraud?
8 What is "clear and convincing" evidence and how does this standard differ from "preponderance of the evidence"?
9 How does a fraud case change when the defendant is the plaintiff's fiduciary?

10 Actions that are classified as fraud can also be crimes. Explain the interplay between civil fraud and criminal fraud.

11 The Restatement of Torts limits actions for negligent misrepresentation to statements made by a defendant during the course of his business. Is this limitation too strict? Why would the drafters of the Restatement create this restriction?

12 What are the elements of negligent misrepresentation?

13 Why is there a requirement of the plaintiff's "reasonable reliance" on the defendant's statement in a negligent misrepresentation case?

14 Explain how the basic elements of a tort case (duty, breach, causation, and damages) are satisfied in a negligent misrepresentation case.

15 What is privity?

16 Opinions are usually not classified as negligent misrepresentations. Why? Are there situations in which an opinion can be actionable as a negligent misrepresentation? Explain.

17 What are some of the specifics that should be raised in a complaint alleging negligent misrepresentation?

18 Explain the defenses available in misrepresentation cases.

19 What is interference with contract? What are the elements of this tort?

20 Should interference with contract remain an actionable tort? Craft an argument against the continued existence of this tort.

21 Explain the public and private enforcement provisions of most states' deceptive trade practices acts.

Applying What You Have Learned

1 Should the contract between an attorney and her client receive the same level of protection as a typical business contract? Why or why not?

2 Draft an answer to the complaint presented in the "Forms and Court Documents" section of this chapter.

3 Draft a complaint for negligent misrepresentation using the facts presented in the beginning of this chapter in "Shareholder's Suit," with one important change: Instead of owning 1,000 shares of End-Run Corporation, Tom is now a major investor who has reviewed the bogus financial statements and has been induced by them to purchase a 51 percent share in the company. How do you address these issues in your complaint?

4 How does your state define *negligent misrepresentation?*

5 Does your state recognize the tort of interference with contract?

6 How does your state define *deceptive trade practices?*

Endnotes

[1] *Standard Oil Co. v. Hunt*, 121 S.E. 184 (1924).

[2] *Coley v. North Carolina National Bank*, 41 N.C. App. 121, 254 S.E.2d 217 (1979).

[3] *Patuxent Development Co. v. Bearden*, 227 N.C. 124, 128, 41 S.E.2d 85 (1947).

[4] *AMPAT/Midwest, Inc. v. Illinois Tool Works, Inc.*, 896 F.2d 1035, 1040 (7th Cir. 1990).

[5] *Board of Ed. v. A, C and S, Inc.*, 546 N.E.2d 580 (1989).

[6] Restatement (Second) of Torts §552, comment a.

[7] "Just in case you had any doubts — there is no tort of negligent misrepresentation in New York." Holahan 13 Pace L. Rev. 763 (1993).

[8] James & Gray, Misrepresentation, 37 M. L. Rev. 286 (1977).

[9] Am. Jur. 2d, Fraud and Deceit §143.

[10] *Bily v. Arthur Young & Co.*, 11 Cal. Rptr. 2d 51 (1992).

[11] *Baumann v. Florance*, 267 App. Div. 113, 114, 44 N.Y.S.2d 706, 707 (3d Dept. 1943).

[12] *Riley v. Bell*, 95 N.W. 170 (1903).

[13] *Wilson v. Murch*, 354 S.W.2d 332 (1962).

[14] *Hosford v. McKissack*, 589 So. 2d 108 (1991).

[15] *National Bank of Pawnee v. Hamilton*, 202 Ill. App. 516 (1916).

[16] *Vettleson v. Special School Dist. No. 1*, 361 N.W.2d 425 (1985).

[17] *Lumley v. Gye*, 2 El & Bl 216, 118 Eng. Rep. 749 (1853).

[18] *Petroleum Energy, Inc. v. Mid-America Petroleum, Inc.*, 775 F. Supp. 1420 (D. Kan. 1991).

[19] *Financial Marketing Services, Inc. v. Hawkeye Bank & Trust of Des Moines*, 588 N.W.2d 450 (1999).

[20] *Edward Vantine Studios, Inc. v. Fraternal Composite Service, Inc.*, 373 N.W.2d 512 (1985).

[21] Am. Jur. 2d Interference §37.

[22] *Diversey Corp. v. Chem-Source Corp.*, 965 P.2d 332 (1998).

[23] *IntelliSec v. Firecom, Inc.*, 2001 WL 218940 5 (E.D.N.Y. 2001).

[24] Am. Jur. 2d, Consumer §282.

[25] *Insurance Co. of North America v. Morris*, 981 S.W.2d 667 (1998).

Appendix A

CLIENT MATERIAL/DOCUMENTS

Clarence D. Arrow
Attorney at Law

CLIENT INTERVIEW — PERSONAL INJURY CASE

CLIENT'S NAME: Charles Allen Chumley
    ADDRESS: 17 Robin Hood Lane
    PHONE # WORK: *N/A, out of work since the accident*
    PHONE # HOME: 555-1212
HOW LONG AT PRESENT ADDRESS? *27 years*
WITH WHOM DOES CLIENT LIVE: *No one*
    SPOUSE: *Julia Lynn Chumley, killed in accident*
    CHILDREN: *Michael Allen Chumley*   AGE: *26*
               John Page Chumley   AGE: *24*

OTHER PRIOR RESIDENCES: *Lived in Akron, Ohio, until transferred here by Knight Manufacturing Co., 27 years ago*
PERSONS CLIENT SUPPORTS: *N/A, both children are grown and have moved out on their own*
CLIENT'S AGE: 57
CLIENT'S DATE OF BIRTH: May 5, 1946
CLIENT'S SOCIAL SECURITY NUMBER: 555-55-5555
CLIENT'S PLACE OF BIRTH: Akron, Ohio
CLIENT'S EDUCATIONAL BACKGROUND: *High school only*

CLIENT'S EMPLOYMENT HISTORY: *After leaving the military, he joined Knight Manufacturing Company as a "day press operator" and has slowly worked his way up to senior supervisor. Other than part-time jobs in high school, this is the only job he's ever had.*

CLIENT'S CURRENT EMPLOYMENT: Senior Supervisor Product Line
    EMPLOYER: Knight Manufacturing Company
    ADDRESS: 1001 Furniture Lane
    SUPERVISOR: Charles Dickens
    TYPE OF WORK: *Supervises extruded plastic pieces for formed furniture*
    LENGTH OF EMPLOYMENT: 27 years

PRESENT JOB STILL AVAILABLE? *Yes, employers have told him that he can return to work as soon as he is able.*
PAY: $32,000 per year

MILITARY HISTORY: *Served in Army from 1964 to 1976. Left as a Chief Petty Officer.*

CLIENT EVER TREATED BY PSYCHIATRIST OR BEEN IN MENTAL INSTITUTION? *No*
PHYSICAL AILMENTS? *Suffers from severe pain, has difficulty walking, diabetes, memory loss, complications from several surgeries, some loss of brain function. (See medicals for additional details; client can't recall everything.)*
PHYSICAL AILMENTS OF FAMILY MEMBERS? *Family has always been in good health. **No family history of diabetes.***
OTHER NAMES BY WHICH CLIENT HAS BEEN KNOWN? *"Chief," since his days in the military.*
BRIEF EXPLANATION OF WHAT HAPPENED: *Client says that he was crossing at a railroad/street intersection near his home and his car was hit (on driver's side) by train. Wife was killed. He was severely injured. No memory of actual accident. Memory loss of several weeks prior to accident. In coma following accident.*
DATE OF INCIDENT: **AUGUST 23, LAST YEAR.** *(Should be all right as far as Statute of Limitations goes.)*
PRIOR ACCIDENTS/LAWSUITS? *Client says never been in an accident, never been sued or brought suit before in his life.*

STATE OF PLACID
COUNTY OF BARNES

REPRESENTATION CONTRACT

THIS AGREEMENT, made and entered into this the 2nd day of February, 2003, between Charles Allen Chumley, hereinafter referred to as "Client"; and CLARENCE D. ARROW AND ASSOCIATES, P.A., hereinafter referred to as "Attorneys";

WITNESSETH:

WHEREAS, Client has a claim against National Railroad Company, Inc., and others, arising out of an accident that occurred on or about the 23rd day of August, last year, and desires to employ the Attorneys on a contingent fee basis;

NOW, THEREFORE, the Attorneys agree to represent, through trial court, as attorney for the Client and the Client agrees to pay the Attorneys

Thirty-Three and One-Third percent (33⅓%) of the amount recovered or which may be recovered in this matter, whether by compromise or settlement at any time before suit is instituted or by compromise, settlement or judgment after suit is instituted, plus expenses incurred in the preparation of the case. Both parties agree that neither party will compromise or settle this action without consent of the other party.

This the 2nd day of February, 2003.

By: Clarence D. Arrow
Attorney at Law
Clarence D. Arrow and Associates, P.A.

To: Chumley File
File Number 03-00045
From: C. Arrow
Re: Billing Info

Note that this is a standard contingency fee case. Client will have to pay court and other expenses. Please note this as a contingency fee in our billing software.

Client Expenses

Item	Amount	Paid
Copying client material at first meeting	22 pages	Not charged

STATE OF PLACID
BARNES COUNTY

AUTHORIZATION FOR RELEASE OF MEDICAL RECORDS

I, Charles Allen Chumley, hereby authorize all physicians, physician's assistants, hospital, and other medical and/or rescue squad and ambulance personnel having examined or treated me, and all other persons or companies possessing records or knowledge relating to such examination or treatment, to disclose or release the same upon request to any attorney or legal assistant of Clarence D. Arrow and Associates, P.A. (hereafter "the firm"), 1001 Burkemont Ave., Placid City, Placid 10000.

Information subject to this Release shall include that contained in all medical records including, but not limited to, rescue squad and ambulance records, emergency room reports, admission summaries, discharge summaries, doctors' orders, nurses' notes, temperature/pulse/respiration charts, anesthesia records, medication summaries, operative notes, consultation requests and reports, laboratory reports, radiology requests and reports, drug requests and reports, pharmaceutical records, and any and all other record of any kind whatsoever pertaining to me, including any and all x-rays, CAT scans, MRIs, and myelograms, and the reports from such tests: This request is made under further provisions of HIPAA. The undersigned expressly waives any privacy or confidentiality issues under HIPAA and further expressly consents under that Act to this release of Personal Health Information (PHI) to attorney.

I understand that the firm is not responsible for the costs of any copies or other expenses whatsoever for these matters. I understand and agree that I will arrange for payment for all copies or other expenses that may be incurred pursuant to P.C.A. §21-09-1245 or other.

A photocopy of the signed original of this Authorization for Release of Medical Records shall be sufficient and acceptable to all persons and entities from whom information or records are requested.

This the 2nd day of February, 2003.

Charles A. Chumley	Charles Chumley
Signature of Patient	Printed Full Name of Patient

555-55-5555	May 5, 1946
Social Security Number of Patient	Date of Birth of Patient

Appendix B

CORRESPONDENCE

CLARENCE D. ARROW & ASSOCIATES, P.A.
ATTORNEYS AT LAW
1001 BURKEMONT AVE.
PLACID CITY, PLACID 10000

CLARENCE D. ARROW, ESQ.

TELEPHONE (555) 555-1212
Fax (555) 555-1213

Charles Chumley
17 Robin Hood Lane
Cling, PL 10001

RE: Contract of Representation and Follow-up Materials

Dear Mr. Chumley:

It was a pleasure to meet with you today. As we discussed during our meeting, there are some follow-up materials that we will need from you in order to continue our investigation of your claim against National Railroad Company, Inc., and others. Here is a list of the items that we need you to locate:

- Your income tax returns for the last three years
- Your personal calendar showing your appointments and movements up to the date of the accident
- Your job performance evaluations from Knight Manufacturing, Inc.
- The damage estimate for the damage to your auto

If you would like my paralegal, Paula, to come by your house and pick up these items, please feel free to give her a call at our main office number.

We look forward to serving you in this matter. If you have any questions about this case, you can reach Paula or me at the above telephone number.

Sincerely,

Clarence D. Arrow
Clarence D. Arrow & Associates, P.A.

CLARENCE D. ARROW & ASSOCIATES, P.A.
ATTORNEYS AT LAW
1001 BURKEMONT AVE.
PLACID CITY, PLACID 10000

CLARENCE D. ARROW, ESQ.   TELEPHONE (555) 555-1212
                                                Fax (555) 555-1213

Matthew Mender, M.D.
Mender Clinic
17 Healing Lane
Placid City, PL 10000

RE: Patient — Charles A. Chumley
D/A: August 23rd, last year

Dear Dr. Mender:

We represent Mr. Charles Chumley in connection with personal injuries he sustained in an accident occurring on the above date. It is our understanding that you treated our client for these injuries. Please send us a narrative medical report describing those injuries, the treatment rendered by you, and the prognosis.

Also, please send us an itemized copy of your bill for such treatment.

A properly executed medical authorization is enclosed.

Thank you for your attention to this matter.

Sincerely,

Clarence D. Arrow
Clarence D. Arrow & Associates, P.A.

Appendix C

PLEADINGS

Charles Chumley, Plaintiff	)))	
	)	Complaint
vs.	)	Jury Trial Demanded
	)	
National Railroad Company, Inc.,	)	
Stanley W. Blue, and	)	
The Town of Cling, Defendants		

Plaintiff, by and through his attorneys, complains of the defendant as follows:

1.

Plaintiff is, and all times hereafter was, a citizen and resident of the Town of CLING, County of BARNES, State of Placid.

2.

Plaintiff alleges upon information and belief that the defendant National Railroad Company (Railroad) is, and at all times hereafter was, a corporation organized and existing under the laws of the State of Placid, licensed to do business, and in fact doing business, in the State of Placid and having a registered agent for the service of process by the name of Richard Robin located at 230 N. Elm Street, Suite 2000, Greensboro, Placid, 27401.

3.

Plaintiff alleges upon information and belief that the defendant Town of CLING (Town) is a duly chartered municipality in the County of BARNES and the State of Placid.

4.

Plaintiff alleges upon information and belief that the defendant STANLEY W. BLUE is a citizen and resident of the County of Barnes, State of Placid.

5.

That at all times relevant to this Complaint the defendant STANLEY W. BLUE was an agent, servant, and employee of the defendant National Railroad Company (Railroad) and was acting within the course and scope of his employment with it.

6.

The plaintiff is informed and believes and therefore alleges that the Town has waived any sovereign immunity, which it otherwise might have through the purchase of liability insurance, thereby affording its residents and residents of other communities the right to sue for negligent acts, which it might commit.

7.

Railroad, at the time of the accident, owned, maintained, and used a set of railroad tracks laid in an east-west direction and passing through the Town.

8.

Morgan Street is a public street in the Town that runs in a north-south direction crossing the tracks.

9.

Plaintiff alleges, upon information and belief, that at the time of the accident, Railroad owned, maintained, and used the railroad tracks at railroad crossing number 728339E, which tracks cross and intersect with Morgan Street, in the Town of CLING, County of BARNES, Placid.

10.

On August 23, 2002, at approximately 4:30 P.M., plaintiff was driving his automobile south on Morgan Street approaching the railroad crossing. A train belonging to and being operated by Railroad, its agents, servants, and employees, was approaching the crossing from an easterly direction.

11.

At the crossing in question at the time of the accident, there were no mechanical devices to warn motorists of an approaching train; no blinking lights, automatic gates, bells or gongs, or stop bars were installed at the crossing.

12.

The northeast quadrant of the grade crossing, at the time of the accident, contained vegetation and trees in such a position that they obstructed and/ or severely restricted the view of the tracks or an approaching train by a motorist approaching the crossing. Upon information and belief, defendants, Railroad, Town, and STANLEY W. BLUE, were under a duty to maintain the area in question.

13.

That as the plaintiff approached the crossing, he stopped and looked both ways; however, he was unable to see the train approaching because of the vegetation and overgrowth which both the Town and the Railroad had negligently allowed to remain upon the right-of-way until such time as he was on the tracks and a collision was inevitable.

14.

Railroad's train struck plaintiff's automobile with great force as plaintiff attempted to cross the railroad track, knocked the car off the tracks in a southwesterly direction and dragged the car, which finally stopped approximately 100 yards from the point of impact.

15.

The Town and Railroad owed to the plaintiff a duty of due care to reasonably and safely maintain the tracks and the area surrounding such tracks, particularly at crossings, in order to provide adequate sight distance for motorists operating automobiles on streets that intersect such crossings.

16.

The Town breached this duty of due care by the following acts of negligence:

a. It failed to close the crossing pursuant to state law, when it knew, or in the exercise of due care should have known, that the crossing constituted an unreasonable hazard to vehicular or pedestrian traffic;

b. It failed to require the installation, construction, erection, or improvement, of warning signs, gates, lights, stop bars, or such other safety devices when it knew or should have known in the exercise of reasonable care that such devices were necessary;

c. It allowed the crossing to remain in use with absolutely no safety devices with total, wanton, and reckless disregard for the safety of vehicular and pedestrian traffic;

d. It allowed the vegetation and trees adjacent to the tracks to obstruct the view by motorists of the tracks and approaching trains when it knew, or in the exercise of due care should have known, that such vegetation and trees constituted an unreasonable hazard to vehicular and pedestrian traffic;

e. It failed to keep the public street free from unnecessary obstructions in violation of State law.

17.

Defendant STANLEY W. BLUE, while in the course and scope of his employment with defendant Railroad, was negligent, reckless, and careless in that he, among other things:

a. Permitted the crossing to remain in such a condition as to endanger the passage or transportation of persons or property across such crossing in violation of state law;

b. Failed to take such measures as to reasonably warn motorists of oncoming trains when it knew, or in the exercise of due care should have known, that the crossing was ultra-hazardous;

c. Failed to give the plaintiff a timely and reasonable warning of the approaching train;

d. Failed to keep a proper lookout for approaching motorists and to take action to avoid the collision between the plaintiff's automobile and the train;

e. Failed to require the installation, construction, erection, or improvement, of warning signs, gates, lights, stop bars, or such other safety devices when it knew or should have known in the exercise of reasonable care that such devices were necessary;

f. Allowed the crossing to remain in use with absolutely no safety devices with total, wanton, and reckless disregard for the safety of vehicular and pedestrian traffic;

g. Allowed the vegetation and trees adjacent to the tracks to obstruct the view by motorists of the tracks and approaching trains when it knew, or in the exercise of due care should have known, that such vegetation and trees constituted an unreasonable hazard to vehicular and pedestrian traffic;

h. Operated its train through a blind or obstructed crossing at an unreasonable rate of speed for the conditions;

i. Given the obstructed nature of the crossing, failed to give adequate warning of the approaching train;

j. Failed to maintain its tracks, crossings, and right-of-way in a condition that would allow for the necessary sight distance of approaching trains.

18.

Defendant Railroad was negligent, reckless, and careless in that it, among other things:

a. Permitted the crossing to remain in such condition as to endanger the passage or transportation of persons or property across such crossing in violation of state law;

b. Failed to take such measures as to reasonably warn motorists of oncoming trains when it knew, or in the exercise of due care should have known, that the crossing was ultra-hazardous;

c. Failed to give the plaintiff a timely and reasonable warning of the approaching train;

d. Failed to keep a proper lookout for approaching motorists and to take action to avoid the collision between the plaintiff's automobile and the train;

e. Failed to require the installation, construction, erection, or improvement, of warning signs, gates, lights, stop bars, or such other safety devices when it knew or should have known in the exercise of reasonable care that such devices were necessary;

f. Allowed the crossing to remain in use with absolutely no safety devices with total, wanton, and reckless disregard for the safety of vehicular and pedestrian traffic;

g. Allowed the vegetation and trees adjacent to the tracks to obstruct the view by motorists of the tracks and approaching trains when it knew, or in the exercise of due care should have known, that such vegetation and trees constituted an unreasonable hazard to vehicular and pedestrian traffic;

h. Operated its train through a blind or obstructed crossing at an unreasonable rate of speed for the conditions;

i. Given the obstructed nature of the crossing, failed to give adequate warning of the approaching train;

j. Failed to maintain its tracks, crossings, and right-of-way in a condition that would allow for the necessary sight distance of approaching trains.

19.

That the negligence of the defendants Town of CLING, National Railway, and STANLEY W. BLUE joined and concurred and combined in point of time and place proximately to cause the collision between plaintiff's vehicle and Railroad's train and plaintiff's resulting serious, painful, and permanent injuries and damages, all of which exceed the sum of Ten Thousand Dollars ($10,000.00), and which include, without limitation, the following:

(1) bodily injury and resulting pain and suffering;

(2) medical expenses, including the costs of therapy;

(3) loss of earnings and earning capacity;

(4) punitive damages as a result of the defendants' reckless and wanton conduct.

WHEREFORE, the plaintiff prays the Court as follows:

1. That the plaintiff have and recover from the defendants, jointly and severally, a sum in excess of Ten Thousand Dollars ($10,000.00) for compensatory and punitive damages as alleged above.

2. That the plaintiff have and recover the costs of this action.

3. For a trial by jury.

4. For such other and further relief as to the Court may seem just and proper.

This the _____day of _____, 2003.

Clarence D. Arrow & Associates, P.A.

By: _____
Clarence D. Arrow, Esq.
State Bar No. 0000001
1001 Burkemont Ave.
Placid City, PL 10000
(555) 555-1212
Attorney for the Plaintiff

STATE OF PLACID		IN THE SUPERIOR COURT
COUNTY OF BARNES		FILE NUMBER: _____

Charles Chumley,	)	
Plaintiff	)	
	)	Answer of National Railroad
vs.	)	Company, Inc. and Stanley W. Blue
	)	
National Railroad Company, Inc.,	)	
Stanley W. Blue, and	)	
The Town of Cling,		
Defendants		

COMES NOW the Defendants National Railroad Company, Inc. (hereafter "Defendant Railroad"), and Stanley W. Blue (hereafter "Defendant Blue") and, answering the Complaint herein, by alleging and saying as follows:

1. Upon information and belief, admitted.
2. Admitted.
3. Upon information and belief, admitted.
4. Admitted.
5. Admitted.
6. These Defendants are without sufficient information or knowledge to enable them to form a belief as to the veracity of the facts alleged in paragraph 6, and this paragraph is therefore denied.
7. Admitted.
8. Admitted.
9. Denied.
10. It is admitted that the Plaintiff was driving an automobile on August 23 of last year and that he was driving in a southerly direction on Morgan Street. It is also admitted that he approached an intersection with Morgan Street and a railroad that belonged to and was operated by Defendant Railroad and its employees. It is further admitted that a train, owned and operated by Defendant Railroad, was heading in a westerly direction toward this same intersection at the date and time alleged. Except as herein admitted, denied.
11. It is admitted that there were cross buck railroad signs positioned at the intersection. These signs were properly installed and clearly visible to motorists crossing the intersection from either the north or the south on Morgan Street. These cross buck signs were adequate warning for reasonable and prudent motorists. It is further admitted that there were no additional warning signs, mechanical gates, or flashing lights to warn motorists of the intersection of Morgan Street with the railroad. Except as herein admitted, denied.
12. Denied.
13. Denied.
14. It is admitted that there was a collision between the Plaintiff's automobile and the Railroad's train. It is further admitted that the Plaintiff's automobile traveled approximately 100 yards in a southwesterly direction immediately after the collision. Except as herein admitted, denied.

15. It is admitted that the Defendants Railroad and Town of Cling had a duty to maintain the railroad tracks and specific areas around the track in a reasonable and safe manner. Except as herein admitted, denied.
16. a. Denied.
    b. Denied.
    c. Denied.
    d. Denied.
    e. Denied.
17. a. Denied.
    b. Denied.
    c. Denied.
    d. Denied.
    e. Denied.
    f. Denied.
    g. Denied.
    h. Denied.
    i. Denied.
    j. Denied.
18. a. Denied.
    b. Denied.
    c. Denied.
    d. Denied.
    e. Denied.
    f. Denied.
    g. Denied.
    h. Denied.
    i. Denied.
    j. Denied.
19. Denied.

Defendant Railroad's and Defendant Blue's First Affirmative Defense

These Defendants show that the Plaintiff's own negligence was either a sole or contributing proximate cause of the collision that resulted in all of the injuries for which the Plaintiff now seeks recovery from these Defendants. Plaintiff's contributory/comparative negligence is hereby pled as a complete bar/partial bar to his recovery against these Defendants.

This the _____day of _____, 2003.

_____

Perry E. Masson, Esq.
State Bar No. 111111111
11 Hamilton Burger Lane
Placid City, PL 10000
(555) 333-1212
Attorney for the Defendants National Railway
Company, Inc. & Stanley W. Blue

STATE OF PLACID   IN THE SUPERIOR COURT
COUNTY OF BARNES   FILE NUMBER: _____

Charles Chumley,   )
Plaintiff   )
)   Answer of Town of Cling
vs.   )
)
National Railroad Company, Inc.,)
Stanley W. Blue, and   )
The Town of Cling,
Defendants

Note: This Answer was substantially identical to National Railroad Company's
Answer and will therefore be excluded from this section.

Appendix D

DISCOVERY

Charles Chumley,   )

Plaintiff   )

)   PLAINTIFF'S FIRST

vs.   )   INTERROGATORIES AND

)   REQUEST FOR PRODUCT OF

National Railroad Company, Inc.,)   DOCUMENTS

Stanley W. Blue, and   )

The Town of Cling,

Defendants

Definitions

For the purpose of this set of Interrogatories, each undefined work shall have its usual and generally accepted meaning. Each defined word, and all variations thereof, shall have the meanings set forth below:

1. "Document"—any paper, file, tape, or similar material upon which verbal, graphic, or pictorial information or image is written, printed, typed, drawn, punched, produced, or reproduced in any fashion, including but not limited to all records, reports, correspondence, memoranda, notes, agreements, studies, minutes, photographs, drawings, sketches, maps, charts, brochures, photocopies, any computer cards, and tapes.
2. "He" and "his" refers to all genders.
3. "Identify" (or "state the identity of"):
   a. With respect to a document, means set forth the following information, if known:
      (i)   a general description thereof (e.g., letter, memorandum, report, etc.);
      (ii) a brief summary of its contents;
      (iii) the name and address of the custodian of the original, or, if unavailable, of the custodian of a copy;
      (iv) the name and address of the person(s), if any, who drafted, prepared, compiled, or signed it;

- (v) any other descriptive information necessary in order to adequately describe it in a Subpoena Duces Tecum, or any motion or request for production thereof; and
- (vi) a statement of whether or not the Plaintiff will voluntarily make it available to the Defendant for copying, and, if not, a statement of the specific reasons for not being willing or able to do so.

b. With respect to any oral communication (including but not limited to conversations, discussions, or oral agreements), "identify" (or "state the identity of") means state the following current or last known information:
- (i) its type or nature (e.g., in person, by telephone, etc.);
- (ii) its date;
- (iii) the identity of all present and/or participating; and
- (iv) a summary of what was said to whom and by whom.

c. With respect to an individual, "identify" (or "state the identity of") means state the following current or last known information:
- (i) his name;
- (ii) his relationship to the Plaintiff at the time relative to the Interrogatory being answered;
- (iii) his employer;
- (iv) his employment position;
- (v) his business address and telephone number; and
- (vi) his residence address.

d. With respect to an association, partnership, or corporation, municipality, State or Federal agency, "identify" (or "state the identity of") means state the following current or last known information:
- (i) its name;
- (ii) its type or nature (e.g., corporation, partnership, joint venture, etc.);
- (iii) the nature of its business or primary activities;
- (iv) its address; and
- (v) its telephone number.

4. "Person" — any natural or artificial being including but not limited to any individual, corporation, partnership, voluntary association, municipality, government, State or Federal agency.

5. "Occurrence" — the combined events and incidents that caused damage to the Plaintiff. The events leading up to and including the alleged misconduct of the Defendant.

Pursuant to Rule 33 of the State Rules of Civil Procedure, the following questions must be answered fully and under oath, in the space following each question (and on attached pages if the space provided is insufficient), and the sworn answers served on the undersigned attorney within thirty (30) days of service hereof.

These questions and the requests for production shall be continuing in nature so as to require supplemental answers as additional information becomes available as provided in the Rules of Civil Procedure.

1. Please describe in as much detail as possible the weather condition at the time and place of the alleged occurrence, including in your answer details of light, temperature, humidity, cloud cover, wind velocity, wind direction, and type of precipitation, if any.
2. Please describe as completely as you can the lighting conditions at the time and place of the alleged occurrence, including the amount of natural light and/or the amount of artificial lighting.
3. Please state what precautions, if any, were taken by you, or any agent or employee of the Defendant, prior to the Plaintiff's alleged occurrence, to prevent injuries to persons in the position of the Plaintiff.
4. Please describe all observations known by you to have been made of any hazard or danger that was involved in the alleged occurrence, including:
   a. the name and address of each person making each such observation;
   b. the date each such observation was made;
   c. the substance of each such observation.
5. Please describe all comments or complaints known by you to have been made regarding any hazard or danger that was involved in the alleged occurrence, including:

6. Please list all governmental standards and regulations governing conditions or activities involved in the alleged occurrence.
7. Please describe each standard and regulation listed in response to the preceding interrogatory, including:
   a. the government body responsible for each standard and regulation;
   b. the formal citation for each standard and regulation;
   c. the content of each such standard and regulation;
   d. the manner in which you became aware of each such standard and regulation;
   e. the date on which you became aware of each such standard and regulation.
8. Please describe each violation or noncompliance with a governmental standard or regulation governing conditions involved in the alleged occurrence, including:
   a. the formal citation for each such governmental standard or regulation that was violated or with which conditions did not comply;
   b. a description of the act or omission constituting each such violation or noncompliance;
   c. the date of each such act or omission.
9. Please list all industry, professional, and trade association standards and regulations governing conditions or activities involved in the alleged occurrence.
10. Please describe each standard and regulation listed in response to the preceding interrogatory, including:
    a. the body responsible for each standard and regulation;
    b. the formal citation of each standard and regulation;
    c. the content of each such standard and regulation;

    d. the manner in which you became aware of each such standard and regulation;

    e. the date on which you became aware of each such standard and regulation.

11. Please describe each violation or noncompliance with an industry, professional, or trade association standard or regulation governing conditions involved in the occurrence, including:

    a. the formal citation for each such standard or regulation that was violated or with which conditions did not comply;

    b. a description of the act or omission constituting each such violation or noncompliance;

    c. the date of each such act or omission.

12. Identify the operating rules, safety rules, and all other rules, bulletins, and writings of the Defendant that governed the conduct of the Defendant's employees at the time and place of the above-specified incident.

13. Identify the Telegraphic Accident Report prepared by the Defendant, its agents, servants, or employees in the ordinary course of Defendant's business and concerning the above-specified personal injury and/or accident.

14. Identify any (Repair) (Maintenance) (I.C.C. Inspection Reports) (Safety Appliance Reports) for a period of 12 months prior to the above-specified injury and/or accident to a period of 3 months subsequent to said injury or accident and specifically:

15. Identify any photographs taken prior to any changes in conditions that reflect the condition of same at the time of or immediately after the subject accident.

16. Identify the track survey kept in the ordinary course of the Defendant's business, reflecting the area of the subject accident. The request is for the last track survey prepared prior to the time of the subject accident and/or injury.

17. Identify the minutes and records of the meeting of the Defendant's safety committee and all "safety items" or similar reports kept or submitted in the ordinary course of the Defendant's business for three (3) years prior to the incident complained of.

18. Identify each member of the crew of Defendant's train involved in the subject accident and the respective crew titles of each.

19. Identify other persons aboard Defendant's train at the time of the subject accident who had any duties of any nature aboard said train, and state with respect to each, their job classification and the nature of their duties aboard said train.

20. Identify all other officers, agents, or employees of Defendant aboard Defendant's train at the time of the subject accident and the functions, if any, of each of such employees on said train.

21. State the location of each person listed in 18, 19, and 20 above at the time the subject accident occurred and the 60 seconds prior thereto.

22. State the name or designation, and location, of any brake control apparatus actually utilized to affect the movement of the train in question for

60 seconds before and 60 seconds after the time of the subject collision and the names of all persons who activated each such apparatus.

23. State the location (with reference to the roadway) of lead diesel unit, at the time the brakes on the train were first applied at or near the time of the collision; and
    a. Describe the type of brake application then made and the distance from the point of impact. (If subsequent brake application of a different type was made, state such location at the time and the type of application then made.)
24. State whether Defendant's railroad track was straight or curved within one mile of each side of the crossing where the subject accident occurred, and, if curved, state for what distance in each direction, and the direction of the curvature of the tracks.
25. State who owned and maintained the railroad track in question.
26. State whether you have in your possession photographs taken of and at the scene of the subject accident showing physical position or location of any warning signs, appliances, vehicles, or railroad equipment as same existed immediately after the happening of the accident and prior to any changes in their respective appearances, locations, or conditions.
27. State the exact width of the public roadway from edge to edge that the railroad tracks crossed upon or over at this crossing.
28. State the kind, type, and exact size and location of each and every fixed warning sign located at or in the vicinity of or approaches to the crossing at the time and place involved.
29. State the exact distance (or if not known, the approximate distance) traveled by the leading point of the Defendant's train from the following points until it came to a stop after the collision:
    a. From the first edge of the roadway passed by the lead unit or car;
    b. From the point of impact;
    c. From the last edge of the roadway passed by the lead unit or car;
    d. From the point where the last brake application prior to impact was made.
30. For the period of three months prior to the date of the subject accident, describe any inspections or repairs of any kind made to the brakes or brake system of any cars in Defendant's train, including each diesel unit, including:
    a. The date and kind of each such repair;
    b. The name and current address of each person making such repairs;
    c. The reason or reasons for each of such repairs.
31. State the exact time and date that an inspection was last made (prior to the occurrence of this accident) of the brake system or brakes on Defendant's train involved in the subject accident and the name and current address of each person who made such inspection.
    a. Give the same information for the first inspection after this accident.
32. State the speed of Defendant's train (if not known, give approximate speed) on the day of the subject accident at the following locations:
    a. One-half mile prior to the crossing;
    b. One thousand feet prior to the crossing;

    c.   Five hundred feet prior to the crossing;

    d.   Fifty feet prior to the crossing;

    e.   At the initial edge of the crossing;

    f.   At impact point.

33. State the distance required to stop a train of similar equipment and containing the same number of cars as the train involved in the subject accident, on similar track, with an emergency application of the brakes at the following speeds:

    a.   5 miles per hour;

    b.   10 miles per hour;

    c.   15 miles per hour;

    d.   20 miles per hour;

    e.   At the speed that the train was going 50 feet from the subject crossing;

    f.   At the speed that the train was going at the initial edge of the subject crossing.

34. State whether or not Defendant's train was moved at all after it first came to a stop following the impact of the subject accident and prior to full investigation by police and railroad crew; if so, state whether it was moved forward or backward, why it was moved forward or backward, and how far it was moved forward or backward.

35. State the name and current address of any Defendant's officers, agents, or employees who have actually inspected, or who have had the duty to inspect:

    a.   Any signal devices at this crossing for the time one year prior to the subject accident to date;

    b.   The physical condition of the crossing and its approaches or adjacent properties for the time one year prior to the subject accident to date.

36. State the names and last known addresses of each and every person known by you, your agents, servants, employees, or attorneys, to have been an eyewitness to the accident out of which this cause arose.

37. State the name and last known addresses of all persons known to you, your agents, servants, employees, or attorneys, who have any knowledge of the circumstances leading up to or surrounding the accident out of which the above cause arose, but are not eyewitnesses.

38. State the names and last known addresses of all persons from whom you, your agents, servants, employees, attorneys, or investigator have taken any written statements, or court reporters' statements in connection with any of the circumstances leading up to or surrounding the occurrence of the subject accident.

39. State whether or not at the time and on the day of the subject accident there were in effect any written side track agreements or other agreements (with respect to any side tracks located within one mile of the crossing where the accident occurred) between Defendant, or its predecessors, and any person or persons, firm, corporation, partnership, or other business association, and, if so, state with respect thereto the following:

    a.   The date of each such agreement;

    b.   The names of the parties to each such agreement;

    c. The names and addresses of the persons having custody or control of such agreements;

    d. The exact location of any side track forming the subject matter of any such agreements.

40. State the date on which the last inspection (prior to the accident) was made by Defendant, through any of its officers, agents, or employees:

    a. Of the crossing;

    b. Of the warning devices thereat.

41. State the names and current residence addresses of every person who made or participated in the last inspection of the crossing or warning devices as specified in the answer above.

42. State the purpose and nature of the last inspection made of the crossing or warning devices as specified in the two answers above.

43. State the name and current address of any employees to whom you administered discipline of any description in connection with the subject accident or their actions relating thereto.

44. If you had received any communication whatsoever prior to this accident, from any person or entity whatsoever relating to the adequacy or performance of any signs or warning signals at this crossing, please state:

    a. The name and current address of the sender;

    b. The date received;

    c. The form (written or verbal, etc.);

    d. The name and address of Defendant's officer, agent, or employee who received it.

45. If you had received any communication whatsoever prior to this accident, from any person or entity whatsoever relating to the adequacy or performance of any signs or warning signals at this crossing, please state:

    a. The name and current address of the sender;

    b. The date received;

    c. The form (written or verbal, etc.);

    d. The name and address of defendant's officer, agent, or employee who received it.

46. State the cost or approximate cost of installing automatic crossing protection at the subject crossing at or about the time of the subject accident, and, specifically, the cost of:

    a. Lights and bells (if not already installed);

    b. Lights, gates, and bells (if not already installed).

47. Please state for a period of three (3) years prior to the subject accident the names and current addresses of all defendant's employees who made any report to defendant (including incident reports and safety items at safety meetings) of safety problems, incidents, or hazards at the subject crossing.

48. Give a complete description of the horn or whistle on defendant's locomotives described above at the time of the subject accident, including but not limited to:

    a. The date of installation or approximate date thereof;

    b. The make and model number and the name of the manufacturer.

49. State which of the above-identified locomotives' horns were actually utilized by defendant for warning purposes at the time involved.
50. Was the defendant, at the time of the subject accident, a member of the American Association of Railroads (A.A.R.) and, if so, please:
    a. Describe and identify A.A.R. recommendations and/or standards as of the time of the subject accident pertaining to:
    b. Crossing protection for the type of crossing herein involved;
    c. Warning equipment on locomotives operating over crossings such as that located at the place of the subject accident herein.

This the _____ day of _____, 2003.
Clarence D. Arrow & Associates, P.A.

_____

Clarence D. Arrow, Esq.
State Bar No. 0000001
1001 Burkemont Ave.
Placid City, PL 10000
(555) 555-1212
Attorney for the Plaintiff

CERTIFICATE OF SERVICE

This is to certify that the undersigned has this date served the foregoing upon all other parties to this cause in the following manner:

- By delivering a copy thereof to the attorneys of record for said parties or to partners or employees at the office of such attorneys.
- By depositing a copy thereof in a postpaid wrapper in a post office or official depository under the exclusive care and custody of the United States Post Office Department properly addressed to the attorneys of record for said parties.

This the _____ day of _____, 2003.

Clarence D. Arrow & Associates, P.A.

_____

Clarence D. Arrow, Esq.
State Bar No. 0000001
1001 Burkemont Ave.
Placid City, PL 10000
(555) 555-1212
Attorney for the Plaintiff

Exhibits provided in response to Interrogatories:

Police report
Photos
        Damage to plaintiff's car (2)
        RR crossing (8)

Photos and Diagrams

This section contains photos of Mr. and Mrs. Chumley in happier times and a diagram of the accident scene.

Appendix E

MEDICAL

Medical Bill Totals for Charles Chumley

Mission Hospital	$219,380.01
Mission Clinic	$2,677.94
EMS	$65.50
Carter Surgical Associates	$12,935.00
Barnes Radiology	$4,561.00
Barnes Rehabilitation Hospital	$83,494.41
Barnes Bone and Joint Clinic	$6,151.20
Medical Internist's Association	$23,118.27
Doctor's Family Care	$760.00
Barnes Diabetes Medical Assoc.	$12,398.45
Joseph Frazier, M.D.	$5,692.02
Total	$371,233.80

BARNES REHABILITATION HOSPITAL
PLACID CITY, PL 10000

HISTORY AND EXAMINATION NOTES

PATIENT NAME: Chumley, Charles
ADMISSION DATE: 12-02-02
HOSPITAL NUMBER: 003-03-9087
HOSPITAL UNIT: HEAD TRAUMA

The medical records have been reviewed and the admitting Physician Assistant and Dr. Frazier have examined the patient.

Date of birth: 5-5-46

INFORMATION PROVIDED BY: Patient, patient's two sons, records from Mission Hospital.

PROFILE: This is the first admission to BRH of this 56-year-old, right-handed male, who previously lived with his wife, Julia, in Cling, Placid. Patient's wife was killed in the accident in which he received his injuries. The patient has a high school education. He worked at Knight Manufacturing Co. for 25+ years. His hobbies included playing golf and walking. He also enjoys watching professional football.

CHIEF COMPLAINT: "I was in an accident with a train and was in a coma for a couple of months."

HISTORY OF PRESENT ILLNESS: The patient was involved in an automobile-train accident in August of this year. The patient suffered multiple traumas. He was initially admitted to Cling Hospital immediately after the accident, but was then transferred to Mission Memorial. The patient's injuries included intraperitoneal hemorrhage, severely displaced left tibial plateau fracture, left hemo-pneumothorax, left elbow lacerations and a closed head injury. The patient underwent an ORIF for his left tibial plateau fracture as well as exploratory laparotomy with a splenectomy. The patient also had five broken ribs and a left hip fracture. The patient has a tracheostomy placed on August 30, 2002. The patient's hospital course was complicated by resistant organisms in the sputum causing acute and chronic bronchitis. The Infectious Disease Consultants for this followed him. The patient was also followed by Dr. Wellby for his pulmonary difficulties.

The patient's hospital course was also complicated by the inability to pass a G-tube secondary to the patient's significant abdominal trauma. The patient has fistula development with infections of the fistula. The patient, therefore, required central hyper-alimentation. The patient has been receiving this via triple lumen catheter. Catheter was placed on October 14. The patient has tolerated this well and, in fact, has been able to eat some by mouth, having had a videofluoroscopy done on November 5.

PAST MEDICAL HISTORY: The patient has suffered the usual childhood diseases without sequelae.

Medically, the patient was diagnosed as having hypertension and was started on medication approximately one month prior to his injury. Trauma history—none, confirmed by both sons.

HABITS: Patient quit smoking about ten years ago. Previous to that, he smoked about 1½ packs per day for 30+ years. The patient did not consume alcoholic beverages. He usually drinks sweet tea, diet soft drinks, and water.

ALLERGIES: NONE.

Glossary

Affirm The appellate court agrees with the verdict, or some ruling, entered in the trial and votes to keep that decision in place.

Answer The name of the document that the defendant serves on the plaintiff, outlining his defenses and any claims he may have against the plaintiff.

Assault When the defendant causes the plaintiff to have fear or apprehension of a harmful or offensive contact.

Battery When the defendant causes harmful or offensive contact to the plaintiff.

Breach When the defendant fails to live up to a legal standard, or violates a duty.

Case law The body of cases decided by judges who have interpreted statutes and prior cases.

Cause of action A legal injury on which a lawsuit can be based.

Certiorari (cert.) The power of a court to decide which cases it will hear and which it will not.

Chattel Personal property, including animals.

Clear and convincing evidence A level of proof higher than mere preponderance of the evidence. In most civil trials preponderance of the evidence is sufficient.

Clear and convincing proof A measure of proof that is higher than preponderance of the evidence. Clear and convincing proof is evidence that is likely to be true under the facts. This standard of proof is less than beyond a reasonable doubt but higher than preponderance of the evidence.

Collateral source rule An evidentiary rule that permits the jury to be told about the plaintiff's other sources of compensation, such as insurance, worker's compensation, etc.

Comparative negligence An approach to negligence cases that balances the negligence of the defendant against the negligence of the plaintiff and permits a reduced recovery for the plaintiff in proportion to the plaintiff's negligence.

Compensatory damages An award by a judge or jury designed to compensate the plaintiff for his physical or financial losses.

Complaint The first pleading in a suit, in which the plaintiff sets out his cause of action against the defendant and requests some form of remedy to be awarded by the court.

Compulsion An overwhelming or irresistible impulse to perform some action.

Contributory negligence A defense available in only a few jurisdictions that provides that a plaintiff who is even partially at fault is barred from any recovery.

Conversion Exercising control over property and removing it from the possession of the rightful owner.

Custom A practice that has acquired a legal status over time such that failing to follow the practice would result in liability.

Damages Money that a court orders the losing side in a civil case to pay to the other side.

Declaratory judgment A court order that specifies the duties and obligations of a party.

Defamation An attack on the reputation or character of another.

Defendant The legal title of the person who is served with the complaint.

Duress When the defendant uses force, threat, or intimidation to overcome the plaintiff's will or to compel the plaintiff to perform (or not to perform) some action.

Duty An obligation imposed by statute or common law.

Elements The points raised by the plaintiff in his complaint that must also be proved at trial; failure to prove these points will often result in a dismissal of the plaintiff's case.

Equity   The court's authority to order individuals and corporations to perform (or not to perform) certain activities because they are unjust.

Excessive force   Force used in self-defense that is clearly disproportionate to the threat posed by another.

Exclusion   The persons, types of losses, or damages not covered by an insurance policy.

Fair market value   The amount that a willing buyer would pay for an item that a willing seller would be willing to accept.

Fiduciary   A relationship in which one person, or entity, is obligated to act in a trustworthy relationship to the other. A fiduciary has the duty to act in the best interests of the other. A common example of a fiduciary relationship is the attorney-client relationship.

Foreseeability   The legal requirement that the plaintiff be a person who would likely be injured by the defendant's conduct.

Foreseeable   The outcome that a person should have known or been able to anticipate or predict based on certain facts.

General damages   Those awards that are closely tied to the defendant's negligence.*

Guilt   The jury's determination that the defendant in a criminal case is responsible for committing a crime.

Immunity   An exception or privilege granted by the law to an action that ordinarily would result in a cause of action.

Indemnify   To compensate a person who has suffered a loss.

Indictment   Official document issued by the grand jury, accusing the defendant of a criminal act.

Informed consent   An agreement by a person to allow some type of action after having been fully informed and after making a knowing and intelligent decision to allow the action.

Injunction   A court order that demands a certain action, or that prohibits a certain action.

Intentional tort   A civil action based on a defendant's purposeful, intentional act that causes harm, as opposed to a defendant who causes harm through negligence.

Intervening cause   Any event that occurs after the initial plaintiff's injury that contributes to or aggravates those injuries.

* Restatement (second) of Torts, §621 (1977).

Invitee   A person who has a business purpose in coming onto the property.

Last clear chance   A claim by a plaintiff in a contributory negligence allegation that the defendant was the person who had the last opportunity to avoid the event that caused the plaintiff's injuries and therefore the defendant should remain liable for the injuries, despite any negligence by the plaintiff.

Legal malpractice   Professional negligence committed by an attorney during the course of her representation of a client.

Liable   A finding that one of the parties in a civil case is obligated to pay damages to the other party.

Libel   Written defamation.

Licensee   Person who enters another person's premises for convenience, curiosity, or entertainment.

Loss of consortium   A claim filed by the spouse of an injured party for the loss of companionship in the marriage caused by the injuries.

Malice   Reckless or false statements. Legal malice is a court-created doctrine that supplies the element by assuming that certain phrases could only have been motivated by ill will. Examples would include falsely accusing someone of a crime or other despicable act.

Malpractice   The failure of a professional to exercise an adequate degree of skill, expertise, and knowledge for an adequate benefit of the client/patient; otherwise known as professional negligence.

Material fact   A fact that is basic to a contract, one that the parties consider to be an essential ingredient of the negotiations.

Mitigation of damages   The responsibility of the plaintiff to lessen his potential injuries or losses by taking reasonable actions to seek medical treatment or take other precautions when a reasonable person in the same situation would have done so.

Motion for directed verdict   A motion brought by the defense at the end of the plaintiff's case, asking that the case be dismissed because the plaintiff has failed to prove the claims raised in the complaint.

Mutual combat   When the parties to a fight voluntarily engage in violence.

Negligence per se   Negligence in and of itself; the principle that the violation of a safety statute establishes a presumption of breach of duty in a negligence action.

No-fault insurance   A type of insurance that requires an insurance company to pay for the insured's damages regardless of who was at fault in causing the damage.

Nuisance   A cause of action that is authorized when the defendant's behavior results in a loss of enjoyment or value in the plaintiff's property.

Per diem   By the day or daily.

Physician-patient relationship   The legally recognized relationship between a physician and patient in which the physician brings to bear her skill in the care and treatment of the patient; this relationship also triggers evidentiary privileges that protect the patient's communications with the physician from compulsory revelation.

Plaintiff   The legal title of the person who brings a complaint.

Pleadings   Documents that describe the legal injuries and counterclaims raised by the parties in a civil case.

Policy   A written insurance contract.

Premium   The insured's payment to the insurance company.

Prima facie   (Latin) "at first sight"; the party has presented adequate evidence to prove a particular point.

Privilege   A protection or advantage given to a class of persons for actions taken by them.

Privity   The direct relationship between the parties to a contract that arises from their involvement in creating the contract.

Products liability   Also known as "product liability," the liability assessed against a manufacturer, seller, wholesaler, etc., for placing a dangerous or defective product on the market that causes injury or damage.

Professional   Someone who either through education, training, or a combination of both, possesses skills that an average person does not.

Proximate causation   The facts that show the defendant's legal responsibility for the injuries to the plaintiff, also known as legal cause.

Proximate cause   Proof that the defendant's actions were the legal cause of the plaintiff's injuries (see Chapter 7).

Ratification   The process of confirming and accepting a previous action; a void contract can be ratified after the fact to make it legally enforceable.

Reasonable person standard   The standard used by the court to provide a yardstick by which it can evaluate the defendant's actions in a particular case.

Release   Surrender or give up a legal right to sue another; the document or court filing in which this right is surrendered.

Remand   The appellate court requires additional information or an evidentiary hearing; it cannot conduct such a hearing itself, so it sends the case back to the trial court for the hearing, and then considers the appeal based on that hearing.

Res ipsa loquitur   (Latin) "the thing speaks for itself"; the principle that under certain circumstances, such as when the type of accident is one that would not ordinarily occur without some form of negligence, the defendant's negligence can be presumed.

Respondeat superior   Liability imposed on an employer for the actions of the employee, when the employee is carrying out his duties for the employer.

Reverse   To reverse a decision is to set it aside; an appellate court disagrees with the verdict, or some ruling, in the trial, and overturns that decision.

Self-defense   When a person uses force (sometimes deadly force) to protect himself from an attack.

Slander   Spoken defamation.

Special damages   Those damages, such as medical bills, closely tied to the plaintiff's injuries and for which a specific amount can usually be calculated.

Specialist   One who has become an expert in a particular field through education, training, or both.

Stacking   The policy limits of one policy are added to the policy limits of one or more other policies, increasing the available funds to the sum of all policies.

Standard of care   The standard used to determine if a party has acted negligently in a particular case.

Stare decisis The principle that courts will reach similar results as in prior cases involving similar facts and legal issues.

Strict liability A finding of liability regardless of fault.

Subrogation In claiming a legal right or a debt, the substitution of one person for another.

Sudden emergency A doctrine that relieves a person of the normal standard of care because of a swiftly developing and dangerous event.

Superseding cause An event that occurs after the initial plaintiff's injury that replaces one act of negligence with another.

Thermography An assessment tool that can monitor temperature changes in the skin; often used by plaintiffs' attorneys as a way of showing that there is greater blood flow in an injured area and thereby providing a "picture of the pain."

Trespasser A person who is on the property of another without permission.

Ultra-hazardous A condition of special or unusual dangerousness.

Verdict The jury's final decision in the case in which they decide questions of fact raised in the case.

Voir dire (French) "Look speak"; the process of questioning a juror to discover bias or prejudice or if she would make an acceptable juror to hear a case.

Warranty A pledge, assurance, or guarantee that a particular fact is true.

Index